Union Catalog of Clemens Letters

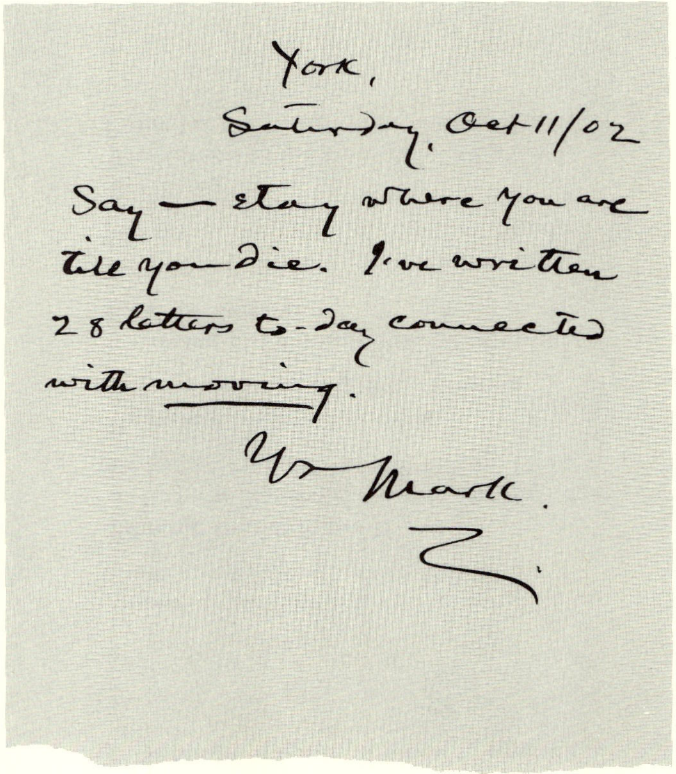
York,
Saturday, Oct 11/02
Say — stay where you are till you die. I've written 28 letters to-day connected with *moving*.
Yr Mark.
Z.

Union Catalog of Clemens Letters

EDITED BY PAUL MACHLIS

A publication of the Mark Twain Project of The Bancroft Library

University of California Press
Berkeley Los Angeles London

Samuel L. Clemens to William D. Howells, 11 October 1902, reproduced by permission of the Houghton Library, Harvard University

University of California Publications:
Catalog and Bibliographies, Volume 1

University of California Press
Berkeley and Los Angeles, California

University of California Press, Ltd.
London, England

ISBN 0-520-09688-6
Library of Congress Catalog Card Number: 85-20895

Printed in the United States of America

Library of Congress Cataloging-in-Publication Data

Main entry under title:
Union catalog of Clemens letters.

(University of California publications. Catalogs and bibliographies; v. 1)
"A publication of the Mark Twain Project of the Bancroft Library."
1. Twain, Mark, 1835–1910—Correspondence—Union lists. 2. Twain, Mark, 1835–1910—Manuscripts—Union lists. 3. Manuscripts, American—Union lists. 4. Catalogs, Union—United States. I. Machlis, Paul. II. Series.
Z6616.T926U54 1986 [PS1331] 016.818'409 [B] 85-20895
ISBN 0-520-09688-6 (alk. paper)

Contents

Preface

One hundred years after the publication of _Adventures of Huckleberry Finn_, the life and works of Mark Twain (_Samuel L. Clemens_) remain of immense interest to the international public as well as to students of American literature and history. A steady stream of new editions, biographical research, literary criticism, and adaptations--on stage, screen, television, and in print--attests to the sustained power of his writings. And the Mark Twain Project continues to issue scholarly and popular editions of the collected works and papers, with substantial public and private support.

To make these editions as complete and accurate as possible is the immediate goal of the _Union Catalog of Clemens Letters_. The cataloging and sorting of over ten thousand letters contributes to the accuracy and thoroughness of the editorial enterprise, not only for volumes of the letters themselves, but for the series of notebooks, novels, and other writings whose texts are inevitably illuminated by the author's letters. This publication of the catalog is intended to extend that assistance to the greater scholarly community. Mark Twain scholars may easily learn of letters relevant to particular periods of the author's life, residences from which he wrote, or persons to whom he wrote. The listings of letters owned by various institutions will assist scholars in the use of materials that can rarely receive such specific cataloging by the repositories owning them. Beyond the realm of Mark Twain studies, it is hoped that the catalog will assist students of American history and publishing for whom the life and works of Samuel L. Clemens contain relevant documentary material.

This work represents the contributions of many people, and it is not possible to acknowledge each individually. Of nearly two thousand library curators and collectors approached, many hundreds have responded with new information about Mark Twain materials. Numerous scholars using the Mark Twain Papers have offered suggestions and corrections, and experts have assisted with each stage of computing, production, and style.

The catalog owes its existence to Robert H. Hirst, Head of the Mark Twain Project. Shortly after assuming his post in 1980, he recognized the need to conduct a truly exhaustive search for the materials to be edited and to prepare adequate tools of documentary control. With the certainty of postponing the immediate publication of volumes, but with the expectation of vastly improving both the quality and rate of publication in the long range, he won the approval of the Project's supporters for the work necessary to find and catalog widely scattered documents, and during the past four years, a significant part of the Project's resources have indeed been applied to this goal.

The most important contribution to the completion of this work was the ongoing assistance of my colleagues at the Mark Twain Project: Robert H. Hirst, Michael B. Frank, Kenneth M.

Sanderson, Victor Fischer, Dahlia Armon, Harriet Elinor Smith, Robert Pack Browning, Richard Bucci, Janet Leigh, and Sunny Gottberg. Each has contributed to the overall planning of the catalog as well as to the accuracy of the catalog entries. Ken Sanderson in particular has played an essential role in nearly every aspect of catalog design, implementation, and publication. Help with letter files, catalog entries, and checking was provided by student assistants Susan Gillman, Penny Johnson, Elizabeth Bishop, David Suchoff, Deborah Dyson, Renee Contratto, Eric Chacon-Arce, and David Goodwin. Penny Johnson provided valuable assistance in the initial stages of the catalog. The chief contribution, however, was made by Susan Gillman, who was essentially a co-editor on the preliminary (1982) version of the catalog through her work of creating thousands of entries, proofreading the catalog against document files, solving innumerable problems of letter identification, and helping with the planning of various aspects of the catalog.

Gracious, expert, and prompt assistance with the complexities of the larger Mark Twain holdings was provided by: Ruth Blair (Connecticut Historical Society), Lisa Browar (Vassar College), Herbert Cahoon (Pierpont Morgan Library), Bridget P. Carr (Houghton Library, Harvard University), Rita S. Faulders (St. John's Seminary), Carol Herron (James S. Copley Library), Sara S. Hodson (Henry E. Huntington Library), James H. Hutson (Library of Congress), Wynn Lee (Mark Twain Memorial), Marguerite L. Levine (American Foundation for the Blind), Kenneth A. Lohf (Columbia University), Jean F. Preston (Princeton University), Diana Royce (Stowe-Day Memorial Library and Historical Foundation), Judy H. Sahak (Honnold Library), David E. Schoonover and Mary Angelotti (Yale University), John D. Stinson (New York Public Library), Henry Sweets (Mark Twain Museum), Lola L. Szladits (New York Public Library, Albert A. and Henry W. Berg Collection), Saundra Taylor (Indiana University, Lilly Library), and Suzan Thompson (University of Virginia). Todd M. Axelrod, Robert Daley, Victor Jacobs, Theodore A. Koundakjian, and Thomas A. Tenney have contributed significantly to the accuracy and completeness of the catalog. James R.K. Kantor, Sondra Shair, and Kathleen Leles assisted with important aspects of the work. Kimberly McGarrity was a source of continual support and encouragement.

The catalog was designed by Sandy Drooker and the editor. University of California Press publication was coordinated by Rose Anne White, Series Manager, and Alain Henon, Managing Editor, of the Press's Serials Division. John Lowe, David Loy, and Mary Engle handled all aspects of production of master copies for both the printed volume and the microfiche, including the control of pagination and headings, on the Department of Library Automation (University of California) XEROX 6670 laser printer. The production of catalog files on the UNIX operating system was greatly aided by the staff of the University of California Computing Center, in particular Bill Tuthill, Bill Wells, Cliff Frost, Les Julian, and John Kephart. Michael D. Cooper, professor in the University's School of Library and Information Studies, provided models for programs used in the project, assisted with design, and provided essential help during the initial stages of implementation.

This volume is published as part of the ongoing activities of the Mark Twain Project funded by the National Endowment for the Humanities, the University of California (Berkeley) Library (Joseph D. Rosenthal, Librarian), The Bancroft Library, and private contributors. Special funding in the initial stages was provided by the Humanities Computing Service (Ann Hernandez, Director) and The Bancroft Library, whose Director, James D. Hart, has worked tirelessly in support of the Mark Twain Project and other scholarship in the humanities.

Guide

THE UNION CATALOG OF CLEMENS LETTERS is a record of documents, each of which meets three criteria:

It was written by, or on behalf of, Samuel L. Clemens (Mark Twain); Olivia L. Clemens; their daughters Olivia Susan (Susy), Clara, or Jean Clemens; or Isabel V. Lyon, Clemens's secretary from 1904 to 1909.

It was written during the author's lifetime (i.e., before 22 April 1910).

At least some fragment of the text has been found by the Mark Twain Project editors.

Excluded from the catalog, therefore, are letters written after 21 April 1910 by Clara Clemens (Gabrilowitsch, later Samossoud) and Isabel V. Lyon. Also excluded are the many letters for which no part of the text has been found, either because the letter has been destroyed, lost, or made otherwise inaccessible.

Excluded also are most published works or works intended for publication that happen to use the letter form. Otherwise, the catalog defines the term letter broadly to include not only the conventional written or telegraphed messages, but also autographs and inscriptions when they are dated or addressed, form letters, unfinished or unsent letters, and envelopes for which the letter itself seems not to survive.

CATALOG ENTRIES contain the following elements:

ADDRESSEES generally appear as last name, separated by a comma from the first name and middle initial. Cross-references are provided for alternate names for married women, pseudonymns, and other cases of alternate names.

DATES appear as year, month, and day, separated by periods, thus "1888.02.05" for 5 February 1888. Asterisks indicate unknown elements, thus "1888.02.**" for an unidentified day in February 1888. The date may be preceded by "aft" (after), "bef" (before), "o/a" (on or after), "o/b" (on or before), "ca" (circa), "pm" (postmarked), or "bet" (between, as in "bet 1888.02.01 & 1888.02.05").

WRITERS appear as two- or three-letter abbreviations, thus "SLC" for "Samuel L. Clemens." Two writers linked by "per" indicate that the second wrote on behalf of the first, thus "SLC per IVL"; when linked by "for" (in the Writer List only), the first wrote on behalf of the second, thus "IVL for SLC." "CC" represents Clara L. Clemens and "OLC" represents

Olivia L. Clemens throughout each of their lives, before and after marriage.

PLACES of writing appear in two parts, separated by a period. The first part is a two-letter abbreviation for a state or country (consisting of standard U.S. postal codes for states, and codes of the same type, usually the initial letters of a country's name, for countries). The second part is the name of a city, thus "FR.Paris." For letters written at sea, the name of a ship is preceded by "SH," thus "SH.Minnehaha." "NY.New York" has been assigned to letters written from the area now known as Manhattan; other New York City entries are listed under names of boroughs, with the exception of letters from Riverdale, listed as "NY.Riverdale."

CUES identify the document by quoting the first several words of the text that seem likely to distinguish it from other similar letters. These words usually come from the beginning of the text proper, omitting such things as dateline and salutation.

SOURCES of the most authoritative text of a letter are represented by 1) standard library symbols, thus "NN" for the New York Public Library; 2) symbols modeled after them, thus "YuB2" for the Tesla Museum, Belgrade; or 3) three-digit symbols for printed transcripts, thus "131" for the <u>New York Times</u>. Symbols in the first two classes may be followed by "(dr)" for a draft, "(ph)" for a photocopy of the manuscript, or "(tr)" for a non-printed transcript. Otherwise, the source text is the holograph that was sent or intended to be sent to the addressee. Telegrams completed at either the issuing or receiving office are considered to be manuscript documents, per unidentified amanuensis. In most cases, symbols for printed sources are followed by a colon and additional bibliographical information, thus "131:1895.01.01" for the 1 January 1895 issue of the <u>New York Times</u>. The numbers following the colon represent page numbers for books; dates of publication for serials and book dealer catalogs; dates of sale for auction house catalogs; and issue numbers for other serials and book dealer catalogs. An "f" following the bibliographical information indicates that the printing contains a photographic facsimile of part or all of the letter text. Two sources are provided when each has been determined to be essential to the restoration of the complete letter text. When the manuscript is divided between two sources, a cue will appear on the same line as each source, representing the part of the text at each one. When a letter text survives only in various transcripts, the most generally available source is listed, and the note "other sources" signals the existence of possibly supplementary versions.

ENTRY NUMBERS are five-digit, arbitarily assigned, unique identification points for documents.

NOTES describe various features of letters, most of which are self-explanatory. Certain conventions have been required to reduce the length of notes: thus "on Smith Oct 14" means "written on Smith's letter to SLC of October 14" and the year of Smith's letter is identical to that of the Clemens letter written on it; "on Oct 14 to Smith" means "written on SLC's letter to Smith of October 14," and again the year of Clemens's letter to Smith is the same as the year of the letter to which the note applies.

SIX LISTS of these catalog entries provide access by the key elements of addressee, writer (if other than SLC), date, place, source (subsorted by date), and source (subsorted by addressee). The latter five lists are supplied in microfiche. The left-to-right order of columns differs with each list, and represents in each case the order of primary and secondary sorting of entries. Note that the Writer List is sorted by writer abbreviation, thus "OLC" follows "IVL." Note also that in the Source-Date and Source-Addressee Lists, "CU-MARK(dr)," "CU-MARK(ph)," and "CU-MARK(tr)" are treated as distinct sources following "CU-MARK." For all other sources, however, entries for drafts, photocopies, and transcripts are interfiled (by date or addressee) with entries for manuscripts. A letter addressed to two persons will be listed twice in the Addressee List, once under each name; a letter written in two places appears twice in the Place List; a letter by two writers appears twice in the Writer List (but note that this list excludes all letters written solely by SLC); a letter written on two dates appears twice in the Date List; and a letter dispersed among two owners appears twice in the Source-Date and Source-Addressee Lists. A letter with a single source and addressed to two persons, however, will be listed only once in the Source-Addressee List, by its source, and then by the first addressee name. Similarly, a letter written on two dates and with a single source appears only once in the Source-Date List. For those letters exceeding the catalog's format of two writers or addressees, additional entries have been created to provide complete access. In these cases, additional entries (with different entry numbers) refer to the same letter text; each will contain a note such as "also by OLC" or "also to William D. Howells" to indicate that the entry is linked to another entry for that text.

The following characteristics of typography and sorting should be noted: umlauts, accents, other diacritical marks, and alternate type fonts were not available in this computer format; asterisks and other punctuation marks sort before numbers, thus "****.**.**" (meaning an unknown date) precedes identified dates in the Date List and lists subsorted by date; numbers sort before letters of the alphabet, thus source "NN7" precedes "NNAF"; and addressee names (as well as other words) beginning with "Mc" are <u>not</u> sorted as if they begin with "Mac."

THE APPENDIXES contain four aids to the use of the catalog:

The ABBREVIATIONS list contains abbreviations used in the catalog (with the exception of source symbols) as well as the names of writers, states, and countries for which abbreviations have been assigned.

The CITIES AND SHIPS list gives city and ship names alphabetically so that users of the Place List may learn the appropriate forms of particular place names.

The SOURCE NAMES list contains names of sources in alphabetical order, each followed by the symbol used for that source in the catalog. Added entries have been provided for titles of books and for variant forms of source names. Sources such as the "University of Colorado" are listed here under "University," and no double entry has been provided for "Colorado"; this conforms to _Symbols of American Libraries_ (12th ed., Washington: Library of Congress, 1980), which provides information about the construction of symbols.

The SOURCE SYMBOLS list is an alphabetical list of source symbols followed by full names and addresses for most collections and bibliographical information for printed sources.

Users of this catalog are urged to submit corrections to the Editor, Mark Twain Project, The Bancroft Library, University of California, Berkeley, CA 94720. Information about supplements to the catalog will be provided upon request.

Addressee List

ADDRESSEE	DATE	WRITER	PLACE	CUE	SOURCE	NUMBER/NOTES
Abbey, Henry	1869.08.21	SLC	NY.Buffalo	Yes, I have	CU-MARK(ph)	00337
Abbott, E.T.	1901.01.22	SLC	NY.New York	I was very	ViU(tr)	05977
Abell, E.W.	1889.09.22	SLC	CT.Hartford	The book has	CU-MARK(ph)	03942
Aberdeen, Earl of	*	*	*	*	*	11127 see Gordon, John C.
Aberdeen, University of	1894.**.**	SLC	Unknown	Mr. C. desires	CU-MARK(dr)	04663
Accident Insurance Co.	1908.08.**	SLC	NY.New York	I shall be	CU-MARK(dr)	08067
Ackerman, Edward P.	1871.07.31	SLC	NY.Elmira	My friend Beecher	NN	00641
Acklom, A.J. & Acklom, Mr.	1896.03.07	SLC	II.Jaipur	Thank you ever	ViU	05027
Acklom, Mr.	1896.03.07	SLC	II.Jaipur	Your telegram came	ViU	05028
Acklom, Mr. & Acklom, A.J.	1896.03.07	SLC	II.Jaipur	Thank you ever	ViU	05027
Adams, Charles F.	1877.12.20	SLC	CT.Hartford	I thank you	ViU	01513
Adams, John	1898.12.05	SLC	AU.Vienna	Like it? Most	CLU-S/C	05159
Adams, John D.	1895.01.23	SLC	FR.Paris	I enclose a	WU(ph)	04837
Adams, John D.	1895.05.10	SLC	FR.Paris	The proofs (for	ViU	04876
Adams, John D.	1895.06.13	SLC	NY.Elmira	Proof of "Mental	NHemH	05005
Adams, John D.	1895.07.03	SLC	NY.Elmira	I'm glad we	NHemH	04969
Adams, J.Q.	o/a 1906.03.31	SLC per IVL	NY.New York	Come--am normally	CU-MARK(dr)	07408 on Adams Mar 31
Adams, L.T.	1879.10.29	SLC	CT.Hartford	Being under the	CU-MARK	01704 dr of Oct 29 to Baker enc
Adams, Maude	****.**.**	SLC	NY.New York	The essential point	CU-MARK	09061
Adams, Samuel H.	1906.08.31	SLC	NH.Dublin	I think that	NN-B(tr)	07513 other sources
Agnew, Cornelius R.	1875.06.07	SLC	CT.Hartford	We have canvassed	OKentU	01238
Agnew, Cornelius R.	1875.06.23	SLC	CT.Hartford	I shipped the	OKentU	01243
Agnew, Cornelius R.	1875.06.30	SLC	CT.Hartford	Yours just received	OKentU	01245

ADDRESSEE		DATE	WRITER	PLACE	CUE	SOURCE	NUMBER/NOTES
Agnew, Cornelius R.		1875.11.26	OLC	CT.Hartford	Mr Clemens has	OKentU	01284
Agnew, Joy	ca	1907.08.31	SLC	NY.Tuxedo Park	Unto you greeting	CU-MARK(tr)	07821 SLC tr
Akers, Elizabeth C.		1900.07.08	SLC	EN.London	The story is	MeWC	08908
Akers, Elizabeth C.		1901.07.17	SLC	NY.Saranac Lake	Of your suggested	MeWC	06091
Akers, Elizabeth C.		1901.07.30	SLC	NY.Saranac Lake	Thirty-five years	MeWC	06100
Akers, Elizabeth C.		1905.02.04	SLC per IVL	NY.New York	Mrs. Clemens and	MeWC	08920
Albany Journal		1885.07.11	SLC	NY.Elmira	What is said	CU-MARK(tr)	03256
Albright, Joseph J.	pm	1874.07.17	SLC	NY.Elmira	This certificate	NBuHi	01112
Alden, Henry M.		1889.05.16	SLC	CT.Hartford	I wish to	CU-MARK	03892
Alden, Henry M.		1891.05.11	SLC	CT.Hartford	See if this	CU-MARK(ph)	04204
Alden, Henry M.		1892.10.13	SLC	IT.Florence	I am going P.S. No, upon	107:1926.02.17 CU-MARK(ph)	10567
Alden, Henry M.		1892.11.24	SLC	IT.Florence	I sent you	157:1924.03.03	09770
Alden, Henry M.		1894.12.10	SLC	FR.Paris	I'm afraid I've	ViU	04823
Alden, Henry M.		1895.05.30	SLC	NY.Elmira	I am laid	107:1925.11.18	09456 other sources
Alden, Henry M.		1898.11.02	SLC	AU.Vienna	That little thing	CtY	05456
Alden, Henry M.		1899.10.30	SLC	EN.London	Yes, I got	CU-MARK(tr)	05696
Alden, Henry M. & Gilder, Richard W.		1903.07.21	SLC	NY.Elmira	Although I have	NN-B	08234 also to others
Alden, Henry M.		1906.11.**	SLC	NY.New York	it is a	114:800	07559
Alden, William L.		1887.05.28	SLC	CT.Hartford	I thank you	ViU	03574
Alden, William L.		1905.01.28	SLC	NY.New York	I thank you	ViU	06987
Aldrich, Lilian W.		****.**.**	CC	NY.New York	I am sure	MH-H	08721
Aldrich, Lilian W.		****.**.**	OLC	CT.Hartford	I find Mr	MH-H	08252
Aldrich, Lilian W.		1874.03.09	SLC	CT.Hartford	With regards not	MH-H	10843 inscription
Aldrich, Lilian W.		1883.12.14	OLC	CT.Hartford	I have put	MH-H	02862
Aldrich, Lilian W.		1883.12.23	OLC	CT.Hartford	It is shameful	MH-H	02873
Aldrich, Lilian W.		1884.01.21	OLC	CT.Hartford	I was glad	MH-H	02895

Aldrich, Lilian W.		1884.04.20	OLC	CT.Hartford	I should like	MH-H	08830
Aldrich, Lilian W.		1884.11.02	OLC	CT.Hartford	I regret that	MH-H	03017
Aldrich, Lilian W.		1886.02.07	SLC	CT.Hartford	Your note has	MH-H	03366
Aldrich, Lilian W. & Aldrich, Thomas B.		1900.10.22	SLC	NY.New York	It is lovely	MH-H	05881
Aldrich, Lilian W.		1900.12.19	OLC	NY.New York	Thank you heartily	MH-H	10593
Aldrich, Lilian W.		1901.**.**	CC	NY.New York	It is lovely	MH-H	05944
Aldrich, Lilian W.		1901.01.08	OLC	NY.New York	I have had	MH-H	05960
Aldrich, Lilian W.		1901.01.20	OLC	NY.New York	To think that	MH-H	05967
Aldrich, Lilian W.		1901.01.31	OLC	NY.New York	Mr Aldrich says	MH-H	05986
Aldrich, Lilian W.		1901.02.06	OLC	NY.New York	We were disapointed	MH-H	05989
Aldrich, Lilian W. & Aldrich, Thomas B.		1901.12.21	SLC	NY.Riverdale	With affectionate	MH-H	06192
Aldrich, Lilian W. & Aldrich, Thomas B.	ca	1904.06.21	SLC	IT.Florence	For what you	MH-H	06884 form letter
Aldrich, Lilian W. & Aldrich, Thomas B.		1905.05.17	SLC	MA.Boston	I came from	MH-H	07044
Aldrich, Lilian W.		1905.09.16	SLC	NH.Dublin	You don't need	MH-H	07136
Aldrich, Lilian W. & Aldrich, Thomas B.		1905.12.14	SLC	NY.New York	To you, &	MH-H	07253 form letter
Aldrich, Lilian W. & Aldrich, Thomas B.		1906.01.11	SLC	NY.New York	A happy voyage	MH-H	07303 telegram
Aldrich, Lilian W. & Aldrich, Thomas B.		1906.04.26	SLC	NY.New York	I rejoice with	MH-H	07435
Aldrich, Lilian W.		1907.03.21	SLC	NY.New York	I have just	CU-MARK(dr) MH-H	07676 telegram
Aldrich, Lilian W.		1907.03.29	SLC	NY.New York	I cannot realize	MH-H	07681
Aldrich, Lilian W.		1908.06.15	SLC	NY.New York	It is lovely	MH-H	08031
Aldrich, Lilian W.		1909.12.26	SLC	CT.Redding	To all friends	MH-H	08519 form letter
Aldrich, Thomas B.		****.**.**	OLC	Unknown	P.S. I find	MH-H	01746
Aldrich, Thomas B.		****.**.**	SLC	Unknown	I know how	VtMiM	07546
Aldrich, Thomas B.		1871.01.15	SLC	NY.Buffalo	You stated, in	MoSW	00559

ADDRESSEE	DATE	WRITER	PLACE	CUE	SOURCE	NUMBER/NOTES
Aldrich, Thomas B.	1871.01.22	SLC	NY.Buffalo	Please do not	MH-H	00560
Aldrich, Thomas B.	1871.01.27	SLC	NY.Buffalo	No indeed, don't	MH-H	00567
Aldrich, Thomas B.	1874.03.08 & 1874.03.16	SLC	CT.Hartford	My boy, you	MoSW	01063
Aldrich, Thomas B.	1874.03.24	SLC	CT.Hartford	All right, my next book	MH-H IC3	01068
Aldrich, Thomas B.	1874.03.25	SLC	CT.Hartford	You see (page	MH-H	01069
Aldrich, Thomas B.	1874.06.08	SLC	NY.Elmira	Many thanks for I hoped you	IC3 MH-H	10331 misdated, see July
Aldrich, Thomas B.	1874.07.08	SLC	NY.Elmira	I hoped you Many thanks for	MH-H IC3	01108 misdated June
Aldrich, Thomas B.	1874.12.18	SLC	CT.Hartford	I read the	VtMiM	01166
Aldrich, Thomas B.	1874.12.31	SLC	CT.Hartford	We implore the	MH-H	01171
Aldrich, Thomas B.	1875.10.20	SLC	CT.Hartford	Welcome back! I	MiD	01274
Aldrich, Thomas B.	1876.01.28	SLC	CT.Hartford	I'm perfectly delighted	NN5	01303
Aldrich, Thomas B.	1877.06.03	SLC	CT.Hartford	Behold I have	VtMiM	01437
Aldrich, Thomas B.	ca 1877.11.17	SLC	CT.Hartford	Your book came	VtMiM	01507
Aldrich, Thomas B.	1879.05.25	SLC	FR.Paris	Tauchnitz replies	IC3	01658
Aldrich, Thomas B.	1879.11.07	SLC	CT.Hartford	On my return	MH-H	01709
Aldrich, Thomas B.	1880.01.08	SLC	CT.Hartford	Been expecting you	MH-H	01752
Aldrich, Thomas B.	1880.09.15	SLC	NY.Elmira	Thank you ever	VtMiM	01834
Aldrich, Thomas B.	1881.09.19	SLC	NY.Elmira	This is one	MH-H	02037
Aldrich, Thomas B.	1881.11.02	SLC	CT.Hartford	I did write	MH-H	02080
Aldrich, Thomas B.	1884.04.10	SLC	NY.New York	Won't you please	MH-H	02949
Aldrich, Thomas B.	1884.04.22	SLC	CT.Hartford	I never had	MH-H	08831
Aldrich, Thomas B.	1884.10.29	SLC	CT.Hartford	Your note came	MH-H	03013
Aldrich, Thomas B.	1889.11.19	SLC	CT.Hartford	It's a lovely	MH-H	03972
Aldrich, Thomas B.	1891.02.21	SLC	CT.Hartford	I thank you	MH-H	04173
Aldrich, Thomas B.	1893.12.06	SLC	NY.New York	If I had	MH-H	04520
Aldrich, Thomas B.	1898.06.29	SLC	AU.Kaltenleut.	It is odd	MH-H	05406
Aldrich, Thomas B.	1898.06.30	SLC	AU.Kaltenleut.	Why, it has	MH-H	05407

Aldrich, Thomas B. & Aldrich, Lilian W.		1900.10.22	SLC	NY.New York	It is lovely	MH-H	05881
Aldrich, Thomas B.		1900.10.27	OLC	NY.New York	We are here	MH-H	05888
Aldrich, Thomas B.		1900.11.13	SLC	NY.New York	I thank you	MH-H	05904
Aldrich, Thomas B.	pm	1901.02.14	SLC	NY.New York	The nation! You	MH-H	10117 on envelope
Aldrich, Thomas B. & Aldrich, Lilian W.		1901.12.21	SLC	NY.Riverdale	With affectionate	MH-H	06192
Aldrich, Thomas B.		1901.12.30	SLC	NY.Riverdale	Fore George I	MH-H	06199
Aldrich, Thomas B.		1902.09.11	SLC	ME.York Harbor	Mrs. Clemens, who	MH-H	06430
Aldrich, Thomas B.		1902.12.07	SLC	NY.Riverdale	Three of us	MH-H	06504
Aldrich, Thomas B.		1902.12.22	SLC	NY.Riverdale	I know of	MH-H	06524
Aldrich, Thomas B.		1903.01.23	SLC	NY.Riverdale	Be Jazes! as	MH-H	06571
Aldrich, Thomas B.		1904.02.14	SLC	IT.Florence	The publishers sent	MH-H	06793
Aldrich, Thomas B.		1904.03.21	SLC	IT.Florence	I know--&	MH-H	06812
Aldrich, Thomas B.	pm	1904.03.29	SLC	IT.Florence	*	MH-H	10152 envelope only
Aldrich, Thomas B.		1904.06.06	SLC	IT.Florence	We are crushed	MH-H	06856
Aldrich, Thomas B. & Aldrich, Lilian W.	ca	1904.06.21	SLC	IT.Florence	For what you	MH-H	06884 form letter
Aldrich, Thomas B. & Aldrich, Lilian W.		1905.05.17	SLC	MA.Boston	I came from	MH-H	07044
Aldrich, Thomas B.		1905.10.27	SLC	MA.Boston	with the love	MH-H	10845 inscription
Aldrich, Thomas B. & Aldrich, Lilian W.		1905.12.14	SLC	NY.New York	To you, &	MH-H	07253 form letter
Aldrich, Thomas B.		1905.12.26	SLC	NY.New York	I am very	MH-H	07272
Aldrich, Thomas B. & Aldrich, Lilian W.		1906.01.11	SLC	NY.New York	A happy voyage	MH-H	07303 telegram
Aldrich, Thomas B. & Aldrich, Lilian W.		1906.04.26	SLC	NY.New York	I rejoice with	MH-H	07435
Aldrich, Thomas B.		1906.10.02	SLC	NH.Dublin	I have just	MH-H	07534
Aldrich, Thomas B.		1906.10.26	SLC	NY.New York	It is with	MH-H	07556
Aldrich, Thomas B.	o/a	1906.11.08	SLC	NY.New York	Opened & read	CU-MARK	07565

ADDRESSEE	DATE	WRITER	PLACE	CUE	SOURCE	NUMBER/NOTES
Aldrich, Thomas B.	1906.12.01	SLC per ABP	NY.New York	Mr. Clemens asked	MAnP(tr)	07580
Alexander, Eben	1894.06.18	SLC	FR.Paris	Your kind favor	CU-MARK(ph)	04740
Alexander, Elizabeth A.	1908.12.30	SLC	CT.Redding	Good! Ever since	NjP	08192
Alexander, John W.	1888.08.10	SLC	NY.Elmira	I am with	NjP	03749
Alexander, John W.	1901.03.21	SLC	NY.New York	Is it strictly	NjP	06022
Alexander, John W.	1901.04.21	SLC	NY.Saranac Lake	I do not	NjP	06040
Alexander, John W.	1902.10.24	SLC	NY.Riverdale	I very much	Mo2	08884
Alexander, John W.	1903.04.10	SLC	NY.Riverdale	I have an	NjP	06620
Alexander, William V.	1903.09.26	OLC	NY.Elmira	As Mr Clemens	ViU	06732
Allen, Elizabeth A.	*	*	*	*	*	11129 see Akers, Elizabeth C.
Allen, Helen S.	****.**.**	SLC	Unknown	with apologies from	ODa2	10383 inscription
Allen, Helen S.	1908.04.25	SLC	NY.New York	I miss you	NN-B	08280
Allen, Helen S.	1909.10.16	SLC	CT.Redding	with the love	110:1965.09.30	10381 inscription
Allen, Helen S.	1909.11.25	SLC	BE.Hamilton	Helen Dear. This	116:1970.06.11	08499 inscription
Allen, Helen S.	1910.02.14	SLC	BE.Hamilton	I know a	138:1913.08	11111 poem inscription
Allen, Helen S.	1910.03.06	SLC	BE.Hamilton	Received of S.L.C.	ODa2	09914
Allen, Henry S.	1891.05.02	SLC per FGW	CT.Hartford	Mr. Clemens desires	CU-MARK(tr)	08620 FGW tr
Allen, Horace N.	1901.12.04	SLC	NY.Riverdale	I am very	NN	06180
Allen, Horace N.	1901.12.30	SLC	NY.Riverdale	Your letter	NN	06200
Allen, Horace N.	1902.01.02	SLC	NY.Riverdale	It is a	NN	06215
Allen, Mrs. William	1910.01.31	SLC	BE.Hamilton	We ought never	ODa2	10382 inscription
Allen, William H.	****.**.**	SLC	CT.Redding	*	CU-MARK	09479 envelope only
Allison, Henry D.	1906.09.** or 1906.10.**	SLC	NH.Dublin	Let us save	CU-MARK(ph)	09430 inscription

American Academy A&L		1905.01.24	SLC per IVL	NY.New York	I cast my	NNAL	06984
American Civic Alliance		1909.11.18	SLC per ABP	CT.Redding	Mr. Clemens directs	CU-MARK(tr)	08493
American Publishing Co.		1876.04.12	SLC	CT.Hartford	Statement rec'd--but	MoPeS	01321
American Publishing Co.		1876.06.24	SLC	NY.Elmira	I have just	CtHC	01346
American Publishing Co.		1876.08.01	SLC	NY.Elmira	Please send me	N	01352
American Publishing Co.		1877.05.12	SLC	CT.Hartford	Please send Cloth	Mo2	01429
American Publishing Co.		1881.03.23	SLC	CT.Hartford	Send me several	MoPeS	01930
American Publishing Co.		1883.05.17	SLC	CT.Hartford	Please send A	CtY	02387
American Publishing Co.		1884.08.11	SLC	NY.Elmira	Unless you bring	ViU	01520
American Publishing Co.		1895.07.01	OLC	NY.Elmira	Until further orders	CtY	04919
American Publishing Co.	bef	1897.03.24	SLC	EN.London	My cable address	CtY	05189
American Publishing Co.		1903.04.28	SLC	NY.Riverdale	War suspended. Truce	CtY	06635
American Publishing Co.	aft	1903.06.10	SLC	NY.Riverdale	In the 2	CtHi	10877
American Publishing Co.		1903.10.23	SLC & OLC	NY.New York	Until further notice	CtY	06754
Anderson, Edwin H.	o/a	1903.04.20	SLC	Unknown	The Harpers considered	CU-MARK(dr)	06624 on Anderson Apr 20
Andrews, Charles B.		1880.02.07	SLC	CT.Hartford	Your Excellency's name	CtLHi	01759
Andrews, Daisy	o/a	1906.08.27	SLC per IVL	NH.Dublin	I hereby authorize	CU-MARK(dr)	07505 on Megrue Aug 27
Andrews, William S.		1873.09.10	SLC	EN.London	I am moving	VtMiM	00960
Andrews, William S.		1874.03.28	SLC	CT.Hartford	Dialect is your	VtMiM	01070
Anhalt, Lawrence J.		1903.03.20	SLC	NY.Riverdale	I could not	CU-MARK(tr)	06603 SLC tr
Anhalt, Lawrence J.		1903.03.31	SLC	NY.Riverdale	No, there are	CU-MARK(tr)	06611 SLC tr
Ann, Alfred E.		1900.02.**	SLC	EN.London	We ought never	CU-MARK(ph)	08856
Ann, Alfred E.		1900.02.23	SLC	EN.London	Upon sober second	CU-MARK	05761
Anongma, Miss		1907.10.23	SLC per IVL	NY.Tuxedo Park	This is to	CU-MARK(tr)	07856 IVL tr

ADDRESSEE		DATE	WRITER	PLACE	CUE	SOURCE	NUMBER/NOTES
Anthony, Alfred W.		****.**.**	SLC	CT.Hartford	With pleasure	CU-MARK(ph)	10972 inscription
Anthony, A.V.S.		1881.03.03	SLC	CT.Hartford	Been away till	CU-MARK(ph)	01920
Anthony, A.V.S.		1881.03.09	SLC	CT.Hartford	It makes me	CU-MARK(tr)	01926
Anthony, A.V.S.		1881.04.28	SLC	CT.Hartford	Yes, I'll hand	CU-MARK	01939
Anthony, A.V.S.		1881.06.03	SLC	CT.Hartford	Are you a	PHi	01967
Anthony, A.V.S.		1882.01.04	SLC	CT.Hartford	with sentiments of	122:1936.01.29	09318 inscription
Anthony, A.V.S.		1883.10.04	SLC	CT.Hartford	We the Clemenses	MH-H	02847
Anthony, Edward		1907.10.02	SLC per IVL	NY.Tuxedo Park	Mr. Clemens asks me	CU-MARK(dr)	07840 on Anthony Sept 29
Apfelstedt, Paul		1877.08.02	SLC	CT.Hartford	From my study	ViU	01460 date uncertain
Appleton (D.) & Co.	bet &	1870.05.20 1870.07.04	SLC	NY.Elmira	The terms of	157:1914.06.03	09767
Appleton, D.F.		1877.12.05	SLC	CT.Hartford	Remembering Mr. Curtis's	109:84	01508
Appleton, Henry C. or Appleton, William W.		1901.07.30	SLC	NY.Saranac Lake	I, also, think	NNC	06101
Appleton, William W. or Appleton, Henry C.		1901.07.30	SLC	NY.Saranac Lake	I, also, think	NNC	06101
Archer, Sally & Parsons, Floyd		****.**.**	SLC	Unknown	Yes, I received	CU-MARK	08744
Archer, William		1900.08.02	SLC	EN.London	Your letter has	TxU	05847
Archer, William		1900.08.08	SLC	EN.London	We of this	Uk	05848
Archer, William	pm	1904.06.22	SLC	IT.Florence	For what you	Uk	06878 form letter
Armstrong Association		1906.01.22	SLC	NY.New York	Please admit my	CU-MARK	08775
Armsworth, H.H.		1901.08.31	SLC	NY.Saranac Lake	It may not	CU-MARK	06128
Arnot, Matthias H.	bet &	1890.03.29 1890.04.03	SLC	CT.Hartford	No--No, I	CU-MARK	04035
Arnot, Matthias H.		1890.08.09	SLC	NY.Tannersville	This enclosed letter	CU-MARK(tr)	09085 SLC tr
Arnot, Matthias H.		1891.04.27	SLC	CT.Hartford	I have in	CU-MARK(tr)	04196
Ashcroft, Ralph W.	pm	1904.10.24	SLC	NY.New York	These are the	MiD	06933 on envelope

Ashcroft, Ralph W.	o/a	1905.08.28	SLC per IVL	NH.Dublin	Mr. Clemens's advice	CU-MARK(dr)	07118 on Ashcroft Aug 28
Ashcroft, Ralph W.		1905.09.02	SLC per IVL	NH.Dublin	Do not put	CU-MARK(tr)	07126 IVL tr
Ashcroft, Ralph W.		1906.09.27	SLC	NY.New York	The Colonel has	CU-MARK(ph)	07531
Ashcroft, Ralph W.		1907.06.19	SLC	EN.London	I have arranged	CU-MARK	07759 on Unwin June 19
Ashcroft, Ralph W.	o/a	1907.06.22	SLC	EN.London	Explain to Sir	CU-MARK	07766 on Reid June 22
Ashcroft, Ralph W.		1907.07.05	SLC	EN.London	Ashcroft, the puzzle	CU-MARK(tr)	11065
Ashcroft, Ralph W.	ca	1908.10.07	SLC	CT.Redding	Greeting and Salutation	InU-Li	10824 form letter
Associated Press		1909.12.24	SLC	CT.Redding	I hear the	MoSW	08516
Astor, Nancy L.		1908.04.28	SLC	NY.New York	I am very	Uk4	07988
Atchison, Charles L.		1900.09.25	SLC	EN.London	I do not	Uk(tr)	05868
Atlantic & Pacific Tel.	o/a	1881.02.01	SLC	CT.Hartford	All right--I	CU-MARK	09592 on Atlantic bill o/a Feb 1
Atterbury, J.W.		1886.01.20	SLC	CT.Hartford	I cannot think	MoHM	03358
Austin, Kate V.		1878.01.12	SLC	NY.Elmira	Your letter has	Mo2	01523
Australian public		1881.07.24	SLC	CT.Branford	During the present	162:1881.10.15	01990
Author's Club Secretary		1896.09.17	SLC	EN.London	For economical reasons	NPla2	05113
Avebury, Baron		*	*	*	*	*	11128 see Lubbock, John
B., Mrs.	ca	1909.01.18	IVL per MLH	CT.Redding	Miss L. asks	CtHMTH(dr)	08296 for SLC
Bacheller & Johnson		1895.01.16	SLC	FR.Paris	I shall be	105:1965.10.26	04835
Bacheller & Johnson		1895.01.23	SLC	FR.Paris	If I had	CU-MARK(ph)	04838
Bacheller, Irving		1887.01.25	SLC	CT.Hartford	Enclosed please find	CU-MARK(tr)	03520
Bacheller, Irving		1900.12.14	SLC	NY.New York	The book has	ViU	05931
Bacheller, Irving		1900.12.21	SLC	NY.New York	It is with	ViU	08605

ADDRESSEE	DATE	WRITER	PLACE	CUE	SOURCE	NUMBER/NOTES
Bacon, Robert	1905.11.28	SLC	NY.New York	For lack of	ViU	07222
Bacon, Robert	1905.12.06	SLC	NY.New York	I am very	ViU	07235
Bacon, Robert	1905.12.15	SLC	NY.New York	I am expecting	ViU	07256
Badeau, Adam	1873.06.15	SLC	EN.London	Mrs. Clemens was	MH-H	00927
Badeau, Adam	1873.07.04	SLC	EN.London	Either the 11th	NRU	00942
Badlam, Alexander	1889.02.09	SLC	CT.Hartford	Yes, that was	CU-MARK	03860
Bagby, George W.	1881.01.07	SLC	CT.Hartford	Unfortunately I am	ViHi	01995
Baillie, J.E.	1874.02.13	SLC	CT.Hartford	I am sorry	UkL6	01047
Bainton, George	1888.10.15	SLC	CT.Hartford	Your inquiry has	Mo2	03791
Baird, Loni & Whitmore, Franklin G.	ca 1900.04.08	SLC & OLC	EN.London	Regarding the main	CU-MARK	08719
Baker, Edith E.	1907.05.02	SLC	NY.New York	I am back	CU-MARK(ph)	07706
Baker, George	1879.10.27	SLC	CT.Hartford	We reached America	CU-MARK(dr)	02408 dr enc in Oct 29 to Adams
Baker, George B.	aft 1906.10.21	SLC per IVL	NY.New York	I am seldom	CU-MARK(dr)	07550
Baldwin, James M.	1900.06.05	SLC	EN.London	I shall like	UkOxU	05813
Baldwin, James M.	1900.06.06	SLC	EN.London	The nine train	174:111	05815
Baldwin, James M.	1900.06.07	SLC	EN.London	I am sending	UkOxU	05817
Baldwin, Mrs. W.	bet 1892.09.23 & 1893.06.14	SLC	IT.Florence	I accept with	NNPM	08603
Baldwin, Wilberforce W.	bet 1892.09.23 & 1893.06.14	JC	IT.Florence	I am out	NNPM	08602
Baldwin, Wilberforce W.	1892.12.11	SLC	IT.Florence	I shall see	NNPM	04305
Baldwin, Wilberforce W.	1892.12.28	SLC	IT.Florence	Mrs. Clemens is	NNPM	04315
Baldwin, Wilberforce W.	pm 1893.06.04	SLC	IT.Florence	Please come out	NNPM	04411
Baldwin, Wilberforce W.	bet 1903.11.** & 1904.06.**	CC	IT.Florence	we shall be	NNPM	08600 fragment
Baldwin, Wilberforce W.	bet 1903.11.** & 1904.06.**	CC	IT.Florence	It does seem	NNPM	08601
Baldwin, Wilberforce W.	bet 1903.11.** & 1904.06.**	SLC	IT.Florence	I hope you	297:102	08599

Baldwin, Wilberforce W.		1904.05.19	SLC	IT.Florence	Mrs. Clemens, with	NNPM	06837
Baldwin, Wilberforce W.		1904.06.06	SLC	IT.Florence	She passed peacefully	NNPM	06857 telegram
Baldwin, Wilberforce W.	pm	1904.06.22	SLC	IT.Florence	For what you	NNPM	06882 form letter
Ballantine, Sergeant		****.**.**	SLC	Unknown	Paper and stamp	296:196	08738
Bancroft, Hubert H.		1905.05.27	SLC	NH.Dublin	I thank you	CU-MARK	07049
Bancroft, John H.		1870.**.**	SLC	NY.Buffalo	Master Jno. H.	107:1914.04.23	02794
Bangs, John K.	to	1899.03.01 1899.03.12	SLC	AU.Vienna	I am very	NN-B	05600
Bangs, John K.		1899.04.27	SLC	AU.Vienna	Do you think	140:205	05208
Bangs, John K.		1900.10.22	SLC	NY.New York	After Wednesday I	WU	05882
Bangs, John K.		1900.11.20	SLC	NY.New York	My wife has	NNC	05911
Bangs, John K.		1902.01.09	SLC	NY.Riverdale	As regards that	CU-MARK	06228 typed form letter
Barber, Julia L.		1907.04.**	SLC	Unknown	To be good	107:1916.03.20	09542 inscription
Barbour, Thomas S.		1905.09.22	SLC	NH.Dublin	Am sending something	InU-Li	10820
Barbour, Thomas S.		1905.09.23	SLC per IVL	NH.Dublin	Mr. Clemens directs	CU-MARK(tr)	07146 IVL tr
Barbour, Thomas S.	o/a	1905.10.14	SLC per IVL	NH.Dublin	Perhaps it would	CU-MARK(dr)	07175 on Barbour Oct 14
Barbour, Thomas S.		1905.10.27	SLC	MA.Boston	I shall go	WU	07188
Barbour, Thomas S.	o/a	1905.11.23	SLC per IVL	NY.New York	Put it in	CU-MARK(dr)	07217 on Barbour Nov 23
Barbour, Thomas S.		1906.01.08	SLC	NY.New York	I have retired	NN-B	08249
Barbour, Thomas S.	ca	1906.01.08	SLC	NY.New York	What to do	CU-MARK(dr)	08674
Barbour, Thomas S.		1906.02.10	SLC per IVL	NY.New York	I am so	NN-B	08251
Barker, Darwin R.		1880.11.15	SLC	CT.Hartford	I have received	NFred	01853
Barnes, A.M.		1892.12.23	SLC	IT.Florence	It is carefully	155:1976.02.24	10448
Barnes, George E.		1869.09.21	SLC	NY.Buffalo	I have been	MHi	00354

ADDRESSEE		DATE	WRITER	PLACE	CUE	SOURCE	NUMBER/NOTES
Barnes, Henry B.		1885.01.25	SLC	CT.Hartford	It would give	CtY	03133
Barnes, Henry B.		1886.11.20	SLC	CT.Hartford	Yes, I would	CtY	03483
Barnes, Henry B.		1886.12.06	SLC	CT.Hartford	Those original "terms"	CtY	03493
Barnett, C.W.		1899.10.25	SLC	EN.London	These have the	UkL6	05694
Barnett, H. Walter		1895.10.03	SLC	AS.Melbourne	My wife is	TxU	04966
Barnum & Bailey		1910.04.03	SLC	BE.Hamilton	I am very	138:1913.08	11112
Barnum, Phineas T.		1874.02.19	SLC	CT.Hartford	It is an	IC4	01051
Barnum, Phineas T.		1875.02.03	SLC	CT.Hartford	I have been	TxU	01188
Barnum, Phineas T.		1875.05.24	SLC	CT.Hartford	I was delighted	CtB	01236
Barnum, Phineas T.		1875.06.07	SLC	CT.Hartford	If nothing happens	ViU	01240
Barr, Robert	ca	1897.09.18	SLC	SW.Weggis	I read through	164:1982.10.03	10600
Barr, Robert	pm	1897.09.18	SLC	SW.Weggis	Many thanks for	CU-MARK(ph)	10669
Barr, Robert		1897.09.29	SLC	AU.Vienna	I like your	CU-MARK(ph)	05293
Barrett, Arabel M.		1892.12.18	SLC	IT.Florence	I am always	MWelC	04484
Barrett, Kate W.		1906.03.23	SLC	NY.New York	If I dared	NN-B(tr)	07399
Barrett, Oliver R.		1890.02.19	SLC	CT.Hartford	You must make	TxU	04020
Barrie, James M.		****.12.26	SLC	NY.New York	Merry Christmas, O	CtY	10937
Barrows, Mr.		1898.04.12	SLC	AU.Vienna	In answer to	CU-MARK	08638 unsent
Bartholdi Pedestal Fund	bef	1883.12.04	SLC	Unknown	You know my	131:1883.12.04	02861
Bartlett, Matthew H.		1877.10.**	SLC	CT.Hartford	who has robbed	CtHMTH	09280 inscription
Bartlett, Matthew H.		1881.10.**	SLC	CT.Hartford	With compts of	TxAu3	11172 inscription
Bartlett, Miss		****.**.**	SLC	CT.Hartford	Mrs. Clemens &	CtHC	07451
Barton, J.H.		1872.01.04	SLC	OH.Dayton	It seems an	CU-MARK	00705 enc in Jan 4 to OLC
Bassett, Norman D.		1906.04.**	SLC	NY.New York	Few things are	WU	10736 inscription
Bates, Blanche		1903.10.23	SLC	NY.New York	None genuine without	260:1958.07.15	06755 inscription

Bath Club Secretary		1907.06.19	SLC per RWA	EN.London	Mr. Clemens directs	CU-MARK(tr)	07757 RWA tr
Battarns, Mr. & West Point Mess	o/a	1907.01.22	SLC per IVL	NY.New York	I thank you	CU-MARK(dr)	10965
Baudius, Mrs. W.		1899.05.25	SLC	AU.Vienna	with the kindest	105:1944.03.23	09431 inscription; other sources
Baxter, Sylvester		****.**.**	SLC	Unknown	Compliments of S.L.	107:1925.12.11	09554 inscription
Baxter, Sylvester		1887.05.28	SLC	CT.Hartford	You did not	MB	03577
Baxter, Sylvester		1889.11.14	SLC	CT.Hartford	I was Howells's	NN-B	02698
Baxter, Sylvester		1889.11.20	SLC	CT.Hartford	Another throne has	NN-B	02699
Baxter, Sylvester		1889.11.22	SLC	CT.Hartford	I am telegraphing	NN-B	02700
Baxter, Sylvester		1889.11.24	SLC	CT.Hartford	It is a	NN-B	02701
Baxter, Sylvester		1889.11.26	SLC	CT.Hartford	Pictures--a good	NN-B	02702
Baxter, Sylvester		1889.12.03	SLC	CT.Hartford	No, I am	NN-B	02703
Baxter, Sylvester		1889.12.19	SLC	CT.Hartford	It was an	NN-B	02705
Baxter, Sylvester		1900.10.26	SLC	NY.New York	It was a	114:701	05886
Beach, Emeline B.		1867.12.05	SLC	DC.Washington	I suppose I	CCamarSJ	00169
Beach, Emeline B.		1868.01.08	SLC	DC.Washington	It is singular	CCamarSJ	00174
Beach, Emeline B.		1868.01.31	SLC	DC.Washington	It is all	CCamarSJ	00187
Beach, Emeline B.		1868.02.10	SLC	DC.Washington	Shipmate, Avast!	CCamarSJ	00192
Beach, Emeline B.		1874.02.04	SLC	CT.Hartford	Welcome home--I	CCamarSJ	01044
Beach, Emeline B.	aft	1905.02.28	SLC	NY.New York	The letter has	CCamarSJ	07010
Beach, Miss		1886.10.17	OLC	CT.Hartford	Here we are	ViU	03468
Beach, Moses S.		1871.11.16	SLC	ME.Portland	My wife has	ViU	00675
Beale, Mary H.		1879.09.08	SLC	NY.Elmira	my correspondence is	116:1983.11.03	10601 other sources
Bean, George L.		1907.12.18	SLC per IVL	NY.New York	Mr. Clemens asks	UPB	10867
Bean, Vernon L.		1900.10.27	SLC	NY.New York	And so that	CU-MARK(ph)	10572
Beard, Beatrice A.	ca	1908.**.**	SLC	Unknown	Mark Twain	111:373	09380 inscription

ADDRESSEE	DATE	WRITER	PLACE	CUE	SOURCE	NUMBER/NOTES
Beard, Daniel C.	****.**.**	SLC	Unknown	This to Beard	DLC	08739 on envelope
Beard, Daniel C.	1889.08.28	SLC	NY.Elmira	I have examined	DLC	03933
Beard, Daniel C.	1889.11.11	SLC	CT.Hartford	Hold me under	NBmtT	03965
Beard, Daniel C.	1902.01.18	SLC	NY.Riverdale	I cannot tell	DLC	06247
Beard, Daniel C.	1902.12.12	SLC	NY.Riverdale	You are right	DLC	06513
Beard, Daniel C.	o/a 1906.04.16	SLC per IVL	NY.New York	Will try to	CU-MARK(dr)	07431 on Beard Apr 16
Beardsley, Lillian R.	1906.08.28	SLC	NH.Dublin	I know it	NN-B(tr)	07507 other sources
Beck, James M.	1909.04.25	SLC	CT.Redding	The truth is	CU-MARK	08389
Becke, Louis	1895.09.24	SLC	AS.Sydney	I am still	AuSN-M	04963
Beckwith, Carroll	ca 1893.**.**	SLC	NY.New York	I'll be there	324:1930.12.05	04317
Beecher, Henry W.	1885.09.11	SLC	NY.Elmira	My nephew Webster	CU-MARK	03288
Beecher, Julia J.	1880.05.30	SLC	CT.Hartford	I have arranged	NEImC	01809
Beecher, Julia J.	1895.07.02	SLC	NY.Elmira	Contract with Mrs.	MoCoJ NEImC	04923 stone inscription NEImC
Beemer, Josephine	aft 1884.04.28	SLC	CT.Hartford	It was not	NPV	10870 on Beemer Apr 28
Belais, Diana	ca 1909.01.18	SLC per MLH	CT.Redding	Mr. C. has	CtHMTH(dr)	08319
Belknap, William W.	1874.08.28	SLC	NY.Elmira	I believe I	ViU	01119
Belknap, William W.	1874.09.05	SLC	NY.Elmira	Your letter is	ViU	01123
Belknap, William W.	1874.09.24	SLC	CT.Hartford	It isn't that	ViU	01132
Bell, Arthur	****.01.10	SLC	CT.Hartford	No--shall lecture	CStoC	09411 deposit
Bell, C.F. Moberly	1900.03.03	SLC	EN.London	The representative of	C4	05768
Bell, C.F. Moberly	1900.04.06	SLC	EN.London	Although you are	C4	05787
Bell, C.F. Moberly	bet 1900.07.** & 1900.09.**	SLC	EN.London	Don't give me	CU-MARK	05828 essay enc
Bell, C.F. Moberly	1901.08.26	SLC	NY.Saranac Lake	Please give me	C4	06118

Bell, C.F. Moberly		1907.05.03	SLC	NY.New York	I perceive your	CU-MARK(dr)	07708 telegram
Bell, Curtis		1893.12.31	SLC	NY.New York	Thank you ever	NN-B	04655
Bell, MacKenzie		1890.06.25	SLC per FGW	CT.Hartford	In reply to	CLU-S/C	04055
Bella		1866.12.04	SLC	CA.San Francisco	By some strange	CU-MARK	00114
Bella		1866.12.04	SLC	CA.San Francisco	I have had	CU-MARK	00113
Bellows, Mrs.		1905.04.25	SLC	NY.New York	with greetings &	ViU	11095 inscription
Belt, Samuel E.	o/a	1905.02.12	SLC per IVL	NY.New York	Mr. Clemens wishes	CU-MARK(dr)	06999 on Belt Feb 12
Benedict, E.C.	o/a	1905.02.12	SLC per IVL	NY.New York	Mr. Clemens has	CU-MARK(dr)	06998 on Dix Feb 9
Benjamin, Anne E.		1906.08.29	SLC	NH.Dublin	I am going	MFai	07511
Benjamin, Beatrice M.		1902.03.18	SLC	FL.Miami	It was lovely	NN3	06305
Benjamin, Beatrice M.		1903.07.**	SLC	NY.Elmira	I think the	155:1975.02.18	10458
Benjamin, Beatrice M.		1903.09.18	SLC	NY.Elmira	Yes, I should	C4	06726
Benjamin, Beatrice M.		1905.03.07	SLC	NY.New York	Thank you for	NN3	07014
Benjamin, Beatrice M.		1908.06.**	SLC	Unknown	Save yourself, dear	NN3	09473 on "Endless chain prayer"
Benjamin, Beatrice M.		1909.02.11	SLC	CT.Redding	Oh, come, dear	NN3	08346
Benjamin, Beatrice M.		1909.10.27	SLC	CT.Redding	This isn't to	CU-MARK(ph)	08477
Benjamin, Beatrice M.		1909.10.29	SLC	CT.Redding	It is unbearable	NN3	08479
Benjamin, Beatrice M.		1909.11.07	SLC	CT.Redding	After all, I	NN3	08482
Benjamin, Lou W.		1886.04.10	SLC	CT.Hartford	You are right	CU-MARK(ph)	03382
Benjamin, William E.		****.**.**	SLC	NY.New York	I am glad	CCamarSJ	08741
Benjamin, William E.		1902.03.12	SLC	NY.Riverdale	I thank you	MFai	06294
Benjamin, William E.		1902.03.21	OLC	NY.Riverdale	Thank you very	MFai	06309
Benjamin, William E.		1902.04.08	OLC	NY.Riverdale	Indeed I do	MFai	06319
Benjamin, William E.		1905.06.01	SLC	NH.Dublin	I am very	MFai	07056
Bennett, James G.		1897.06.19	SLC	EN.London	I was glad	211:355	05236

ADDRESSEE	DATE	WRITER	PLACE	CUE	SOURCE	NUMBER/NOTES
Bennett, James G.	1897.06.19	SLC	EN.London	I concealed this	CU-MARK(tr)	08637
Bennett, James G.	1897.06.24	SLC	EN.London	When my family	VtMiM	05232
Bennett, James G.	1897.06.25	SLC	EN.London	I enclose a	CU-MARK(tr)	08636
Bennett, James G. Jr.	1875.11.17	SLC	CT.Hartford	The book I	CU-MARK(ph)	10499
Bennett, John	1872.11.07	SLC	Unknown	with the warm	CtHMTH	10432 inscription
Bennett, Mark	1903.09.01	SLC	NY.Elmira	Your kind favor	CU-MARK(ph)	06721
Bennett, Mr.	1896.01.28	SLC	II.Bombay	I am most	C4	05014
Bensley, Martha	1906.06.14	SLC	NH.Dublin	I am sending	CU-MARK(tr)	07459
Benson, Florence	1907.12.01	SLC	NY.New York	Thank you for	MCo	07872
Benthergsen, Mr.	1901.10.25	SLC	NY.Riverdale	Yes, I accept	415:134	06164
Bentley, George	1873.10.13	SLC	EN.London	Did my clerk	ViU	00974
Bentley, George	1873.10.15 & 1873.10.30	SLC	EN.London & SH.Batavia	Two engagements (both)	ViU	00975
Bentley, George	1876.04.26	SLC	CT.Hartford	You remember a	ViU	01326 misaddressed to Richard Bentley
Bentley, George	1876.07.06	SLC	CT.Hartford	Your favor June	ViU	01348 misaddressed to Richard Bentley
Bentley, George	1877.09.15	SLC	CT.Hartford	I sent you	ViU	01480
Bentley, Margaret A.	1887.07.07	SLC	NY.Elmira	I had not	CAlb2	03594
Bentley, Richard	*	*	*	*	*	10327 see Bentley, George
Benton, Joel	1870.02.20	SLC	NY.Buffalo	No, I write	NPV	00428 date uncertain
Bergheim, Samuel M.	1903.02.06	SLC per IVL	NY.Riverdale	Your letter of	CU-MARK	06577
Berkshire Eagle eds.	1879.09.23	SLC	NY.Elmira	I can only	112:1879.10.16	10860
Bernhardt, Sarah	1905.12.17	SLC	Unknown	Ah, Madame the	122:1934.02.15	09377 inscription; other sources
Berry, Earl O.	bef 1871.01.06	SLC	NY.Buffalo	please see to	ViU	00556

Bertram, James	o/a 1905.12.19	SLC per IVL	NY.New York	Very glad to	CU-MARK(dr)	07264 on Bertram Dec 19
Besant, Walter	****.**.**	SLC	Unknown	This is only	CU-MARK(ph)	08772
Besant, Walter	1898.02.22	SLC	AU.Vienna	It makes me	NN-B	05487
Besant, Walter	1898.04.08	SLC	AU.Vienna	I should like	CU-MARK(ph)	03817
Bess, Frederick B.	o/a 1905.06.26	SLC per IVL	NH.Dublin	If Mr. Clemens	CU-MARK(dr)	07071 on Bess June 26
Bessie	1889.08.24	JC	NY.Elmira	I went to	Mo4	02440
Bickers, Mr.	1896.03.07	SLC	II.Jaipur	It is decided	CU-MARK(ph)	05029
Bickers, Mr.	1896.03.13	SLC	II.Jaipur	This time I	CU-MARK(ph)	05032
Bigelow, Edith E. & Bigelow, Poultney	1899.04.02	SLC	AU.Vienna	We are beginning	N7(tr)	05573
Bigelow, Poultney	1891.11.09	SLC	GE.Berlin	Thank you for	N7(tr)	04250
Bigelow, Poultney	1892.05.06	SLC	IT.Florence	Did I have	N7(tr)	04288
Bigelow, Poultney	1893.08.01	SLC	AU.Krankenheil	It is a	N7(tr)	04429
Bigelow, Poultney	1894.01.14	SLC	NY.New York	Thank you cordially	N7	04672
Bigelow, Poultney	1894.02.11	SLC	NY.New York	Your heart will	N7(tr)	04691
Bigelow, Poultney	1895.04.25	SLC	FR.Paris	Thank you ever	N7(tr)	04870
Bigelow, Poultney	1895.05.02	SLC	FR.Paris	My! I wish	N7(tr)	04875
Bigelow, Poultney	1896.07.16	SLC	AF.Capetown	We reached here	N7	05085
Bigelow, Poultney	1896.10.**	SLC	EN.London	Private. (Which is	N7(tr)	05122
Bigelow, Poultney	1898.07.29	SLC	AU.Kaltenleut.	I want to	N7(tr)	05417
Bigelow, Poultney	1898.12.19	SLC	AU.Vienna	I was astonished	N7(tr)	05481
Bigelow, Poultney	1899.**.**	SLC	EN.London	Goodbye & pleasant	N7(tr)	05527
Bigelow, Poultney	1899.03.**	SLC	AU.Vienna	I am mailing	N7(tr)	05553
Bigelow, Poultney	1899.03.22	SLC	AU.Vienna	Of course I	N7(tr)	05565
Bigelow, Poultney & Bigelow, Edith E.	1899.04.02	SLC	AU.Vienna	We are beginning	N7(tr)	05573
Bigelow, Poultney	1899.06.01	SLC	EN.London	All right--make	N7(tr)	05628

ADDRESSEE	DATE	WRITER	PLACE	CUE	SOURCE	NUMBER/NOTES
Bigelow, Poultney	bet 1899.07.10 & 1899.09.27	SLC	SE.Sanna	We are well	N7	05661
Bigelow, Poultney	1899.07.30	SLC	SE.Sanna	I've lost your	N7(tr)	05659
Bigelow, Poultney	1899.09.01	SLC	SE.Sanna	We are progressing	N7(tr)	05669
Bigelow, Poultney	1899.10.14	SLC	EN.London	Don't give that	N7(tr)	05689
Bigelow, Poultney	bef 1899.11.10	SLC	EN.London	P.S. Too bad!	N7	10947
Bigelow, Poultney	bef 1899.11.10	SLC	EN.London	Shall be delighted	N7	05702
Bigelow, Poultney	1900.**.**	SLC	Unknown	Hochwohgeboren	N7	05733
Bigelow, Poultney	1900.**.**	SLC	Unknown	Yes, tell him	N7	05732
Bigelow, Poultney	1900.**.**	SLC	Unknown	You are going	N7	05734
Bigelow, Poultney	1900.**.**	SLC	Unknown	You are to	N7	05731
Bigelow, Poultney	1900.01.18	SLC	EN.London	Please tell me	143:f	05749
Bigelow, Poultney	1900.01.18	SLC	EN.London	Will you transact	CU-MARK	05750 on Harper Jan 6
Bigelow, Poultney	1900.02.03	SLC	EN.London	We shall be	N7	05756
Bigelow, Poultney	1900.05.10	SLC	EN.London	If the right	N7	05804
Bigelow, Poultney	1900.07.25	SLC	EN.London	Come out &	N7	05836
Bigelow, Poultney	1900.09.26	SLC	EN.London	Hurry along with	143:469f	05869
Bigelow, Poultney	1900.11.20	SLC	NY.New York	Man sagt du	ViU	05913
Bigelow, Poultney	1902.03.12	SLC	NY.Riverdale	I thanked you	CU-MARK(tr)	06295
Bigelow, Poultney	1902.05.02	SLC	NY.Riverdale	Land!--I don't	N7	06331
Bigelow, Poultney	1902.10.27	SLC	NY.Riverdale	All success to	N7(tr)	06474
Bigelow, Poultney	1902.11.15	SLC	NY.Riverdale	Welcome!--welcome!	N7(tr)	06488
Bigelow, Poultney	1903.01.17	SLC	NY.Riverdale	Our house has	N7(tr)	06567
Bigelow, Poultney	1903.02.21	SLC	NY.Riverdale	Forgive me! Great	N7(tr)	06584
Bigelow, Poultney	1903.04.17	SLC	NY.Riverdale	I am in	N7(tr)	06622
Bigelow, Poultney	1904.05.04	SLC	IT.Florence	Indeed, I should	N7(tr)	06827
Bigelow, Poultney	1909.05.18	SLC	CT.Redding	Come, by all	N7	08398
Bigelow, Poultney	1909.05.27	SLC	CT.Redding	Indeed yes, the	N7(tr)	08405

Biggs, Andrew C.	o/a	1905.01.11	SLC	NY.New York	Questions Pertaining to	CU-MARK	06981 on petition
Bill, George L.		1888.12.25	SLC	Unknown	with the compliments	105:1939.12.08	09654 inscription
Billings, John S.		1907.03.22	SLC	NY.New York	This is a	NN	07677
Billings, Josh		*	*	*	*	*	10305 see Shaw, Henry W.
Billings, Mrs. David		1888.08.24	SLC & OLC	NY.Elmira	That is exactly	NN-B	02685
Bingham, Theodore A.		1907.10.15	SLC per IVL	NY.Tuxedo Park	Here is a	CU-MARK(tr)	07853
Bingham, Theodore A.		1908.09.18	SLC	CT.Redding	A couple of	CU-MARK	08098
Bird, C. Gladstone		1908.05.14	SLC per ABP	NY.New York	Some weeks ago	CU-MARK(ph)	07998
Bishop, J.L.		1900.09.12	SLC	EN.London	1. "The Man	CU-MARK(tr)	05862
Bissell (Geo. P.) & Co.		1876.06.29	SLC	NY.Elmira	Make check payable	CU-MARK	09063 on tax bill
Bissell (Geo. P.) & Co.		1877.05.15	SLC per CEP	CT.Hartford	I hereby authorize	CtHMTH	01431
Bissell (Geo. P.) & Co.		1878.02.09	SLC	GE.Munich	Please pay to	CtHMTH	10330 misdated, see 1879
Bissell (Geo. P.) & Co.		1878.05.23	SLC	GE.Heidelberg	Please pay to	CtHMTH	10474 enc in May 23 to Twichell
Bissell (Geo. P.) & Co.		1879.02.09	SLC	GE.Munich	Please pay to	CtHMTH	01630 misdated 1878
Bissell (Geo. P.) & Co. & Cleveland, E.S.		1879.09.08	SLC	NY.Elmira	Please pay to	CtHMTH	09186
Bissell (Geo. P.) & Co.		1879.10.13	SLC	NY.Elmira	Please pay to	CtHMTH	01698
Bixby, Horace E.	bet &	1870.01.01 1870.01.05	SLC	NY.Elmira	Thirty tons of	152:1882.05.07	00400
Black, John C.		1885.07.08	SLC	NY.Elmira	I have not	CU-MARK(tr)	03255
Blackmer, Helen K.	ca	1908.09.21	SLC	CT.Redding	I accept with	CU-MARK(dr)	08109
Blackmer, Helen K.		1909.03.03	SLC	CT.Redding	I thank you	CtY	08359
Blackmer, Helen K.		1909.03.13	SLC	CT.Redding	Saturday April 10	CtY	08373

ADDRESSEE	DATE	WRITER	PLACE	CUE	SOURCE	NUMBER/NOTES
Blackmer, Helen K.	1909.10.13	SLC	CT.Redding	It's congratulations	CtY	08468
Blackmer, Helen K.	1909.10.30	SLC	CT.Redding	To-day you will	CtY	08481
Blackmer, Margaret	aft 1907.11.11	SLC	Unknown	This is only	NN-B	09266 inscription
Blackmer, Margaret	1908.03.02	SLC	BE.Hamilton	I saw the	CtY	07954
Blackmer, Margaret	1908.04.14	SLC	NY.New York	Dear Margaret, we	CtY	07974
Blackmer, Margaret	1908.04.15	SLC	NY.New York	I have your	CtY	07975
Blackmer, Margaret	1908.05.25	SLC	NY.New York	Did I tell	CtY	08009
Blackmer, Margaret	1908.06.20	SLC	CT.Redding	I thank you	CtY	08039
Blackmer, Margaret	1908.07.07	SLC	CT.Redding	I was wondering	CtY	08049
Blackmer, Margaret	1908.08.13	SLC	CT.Redding	It's a charming	CtY	08084
Blackmer, Margaret	1908.09.18	SLC	CT.Redding	I am so	CtY	08106
Blackmer, Margaret	1908.10.06	SLC	CT.Redding	You dear Margaret	CtY	08123
Blackmer, Margaret	1908.10.07	SLC	CT.Redding	Oh, you dear	CtY	08127
Blackmer, Margaret	1908.10.11	SLC	CT.Redding	I clear forgot	CtY	08134
Blackmer, Margaret	1908.10.24 to 1908.10.29	SLC	CT.Redding	Dear heart, you wouldn't	CtY	08143
Blackmer, Margaret	1908.11.01	SLC	CT.Redding	You sweet Margaret	CU-MARK(tr)	08152
Blackmer, Margaret	1908.11.29	SLC	CT.Redding	You "suppose" I	CtY	07372
Blackmer, Margaret	1909.01.03	SLC	CT.Redding	I wonder where	CtY	08307
Blackmer, Margaret	1909.02.05	SLC	CT.Redding	Good! I've heard	CtY	08341
Blackmer, Margaret	1909.02.20	SLC	CT.Redding	Attention, you dear	CtY	08352
Blackmer, Margaret	1909.09.15	SLC	CT.Redding	You thoughtless little	CtY	08453
Blackmer, Margaret	1909.11.18	SLC	CT.Redding	I don't seem	CtY	08495
Blackmer, Margaret	pm 1910.01.17	SLC	BE.Hamilton	To all friends	CtY	08541 form letter
Blackmer, Margaret	1910.01.26	SLC	BE.Hamilton	So you have	CtY	08551
Blackwood, William	1897.11.07	SLC per OLC	AU.Vienna	I want to	UkENL	05311
Bladen, Charles H.	bef 1876.10.26	SLC	CT.Hartford	By the inclosed	131:1876.10.29	01380
Blaine, James G.	1875.10.11	SLC	CT.Hartford	I think I	DLC	00552

Blair, J.C.	1884.01.29	SLC	CT.Hartford	Your pockets are	CU-MARK(ph)	02898
Blake, D.E.	****.**.**	SLC	Unknown	It may not	CCC	00314 form letter
Blamire, Joseph L.	1872.06.21	SLC	CT.Hartford	We are very	ViU	00758
Blamire, Joseph L.	1872.06.23	SLC	CT.Hartford	I enclose preface	ViU	00759
Blamire, Joseph L.	1872.07.10	SLC	CT.New Saybrook	Am spending the	UkL5	00764
Blamire, Joseph L.	1872.07.21	SLC	CT.New Saybrook	I snatched this	ViU	00772 preface enc
Bland, Henry M.	o/a 1907.01.30	SLC per IVL	NY.New York	not likely to	CU-MARK(dr)	07660 on Bland Jan 30
Blasdel, Henry G. & Helm, Alfred	1866.11.01	SLC	NV.Virginia City	Your kind and	431:1866.11.04	00109 also to Gilbert & Rice
Blasdel, Henry G. & Low, Frederick F.	1866.12.06	SLC	CA.San Francisco	I cannot too	417:1866.12.08	00115 also to French & Hoffman
Bliss, Elisha	****.**.**	SLC	Unknown	Truly yours	105:1945.05.07	09422 inscription
Bliss, Elisha	****.**.**	SLC	Unknown	*	CtHMTH	10657 envelope only
Bliss, Elisha	1867.12.02	SLC	DC.Washington	I only received	CU-MARK	00165
Bliss, Elisha	1868.01.27	SLC	NY.New York	Your favor of	CU-MARK	00185
Bliss, Elisha	1868.02.04 & 1868.02.06	SLC	DC.Washington	If you ever	CU-MARK	00189
Bliss, Elisha	1868.05.05	SLC	CA.San Francisco	The Alta people	CU-MARK(tr)	02731
Bliss, Elisha	1868.05.28	SLC	CA.San Francisco	H.H. Bancroft	ViU	02733
Bliss, Elisha	1868.06.23	SLC	CA.San Francisco	The book is	PPiU	02736
Bliss, Elisha	1868.07.05	SLC	CA.San Francisco	I waited over	C4	02739
Bliss, Elisha	1868.09.03	SLC	NY.Elmira	Enclosed you will	CU-MARK(tr)	02748
Bliss, Elisha	1869.02.14	SLC	OH.Ravenna	I got your	PPiU	00251
Bliss, Elisha	1869.03.30	SLC	NY.Elmira	I sent the	CU-MARK	00279
Bliss, Elisha	1869.04.11	SLC	NY.Elmira	All the names	Mo4	00288
Bliss, Elisha	1869.04.12	SLC	NY.Elmira	I think St	CU-MARK	00281

ADDRESSEE	DATE	WRITER	PLACE	CUE	SOURCE	NUMBER/NOTES
Bliss, Elisha	1869.04.15	SLC	NY.Elmira	Yes, on page	CtY	00283
Bliss, Elisha	1869.04.20	SLC	NY.Elmira	I wish you	CU-MARK	00286
Bliss, Elisha	1869.04.29	SLC	NY.Elmira	All right. I	CU-MARK	00290
Bliss, Elisha	1869.07.12	SLC	NY.Elmira	The circular for	MoSw2	00326
Bliss, Elisha	1869.07.22	SLC	NY.Elmira	Mr Bliss, are	CSj2	00327
Bliss, Elisha	1869.08.01	SLC	NY.Elmira	I had some	CU-MARK(tr)	00328
Bliss, Elisha	1869.08.12	SLC	NY.Buffalo	Your splendid letter	CU-MARK	00330
Bliss, Elisha	1869.08.14	SLC	NY.Buffalo	I enclose the	NBuHi	00331
Bliss, Elisha	1869.08.15	SLC	NY.Buffalo	There is a	WU(tr)	00333
Bliss, Elisha	1869.09.02	SLC	NY.Buffalo	Have you an	CU-MARK	00342
Bliss, Elisha	1869.09.03	SLC	NY.Buffalo	I "cave." You	CU-MARK	00344
Bliss, Elisha	1869.09.07	SLC	NY.Buffalo	I guess Mr.	CU-MARK	00348
Bliss, Elisha	1869.09.07	SLC	NY.Buffalo	Mrs. Wm. Barstow	TxEU	08611
Bliss, Elisha	1869.09.21	SLC	NY.Buffalo	The Editor of	105:1938.11.09	00355
Bliss, Elisha	1869.09.27	SLC	NY.Buffalo	Arnold called on	CU-MARK	00358
Bliss, Elisha	1869.12.28	SLC	NY.New York	My room-rate in	CU-MARK(ph)	00396
Bliss, Elisha	1870.01.22	SLC	NY.Elmira	Our boys in	CU-MARK	00415
Bliss, Elisha	1870.01.28	SLC	NY.Elmira	I want you	CU-MARK	00418
Bliss, Elisha	1870.02.23	SLC	NY.Buffalo	Why bless your	CU-MARK	00431
Bliss, Elisha	1870.03.03	SLC	NY.Buffalo	Won't you send	CU-MARK	00438
Bliss, Elisha	1870.03.11	SLC	NY.Buffalo	I turned the	NN-B	00443
Bliss, Elisha	1870.04.23	SLC	NY.Buffalo	All right--the	CU-MARK	00459
Bliss, Elisha	1870.05.05	SLC	NY.Elmira	We return home	WU(tr)	00461
Bliss, Elisha	1870.05.07	SLC	NY.Elmira	I have just	CU-MARK	00462
Bliss, Elisha	1870.05.20	SLC	NY.Buffalo	Appleton wants me	C4	00465
Bliss, Elisha	1870.05.30	SLC	NY.Buffalo	Will you send	CtY	00473
Bliss, Elisha	1870.06.09	SLC	NY.Elmira	Please have the	CtHMTH	00478
Bliss, Elisha	1870.06.27	SLC	NY.Elmira	Yes the "Reading	WU(tr)	00483
Bliss, Elisha	1870.07.04	SLC	NY.Elmira	Mr Langdon is	C4	00486

Bliss, Elisha	1870.07.18	SLC	NY.Elmira	Mr. Langdon is	NN-B	00490
Bliss, Elisha	1870.08.02	SLC	NY.Elmira	You know I	OC	00494
Bliss, Elisha	1870.08.05	SLC	NY.Elmira	The physicians pronounce	155:1984.07.16	10994
Bliss, Elisha	1870.08.11	SLC	NY.Elmira	I meant to	OC	00496
Bliss, Elisha	1870.09.04	SLC	NY.Buffalo	During past week	CU-MARK	00502
Bliss, Elisha	aft 1870.09.19	SLC	NY.Buffalo	I turn this	CCC	00508
Bliss, Elisha	1870.09.22	SLC	NY.Buffalo	My map is	CU-MARK	00509
Bliss, Elisha	aft 1870.09.29	SLC	Unknown	I have no	CU-MARK	00543
Bliss, Elisha	1870.10.13	SLC	NY.Buffalo	I have a	MB	00511
Bliss, Elisha	1870.10.26	SLC	NY.Buffalo	My man took	CU-MARK(ph)	00514
Bliss, Elisha	1870.10.28	SLC	NY.Buffalo	Please forward a	NN-B	00516
Bliss, Elisha	1870.10.29	SLC	NY.Buffalo	I got the	C4	00517
Bliss, Elisha	1870.10.31	SLC	NY.Buffalo	Oh, I didn't	CU-MARK(ph)	00519
Bliss, Elisha	1870.11.05	SLC	NY.Buffalo	It is a	NN-B	00523
Bliss, Elisha	1870.11.07	SLC	NY.Buffalo	This is to	CU-MARK	00527
Bliss, Elisha	1870.11.22	SLC	NY.Buffalo	Please send this	CtY	00542
Bliss, Elisha	1870.11.28	SLC	NY.Buffalo	My brother expects	CU-MARK	00545
Bliss, Elisha	1870.12.02	SLC	NY.Buffalo	I'll tell you	NN5	00548
Bliss, Elisha	1870.12.17	SLC	NY.Buffalo	Got homesick. Will	NN-B	00550 telegram
Bliss, Elisha	1870.12.22	SLC	NY.Buffalo	This is to To-day I arranged	CtY ViU	02785
Bliss, Elisha	1871.01.03	SLC	NY.Buffalo	No, if this	CU-MARK	00553
Bliss, Elisha	1871.01.04 & 1871.01.05	SLC	NY.Buffalo	The curious the one about	CU-MARK 107:1927.02.14	00555
Bliss, Elisha	1871.01.05	SLC	NY.Buffalo	I wish you	MGlHi	04138
Bliss, Elisha	1871.01.24	SLC	NY.Buffalo	Orion says you	CU-MARK(ph)	00562
Bliss, Elisha	1871.01.27	SLC	NY.Buffalo	Tell you what	CU-MARK	00568
Bliss, Elisha or Bliss, Frank E.	1871.01.31	SLC	NY.Buffalo	Have an appointment	CU-MARK	00571 telegram
Bliss, Elisha	1871.02.15	SLC	NY.Buffalo	This is to	CU-MARK	00576

ADDRESSEE	DATE	WRITER	PLACE	CUE	SOURCE	NUMBER/NOTES
Bliss, Elisha	1871.03.17	SLC	NY.Buffalo	Out of this	NN-B	02455
Bliss, Elisha & Clemens, Orion	1871.03.20	SLC	NY.Elmira	We are all	CU-MARK	00595
Bliss, Elisha	1871.05.03	SLC	NY.Elmira	My friend Ned	CU-MARK	00610
Bliss, Elisha	1871.05.15	SLC	NY.Elmira	Yrs rec'd enclosing	ViU	00612
Bliss, Elisha	1871.06.21	SLC	NY.Elmira	Here are three	CU-MARK	00618
Bliss, Elisha	bet 1871.10.01 & 1872.01.30	SLC	Unknown	If he does	120:1925.02	09924
Bliss, Elisha	1871.10.19	SLC	PA.Wilkes-Barre	I brought the	C4	00665
Bliss, Elisha	1871.11.12	SLC	MA.Boston	Please send copies	CU-MARK	00672
Bliss, Elisha	1871.12.01	SLC	Unknown	Here is a	CU-MARK	00723
Bliss, Elisha	1872.03.20	SLC	NY.Elmira	The more I	CU-MARK	00737
Bliss, Elisha	1872.03.21	SLC	NY.Elmira	At last I	CtY	00738
Bliss, Elisha	1872.07.20	SLC	CT.New Saybrook	Been looking for	ViU	00770
Bliss, Elisha	1872.07.28	SLC	CT.New Saybrook	I shall be	NN	00781
Bliss, Elisha	1872.08.07	SLC	CT.New Saybrook	This is to	CtY	00787
Bliss, Elisha	1872.09.28	SLC	EN.London	I have been	CU-MARK	00816
Bliss, Elisha	1873.02.25	SLC	CT.Hartford	Stir Frank up	CtY	00875
Bliss, Elisha	1873.02.26	SLC	CT.Hartford	All right. Make	CU-MARK	00876
Bliss, Elisha	1873.02.28	SLC	CT.Hartford	so infatuated that	255:130	09999
Bliss, Elisha	1873.03.04	SLC	CT.Hartford	Statement rec'd for	ViU	00881
Bliss, Elisha	1873.03.26	SLC	CT.Hartford	I leave in	CU-MARK	00890
Bliss, Elisha	1873.05.03	SLC	CT.Hartford	We shall doubtless	WU(tr)	00912
Bliss, Elisha	1873.06.18	SLC	EN.London	Have begun to	NN-B	00928
Bliss, Elisha	1873.07.07	SLC	EN.London	Finally concluded not	ViU	00948 pamphlet preface enc
Bliss, Elisha	1873.07.10	SLC	EN.London	Publish if you	CU-MARK(tr)	10976
Bliss, Elisha	1873.07.16	SLC per SCT	EN.London	We shall issue	CtY	00953
Bliss, Elisha	1873.07.27	SLC	SK.Edinburgh	Confound it. I	CtY	00956
Bliss, Elisha	1873.08.02	SLC	SK.Edinburgh	Have just telegraphed	111:169	05816

Bliss, Elisha		1873.08.02	SLC	SK.Edinburgh	Stop that pamphlet	CU-MARK(tr)	08826 telegram; SLC tr
Bliss, Elisha		1873.11.05	SLC	CT.Hartford	Please send very	ViU	00979
Bliss, Elisha		1874.02.19	SLC	CT.Hartford	Through being my	WU(tr)	01052 other sources
Bliss, Elisha		1874.05.22	SLC	NY.Elmira	I have mislaid	CtY	01093
Bliss, Elisha	aft	1875.02.11	SLC	CT.Hartford	Suppose you write	NN-B	02486
Bliss, Elisha	bet &	1875.02.26 1875.03.**	SLC	CT.Hartford	From London I	CU-MARK	01199
Bliss, Elisha		1875.03.01	SLC	CT.Hartford	I've put off	CU-MARK	01200
Bliss, Elisha		1875.03.24	SLC	CT.Hartford	Called twice to	CU-MARK	01214
Bliss, Elisha	bef	1875.07.21	SLC	CT.Hartford	Bliss please print	CtY	01252
Bliss, Elisha		1875.11.05	SLC	CT.Hartford	You may let	CU-MARK	01280
Bliss, Elisha		1875.11.18	SLC	CT.Hartford	Please send me	MoPeS	01281
Bliss, Elisha		1876.02.17	SLC	CT.Hartford	Please send--	ViU	01308
Bliss, Elisha		1876.03.19	SLC	CT.Hartford	It is going	CtY	01315
Bliss, Elisha	o/a	1876.04.15	SLC	CT.Hartford	Please send these	CtY	01322 on Spofford Apr 15
Bliss, Elisha		1876.05.16	SLC	CT.Hartford	Are the pictures	MoPeS	01335
Bliss, Elisha	ca	1876.06.01	SLC	CT.Hartford	Will this do	CLU-S/C	01337
Bliss, Elisha		1876.06.24	SLC	NY.Elmira	I am ready	CtY	01345
Bliss, Elisha		1876.07.22	SLC	NY.Elmira	Of course I	CU-MARK	01349
Bliss, Elisha		1876.08.08	SLC	NY.Elmira	Everything O.K. So	CU-MARK	01356
Bliss, Elisha		1876.09.14	SLC	CT.Hartford	Don't forget to	DGU	02167
Bliss, Elisha or Bliss, Frank E.		1877.01.24	SLC	CT.Hartford	Statement & check	MoPeS	01163
Bliss, Elisha		1877.08.06	SLC	NY.Elmira	I guess you	C4	01465
Bliss, Elisha		1880.03.20	SLC	CT.Hartford	I like the	NN-B	02540
Bliss, Elisha		1880.04.21	SLC	CT.Hartford	Wm A. Seaver	CtY	01788 on Seaver Apr 20

ADDRESSEE		DATE	WRITER	PLACE	CUE	SOURCE	NUMBER/NOTES
Bliss, Frank E.		****.**.**	SLC	Unknown	Of course I	CU-MARK(tr)	08773
Bliss, Frank E.		1869.01.07	SLC	IL.Chicago	I am glad	CtY	00221
Bliss, Frank E.		1869.02.01	SLC	IL.Jacksonville	I shall be	NN-B	02446
Bliss, Frank E.		1870.09.15	SLC	NY.Buffalo	We are obliged	CtHMTH	00505
Bliss, Frank E. or Bliss, Elisha		1871.01.31	SLC	NY.Buffalo	Have an appointment	CU-MARK	00571 telegram
Bliss, Frank E.	ca	1872.04.06	SLC	NY.Elmira	Please send James	105:1954.03.23	09424
Bliss, Frank E.		1872.04.19	SLC	NY.Elmira	What is your	WU(tr)	00741
Bliss, Frank E.		1872.05.15	SLC	NY.Elmira	Please send another	CtY	00749
Bliss, Frank E.		1872.05.26	SLC	NY.Elmira	Please send 1/2	C4	00753
Bliss, Frank E.		1872.07.11	SLC	CT.New Saybrook	Is your father	134:1930.11.16	00765
Bliss, Frank E.		1872.07.12	SLC	CT.New Saybrook	This is from	MoPeS	00767 on Pamela Moffett July 8
Bliss, Frank E.	ca	1873.07.07	SLC	EN.London	Use as much	CtY	11061 on essay
Bliss, Frank E.	o/a	1876.01.01	SLC	CT.Hartford	Please return it	CU-MARK	05326
Bliss, Frank E. or Bliss, Elisha		1877.01.24	SLC	CT.Hartford	Statement & check	MoPeS	01163
Bliss, Frank E.		1878.01.24	SLC	CT.Hartford	You've done exceedingly	110:1972.02.03	10340
Bliss, Frank E.		1878.06.16	SLC	GE.Heidelberg	I have been	CU-MARK(ph)	01571
Bliss, Frank E.		1878.07.13	SLC	GE.Heidelberg	Yours of June	WU(tr)	01576 other sources
Bliss, Frank E.		1878.08.20	SLC	SW.Lucerne	I find it	NN-B	02525
Bliss, Frank E.		1879.02.09	SLC	GE.Munich	Yes, I'm still	WU(tr)	01629
Bliss, Frank E.		1879.04.15	SLC	FR.Paris	I have been	NN-B	02531
Bliss, Frank E.		1879.05.10	SLC	FR.Paris	I received a	NjP	01653
B iss, Frank E.		1879.06.10	SLC	FR.Paris	Brown sent you	C4	01665
Bliss, Frank E.		1879.06.10	SLC	FR.Paris	All right--have	WU(tr)	01664
Bliss, Frank E.		1879.06.13	SLC	FR.Paris	P.S.--Perhaps	C4	01668
Bliss, Frank E.		1879.06.15	SLC	FR.Paris	I think I	C4	01670
Bliss, Frank E.		1879.06.17	SLC	FR.Paris	Please process that	C4	01671

Bliss, Frank E.		1879.09.06	SLC	NY.Elmira	When you return	C4	01683 date uncertain
Bliss, Frank E.		1879.09.08	SLC	NY.Elmira	A stranger writes	WU(tr)	01684
Bliss, Frank E.		1879.09.16	SLC	NY.Elmira	I told Brown	C4	01691
Bliss, Frank E.		1880.05.08	SLC	CT.Hartford	Of course I	C4	01801
Bliss, Frank E.	ca	1880.05.20	SLC	CT.Hartford	Evidently this should	CU-MARK	09196 on Chatto & Windus May 3
Bliss, Frank E.		1880.10.23	SLC	CT.Hartford	This is to	WU(tr)	01844 other sources
Bliss, Frank E.		1880.12.24	SLC	CT.Hartford	Please send Innocents	NBuU-PO	01877
Bliss, Frank E.		1881.04.08	SLC	CT.Hartford	Your ck for	Mo2	02414
Bliss, Frank E.		1881.04.15	SLC	CT.Hartford	Will you please	CAlb2	01936
Bliss, Frank E.		1881.05.30	SLC	CT.Hartford	The 1st of	WU(tr)	01960
Bliss, Frank E.		1881.06.16	SLC	CT.Branford	Please deliver to Mr.	ODa2	11208
Bliss, Frank E.		1882.09.09	SLC	NY.Elmira	I am pretty	WU(tr)	02266
Bliss, Frank E.		1884.02.07	SLC	CT.Hartford	By the middle	107:1925.03.03	02910
Bliss, Frank E.	o/a	1884.05.11	SLC	CT.Hartford	Please send him	CtHMTH	02974 on Wallihan May 11
Bliss, Frank E.		1888.10.09	SLC per FGW	CT.Hartford	I am directed	ViU CtY	03787 CtY enc
Bliss, Frank E.		1890.04.25	SLC	CT.Hartford	From your description	CSj2	09176
Bliss, Frank E.		1892.10.31	SLC	IT.Florence	I hear you	CtY	08926
Bliss, Frank E.		1893.03.08	SLC	IT.Florence	I have yours	NN-B	04635
Bliss, Frank E.		1894.08.**	SLC	Unknown	I lost that	229:1956.05	08934 other sources
Bliss, Frank E.		1894.10.13	SLC	FR.Rouen	Your telegraph has	CtMy2	04798
Bliss, Frank E.		1894.10.29	SLC	FR.Rouen	Please send a	WU(tr)	04804
Bliss, Frank E.		1894.12.09	SLC	FR.Paris	What does this	CtY	04820 on printed advertisement
Bliss, Frank E.		1895.05.30	SLC	NY.Elmira	It is a	CCC	04881
Bliss, Frank E.		1895.07.01	SLC	NY.Elmira	Yours of June	WU(tr)	04920

ADDRESSEE	DATE	WRITER	PLACE	CUE	SOURCE	NUMBER/NOTES
Bliss, Frank E.	1896.10.21	SLC	EN.London	As I understand	C4	05134
Bliss, Frank E.	1897.01.19	SLC	EN.London	Please refer to	NN-B	05501
Bliss, Frank E.	1897.03.19	SLC	EN.London	I enclose renewal	NN-B	05187
Bliss, Frank E.	1897.03.26	SLC	EN.London	I have done	CtY	05191
Bliss, Frank E.	bet 1897.05.01 & 1897.07.31	SLC	Unknown	Bliss, make a	MoPeS	02359
Bliss, Frank E.	1897.05.03 & 1897.05.05	SLC	EN.London	Now you're speaking	NN-B	05511
Bliss, Frank E.	1897.05.31	SLC	EN.London	I as author	DLC	04430 on May 31 to Spofford
Bliss, Frank E.	1897.07.02	SLC	EN.London	Here's a photo	C4	05249
Bliss, Frank E.	1897.07.27	SLC	SW.Weggis	Following equator	NN-B	05518 telegram
Bliss, Frank E.	1897.11.03	SLC	AU.Vienna	The chambermaid mislaid	ODa2	05305
Bliss, Frank E.	1897.11.04	SLC	AU.Vienna	Your cablegram P.S. I percieve	CU-MARK CtY	05307
Bliss, Frank E.	1897.11.04	SLC	AU.Vienna	Lie. Wrote no such	CU-MARK(ph)	05309 telegram
Bliss, Frank E.	1897.11.26	SLC	AU.Vienna	Fortunately I have	CtY	05316 fragment
Bliss, Frank E.	1897.12.16	SLC	AU.Vienna	I supposed I	OrPR	05323
Bliss, Frank E.	1898.**.**	SLC	Unknown	sick-nurse, Mrs.	157:1923.02.13	09857
Bliss, Frank E.	1898.02.11	SLC	AU.Vienna	Considering all the	C4	05348
Bliss, Frank E.	1898.02.27	SLC	AU.Vienna	The statement to	Mo2	08850
Bliss, Frank E.	1898.03.25	SLC	AU.Vienna	Oh, as to	TxU	05370
Bliss, Frank E.	1898.03.30	SLC	AU.Vienna	The book for	CU-MARK(tr)	05371
Bliss, Frank E.	1898.06.18	SLC	AU.Kaltenleut.	P.S. Another article	ODa2	11197
Bliss, Frank F.	1898.06.21	SLC	AU.Kaltenleut.	If there are	WU(tr)	05402
Bliss, Frank E.	1898.07.20	SLC	AU.Kaltenleut.	Yes it was	WU(tr)	05412 other sources
Bliss, Frank E.	1898.08.28	SLC	AU.Kaltenleut.	I have yours P.S. The contract	CtY WU	05424 WU ph
Bliss, Frank E.	1898.10.18	SLC	AU.Vienna	The 3 books	WU(tr)	05449

Bliss, Frank E.		1898.11.17	SLC	AU.Vienna	I put in	CU-MARK	05470
Bliss, Frank E.		1898.12.10	SLC	AU.Vienna	I must give	NSyU	05478
Bliss, Frank E.	ca	1899.01.01	SLC	AU.Vienna	I told you	NNC	05472
Bliss, Frank E.		1899.02.02	SLC	AU.Vienna	Yes I like	449:f	05539
Bliss, Frank E.		1899.02.27	SLC	AU.Vienna	The enclosed has	ODa2	05552
Bliss, Frank E.		1899.03.31	SLC	AU.Vienna	I want set	CtHMTH	05571
Bliss, Frank E.		1899.04.15	SLC	AU.Vienna	If Mr. Adolph	WU(tr)	05576
Bliss, Frank E.		1899.04.22	SLC	AU.Vienna	I am very	CtMy2	05581
Bliss, Frank E.	ca	1899.10.**	SLC	EN.London	Must I sign	NN-B(dr)	08750 telegram
Bliss, Frank E.		1899.10.01	SLC	EN.London	We reached England	ViU	05683
Bliss, Frank E.	o/a	1899.10.01	SLC	EN.London	Confidential, Bliss	CtY	05684 on tr of Oct 1 to Harper
Bliss, Frank E.		1900.01.16	SLC	EN.London	Yes, date the	PP	05748
Bliss, Frank E.		1900.02.22	SLC	EN.London	I suppose that	CtY	05760
Bliss, Frank E.		1900.03.21	SLC	EN.London	All right--I	F2	08613
Bliss, Frank E.		1900.03.30	SLC	EN.London	Correct the	CtY	05786 on printed page
Bliss, Frank E.		1900.04.25	SLC	EN.London	Col. Harvey has	CtY	11058
Bliss, Frank E.		1900.09.18	SLC	EN.London	You haven't sent	CtHMTH	05864
Bliss, Frank E.		1900.10.25	SLC	NY.New York	Mrs. Clemens says	CtY	05885
Bliss, Frank E.		1900.11.01	SLC	NY.New York	Do you remember	212:1946.03.23	05893 other sources
Bliss, Frank E.		1900.11.16	SLC	NY.New York	Frank Doubleday (whom	CU-MARK(ph)	05909
Bliss, Frank E.	ca	1901.**.**	SLC	Unknown	This duffer has	157:1918.12.12	09860 on Wise ca 1901
Bliss, Frank E.		1901.03.**	SLC	NY.New York	10,000 sets pay	WU(tr)	06010
Bliss, Frank E.		1901.03.18	SLC	NY.New York	I expect the	WU(tr)	06019
Bliss, Frank E.	o/a	1901.03.25	SLC	NY.New York	Please send him	CtY	06026 on Gurlitz Mar 25

ADDRESSEE	DATE	WRITER	PLACE	CUE	SOURCE	NUMBER/NOTES
Bliss, Frank E.	1901.03.27	SLC	NY.New York	I have been	WU(tr)	06029
Bliss, Frank E.	o/a 1901.04.04	SLC	NY.New York	Come! this is	CU-MARK(tr)	06032 on Bliss Apr 4
Bliss, Frank E.	1901.04.16	SLC	NY.New York	Understand, Bliss, that	TxU	06038
Bliss, Frank E.	1901.05.14	SLC	NY.New York	This is Col	CtY	06056 on May 4 to Harvey
Bliss, Frank E.	1901.05.20	SLC	NY.New York	You have correctly	CtY	11060 on Bliss May 15
Bliss, Frank E.	1901.06.21 & 1901.09.19	SLC	NY.Saranac Lake	This man seems	CU-MARK(ph)	05912
Bliss, Frank E.	1901.07.13	SLC	NY.Saranac Lake	I can't quite	WU(tr)	06088
Bliss, Frank E.	1901.08.26	SLC	NY.Saranac Lake	The thing I	TxU	06119
Bliss, Frank E.	1901.08.29	SLC	NY.Saranac Lake	No, upon reflection	TxU	06126
Bliss, Frank E.	1901.09.08	SLC	NY.Saranac Lake	The lynching-book	TxU	06131
Bliss, Frank E.	1901.10.27	SLC	NY.Riverdale	Come! With the	CLU-C	06168
Bliss, Frank E.	1902.01.10	SLC	NY.Riverdale	This is my	MoSW	06240
Bliss, Frank E.	1902.02.04	SLC	NY.Riverdale	There is a	CtMy2	06266
Bliss, Frank E.	1902.02.15	SLC	NY.Riverdale	I suppose Newbegin	CtY	06278
Bliss, Frank E.	1902.03.12	SLC	NY.Riverdale	This is four	CtY	06296 on tr of Mar 8 to Harvey
Bliss, Frank E.	1902.06.10	SLC	NY.Riverdale	1. The Publishers	122:1936.01.29	06356
Bliss, Frank E.	1902.08.**	SLC	ME.York Harbor	Don't send me	C4	06396
Bliss, Frank E.	1902.09.23	SLC	ME.York Harbor	Do you keep	CU-MARK	06437
Bliss, Frank E.	1902.10.08	SLC	ME.York Harbor	If there is	WU(tr)	06456
Bliss, Frank E.	1902.12.25	SLC	NY.Riverdale	You needn't hurry	WU(tr)	06526
Bliss, Frank E.	1903.01.09	SLC	NY.Riverdale	Yes, you can	ViU	06552
Bliss, Frank E.	1903.02.25	SLC per IVL	NY.Riverdale	I have this	CtY	06585 on Rogers Feb 24
Bliss, Frank E.	1903.03.04	SLC	NY.Riverdale	Church Manual of	CtMy2	06591
Bliss, Frank E.	1903.04.28	SLC	NY.Riverdale	Yours of the	WU(tr)	06636

Bliss, Frank E.		1903.05.11	SLC	NY.Riverdale	Frank, if you	CtY	06655
Bliss, Frank E. & Jacobs, Ward		1903.06.25	SLC	NY.Riverdale	I forgot one	CtHi	06684
Bliss, Frank E.	o/a	1903.07.29	SLC	NY.Elmira	I agree with	CtY	06715 on Bliss July 29
Bliss, Frank E.	o/a	1903.07.29	SLC	Unknown	What obstacles?	CU-MARK	06716 on Bliss to OLC July 29
Bliss, Frank E.		1904.09.09	SLC	NY.New York	As I understand	WU(tr)	06918
Bliss, Walter		1898.01.09	SLC per OLC	AU.Vienna	Mr Clemens asks	MoPeS	05333
Bloxham, E.T.	o/a	1905.12.07	SLC per IVL	NY.New York	Mr. Clemens wishes	CU-MARK(dr)	07237 on Bloxham Dec 7
Blumenfeld, R.D.		1901.12.17	SLC	NY.Riverdale	I have had	181:168	06189
Boardman, Jenny S.		1887.03.25	SLC	CT.Hartford	You have spirited	NN-B	02656
Boas, Rebecca P.		1885.01.09	SLC	MO.St. Louis	I shall certainly	C4	03108
Bodley, J.E.C.		****.**.**	SLC	Unknown	I am desperately	UkOxU	08751
Bohon, Isabella S.		1904.07.20	SLC	MA.Lee	No, some of	IU-R	06894 misdated July 21; on form letter
Bohon, Isabella S.	o/a	1907.07.29	SLC per IVL	NY.Tuxedo Park	Mr. Clemens has	CU-MARK(dr)	07791 on Bohon July 29
Bok, Edward W.		****.**.**	SLC	Unknown	It is very	183:102f	09198 inscription
Bok, Edward W.		****.**.**	SLC	Unknown	No, No--it	184:205	08743
Bok, Edward W.		****.**.**	SLC	Unknown	Of course, I	184:383	08771
Bok, Edward W.		1882.02.24	SLC	CT.Hartford	I hope I	184:204	02166 typed
Bok, Edward W.		1891.04.24	SLC	CT.Hartford	If you will	ODa2	04194
Bok, Edward W.		1898.09.02	SLC	AU.Kaltenleut.	I have partly-written	ViU	05431
Bok, Edward W.		1898.10.10	SLC	AU.Kaltenleut.	A good deal	ViU	05446 mislabeled Vienna

ADDRESSEE	DATE	WRITER	PLACE	CUE	SOURCE	NUMBER/NOTES
Bok, Edward W.	1902.10.18	SLC	NY.New York	I wish I	ViU	06465
Bok, Edward W.	1902.11.22	SLC per IVL	NY.Riverdale	It is a	ViU	06490
Bok, Edward W.	1903.07.08	SLC	NY.Elmira	Photographs with	ViU	06695
Bok, Edward W.	1903.07.17	SLC	NY.Elmira	The pictures of	ViU	06701
Bok, Edward W.	1903.07.18	SLC	NY.Elmira	Please strike out	ViU	06703
Bok, Edward W. & Collier, Robert	1903.07.21	SLC	NY.Elmira	Although I have	NN-B	11122 also to others
Bok, Edward W.	1903.09.01	SLC	NY.Elmira	There is a	ViU	06723
Bok, Edward W.	1903.09.19	SLC	NY.Elmira	Whenever it is	ViU	06727
Bok, Edward W.	1903.09.26	OLC	NY.Elmira	As Mr Clemens	ViU	06731
Bok, William J.	1888.07.25	SLC per FGW	CT.Hartford	No--no, I	CtHMTH(dr)	09825 enc in July 25 to FGW
Bolles, George A.	****.06.18	SLC	Unknown	Your note arrived	MH-H	08688
Bolton, Sarah K.	****.**.**	SLC	Unknown	Some day, dear	MWA	05007
Bolton, Sarah K.	1886.10.23	SLC	CT.Hartford	I am called	MWA	01973
Bolton, Sarah K.	1886.11.03	SLC	CT.Hartford	Please keep the	MWA	02005
Bolton, Sarah K.	1886.11.13	SLC	CT.Hartford	I don't imagine	MWA	01976
Bolton, Sarah K.	1887.07.07	SLC	NY.Elmira	You have made	MWA	02106
Bolton, Sarah K.	1888.09.20	SLC	NY.Elmira	Supscription-books	MWA	05042
Boone, T.W.M.	1880.09.03	SLC	NY.Elmira	I desire to	ArU	03341
Booth, Edwin	1877.04.07	SLC	CT.Hartford	I have called	VtMiM	01411
Booth, Edwina	1877.04.08	SLC	CT.Hartford	Some day, Miss	ViU	09285 inscription
Booth, Edwina	1894.02.03	SLC	NY.New York	If I had	CU-MARK(ph)	10568
Booth, Etta	1877.09.10	SLC	CT.Hartford	Your letter has	CU-MARK	01479
Booth, Hattie	1870.03.18	SLC	NY.Buffalo	I do it	CtHSD	00445
Booth, Mary M.	1880.06.11	SLC	CT.Hartford	I think yours	105:1947.05.12f	01811 inscription
Booth, Mr.	****.**.**	SLC	Unknown	Mr. Booth, if	107:1924.03.10	09454
Bostelmann, John C.	1889.09.13	SLC	NY.Elmira	I enclose check	CU-MARK(tr)	03939

Boston Advertiser ed.		1874.06.16	SLC	NY.Elmira	Last year, in	NN-B 189:1874.06.23	02471
Boston Herald ed.		1885.07.06	SLC	NY.Elmira	I want to	CU-MARK	03254
Bouchere, Elise de		1900.10.02	SLC	EN.London	with the kindest	122:1931.04.29	09269 inscription
Boucicault, Aubrey	o/a	1906.06.22	SLC per IVL	NH.Dublin	Mr. Clemens is	CU-MARK(dr)	07466 on Boucicault June 22
Bouton, J.W.		1883.02.18	SLC	CT.Hartford	Draw & be	CU-MARK	02347
Bowen, Clarence W.		1889.04.08	SLC	CT.Hartford	I accept with	MWA	03881
Bowen, Clarence W.		1889.04.28	SLC	CT.Hartford	At the last	MWA	03887
Bowen, Clarence W.		1890.01.24	SLC	CT.Hartford	My hand is	MWA	04006
Bowen, Dora C.		1900.06.06	SLC	EN.London	Yes, I really	TxU	05814
Bowen, Herbert E.		1903.01.04	SLC	NY.Riverdale	It seems to	ViU	06549
Bowen, Marjorie		1907.03.25	SLC	NY.New York	Indeed I shall	CU-MARK(ph)	07680
Bowen, Marjorie		1907.05.27	SLC	NY.Tuxedo Park	I shall be	297:130f	07733
Bowen, Marjorie		1907.06.18	SLC per RWA	EN.London	Mr. Clemens bids	CU-MARK(tr)	07743 RWA tr
Bowen, William		1866.05.07	SLC	HI.Maui	I have been	TxU(ph)	00100
Bowen, William		1866.08.25	SLC	CA.San Francisco	There has been	TxU	00106
Bowen, William		1867.06.07	SLC	NY.New York	We leave tomorrow have to write	CU-MARK(tr) TxU	00133
Bowen, William		1868.01.25	SLC	NY.New York	I have just	TxU	00184
Bowen, William		1870.02.06	SLC	NY.Buffalo	My heart goes	TxU	02464
Bowen, William	ca	1870.06.01	SLC	Unknown	Been too busy	CU-MARK(ph)	02136
Bowen, William		1871.07.23	SLC	NY.Elmira	I have been	ViU	00639
Bowen, William		1873.01.17	SLC	CT.Hartford	I am deeply	TxU	00858 date uncertain
Bowen, William		1873.03.20	SLC	CT.Hartford	Am very much	TxU	00888
Bowen, William		1873.03.28	SLC	CT.Hartford	Bless your heart	TxU	00891
Bowen, William		1873.11.07	SLC	CT.Hartford	Have just got	TxU	00981
Bowen, William	ca	1874.02.25	SLC	CT.Hartford	frag. promises to	TxU	01054 fragment

ADDRESSEE	DATE	WRITER	PLACE	CUE	SOURCE	NUMBER/NOTES
Bowen, William	aft 1874.05.05	SLC	NY.Elmira	Glad to hear	CU-MARK(ph)	01083
Bowen, William	1876.08.31	SLC	NY.Elmira	Damnation, (if you	CU-MARK	01360 unsent
Bowen, William	1888.10.06	SLC	CT.Hartforc	I want you	TxU	03783 telegram
Bowen, William	1888.11.04	SLC	CT.Hartford	I received your	TxU	03826
Bowen, William	1888.12.29	SLC	CT.Hartford	I am exceedingly	TxU	03810
Bowen, William	bef 1889.12.07	SLC	CT.Hartford	Will that do	TxU	03984
Bowes, Margaret I.	1910.01.26	SLC	BE.Hamilton	I am so	CU-MARK(tr)	08552
Bowker, Bessie S.	1900.04.19	SLC	EN.London	There isn't a	MiU	05793
Bowker, Richard R.	aft 1885.07.23	SLC	Unknown	It is a	DLC	11152
Bowker, Richard R.	bef 1885.07.23	SLC	Unknown	If you will	DLC	11151
Bowker, Richard R.	1889.10.09	SLC	CT.Hartford	I have worked	NN	03949
Bowker, Richard R.	pm 1889.12.02	SLC	CT.Hartford	Blessed are the	NN	03981
Bowker, Richard R.	1899.12.04	SLC	EN.London	Indeed I should	NN	05716
Bowker, Richard R.	1906.02.04	SLC per IVL	NY.New York	Mr. Clemens requests	NN	07327
Bowker, Richard R.	1908.12.22	SLC	CT.Redding	I am somewhat	NN	08186
Bowles, Samuel	1869.06.22	SLC	CT.Hartford	Since I have	282:1918.04.23	09743
Bowney, E.M.	1907.08.**	SLC	NY.Tuxedo Park	On the whole	226:183	09258 inscription
Bowring & Co.	1907.07.30	SLC per RWA	Unknown	I shall be	CU-MARK(tr)	07795 RWA tr
Bowser, David W.	1880.03.20	SLC	CT.Hartford	I haven't read	TxU	01772
Bowser, David W.	o/a 1880.03.30	SLC	CT.Hartford	Now, Master Wattie	TxU	01777 on Howells Mar 30
Bowser, David W.	1880.12.22	SLC	CT.Hartford	I certainly owe	TxU	02124
Bowser, David W.	1881.11.16	SLC	CT.Hartford	Many thanks for	TxU	02087
Bowser, David W.	1882.01.10	SLC	CT.Hartford	My boy, I clear	TxU	02147
Boyesen, Elizabeth K.	1889.03.03	SLC	CT.Hartford	It's entirely sufficient	CU-MARK	03869
Boyesen, Hjalmar H.	1879.11.06	SLC	CT.Hartford	Met a fine	CU-MARK(ph)	01707
Boyesen, Hjalmar H.	1880.04.23	SLC	CT.Hartford	I thank you	ViU	01792

Boyesen, Hjalmar H.		1881.10.26	SLC	CT.Hartford	I shall have	122:1936.01.14	02067 other sources
Boyesen, Hjalmar H.		1882.01.11	SLC	CT.Hartford	I was mightily	ViU	02149
Boyesen, Hjalmar H.		1887.10.21	SLC	CT.Hartford	Truly Yours	157:1924.11.06	09789 inscription
Boyesen, Hjalmar H.		1887.11.07	SLC	CT.Hartford	Won't you please	Sw2	03665
Boyle, Virginia F.		1901.09.16	SLC	NY.Saranac Lake	They arrived last	CU-MARK(ph)	06137
Boyle, Virginia F.		1902.01.06	SLC	NY.Riverdale	I am not	CU-MARK(ph)	06221
Boyle, Virginia F.	ca	1904.06.21	SLC	IT.Florence	For what you	CU-MARK(ph)	06844 form letter
Boyle, Virginia F.		1905.07.17	SLC	NH.Dublin	We are here	CU-MARK(ph)	07086
Brachmann, Elisabeth		1902.04.14	SLC	NY.Riverdale	Don't let Chatto	CLjC	10673 misdated Aug
Brachmann, Elisabeth		1902.08.14	SLC	NY.Riverdale	Don't let Chatto	CLjC	10677 misdated, see Apr
Brachmann, Elisabeth	pm	1902.09.26	SLC	ME.York Harbor	I shall be	CU-MARK(ph)	10158
Braekstad, Hans L.		1899.08.24	SLC	SE.Sanna	Unhappily for me	NoOU	05665
Bramhall, Mrs. L.C.U.	o/a	1905.12.04	SLC per IVL	NY.New York	Not seen Mrs.	CU-MARK(dr)	07230 on Bramhall Dec 4
Breckenridge, Marjorie		****.**.**	SLC	CT.Redding	I can't, Marjorie	MiK2	08690
Breckenridge, Marjorie		1908.04.19	SLC	NY.New York	Marjorie dear, we all	MiK2	07980
Breckenridge, Marjorie		1908.10.07	SLC	CT.Redding	Indeed you are	MiK2	08126
Breckenridge, Marjorie		1908.12.01	SLC	CT.Redding	You see I	MiK2	08167
Breckenridge, Marjorie		1909.05.26	SLC	CT.Redding	The summer is	MiK2	08402
Bree, Malvine	pm	1898.05.29	CC	AU.Kaltenleut.	Konnen Sie	CU-MARK(ph)	10944 also by SLC & OLC
Bree, Malvine	pm	1898.05.29	SLC & OLC	AU.Kaltenleut.	Konnen Sie	CU-MARK(ph)	05217 also by CC
Bree, Malvine		1898.12.24	CC	AU.Vienna	from her pupil	CU-MARK(ph)	10945 inscription
Bree, Malvine		1903.**.**	CC	Unknown	Es thut mir	CU-MARK(tr)	06537
Bree, Malvine		1903.**.**	CC	Unknown	Kommen Sie bald	CU-MARK(tr)	06536

ADDRESSEE	DATE	WRITER	PLACE	CUE	SOURCE	NUMBER/NOTES
Bree, Malvine	1903.06.23	CC	NY.Riverdale	Habe ich oder	CU-MARK(tr)	06681
Bridge, Cyprian A.	1895.12.23	SLC	AS.Sydney	We sail in	NNC	04984
Bridges, Robert	1902.02.18	SLC	NY.Riverdale	I thank you	PCarlD	06280
Brigham, Warren L.	1870.12.01	SLC	NY.Buffalo	I am sorry	MBAt	07285
Brittain, Harry E.	1907.06.18	SLC per RWA	EN.London	Mr. Clemens has	CU-MARK(tr)	07744 RWA tr
Brockley, Nettie	1908.12.**	SLC per IVL	CT.Redding	Indeed yes, dear	CU-MARK(tr)	08166
Bronson, Katherine C.	1892.05.25	SLC	IT.Venice	You are wonderfully	ViU	04294
Bronson, Katherine C.	1893.02.20	SLC	IT.Florence	Mrs. Clemens sends	CU-MARK(ph)	04341
Bronson, Miss	1894.07.04	SLC	FR.La Bourboule	Do lay this	CU-MARK(ph)	04751 inscription
Brooklyn Daily Eagle	1867.12.30	SLC	NY.New York	In your issue	194:1867.12.31	11062
Brooklyn Daily Eagle	1869.12.03	SLC	NY.Brooklyn	I was to	194:1869.12.04	02283
Brooks, Mrs.	****.**.**	SLC	CT.Hartford	Livy is getting	ViU	08694
Brooks, Noah	1883.07.23	SLC	NY.Elmira	When you wrote	CU-MARK	02351
Brooks, Samuel	o/a 1906.10.10	SLC per IVL	Unknown	That was in	CU-MARK(dr)	07541 on Brooks Oct 10
Brooks, Shirley	1873.09.23	SLC	EN.London	May I send	NNPM	00963
Brooks, Shirley	1873.12.12	SLC	EN.London	The fog got	ViU	01002
Brown & Gross	1887.01.15	SLC	CT.Hartford	Please order &	CU-MARK(ph)	10566
Brown & Gross	bef 1888.08.07	SLC	NY.Elmira	Please get me	305:1912.05.08	09742 on printed prospectus
Brown, Charles R.	o/a 1887.09.02	SLC	NY.Elmira	I have received	CU-MARK	03622
Brown, John	1873.09.22 & 1873.09.25	SLC	EN.London	Of all the	CU-MARK(ph)	03362
Brown, John	1873.10.30	SLC	SH.Batavia	We have plowed	CLjC	00978
Brown, John	1874.02.28	SLC	CT.Hartford	My dear friend	CtY	01056
Brown, John	1874.04.27	SLC	NY.Elmira	This town is	CU-MARK(ph)	01080
Brown, John	1874.06.15	SLC	NY.Elmira	The letters have	NN-B	02470
Brown, John	1874.09.04	SLC	NY.Elmira	I have been	CU-MARK(ph)	01122 other sources

Brown, John	aft	1875.10.25	SLC & OLC	CT.Hartford	We had grown	UkENL	01279
Brown, John		1876.06.22	SLC & OLC	NY.Elmira	Dear friend the	CU-MARK(ph)	01343
Brown, John		1876.12.05	SLC	CT.Hartford	I want to	UkENL	02465
Brown, John	&	1877.08.25 1877.08.27	SLC	NY.Elmira	I thought I	NN-B	01473
Brown, John		1879.08.21	SLC	EN.Liverpool	During all the	CU-MARK(ph)	01682
Brown, John	to	1880.08.14 1880.08.15	SLC	NY.Elmira	A couple of	CU-MARK(ph)	02814
Brown, John Jr.		1882.06.01	SLC	CT.Hartford	I was three	UkENL	02212
Brown, John Jr.		1882.10.29	SLC	CT.Hartford	I am a	UkENL	08906
Brown, John Jr.		1882.12.16	SLC	CT.Hartford	You may be	UkENL	08905 typed
Brown, John Jr.		1890.02.11	SLC	CT.Hartford	Both copies came	195:361	04015
Brown, John Jr.		1906.03.26	SLC	NY.New York	With this I	UkENL	07402
Brown, John Jr.		1908.06.20	SLC	CT.Redding	I have economised	UkENL	08036
Brown, John Jr.		1909.08.05	SLC	CT.Redding	Don't you think	UkENL	08438
Brown, John Jr.		1909.09.**	SLC	CT.Redding	It was too	UkENL	08447
Brown, Walter L.		1886.06.14	SLC	CT.Hartford	It is a	WU(ph)	03409
Brownell, Louise	pm	1891.04.20	SC	PA.Bryn Mawr	It breaks my	NCH	09128
Brownell, Louise	pm	1891.04.29	SC	CT.Hartford	Mamma knows I	NCH	09129
Brownell, Louise	ca	1891.09.07	SC	SW.Lucerne	I have been	NCH	09134
Brownell, Louise	ca	1891.09.07	SC	SW.Lucerne	My darling I	NCH	09135
Brownell, Louise	ca	1891.10.**	SC	GE.Berlin	I am afraid	NCH	09132
Brownell, Louise	ca	1891.10.**	SC	Unknown	Ever since I	NCH	09131
Brownell, Louise	ca	1891.10.**	SC	Unknown	Your letter of	NCH	09133
Brownell, Louise		1891.10.02	SC	SW.Ouchy	At last a	NCH	09130
Brownell, Louise		1891.10.03	SC	SW.Lucerne	Your letter which	NCH	09138
Brownell, Louise		1891.10.31	SC	GE.Berlin	Your precious last	NCH	09136
Brownell, Louise	pm	1891.11.12	SC	GE.Berlin	*	NCH	09137 envelope only

ADDRESSEE		DATE	WRITER	PLACE	CUE	SOURCE	NUMBER/NOTES
Brownell, Louise		1892.04.08	SC	AU.Trent	I have been	NCH	09139
Brownell, Louise	ca	1892.04.20	SC	IT.Rome	I really don't	NCH	09142
Brownell, Louise	pm	1892.04.21	SC	IT.Rome	Two letters have	NCH	09140
Brownell, Louise	pm	1892.04.29	SC	IT.Rome	A little tired	NCH	09141
Brownell, Louise	pm	1892.05.29	SC	IT.Venice	We have been	NCH	09143
Brownell, Louise		1892.08.**	SC	GE.Nauheim	The most lovely	NCH	09145
Brownell, Louise	pm	1892.08.18	SC	GE.Frankfurt	*	NCH	09144 envelope only
Brownell, Louise	pm	1892.09.09	SC	GE.Bad-Nauheim	I must send	NCH	09146
Brownell, Louise	pm	1892.09.19	SC	Unknown	I have tried	NCH	09147
Brownell, Louise	pm	1892.09.25	SC	IT.Florence	This our first	NCH	09148
Brownell, Louise	ca	1892.09.27	SC	IT.Florence	I am thinking	NCH	10425
Brownell, Louise	pm	1892.10.14	SC	IT.Florence	I cannot tell	NCH	09149
Brownell, Louise	pm	1892.11.07	SC	IT.Florence	There has been	NCH	09150
Brownell, Louise	pm	1892.11.13	SC	IT.Florence	I was so	NCH	09151
Brownell, Louise	pm	1892.11.18	SC	IT.Florence	Your past three	NCH	09152
Brownell, Louise	pm	1892.12.27	SC	IT.Florence	Your New Year's	NCH	09153
Brownell, Louise	pm	1892.12.31	SC	IT.Florence	Such a beautiful	NCH	09154
Brownell, Louise	pm	1893.01.**	SC	IT.Florence	Such a love	NCH	09155
Brownell, Louise		1893.03.**	SC	GE.Franzensbad	It is true	NCH	09157
Brownell, Louise	pm	1893.03.05	SC	IT.Florence	It is so	NCH	09156
Brownell, Louise		1893.04.**	SC	IT.Florence	At last a	NCH	09160
Brownell, Louise	pm	1893.04.03	SC	IT.Venice	Your letter telling	NCH	09158
Brownell, Louise	pm	1893.04.06	SC	IT.Venice	I believe I	NCH	09159
Brownell, Louise	pm	1893.06.08	SC	IT.Florence	I was so	NCH	09161
Brownell, Louise	pm	1893.06.13	SC	IT.Florence	We are in	NCH	09162
Brownell, Louise	pm	1893.06.21	SC	IT.Florence	Your beautiful letter	NCH	09163
Brownell, Louise		1893.06.28	SC	Unknown	In the above	NCH	09166 poem enc
Brownell, Louise	pm	1893.09.03	SC	GE.Franzensbad	I have carried	NCH	09164

Brownell, Louise		1894.07.29	SC	FR.Fontainebleau	I don't know	NCH	09167
Bruce-Joy, A.		1907.07.30	SLC per RWA	Unknown	Your letter of	CU-MARK(tr)	07796 RWA tr
Brunswick-Balke-C. Co.	o/a	1906.04.02	SLC per IVL	NY.New York	Thanks for tickets	CU-MARK(dr)	07410 on Co. Apr 2
Brush, Louis		****.**.**	SLC	Unknown	With best regards	107:1927.02.28	09564 inscription
Brush, Louis		1874.02.**	SLC	CT.Hartford	With compts of	NN-B	09811 inscription
Brush, Nancy D.		****.**.**	JC	NY.New York	Dr. Peterson opened	DSI	09070 fragment
Brush, Nancy D.		****.**.**	JC	Unknown	I am delighted	DSI	09073
Brush, Nancy D.		1906.01.11	JC	NY.New York	What does this	DSI	07302
Brush, Nancy D.		1906.02.11	JC	NY.New York	Thank you very	DSI	07339
Brush, Nancy D.		1906.10.21	JC	NY.New York	I am still	DSI	07552
Brush, Nancy D.		1907.01.16	JC	CT.Greenwich	I am behind	DSI	07628
Brush, Nancy D.		1907.02.11	JC	NY.Katonah	I was delighted	DSI	07651
Brush, Nancy D.		1907.04.24	JC	NY.Katonah	I was mighty	DSI	07697
Brush, Nancy D.		1907.06.24	JC	NY.Katonah	Until very recently	DSI	07769
Brush, Nancy D.		1907.08.07	JC	NY.Katonah	I don't know	DSI	07809
Brush, Nancy D.		1907.10.02	JC	NY.Katonah	I feel that	DSI	07842
Brush, Nancy D.		1907.10.31	JC	NY.Katonah	Your second letter	DSI	07859
Brush, Nancy D.		1907.11.07	JC	NY.Katonah	I haven't much	DSI	07861
Brush, Nancy D.		1907.11.15	JC	NY.Katonah	I am one	DSI	07862
Brush, Nancy D.		1907.11.23	JC	NY.Katonah	What is Gerry	DSI	07868
Brush, Nancy D.		1907.11.29	JC	NY.Katonah	You careless child	DSI	07871
Brush, Nancy D.		1907.12.05	JC	NY.Katonah	Your letters are	DSI	07883
Brush, Nancy D.		1907.12.09	JC	NY.Katonah	I am sending	DSI	07884
Brush, Nancy D.		1907.12.23	JC	NY.Katonah	I am behind	DSI	07893
Brush, Nancy D.		1907.12.26	JC	NY.Katonah	This is just	DSI	07896
Brush, Nancy D.		1908.01.02	JC	NY.Katonah	Yes, Gerry did	DSI	07910

ADDRESSEE	DATE	WRITER	PLACE	CUE	SOURCE	NUMBER/NOTES
Brush, Nancy D.	1908.01.06	JC	CT.Greenwich	The promised tracing	DSI	07909
Brush, Nancy D.	1908.01.29	JC	CT.Greenwich	I had a	DSI	07927
Brush, Nancy D.	1908.02.09	JC	CT.Greenwich	This is Sunday	DSI	07933
Brush, Nancy D.	1908.02.17	JC	CT.Greenwich	I am inutterably	DSI	07940
Brush, Nancy D.	1908.02.23	JC	CT.Greenwich	I am rushing	DSI(tr)	07947
Brush, Nancy D.	1908.03.02	JC	CT.Greenwich	Tonight I can	DSI	07955
Brush, Nancy D.	1908.03.10	JC	CT.Greenwich	The day after	DSI	07959
Brush, Nancy D.	1908.03.29	JC	CT.Greenwich	My head is	DSI	07966
Brush, Nancy D.	1908.04.05	JC	CT.Greenwich	I feel pretty	DSI	07970
Brush, Nancy D.	1908.04.15	JC	CT.Greenwich	I first meant	DSI	07976
Brush, Nancy D.	1908.04.26	JC	CT.Greenwich	Spring is here	DSI	07986
Brush, Nancy D.	1908.05.06	JC	CT.Greenwich	Your letter must	DSI	07992
Brush, Nancy D.	1908.05.20	JC	MA.Gloucester	I just heard	DSI	08002
Brush, Nancy D.	1908.06.29	JC	MA.Gloucester	You don't know	DSI	08045
Brush, Nancy D.	ca 1908.07.**	JC	MA.Gloucester	P.S. Father came	DSI	09072
Brush, Nancy D.	1908.07.08	JC	MA.Gloucester	I have just	DSI	08054
Brush, Nancy D.	1908.07.23	JC	MA.Gloucester	I haven't heard	DSI	08059
Brush, Nancy D.	1908.08.01	JC	MA.Gloucester	I am late	DSI	08071
Brush, Nancy D.	1908.08.09	JC	MA.Gloucester	I have just	DSI	08078
Brush, Nancy D.	1908.08.27	JC	MA.Gloucester	I asked Galla	DSI	08094
Brush, Nancy D.	1908.09.10	JC	MA.Gloucester	Just a few	DSI	08101
Brush, Nancy D.	1909.06.13	JC	CT.Redding	Couldn't you find	DSI	08420
Brush, Nancy D.	1909.07.08	JC	CT.Redding	Did you think	DSI	08432
Brush, Nancy D.	1909.07.29	JC	CT.Redding	You were right	DSI	08437
Brush, Nancy D.	1909.09.22	JC	CT.Redding	Is she the	DSI	08459
Brush, Nancy D.	1909.11.10	JC	CT.Redding	I sent someone	DSI	08489
Brush, Nancy D.	1909.11.28	JC	CT.Redding	We had a	DSI	08501
Bryan, William L.	1907.03.29	SLC	NY.New York	Assuming that I	CU-MARK(tr)	07679
Bryce, James	1900.03.21	SLC	EN.London	Presently some gentleman	UkOxU	05778

Bryce, Lloyd S.	1894.10.13	SLC	FR.Rouen	Your kind note	CtY	04797
Bryce, Lloyd S.	1894.11.30	SLC	FR.Paris	I am located	CU-MARK(tr)	04816
Bryce, Lloyd S.	1895.03.09	SLC	NY.New York	I find a	ViU	04847
Buckley, Miss	1895.09.15	SLC	AS.Melbourne	I am so	ODa2	04961
Buckus, Samuel W.	1891.05.29	SLC per FGW	CT.Hartford	In compliance with	CU-MARK(tr)	01172 FGW tr
Buel, Clarence C.	1886.02.26	SLC	CT.Hartford	Yes--that's the	NN-B	03373
Buel, Clarence C.	1888.08.12	SLC	NY.Elmira	I'll tell you	NN-B	03589 also to Gilder & Johnson
Buel, Clarence C.	1891.08.15	SLC	GE.Marienbad	Obliged to decline	CU-MARK(tr)	10936 telegram; SLC tr
Buel, Clarence C.	1891.08.16	SLC	GE.Marienbad	I had to	CU-MARK(ph)	04223
Buel, Clarence C.	1893.12.13	SLC	NY.New York	My voice has	ViU	04525
Buel, Clarence C.	1893.12.14	SLC	NY.New York	I am still	Mo2	04527
Buel, Clarence C.	1895.04.02 to 1895.04.03	SLC	SH.Paris	Before I left	CU-MARK(ph)	04858
Buel, Clarence C. & Carey, William	1895.08.17	SLC	CN.Vancouver	This is to	Mo2	02400 to six editors
Buel, Clarence C.	1905.12.29	SLC per IVL	NY.New York	This letter from	ViU	07276
Buffalo Express readers	1870.03.07	SLC	NY.Buffalo	The paragraph now	196:1870.03.08	05162
Bunce, Edward M.	****.**.**	SLC	CT.Hartford	Look here, you	NNC	08700
Bunce, Edward M.	1896.10.16	SLC	EN.London	It is with	CtHMTH	05131
Bunce, Mrs. Edward M.	1890.10.25	OLC	CT.Hartford	Thank you so	MiMtpT	08907
Bunce, Mrs. Edward M.	1898.12.02	SLC	AU.Vienna	It falls like	CtHMTH	05474
Bunce, Nellie	1888.06.09	SLC	CT.Hartford	I thank Will	CtHMTH	03723
Bunce, Nellie	1889.09.07	SLC	NY.Elmira	How well I	CtHMTH	03938
Bunn, W.M.	1887.12.23	SLC	CT.Hartford	Two days' notice	CtY	03681
Bunner, Alice L.	1899.06.06	SLC	EN.Broadstairs	Unfortunately I am	ViU	05633
Burbank, Alfred P.	1887.09.08	SLC	NY.Elmira	Alas & alas	CU-MARK	03645
Burbank, Alfred P.	1887.10.**	SLC	Unknown	Go to Sheol	CU-MARK(dr)	03656

ADDRESSEE	DATE	WRITER	PLACE	CUE	SOURCE	NUMBER/NOTES
Burdette, Robert J.	1881.12.20	SLC	CT.Hartford	With the kindest	CtHMTH	09317 inscription
Burdette, Robert J.	o/a 1890.04.19	SLC	CT.Hartford	You will have	197:136	04034
Burgess, Gilbert	1897.03.03	SLC	EN.London	It is most	MiD	05182
Burgess, Mr.	1884.10.28	SLC	CT.Hartford	I am most	CU-MARK(ph)	10564
Burke, Billie	1907.12.05	SLC per IVL	NY.New York	It was lovely	CU-MARK(tr)	07882
Burlingame, Anson or Burlingame, Edward L.	1866.07.07	SLC	HI.Honolulu	Yours Truly	DLC	10786 inscription
Burlingame, Anson	1868.02.18 or 1868.02.19	SLC	DC.Washington	Don't neglect or	297:18	00194
Burlingame, Anson	1868.02.19	SLC	DC.Washington	This is to	DLC	00195
Burlingame, Edward L. or Burlingame, Anson	1866.07.07	SLC	HI.Honolulu	Yours Truly	DLC	10786 inscription
Burlingame, Edward L.	1868.10.07	SLC	CT.Hartford	I am here	297:18	02757
Burns, Marie E.	o/a 1906.04.08	SLC per IVL	NY.New York	In the circumstances	CU-MARK(dr)	07419 on Burns Apr 8
Burrage, Charles D.	1905.02.11	SLC	NY.New York	You wrote me a very	ODa2	11195
Burrough, Frank E.	1900.12.15	SLC	NY.New York	I should say	MoCgS	05932
Burrough, Jacob H.	1876.11.01	SLC	CT.Hartford	As you describe	MoCgS	01384
Burton, Mr.	****.**.**	SLC	Unknown	I wish I	CtHSD	07433
Burton, Nathaniel J.	1881.12.28	SLC	CT.Hartford	You can nest	CU-MARK	02127
Bustard, A.A.	o/a 1906.03.14	SLC per IVL	NY.New York	It was privately	CU-MARK(dr)	07382 on Bustard Mar 14
Butes, Dorothy	1907.04.22	SLC	NY.New York	On the whole	CU-MARK(ph)	10554 inscription
Butes, Dorothy	1907.05.**	SLC	NY.Tuxedo Park	Your letter has	NNC	07702
Butes, Dorothy	1908.07.25	SLC	CT.Redding	Goodbye you dear	CU-MARK	08058
Butler, Nicholas M.	1908.10.12	SLC	CT.Redding	I gladly join	CU-MARK(tr)	08135
Butters, Henry	ca 1904.**.**	SLC	Unknown	I suppose you	CU-MARK	08717
Byng, Emily G.	1909.07.**	SLC	CT.Redding	with the compliments	116:1972.01.27	09933 inscription
Bynner, Witter	1906.10.05	SLC	NH.Dublin	You have certainly	MH-H	07538

Bynner, Witter	1907.**.**	SLC	NY.New York	Of all sad	CU-MARK(tr)	07610 inscription
C. & Co.	aft 1904.**.**	SLC per IVL	Unknown	I have no	CU-MARK(tr)	06541
Cable, George W.	****.**.**	CC	NY.New York	It was extremely	LNT	10726
Cable, George W.	1881.07.17	SLC	CT.Branford	The book has	LNT	01985
Cable, George W.	1882.06.20	SLC	CT.Hartford	Confound it, the	LNT	02222
Cable, George W.	1882.09.29	SLC	NY.New York	I've rushed in	LNT	02281
Cable, George W.	1882.10.05	SLC	CT.Hartford	Did you get	LNT	02286 typed
Cable, George W.	1882.10.12	SLC	CT.Hartford	The portrait has	LNT	02290 typed
Cable, George W.	1882.10.16	SLC	CT.Hartford	All right to	LNT	02291 typed
Cable, George W.	1882.11.11	SLC	CT.Hartford	The books all	LNT	02303 typed
Cable, George W.	1883.01.15	SLC	CT.Hartford	I have just	LNT	02336
Cable, George W.	1883.03.09	SLC	CT.Hartford	Roswell Smith has	LNT	02354
Cable, George W.	1883.03.10	SLC	CT.Hartford	In behalf of	LNT	02357 group letter
Cable, George W.	1883.03.17	SLC	CT.Hartford	You are to	LNT	02361
Cable, George W.	1883.03.23	SLC	CT.Hartford	Suppose you repeat	LNT	10710 telegram
Cable, George W.	1883.03.23	SLC	CT.Hartford	Mrs. Clemens and	LNT	02363 typed
Cable, George W.	1883.03.26	SLC	CT.Hartford	You are to	LNT	10711 telegram
Cable, George W.	1883.03.27	SLC	CT.Hartford	No that won't	LNT	10712 telegram
Cable, George W.	1883.04.16	SLC	CT.Hartford	There is not	LNT	02371 typed
Cable, George W.	1883.06.04	SLC	CT.Hartford	The girls were	LNT	08821 typed
Cable, George W.	1885.01.23	OLC	CT.Hartford	This letter was	LNT	10725
Cable, George W.	1885.03.02	OLC	CT.Hartford	This document has	LNT	03182

ADDRESSEE	DATE	WRITER	PLACE	CUE	SOURCE	NUMBER/NOTES
Cable, George W.	1885.05.17	SLC	CT.Hartford	Your letter came	LNT	03229
Cable, George W.	1889.06.11	SLC	CT.Hartford	They are lost	LNT	03900
Cable, George W.	1895.06.25	SLC	NY.Elmira	You make me	LNT	04897
Cable, George W.	1901.10.15	SLC	NY.Riverdale	Your book came	LNT	06156
Cable, George W.	1902.01.09	SLC	NY.Riverdale	As regards that	CU-MARK	06229 typed form letter
Cable, Louise S.	1884.01.30	SLC	CT.Hartford	Your husband will	LNT	09227 telegram
Cable, Louise S.	1884.02.01	OLC	CT.Hartford	Mr Cable has	LNT	02902
Cable, Louise S.	1884.02.05	OLC	CT.Hartford	Still a good	LNT	10720
Cable, Louise S.	1884.02.06	OLC	CT.Hartford	I am going	LNT	02909
Cable, Louise S.	1884.02.07	OLC	CT.Hartford	I congratulate you	LNT	02911
Cadieu, Florence W.	1906.03.15	SLC	NY.New York	On the whole it is	ODa2	11188 inscription
Cadley, Peter	o/a 1905.12.25	SLC per IVL	NY.New York	Don't remember where	CU-MARK(dr)	07274
Cake, Lu B.	o/a 1906.02.16	SLC per IVL	NY.New York	very little time	CU-MARK(dr)	07346 on Cake Feb 16
Caldwell, S.L.	1885.04.11	SLC	CT.Hartford	In answer to	NPV	03212
Caldwell, William A.	1906.02.05	SLC	NY.New York	No, it isn't	NN-B(tr)	07328
California Pioneers	1869.10.11	SLC	NY.Elmira	Circumstances render it	317:1869.10.14	00363 other sources
Campbell-Bannerman, H.	ca 1905.11.30	SLC	NY.New York	Just a line	CU-MARK(tr)	07226
Campbell-Bannerman, H.	1906.09.07	SLC	NH.Dublin	Congratulations, not	VtMiM	07519 telegram
Canfield, James H.	****.**.**	SLC	Unknown	It was always	206:1885.03.18	07833
Canfield, Von Beck	o/a 1909.03.19	SLC per IVL	CT.Redding	Don't think I	CU-MARK(dr)	08374 on Canfield Mar 19
Cannon, Joseph G.	1906.12.07	SLC	DC.Washington	Please get me	114:801	07586 other sources
Capper, Mrs. Louie P.	o/a 1907.02.21	SLC per IVL	NY.New York	Has seen the	CU-MARK(dr)	07657 on Capper Feb 21
Cardner, Iretus G.	1870.10.26	SLC	NY.Buffalo	How men do	ODa2	00515

Cardner, Iretus G.	1870.11.02	SLC	NY.Buffalo	Yours of 29th	CU-MARK(ph)	00521
Carey, Mr.	1897.06.14	SLC	EN.London	Oh, bless your	CCC	05226
Carey, William	****.**.**	SLC	Unknown	and if Gilder	230:230	08984
Carey, William	1893.09.**	SLC	Unknown	Land, I never	NN-B	04652
Carey, William & Buel, Clarence C.	1895.08.17	SLC	CN.Vancouver	This is to	Mo2	02400 to six editors
Carey, William	1901.02.20	SLC	NY.New York	Carey says he	CtHSD	06006
Carleton, Henry G.	1884.04.15	SLC	CT.Hartford	I think you	MWiW-C	02968
Carleton, Will	1902.11.28	SLC	NY.New York	Done by Truly	305:1913.05.12	09760 engraved inscription
Carnegie, Andrew	****.**.**	SLC	NY.New York	You can take	188:295	08593
Carnegie, Andrew	****.**.**	SLC	NY.New York	I am in	DLC	08594
Carnegie, Andrew	****.**.**	SLC	NY.New York	I don't know	DLC	08592
Carnegie, Andrew	****.**.**	SLC	NY.New York	Mr. Gilder has	DLC	08591
Carnegie, Andrew	1890.03.17	SLC	CT.Hartford	I wish to	NN	04027
Carnegie, Andrew	1890.04.23	SLC	CT.Hartford	I was sorry	NN	04043
Carnegie, Andrew	1890.05.01	SLC	CT.Hartford	Oh, I am	NN	04044
Carnegie, Andrew	1893.**.**	SLC	NY.New York	I mean to	NN	08486
Carnegie, Andrew	1893.01.28	SLC	IT.Florence	Won't you let	137:19f	03592
Carnegie, Andrew	1893.04.05	SLC	NY.New York	I am coming	NN	04363
Carnegie, Andrew	1893.04.07	SLC	NY.New York	Many thanks to	NN	04365
Carnegie, Andrew	1897.07.07	SLC	EN.London	We are leaving	297:165	05252
Carnegie, Andrew	1900.05.17	SLC	EN.London	Where are you	DLC	05806
Carnegie, Andrew	1900.07.08	SLC	EN.London	It is a	DLC	05832
Carnegie, Andrew	1901.02.06	SLC	NY.New York	You seem to	DLC	05990
Carnegie, Andrew	1901.11.21	SLC	NY.Riverdale	I find I	DLC	06173
Carnegie, Andrew	1904.11.03	SLC	NY.New York	In our sad	NN	06944
Carnegie, Andrew	1905.**.**	SLC	Unknown	I saw Esau	CU-MARK	06966 inscription
Carnegie, Andrew	1905.04.28	SLC	NY.New York	For thirty-eight years	MoSW	07035

ADDRESSEE	DATE	WRITER	PLACE	CUE	SOURCE	NUMBER/NOTES
Carnegie, Andrew	1905.12.02	SLC	NY.New York	What is your	DLC	11154
Carnegie, Andrew	1905.12.06	SLC	NY.New York	Any one of	297:107	07242
Carnegie, Andrew	1906.02.01	SLC	NY.New York	I am requested	DLC	11155
Carnegie, Andrew	1906.02.10	SLC	NY.New York	The whisky arrived	DLC	07337
Carnegie, Andrew	1906.11.26	SLC	NY.New York	I should be	DLC	11156 typed
Carnegie, Andrew & Carnegie, Louise W.	1906.12.31	SLC	NY.New York	a Happy New	NN	07604
Carnegie, Andrew	1907.07.04	SLC	EN.London	I was very	DLC	07776
Carnegie, Andrew	1908.01.22	SLC	NY.New York	I have had	DLC	08897
Carnegie, Andrew	1908.04.28	SLC	NY.New York	The whisky came	DLC	11157
Carnegie, Andrew	1909.03.26	SLC	CT.Redding	Many thanks for	DLC	11158
Carnegie, Andrew	1910.02.04	SLC	BE.Hamilton	This will introduce	297:168	08554
Carnegie, Louise W.	1903.03.31	SLC	NY.Riverdale	That was perfectly	NN	06612
Carnegie, Louise W.	1904.**.**	SLC	IT.Florence	We can't call	NN	06776
Carnegie, Louise W.	1905.**.**	SLC	NY.New York	This which I	NN	06975
Carnegie, Louise W. & Carnegie, Andrew	1906.12.31	SLC	NY.New York	a Happy New	NN	07604
Carnegie, Margaret	1900.05.28	SLC	EN.London	You are so	NN	05810
Carpenter, John R.	1904.02.14	SLC	IT.Florence	Your kind letter	CU-MARK	06792
Carpenter, William P.	1869.09.23	SLC	NY.Buffalo	I have forwarded	NNC	00357
Carr, Richard C.	1908.04.17	SLC	NY.New York	I have not	Mo2	08898
Carter, John H.	1881.06.11	SLC	CT.Hartford	You can use	OMC	10700
Casey, Charles	1885.03.02	SLC	CT.Hartford	That is a	CU-MARK(ph)	08833
Casey, Charles	1885.03.11	SLC	CT.Hartford	I hurried all	ODa2	03187
Cate, Garth W.	1906.11.25	SLC	NY.New York	Taking the pledge will	ODa2	11189 inscription
Cates, Lamotte	1902.06.07	SLC	MO.St. Louis	with the best	120:1938.01	09906 inscription; other sources
Caulfield, Edward B.	1903.11.**	SLC	IT.Florence	I waited till	CtHMTH	10950
Caulfield, Edward B.	1903.11.**	SLC	IT.Florence	Shall we call	CtHMTH	06756

Caulfield, Edward B.	bet 1903.11.** & 1903.12.**	SLC	IT.Florence	I knew there	ViU	06762
Caulfield, Edward B.	1904.01.04	SLC per IVL	IT.Florence	I hope you	Mo2	08887
Ceall, D.	1906.02.10	SLC	NY.New York	I thank you	NN-B(tr)	07338
Cecchi, Sebastiano	1905.**.**	SLC per IVL	Unknown	In the bearer	CU-MARK	06974
Century ed.	****.**.**	SLC	AU.Vienna	In the back	267:324	09501 on envelope
Century ed.	****.**.**	SLC	CT.Hartford	Glass--Handle with	WU(ph)	09059 on envelope
Century ed.	****.**.**	SLC	Unknown	Don't you think	Mo2	08291
Century ed.	1889.08.07	SLC	NY.Elmira	I've done as	ViU	03926
Century ed.	1897.08.30	SLC	SW.Weggis	You might find	CU-MARK(ph)	05282
Chaikovsky, Nikolai V.	o/a 1906.03.27	SLC	NY.New York	I thank you	131:1906.03.30	07405
Chaikovsky, Nikolai V.	1907.04.16	SLC per IVL	NY.New York	Mr. Clemens asks me	CU-MARK(dr)	10748 on Chaikovsky Apr 11
Chalmers, Jeanne	1894.01.26	SLC	MA.Boston	I tried to	176:56	04678
Chamberlain, Henry R.	1901.02.20	SLC	NY.New York	Laffan says that the	AuSN-M	10662 typed
Chamberlaine, Augustus	o/a 1905.07.30	SLC per IVL	NH.Dublin	Perhaps Jean will	CU-MARK(dr)	07092 on Chamberlaine July 30
Chamberlaine, Augustus	o/a 1905.09.28	SLC per IVL	NH.Dublin	Mr. Clemens not	CU-MARK(dr)	07150 on Chamberlaine Sept 28
Chamberlin, John R.	o/a 1907.12.11	SLC per IVL	NY.New York	I acknowledge receipt	CU-MARK(dr)	07887 on Chamberlin Dec 11
Chambers, Julius	1891.05.20	SLC	CT.Hartford	But you do	CU-MARK(tr)	04208 SLC tr
Chambers, Julius	1891.05.22	SLC	Unknown	No, upon reflection	CU-MARK(tr)	04210 SLC tr
Chambers, Julius	1900.11.19	SLC	Unknown	Yours of two	157:1916.01.20	09803

ADDRESSEE	DATE	WRITER	PLACE	CUE	SOURCE	NUMBER/NOTES
Chambers, Julius	1902.03.02	SLC	NY.Riverdale	My address is	157:1916.01.20	09802 other sources
Chambers, Robert W.	1902.11.28	SLC	NY.New York	Done by Truly	155:1962.10.29	10457 engraved inscription
Chapin, Adele	1896.05.30	SLC	AF.Bloemfontein	Do you know	203:121	05060
Chapin, Frederic	o/a 1905.11.03	SLC per IVL	NY.New York	Your favor of	CU-MARK(dr)	07193 on Chapin Nov 3
Chapin, Frederic	o/a 1906.07.25	SLC per IVL	NH.Dublin	now the sailing	CU-MARK(dr)	07479 on Chapin July 22
Chapin, Frederic	o/a 1906.08.19	SLC per IVL	NH.Dublin	If there is	CU-MARK(dr)	07502 on Chapin Aug 19
Chapin, Frederic	o/a 1906.09.12	SLC per IVL	NH.Dublin	Mr. Clemens is	CU-MARK(dr)	07521 on Chapin Sept 12
Chapman, John W.	1887.02.12	SLC	CT.Hartford	I never saw	171:1932.12	03527
Chapman, John W.	1887.02.15	SLC	CT.Hartford	I thank you	171:1932.12	03529
Chattanooga Republican	1891.03.10	SLC	CT.Hartford	The original of	204:1891.03.15	04380
Chatto & Windus	****.**.**	SLC	Unknown	Please send me	NN-B	09057
Chatto & Windus	1874.04.08	SLC	CT.Hartford	Dod Grile (Mr.	MB	01072
Chatto & Windus	1878.01.21	SLC	CT.Hartford	Please have these	107:1926.04.01	02324 date uncertain
Chatto & Windus	1878.09.08	SLC	SW.Geneva	Please do me	M2	03446
Chatto & Windus	1878.10.14	SLC	IT.Venice	Please mail a	AuMS	01601
Chatto & Windus	1880.04.20	SLC	CT.Hartford	Mr. Conway is	NN-B	02541 enc in Apr 20 to Conway
Chatto & Windus	1880.04.25	SLC	CT.Hartford	It is too	Uk4	00779 deposit
Chatto & Windus	1880.05.01	SLC	CT.Hartford	I never attend	Uk4	00783 deposit
Chatto & Windus	1880.12.01	SLC	CT.Hartford	Yours of Dec.	IU-R	01863
Chatto & Windus	1881.08.25	SLC	MA.Boston	I will take	Uk4	01591 per unknown amanuensis; deposit

Chatto & Windus	1881.10.07	SLC	CT.Hartford	Your notes for	Uk	02046
Chatto & Windus	1881.11.27	SLC	CN.Montreal	I am here	Uk4	02100 deposit
Chatto & Windus	1882.05.29	SLC	CT.Hartford	Your note for	Uk4	01623 typed; deposit
Chatto & Windus	1883.02.28	SLC	CT.Hartford	This is to	Uk4(tr)	01648 deposit
Chatto & Windus	1884.11.05	SLC	CT.Hartford	I find your	ViU	03020
Chatto & Windus	1885.09.08	SLC	NY.Elmira	Your favor of	Uk4	03286 deposit
Chatto & Windus	1886.07.12	SLC	NY.Elmira	It was a	Uk4	01506 deposit
Chatto & Windus	1887.09.19	SLC	CT.Hartford	I have just	Uk4	09055 deposit
Chatto & Windus	1887.12.29	SLC	CT.Hartford	It occurs to	TxU	03687
Chatto & Windus	1889.11.** or 1889.12.**	SLC	CT.Hartford	All right	NN-B	02707 on proofsheets
Chatto & Windus	aft 1889.12.15	SLC	CT.Hartford	It is very	NN-B	02708
Chatto & Windus	1890.02.12	SLC	NY.New York	You have done	Uk4	09481 telegram; deposit
Chatto & Windus	aft 1891.03.17	SLC	CT.Hartford	I have referred	Uk4	09492 on Tauchnitz Mar 17; deposit
Chatto & Windus	1891.07.12	SLC	FR.Aix-les-Bains	Your welcome favor	Uk4	00972 deposit
Chatto & Windus	1891.10.07	SLC	GE.Frankfurt	Please send me	ViU	04243
Chatto & Windus	1891.10.09	SLC	GE.Berlin	I have had	NN-B	04596
Chatto & Windus	1891.10.16	SLC	GE.Berlin	Being badly crippled	MoHM	04244
Chatto & Windus	1891.11.22	SLC	GE.Berlin	Yes, that is	NSyU	04255
Chatto & Windus	1891.12.20	OLC	GE.Berlin	I venture to	NN-B	05582
Chatto & Windus	1891.12.22	SLC	GE.Berlin	Please have 4	Uk4	01168 deposit
Chatto & Windus	1891.12.27	OLC	GE.Berlin	Thank you for	NN-B	05966
Chatto & Windus	1892.01.27	SLC	GE.Berlin	I am 2	Uk	04268

ADDRESSEE	DATE	WRITER	PLACE	CUE	SOURCE	NUMBER/NOTES
Chatto & Windus	1892.03.27	SLC	IT.Rome	We have just	C4	04279
Chatto & Windus	1892.07.29	SLC	GE.Bad-Nauheim	Yesterday I began	107:1925.04.16	09635
Chatto & Windus	1892.10.13	SLC	IT.Florence	Won't you please	KyLoU	04659
Chatto & Windus	1892.11.10	SLC	IT.Florence	The Finger-Prints has	NN-B	04623
Chatto & Windus	1892.12.16	SLC	IT.Florence	Please send me	Mo2	02454
Chatto & Windus	bef 1893.02.17	SLC	IT.Florence	Won't you please	CAlb2	04340 on Hafen Feb 11
Chatto & Windus	1893.03.06	SLC	IT.Florence	I thank you	KyLoU	04348
Chatto & Windus	1893.04.30	OLC	IT.Florence	The exquisite Joan	NN-B	05951
Chatto & Windus	1893.05.23	SLC	SH.Kaiser Wilh.	Please send a	ViU Uk4	04405 ViU tr; Uk4 deposit
Chatto & Windus	1893.06.12	SLC	FR.Paris	I wish to	122:1936.11.17	09954
Chatto & Windus	1893.06.12	SLC	IT.Florence	We take wing	Uk4	04415 deposit
Chatto & Windus	1893.07.30	SLC	AU.Krankenheil	As usual, you	Mo2	08931
Chatto & Windus	1893.08.05	SLC	AU.Krankenheil	Please send me	InU-Li	04431
Chatto & Windus	1893.08.18	SLC	AU.Krankenheil	Yes, sirs, you	OC	04436
Chatto & Windus	1894.06.17	SLC	FR.Paris	You will soon	Uk4	04739 deposit
Chatto & Windus	1894.07.02	SLC	FR.La Bourboule	I sail for	CtY	05251
Chatto & Windus	1894.07.04	SLC	FR.La Bourboule	Your telegram arrived	NN-B	04912
Chatto & Windus	1894.07.06	OLC	FR.La Bourboule	I rec'd safely	Uk4	01229 deposit
Chatto & Windus	1894.08.28	SLC	FR.Etretat	Oh, my God	MoHM	04783
Chatto & Windus	1894.09.12	SLC	FR.Etretat	The cablegram has	MoHM	04787
Chatto & Windus	1895.01.03	SLC	FR.Paris	Many thousand thanks	MoHM	04831
Chatto & Windus	1895.01.07	SLC	FR.Paris	All authorities of	MoHM	04832 on Scott Dec 26
Chatto & Windus	1895.04.04	SLC	EN.London	please pay S.	ViU	04861
Chatto & Windus	1895.06.**	OLC	NY.Elmira	Your check for	Uk4	09508 deposit

Chatto & Windus		1895.11.19	SLC	AU.Vienna	I think we	NN-B	10308 misdated, see 1897
Chatto & Windus		1896.**.**	CC	Unknown	My Father would	NN-B	05952
Chatto & Windus		1896.03.10	OLC	II.Jaipur	Will you kindly	NN-B	06003
Chatto & Windus	o/a	1896.07.15	SLC	Unknown	Will you answer	CU-MARK	05084 on Siegel to Harper July 8
Chatto & Windus		1896.07.31	SLC	EN.Southampton	Please forward all	NN-B	05237 telegram
Chatto & Windus		1896.08.07	CC	EN.Weybridge	Will you kindly	NN-B	06047
Chatto & Windus		1896.08.14	SLC	EN.Guildford	We may sail	NN-B	05240 telegram
Chatto & Windus		1896.10.20	SLC	EN.London	Please look it	MoHM	05132
Chatto & Windus		1896.10.26	SLC	EN.London	I suppose you	MoHM	05135
Chatto & Windus		1896.10.27	SLC	EN.London	Did you receive	MoHM	05137
Chatto & Windus		1896.10.29	SLC	EN.London	1. Please send me	ViU	05138
Chatto & Windus		1896.10.31	SLC	EN.London	Am very much	ViU	05140
Chatto & Windus		1896.11.13	SLC	Unknown	Please send me	NN-B	05244
Chatto & Windus		1896.11.17	SLC	EN.London	I have finished	MoHM	05143
Chatto & Windus		1896.11.18	SLC	EN.London	Can you shove	CSmH	05146
Chatto & Windus		1896.11.18	SLC	EN.London	I think it	MoHM	05145
Chatto & Windus		1896.12.**	SLC per OLC	EN.London	Will you kindly	NN-B	06095
Chatto & Windus		1896.12.18	SLC per OLC	EN.London	Will you kindly	NN-B	06103
Chatto & Windus		1896.12.23	OLC	EN.London	Will you kindly	NN-B	06116
Chatto & Windus		1896.12.24	SLC	EN.London	I would like	NN-B	05245
Chatto & Windus		1897.02.01	SLC	EN.London	I've got just	NN-B	05503
Chatto & Windus		1897.02.03	OLC	EN.London	Will you kindly	NN-B	06140
Chatto & Windus		1897.02.11	SLC	EN.London	something that will	107:1929.04.18	09567
Chatto & Windus		1897.03.09	OLC	EN.London	Will you please	NN-B	06171
Chatto & Windus	pm	1897.03.23	SLC	EN.London	R. writes me	UPB	10866

ADDRESSEE	DATE	WRITER	PLACE	CUE	SOURCE	NUMBER/NOTES
Chatto & Windus	1897.03.25	SLC	EN.London	The Personal	KyLoU	05190
Chatto & Windus	1897.04.01	OLC	EN.London	Will you send	NN-B	06203
Chatto & Windus	1897.04.14	SLC	EN.London	Thank you ever	NN-B	05508
Chatto & Windus	1897.04.16 or 1897.04.18	SLC	EN.London	Good. And now	NN-B	05509
Chatto & Windus	1897.04.24	SLC	EN.London	Stoker will go	NN-B	05510
Chatto & Windus	1897.05.07	SLC	EN.London	Please send me	NN-B	05500
Chatto & Windus	1897.06.15	SLC	EN.London	Please send for	ViU	05228
Chatto & Windus	1897.07.**	SLC	EN.London	The rest of	107:1928.03.13	09180
Chatto & Windus	1897.07.19	SLC	SW.Weggis	If the printer	NN-B	05517
Chatto & Windus	1897.07.22	SLC	SW.Weggis	They don't pay P.S. July	CU-MARK IU-R	08644
Chatto & Windus	1897.07.22	SLC	SW.Weggis	Let us drop	CU-MARK	05267
Chatto & Windus	1897.07.25	SLC	SW.Weggis	I give it	ViU	05271
Chatto & Windus	1897.07.31	SLC	SW.Weggis	Ah, but why	NN-B	05519
Chatto & Windus	1897.08.**	SLC	SW.Weggis	You can send	ViU	05276
Chatto & Windus	1897.09.03	SLC	SW.Weggis	Your letter caught	MoHM	05287
Chatto & Windus	1897.09.15	SLC	SW.Weggis	When you receive	Mo2	08848
Chatto & Windus	1897.09.29	SLC	AU.Vienna	Please send the	ViU	05292
Chatto & Windus	1897.10.02	CC	AU.Vienna	Will you please	NN-B	06256
Chatto & Windus	1897.10.03	SLC	AU.Vienna	rest of the	105:1946.11.04	04278
Chatto & Windus	1897.10.23	SLC	AU.Vienna	When the book	CU-MARK(tr)	05300
Chatto & Windus	1897.11.**	OLC	AU.Vienna	Mr Clemens would	NN-B	06269
Chatto & Windus	1897.11.03	SLC	AU.Vienna	Bliss's canvassing copy	UPB	10863
Chatto & Windus	1897.11.11	SLC	AU.Vienna	Another name. When	NN-B	05523
Chatto & Windus	1897.11.19	SLC	AU.Vienna	I think we	NN-B	05002 misdated 1895
Chatto & Windus	ca 1897.12.01	OLC	AU.Vienna	Will you kindly	NN-B	06287
Chatto & Windus	1897.12.02	OLC	AU.Vienna	Will you kindly	NN-B	06332
Chatto & Windus	1897.12.09	OLC	AU.Vienna	Regarding "The	NN-B	06336

Chatto & Windus	pm	1897.12.23	SLC	AU.Vienna	You may make	Uk4	01260 deposit
Chatto & Windus		1898.01.10	OLC	AU.Vienna	The statement of	Uk4	01398 deposit
Chatto & Windus		1898.01.12	OLC	AU.Vienna	Mr Clemens wishes	NN-B	06342
Chatto & Windus		1898.01.19	OLC	AU.Vienna	Mr Clemens wishes	NN-B	06355
Chatto & Windus		1898.02.08	SLC	AU.Vienna	When you declined	ViU	05346
Chatto & Windus		1898.02.17	SLC	AU.Vienna	I have written	CU-MARK	05350
Chatto & Windus		1898.02.26	SLC	AU.Vienna	I guess we've	ViU	05354
Chatto & Windus		1898.04.13	OLC	AU.Vienna	Will you kindly	NN-B	06387
Chatto & Windus		1898.04.21	OLC	AU.Vienna	Thank you very	NN-B	06428
Chatto & Windus		1898.05.06	OLC	AU.Vienna	Mr Clemens cabled	MoHM	05383
Chatto & Windus		1898.05.06	SLC	AU.Vienna	Now, then, I	MoHM	05384
Chatto & Windus		1898.05.07	SLC	AU.Vienna	Return the thick	MoHM	05385 telegram
Chatto & Windus		1898.05.13	SLC	AU.Vienna	The books came	MoHM	05388
Chatto & Windus		1898.05.17	SLC	AU.Vienna	Please send this	NN-B	05489
Chatto & Windus		1898.06.28	SLC	AU.Kaltenleut.	I am writing	205:1931.06.18	10087
Chatto & Windus		1898.06.29	SLC	AU.Kaltenleut.	Meantime tell me	NN-B	05491
Chatto & Windus		1898.07.06	SLC	AU.Kaltenleut.	The book-trade	MoHM	05408
Chatto & Windus		1898.07.26	SLC	AU.Kaltenleut.	Please send me	Me2	05415
Chatto & Windus	bef	1898.08.15	CC	AU.Kaltenleut.	Will you kindly	NN-B	06479
Chatto & Windus		1898.09.13	OLC	AU.Kaltenleut.	Mr Clemens wishes	NN-B	06689
Chatto & Windus		1898.09.24	OLC	AU.Kaltenleut.	Thank you heartily	NN-B	06707
Chatto & Windus		1898.09.26	SLC	AU.Kaltenleut.	The books came	NN-B	05494
Chatto & Windus		1898.10.12	SLC	AU.Kaltenleut.	Please have my	NN-B	05496
Chatto & Windus		1898.11.13	SLC	AU.Vienna	Confound it, this	Uk4	01289 poem enc; deposit
Chatto & Windus	pm	1898.11.19	SLC	AU.Vienna	I agree to	Uk4	01390 deposit
Chatto & Windus		1899.02.07	SLC	AU.Vienna	A friend of	CU-MARK	05544

ADDRESSEE	DATE	WRITER	PLACE	CUE	SOURCE	NUMBER/NOTES
Chatto & Windus	1899.03.16	SLC	AU.Vienna	You are like	TxU	05564
Chatto & Windus	1899.04.02	SLC	AU.Vienna	I have no	NN-B	05602 on Fruhauf Mar 31
Chatto & Windus	1899.04.10	SLC	AU.Vienna	Please send me	NN-B	05604
Chatto & Windus	1899.04.11	SLC	AU.Vienna	I have just	Uk4	09484 deposit
Chatto & Windus	1899.04.25	SLC	AU.Vienna	Bliss seems to	NN-B	05605
Chatto & Windus	1899.05.04	SLC	AU.Vienna	Please find Madame	NN-B	05606 telegram
Chatto & Windus	1899.05.23	SLC	AU.Vienna	Shall reach Prince	NN-B	05608 telegram
Chatto & Windus	1899.05.25	SLC	AU.Vienna	Yes take Prince	NN-B	05609 telegram
Chatto & Windus	1899.05.31	SLC	FR.Calais	Shall arrive by	NN-B	05610 telegram
Chatto & Windus	1899.06.04	SLC	EN.Broadstairs	Please forward letters	ViU	05632
Chatto & Windus	1899.06.09	SLC	EN.London	Can't you get	NN-B	05613
Chatto & Windus	aft 1899.06.09	SLC	EN.London	After reflection, Mrs.	NN-B	05614
Chatto & Windus	1899.06.18	SLC	EN.London	I am invited	NN-B	05615
Chatto & Windus	1899.06.18	SLC	EN.London	This is all	Uk4	09489 on printed notice; deposit
Chatto & Windus	1899.07.16	SLC	SE.Sanna	Please send me	CU-MARK(ph)	10570
Chatto & Windus	1899.08.20	CC & OLC	SE.Sanna	Will you kindly (CC) I shall be (OLC)	NN-B	06890
Chatto & Windus	1899.08.23	OLC	SE.Sanna	I am going	NN-B	06993
Chatto & Windus	1899.09.07	SLC per OLC	SE.Sanna	As Mr Clemens	Uk4	01404 deposit
Chatto & Windus	1899.09.17	OLC	SE.Sanna	Will you kindly	KyLoU	05678
Chatto & Windus	1900.04.02	SLC	EN.London	I have today	Uk4	00844 deposit
Chatto & Windus	1901.01.25	SLC	NY.New York	I have told	Uk4	09491 Mothere Nov 6 1900 enc; deposit

Chatto & Windus	1901.11.24	SLC	NY.Riverdale	Please send me	MoHM	06178
Chatto & Windus	1902.04.19	SLC	NY.Riverdale	The above is	Uk4	10596 on Chatto & Windus Apr 10; deposit
Chatto & Windus	1902.11.22	SLC per IVL	NY.Riverdale	Please write this	Uk4	01410 deposit
Chatto & Windus	1907.06.03	SLC per IVL	NY.Tuxedo Park	Mr. Clemens asks	Uk4	01478 deposit
Chatto, Andrew	****.**.**	SLC	Unknown	Please answer him	107:1925.02.24	09552
Chatto, Andrew	****.**.**	SLC	Unknown	If I shall	425:1916.06.29	09490
Chatto, Andrew	1877.11.07	SLC per FCH	CT.Hartford	It is a	ViU	01502
Chatto, Andrew	1877.12.10	SLC per FCH	CT.Hartford	Thanks for the	NN-B	02519
Chatto, Andrew	1878.02.06	SLC	CT.Hartford	A member of	110:1966.05.31	10856 per unknown amanuensis
Chatto, Andrew	1878.06.03	SLC	GE.Heidelberg	Won't you please	CLjC	01567
Chatto, Andrew	1879.03.24	SLC	FR.Paris	Do you see	NjP	01643 fragment
Chatto, Andrew	1879.04.25	SLC	FR.Paris	While we wait	CU-MARK(ph)	01650
Chatto, Andrew	1879.05.29	SLC	FR.Paris	Please send a	NN-B	02532 fragment
Chatto, Andrew	1879.08.19	SLC	EN.Windermere	In a picture-shop	NN-B	02533
Chatto, Andrew	1880.03.27	SLC	CT.Hartford	Yours just received	Uk4	00743 deposit
Chatto, Andrew	1881.11.11	SLC	CT.Hartford	Yours of the	NN-B	02556 fragment
Chatto, Andrew	1882.03.03	SLC	CT.Hartford	Baron Tauchnitz wrote	CtY	02169 typed
Chatto, Andrew	1882.06.10	SLC	CT.Hartford	Will you please	NN-B	02563 typed
Chatto, Andrew	1882.07.03	SLC	CT.Hartford	I see by	CU-MARK	02229
Chatto, Andrew	1882.10.27	SLC	CT.Hartford	Here are some	NN-B	02566 typed

ADDRESSEE	DATE	WRITER	PLACE	CUE	SOURCE	NUMBER/NOTES
Chatto, Andrew	1883.06.11	SLC	CT.Hartford	I hereby agree	Uk4	00813 deposit
Chatto, Andrew	1883.09.01	SLC	NY.Elmira	I can't read	Uk	02829 mislabeled Hartford
Chatto, Andrew	1883.11.12	SLC	CT.Hartford	Your recent letter	Uk4	00863 typed; deposit
Chatto, Andrew	1884.03.03	SLC	CT.Hartford	Here's another of	ViU	02932
Chatto, Andrew	1884.04.01	SLC	CT.Hartford	Chas. L. Webster	122:1934.02.15	02945
Chatto, Andrew	1884.12.04	SLC	MI.Muskegon	For the first	297:24	03045 other sources
Chatto, Andrew	1885.03.11	SLC	CT.Hartford	I have been	Uk4	01672 deposit
Chatto, Andrew	1886.06.02	SLC	CT.Hartford	All authority over	Uk4	00866 deposit
Chatto, Andrew	1886.09.14	SLC	NY.Elmira	The notes &	Uk4	01675 deposit
Chatto, Andrew	1887.02.15	SLC	CT.Hartford	That was only	Uk4	01775 deposit
Chatto, Andrew	1887.09.19	SLC	CT.Hartford	It's a quite	Uk4	01851 deposit
Chatto, Andrew	1887.12.05	SLC	CT.Hartford	Look here, I	CU-MARK	03675
Chatto, Andrew	1888.01.08	SLC	CT.Hartford	I am very	Uk4	00919 deposit
Chatto, Andrew	1888.01.16	SLC	CT.Hartford	Our Mr. Hall	Uk4	00678 deposit
Chatto, Andrew	1888.02.14	SLC	NY.New York	The electros of	OC	03704
Chatto, Andrew	1888.03.07	SLC	CT.Hartford	I guess the	Uk4	01424 contract enc; deposit
Chatto, Andrew	1888.06.06	SLC	CT.Hartford	Everything proposed in	Uk4	00703 deposit
Chatto, Andrew	1888.07.15	SLC	NY.Elmira	I don't think	ViU	03732
Chatto, Andrew	1888.09.17	SLC	NY.Elmira	Your notes &	Uk	03766
Chatto, Andrew	1889.06.22	SLC	NY.New York	As soon as	TxU	03903
Chatto, Andrew	1889.07.16	SLC	CT.Hartford	Your statements and	Uk4	03913 deposit

Chatto, Andrew		1889.08.21	SLC	NY.Elmira	Enclosed is the	Uk4	01442 deposit
Chatto, Andrew	aft	1889.12.18	SLC	CT.Hartford	Respectfully submitted	Uk4	01299 on Moore Dec 18; deposit
Chatto, Andrew		1891.03.29	SLC	CT.Hartford	Do you know	Uk4	01209 deposit
Chatto, Andrew		1891.07.08	SLC	FR.Aix-les-Bains	Please send me	122:1936.11.17	09895
Chatto, Andrew		1891.07.18	SLC	FR.Aix-les-Bains	Thank you ever	Uk4	00946 deposit
Chatto, Andrew		1891.07.25	SLC	FR.Aix-les-Bains	You sent me	Uk4	01042 deposit
Chatto, Andrew		1891.08.15	SLC	GE.Marienbad	Yes, the newspaper	Uk4	01131 deposit
Chatto, Andrew		1894.12.15	SLC	FR.Paris	My youngest daughter	250:1977.07	04824
Chatto, Andrew		1895.05.07	SLC	FR.Paris	I am very	Uk4(tr)	01599 deposit
Chatto, Andrew		1896.06.18	SLC	AF.Port Eliz.	I see your	KyLoU	05075
Chatto, Andrew	bet &	1896.08.07 1896.08.14	SLC per CC	EN.Guildford	My Father has	NN-B	06077
Chatto, Andrew		1896.08.11	SLC	EN.Guildford	We've got ourselves	CU-MARK(ph)	05092
Chatto, Andrew		1896.08.19	SLC	EN.Guildford	P.S. These wholly	NN-B	05241
Chatto, Andrew	bet &	1896.10.04 1896.10.18	SLC	EN.London	To-morrow or next	MoHM	08842
Chatto, Andrew	bef	1897.02.03	SLC	EN.London	If the books	NN-B	05504
Chatto, Andrew	bef	1897.05.21	SLC	EN.London	Please, does this	NN-B	05513
Chatto, Andrew		1897.07.30	SLC	SW.Weggis	Yours of the	NBuU-PO	05274
Chatto, Andrew		1897.08.09	SLC	SW.Weggis	These letter batches	NN-B	05521
Chatto, Andrew		1897.12.18	SLC	AU.Vienna	Please send a	NN-B	05524
Chatto, Andrew		1898.06.13	CC	AU.Kaltenleut.	My Father sends	NN-B	06447
Chatto, Andrew		1899.06.01	OLC	EN.London	I want to	NN-B	06774
Chatto, Andrew		1899.06.30	OLC	EN.London	I want to	NN-B	06818
Chatto, Andrew		1899.09.24	SLC	SE.Sanna	Many people will	NN-B	05620
Chatto, Andrew		1900.**.**	SLC	Unknown	I am sending	MB	05738

ADDRESSEE		DATE	WRITER	PLACE	CUE	SOURCE	NUMBER/NOTES
Chatto, Andrew		1900.09.02	SLC	EN.London	with the kindest	ViU	11091 inscription
Chatto, Andrew	pm	1904.06.23	SLC	IT.Florence	For what you	KyLoU	06880 form letter
Chatto, Andrew Jr.		1896.11.13	SLC	EN.London	You know about	UkCo2	02719
Chatto, Andrew Jr.		1896.11.17	CC	EN.London	We are exceedingly	UkCo2	02721
Chatto, Andrew Jr.		1896.11.22	SLC	EN.London	I do not	UkCo2	02720
Chatto, Andrew Jr.		1896.11.23	JC	EN.London	As you will	UkCo2	02723
Chatto, Andrew Jr.		1896.11.30	OLC	EN.London	Enclosed please find	UkCo2	02742
Cheiro or Hamon, Louis		1895.**.**	SLC	Unknown	Cheiro has exposed	244:133	09120 inscription
Cheney, Frank W.	ca	1878.02.23	SLC	CT.Hartford	He sent the	CtHMTH	01534
Cheney, Mary B.		1898.10.07	OLC	AU.Kaltenleut.	Your letter was	CtHMTH	05445
Cheney, Mary B.		1900.02.25	OLC	EN.London	Ever since Milly	CU-MARK(ph)	05763
Cheney, Mary B.		1904.07.21	SLC	MA.Lee	She was indeed	CtHMTH	06895
Chester, J.		1886.09.10	SLC	NY.Elmira	No, I most	CU-MARK	03454
Chetterling, H.W.	o/a	1905.12.07	SLC per IVL	NY.New York	would answer the	CU-MARK(dr)	07238 on Chetterling Dec 7
Chicago Press Club		*	*	*	*	*	11169 see Press Club of Chicago
Child & Co.		1896.02.08	SLC	II.Calcutta	This is the	CU-MARK(ph)	05019
Childhood's Appeal ed.		1880.11.30	SLC	CT.Hartford	I do it	208:1880.12.09	02134
Chiles, William H.	pm	1902.**.**	SLC	NY.Elmira	*	213:1979	10130 envelope only
Chipchase, J.		1885.03.02	SLC	DC.Washington	I take my	CU-MARK	03181
Choate (Warren) & Co.		1875.02.26	SLC	CT.Hartford	I am not	CU-MARK(ph)	01197
Cholmeley-Jones, J.		1908.08.**	SLC	CT.Redding	with the best wishes	ODa2	11217 inscription
Cholmondeley, Reginald		1881.07.24	SLC	CT.Branford	Being dead I	CU-MARK(tr)	01987
Cholmondeley, Reginald		1885.03.28	SLC	CT.Hartford	Yes indeed feuds	CU-MARK(tr)	03198
Christ Church Dean		1907.06.19	SLC per RWA	EN.London	Mr. S.L. Clemens begs	CU-MARK(tr)	07748 RWA tr

Christ, Fred V.		1908.08.28	SLC	CT.Redding	You say: "I	CtY	08092
Christensen, Christen		1888.10.09	SLC	CT.Hartford	I shall be	Dn	03786
Christensen, Margaret		1907.01.18	SLC	NY.New York	I thank you	CU-MARK(ph)	07631
Christian Union ed.	aft	1885.06.11	SLC	Unknown	I have just	209:1885.07.16	00089
Christiancy, H.C.		1887.12.18	SLC	CT.Hartford	As I understand	CU-MARK	03678
Chronicle editor		1896.11.18	SLC	EN.London	I find this	CSmH	05144
Church, Francis P.		1870.02.09	SLC	NY.Buffalo	a generous father-in-law	309:3:364	00422
Church, Francis P.		1870.03.11	SLC	NY.Buffalo	If I can	309:3:364	00442
Church, Francis P.		1870.04.02	SLC	NY.Buffalo	My own paper	196:1870.04.12	00453
Church, Francis P.		1870.10.18	SLC	NY.Buffalo	The matter referred	309:3:255f	00513
Church, Francis P.		1870.12.23	SLC	NY.Buffalo	Oh, please don't	309:3:366	02786
Church, Frederick E.		1887.06.11	SLC	CT.Hartford	It was an	CU-MARK	03582
Church, Frederick E.		1891.03.27	SLC	CT.Hartford	It is most	NHudO	04185
Church, William C.		1868.02.22	SLC	DC.Washington	Confound it, when	309:3:364	00020
Cist, Louis J.		1876.08.01	SLC	NY.Elmira	No, I do	CtY	01353
Clagett, William H.		1862.02.28	SLC	NV.Carson City	The expressman has	ViU	00037
Clagett, William H.	to	1862.03.08 1862.03.09	SLC	NV.Carson City	As a good	ViU	00039
Clagett, William H.		1862.04.18	SLC	NV.Esmeralda	Yours of the	ViU	00044
Clagett, William H.		1862.09.09	SLC	NV.Esmeralda	Orion enclosed your	ViU	00059
Clark	ca	1883.08.22	SLC	NY.Elmira	Your telegram much	CU-MARK(dr)	08596 telegram
Clark, Champ		1909.06.05	SLC	CT.Redding	Is the new	ViU(tr)	08415 SLC tr
Clark, Charles H.	aft	1878.01.12	SLC	CT.Hartford	The only millionaire	110:1970.06.04	01524 addressee & date uncertain
Clark, Charles H.		1880.03.06	SLC	CT.Hartford	I haven't ever	CtHMTH	08597
Clark, Charles H.		1884.06.24	SLC	NY.Elmira	We watch the	CtHMTH	02994
Clark, Charles H.		1886.01.03	SLC	CT.Hartford	You perceive that	CtHT-W	03352
Clark, Charles H.		1887.08.13	SLC	NY.Elmira	I will inquire	CtHT-W	03625

ADDRESSEE	DATE	WRITER	PLACE	CUE	SOURCE	NUMBER/NOTES
Clark, Charles H.	1888.07.02	SLC	NY.Elmira	Thanks for your	CU-MARK	03728
Clark, Charles H.	1900.10.21	SLC	NY.New York	Bunce, Robinson, and	CU-MARK(tr)	05879 telegram
Clark, Charles H.	1903.03.23	SLC	NY.Riverdale	Do not trouble	CU-MARK	06607
Clark, Charles H.	1906.02.26	SLC per IVL	NY.New York	Will you assemble	TxU(tr)	07357 telegram; IVL tr
Clark, Charles H.	1906.03.04	SLC	NY.New York	This is the	NN-B(tr)	07362
Clark, Charles H.	o/a 1906.03.09	SLC per IVL	NY.New York	All right--got	CU-MARK(dr)	07373 on Clark Mar 9
Clark, Charles H.	o/a 1906.03.14	SLC per IVL	NY.New York	We've gotten through	CU-MARK(dr)	07383 on Clark Mar 14
Clark, Charles H.	1907.01.22	SLC per IVL	NY.New York	I thank you	CU-MARK(tr)	07633 IVL tr
Clark, Charles H.	o/a 1908.12.02	SLC per IVL	CT.Redding	I remember the	CU-MARK(dr)	08168 on Clark Dec 2
Clark, Francis D.	1876.01.05	SLC	CT.Hartford	Your courteous	170:30	01294
Clark, Francis D.	1877.08.20	SLC	NY.Elmira	Your favor of	CSfCP	10338
Clarke, Archibald	1900.10.05	SLC	Unknown	with compliments of	ViU	11090 inscription
Clarke, Edward E.	1906.02.**	SLC	NY.New York	I have found	114:789	07323
Clarke, Edward E.	o/a 1906.05.30	SLC per IVL	NH.Dublin	Mr. Clemenes requests	CU-MARK(dr)	07446 on Clarke May 30
Clarke, William F. & Dodge, Mary M.	1895.08.17	SLC	CN.Vancouver	This is to	Mo2	02405 to six editors
Clemens, Bryan M.	****.**.**	SLC	Unknown	*	Mo2	11002 envelope only
Clemens, Bryan M.	1897.06.30	OLC	EN.London	If you and	Mo2	08847
Clemens, Bryan M.	1897.12.18	OLC	AU.Vienna	My Mr Clemens	Mo2	08849
Clemens, Clara L.	****.**.**	OLC	Unknown	Good night my	CU-MARK(tr)	08628
Clemens, Clara L.	****.**.**	OLC	Unknown	Good night my	CU-MARK(tr)	08639
Clemens, Clara L.	****.**.**	OLC	Unknown	Well! Clara, so	CU-MARK(tr)	08655
Clemens, Clara L.	****.**.**	SLC	Unknown	from one of	323:8	09245 inscription

Clemens, Clara L.		****.**.**	SLC	Unknown	Take my bedroom	CtHMTH(tr)	08627
Clemens, Clara L.		1877.07.19	SLC	NY.New York	Bay Clemens, I have	Mo4	01454
Clemens, Clara L.		1880.12.25	SLC	Unknown	from Papa. Christmas	454:1951.05	09528 inscription
Clemens, Clara L.		1882.06.08	SLC	CT.Hartford	This is the	CCamarSJ	10639 inscription
Clemens, Clara L.		1884.11.23	SLC	NY.New York	I enjoy your	CU-MARK	03034
Clemens, Clara L.		1884.12.14	SLC	MI.Grand Rapids	Wie geht es	ViU(tr)	03058
Clemens, Clara L.		1889.07.15	SLC	CT.Hartford	Clara dear, I	CU-MARK(tr)	03911
Clemens, Clara L.		1890.07.20	SLC	CT.Hartford	Clara dear, I hope	CU-MARK(tr)	04064
Clemens, Clara L. & Clemens, Olivia L.	pm	1890.07.21	SLC	CT.Hartford	he is on	CU-MARK	04066 fragment
Clemens, Clara L.		1890.09.30	SC	NY.New York	I am sitting	CU-MARK(tr)	04097
Clemens, Clara L. & Clemens, Susy		1891.06.28	SLC	FR.Aix-les-Bains	I love you	CU-MARK	04216
Clemens, Clara L. & Clemens, Susy		1891.06.29	SLC	FR.Aix-les-Bains	Mamma is a	CU-MARK	04217
Clemens, Clara L. & Clemens, Susy		1891.07.03	SLC & JC	FR.Aix-les-Bains	Day before yesterday	CU-MARK	04219
Clemens, Clara L.		1891.09.29	SLC	SW.Rhone River	The vast stone	CU-MARK	04237
Clemens, Clara L.		1892.03.05	OLC	FR.Menton	How I do	CU-MARK(tr)	04272
Clemens, Clara L.		1892.03.22	SLC	FR.Menton	Yes, if you	CU-MARK	04277
Clemens, Clara L.		1892.06.10	SLC	GE.Bad-Nauheim	Clara dear, we	CU-MARK	04296
Clemens, Clara L.		1892.06.12	SLC	GE.Bad-Nauheim	Clara dear, I can	CU-MARK(tr)	04298
Clemens, Clara L.		1892.10.06	SLC	IT.Florence	I have just	CU-MARK	00244
Clemens, Clara L.		1892.10.07	OLC	IT.Florence	I did not	CU-MARK(tr)	00382
Clemens, Clara L.	aft	1892.10.07	SC	IT.Florence	I have missed	CU-MARK(tr)	08922
Clemens, Clara L.		1892.10.14	SLC	IT.Florence	Clara dear, if	CU-MARK	00611
Clemens, Clara L.		1892.10.21	SLC	IT.Florence	Dear old Ben	CU-MARK	00658
Clemens, Clara L.		1892.11.04	SC	IT.Florence	Mamma wants me	CU-MARK(tr)	02722
Clemens, Clara L.		1892.11.05	SLC	IT.Florence	Why, you are	CU-MARK	02399
Clemens, Clara L.		1892.11.10	SLC	IT.Florence	I must write	CU-MARK	02404

ADDRESSEE	DATE	WRITER	PLACE	CUE	SOURCE	NUMBER/NOTES
Clemens, Clara L.	1892.11.16	OLC	IT.Florence	A letter reached	CU-MARK(tr)	02407
Clemens, Clara L.	1892.11.16	SLC	IT.Florence	Now didn't you	CU-MARK	02406
Clemens, Clara L.	1892.12.**	SC	IT.Florence	Lately you haven't	CU-MARK(tr)	04548
Clemens, Clara L.	1892.12.01	OLC	IT.Florence	Susy and I	CU-MARK(tr)	00832
Clemens, Clara L.	1892.12.06	SC	IT.Florence	You are having	CU-MARK(tr)	02410
Clemens, Clara L.	1892.12.11	OLC	IT.Florence	I am in	CU-MARK(tr)	04306
Clemens, Clara L.	1892.12.15	SLC	IT.Florence	Ben dear, I	CU-MARK(tr)	04307
Clemens, Clara L.	1892.12.19	SLC	IT.Florence	I send you	CU-MARK(tr)	04310
Clemens, Clara L.	1892.12.20	OLC	IT.Florence	A Merry Christmas	CU-MARK(tr)	04311
Clemens, Clara L.	1892.12.22	SC	IT.Florence	I believe I	CU-MARK(tr)	04312
Clemens, Clara L.	1892.12.25	SLC	IT.Florence	I thank you	CU-MARK	04313
Clemens, Clara L.	ca 1893.01.**	SLC	IT.Florence	*	ViU	10195 envelope only
Clemens, Clara L.	1893.01.05	OLC	IT.Florence	I am truly	CU-MARK(tr)	04323
Clemens, Clara L.	1893.01.09	SLC	IT.Florence	Ah, Ben, dear	CU-MARK(tr)	04324
Clemens, Clara L.	1893.01.15	OLC	IT.Florence	I hope you	CU-MARK(tr)	04326
Clemens, Clara L.	1893.01.21	SLC	IT.Florence	Clara dear, your	CU-MARK(tr)	04328
Clemens, Clara L.	1893.01.24	SC	IT.Florence	I am writing	CU-MARK(tr)	04329
Clemens, Clara L.	1893.01.26	OLC	IT.Florence	I am so	CU-MARK(tr)	04330
Clemens, Clara L.	1893.02.02	SC	IT.Florence	I do wish	CU-MARK(tr)	04333
Clemens, Clara L.	1893.02.05	SLC	IT.Florence	It is lonesome	CU-MARK(tr)	04335
Clemens, Clara L.	1893.02.22	OLC	IT.Florence	Your letter came	CU-MARK(tr)	04342
Clemens, Clara L.	1893.02.28	SC	IT.Florence	What has happened	CU-MARK(tr)	04345
Clemens, Clara L.	1893.03.**	SC	IT.Florence	I don't know	CU-MARK(tr)	04346
Clemens, Clara L.	1893.03.12	SLC	IT.Florence	Ben, dear, the	CU-MARK(tr)	04350
Clemens, Clara L.	1893.03.23	SC	IT.Florence	I am so	CU-MARK(tr)	04358
Clemens, Clara L.	1893.03.26	SC	IT.Florence	The time for	CU-MARK(tr)	04360
Clemens, Clara L.	1893.04.10	SC	IT.Venice	Mamma wants me	CU-MARK(tr)	04369
Clemens, Clara L.	1893.04.15	SC	IT.Venice	Venice is so	CU-MARK(tr)	04376
Clemens, Clara L.	1893.04.29	SC	IT.Florence	I am going	CU-MARK(tr)	04389

Clemens, Clara L.		1893.08.08	SC	GE.Franzensbad	Thank you so	CU-MARK(tr)	04432
Clemens, Clara L.		1893.08.27	JC	GE.Munich	We are downhearted	CU-MARK(tr)	04439
Clemens, Clara L.		1893.09.10	SLC	NY.New York	I've been missing	CU-MARK	04442
Clemens, Clara L.		1893.09.13	SLC	NY.New York	Dear Benkins, bless	CU-MARK(tr)	04445
Clemens, Clara L.		1893.09.15	SLC	NY.New York	Clara, sweetheart, you	CU-MARK	04450
Clemens, Clara L.		1893.09.17	SLC	NJ.Madison	Clara dear, I arrived	CU-MARK	04452
Clemens, Clara L.		1893.09.21	SLC	NY.New York	Clara dear, why	CU-MARK	04457
Clemens, Clara L.		1893.09.23	SLC	NY.New York	Benny dear, whenever	CU-MARK	04459
Clemens, Clara L.		1893.09.26	SLC	NY.New York	Benny dear, this	CU-MARK	04460
Clemens, Clara L.		1893.09.30	SLC	NY.New York	Benny dear, I've got	CU-MARK	04464
Clemens, Clara L.		1893.10.**	SC	GE.Franzensbad	And so you	CU-MARK(tr)	04465
Clemens, Clara L.		1893.10.03	SLC	NY.New York	Well, dear Ben	CU-MARK	04467
Clemens, Clara L.		1893.10.05	OLC & SC	GE.Hamburg	Your letter telling	CU-MARK(tr)	04470
Clemens, Clara L.		1893.10.05	SLC	NY.New York	It was a	CU-MARK	04469
Clemens, Clara L.		1893.10.15	OLC	GE.Hamburg	No it would	CU-MARK(tr)	04473
Clemens, Clara L. or Clemens, Olivia L.	ca	1893.10.17	SLC	NY.New York	I have been	293:86	06177
Clemens, Clara L.		1893.10.18	SLC	NY.New York	Clarchen dear, it	CU-MARK	04477
Clemens, Clara L.		1893.11.**	SC	FR.Paris	I do wish	CU-MARK(tr)	04485
Clemens, Clara L.		1893.11.02	SLC	NY.New York	Clara dear, be	CU-MARK(tr)	04486
Clemens, Clara L.		1893.11.14	SC	FR.Paris	Your letter from	CU-MARK(tr)	04502
Clemens, Clara L.		1893.11.19	SC	FR.Paris	I cannot be	CU-MARK(tr)	04506
Clemens, Clara L.		1893.11.23	SC	FR.Paris	Thank you many	CU-MARK(tr)	04507
Clemens, Clara L.		1893.11.27	OLC	FR.Paris	It is my	CU-MARK(tr)	04509
Clemens, Clara L.		1894.02.02	SLC	NY.New York	Come now, you	CU-MARK	04686
Clemens, Clara L.		1894.02.05	SLC	NY.New York	I was intending	CU-MARK	04688
Clemens, Clara L.		1894.07.01	OLC	FR.La Bourboule	Your dispatch has	CU-MARK(tr)	04750
Clemens, Clara L.		1894.07.04	SLC	FR.La Bourboule	Clara dear, yours	CU-MARK	04752
Clemens, Clara L.		1894.07.18	OLC	FR.La Bourboule	Your pencil note	CU-MARK(tr)	04757

ADDRESSEE	DATE	WRITER	PLACE	CUE	SOURCE	NUMBER/NOTES
Clemens, Clara L.	1894.08.03	SLC	NY.New York	You dear old	CU-MARK	04773
Clemens, Clara L.	1894.08.05	OLC	FR.Etretat	I enclose you	CU-MARK(tr)	04771
Clemens, Clara L.	1894.08.10	SC	FR.Etretat	I am ashamed	CU-MARK(tr)	04779
Clemens, Clara L.	1894.08.16	OLC	FR.Etretat	Be sure and	CU-MARK(tr)	04781
Clemens, Clara L.	1894.08.25	OLC	FR.Etretat	I get no	CU-MARK(tr)	04782
Clemens, Clara L.	1895.**.**	SC	CT.Hartford	I am in	CU-MARK(tr)	04828
Clemens, Clara L.	1895.07.30	SC	NY.Elmira	Your letters are	CU-MARK(tr)	04937
Clemens, Clara L.	1895.08.10	SC	NY.Elmira	I will try	CU-MARK(tr)	04941
Clemens, Clara L.	1895.09.13	SC	NY.Elmira	I was intensely	CU-MARK(tr)	04960
Clemens, Clara L.	1895.09.16	SC	NY.Elmira	I am thinking	CU-MARK(tr)	04962
Clemens, Clara L.	1895.12.30	SC	NY.Elmira	Your letters are	CU-MARK(tr)	04985
Clemens, Clara L.	1896.**.**	SC	NJ.Orange	I am sitting	CU-MARK(tr)	05006
Clemens, Clara L.	1896.05.22	SLC	AF.Johannesburg	I go your	CU-MARK	05052
Clemens, Clara L.	1896.06.08	SLC	AF.Kingwilliams.	Dear dear Ben	CtHMTH	05070
Clemens, Clara L.	1898.10.17	SLC	AU.Vienna	Well, Benny dear	CU-MARK	05448
Clemens, Clara L.	1899.06.15	SLC	EN.London	No, Oom Paul	CU-MARK(tr)	05639 four postcards
Clemens, Clara L.	1899.07.12	SLC	SE.Sanna	This is the	CU-MARK	05653
Clemens, Clara L.	1901.06.21	OLC	Unknown	What a help	CU-MARK(tr)	06078
Clemens, Clara L.	1901.06.29	SLC	NY.Saranac Lake	What does the	CU-MARK(tr)	06082
Clemens, Clara L.	1901.07.04	OLC	NY.Saranac Lake	It does worry	CU-MARK(tr)	06083
Clemens, Clara L.	1901.09.25	OLC	NY.Elmira	A bright beautiful	CU-MARK(tr)	06142
Clemens, Clara L.	ca 1902.01.01	OLC	NY.Riverdale	Shall I send	ViU	06212
Clemens, Clara L.	1902.01.20 & 1902.01.21	SLC & OLC	NY.Elmira	Clara dear, Mrs. Clemens	CU-MARK(tr)	06250
Clemens, Clara L.	1902.03.18	SLC	FL.Miami	Clara dear, I desire	MiD	06306
Clemens, Clara L.	bet 1903.05.14 & 1903.06.20	SLC	NY.Riverdale	Dear Benny, this	MoKiU	06661 ten notes & drawings
Clemens, Clara L.	bet 1903.06.** & 1903.07.**	OLC	NY.Elmira	I am very	CU-MARK(tr)	06694

Clemens, Clara L.	bet 1903.06.** & 1903.07.**	SLC	NY.Elmira	Jean thinks you	CU-MARK(tr)	06711
Clemens, Clara L.	1903.07.02	SLC	NY.Elmira	Clara dear, if	CU-MARK(tr)	06686
Clemens, Clara L.	1903.07.02	SLC	NY.Elmira	Clara dear, your	CU-MARK(tr)	06687
Clemens, Clara L.	1903.07.05	OLC	NY.Elmira	It is raining	CU-MARK(tr)	06693
Clemens, Clara L.	1903.07.05	SLC	NY.Elmira	Ah, you poor	CU-MARK(tr)	06692
Clemens, Clara L.	1903.07.10	OLC	NY.Elmira	I have very	CU-MARK(tr)	06696
Clemens, Clara L.	1903.07.17	SLC	NY.Elmira	You dear little	CU-MARK(tr)	06700
Clemens, Clara L.	1903.07.29	OLC	NY.Elmira	Your letter did	CU-MARK(tr)	06712
Clemens, Clara L.	bet 1903.08.** & 1903.09.**	SLC	NY.New York	Dear Ben, I expect	CU-MARK	06720
Clemens, Clara L.	1903.09.24	SLC	NY.New York	Benny dear, I am	CU-MARK(tr)	06730
Clemens, Clara L.	1903.10.13	SLC	NY.New York	Benny dear, I have	CU-MARK(tr)	06740
Clemens, Clara L.	1904.**.**	SLC	Unknown	This enlargement will	CCamarSJ	10649 inscription
Clemens, Clara L.	1904.07.26	SLC	MA.Lee	You dear little	CtHMTH	06903
Clemens, Clara L.	1904.11.27	SLC	Unknown	with the love	C2	10731 inscription
Clemens, Clara L.	1905.05.20	SLC	NH.Dublin	Clarchen dear, to get	CU-MARK(tr)	07046
Clemens, Clara L.	1905.06.08	SLC	NH.Dublin	Ah, you dear	CU-MARK(tr)	07060
Clemens, Clara L.	1905.06.11	SLC	NH.Dublin	Clarchen dear, I've	CU-MARK(tr)	07061
Clemens, Clara L.	1905.06.18	SLC	NH.Dublin	It's raining, dear	CU-MARK(tr)	07063
Clemens, Clara L.	1905.06.29	SLC	NH.Dublin	Ah dear heart	CU-MARK(tr)	07073
Clemens, Clara L.	1905.07.16	SLC	NH.Dublin	Clarchen dear, Jean	CU-MARK(tr)	07087
Clemens, Clara L.	1905.07.16	SLC	NH.Dublin	You dear, read	CU-MARK(tr)	07084
Clemens, Clara L.	1905.08.03	SLC	NH.Dublin	Ben dear, do	CU-MARK(tr)	07097
Clemens, Clara L.	1905.08.28	SLC	MA.Boston	I arrived unfatigued	CU-MARK(tr)	07119
Clemens, Clara L.	1905.09.02	SLC	NH.Dublin	Dear Ashcat, I	CU-MARK(tr)	07125
Clemens, Clara L.	1905.09.03	SLC	NH.Dublin	Clarchen dear, in my	CU-MARK(tr)	07127
Clemens, Clara L.	1905.09.15	SLC	NH.Dublin	Clarchen dear, I have	CU-MARK(tr) NTRS	07134 NTRS envelope

ADDRESSEE	DATE	WRITER	PLACE	CUE	SOURCE	NUMBER/NOTES
Clemens, Clara L.	1905.10.01	SLC	NH.Dublin	Oh, you poor	CU-MARK(tr)	07156
Clemens, Clara L.	1905.10.03	SLC	NH.Dublin	Why, you poor Clara dear, you	CU-MARK(tr) NTRS	07159
Clemens, Clara L.	1905.10.06	SLC	NH.Dublin	Why, you little	CU-MARK(tr)	07163
Clemens, Clara L.	1905.10.11	SLC	NH.Dublin	Clara, you little	CU-MARK(tr)	07171
Clemens, Clara L.	1905.10.15	SLC	NH.Dublin	In my bedroom	CU-MARK(tr)	07177
Clemens, Clara L.	1905.10.18	SLC	NH.Dublin	It shall be	CU-MARK(tr)	07179
Clemens, Clara L.	1905.10.20	SLC	NH.Dublin	Clarchen dear, I wish	CU-MARK(tr)	07184
Clemens, Clara L.	1906.02.18	SLC	NY.New York	Well, dear ashcat	CU-MARK(tr)	07349
Clemens, Clara L.	1906.04.08	SLC	NY.New York	I am so	CU-MARK(ph)	07420
Clemens, Clara L.	1906.06.09	SLC	NH.Dublin	Clarchen dear, many	CU-MARK(tr)	07454
Clemens, Clara L.	1906.06.20	SLC	NH.Dublin	Clara dear, if	CU-MARK(tr)	07462
Clemens, Clara L.	1906.07.**	SLC	NH.Dublin	Clarchen dear, it	CU-MARK(tr)	07468
Clemens, Clara L.	1906.07.02	SLC	MA.Fairhaven	Clara dear, I spent	CU-MARK(tr)	07471
Clemens, Clara L.	1906.07.27	SLC	NH.Dublin	It's a darling	CU-MARK(tr)	07483
Clemens, Clara L.	1906.08.03	SLC	NH.Dublin	Clarchen dear, I first	CU-MARK(tr)	07489
Clemens, Clara L.	1906.08.28	SLC	NH.Dublin	Dear Ashcat, I	CU-MARK(tr)	07510
Clemens, Clara L.	1906.09.04	SLC	NH.Dublin	I am so	CU-MARK(tr)	07517
Clemens, Clara L.	1906.10.02	SLC	NH.Dublin	Clara dear, perhaps	CU-MARK(tr)	07533
Clemens, Clara L.	1906.10.09	SLC	NH.Dublin	Clara dear I hope	CU-MARK(tr)	07539
Clemens, Clara L.	1907.02.24	SLC	NY.New York	I shall watch	CU-MARK(tr)	07662
Clemens, Clara L.	1907.03.05	SLC	NY.New York	Remember, the audience	CU-MARK(tr)	07671
Clemens, Clara L.	1907.03.12	SLC	NY.New York	Clara dear, your	CU-MARK(tr)	07675
Clemens, Clara L.	1907.05.02	SLC	NY.New York	O dear Ashcat	CU-MARK(tr)	07705
Clemens, Clara L.	1907.06.**	SLC	Unknown	They all pattern	CU-MARK	08676 telegram
Clemens, Clara L.	1907.06.30	SLC	EN.London	Clarchen dear, I	CU-MARK(tr)	07773
Clemens, Clara L.	1907.07.12	SLC	EN.London	Clarchen dear, we sail	CU-MARK(tr)	07783
Clemens, Clara L.	1907.07.27	SLC	NY.Tuxedo Park	Clara dear, Clara	CtHMTH	07790
Clemens, Clara L.	1907.08.**	SLC	NY.Tuxedo Park	Oh, Clara dear	CU-MARK	07804

Clemens, Clara L.	1907.09.05	SLC	NY.Tuxedo Park	I, also, should	CtHMTH	07830
Clemens, Clara L.	aft 1907.12.15	SLC	Unknown	Sunday night I	CtHMTH(tr)	07891
Clemens, Clara L.	1908.01.27	SLC	BE.Hamilton	Clara dear, we arrived	CU-MARK(tr)	07926
Clemens, Clara L.	1908.02.29	SLC	BE.Hamilton	Clara dear, there	CU-MARK(tr)	07951
Clemens, Clara L.	1908.03.23	SLC	BE.Hamilton	Dear heart, it	CU-MARK	07962
Clemens, Clara L.	1908.04.05	SLC	BE.Hamilton	Clarchen dear, I hope	MiD	07969
Clemens, Clara L.	1908.05.19	SLC	NY.New York	Clarchen dear, you are	CU-MARK(tr)	08001
Clemens, Clara L.	1908.06.03	SLC	NY.New York	Well, Clarchen dear	CU-MARK(tr)	08017
Clemens, Clara L.	1908.06.20	SLC	CT.Redding	Clara dear, I have	CU-MARK(tr)	08037
Clemens, Clara L.	1908.07.18	SLC	CT.Redding	Clara dear, the enclosed	CSmH	08055
Clemens, Clara L.	1908.07.30	SLC	CT.Redding	I place with	C4(tr)	08066
Clemens, Clara L.	1908.09.21	JC	MA.Gloucester	Reach city at	CU-MARK	08108 telegram
Clemens, Clara L.	1908.10.06	SLC	CT.Redding	Clarchen dear, your	CtHMTH	08121
Clemens, Clara L.	1908.10.24	SLC	NJ.Deal	Clara dear, I saw	CU-MARK(ph)	04132
Clemens, Clara L.	1908.12.12	SLC	CT.Redding	Clarchen dear, you	MoHM	08179
Clemens, Clara L.	1909.03.11	SLC	CT.Redding	Clara dear, I am	CU-MARK(tr)	08370
Clemens, Clara L.	1909.07.18	SLC	CT.Redding	Clarchen dear Jean	CU-MARK(tr)	08435
Clemens, Clara L.	1909.10.**	SLC	CT.Redding	It is very	CU-MARK(dr)	08463
Clemens, Clara L.	1909.11.26	SLC	BE.Hamilton	I do hope	CU-MARK(tr)	08500
Clemens, Clara L.	1909.12.06	SLC	BE.Hamilton	Clara dear, I	CU-MARK(tr)	08506
Clemens, Clara L.	1909.12.29	SLC	CT.Redding	O, Clara, Clara	CSmH(tr)	08527 SLC tr
Clemens, Clara L.	1910.02.21	SLC	BE.Hamilton	Clara dear, your	294:115	08561
Clemens, Clara L.	1910.03.06	SLC	BE.Hamilton	Clara dear, yours	ViU	08567
Clemens, Clara L.	1910.03.12	SLC	BE.Hamilton	Clarchen dear, it	MoHM	08569
Clemens, Clara L. & Gabrilowitsch, Ossip	1910.03.12	SLC	BE.Hamilton	Clara dear, last	CU-MARK(tr)	08568
Clemens, Clara L.	1910.03.24	SLC	BE.Hamilton	Clara dearest, I hope	CU-MARK(tr)	08574
Clemens, Clara L.	1910.04.21	SLC	CT.Redding	You did not	ViU	08581 unsent

ADDRESSEE		DATE	WRITER	PLACE	CUE	SOURCE	NUMBER/NOTES
Clemens, Henry		1856.08.05	SLC	IA.Keokuk	Annie is well	NPV	00012
Clemens, James R.		****.**.**	JC	Unknown	The waiter put	Mo2	08411
Clemens, James R.		****.**.**	OLC	EN.London	I am so	Mo2	10534
Clemens, James R.		****.**.**	OLC	Unknown	I am so	Mo2	08410
Clemens, James R.		****.**.**	OLC	Unknown	We are extremely	Mo2	08409
Clemens, James R.		****.**.**	SLC	Unknown	*	Mo2	11003 envelope only
Clemens, James R. & Clemens, Katharine B.	ca	****.12.25	SLC	Unknown	Love and Christmas	Mo2(tr)	08390
Clemens, James R.	ca	1897.**.**	OLC	EN.London	Miss Mac Greggor	Mo2	08406
Clemens, James R.		1897.03.05	SLC	EN.London	Your note has	Mo2	05184
Clemens, James R.		1897.03.25	SLC	EN.London	Most unfortunately that	Mo2	08843
Clemens, James R.		1897.04.01	OLC	EN.London	Will you come	Mo2	10513
Clemens, James R.	pm	1897.04.08	SLC	EN.London	*	Mo2	11000 envelope only
Clemens, James R.		1897.05.06	SLC	EN.London	I was told	Mo2	08845
Clemens, James R.		1897.06.02	SLC	EN.London	P.S. If you	Mo2	05220
Clemens, James R.		1897.06.02	SLC	EN.London	Will you meet	Mo2	05222
Clemens, James R.		1897.06.03	SLC	EN.London	All right, I	Mo2	05225
Clemens, James R.		1897.06.25	SLC	EN.London	I find that	Mo2	05234
Clemens, James R.		1897.10.21	SLC	AU.Vienna	We were very	Mo2	05299
Clemens, James R.	bet &	1897.12.** 1899.05.**	OLC	Unknown	*	Mo2	10060 envelope only
Clemens, James R.		1898.06.29	SLC	AU.Kaltenleut.	When you &	Mo2	05405
Clemens, James R.		1898.07.20	SLC	AU.Kaltenleut.	Let us appoint	Mo2	08852
Clemens, James R.		1898.09.10	CC	AU.Kaltenleut.	Ordered by my	Mo2	11016
Clemens, James R.	pm	1898.09.14	SLC	AU.Kaltenleut.	*	Mo2	11001 envelope only
Clemens, James R.		1899.03.05	SLC	AU.Vienna	We were very	Mo2	05555
Clemens, James R.		1899.03.29	OLC	AU.Vienna	I cannot tell	Mo2	08854
Clemens, James R. & Clemens, Katharine B.		1899.05.03	SLC	EN.London	Congratulations	Mo2	08855 telegram

Clemens, James R.		1899.05.24	SLC	AU.Vienna	Dinner guests are	Mo2	05594
Clemens, James R.	bet &	1899.10.01 1900.06.06	SLC	EN.London	James, I want	Mo2	08311
Clemens, James R.		1900.01.12	SLC	EN.London	Are you home	Mo2	05746
Clemens, James R. & Clemens, Katharine B.	o/a	1900.03.27	OLC	EN.London	With affectionate	Mo2	10949 inscription
Clemens, James R. & Clemens, Katharine B.		1900.03.28	SLC	EN.London	We send love	Mo2	08858 telegram
Clemens, James R.		1900.03.30	OLC	EN.London	I am sure	Mo2	08859
Clemens, James R.	pm	1900.04.04	OLC	EN.London	My Mr Clemens	Mo2	08860
Clemens, James R.		1900.07.12	SLC	EN.London	Those were the	Mo2	05834
Clemens, James R.		1900.07.18	SLC	EN.London	The bill for	Mo2	05835
Clemens, James R.	pm	1900.07.25	OLC	EN.London	My Mr Clemens	Mo2	08865
Clemens, James R.		1900.07.25	SLC	EN.London	Since you were	Mo2	05837
Clemens, James R.		1902.05.23	SLC	NY.Riverdale	I am thanking	Mo2	06343
Clemens, James R.		1902.06.06	SLC	MO.St. Louis	May my namesake	Mo2	09370 inscription
Clemens, James R.		1902.06.10	SLC	NY.Riverdale	I arrived unfatigued	Mo2	06357
Clemens, James R.		1902.06.13	SLC	NY.Riverdale	Can Mrs. Clemens	Mo2	06363
Clemens, James R.		1902.06.29	SLC	ME.York Harbor	We arrived here	Mo2	06379
Clemens, James R.		1902.07.27	OLC	ME.York Harbor	Indeed we send	Mo2	08882
Clemens, James R. & Clemens, Katharine B.		1902.08.22	SLC	ME.York Harbor	To-day, for the	Mo2	06413
Clemens, James R.	o/a	1902.09.15	SLC	ME.York Harbor	By the handwriting	Mo2	08883 on Howells Sept 15
Clemens, James R.		1902.10.23	SLC	NY.Riverdale	The pipes came	Mo2	06472
Clemens, James R.		1908.09.03	SLC	CT.Redding	Shall be very	Mo2	08902 telegram
Clemens, Jane family & Clemens, Jane L.	or	1862.01.30 1862.02.01	SLC	Unknown	In the little	NPV	00038
Clemens, Jane family & Clemens, Jane L.		1866.11.02	SLC	NV.Virginia City	You know the	NPV	00110 misdated Nov 1

ADDRESSEE	DATE	WRITER	PLACE	CUE	SOURCE	NUMBER/NOTES
Clemens, Jane family & Clemens, Jane L.	1866.12.04	SLC	CA.San Francisco	I have written	NPV 114:122	00112
Clemens, Jane family & Clemens, Jane L.	1866.12.14	SLC	CA.San Francisco	I sail to-morrow	NPV	00116
Clemens, Jane family & Clemens, Jane L.	1867.04.15	SLC	NY.New York	I need not	ViU	00122
Clemens, Jane family & Clemens, Jane L.	1867.04.19	SLC	NY.New York	Direct my letters	CU-MARK ViU	00123 ViU envelope
Clemens, Jane family & Clemens, Jane L.	1867.05.01	SLC	NY.New York	Don't expect me	NPV	00126
Clemens, Jane family & Clemens, Jane L.	1867.05.20	SLC	NY.New York	Don't--don't ask	CU-MARK	00130
Clemens, Jane family & Clemens, Jane L.	1867.06.01	SLC	NY.New York	I know I	NPV	00132
Clemens, Jane family & Clemens, Jane L.	1867.06.07	SLC	NY.New York	I suppose we	NPV	00134
Clemens, Jane family & Clemens, Jane L.	1867.06.20 to 1867.07.05	SLC	PO.Azores to FR.Marseilles	We are having	NPV	00139
Clemens, Jane family & Clemens, Jane L.	1867.07.12	SLC	FR.Marseilles	I started to	NPV	00140
Clemens, Jane family & Clemens, Jane L.	1867.07.15	SLC	IT.Genoa	I am just	NPV	00141
Clemens, Jane family & Clemens, Jane L.	1867.08.09	SLC	IT.Naples	I can't write	CU-MARK	00144
Clemens, Jane family & Clemens, Jane L.	1867.08.25	SLC	RU.Yalta	We have been	NPV	00145
Clemens, Jane family & Clemens, Jane L.	1867.09.01	SLC	TU.Constantinop.	All well. Do	NPV	00146
Clemens, Jane family & Clemens, Jane L.	1867.09.11	SLC	SY.Beirut	We are here	NPV	00148
Clemens, Jane family & Clemens, Jane L.	1867.10.12 to 1867.10.17	SLC	IT.Cagliari to SP.Gibralter	We have just	NPV	00151
Clemens, Jane family & Clemens, Jane L.	1867.10.24	SLC	SP.Cadiz	We left Gibraltar	NPV	00152
Clemens, Jane family & Clemens, Jane L.	1867.11.19	SLC	NY.New York	The Quaker City	NPV	00155
Clemens, Jane family & Clemens, Jane L.	1867.11.20	SLC	NY.New York	I am ashamed	NPV	00156

Clemens, Jane family & Clemens, Jane L.	1867.11.25	SLC	DC.Washington	Tired & sleepy	NPV	00162
Clemens, Jane family & Clemens, Jane L.	1867.12.10	SLC	DC.Washington	I called on	NPV	00171
Clemens, Jane family & Clemens, Jane L.	1868.01.13	SLC	DC.Washington	I thought you	NPV	00179
Clemens, Jane family & Clemens, Jane L.	1868.02.21	SLC	DC.Washington	I was as	NPV	00197
Clemens, Jane family & Clemens, Jane L.	1868.03.15	SLC	SH.Henry Chaun.	I have nothing	NPV	00201
Clemens, Jane family & Clemens, Jane L.	1868.06.07	SLC	CA.San Francisco	A son of	CU-MARK	02734
Clemens, Jane family & Clemens, Jane L.	1868.08.24 & 1868.08.25	SLC	NY.Elmira	You see I	NPV	02747
Clemens, Jane family & Clemens, Jane L.	1868.11.18	SLC	OH.Cleveland	Have received letters	NPV	02763
Clemens, Jane family & Clemens, Jane L.	1868.11.20	SLC	OH.Cleveland	I played against	NPV	02766
Clemens, Jane family & Clemens, Jane L.	1868.12.10	SLC	NY.New York	I didn't move	NPV	02728
Clemens, Jane family & Clemens, Jane L.	1869.02.05	SLC	NY.Elmira	This is to	Mo4	00245
Clemens, Jane family & Clemens, Jane L.	1869.02.27	SLC	NY.Lockport	I enclose $20	NPV	00262
Clemens, Jane family & Clemens, Jane L.	bet 1869.04.07 & 1869.04.10	SLC	NY.Elmira	of it, for	Mo4	00285 fragment
Clemens, Jane family & Clemens, Jane L.	1869.06.04	SLC	NY.Elmira	Livy sends you	NPV	00315
Clemens, Jane family & Clemens, Jane L.	1869.12.15	SLC	MA.Boston	I arrived here	NPV	00389
Clemens, Jane family & Clemens, Jane L.	1870.03.26	SLC	NY.Buffalo	The coffin of	NPV	00449
Clemens, Jane family & Clemens, Jane L.	1871.02.17	SLC	NY.Buffalo	By means of	NPV	00577
Clemens, Jane family & Clemens, Jane L.	1871.03.15	SLC	NY.Buffalo	Livy sits up	NPV	00591
Clemens, Jane family & Clemens, Jane L.	1872.12.05	SLC	CT.Hartford	Livy is so	NPV	00840

ADDRESSEE	DATE	WRITER	PLACE	CUE	SOURCE	NUMBER/NOTES
Clemens, Jane family & Clemens, Jane L.	1872.12.20	SLC & OLC	CT.Hartford	A Merry Christmas	NPV	00847
Clemens, Jane L.	****.**.**	SLC	Unknown	This modest little	CtHMTH	07442
Clemens, Jane L.	1853.08.24	SLC	NY.New York	You will doubtless	247:1853.09.08	02711 other sources
Clemens, Jane L.	1853.08.31	SLC	NY.New York	New York is	245:1853.09.10	02712 other sources
Clemens, Jane L. & Moffett, Pamela A.	1856.06.10	SLC	IA.Keokuk	I have nothing	NPV	00011
Clemens, Jane L. & Moffett, Pamela A.	1861.09.19 to 1861.09.24	SLC	NV.Carson City	The level ranks	114:56	00029
Clemens, Jane L. & Moffett, Pamela A.	1861.10.25	SLC	NV.Carson City	I have just	NPV	00030
Clemens, Jane L.	1861.10.26	SLC	NV.Carson City	You ask me	275:1861.11.20	00031
Clemens, Jane L.	1862.01.30	SLC	NV.Carson City	How sleep the	275:1862.03.06	00034
Clemens, Jane L. & Clemens, Jane family	1862.01.30 or 1862.02.01	SLC	Unknown	In the little	NPV	00038
Clemens, Jane L. & Moffett, Pamela A.	1862.02.08 to 1862.02.09	SLC	NV.Carson City	By George, Pamela	NPV	00036
Clemens, Jane L.	1862.03.20	SLC	NV.Carson City	Lo! the poor	275:1862.06.25	00040
Clemens, Jane L.	1862.04.02	SLC	NV.Carson City	Yours of March	NPV	00041
Clemens, Jane L. & Moffett, Pamela A.	1863.02.16	SLC	NV.Virginia City	I suppose I	NPV	00061
Clemens, Jane L. & Moffett, Pamela A.	1863.04.11 to 1863.04.12	SLC	NV.Virginia City	It is very of great, dark	NPV CU-MARK	00063
Clemens, Jane L.	bet 1863.04.17 & 1863.04.24	SLC	NV.Virginia City	ladies at the	NPV	00064 fragment
Clemens, Jane L. & Moffett, Pamela A.	1863.05.**	SLC	CA.San Francisco	No 1--$20	CU-MARK	00065
Clemens, Jane L. & Moffett, Pamela A.	1863.06.01	SLC	CA.San Francisco	The Unreliable &	NPV	00066
Clemens, Jane L. & Moffett, Pamela A.	1863.06.04	SLC	CA.San Francisco	My visit to	CU-MARK	00067
Clemens, Jane L. & Moffett, Pamela A.	1863.07.18	SLC	NV.Virginia City	Ma, you are	CU-MARK	00069
Clemens, Jane L. & Moffett, Pamela A.	1863.08.05	SLC	NV.Virginia City	I got burned	CU-MARK	00070

Clemens, Jane L. & Moffett, Pamela A.	1863.08.19	SLC	NV.Steamboat Sp.	Ma, you have	NPV	00071
Clemens, Jane L.	bet 1864.01.01 & 1864.01.09	SLC	NV.Virginia City	ment. It was I can't write	NPV CU-MARK	00072 fragment
Clemens, Jane L. & Moffett, Pamela A.	1864.01.10	SLC	NV.Carson City	2 P.M. Sunday	CU-MARK	00073
Clemens, Jane L. & Moffett, Pamela A.	1864.05.16	SLC	NV.Virginia City	I had rather	CU-MARK(tr)	00077
Clemens, Jane L.	1864.08.13	SLC	CA.San Francisco	The place where You have	NPV CU-MARK(tr)	10993
Clemens, Jane L. & Moffett, Pamela A.	1864.09.25	SLC	CA.San Francisco	You can see	NPV	00087
Clemens, Jane L. & Moffett, Pamela A.	1866.01.20	SLC	CA.San Francisco	Ma's last letter	CU-MARK	00094
Clemens, Jane L. & Moffett, Pamela A.	1866.03.05	SLC	CA.San Francisco	I start to	NPV	00096
Clemens, Jane L. & Moffett, Pamela A.	1866.04.03	SLC	HI.Honolulu	I have been	NPV	00097
Clemens, Jane L. & Moffett, Pamela A.	1866.05.04	SLC	HI.Maui	11 o'clock at	NPV	00099
Clemens, Jane L. & Moffett, Pamela A.	1866.06.21	SLC	HI.Honolulu	I expect I	NPV	00102
Clemens, Jane L. & Moffett, Pamela A.	1866.06.27	SLC	HI.Honolulu	I enjoy being	NPV	00103
Clemens, Jane L. & Moffett, Pamela A.	1866.07.30 to 1866.08.20	SLC	SH.Smyrniote & CA.San Francisco	I write, now	NPV	00105
Clemens, Jane L. & Clemens, Jane family	1866.11.02	SLC	NV.Virginia City	You know the	NPV	00110 misdated Nov 1
Clemens, Jane L. & Clemens, Jane family	1866.12.04	SLC	CA.San Francisco	I have written	NPV 114:122	00112
Clemens, Jane L. & Clemens, Jane family	1866.12.14	SLC	CA.San Francisco	I sail to-morrow	NPV	00116
Clemens, Jane L. & Clemens, Jane family	1867.04.15	SLC	NY.New York	I need not	ViU	00122
Clemens, Jane L. & Clemens, Jane family	1867.04.19	SLC	NY.New York	Direct my letters	CU-MARK ViU	00123 ViU envelope
Clemens, Jane L.	1867.05.01	SLC	NY.New York	The dearest Friend	ViU	09410 inscription

ADDRESSEE	DATE	WRITER	PLACE	CUE	SOURCE	NUMBER/NOTES
Clemens, Jane L. & Clemens, Jane family	1867.05.01	SLC	NY.New York	Don't expect me	NPV	00126
Clemens, Jane L. & Clemens, Jane family	1867.05.20	SLC	NY.New York	Don't--don't ask	CU-MARK	00130
Clemens, Jane L. & Clemens, Jane family	1867.06.01	SLC	NY.New York	I know I	NPV	00132
Clemens, Jane L. & Clemens, Jane family	1867.06.07	SLC	NY.New York	I suppose we	NPV	00134
Clemens, Jane L. & Clemens, Jane family	1867.06.20 to 1867.07.05	SLC	PO.Azores to FR.Marseilles	We are having	NPV	00139
Clemens, Jane L. & Clemens, Jane family	1867.07.12	SLC	FR.Marseilles	I started to	NPV	00140
Clemens, Jane L. & Clemens, Jane family	1867.07.15	SLC	IT.Genoa	I am just	NPV	00141
Clemens, Jane L. & Clemens, Jane family	1867.08.09	SLC	IT.Naples	I can't write	CU-MARK	00144
Clemens, Jane L. & Clemens, Jane family	1867.08.25	SLC	RU.Yalta	We have been	NPV	00145
Clemens, Jane L. & Clemens, Jane family	1867.09.01	SLC	TU.Constantinop.	All well. Do	NPV	00146
Clemens, Jane L. & Clemens, Jane family	1867.09.11	SLC	SY.Beirut	We are here	NPV	00148
Clemens, Jane L. & Clemens, Jane family	1867.10.12 to 1867.10.17	SLC	IT.Cagliari to SP.Gibralter	We have just	NPV	00151
Clemens, Jane L. & Clemens, Jane family	1867.10.24	SLC	SP.Cadiz	We left Gibraltar	NPV	00152
Clemens, Jane L. & Clemens, Jane family	1867.11.19	SLC	NY.New York	The Quaker City	NPV	00155
Clemens, Jane L. & Clemens, Jane family	1867.11.20	SLC	NY.New York	I am ashamed	NPV	00156
Clemens, Jane L. & Clemens, Jane family	1867.11.25	SLC	DC.Washington	Tired & sleepy	NPV	00162
Clemens, Jane L. & Clemens, Jane family	1867.12.10	SLC	DC.Washington	I called on	NPV	00171
Clemens, Jane L. & Moffett, Pamela A.	1868.01.08	SLC	DC.Washington	And so the	NPV	00175
Clemens, Jane L. & Moffett, Pamela A.	1868.01.09	SLC	DC.Washington	That infernal lecture	NPV	00176

Clemens, Jane L. & Clemens, Jane family		1868.01.13	SLC	DC.Washington	I thought you	NPV	00179
Clemens, Jane L. & Moffett, Pamela A.		1868.01.24	SLC	CT.Hartford	This is a	NPV	00182
Clemens, Jane L. & Moffett, Pamela A.		1868.02.06	SLC	DC.Washington	For two months	NPV	00190
Clemens, Jane L. & Clemens, Jane family		1868.02.21	SLC	DC.Washington	I was as	NPV	00197
Clemens, Jane L. & Clemens, Jane family		1868.03.15	SLC	SH.Henry Chaun.	I have nothing	NPV	00201
Clemens, Jane L. & Clemens, Jane family		1868.06.07	SLC	CA.San Francisco	A son of	CU-MARK	02734
Clemens, Jane L. & Clemens, Jane family	&	1868.08.24 1868.08.25	SLC	NY.Elmira	You see I	NPV	02747
Clemens, Jane L.		1868.11.03	SLC	NY.New York	I have just	NPV	02762
Clemens, Jane L. & Clemens, Jane family		1868.11.18	SLC	OH.Cleveland	Have received letters	NPV	02763
Clemens, Jane L. & Clemens, Jane family		1868.11.20	SLC	OH.Cleveland	I played against	NPV	02766
Clemens, Jane L. & Clemens, Jane family		1868.12.10	SLC	NY.New York	I didn't move	NPV	02728
Clemens, Jane L. & Clemens, Jane family		1869.02.05	SLC	NY.Elmira	This is to	Mo4	00245
Clemens, Jane L. & Clemens, Jane family		1869.02.27	SLC	NY.Lockport	I enclose $20	NPV	00262
Clemens, Jane L. & Clemens, Jane family	bet &	1869.04.07 1869.04.10	SLC	NY.Elmira	of it, for	Mo4	00285 fragment
Clemens, Jane L.		1869.05.10	SLC	CT.Hartford	Well, I did	CU-MARK	00294
Clemens, Jane L. & Clemens, Jane family		1869.06.04	SLC	NY.Elmira	Livy sends you	NPV	00315
Clemens, Jane L. & Moffett, Pamela A.		1869.06.26	SLC	NY.Elmira	I shipped my	CU-MARK	00322
Clemens, Jane L. & Clemens, Jane family		1869.12.15	SLC	MA.Boston	I arrived here	NPV	00389
Clemens, Jane L. & Clemens, Jane family		1870.03.26	SLC	NY.Buffalo	The coffin of	NPV	00449
Clemens, Jane L. & Moffett, Pamela A.		1870.06.25	SLC	NY.Elmira	We were called	NPV	00481

ADDRESSEE	DATE	WRITER	PLACE	CUE	SOURCE	NUMBER/NOTES
Clemens, Jane L. & Moffett, Pamela A.	1870.07.27	SLC	NY.Elmira	Mr Langdon is	NPV	00492
Clemens, Jane L. & Clemens, Jane family	1871.02.17	SLC	NY.Buffalo	By means of	NPV	00577
Clemens, Jane L. & Clemens, Jane family	1871.03.15	SLC	NY.Buffalo	Livy sits up	NPV	00591
Clemens, Jane L.	1871.06.11	SLC	NY.Elmira	I saw Pamela	Mo4	00615
Clemens, Jane L.	1871.12.28	SLC	IL.Danville	Enclosed I send	NPV	00697
Clemens, Jane L. & Moffett, Pamela A.	1872.11.06	SLC	EN.London	I have been	NPV	00829
Clemens, Jane L. & Moffett, Pamela A.	1872.11.26	SLC	CT.Hartford	Very glad to	NPV	00835 on Mollie Clemens Nov 26
Clemens, Jane L. & Clemens, Jane family	1872.12.05	SLC	CT.Hartford	Livy is so	NPV	00840
Clemens, Jane L. & Clemens, Jane family	1872.12.20	SLC & OLC	CT.Hartford	A Merry Christmas	NPV	00847
Clemens, Jane L. & Moffett, Pamela A.	1873.06.15	OLC	EN.London	We are so	NPV	00926
Clemens, Jane L. & Moffett, Pamela A.	1873.07.**	OLC	EN.London	We have not	NPV	00939
Clemens, Jane L. & Moffett, Pamela A.	1873.08.15	OLC	SK.Edinburgh	Your letter was	NPV	00793
Clemens, Jane L.	1873.11.06	SLC	CT.Hartford	I meant to	CU-MARK(tr)	00980
Clemens, Jane L.	1873.12.25	OLC	CT.Hartford	Mrs Jane Clemens	ViU	11107 inscription
Clemens, Jane L.	1874.05.10	SLC	NY.Elmira	Orion & Mollie	NPV	01087
Clemens, Jane L.	1874.07.11	SLC	NY.Elmira	We have been	CU-MARK	01109
Clemens, Jane L. & Moffett, Pamela A.	1874.08.15	SLC	NY.Elmira	I came away	114:220	01117
Clemens, Jane L.	aft 1874.11.16	SLC	CT.Hartford	Livy is tolerable	CU-MARK	09071 on Watterson Nov 12
Clemens, Jane L. & Moffett, Pamela A.	1875.04.25	SLC	CT.Hartford	We want to	CU-MARK	01224 date uncertain
Clemens, Jane L.	1875.12.22	SLC	CT.Hartford	P.S. to letter	NPV	00397

Clemens, Jane L. & Clemens, Mollie		1877.08.30	SLC	NY.Elmira	I write for	CU-MARK	01476
Clemens, Jane L.		1878.02.17	SLC	CT.Hartford	I suppose I	NPV	01530
Clemens, Jane L.		1878.02.23	SLC	CT.Hartford	Orion wrote me	CU-MARK	01535
Clemens, Jane L. & Moffett, Pamela A.		1878.04.07	SLC	NY.Elmira	I have told	NPV 114:325	01553
Clemens, Jane L. & Moffett, Pamela A.		1878.07.01	SLC	GE.Heidelberg	The letter came	CU-MARK(tr)	01575
Clemens, Jane L. & Moffett, Pamela A.		1878.08.20	SLC	SW.Lucerne	We came into	CU-MARK	01587
Clemens, Jane L.	&	1878.09.04 1878.09.08	SLC & OLC	SW.Geneva	Your letter enclosing	CU-MARK	01592
Clemens, Jane L. & Moffett, Pamela A.		1878.12.01	SLC	GE.Munich	I broke the	CU-MARK	01610
Clemens, Jane L. & Moffett, Pamela A.	bet &	1879.02.14 1879.02.27	SLC	GE.Munich	that finest character	CU-MARK(tr)	09211
Clemens, Jane L. & Moffett, Pamela A.		1879.05.29	SLC	FR.Paris	I have just	NPV	01661
Clemens, Jane L.		1880.01.07	SLC	CT.Hartford	I have been	NPV	01751
Clemens, Jane L. & Moffett, Pamela A.		1880.04.11	SLC	CT.Hartford	We leave for	NPV	01783
Clemens, Jane L. & Moffett, Pamela A.		1880.04.21	SLC	CT.Hartford	I don't know	NPV	01789
Clemens, Jane L. & Moffett, Pamela A.		1880.05.14	SLC	CT.Hartford	My advice to	NPV	01804
Clemens, Jane L.	ca	1880.08.01	SLC & JC	CT.Hartford	Lovingly your	CU-MARK(tr)	09127
Clemens, Jane L.		1881.01.09	SLC	CT.Hartford	Ten or twelve	NPV	01886
Clemens, Jane L. & Moffett, Pamela A.		1881.05.02	SLC	CT.Hartford	I believe there	NPV	01946
Clemens, Jane L.		1881.09.19	SLC	NY.Elmira	I was exceedingly	NPV	02038
Clemens, Jane L.		1881.12.**	SLC	CT.Hartford	To Mrs. Jane	ViU	09315 inscription
Clemens, Jane L. & Webster, Charles L.		1882.01.21	SLC	CT.Hartford	Suppose you put	NPV	02152
Clemens, Jane L.		1882.05.29	SLC	CT.Hartford	I am glad	NPV	02192

ADDRESSEE		DATE	WRITER	PLACE	CUE	SOURCE	NUMBER/NOTES
Clemens, Jane L.		1882.07.**	SLC	CT.Hartford	It is a	295:188	02228
Clemens, Jane L.		1882.10.09	SLC	CT.Hartford	Liva has gone	CU-MARK	02289 typed
Clemens, Jane L. & Clemens, Orion		1883.07.21	SLC	NY.Elmira	I don't know	CU-MARK	02616 also to Mollie Clemens
Clemens, Jane L.		1883.08.16	SLC	NY.Elmira	We expect to	CU-MARK	02822
Clemens, Jane L.		1883.09.15	SLC	CT.Hartford	I am afraid	NPV	10939
Clemens, Jane L. & Clemens, Orion		1883.12.19	SLC	CT.Hartford	Merry Christmas from	CU-MARK	02866 also to Mollie Clemens
Clemens, Jane L.		1884.04.15	SLC	CT.Hartford	I believe there	NPV	02953
Clemens, Jane L.		1885.06.08	SLC	NY.New York	This is Clara's	NPV	03238
Clemens, Jane L.		1885.06.26	SLC	NY.Elmira	Here is a	NPV	03245
Clemens, Jane L.		1885.10.30	SLC	CT.Hartford	I suppose I	NPV	03299
Clemens, Jane L.	pm	1885.11.16	SLC	CT.Hartford	*	CU-MARK	10078 envelope only
Clemens, Jane L.		1885.12.06	OLC	CT.Hartford	We rec'd a	CU-MARK	03324
Clemens, Jane L.		1885.12.18	SLC	CT.Hartford	I do hope	NPV	03335
Clemens, Jane L.		1886.08.07	SLC	NY.Elmira	I heard that	NPV	03436
Clemens, Jane L.		1887.07.24	SLC	NY.Elmira	Jean will be	NPV	03611
Clemens, Jane L.		1887.12.18	SLC	CT.Hartford	Will you take	CU-MARK	02548 also to Orion & Mollie Clemens
Clemens, Jane L.		1889.04.03	SLC	CT.Hartford	All the family	CU-MARK	03879
Clemens, Jane L. (Jean)		*	*	*	*	*	11135 see Clemens, Jean
Clemens, Jean		****.**.**	SLC	MA.Fairhaven	Jean dear, I got	CU-MARK(tr)	08667
Clemens, Jean		****.**.**	SLC	NY.New York	Oh, great Scott	Mo4	03993
Clemens, Jean		****.**.**	SLC	Unknown	It is your	CtHMTH(tr)	08986
Clemens, Jean		1884.12.14	SLC	MI.Grand Rapids	Ofters denk ich	CU-MARK	03060
Clemens, Jean		1890.07.20	SLC	CT.Hartford	Jean dear, Max	CU-MARK(tr)	04065
Clemens, Jean		1892.06.14	SLC	GE.Bremen	I am up	153:946	04299

Clemens, Jean		1893.09.13	SLC	NY.New York	Oh yes, bless	CU-MARK	04446
Clemens, Jean		1893.12.28	SLC	NY.New York	I am glad	CU-MARK	04541
Clemens, Jean		1894.02.**	SLC	MA.Fairhaven	Jean dear, I	CU-MARK	04682
Clemens, Jean	&	1896.02.16 1896.02.18	OLC	II.Darjeeling	Look on the	ViU(tr)	05022
Clemens, Jean	&	1896.03.10 1896.03.12	OLC	II.Jaipur	We are having	ViU(tr)	05030
Clemens, Jean		1903.07.26	SLC	NY.Elmira	on a Birthday	308:177	10371 inscription
Clemens, Jean		1903.08.12	SLC	NY.New York	I have just	CU-MARK(tr)	06719
Clemens, Jean & Lyon, Isabel V.	pm	1904.10.18	SLC	NY.New York	All right, Jean	NRU	06931 on envelope
Clemens, Jean		1904.10.27	SLC	NY.New York	Let Miss Lyon	CU-MARK	06937
Clemens, Jean		1904.11.25	SLC	NY.New York	No, dear, they	CU-MARK	06956
Clemens, Jean		1906.06.28	SLC	NY.New York	Jean dear, it	CU-MARK(tr)	07463
Clemens, Jean		1906.07.10	SLC	NY.New York	Jean dear, I spend	CU-MARK(tr)	07477
Clemens, Jean	o/a	1906.08.**	SLC	Unknown	With the deep	WRI2	10952 inscription
Clemens, Jean		1906.09.23	SLC	CT.Norfolk	It was grand	CU-MARK(tr)	07529
Clemens, Jean		1906.10.29	SLC	NY.New York	I am so	CU-MARK(tr)	07558
Clemens, Jean		1906.11.08	SLC	NY.New York	It is a	NN-B(tr)	07563
Clemens, Jean		1906.11.13	SLC	NY.New York	Jean dear, since	CU-MARK(tr)	07568
Clemens, Jean		1906.12.07	SLC	DC.Washington	Jean dear, I came	CU-MARK(tr)	07582
Clemens, Jean		1907.**.**	SLC	NY.New York	Jean dear, here	NN-B	08273
Clemens, Jean		1907.01.01	SLC	NY.New York	Jean dear, we had	ViU	07618
Clemens, Jean		1907.01.11	SLC	NY.New York	Dear Jean, I	CU-MARK(tr)	07625
Clemens, Jean		1907.01.17	SLC	NY.New York	Why yes, dear	CU-MARK(tr)	07615
Clemens, Jean		1907.01.26	SLC	NY.New York	It is good	CU-MARK(tr)	07635
Clemens, Jean		1907.01.27	SLC	BE.Hamilton	Jean dear, we have	CtHMTH	10586 misdated, see 1908
Clemens, Jean		1907.02.14	SLC	NY.New York	I am very	CU-MARK(tr)	07649

ADDRESSEE	DATE	WRITER	PLACE	CUE	SOURCE	NUMBER/NOTES
Clemens, Jean	1907.02.21	SLC	NY.New York	Jean dear, Ashcroft's	CU-MARK(tr)	07659
Clemens, Jean	1907.02.25	SLC	NY.New York	Your news about	NN-B(tr)	07664
Clemens, Jean	1907.03.05	SLC	NY.New York	O dear me	CU-MARK(tr)	07670
Clemens, Jean	1907.04.22	SLC	NY.New York	I've been to	CU-MARK(tr)	07696
Clemens, Jean	1907.05.14	SLC	NY.Tuxedo Park	Oh, you dear	CU-MARK(tr)	07720
Clemens, Jean	1907.05.26	SLC	NY.Tuxedo Park	It saddened me	CU-MARK(tr)	07730
Clemens, Jean	1907.06.**	SLC	NY.Tuxedo Park	If your mother	CtHMTH(tr)	07739
Clemens, Jean	1907.06.23	SLC	EN.London	I have been	CU-MARK(tr)	07767
Clemens, Jean	1907.06.30	SLC	EN.London	Jean dear, I	MoHM	07771
Clemens, Jean	1907.07.04	SLC	EN.London	Just a line	CU-MARK(tr)	07778
Clemens, Jean	1907.07.12	SLC	EN.London	Jean dear, we sail	CU-MARK(tr)	07782
Clemens, Jean	1907.08.25	SLC	NY.Tuxedo Park	Dearest Jean, I hope	CU-MARK(tr)	07818
Clemens, Jean	1907.09.21	SLC	NY.Tuxedo Park	Jean dear, I am	CU-MARK(tr)	07837
Clemens, Jean	1907.10.04	SLC	NY.Tuxedo Park	Jean dear it is	CtY	07843
Clemens, Jean	1907.10.08	SLC	NY.Tuxedo Park	Jean dear, I hear	CU-MARK(tr)	07849
Clemens, Jean	1907.11.15	SLC	NY.New York	Jean dear, you may	CU-MARK(tr)	07863
Clemens, Jean	1907.12.01	SLC	NY.New York	Oh, Jean dear	CU-MARK(tr)	07877
Clemens, Jean	1907.12.02	SLC	NY.New York	Dear Jean I will	CU-MARK(tr)	07878
Clemens, Jean	1907.12.21	SLC	NY.New York	Dear Jean this is	CU-MARK(tr)	07892
Clemens, Jean	1908.01.27	SLC	BE.Hamilton	Jean dear, we have	CtHMTH	07637 misdated 1907
Clemens, Jean	1908.02.14	SLC	NY.New York	I must snatch	CU-MARK(tr)	07938
Clemens, Jean	1908.03.02	SLC	BE.Hamilton	Jean dear, there	CU-MARK(tr)	07952
Clemens, Jean	1908.03.10	SLC	BE.Hamilton	Jean dear, we are	CU-MARK(tr)	07956
Clemens, Jean	1908.03.23	SLC	BE.Hamilton	There is nothing	CU-MARK(tr)	07963
Clemens, Jean	1908.05.15	SLC	NY.New York	It is a	CU-MARK(tr)	07999
Clemens, Jean	1908.05.20	SLC	NY.New York	Jean dear, welcome	CU-MARK(tr)	08005
Clemens, Jean	1908.05.22	SLC	NY.New York	Your beautiful letter	CU-MARK(tr)	08006
Clemens, Jean	1908.06.05	SLC	NY.New York	Dear Jean, consound	CU-MARK(tr)	08021
Clemens, Jean	1908.06.14	SLC	NY.New York	The time is	CU-MARK(tr)	08028

Clemens, Jean		1908.06.19	SLC	CT.Redding	I like the	CU-MARK(tr)	08035
Clemens, Jean		1908.07.02	SLC	CT.Redding	Dear Jean I am	CU-MARK(tr)	08051
Clemens, Jean		1908.07.28	SLC	CT.Redding	Dear Jean it	CU-MARK(tr)	08062
Clemens, Jean		1908.08.09	SLC	CT.Redding	Jean dear, don't	CU-MARK(tr)	08077
Clemens, Jean		1908.10.02	SLC	CT.Redding	Jean dear, it was	CU-MARK(tr)	08118
Clemens, Jean		1908.10.12	SLC	CT.Redding	Oh Jean dear	NN-B(tr)	08136 other sources
Clemens, Jean		1908.10.23	SLC	NJ.Deal	I came down	NN-B(tr)	08141 other sources
Clemens, Jean		1908.11.04	SLC	CT.Redding	Jean dear, an	NN-B(tr)	08153
Clemens, Jean		1908.11.30	SLC	CT.Redding	Jean dear, I have	NN-B(tr)	08289
Clemens, Jean		1908.12.17	SLC	CT.Redding	You sail January	CU-MARK(tr)	08182 telegram
Clemens, Jean		1909.01.02	SLC	CT.Redding	Happy New Year	InU-Li	08306
Clemens, Jean		1909.02.08	SLC	CT.Redding	Your letter has	MiD	08342
Clemens, Jean		1909.02.26	SLC	CT.Redding	You dear Jean	CU-MARK(tr)	08355
Clemens, Jean		1909.03.03	SLC	CT.Redding	Jean dear, I think	CU-MARK(tr)	08358
Clemens, Jean		1909.04.19	SLC	CT.Redding	Dear child you	CU-MARK(tr)	08385
Clemens, Jean		1909.12.06	SLC	BE.Hamilton	Oh, you dear	CU-MARK	08507
Clemens, Katharine B.		****.**.**	OLC	Unknown	*	Mo2	10154 envelope only
Clemens, Katharine B.		****.**.**	OLC	Unknown	with congratulations to	Mo2	08417
Clemens, Katharine B. & Clemens, James R.	ca	****.12.25	SLC	Unknown	Love and Christmas	Mo2(tr)	08390
Clemens, Katharine B.		1899.03.29	SLC & OLC	AU.Vienna	Our kinsman has	Mo2	05570
Clemens, Katharine B. & Clemens, James R.		1899.05.03	SLC	EN.London	Congratulations	Mo2	08855 telegram
Clemens, Katharine B.		1899.06.24	OLC	EN.London	If you have	Mo2	02479
Clemens, Katharine B.		1899.12.08	OLC	EN.London	Your letter has	Mo2	08853
Clemens, Katharine B. & Clemens, James R.	o/a	1900.03.27	OLC	EN.London	With affectionate	Mo2	10949 inscription

ADDRESSEE	DATE	WRITER	PLACE	CUE	SOURCE	NUMBER/NOTES
Clemens, Katharine B. & Clemens, James R.	1900.03.28	SLC	EN.London	We send love	Mo2	08858 telegram
Clemens, Katharine B.	1900.05.01	OLC	EN.London	I wonder how	Mo2	08862
Clemens, Katharine B.	bet 1900.05.10 & 1900.05.24	OLC	EN.London	I am so	Mo2	08861
Clemens, Katharine B.	1900.05.29	OLC	EN.London	Mr Clemens and	Mo2	08863
Clemens, Katharine B.	1900.06.13	SLC	EN.London	I am very	Mo2	05820
Clemens, Katharine B.	1900.07.12	OLC	EN.London	I was so	Mo2	02663
Clemens, Katharine B.	1900.07.15	JC	EN.London	I am so	Mo2	08864
Clemens, Katharine B.	1900.08.22	OLC	EN.London	Can you &	Mo2	08866
Clemens, Katharine B.	1900.10.06	OLC	EN.London	*	Mo2	10114 envelope only
Clemens, Katharine B.	1902.05.04	OLC	NY.Riverdale	It was indeed	Mo2	08878
Clemens, Katharine B.	1902.05.17	OLC	NY.Riverdale	Your kind letter	Mo2	06340
Clemens, Katharine B.	1902.05.27	OLC	NY.Riverdale	How I wish	Mo2	08879
Clemens, Katharine B.	1902.06.**	SLC	Unknown	with the love	Mo2	09369 inscription
Clemens, Katharine B. & Clemens, James R.	1902.08.22	SLC	ME.York Harbor	To-day, for the	Mo2	06413
Clemens, Katharine B.	1902.08.27	SLC	ME.York Harbor	Your kind good	Mo2	06416
Clemens, Katharine B.	1902.09.26	SLC	ME.York Harbor	Livy was very	Mo2	06443
Clemens, Katharine B.	1905.08.31	SLC	NH.Dublin	I am just	Mo2	07121
Clemens, Katharine B.	1906.10.16	SLC	NH.Dublin	Your letter has	Mo2	07549
Clemens, Katharine B.	1907.10.05	SLC per IVL	NY.Tuxedo Park	Mr. Clemens asks	Mo2	08894
Clemens, Katharine B.	1908.08.13	SLC per IVL	CT.Redding	Mr. Clemens asks	Mo2	08900
Clemens, Katharine B.	1908.08.20	SLC per IVL	CT.Redding	Mr Clemens asks	Mo2	08901
Clemens, Katharine B.	1910.01.16	SLC per ABP	CT.Redding	To all friends	CU-MARK(ph)	08538 form letter
Clemens, Katharine B.	pm 1910.03.16	SLC per ABP	CT.Redding	To all friends	Mo2	11005 form letter
Clemens, Katharine B.	1910.03.24	SLC	BE.Hamilton	I am grateful	Mo2	08575

Clemens, Mary E.	*	*	*	*	*	11137 see Clemens, Mollie
Clemens, Mollie & Clemens, Orion	****.**.**	CC	Unknown	I thank you	CU-MARK	08720
Clemens, Mollie & Clemens, Orion	1858.03.09	SLC	MO.St. Louis	I must take	NPV	00014
Clemens, Mollie	1858.06.18	SLC	TN.Memphis	Long before this	CU-MARK	00016
Clemens, Mollie & Clemens, Orion	1861.02.06	SLC	IL.Cairo	After promising Mrs.	NPV	00027
Clemens, Mollie	bet 1861.09.01 & 1861.10.31	SLC	NV.Carson City	will, although I	NPV	02715 fragment
Clemens, Mollie	1862.01.31	SLC	NV.Carson City	Paint-Brush in	CU-MARK	00035 on Orion Clemens Jan 29-31
Clemens, Mollie & Clemens, Orion	1862.10.21	SLC	NV.Virginia City	I wrote by	NPV	00060
Clemens, Mollie	1864.05.20	SLC	NV.Virginia City	I have had	CU-MARK	00078
Clemens, Mollie & Clemens, Orion	1864.05.25	SLC	NV.Virginia City	Don't stump for	CU-MARK	00081
Clemens, Mollie & Clemens, Orion	1864.08.14	SLC	CA.San Francisco	I have managed	CU-MARK	00085
Clemens, Mollie & Clemens, Orion	1864.09.28	SLC	CA.San Francisco	I guess my	CU-MARK	00088
Clemens, Mollie & Clemens, Orion	1865.10.19 to 1865.10.20	SLC	CA.San Francisco	Orion there was	CU-MARK	00092
Clemens, Mollie	1866.05.22	SLC	HI.Honolulu	I have just	NPV	00101
Clemens, Mollie	1867.02.**	SLC	NY.New York	I have tried	NPV	00119
Clemens, Mollie	aft 1870.12.20	SLC	NY.Buffalo	don't know but	NPV	02795 fragment
Clemens, Mollie	1871.03.18	SLC	NY.Buffalo	*	CU-MARK	10080 envelope only
Clemens, Mollie & Clemens, Orion	1871.06.07	SLC	NY.Elmira	I forgot to	CU-MARK	00613
Clemens, Mollie & Clemens, Orion	1871.06.21	SLC	NY.Elmira	Am very glad	CU-MARK	00619

ADDRESSEE	DATE	WRITER	PLACE	CUE	SOURCE	NUMBER/NOTES
Clemens, Mollie & Clemens, Orion	1871.12.24	SLC & OLC	CT.Hartford	I enclose our	CU-MARK	00692
Clemens, Mollie & Clemens, Orion	1872.05.15	SLC	NY.Elmira	We arrived last	CU-MARK	00747
Clemens, Mollie	1872.05.20	SLC	NY.Elmira	Just a hasty	CU-MARK	00751
Clemens, Mollie & Clemens, Orion	1872.05.22	SLC	NY.Elmira	We are delayed	CU-MARK	00752
Clemens, Mollie	1872.07.**	OLC	CT.New Saybrook	More things I	Mo4	00760
Clemens, Mollie	aft 1872.07.06	SLC	CT.New Saybrook	The Boston package	CU-MARK	00762
Clemens, Mollie	1872.07.07	OLC	CT.New Saybrook	We are very	CU-MARK	00763
Clemens, Mollie	1872.07.12	OLC	CT.New Saybrook	I rec'd your	CU-MARK	00766
Clemens, Mollie	pm 1872.07.2*	SLC	CT.New Saybrook	Please send me	CU-MARK	00771
Clemens, Mollie	1872.07.21	SLC	CT.New Saybrook	Send to Moore	Mo4	00775
Clemens, Mollie	pm 1872.07.23	SLC	CT.New Saybrook	Please send me	CU-MARK	00773
Clemens, Mollie	pm 1872.07.25	SLC	CT.New Saybrook	Please send all	CU-MARK	00774
Clemens, Mollie	pm 1872.07.26	OLC	CT.New Saybrook	*	CU-MARK	10427 envelope only
Clemens, Mollie	aft 1872.07.27	OLC	CT.New Saybrook	Daily commissions you	CU-MARK	00780
Clemens, Mollie	aft 1872.07.27	OLC	CT.New Saybrook	Don't forget to	CU-MARK	00702
Clemens, Mollie	pm 1872.07.27	OLC	CT.New Saybrook	I am going	CU-MARK	00778
Clemens, Mollie	1872.07.30	SLC	CT.New Saybrook	The satchel arrived	CU-MARK	00782
Clemens, Mollie	1872.08.02	SLC	CT.New Saybrook	I wish Orion	CU-MARK	00784
Clemens, Mollie	1872.08.05	SLC	CT.New Saybrook	Send carriage to	CU-MARK	00785 telegram
Clemens, Mollie	1872.08.08	SLC	CT.New Saybrook	Please stir up	CU-MARK	00788 telegram
Clemens, Mollie	1872.08.08	SLC	CT.New Saybrook	Please send the	CU-MARK	00789
Clemens, Mollie	1872.08.16	SLC	CT.New Saybrook	Send down all	CU-MARK	00794 telegram
Clemens, Mollie	pm 1872.08.21	OLC	Unknown	I send you	CU-MARK	00797
Clemens, Mollie	pm 1872.08.27	OLC	CT.New Saybrook	I send you	CU-MARK	00798
Clemens, Mollie	1872.08.28	OLC	CT.New Saybrook	Let Mary go	CU-MARK	00799 telegram

Clemens, Mollie & Clemens, Orion		1873.05.05	SLC	CT.Hartford	Your letters received	CU-MARK	00913
Clemens, Mollie	pm	1873.06.23	OLC	EN.London	I am altogether	CU-MARK	00930
Clemens, Mollie & Clemens, Orion	aft	1873.09.10	SLC	EN.London	We got seal-skin	NPV	00962
Clemens, Mollie		1874.01.11 & 1874.01.14	OLC	CT.Hartford	Your letter and	NPV	01039
Clemens, Mollie & Clemens, Orion		1874.06.10	SLC	NY.Elmira	The child was	CU-MARK	01096
Clemens, Mollie		1874.12.27	SLC & OLC	CT.Hartford	I wish that	CU-MARK	01169
Clemens, Mollie		1877.07.29	OLC	NY.Elmira	I was very	CU-MARK(tr)	01435
Clemens, Mollie & Clemens, Jane L.		1877.08.30	SLC	NY.Elmira	I write for	CU-MARK	01476
Clemens, Mollie		1878.12.15	OLC	GE.Munich	I have been	CU-MARK	01615
Clemens, Mollie		1879.12.02	OLC	CT.Hartford	I do feel	CU-MARK	01732
Clemens, Mollie		1880.12.07	OLC	CT.Hartford	I don't know	CU-MARK	01867
Clemens, Mollie		1880.12.08	SLC	CT.Hartford	Here is your	CU-MARK	01866
Clemens, Mollie		1880.12.28	OLC	CT.Hartford	The quilt &	CU-MARK	01883
Clemens, Mollie	ca	1881.07.01	OLC	CT.Branford	We rec'd last	CU-MARK	01979
Clemens, Mollie		1883.07.21	SLC	NY.Elmira	I don't know	CU-MARK	02846 also to Jane & Orion Clemens
Clemens, Mollie	aft	1883.09.30	SLC	Unknown	It is distressing	NPV	02843
Clemens, Mollie		1883.12.19	SLC	CT.Hartford	Merry Christmas from	CU-MARK	02879 also to Jane & Orion Clemens
Clemens, Mollie		1884.12.27	CC	CT.Hartford	I thank you	CU-MARK	03073
Clemens, Mollie		1885.01.11	OLC	CT.Hartford	Think that before	NPV	03112
Clemens, Mollie & Clemens, Orion		1885.03.05	SLC	CT.Hartford	I reached home	NPV	03184
Clemens, Mollie		1886.08.06	SLC	NY.Elmira	What a terrific	NPV	03435
Clemens, Mollie		1887.07.10	SLC	NY.Elmira	This is a	114:488	03599
Clemens, Mollie		1887.07.24	SLC	NY.Elmira	The carriage &	CU-MARK	03612

ADDRESSEE	DATE	WRITER	PLACE	CUE	SOURCE	NUMBER/NOTES
Clemens, Mollie & Clemens, Orion	1887.12.18	SLC	CT.Hartford	Will you take	CU-MARK	03680 also to Jane Clemens
Clemens, Mollie & Clemens, Orion	1890.08.21	SLC	NY.Elmira	Orion, I want	CU-MARK	04083
Clemens, Mollie & Clemens, Orion	1890.08.31	SLC	NY.Tannersville	I am just	CU-MARK	04090
Clemens, Mollie	1890.10.30	SLC	CT.Hartford	All the family	CU-MARK	04108
Clemens, Mollie	1890.12.11	SLC	CT.Hartford	Give these to	CU-MARK(tr)	04119
Clemens, Mollie & Clemens, Orion	1892.08.23	SLC	GE.Bad-Nauheim	Private because no	CU-MARK	01768
Clemens, Mollie	1892.09.04	JC	GE.Bad-Nauheim	I received your	CU-MARK	01917
Clemens, Mollie & Clemens, Orion	1893.02.02	SLC	IT.Florence	Here is another	CU-MARK	04332
Clemens, Mollie & Clemens, Orion	1893.04.24	SLC	IL.Chicago	I have been	NPV	04386
Clemens, Mollie & Clemens, Orion	1893.07.26	SLC	AU.Krankenheil	We have been	CU-MARK(tr)	04425
Clemens, Mollie & Clemens, Orion	1893.11.03	SLC	NY.New York	Clara and I	CU-MARK(tr)	04487
Clemens, Mollie & Clemens, Orion	1893.11.29	SLC	NY.New York	I meant to	CU-MARK	04512 on clipping
Clemens, Mollie & Clemens, Orion	1894.04.12	SLC	SH.New York	I shall arrive	CU-MARK(tr)	04717
Clemens, Mollie	1894.05.08	SLC	NY.New York	Thank you for	CU-MARK(tr)	04730
Clemens, Mollie & Clemens, Orion	1896.09.14	SLC	EN.London	There is nothing	CU-MARK(tr)	05110
Clemens, Mollie & Clemens, Orion	1897.11.05	SLC	AU.Vienna	I believe I	TxU	05310
Clemens, Mollie	1897.12.11	SLC	AU.Vienna	It is 10	CU-MARK(ph)	05320
Clemens, Mollie	1898.05.24	SLC	AU.Kaltenleut.	This post-card picture	IU-R	05392
Clemens, Mrs. John M.	*	*	*	*	*	11134 see Clemens, Jane L.
Clemens, Mrs. Orion	*	*	*	*	*	11136 see Clemens, Mollie
Clemens, Olivia L.	****.**.**	SLC	Unknown	I hope you	105:1956.04.10	09465

Clemens, Olivia L.	1868.09.07	SLC	NY.Elmira	The impulse is	CU-MARK	02750 E#1; date uncertain
Clemens, Olivia L.	1868.09.21	SLC	MO.St. Louis	I cannot frame	CU-MARK	02751 E#2
Clemens, Olivia L.	1868.10.05	SLC	Unknown	P.S.--I suspect	CU-MARK	02770 date uncertain
Clemens, Olivia L.	1868.10.18	SLC	CT.Hartford	You have rebuked	CU-MARK	02759 E#4
Clemens, Olivia L.	1868.10.30	SLC	CT.Hartford	Your welcome letter	CU-MARK	02760 E#5
Clemens, Olivia L.	1868.11.28	SLC	NY.New York	When I found	CU-MARK	02768 E#6
Clemens, Olivia L.	1868.12.04	SLC	NY.New York	A blessed peace	CU-MARK	02724 E#8
Clemens, Olivia L.	1868.12.04	SLC	NY.New York	No! I got	CU-MARK	02725 E#9
Clemens, Olivia L.	1868.12.05 to 1868.12.07	SLC	NY.New York	I feel better	CU-MARK	02726 E#10
Clemens, Olivia L.	1868.12.09	SLC	NY.New York	At 1 o'clock	CU-MARK	02727 E#11
Clemens, Olivia L.	1868.12.12	SLC	NY.Norwich	It is spendid	CU-MARK	00205 E#12
Clemens, Olivia L.	1868.12.19 to 1868.12.20	SLC	NY.Fort Plain	Here at dead	CU-MARK	00206 E#13
Clemens, Olivia L.	1868.12.21 to 1868.12.23	SLC	MI.Detroit	I am almost	CU-MARK	00207 E#14
Clemens, Olivia L.	1868.12.23 to 1868.12.24	SLC	MI.Lansing	Twenty minutes after	CU-MARK	00208 E#15
Clemens, Olivia L.	1868.12.24 to 1868.12.25	SLC	MI.Lansing	I have been	CU-MARK	00210 E#16; place uncertain
Clemens, Olivia L.	1868.12.27	SLC	MI.Tecumseh	I got your	CU-MARK	00211 E#17
Clemens, Olivia L.	1868.12.30	SLC	OH.Cleveland	My dearest Livy	CU-MARK	00213 E#18
Clemens, Olivia L.	1868.12.31	SLC	OH.Cleveland	Your Chirstmas letter	CU-MARK	00214 E#19

ADDRESSEE	DATE	WRITER	PLACE	CUE	SOURCE	NUMBER/NOTES
Clemens, Olivia L.	1869.01.02	SLC	IN.Fort Wayne	I wish I	CU-MARK	00217 E#20
Clemens, Olivia L.	1869.01.06	SLC	IL.Rockford	I was just	CU-MARK	00220 E#22
Clemens, Olivia L.	1869.01.07	SLC	IL.Chicago	that is the	CU-MARK	00224 E#23
Clemens, Olivia L.	1869.01.12	SLC	IL.El Paso	I talked in	CU-MARK	00227 E#25
Clemens, Olivia L.	1869.01.13 to 1869.01.14	SLC	IL.Ottawa	Another botch of	CU-MARK	00231 E#26
Clemens, Olivia L.	1869.01.14	SLC	IA.Davenport	Livy, darling, I greet	CU-MARK	00232 E#27
Clemens, Olivia L.	1869.01.16	SLC	IL.Chicago	I am uncomfortably	CU-MARK	00234 E#28
Clemens, Olivia L.	1869.01.19	SLC	OH.Cleveland	I reached here	CU-MARK	00235 E#29
Clemens, Olivia L.	1869.01.20	SLC	OH.Toledo	It was splendid	CU-MARK	00236 E#30
Clemens, Olivia L.	1869.01.21 to 1869.01.22	SLC	OH.Norwalk	I wrote you	CU-MARK	00237 E#31
Clemens, Olivia L.	1869.01.22	SLC	OH.Cleveland	Oh, Livy darling	CU-MARK	00238 E#32
Clemens, Olivia L.	1869.01.23 to 1869.01.24	SLC	OH.Cleveland	Now, you dear	CU-MARK	00239 E#33
Clemens, Olivia L.	1869.01.24	SLC	OH.Cleveland	It has come	CU-MARK	00241 E#34
Clemens, Olivia L.	1869.01.26	SLC	IL.Batavia	Livy darling, I never	CU-MARK	00242 E#35
Clemens, Olivia L.	1869.01.29	SLC	IL.Galena	Livy darling, I have	CU-MARK	00243 E#37
Clemens, Olivia L.	1869.02.13	SLC	OH.Cleveland	Livy, darling, (10	CU-MARK	00247 E#38
Clemens, Olivia L.	1869.02.13 to 1869.02.14	SLC	OH.Ravenna	I am able	CU-MARK	00250 E#39
Clemens, Olivia L.	1869.02.15	SLC	OH.Ravenna	Livy, darling, how	CU-MARK	00254 E#40
Clemens, Olivia L.	1869.02.17	SLC	PA.Titusville	Livy dear, I don't	CU-MARK	00255 E#41

Clemens, Olivia L.	1869.02.26	SLC	NY.Brooklyn	My Darling Livy, it	CU-MARK	00259 E#43
Clemens, Olivia L.	1869.02.27	SLC	NY.Lockport	Livy dear, it does	CU-MARK	00260 E#44
Clemens, Olivia L.	1869.02.28	SLC	NY.Rochester	I haven't anything	CU-MARK	00263 E#45
Clemens, Olivia L.	1869.03.02	SLC	NY.Rochester	I love you	CU-MARK	00264 E#46
Clemens, Olivia L.	1869.03.04	SLC	NY.Lockport	I am not	CU-MARK	00266 E#47
Clemens, Olivia L.	1869.03.05	SLC	CT.Hartford	What a darling	CU-MARK	00267 E#48
Clemens, Olivia L.	1869.03.06	SLC	CT.Hartford	Livy dear, I have	CU-MARK	00269 E#50
Clemens, Olivia L.	1869.03.06	SLC	CT.Hartford	Livy my darling, when	CU-MARK	00268 E#49
Clemens, Olivia L.	1869.03.08	SLC	CT.Hartford	Livy dear, I am	CU-MARK	00271 E#51
Clemens, Olivia L.	1869.03.08 to 1869.03.09	SLC	CT.Hartford	How this precious	CU-MARK	00272 E#52
Clemens, Olivia L.	1869.03.10	SLC	CT.Hartford	I suppose my	CU-MARK	00274 E#53
Clemens, Olivia L.	1869.03.12	SLC	CT.Hartford	My Darling!--Your	CU-MARK	00275 E#54
Clemens, Olivia L.	1869.03.13	SLC	CT.Hartford	It lacks something	CU-MARK	00277 E#56
Clemens, Olivia L.	1869.05.08	SLC	CT.Hartford	Patience! Fortitude!	CU-MARK	00292 E#62
Clemens, Olivia L.	1869.05.08	SLC	NY.New York	It has been	CU-MARK	00291 E#61
Clemens, Olivia L.	1869.05.09	SLC	CT.Hartford	Break our engagement	CU-MARK	00293 E#64
Clemens, Olivia L.	1869.05.12	SLC	CT.Hartford	Was there ever	CU-MARK	00299 E#67
Clemens, Olivia L.	1869.05.13	SLC	CT.Hartford	Why, you little	CU-MARK	00300 E#68
Clemens, Olivia L.	1869.05.14	SLC	CT.Hartford	A natural impulse	CU-MARK	00302 E#69

ADDRESSEE	DATE	WRITER	PLACE	CUE	SOURCE	NUMBER/NOTES
Clemens, Olivia L.	1869.05.15	SLC	CT.Hartford	I have already	CU-MARK	00301 misdated Thursday; E#70
Clemens, Olivia L.	1869.05.15	SLC	CT.Hartford	It is a	CU-MARK	00303 E#71
Clemens, Olivia L.	1869.05.15	SLC	CT.Hartford	Livy dear, only	CU-MARK	00304 E#72
Clemens, Olivia L.	1869.05.17	SLC	CT.Hartford	I can't resist	CU-MARK	00305 E#73
Clemens, Olivia L.	1869.05.19 to 1869.05.20	SLC	CT.Hartford	Livy dear, I think	CU-MARK	00306 E#75
Clemens, Olivia L.	1869.05.22	SLC	NY.New York	Livy darling, Precious	CU-MARK	00307 date uncertain
Clemens, Olivia L.	1869.05.24	SLC	CT.East Windsor	My precious little	CU-MARK	00309 E#81
Clemens, Olivia L.	1869.06.08	SLC	NY.Elmira	It is the	CU-MARK	00316 E#82
Clemens, Olivia L.	1869.06.21	SLC	CT.Hartford	By the almanac	CU-MARK	00318 E#83
Clemens, Olivia L.	1869.06.23	SLC	NY.New York	Little saint,--dear	CU-MARK	00321 E#84
Clemens, Olivia L.	1869.08.08	SLC	NY.Buffalo	Livy darling, often	CU-MARK	00329 E#90
Clemens, Olivia L.	1869.08.19	SLC	NY.Buffalo	My child, I	CU-MARK	00335 E#101
Clemens, Olivia L.	1869.08.21	SLC	NY.Buffalo	Darling, it is	CU-MARK	00339 E#104
Clemens, Olivia L.	1869.08.25 & 1869.08.26	SLC	NY.Buffalo	My Livy, my	CU-MARK	00341 E#108
Clemens, Olivia L.	1869.09.**	SLC	Unknown	from Saml. L. Clemens	CCamarSJ	09405 inscription
Clemens, Olivia L.	1869.09.02	SLC	NY.Buffalo	Yes, my little	CU-MARK	00343
Clemens, Olivia L.	1869.09.03	SLC	NY.Buffalo	Oh no, my	CU-MARK	00346 E#113
Clemens, Olivia L.	1869.09.06	SLC	NY.Buffalo	Livy darling, I	CU-MARK	00347 E#114 1/2
Clemens, Olivia L.	1869.09.07	SLC	NY.Buffalo	I know a	CU-MARK	00349 E#116

Clemens, Olivia L.	1869.09.08 & 1869.09.09	SLC	NY.Buffalo	Livy, my precious little	CU-MARK	00351 E#117
Clemens, Olivia L.	1869.10.30 to 1869.10.31	SLC	PA.Pittsburgh	I have just	CU-MARK	00365 E#128
Clemens, Olivia L.	1869.11.10	SLC	MA.Boston	I shall spend	CU-MARK	00366 E#133
Clemens, Olivia L.	1869.11.10 to 1869.11.11	SLC	MA.Boston	Darling, it is	CU-MARK	00367 E#134
Clemens, Olivia L.	1869.11.15 & 1869.11.16	SLC	MA.Clinton & MA.Holyoke	I had to	CU-MARK	00368 E#138
Clemens, Olivia L.	1869.11.19	SLC	MA.Boston	Boston, 19th--Livy	CU-MARK	00374 E#141
Clemens, Olivia L.	1869.11.24	SLC	CT.Hartford	I am perplexed	CU-MARK	00377 E#147
Clemens, Olivia L.	1869.11.25	SLC	MA.Boston	Well! here I	CU-MARK	00378 E#148
Clemens, Olivia L.	1869.11.27	SLC	MA.Boston	Oh, you little	CU-MARK	00379 E#149
Clemens, Olivia L.	1869.11.28	SLC	MA.Boston	Livy darling, I thank	CU-MARK	00380 E#150
Clemens, Olivia L.	1869.11.29	SLC	MA.Boston	Don't know whether	CU-MARK	00381
Clemens, Olivia L.	1869.12.14	SLC	MA.Springfield	Livy my peerless	CU-MARK	00387 probably E#155
Clemens, Olivia L.	1869.12.15 & 1869.12.16	SLC	RI.Pawtucket & MA.Boston	My child, I	CU-MARK	00388 E#156
Clemens, Olivia L.	1869.12.18 & 1869.12.19	SLC	MA.Boston	Sweetheart, I wrote	CU-MARK	00391 E#159
Clemens, Olivia L.	1869.12.21	SLC	MA.Boston	Little sweetheart, I	CU-MARK	00392 E#160
Clemens, Olivia L.	1869.12.25	SLC	MA.Boston	A happy Christmas	CU-MARK	00393 E#163
Clemens, Olivia L.	1869.12.27	SLC	CT.New Haven	Sweetheart, it is	CU-MARK	00394 E#166
Clemens, Olivia L.	1870.01.06	SLC	NY.New York	Good luck, sweetheart	CU-MARK	00402 E#168
Clemens, Olivia L.	1870.01.07 & 1870.01.08	SLC	NY.Troy	Darling, I have had	CU-MARK	00403 E#169

ADDRESSEE	DATE	WRITER	PLACE	CUE	SOURCE	NUMBER/NOTES
Clemens, Olivia L.	1870.01.08	SLC	NY.Troy	Sweetheart, this is	CU-MARK	00404 E#170
Clemens, Olivia L.	1870.01.10	SLC	NY.Albany	Had an immense	CU-MARK	00406 E#172
Clemens, Olivia L.	1870.01.10	SLC	NY.Albany	It is snowing	CU-MARK	00407 E#173
Clemens, Olivia L.	1870.01.13	SLC	NY.Cambridge	No, Livy dear	CU-MARK	00408 E#176
Clemens, Olivia L.	1870.01.14	SLC	NY.Troy	Livy darling, I have	CU-MARK	00410 E#177
Clemens, Olivia L.	1870.01.14	SLC	NY.Utica	You dear little	CU-MARK	00411 misdated Jan 15; E#178
Clemens, Olivia L.	1870.01.20	SLC	NY.Hornellsville	My child, I	CU-MARK	00414 E#184
Clemens, Olivia L.	1870.07.06	SLC	DC.Washington	Livy my darling, I have	CU-MARK	00487
Clemens, Olivia L.	1870.07.08	SLC	DC.Washington	Livy my Darling, the	CU-MARK	00488
Clemens, Olivia L.	1870.11.27	SLC	Unknown	From S.L.C.	454:1951.05	09527 inscription
Clemens, Olivia L.	1871.01.12	SLC	OH.Cleveland	Just a line	CU-MARK	00557
Clemens, Olivia L.	1871.08.08 or 1871.08.09	SLC	CT.Hartford	it isn't worth	CU-MARK	00643 fragment
Clemens, Olivia L.	1871.08.10	SLC	CT.Hartford	Livy darling, the	CU-MARK	00644
Clemens, Olivia L.	1871.08.18	SLC	CT.Hartford	Livy darling, one of	CU-MARK	00646
Clemens, Olivia L.	1871.09.08	SLC	DC.Washington	Livy darling, the	CU-MARK	00650
Clemens, Olivia L.	1871.10.14	SLC	NY.New York	We played billiards	CU-MARK	00660
Clemens, Olivia L.	1871.10.15	SLC	PA.Bethlehem	Livy darling, I got	CU-MARK	00661
Clemens, Olivia L.	1871.10.16	SLC	PA.Bethlehem	Livy darling, this is	CU-MARK	00662
Clemens, Olivia L.	1871.10.17	SLC	PA.Allentown	Livy darling, this	CU-MARK	00663
Clemens, Olivia L.	1871.10.18	SLC	PA.Wilkes-Barre	Livy darling, I am in	CU-MARK	00664
Clemens, Olivia L.	1871.10.27	SLC	MA.Great Barr.	Livy Darling--the	Mo4	00667
Clemens, Olivia L.	1871.10.31	SLC	MA.Milford	Livy darling, the same	CU-MARK	00668
Clemens, Olivia L.	1871.11.01	SLC	MA.Boston	Livy darling, it was	CU-MARK	00669
Clemens, Olivia L.	1871.11.09	SLC	MA.Worcester	Livy darling, am just	CU-MARK	00670

Clemens, Olivia L.	1871.11.11	SLC	MA.Boston	Livy darling, I talked	CU-MARK	00671
Clemens, Olivia L.	1871.11.12	SLC	MA.Boston	Livy darling, I missed	CU-MARK	00673
Clemens, Olivia L.	1871.11.15	SLC	MA.Haverhill	Livy darling, it was	CU-MARK	00674
Clemens, Olivia L.	1871.11.16	SLC	ME.Portland	Livy darling--this is	CU-MARK	00676
Clemens, Olivia L.	1871.11.27	SLC	VT.Bennington	Livy darling, good	CU-MARK	00680
Clemens, Olivia L.	1871.12.03	SLC	NY.Homer	Livy darling, send	CU-MARK	00684
Clemens, Olivia L.	1871.12.04	SLC	NY.Geneva	Livy darling, I am thus	CU-MARK	00685
Clemens, Olivia L.	1871.12.05	SLC	NY.Auburn	Old darling, I	CU-MARK	00686
Clemens, Olivia L.	1871.12.16	SLC	IL.Chicago	My dear dear	CU-MARK	00690
Clemens, Olivia L.	1871.12.19	SLC	IL.Chicago	*	CU-MARK	10854 envelope only
Clemens, Olivia L.	1871.12.25	SLC	IL.Chicago	Joy, & peace	CU-MARK	00693
Clemens, Olivia L.	1871.12.26	SLC	IL.Champaign	Livy Darling, it	CU-MARK	00694
Clemens, Olivia L.	1871.12.27	SLC	IL.Tuscola	I made an	CU-MARK	00695
Clemens, Olivia L.	1871.12.28	SLC	IL.Danville	Livy Darling, I am	CU-MARK	00696
Clemens, Olivia L.	1871.12.31	SLC	IL.Paris	Livy darling, I attended	CU-MARK	00700
Clemens, Olivia L.	1872.01.04	SLC	OH.Dayton	Livy, old sweetheart	CU-MARK	00704 Jan 4 to Barton enc
Clemens, Olivia L.	1872.01.07	SLC	OH.Wooster	Livy darling, did these	CU-MARK	00708
Clemens, Olivia L.	1872.01.08	SLC	OH.Salem	Livy darling, I got	CU-MARK	00711
Clemens, Olivia L.	1872.01.09	SLC	OH.Steubenville	Livy Darling, I am	CU-MARK	00712
Clemens, Olivia L.	1872.01.10 to 1872.01.11	SLC	WV.Wheeling & PA.Pittsburgh	Livy darling, it was	CU-MARK	00714
Clemens, Olivia L.	1872.01.12	SLC	PA.Kittanning	Livy darling, this is	CU-MARK	00715
Clemens, Olivia L.	1872.01.13	SLC	PA.Pittsburgh	Livy darling, just been	CU-MARK	00716
Clemens, Olivia L.	1872.01.16	SLC	PA.Pittsburgh	Livy darling, in the	CU-MARK	00718
Clemens, Olivia L.	1872.01.20	SLC	PA.Harrisburg	Livy darling, I am	CU-MARK	00720
Clemens, Olivia L.	1872.08.18	SLC	NY.New York	Livy darling, when	NN-B	00795
Clemens, Olivia L.	1872.08.20	SLC	NY.New York	Livy darling, my	Mo4	00796
Clemens, Olivia L.	1872.08.29	SLC	SH.Scotia	Livy darling, I have	CU-MARK	00800

ADDRESSEE	DATE	WRITER	PLACE	CUE	SOURCE	NUMBER/NOTES
Clemens, Olivia L.	1872.09.01	SLC	EN.Liverpool	Livy darling, I wonder	CU-MARK	00803
Clemens, Olivia L.	1872.09.11	SLC	EN.London	Livy darling, I was	CU-MARK	00805
Clemens, Olivia L.	1872.09.15	SLC	EN.London	Livy, darling, everybody	Mo4	00807
Clemens, Olivia L.	1872.09.15 or 1872.09.16	SLC	EN.London	There was once	CU-MARK	00806
Clemens, Olivia L.	pm 1872.09.16	SLC	EN.London	*	ViU	10141 envelope only
Clemens, Olivia L.	1872.09.22	SLC	EN.London	Livy darling, I am	CU-MARK	00810
Clemens, Olivia L.	1872.09.25	SLC	EN.London	Livy darling, got	CU-MARK	00814
Clemens, Olivia L.	1872.09.28	SLC	EN.London	Livy darling, it has	CU-MARK	00815
Clemens, Olivia L.	1872.10.03	SLC	EN.London	Livy darling, it is	CU-MARK	00817
Clemens, Olivia L.	1872.10.12	SLC	EN.London	I have been	Mo4	00822
Clemens, Olivia L.	1872.10.25	SLC	EN.London	Livy darling, I have	CU-MARK	00823
Clemens, Olivia L.	1872.11.09	SLC	EN.London	Livy darling, it was	CU-MARK	00831
Clemens, Olivia L.	1873.02.02	SLC	NY.New York	It is a	CU-MARK	00872
Clemens, Olivia L.	1873.04.25 to 1873.04.26	SLC	CT.Hartford	Livy darling, as Warner	Mo4	00908
Clemens, Olivia L.	1873.04.26	SLC	CT.Hartford	Livy darling, I have	CU-MARK	00909
Clemens, Olivia L.	1873.05.01	SLC	CT.Hartford	Livy dear, are you	CU-MARK(tr)	00911
Clemens, Olivia L.	1873.11.10	SLC	SH.City of Ches.	Livy darling, you really	CU-MARK	00982
Clemens, Olivia L.	1873.11.14	SLC	SH.City of Ches.	Livy darling, we have	CU-MARK	00983
Clemens, Olivia L.	1873.11.20	SLC	EN.London	Livy darling, it is	CU-MARK	00984
Clemens, Olivia L.	1873.11.21	SLC	EN.London	Livy my darling, I have	CU-MARK	00985
Clemens, Olivia L.	1873.11.23	SLC	EN.London	Sweetheart, it is	CU-MARK	00987
Clemens, Olivia L.	1873.11.24	SLC	EN.London	Livy darling, Dolby	CU-MARK	00988
Clemens, Olivia L.	1873.11.26	SLC	EN.London	Livy darling, old	CU-MARK	00989
Clemens, Olivia L.	1873.12.03	SLC	EN.London	Livy darling, I am as	CU-MARK	00991
Clemens, Olivia L.	1873.12.06	SLC	EN.London	Livy darling, I shall	CU-MARK	00992
Clemens, Olivia L.	1873.12.07	SLC	EN.London	Livy darling, I love	CU-MARK	00993
Clemens, Olivia L.	1873.12.09	SLC	EN.London	Livy darling, I never	CU-MARK	00994

Clemens, Olivia L.	1873.12.11	SLC	EN.London	Livy darling, there's	CU-MARK	00999 on Smalley Dec 9
Clemens, Olivia L.	1873.12.11	SLC	EN.London	Livy my darling, I am	CU-MARK	01000
Clemens, Olivia L.	1873.12.12	SLC	EN.London	My own dear	CU-MARK	01001
Clemens, Olivia L.	1873.12.13	SLC	EN.London	Livy darling, I am	CU-MARK	01004
Clemens, Olivia L.	1873.12.14	SLC	EN.London	My own little	CU-MARK	01005
Clemens, Olivia L.	1873.12.16	SLC	EN.London	Livy my darling, we did	CU-MARK	01007
Clemens, Olivia L.	1873.12.20	SLC	EN.London	Livy darling, I am about	CU-MARK	01010
Clemens, Olivia L.	1873.12.21	SLC	EN.London	Livy darling, I dined	CU-MARK	01011
Clemens, Olivia L.	1873.12.22	SLC	EN.London	Livy my darling, this is	CU-MARK	01014
Clemens, Olivia L.	1873.12.23	SLC	EN.London	Livy darling, Finlay	CU-MARK	01015
Clemens, Olivia L.	1873.12.25	SLC	EN.Salisbury	Livy my darling, I sent	CU-MARK	01017
Clemens, Olivia L.	1873.12.29	SLC	EN.London	Livy darling, I will	CU-MARK	01018
Clemens, Olivia L.	1873.12.31	SLC	EN.London	Livy my darling, I	CU-MARK	01022
Clemens, Olivia L.	1874.01.01	SLC	EN.London	11.30 AM. Horse-guards	CU-MARK	01025
Clemens, Olivia L.	1874.01.02	SLC	EN.London	Livy my darling, I want	CU-MARK	01028
Clemens, Olivia L.	1874.01.03	SLC	EN.London	Livy darling, it is 2	CU-MARK	01029
Clemens, Olivia L.	1874.01.04	SLC	EN.London	Livy darling, Stoddard	CU-MARK	01030
Clemens, Olivia L.	1874.01.04	SLC	EN.London	One more day	CU-MARK	01031
Clemens, Olivia L.	1874.01.05	SLC	EN.London	Got a letter	CU-MARK	01033
Clemens, Olivia L.	1874.07.03	SLC	CT.Hartford	Livy darling, I told	Mo4	01105
Clemens, Olivia L.	1874.11.12	SLC	CT.Ashford	Livy darling, this hotel	CU-MARK	01149
Clemens, Olivia L.	1874.11.12	SLC	CT.Vernon	Livy darling, we started	CU-MARK	01148
Clemens, Olivia L.	1874.11.13	SLC	CT.New Boston	Livy darling, it is	CU-MARK	01150
Clemens, Olivia L.	1874.11.14	SLC	MA.Boston	Livy darling, we had a	CU-MARK	01152
Clemens, Olivia L.	1874.12.**	SLC	Unknown	For Livy Clemens	NvU	09710 inscription
Clemens, Olivia L.	1875.04.18	SLC	MA.Cambridge	We are having	CU-MARK	01220
Clemens, Olivia L.	1875.11.27	SLC	CT.Hartford	Livy darling, six	CU-MARK	01285

ADDRESSEE	DATE	WRITER	PLACE	CUE	SOURCE	NUMBER/NOTES
Clemens, Olivia L.	1876.**.**	SLC	CT.Hartford	To Livy L.	CCamarSJ	10648 inscription
Clemens, Olivia L.	1876.12.03	SLC	NY.New York	Livy darling, I love	CU-MARK	01391
Clemens, Olivia L.	1877.03.11	SLC	MA.Boston	Livy darling we	CU-MARK(tr)	02863 date uncertain
Clemens, Olivia L.	1877.04.23	SLC	NY.New York	Livy, darling, I am	CU-MARK	01414
Clemens, Olivia L.	1877.04.26	SLC	MD.Baltimore	I have just	CU-MARK	01416
Clemens, Olivia L.	1877.04.27	SLC	MD.Baltimore	Livy, My Darling, I had	CU-MARK	01418
Clemens, Olivia L.	1877.05.17	SLC	NY.New York	Livy darling, it is	CU-MARK	01433
Clemens, Olivia L.	1877.07.15	SLC	NY.New York	Livy darling, I took	CU-MARK	01450
Clemens, Olivia L.	1877.07.17	SLC	CT.Hartford	Half any hour	CU-MARK	01453
Clemens, Olivia L.	1877.07.17	SLC	CT.Hartford	If you don't	CU-MARK	01452
Clemens, Olivia L.	1877.07.17	SLC	CT.Hartford	Livy darling, I believed	CU-MARK	05443
Clemens, Olivia L.	1877.07.27	SLC	NY.New York	Now, my darling	CU-MARK	01456
Clemens, Olivia L.	1877.07.30	SLC	NY.New York	Livy, my darling, I	CU-MARK	01459
Clemens, Olivia L.	1878.08.05	SLC	GE.Allerheiligen	Livy darling, we had	Mo4	01583 date uncertain
Clemens, Olivia L.	1878.08.23	SLC	SW.Kandersteg	Livy darling, we had	114:334	01588
Clemens, Olivia L.	1878.08.24	SLC	SW.Leukerbad	Livy darling, Joe	114:334	01589
Clemens, Olivia L.	1878.08.26	SLC	SW.St. Niklaus	Livy darling, we came	114:335	01590
Clemens, Olivia L.	1879.11.11	SLC	IL.Chicago	Livy darling, George	Mo4	01712
Clemens, Olivia L.	1879.11.11	SLC	IL.Chicago	Livy darling, I am	Mo4	01713
Clemens, Olivia L.	1879.11.12	SLC	IL.Chicago	Livy darling, it was a	CU-MARK	01714
Clemens, Olivia L.	1879.11.14	SLC	IL.Chicago	I've just come	CU-MARK	01715
Clemens, Olivia L.	1879.11.27	SLC	CT.Hartford	Livy darling, time	Mo4	02877
Clemens, Olivia L.	1880.10.12	SLC	CT.Hartford	I've been here	Mo4	01839
Clemens, Olivia L.	1881.08.25	SLC	MA.Boston	Livy darling, I will	CCamarSJ	02015
Clemens, Olivia L.	1881.11.27	SLC	CN.Montreal	Livy dear, a mouse	114:409f	02101 rebus letter
Clemens, Olivia L.	1881.11.28	SLC	CN.Montreal	Livy darling, you P.S. On the	Mo4 CU-MARK	02103
Clemens, Olivia L.	1881.11.29	SLC	CN.Montreal	Well, sweetheart, I	CU-MARK	02105

Clemens, Olivia L.	1881.12.01	SLC	CN.Montreal	Livy darling, I was	CU-MARK	02107
Clemens, Olivia L.	1881.12.02	SLC	CN.Quebec	Livy darling, I suppose	CU-MARK	02108
Clemens, Olivia L.	1881.12.04	SLC	CN.Quebec	Livy darling, I received	114:409	02109
Clemens, Olivia L.	1881.12.06	SLC	CN.Montreal	Livy darling, I am	Mo4	02110
Clemens, Olivia L.	1881.12.07	SLC	CN.Montreal	Livy darling, I have	Mo4	02111
Clemens, Olivia L.	1882.04.19	SLC	IN.Indianapolis	Well, Livy darling	CU-MARK	02202
Clemens, Olivia L.	1882.04.21	SLC	SH.Gold Dust	Livy darling, I am	CU-MARK	02203
Clemens, Olivia L.	1882.04.22	SLC	SH.Gold Dust	Livy darling, the	CU-MARK	02204
Clemens, Olivia L.	1882.04.25	SLC	SH.Gold Dust	Well, Livy darling	CU-MARK	02205
Clemens, Olivia L.	1882.04.29	SLC	LA.New Orleans	Livy darling, we are	CU-MARK	02208
Clemens, Olivia L.	1882.05.02	SLC	LA.New Orleans	Livy darling, we are	CU-MARK	02184
Clemens, Olivia L.	1882.05.04	SLC	LA.New Orleans	Well, Livy Darling	CU-MARK	02186
Clemens, Olivia L.	1882.05.06	SLC	LA.New Orleans	Livy darling, it is 7	CU-MARK	02188
Clemens, Olivia L.	1882.05.08	SLC	SH.Baton Rouge	We are moving	CU-MARK	02189
Clemens, Olivia L.	1882.05.17	SLC	IL.Quincy	Livy darling, I am	CU-MARK	02190
Clemens, Olivia L.	1882.05.20	SLC	SH.Baton Rouge	We are in	CU-MARK	02191
Clemens, Olivia L.	1883.**.**	SLC	CT.Hartford	from SLC	ViU	10852 inscription
Clemens, Olivia L.	1883.03.02	SLC	NY.New York	Livy darling, I haven't	CU-MARK	02353
Clemens, Olivia L.	1883.05.08	SLC	MA.Boston	Livy darling, I grew	CU-MARK	02385
Clemens, Olivia L.	1883.05.22	SLC	CN.Montreal	Livy darling, I reached	CU-MARK	02392
Clemens, Olivia L.	1883.05.23	SLC	CN.Ottawa	Livy my dear	CU-MARK	02393
Clemens, Olivia L.	1883.05.24	SLC	CN.Ottawa	Livy darling, I must not	CU-MARK	02394
Clemens, Olivia L.	1883.05.28	SLC	CN.Ottawa	Livy darling, I will	CU-MARK	02397
Clemens, Olivia L.	1883.05.28	SLC	CN.Ottawa	Well, sweetheart, of	CU-MARK	02396
Clemens, Olivia L.	1884.**.**	SLC	Unknown	from S.L. Clemens	260:1963.11	09329 inscription
Clemens, Olivia L. & Clemens, Samuel L.	1884.04.17	CC	CT.Hartford	It does not	MH-H	02958
Clemens, Olivia L. & Clemens, Samuel L.	1884.04.17	SC	CT.Hartford	Jean seems bright	MH-H	02957

ADDRESSEE	DATE	WRITER	PLACE	CUE	SOURCE	NUMBER/NOTES
Clemens, Olivia L.	1884.04.18	CC	CT.Hartford	I have nothing	MH-H	02959
Clemens, Olivia L.	1884.11.12	SLC	MA.Lowell	Livy darling, only	CU-MARK	03024
Clemens, Olivia L.	1884.11.21	SLC	PA.Philadelphia	Livy darling, a most	CU-MARK	03030
Clemens, Olivia L.	1884.11.23	SLC	NY.New York	Livy dear, only	CU-MARK	03032
Clemens, Olivia L.	1884.11.24	SLC	DC.Washington	Splendid times, Livy	CU-MARK	03037
Clemens, Olivia L.	1884.11.28	SLC	DC.Washington	We dined &	CU-MARK	03040
Clemens, Olivia L.	1884.11.29	SLC	MD.Baltimore	Livy darling, Judge	CU-MARK	03041
Clemens, Olivia L.	1884.12.01	SLC	MA.Adams	Livy darling, it is 6.30	CU-MARK	03043
Clemens, Olivia L.	1884.12.03	SLC	NY.Albany	We arrived at	CU-MARK	03044
Clemens, Olivia L.	1884.12.06	SLC	NY.Rochester	Just arrived, Livy	CU-MARK	03049
Clemens, Olivia L.	1884.12.06	SLC	NY.Rochester	Poor Mrs. Sage	CU-MARK	03050
Clemens, Olivia L.	1884.12.07	SLC	NY.Rochester	Livy darling, I got	CU-MARK	03051
Clemens, Olivia L.	1884.12.07	SLC	NY.Rochester	P.S. I have	CU-MARK	08634
Clemens, Olivia L.	1884.12.08	SLC	CN.Toronto	I ate a	CU-MARK	03052
Clemens, Olivia L.	1884.12.09	SLC	CN.Toronto	Livy darling, guess	CU-MARK	03053
Clemens, Olivia L.	1884.12.12	SLC	MI.Ann Arbor	Livy darling, I rushed	CU-MARK	03055
Clemens, Olivia L.	1884.12.13	SLC	MI.Grand Rapids	Only one word	CU-MARK	03056
Clemens, Olivia L.	1884.12.14	SLC	MI.Grand Rapids	Livy dear, I have	CU-MARK	03057
Clemens, Olivia L.	1884.12.15	SLC	OH.Toledo	Livy darling, I arrived	CU-MARK	03061
Clemens, Olivia L.	1884.12.15	SLC	OH.Toledo	P.S. While I	CU-MARK	03062
Clemens, Olivia L.	1884.12.25	SLC	Unknown	with the matured	CCamarSJ	09332 inscription
Clemens, Olivia L.	1884.12.27	SLC	NY.New York	Livy darling, I hope	CU-MARK	03072
Clemens, Olivia L.	1884.12.28	SLC	PA.Pittsburgh	Well, sweetheart, I	CU-MARK	03076
Clemens, Olivia L.	1884.12.29	SLC	PA.Pittsburgh	Well, mamma, dear	CU-MARK	03077
Clemens, Olivia L.	1884.12.30	SLC	OH.Dayton	Livy darling, we got	CU-MARK	03078
Clemens, Olivia L.	1885.01.01	SLC	KY.Paris	Livy darling, we have	CU-MARK	03097
Clemens, Olivia L.	1885.01.02	SLC	KY.Paris	Livy darling, I am just	CU-MARK	03098
Clemens, Olivia L.	1885.01.03	SLC	OH.Cincinnati	Livy darling, we	CU-MARK	03099
Clemens, Olivia L.	1885.01.04	SLC	OH.Cincinnati	Livy darling, it is a	CU-MARK	03101

Clemens, Olivia L.	1885.01.07	SLC	IN.Indianapolis	P.S. (On cars	CU-MARK	03104
Clemens, Olivia L.	1885.01.08	SLC	IN.Indianapolis	We were up	CU-MARK	03107
Clemens, Olivia L.	1885.01.11	SLC	MO.St. Louis	How measureless &	CU-MARK	03111
Clemens, Olivia L.	1885.01.11	SLC	MO.St. Louis	Livy darling, it is a	CU-MARK	03110 misdated Jan 10
Clemens, Olivia L.	1885.01.14	SLC	IA.Keokuk	Livy darling, I'm clear	CU-MARK	03116
Clemens, Olivia L.	1885.01.17 & 1885.01.18	SLC	IL.Chicago	Livy darling, Mr. Wilson	CU-MARK	03120
Clemens, Olivia L.	1885.01.17	SLC	IL.Chicago	Livy darling, Clara	CU-MARK	03119
Clemens, Olivia L.	1885.01.19	SLC	IL.Chicago	Back from Evanston	CU-MARK	03121
Clemens, Olivia L.	1885.01.21	SLC	WI.Madison	Yes, my darling	CU-MARK	03125
Clemens, Olivia L.	1885.01.23	SLC	MN.St. Paul	No, Livy dear	CU-MARK	03131
Clemens, Olivia L.	1885.01.31	SLC	IA.Davenport	More relatives, mama	CU-MARK	03141
Clemens, Olivia L.	1885.02.01	SLC	IL.Chicago	Livy darling, don't	CU-MARK	03148
Clemens, Olivia L.	1885.02.02	SLC	IL.Chicago	This is the	CU-MARK	03149
Clemens, Olivia L.	1885.02.03	SLC	IL.Chicago	Well, Livy darling	CU-MARK	03150
Clemens, Olivia L.	1885.02.04	SLC	IL.Chicago	Livy dear, we hit	CU-MARK	03153
Clemens, Olivia L.	1885.02.05	SLC	IN.South Bend	Livy dear, we are	CU-MARK	03154
Clemens, Olivia L.	1885.02.06	SLC	IN.Lafayette	Livy darling, we are	CU-MARK	03155
Clemens, Olivia L.	1885.02.07	SLC	Unknown	Although I slept	CU-MARK	03156
Clemens, Olivia L.	1885.02.08	SLC	IN.Indianapolis	No, Livy darling	CU-MARK	03158
Clemens, Olivia L.	1885.02.09	SLC	OH.Columbus	Livy dear, you cannot	CU-MARK	03160
Clemens, Olivia L.	1885.02.10	SLC	OH.Columbus	Livy darling, rode	CU-MARK	03161
Clemens, Olivia L.	1885.02.13	SLC	MI.Detroit	Livy darling, if they	CU-MARK	03165
Clemens, Olivia L.	1885.02.15	SLC	CN.Toronto	Livy darling, I did not	CU-MARK	03166
Clemens, Olivia L.	1885.02.17	SLC	Unknown	Yesterday I was	CU-MARK	03171
Clemens, Olivia L.	1885.02.18	SLC	Unknown	This is a	CU-MARK	03173
Clemens, Olivia L.	1885.02.19	SLC	CN.Montreal	Livy darling, do you	CU-MARK	03174
Clemens, Olivia L.	1885.02.20	SLC	Unknown	Ah, my darling	CU-MARK	03176

ADDRESSEE	DATE	WRITER	PLACE	CUE	SOURCE	NUMBER/NOTES
Clemens, Olivia L.	1885.03.02	SLC	DC.Washington	Die Aehnblichkeit	CU-MARK	03180
Clemens, Olivia L.	1885.03.04	SLC	Unknown	We were at	CU-MARK	03183 telegram
Clemens, Olivia L.	1885.03.21	SLC	NY.New York	Gerhardt worked three	CU-MARK	03193 telegram
Clemens, Olivia L.	1885.04.08	SLC	NY.New York	Livy darling, this	CU-MARK	03208
Clemens, Olivia L.	1885.04.09	SLC	PA.Philadelphia	Livy darling, it was	CU-MARK	03210
Clemens, Olivia L.	1885.06.30	SLC	NY.Mt. McGregor	Livy darling, what a	CU-MARK	03248
Clemens, Olivia L.	1885.07.01	SLC	NY.Mt. McGregor	Livy darling, I shall	CU-MARK	03249
Clemens, Olivia L.	1885.07.24	SLC	NY.New York	Livy darling, I reached	CU-MARK	03266
Clemens, Olivia L.	1885.08.04	SLC	NY.New York	Livy darling, New	CU-MARK	03274
Clemens, Olivia L.	1885.08.06	SLC	NY.New York	Livy darling, I have	CU-MARK	03275
Clemens, Olivia L.	1885.08.06	SLC	NY.New York	Livy darling, I have	CU-MARK	03277
Clemens, Olivia L.	1885.11.17	SLC	NY.New York	Livy darling, another	CU-MARK	03309
Clemens, Olivia L.	1885.11.18	SLC	NY.New York	Livy dear, I suppose	CU-MARK	03310
Clemens, Olivia L.	1885.11.21	SLC	NY.New York	Livy darling, I told	CU-MARK	03312
Clemens, Olivia L.	1885.11.25	SLC	NY.New York	Livy darling, I was	CU-MARK	03314
Clemens, Olivia L.	1885.11.27	SLC	CT.Hartford	We have reached	CU-MARK	03315
Clemens, Olivia L.	1885.12.**	SLC	CT.Hartford	from S.L.C.	CCamarSJ	10650 inscription
Clemens, Olivia L.	1885.12.03	SLC	NY.New York	Livy darling, I got	CU-MARK	03323
Clemens, Olivia L.	1886.01.26	SLC	NY.New York	Livy dear, the contracts	CU-MARK	03360
Clemens, Olivia L.	1886.01.28	SLC	DC.Washington	Livy darling, it was	CU-MARK	03361
Clemens, Olivia L.	1886.05.05	SLC	Unknown	It was good	CU-MARK	03389
Clemens, Olivia L.	1886.05.06	SLC	NY.West Point	Livy darling, it is 8.30	CU-MARK	03390
Clemens, Olivia L.	1886.05.10	SLC	MA.Boston	Livy darling, I came	CU-MARK	03393
Clemens, Olivia L.	1886.07.30	SLC	NY.New York	Livy darling, I have	CU-MARK	03430
Clemens, Olivia L.	1886.08.01	SLC	NY.New York	Livy darling, I am	CU-MARK	03431
Clemens, Olivia L.	1886.08.02	SLC	NY.New York	Livy darling, I have 8	CU-MARK	03433
Clemens, Olivia L.	1886.10.26	SLC	NY.New York	Livy dear, only	CU-MARK	03475
Clemens, Olivia L.	1887.02.10	SLC	NY.New York	Livy darling, I finished	CU-MARK	03525

Clemens, Olivia L.		1887.07.26	SLC	NY.New York	Livy darling, I have	CU-MARK	03615
Clemens, Olivia L.		1887.10.04	SLC	NY.New York	Livy darling, the last	CU-MARK	03657
Clemens, Olivia L.		1888.03.16	SLC	NY.New York	I have only	CU-MARK	03709
Clemens, Olivia L.		1888.06.06	SLC	NY.New York	When you see	MoHM	03722 telegram
Clemens, Olivia L.		1888.11.27	SLC	CT.Hartford	Livy darling, I am	CtHMTH	03837
Clemens, Olivia L.		1888.12.31	SLC	CT.Hartford	Happy New Year	CU-MARK(tr)	03815 SLC tr
Clemens, Olivia L.		1889.07.12	SLC	CT.Hartford	It is lovely	CU-MARK	03909
Clemens, Olivia L.		1889.07.17	SLC	CT.Hartford	Livy darling, that	CU-MARK	03915
Clemens, Olivia L.		1889.07.17	SLC	CT.Hartford	Livy darling, this that	CU-MARK	03914
Clemens, Olivia L.		1889.12.06	SLC	CT.Hartford	George put this	CU-MARK	03983 Warner Dec 3 enc
Clemens, Olivia L.		1890.05.21	SLC	NY.New York	Livy darling, I have	CU-MARK	04050
Clemens, Olivia L.		1890.06.14	SLC	DC.Washington	Livy darling, I got your	CU-MARK	04051
Clemens, Olivia L. & Clemens, Clara L.	pm	1890.07.21	SLC	CT.Hartford	he is on	CU-MARK	04066 fragment
Clemens, Olivia L.		1890.08.28	SLC	DC.Washington	Livy darling, I am	CU-MARK	04088
Clemens, Olivia L.		1890.10.24	SLC	PA.Bryn Mawr	Livy darling, it is 20	CU-MARK	04106
Clemens, Olivia L.		1890.11.25	SLC	PA.Bryn Mawr	Just one word	Mo4	08631
Clemens, Olivia L.	&	1890.11.26 1890.11.27	SLC	CT.Hartford	Livy Darling, in two	Mo4	08633
Clemens, Olivia L.		1890.11.29	SLC	CT.Hartford	Mrs. Taft has	CU-MARK	04116
Clemens, Olivia L.		1891.01.13	SLC	DC.Washington	Livy darling, I went	CU-MARK	04157
Clemens, Olivia L.		1891.01.14	SLC	DC.Washington	Well, sweetheart, I	CU-MARK	04158
Clemens, Olivia L.		1891.02.07	SLC	CT.Hartford	Am I to	Mo4	04167
Clemens, Olivia L.		1891.04.18	SLC	CT.Hartford	Livy darling, your	CU-MARK	04191
Clemens, Olivia L.		1891.04.19	SLC	CT.Hartford	Well, sweetheart, I	CU-MARK	04192
Clemens, Olivia L.		1891.04.21	SLC	CT.Hartford	Good! Aunt Sue	CU-MARK	04193
Clemens, Olivia L.		1891.09.20	SLC	SW.Rhone River	On the lake 3.15 p.m., Sunday	114:549 CU-MARK	04227

ADDRESSEE	DATE	WRITER	PLACE	CUE	SOURCE	NUMBER/NOTES
Clemens, Olivia L.	1891.09.21	SLC	SW.Port-de-Gros.	Name of the	CU-MARK	04229
Clemens, Olivia L.	1891.09.22	SLC	SW.Rhone River	Good morning, sweetheart	CU-MARK	04230
Clemens, Olivia L.	1891.09.24 & 1891.09.25	SLC	SW.Rhone River	I salute you	CU-MARK	04233
Clemens, Olivia L.	1891.09.25	SLC	SW.Rhone River	Livy darling, we sailed	CU-MARK	04234
Clemens, Olivia L.	1891.09.26	SLC	FR.La Voulte	Land, Livy darling	CU-MARK	04235
Clemens, Olivia L.	1891.09.28	SLC	SW.Rhone River	Livy darling, I didn't	CU-MARK	04236
Clemens, Olivia L.	1891.09.30	SLC	FR.Arles	Livy darling, I haint	CU-MARK	04238
Clemens, Olivia L.	1891.10.01	SLC	FR.Nimes	Good morning, dear	CU-MARK	04240
Clemens, Olivia L.	1892.11.27	SLC	IT.Florence	If that rich	ViU	09463 inscription
Clemens, Olivia L.	1893.04.04	SLC	NY.New York	Livy darling, Howells	CU-MARK	04362
Clemens, Olivia L.	1893.04.07	SLC	NY.New York	There is a	293:104	04367
Clemens, Olivia L.	1893.04.18	SLC	IL.Chicago	Dear old Sweetheart	CU-MARK	04377
Clemens, Olivia L.	1893.05.06	SLC	NY.Elmira	Livy darling, it's	CU-MARK	04396
Clemens, Olivia L.	1893.05.08	SLC	NY.Elmira	Livy darling, it broke	CU-MARK	04400
Clemens, Olivia L.	1893.08.28	SLC	GE.Leipzig	Livy darling, it has	CU-MARK	04440
Clemens, Olivia L.	1893.09.07	SLC	NY.New York	My darling, your	CU-MARK	04441
Clemens, Olivia L.	1893.09.13	SLC	NY.New York	Livy darling, I was	CU-MARK	04447
Clemens, Olivia L.	1893.09.13	SLC	NY.New York	Livy darling it is	CU-MARK	04444
Clemens, Olivia L.	1893.09.17	SLC	NJ.Madison	The billows of	CU-MARK	04453
Clemens, Olivia L.	1893.09.19	SLC	NY.New York	Mrs Hannahs tells	CU-MARK	04454
Clemens, Olivia L.	1893.09.21	SLC	NY.New York	My darling, I've been	CU-MARK	04456
Clemens, Olivia L.	1893.09.21	SLC	NY.New York	Sweetheart, I am	CU-MARK	04455
Clemens, Olivia L.	1893.09.26	SLC	NY.New York	Livy darling, you easily	Mo4	04461
Clemens, Olivia L.	1893.09.28 & 1893.09.30	SLC	NY.New York	Livy darling, only	CU-MARK	04463
Clemens, Olivia L.	1893.09.28	SLC	NY.New York	My darling, I wonder	CU-MARK	04462
Clemens, Olivia L.	1893.10.03	SLC	NY.New York	Livy darling, this is	CU-MARK	04466
Clemens, Olivia L.	1893.10.05	SLC	NY.New York	Livy darling, if	Mo4	04468

Clemens, Olivia L.	to	1893.10.17 1893.12.17	SLC	NY.New York	Tale of the	CU-MARK	04475
Clemens, Olivia L. or Clemens, Clara L.	ca	1893.10.17	SLC	NY.New York	I have been	293:86	06177
Clemens, Olivia L.		1893.10.18	SLC	NY.New York	I don't seem	Mo4	04476
Clemens, Olivia L.		1893.11.08	SLC	NY.New York	Dear old Sweetheart	CU-MARK	04494
Clemens, Olivia L.		1893.11.10	SLC	NY.New York	Dear Sweetheart, it is	CU-MARK	04495
Clemens, Olivia L.		1893.11.14	SLC	NY.New York	Livy darling, Clara had	CU-MARK	04501
Clemens, Olivia L.		1893.11.18	SLC	NY.New York	I accepted this	CU-MARK	04505 on Irving Nov 17
Clemens, Olivia L.		1893.11.28	SLC	NY.New York	I wonder if	CU-MARK	04511
Clemens, Olivia L.	pm	1893.11.28	SLC	NY.New York	his army of	CU-MARK	04510 fragment
Clemens, Olivia L.		1893.12.02	SLC	NY.New York	Livy darling, I shall	CU-MARK	04516 on Howells Dec 1
Clemens, Olivia L.		1893.12.04	SLC	NY.New York	Livy darling, we had	CU-MARK	04518
Clemens, Olivia L.		1893.12.04	SLC	NY.New York	No, dear old	CU-MARK	04517
Clemens, Olivia L.		1893.12.08	SLC	NY.New York	Livy darling, yesterday	CU-MARK	04522
Clemens, Olivia L.		1893.12.09	SLC	NY.New York	Well, Livy darling	CU-MARK	04523
Clemens, Olivia L.		1893.12.15	SLC	NY.New York	P.S. Dear heart	CU-MARK	04530
Clemens, Olivia L.		1893.12.15	SLC	NY.New York	Oh, dearheart, for	Mo4	04529
Clemens, Olivia L.		1893.12.19	SLC	NY.New York	Livy darling, I went	CU-MARK	04532
Clemens, Olivia L.	&	1893.12.20 1893.12.21	SLC	NY.New York	That is the	CU-MARK	04533 on dr of speech
Clemens, Olivia L.		1893.12.25	SLC	NY.New York	I arrived from	Mo4	04536
Clemens, Olivia L.	&	1893.12.28 1893.12.29	SLC	NY.New York	I hain't got	CU-MARK	04542 on Rogers Dec 28
Clemens, Olivia L.		1893.12.29	SLC	NY.New York	Dear old sweetheart	CU-MARK	04543
Clemens, Olivia L.		1893.12.30	SLC	NY.New York	My best darling	CU-MARK	04545
Clemens, Olivia L.		1894.01.04	SLC	NY.New York	No, dear sweetheart	CU-MARK	04668

ADDRESSEE	DATE	WRITER	PLACE	CUE	SOURCE	NUMBER/NOTES
Clemens, Olivia L.	1894.01.11	SLC	CT.Hartford	Livy darling, I saw	CU-MARK	04669
Clemens, Olivia L.	1894.01.12	SLC	NY.New York	Livy darling, I came	CU-MARK NN5	04671 CU-MARK envelope
Clemens, Olivia L.	1894.01.12	SLC	NY.New York	Waiting here for	CU-MARK	04670
Clemens, Olivia L.	1894.01.13	SLC	NY.New York	Well, Livy darling	CU-MARK	04673
Clemens, Olivia L.	1894.01.15	SLC	NY.New York	Livy darling it now	CU-MARK	04675
Clemens, Olivia L.	1894.01.15	SLC	NY.New York	Livy darling, when	CU-MARK	04674
Clemens, Olivia L.	1894.01.25	SLC	MA.Boston	Livy darling, I am	CU-MARK	04677
Clemens, Olivia L.	1894.01.27 & 1894.01.30	SLC	NY.New York	Oh, Livy darling	CU-MARK	04679
Clemens, Olivia L.	1894.02.02	SLC	NY.New York	Wedding-news: Our	CU-MARK(tr)	04685 telegram; SLC tr
Clemens, Olivia L.	1894.02.07	SLC	NY.New York	Sweetheart, to-morrow is	CU-MARK	04689
Clemens, Olivia L.	1894.02.08 or 1894.02.09	SLC	NY.New York	Ah, Sweetheart confound	CU-MARK	04690
Clemens, Olivia L.	1894.02.11 to 1894.02.13	SLC	NY.New York	So you've gone	CU-MARK	04692
Clemens, Olivia L.	1894.02.15	SLC	NY.New York	Livy darling, we have	CU-MARK	04693
Clemens, Olivia L.	1894.02.20	SLC	NY.New York	New York, &	CU-MARK	04695 fragment
Clemens, Olivia L.	1894.02.23	SLC	MA.Fairhaven	Dear Sweetheart, Mr.	CU-MARK	04697
Clemens, Olivia L.	1894.02.25 to 1894.02.27	SLC	NY.New York	Why no, dearheart	CU-MARK	04699
Clemens, Olivia L.	1894.03.01	SLC	NY.New York	A man said	CU-MARK	04700
Clemens, Olivia L.	1894.03.02	SLC	NY.New York	Dear Sweetheart, I was	CU-MARK	04702
Clemens, Olivia L.	1894.03.02	SLC	NY.New York	Livy darling, this is my	CU-MARK	04701
Clemens, Olivia L.	1894.04.14	SLC	NY.New York	Livy dear, we touched	CU-MARK	04718
Clemens, Olivia L.	1894.04.15	SLC	NY.New York	Ich liebe Dich	CU-MARK	04719
Clemens, Olivia L.	1894.04.16	SLC	NY.New York	Well, dearheart, Mr.	CU-MARK	04720
Clemens, Olivia L.	1894.04.19	SLC	NY.New York	Dear old sweetheart	CU-MARK	04721
Clemens, Olivia L.	1894.04.20	SLC	NY.New York	Well, dearheart, I	CU-MARK	04723
Clemens, Olivia L.	1894.04.22	SLC	NY.New York	Dear old darling	CU-MARK	04724

Clemens, Olivia L.		1894.05.04	SLC	NY.New York	Well, dearheart, I've	CU-MARK	04728
Clemens, Olivia L.		1894.05.16	SLC	EN.London	I shall reach	Mo4	10490
Clemens, Olivia L.		1894.07.06	SLC	FR.Paris	Well, I've been	CU-MARK	04753
Clemens, Olivia L.		1894.07.13	SLC	SH.Paris	Livy darling, we shall	CU-MARK	04754
Clemens, Olivia L.		1894.07.17	SLC	NY.New York	Livy dear, I deposited	CU-MARK	04756
Clemens, Olivia L.		1894.07.20	SLC	NY.New York	Livy darling, Mr. Rogers	CU-MARK	04758
Clemens, Olivia L.		1894.07.23	SLC	NY.Brooklyn	However, it should	CU-MARK	04759 misdated July 22
Clemens, Olivia L.		1894.07.23	SLC	NY.New York	My darling, I note	CU-MARK	04760
Clemens, Olivia L.		1894.07.25	SLC	NY.New York	Dear sweetheart	CU-MARK	04761
Clemens, Olivia L.		1894.07.26	SLC	NY.New York	Good morning &	CU-MARK	04764
Clemens, Olivia L.		1894.07.26	SLC	NY.New York	Livy darling, I could	CU-MARK	04763
Clemens, Olivia L.		1894.07.29	SLC	NY.New York	Bless your dear	CU-MARK	04766
Clemens, Olivia L.		1894.07.31	SLC	NY.New York	Livy dear, I am going	CU-MARK	04767
Clemens, Olivia L.		1894.08.03	SLC	NY.New York	But do not	CU-MARK	04769
Clemens, Olivia L.		1894.08.05	SLC	NY.New York	Livy darling, I went	CU-MARK	04772
Clemens, Olivia L.		1894.08.09	SLC	NY.New York	Livy my darling	CU-MARK	04778
Clemens, Olivia L.	pm	1895.03.11	SLC	NY.New York	Livy darling, I have	CU-MARK	04850
Clemens, Olivia L.	to	1895.03.20 1895.03.21	SLC	CT.Hartford	Livy darling, when I	CU-MARK	04851
Clemens, Olivia L.		1895.03.21	SLC	CT.Hartford	P.S. Hartford is	CU-MARK	04852
Clemens, Olivia L.		1895.06.03	SLC	AF.Bloemfontein	Well, sweetheart, I	CU-MARK	10326 misdated, see 1896
Clemens, Olivia L.		1896.05.15	SLC	AF.Pietermaritz.	Livy darling, we had a	CU-MARK	05044
Clemens, Olivia L.		1896.05.16	SLC	AF.Pietermaritz.	I have just	CU-MARK	05045
Clemens, Olivia L.		1896.05.19	SLC	AF.Johannesburg	Livy dear, I have just	CU-MARK	05047
Clemens, Olivia L.		1896.05.19	SLC	AF.Johannesburg	Livy dear, I've only	CU-MARK	05046
Clemens, Olivia L.	&	1896.05.20 1896.05.21	SLC	AF.Johannesburg	Livy darling I love	CU-MARK	05050

ADDRESSEE	DATE	WRITER	PLACE	CUE	SOURCE	NUMBER/NOTES
Clemens, Olivia L.	1896.05.23 to 1896.05.24	SLC	AF.Pretoria	Livy darling, I had	CU-MARK	08652
Clemens, Olivia L.	1896.05.25	SLC	AF.Pretoria	Livy darling, I am	CU-MARK	05055
Clemens, Olivia L.	1896.05.27	SLC	AF.Pretoria	Livy darling, we are	CU-MARK	05057
Clemens, Olivia L.	1896.05.29	SLC	AF.Johannesburg	Dear, dear, Livy	CU-MARK	05059
Clemens, Olivia L.	1896.06.01	SLC	AF.Bloemfontein	Dear Sweetheart I	CU-MARK	05062
Clemens, Olivia L.	1896.06.03	SLC	AF.Bloemfontein	Well Sweetheart, I	CU-MARK	05064 misdated 1895
Clemens, Olivia L.	1896.06.04	SLC	AF.Queenstown	Well, sweetheart, I	CU-MARK	05065
Clemens, Olivia L.	1896.06.07	SLC	AF.Kingwilliams.	Livy darling it is 5	CU-MARK	05067
Clemens, Olivia L.	1896.06.08	SLC	AF.Kingwilliams.	Livy darling, how would	CU-MARK	05069
Clemens, Olivia L.	1896.06.10	SLC	AF.Kingwilliams.	It is no	CU-MARK	05071
Clemens, Olivia L.	1896.06.12	SLC	AF.East London	Livy darling I have just	CU-MARK	05073
Clemens, Olivia L.	1896.08.16 to 1896.08.17	SLC	EN.Guildford	My darling, you	CU-MARK	05095
Clemens, Olivia L.	1896.08.19	SLC	EN.Guildford	I have spent	CU-MARK	05097
Clemens, Olivia L.	1896.08.19	SLC	EN.Guildford	Oh, my heart-broken	CU-MARK	05096
Clemens, Olivia L.	1896.08.21	SLC	EN.Guildford	Oh, poor Livy	CU-MARK	05098
Clemens, Olivia L.	1896.08.25	SLC	EN.Guildford	Livy darling, your	CU-MARK	05099
Clemens, Olivia L.	1896.08.26 & 1896.08.28	SLC	EN.Guildford	I know what	CU-MARK	05100
Clemens, Olivia L.	1896.08.29 to 1896.08.30	SLC	EN.Guildford	I wonder if	CU-MARK	05102
Clemens, Olivia L.	1896.11.27	SLC	EN.London	We have lost	CU-MARK	05151
Clemens, Olivia L.	o/b 1897.05.18	SLC	EN.London	Livy dear, the book is	CU-MARK	05213
Clemens, Olivia L.	1901.08.02	SLC	NY.New York	Livy darling, please	CU-MARK(tr)	06105
Clemens, Olivia L.	1901.08.03	SLC	SH.Kanawha	Livy darling, we went	CU-MARK(tr)	06106
Clemens, Olivia L.	1901.08.04	SLC	SH.Kanawha	We sail for	CU-MARK(tr)	06107
Clemens, Olivia L.	1901.08.06	SLC	SH.Kanawha	Livy darling, it is	CU-MARK(tr)	06108
Clemens, Olivia L.	1901.08.07	SLC	SH.Kanawha	Livy dearest, the anchor	CU-MARK(tr)	06109
Clemens, Olivia L.	1901.08.09	SLC	SH.Kanawha	Livy darling, I got your	CU-MARK	06110
Clemens, Olivia L.	1901.08.11	SLC	SH.Kanawha	Livy darling, we	CU-MARK	06111

Clemens, Olivia L.	1901.08.13	SLC	SH.Kanawha	There is nothing	CU-MARK	06112
Clemens, Olivia L.	1901.08.14	SLC	SH.Kanawha	Livy darling, I am with	CU-MARK	06114
Clemens, Olivia L.	1901.08.14	SLC	SH.Kanawha	Nothing to say	CU-MARK	06113
Clemens, Olivia L.	1901.08.16	SLC	SH.Kanawha	Livy darling, only	CU-MARK	06115
Clemens, Olivia L.	1901.10.22	SLC	CT.New Haven	I didn't write	CU-MARK	06163
Clemens, Olivia L.	1901.11.27	SLC	NY.Riverdale	Upon the occasion	CCamarSJ	10647 inscription
Clemens, Olivia L.	1901.11.30	SLC	NY.Riverdale	in passing notice	CCamarSJ	10646 inscription
Clemens, Olivia L.	bet 1902.**.** & 1903.**.**	SLC	NY.Riverdale	I do love	293:247	08810
Clemens, Olivia L.	bet 1902.**.** & 1903.**.**	SLC	NY.Riverdale	Arouse! the Spring	CU-MARK	08807
Clemens, Olivia L.	bet 1902.**.** & 1903.**.**	SLC	NY.Riverdale	Dear Livy dear	CU-MARK	08797
Clemens, Olivia L.	bet 1902.**.** & 1903.**.**	SLC	NY.Riverdale	Dearest, we've had	CU-MARK	08800
Clemens, Olivia L.	bet 1902.**.** & 1903.**.**	SLC	NY.Riverdale	Dearheart, in accordance	CU-MARK	08799
Clemens, Olivia L.	bet 1902.**.** & 1903.**.**	SLC	NY.Riverdale	Dearheart, I've done	CU-MARK	08808
Clemens, Olivia L.	bet 1902.**.** & 1903.**.**	SLC	NY.Riverdale	Don't know the	CU-MARK	08794
Clemens, Olivia L.	bet 1902.**.** & 1903.**.**	SLC	NY.Riverdale	Good morning, dear	CU-MARK	08798
Clemens, Olivia L.	bet 1902.**.** & 1903.**.**	SLC	NY.Riverdale	Good-night, dear	CU-MARK	08803
Clemens, Olivia L.	bet 1902.**.** & 1903.**.**	SLC	NY.Riverdale	Honey, I's gwyne	CU-MARK	08804
Clemens, Olivia L.	bet 1902.**.** & 1903.**.**	SLC	NY.Riverdale	I am not	CU-MARK	08795
Clemens, Olivia L.	bet 1902.**.** & 1903.**.**	SLC	NY.Riverdale	Livy darling, Clara	CU-MARK	08792
Clemens, Olivia L.	bet 1902.**.** & 1903.**.**	SLC	NY.Riverdale	Livy darling, I have	CU-MARK	08796
Clemens, Olivia L.	bet 1902.**.** & 1903.**.**	SLC	NY.Riverdale	Livy darling, Mr.	CU-MARK	08793

ADDRESSEE	DATE	WRITER	PLACE	CUE	SOURCE	NUMBER/NOTES
Clemens, Olivia L.	bet 1902.**.** & 1903.**.**	SLC	NY.Riverdale	Livy dear, aren't	CU-MARK	08806
Clemens, Olivia L.	bet 1902.**.** & 1903.**.**	SLC	NY.Riverdale	Livy dear, your daughter	CU-MARK	08802
Clemens, Olivia L.	bet 1902.**.** & 1903.**.**	SLC	NY.Riverdale	Schon ist's wieder	CU-MARK	08801
Clemens, Olivia L.	bet 1902.**.** & 1903.**.**	SLC	NY.Riverdale	There, now, my	CU-MARK	08805
Clemens, Olivia L.	bet 1902.**.** & 1903.**.**	SLC	NY.Riverdale	To the blessed	NN-B	08809
Clemens, Olivia L.	1902.03.14	SLC	GA.Savannah	Livy darling, it is	CU-MARK	06300
Clemens, Olivia L.	1902.03.15	SLC	FL.St. Augustine	Dearheart, we came	CU-MARK	06301
Clemens, Olivia L.	1902.03.16	SLC	FL.Palm Beach	Livy darling, the whole	CU-MARK	06302
Clemens, Olivia L.	1902.03.17	SLC	FL.Palm Beach	Dear heart, we are	CU-MARK	06303
Clemens, Olivia L.	1902.03.19	SLC	SH.Kanawha	Livy darling, we did not	CU-MARK	06307
Clemens, Olivia L.	1902.03.21	SLC	SH.Kanawha	We were intending	CU-MARK	06308
Clemens, Olivia L.	1902.03.22	SLC	SH.Kanawha	We had the	CU-MARK	06310
Clemens, Olivia L.	1902.03.24	SLC	SH.Kanawha	Dearheart, we are	CU-MARK	06311 misdated Mar 23
Clemens, Olivia L.	1902.03.29	SLC	SH.Kanawha	Livy darling, we took	CU-MARK	06313
Clemens, Olivia L.	1902.04.01	SLC	SH.Kanawha	We are homeward	CU-MARK	06315
Clemens, Olivia L.	1902.04.02	SLC	SH.Kanawha	Livy dear, it is decided	CU-MARK	06316
Clemens, Olivia L.	1902.04.04	SLC	SH.Kanawha	We are off	CU-MARK	06317
Clemens, Olivia L.	1902.04.05	SLC	SH.Kanawha	Livy darling it is too	CU-MARK	06318
Clemens, Olivia L.	1902.05.31	SLC	MO.Hannibal	Livy darling, I slept	CU-MARK	06351
Clemens, Olivia L.	1902.11.30	SLC	NY.Elmira	Clara dear, it was	CU-MARK(tr)	06495
Clemens, Olivia L.	1902.12.08	SLC	NY.Riverdale	Livy darling, do you	CU-MARK	06506
Clemens, Olivia L.	1903.01.05	SLC	NY.Riverdale	Mr. Lucy, of	CU-MARK	06551 misdated Dec
Clemens, Olivia L.	1903.01.06	SLC	NY.Riverdale	Good-night, sweetheart	CU-MARK	08777
Clemens, Olivia L.	1903.01.14	SLC	NY.Riverdale	Livy dear, there's	CU-MARK	08778
Clemens, Olivia L.	1903.01.15	SLC	NY.Riverdale	Ship ahoy!	CU-MARK	08779

Clemens, Olivia L.		1903.01.25	SLC	NY.Riverdale	Dearest sweetheart, it	CU-MARK	08780
Clemens, Olivia L.		1903.01.25	SLC	NY.Riverdale	I will write	CU-MARK	08781
Clemens, Olivia L.		1903.01.26	SLC	NY.Riverdale	I am where	CU-MARK	08782
Clemens, Olivia L.		1903.02.02	SLC	NY.Riverdale	It's a long	CU-MARK(tr)	08783
Clemens, Olivia L.		1903.02.02	SLC	Unknown	This is Diana	CU-MARK(ph)	09711 inscription
Clemens, Olivia L.		1903.02.04	SLC	NY.Riverdale	And now the	CU-MARK	08784
Clemens, Olivia L.		1903.02.04	SLC	NY.Riverdale	Dearheart, how wonderful	CU-MARK	08785
Clemens, Olivia L.		1903.02.14	SLC	NY.Riverdale	And so this	CU-MARK	08786
Clemens, Olivia L.		1903.02.27	SLC	NY.Riverdale	The ashcats have	CU-MARK	08787
Clemens, Olivia L.		1903.03.01	SLC	NY.Riverdale	Good-night, Livy darling	CU-MARK	08788
Clemens, Olivia L.		1903.03.31	SLC	NY.Riverdale	Good-night, Livy darling	CU-MARK	08789
Clemens, Olivia L.	bet &	1903.04.** 1903.05.**	SLC	NY.Riverdale	Livy darlint I	CU-MARK	08791
Clemens, Olivia L.		1903.04.04	SLC	NY.Riverdale	Livy darling, here is	CU-MARK	08790
Clemens, Olivia L.		1903.05.17	SLC	MA.Fairhaven	Livy darling, your	CU-MARK	06663
Clemens, Olivia L.		1903.09.20	SLC	NY.New York	Dear, dear sweetheart	CU-MARK	06728
Clemens, Olivia L.		1903.10.10	SLC	NY.New York	With great love	CU-MARK(ph)	10735 inscription
Clemens, Olivia L.		1903.12.05	SLC	NY.Riverdale	Mr. Lucy, of	CU-MARK	10328 misdated, see 1903.01.05
Clemens, Olivia L.	aft	1904.03.01	SLC per IVL	IT.Florence	Mr. Clemens wishes	CU-MARK	06802
Clemens, Olivia L.		1904.04.**	SLC	IT.Florence	Dearheart, I hope	ViU	06820
Clemens, Olivia S.		*	*	*	*	*	11139 see Clemens, Susy
Clemens, Orion & Clemens, Mollie		****.**.**	CC	Unknown	I thank you	CU-MARK	08720
Clemens, Orion	pm	****.02.18	SLC	CT.Hartford	*	CU-MARK	10473 envelope only
Clemens, Orion	 &	1853.10.26 1853.10.28	SLC	PA.Philadelphia	I was at Philadelphia is	NPV 158:1853.11.11	00002

ADDRESSEE	DATE	WRITER	PLACE	CUE	SOURCE	NUMBER/NOTES
Clemens, Orion	1853.11.28	SLC	PA.Philadelphia	I received your	NPV	00003
Clemens, Orion & Clemens, Mollie	1858.03.09	SLC	MO.St. Louis	I must take	NPV	00014
Clemens, Orion	1860.01.27	SLC	Unknown	yourself from the What is a	NPV 153:146	00018 date uncertain
Clemens, Orion	1860.09.28	SLC	LA.New Orleans	I just received	NPV	00025
Clemens, Orion	1860.11.21	SLC	MO.St. Louis	At last, I	CU-MARK	00026
Clemens, Orion & Clemens, Mollie	1861.02.06	SLC	IL.Cairo	After promising Mrs.	NPV	00027
Clemens, Orion	1861.03.18	SLC	MO.St. Louis	Castle and myself Your last has	NPV 114:45	00022
Clemens, Orion	1861.04.26	SLC	SH.Hannibal City	I am on	NPV	00028
Clemens, Orion	bet 1861.10.01 & 1861.11.30	SLC	Unknown	From Hon. Chief	CU-MARK	00033
Clemens, Orion	1862.04.13	SLC	NV.Esmeralda	Wasson got here	NPV	00042
Clemens, Orion	1862.04.17 & 1862.04.19	SLC	NV.Aurora	As to the	CU-MARK	00043
Clemens, Orion	1862.04.24 to 1862.04.25	SLC	NV.Esmeralda	Yours of the	NPV	00045
Clemens, Orion	1862.04.28	SLC	NV.Esmeralda	Well, if Perry	NPV	00046
Clemens, Orion	1862.05.04 & 1862.05.05	SLC	NV.Esmeralda	Well--if you	NPV	00047
Clemens, Orion	1862.05.11 to 1862.05.12	SLC	NV.Esmeralda	To use a	NPV CU-MARK	00048 CU-MARK envelope
Clemens, Orion	1862.05.17	SLC	NV.Esmeralda	If you can't	NPV	00049
Clemens, Orion	1862.06.02	SLC	NV.Esmeralda	The "Monitor" suit	NPV	00050
Clemens, Orion	1862.06.09	SLC	NV.Esmeralda	I have received	NPV	02778
Clemens, Orion	1862.06.22	SLC	NV.Esmeralda	Things are going	ViU	00052
Clemens, Orion	1862.06.25	SLC	NV.Esmeralda	The mail will	NPV CU-MARK	00053 CU-MARK envelope
Clemens, Orion	1862.07.09	SLC	NV.Esmeralda	I am here	CU-MARK	00054
Clemens, Orion	1862.07.23	SLC	NV.Esmeralda	No, I don't	NPV	00055
Clemens, Orion	1862.07.30	SLC	NV.Esmeralda	Your letter to	NPV	00056

Clemens, Orion		1862.08.07	SLC	NV.Esmeralda	Barstow wrote that	NPV	00057
Clemens, Orion & Clemens, Mollie		1862.10.21	SLC	NV.Virginia City	I wrote by	NPV	00060
Clemens, Orion		1863.06.20	SLC	CA.San Francisco	The Echo progresses	CU-MARK	00068
Clemens, Orion		1864.04.14	SLC	NV.Virginia City	I hereby resign	Nv	11066
Clemens, Orion & Clemens, Mollie		1864.05.25	SLC	NV.Virginia City	Don't stump for	CU-MARK	00081
Clemens, Orion		1864.05.26	SLC	NV.Virginia City	Send me two	CU-MARK	00082
Clemens, Orion & Clemens, Mollie		1864.08.14	SLC	CA.San Francisco	I have managed	CU-MARK	00085
Clemens, Orion & Clemens, Mollie		1864.09.28	SLC	CA.San Francisco	I guess my	CU-MARK	00088
Clemens, Orion		1864.10.18	SLC	CA.San Francisco	Capt Blaisdell says	CU-MARK	00090
Clemens, Orion		1864.11.11	SLC	CA.San Francisco	I have been	CU-MARK	00091
Clemens, Orion	pm	1865.05.02	SLC	CA.San Francisco	*	CU-MARK	10792 envelope only
Clemens, Orion & Clemens, Mollie	to	1865.10.19 1865.10.20	SLC	CA.San Francisco	Orion there was	CU-MARK	00092
Clemens, Orion		1865.12.13	SLC	CA.San Francisco	I have just	CU-MARK	00093
Clemens, Orion		1868.02.21	SLC	DC.Washington	I am glad	114:150	00198
Clemens, Orion	or	1868.03.08 1868.03.09	SLC	DC.Washington	I have made	153:359	00199 place uncertain
Clemens, Orion		1870.**.**	SLC	NY.Buffalo	*	CU-MARK	10294 envelope only
Clemens, Orion		1870.04.21	SLC	NY.Buffalo	I enclose (if	CU-MARK	00457
Clemens, Orion	bef	1870.04.21	SLC	NY.Buffalo	Orion, if this	CU-MARK	00456
Clemens, Orion		1870.07.15	SLC	NY.Elmira	Per contract I	CU-MARK	00489
Clemens, Orion		1870.08.01	SLC	NY.Elmira	Pamela has at	CU-MARK	00493
Clemens, Orion	ca to	1870.08.24 1870.08.31	SLC	NY.Buffalo	I find that	114:175	00499
Clemens, Orion	pm	1870.09.03	SLC	NY.Buffalo	Leave it in	CU-MARK	00501 on envelope
Clemens, Orion		1870.09.09	SLC	NY.Buffalo	O here! I	NPV	00504

ADDRESSEE	DATE	WRITER	PLACE	CUE	SOURCE	NUMBER/NOTES
Clemens, Orion	1870.11.05	SLC	NY.Buffalo	Pamela said the I am writing	NPV CU-MARK	00524
Clemens, Orion	1870.11.11	SLC	NY.Buffalo	You have got	CU-MARK	00531
Clemens, Orion	aft 1870.11.18	SLC	NY.Buffalo	I hope you	NPV	00537
Clemens, Orion	1871.02.22	SLC	NY.Buffalo	Return to me	CU-MARK	00579
Clemens, Orion	1871.03.04	SLC	NY.Buffalo	What I wanted	NPV	00583
Clemens, Orion	1871.03.09	SLC	NY.Buffalo	Tell Bliss "all	PBL	00584
Clemens, Orion	1871.03.10	SLC	NY.Buffalo	Have just sent	NN-B	02453
Clemens, Orion	1871.03.11 & 1871.03.13	SLC	NY.Buffalo	Now why do	CU-MARK	00587
Clemens, Orion	1871.03.15	SLC	NY.Buffalo	I am sorry	CU-MARK	00592
Clemens, Orion & Bliss, Elisha	1871.03.20	SLC	NY.Elmira	We are all	CU-MARK	00595
Clemens, Orion	1871.04.04	SLC	NY.Elmira	In moving from	CU-MARK	00598
Clemens, Orion	1871.04.08 & 1871.04.10	SLC	NY.Elmira	If I don't	CU-MARK	00602
Clemens, Orion	1871.04.18	SLC	NY.Elmira	Since Knox has	CU-MARK	00603
Clemens, Orion	1871.04.30	SLC	NY.Elmira	I do not	NPV	00609
Clemens, Orion & Clemens, Mollie	1871.06.07	SLC	NY.Elmira	I forgot to	CU-MARK	00613
Clemens, Orion & Clemens, Mollie	1871.06.21	SLC	NY.Elmira	Am very glad	CU-MARK	00619
Clemens, Orion	1871.06.27	SLC	NY.Elmira	I wrote a	CU-MARK	00622
Clemens, Orion	1871.06.27	SLC	NY.Elmira	If convenient, leave	CU-MARK	00620
Clemens, Orion	1871.06.29	SLC	NY.Elmira	From a remark	CU-MARK	00628
Clemens, Orion	1871.07.02	SLC	NY.Elmira	My MSS? Shall	CU-MARK	00630
Clemens, Orion	1871.07.07	SLC	NY.Elmira	Look in the	NPV	00633
Clemens, Orion	1871.08.31	SLC	NY.Elmira	We have scarcely	CU-MARK	00649
Clemens, Orion	1871.09.16	SLC	NY.Elmira	I believe I	CU-MARK	00652
Clemens, Orion	1871.09.17	SLC	NY.Elmira	Inclose a letter	CU-MARK	00653
Clemens, Orion & Clemens, Mollie	1871.12.24	SLC & OLC	CT.Hartford	I enclose our	CU-MARK	00692
Clemens, Orion	1872.03.07	SLC	CT.Hartford	I cannot let	CU-MARK	00730

Clemens, Orion	1872.03.19	SLC	NY.Elmira	All well &	CU-MARK	00733
Clemens, Orion	1872.03.19	SLC	NY.Elmira	Born, in Elmira	CU-MARK	00734
Clemens, Orion & Clemens, Mollie	1872.05.15	SLC	NY.Elmira	We arrived last	CU-MARK	00747
Clemens, Orion & Clemens, Mollie	1872.05.22	SLC	NY.Elmira	We are delayed	CU-MARK	00752
Clemens, Orion	1872.08.11	SLC	CT.New Saybrook	I shall sail	CU-MARK	00791
Clemens, Orion	1872.08.16 or 1872.08.17	SLC	CT.Hartford	Pay this, if	CU-MARK	10727 on Holz July 18
Clemens, Orion & Clemens, Mollie	1873.05.05	SLC	CT.Hartford	Your letters received	CU-MARK	00913
Clemens, Orion & Clemens, Mollie	aft 1873.09.10	SLC	EN.London	We got seal-skin	NPV	00962
Clemens, Orion	1874.02.04	SLC	CT.Hartford	God knows yours	CU-MARK	01045
Clemens, Orion	1874.03.18	SLC	CT.Hartford	The enclosed letter	CU-MARK	01064
Clemens, Orion	1874.04.10	SLC	CT.Hartford	Am expecting Mollie	CU-MARK	01074
Clemens, Orion	1874.05.10	SLC	NY.Elmira	Everybody gets a	CU-MARK	01089
Clemens, Orion & Clemens, Mollie	1874.06.10	SLC	NY.Elmira	The child was	CU-MARK	01096
Clemens, Orion	1874.06.17	SLC	NY.Elmira	I showed the	CU-MARK	01101
Clemens, Orion	1874.07.29	SLC	NY.Elmira	We had a	CU-MARK	01114
Clemens, Orion	1874.08.28	SLC	NY.Elmira	Yrs containing cheque	CU-MARK	01120
Clemens, Orion	1874.09.21	SLC	CT.Hartford	Yrs containing ck	CU-MARK	01128
Clemens, Orion	1874.12.09	SLC	CT.Hartford	I am trying	NPV	01162 typed
Clemens, Orion	1875.03.01	SLC	CT.Hartford	Hoping that the	CU-MARK	01201
Clemens, Orion	1875.03.27	SLC	CT.Hartford	No, I must	CU-MARK	01216
Clemens, Orion	1875.07.26	SLC	CT.Hartford	All right. I	CU-MARK	01255
Clemens, Orion	1877.05.05	SLC	CT.Hartford	It was my	CU-MARK	01426
Clemens, Orion	pm 1877.05.14	SLC	CT.Hartford	Profanity is more	CU-MARK	01430 on form letter
Clemens, Orion	1877.11.13	SLC	CT.Hartford	*	CU-MARK	10110 envelope only

ADDRESSEE		DATE	WRITER	PLACE	CUE	SOURCE	NUMBER/NOTES
Clemens, Orion		1877.12.10	SLC per FCH	CT.Hartford	Please ask your	CU-MARK	01511
Clemens, Orion		1877.12.19	SLC	CT.Hartford	If I write	CU-MARK	01512 fragment
Clemens, Orion		1878.01.28	SLC	CT.Hartford	Am just back	NPV	01527 fragment
Clemens, Orion		1878.02.21	SLC	CT.Hartford	You make it	CU-MARK	01531
Clemens, Orion		1878.03.23	SLC	CT.Hartford	Every man must	CU-MARK	01547
Clemens, Orion		1879.02.09	SLC	GE.Munich	I enclose draft	CU-MARK	01631
Clemens, Orion		1879.05.29	SLC	FR.Paris	Never mind the	CU-MARK	01662
Clemens, Orion	ca	1879.10.29	SLC	CT.Hartford	I like the	CU-MARK(tr)	01703
Clemens, Orion		1879.11.14	SLC	IL.Chicago	Well, it was	CU-MARK	01716
Clemens, Orion		1880.02.07	SLC	CT.Hartford	Glass received, all	CU-MARK	01760
Clemens, Orion		1880.02.21	SLC	CT.Hartford	Meant to ask	NPV	01761
Clemens, Orion		1880.02.26	SLC	CT.Hartford	I believe I	NPV	01763
Clemens, Orion		1880.02.28	SLC	CT.Hartford	Send me that	NPV	01764
Clemens, Orion		1880.03.05	SLC	CT.Hartford	All right--send	NPV	01766
Clemens, Orion		1880.04.04	SLC	CT.Hartford	Please don't put	NPV	01782
Clemens, Orion	ca	1880.04.26	SLC	CT.Hartford	Let it be	CU-MARK(tr)	09214
Clemens, Orion		1880.05.06	SLC	CT.Hartford	It is a	CU-MARK	01799
Clemens, Orion		1880.05.12	SLC	CT.Hartford	Drop the book	CU-MARK	01802
Clemens, Orion	pm	1880.06.01	SLC	CT.Hartford	*	CU-MARK	09476 envelope only
Clemens, Orion		1880.06.22	SLC	NY.Elmira	Very well, then	CU-MARK	01816
Clemens, Orion		1880.10.24	SLC	CT.Hartford	Bliss is dead	CU-MARK	01845
Clemens, Orion		1880.11.27	SLC	CT.Hartford	We thank Mollie	NPV	01857
Clemens, Orion		1880.12.17	SLC	CT.Hartford	The pig matter	NPV	01874
Clemens, Orion	pm	1881.06.02	SLC	CT.Hartford	But I told	CU-MARK	01966 on form letter
Clemens, Orion		1881.06.04	SLC	CT.Hartford	Good--you are	CU-MARK	01969
Clemens, Orion		1881.10.15	SLC	CT.Hartford	My entire day	CU-MARK	02052
Clemens, Orion		1881.10.26	SLC	Unknown	Yes, but I	NPV	02068

Clemens, Orion		1881.11.11	SLC	CT.Hartford	The nuts came	NPV	02085
Clemens, Orion		1881.11.21	SLC	CT.Hartford	O yes, we	NPV	02093
Clemens, Orion		1882.01.21	SLC	CT.Hartford	All right, shall	CU-MARK	02153 Jan 21 to Hooper enc
Clemens, Orion & Clemens, Orion family		1882.09.05	SLC	NY.Elmira	I am glad	CU-MARK	02263
Clemens, Orion		1882.11.18	SLC	CT.Hartford	In order to	CU-MARK	02307 typed
Clemens, Orion		1883.02.22	SLC	CT.Hartford	Your Dr. George	CU-MARK	02350
Clemens, Orion & Clemens, Jane L.		1883.07.21	SLC	NY.Elmira	I don't know	CU-MARK	02616 also to Mollie Clemens
Clemens, Orion		1883.08.29	SLC	NY.Elmira	It is beautifully	CU-MARK	02826
Clemens, Orion		1883.09.04	SLC	NY.Elmira	Here is something	CU-MARK	02832 Holcombe Aug 29 enc
Clemens, Orion		1883.09.28	SLC	CT.Hartford	Kings rec'd. Quite	NPV	02841
Clemens, Orion & Clemens, Jane L.		1883.12.19	SLC	CT.Hartford	Merry Christmas from	CU-MARK	02866 also to Mollie Clemens
Clemens, Orion		1884.11.03	SLC	CT.Hartford	A lot of	NPV	03019
Clemens, Orion		1884.11.15	SLC	MA.Boston	Don't send telegrams	NPV	03026
Clemens, Orion		1884.11.17	SLC	CT.Hartford	No copy of	NPV	03082
Clemens, Orion		1884.12.26	SLC	CT.Hartford	I am just	NPV	03070
Clemens, Orion		1884.12.28	SLC	PA.Pittsburgh	Pond has got	NPV	03074
Clemens, Orion		1885.01.14	CC	CT.Hartford	I thank you	CU-MARK	03115
Clemens, Orion		1885.01.16	SLC	IL.Chicago	I wish to	NPV	03118
Clemens, Orion	pm	1885.01.17	SLC	IL.Chicago	*	CU-MARK	10097 envelope only
Clemens, Orion		1885.02.**	SLC	Unknown	Don't show that	NPV	10885
Clemens, Orion & Clemens, Mollie		1885.03.05	SLC	CT.Hartford	I reached home	NPV	03184
Clemens, Orion		1885.04.11	SLC	CT.Hartford	Damn Wm Lampton	NPV	03216
Clemens, Orion		1885.05.05	SLC	CT.Hartford	Heiliger Gott im	NPV	03222

ADDRESSEE	DATE	WRITER	PLACE	CUE	SOURCE	NUMBER/NOTES
Clemens, Orion	1885.05.16	SLC	CT.Hartford	I have asked	NPV	03228
Clemens, Orion	1885.05.22	SLC	CT.Hartford	You jump to	NPV	03230 typed
Clemens, Orion	1885.07.11	SLC	NY.Elmira	I'll bet Mollie's	CU-MARK	03257
Clemens, Orion	1885.07.18	SLC	NY.Elmira	Settle it! And	CU-MARK	03261
Clemens, Orion	1885.08.30	SLC	NY.Elmira	I believe there	CU-MARK	03282
Clemens, Orion	1885.09.22	SLC	CT.Hartford	That was what	NPV	03289
Clemens, Orion	o/a 1885.11.15	SLC	CT.Hartford	Answer this for	CU-MARK	03307 on Greening Nov 15
Clemens, Orion	1885.11.28	SLC	CT.Hartford	The enclosed letters	CU-MARK	03316 Nov 24 letters enc
Clemens, Orion	1885.12.08	SLC	CT.Hartford	A ton of	CU-MARK	03329
Clemens, Orion	1886.06.02	SLC	CT.Hartford	To avoid the	CU-MARK	03403
Clemens, Orion	1886.10.06	SLC	CT.Hartford	Yes, buy Pamela's	CU-MARK	03463
Clemens, Orion	1887.03.16	SLC	CT.Hartford	No, don't bother	NPV	03380
Clemens, Orion	1887.05.05	SLC	CT.Hartford	No, just peg	CU-MARK	03566
Clemens, Orion	1887.05.28	SLC	CT.Hartford	Enclosed is for	CU-MARK	03575
Clemens, Orion	1887.09.07	SLC	Unknown	These are secrets	CU-MARK	03643
Clemens, Orion	1887.12.08	SLC	CT.Hartford	I have never	NPV CU-MARK	03676 CU-MARK envelope
Clemens, Orion & Clemens, Mollie	1887.12.18	SLC	CT.Hartford	Will you take	CU-MARK	03680 also to Jane Clemens
Clemens, Orion	1888.01.22	SLC	CT.Hartford	It is an	CU-MARK	03698
Clemens, Orion	1888.07.02	SLC	NY.Elmira	We are sorry	CU-MARK	03727
Clemens, Orion	pm 1888.08.03	SLC	CT.Hartford	*	CU-MARK	10101 envelope only
Clemens, Orion	1888.09.16	SLC	NY.Elmira	My plans were	NPV	03765
Clemens, Orion	1888.09.19	SLC	NY.Elmira	Who is this	CU-MARK	03769
Clemens, Orion	1888.10.03	SLC	CT.Hartford	Keep a sharp	NPV	03781
Clemens, Orion	1888.11.23	SLC	CT.Hartford	I have ordered	NPV	03835

Clemens, Orion	1888.11.29	SLC	CT.Hartford	Jesus Christ!--It	CU-MARK	03838
Clemens, Orion	1889.01.05	SLC	CT.Hartford	At 12.20 this	CU-MARK	03847
Clemens, Orion	1889.07.01	SLC	NY.Elmira	Read it &	CU-MARK	03904
Clemens, Orion	1889.08.02	SLC	NY.Elmira	I have been	CU-MARK	03920
Clemens, Orion	1889.12.16	SLC	CT.Hartford	We all send	CU-MARK	03987
Clemens, Orion	1890.01.08	SLC	CT.Hartford	There is no	CU-MARK	04005
Clemens, Orion	1890.02.27	SLC	CT.Hartford	If all the	CU-MARK	04022
Clemens, Orion & Clemens, Mollie	1890.08.21	SLC	NY.Elmira	Orion, I want	CU-MARK	04083
Clemens, Orion & Clemens, Mollie	1890.08.31	SLC	NY.Tannersville	I am just	CU-MARK	04090
Clemens, Orion	1890.09.01	SLC	NY.Tannersville	I have written	CU-MARK	04091
Clemens, Orion	1891.02.25	SLC	CT.Hartford	I've shook the	CU-MARK	04175
Clemens, Orion	1891.04.30	SLC	CT.Hartford	*	CU-MARK	10165 envelope only
Clemens, Orion	1892.06.28	SLC	IL.Chicago	I reached New	CU-MARK	04302
Clemens, Orion & Clemens, Mollie	1892.08.23	SLC	GE.Bad-Nauheim	Private because no	CU-MARK	01768
Clemens, Orion	1892.09.02	SLC	GE.Bad-Nauheim	Tear up the	CU-MARK	01912
Clemens, Orion & Clemens, Mollie	1893.02.02	SLC	IT.Florence	Here is another	CU-MARK	04332
Clemens, Orion	1893.04.20	SLC	NY.New York	All I wanted	CU-MARK(tr)	04379
Clemens, Orion & Clemens, Mollie	1893.04.24	SLC	IL.Chicago	I have been	NPV	04386
Clemens, Orion	1893.05.01	SLC	NY.New York	I am less	CU-MARK(tr)	04393
Clemens, Orion & Clemens, Mollie	1893.07.26	SLC	AU.Krankenheil	We have been	CU-MARK(tr)	04425
Clemens, Orion & Clemens, Mollie	1893.11.03	SLC	NY.New York	Clara and I	CU-MARK(tr)	04487
Clemens, Orion & Clemens, Mollie	1893.11.29	SLC	NY.New York	I meant to	CU-MARK	04512 on clipping
Clemens, Orion & Clemens, Mollie	1894.04.12	SLC	SH.New York	I shall arrive	CU-MARK(tr)	04717
Clemens, Orion	1894.04.23	SLC	NY.New York	Your uncle Orion	CU-MARK(tr)	04726

ADDRESSEE	DATE	WRITER	PLACE	CUE	SOURCE	NUMBER/NOTES
Clemens, Orion	1894.06.21	SLC	FR.Paris	Ed is right	CU-MARK(tr)	04742
Clemens, Orion	1894.08.07	SLC	NY.New York	You must forgive	CU-MARK	04775
Clemens, Orion	1895.05.26	SLC	NY.Elmira	We are in	CU-MARK(tr)	04880
Clemens, Orion & Clemens, Mollie	1896.09.14	SLC	EN.London	There is nothing	CU-MARK(tr)	05110
Clemens, Orion	1897.03.28	SLC	EN.London	I was greatly	CU-MARK(tr)	05194
Clemens, Orion & Clemens, Mollie	1897.11.05	SLC	AU.Vienna	I believe I	TxU	05310
Clemens, Orion family & Clemens, Orion	1882.09.05	SLC	NY.Elmira	I am glad	CU-MARK	02263
Clemens, Pamela	*	*	*	*	*	10322 see Moffett, Pamela
Clemens, Samuel L.	****.**.**	CC	Unknown	If you want	CU-MARK(tr)	10706
Clemens, Samuel L.	ca 1868.12.15	OLC	NY.Elmira	To think of	456:35	11067
Clemens, Samuel L.	1869.11.13	OLC	NY.Elmira	My dear I	CU-MARK	00372
Clemens, Samuel L.	1871.11.20	OLC	CT.Hartford	Last night you	CU-MARK	00679
Clemens, Samuel L.	1871.11.28	OLC	CT.Hartford	It is too	CU-MARK	00681
Clemens, Samuel L.	1871.11.29	OLC	CT.Hartford	My darling, it is	CU-MARK	00682
Clemens, Samuel L.	1871.12.02 & 1871.12.03	OLC	CT.Hartford	It did me	CU-MARK	00683
Clemens, Samuel L.	1871.12.20	OLC	CT.Hartford	I must not	CU-MARK	00691
Clemens, Samuel L.	1871.12.29	OLC	CT.Hartford	Langdon about well	CU-MARK	00698 telegram
Clemens, Samuel L.	1871.12.30	OLC	CT.Hartford	Your letter from	CU-MARK	00699
Clemens, Samuel L.	1872.01.07	OLC	CT.Hartford	You have seemed	CU-MARK	00709
Clemens, Samuel L.	1872.01.10	OLC	CT.Hartford	I have been	CU-MARK	00713
Clemens, Samuel L.	1874.06.**	OLC	NY.Elmira	Did you send	Mo4	01095
Clemens, Samuel L.	1874.06.**	OLC	NY.Elmira	We have been	Mo4	01094
Clemens, Samuel L.	bet 1877.04.25 & 1877.05.01	OLC	CT.Hartford	Last night, after	ViU(tr)	01421
Clemens, Samuel L.	1877.07.28	OLC	NY.Elmira	I rec'd your	CU-MARK	01457
Clemens, Samuel L.	1877.07.29	OLC	NY.Elmira	Two letters came	CU-MARK	01458

Clemens, Samuel L.		1877.08.12	OLC	NY.Elmira	We are all	CU-MARK	01470
Clemens, Samuel L.	pm	1882.04.19	OLC	CT.Hartford	*	CU-MARK	10428 envelope only
Clemens, Samuel L.	&	1882.04.23 & 1882.04.27	OLC & SC	CT.Hartford	We all miss	CU-MARK	02206
Clemens, Samuel L.		1882.05.03	OLC	CT.Hartford	I rec'd yesterday	Mo4	02185
Clemens, Samuel L.		1882.05.05	OLC	CT.Hartford	A letter from	CU-MARK	02187
Clemens, Samuel L.	pm	1882.05.09	OLC	CT.Hartford	*	CU-MARK	10093 envelope only
Clemens, Samuel L.		1883.05.24	OLC	CT.Hartford	I rec'd today	CU-MARK	02395
Clemens, Samuel L. & Clemens, Olivia L.		1884.04.17	CC	CT.Hartford	It does not	MH-H	02958
Clemens, Samuel L. & Clemens, Olivia L.		1884.04.17	SC	CT.Hartford	Jean seems bright	MH-H	02957
Clemens, Samuel L.		1884.04.18	CC	CT.Hartford	I must tell	MH-H	02960
Clemens, Samuel L.		1884.11.09	SC	CT.Hartford	Cleveland and Buffalo	CU-MARK(tr)	03021
Clemens, Samuel L.	pm	1884.11.11	OLC	CT.Hartford	I was particularly	CU-MARK	03022
Clemens, Samuel L.		1884.11.21	OLC	CT.Hartford	I rather hoped	CU-MARK	03029
Clemens, Samuel L.		1884.11.24	OLC	CT.Hartford	Your dispatch is	CU-MARK	03038
Clemens, Samuel L.	ca	1884.11.30	OLC	CT.Hartford	To our beloved	CU-MARK	03042
Clemens, Samuel L.		1885.01.03	OLC	CT.Hartford	Thirty letters lie	CU-MARK	03100
Clemens, Samuel L.		1885.01.07	CC	CT.Hartford	We do miss	CU-MARK	03106
Clemens, Samuel L.		1885.01.09	OLC	CT.Hartford	Here I am	Mo4	03142
Clemens, Samuel L.		1885.01.16	OLC	CT.Hartford	Last evening Susy	Mo4	03143
Clemens, Samuel L.		1885.01.21	OLC	CT.Hartford	No letter has	CU-MARK	03124
Clemens, Samuel L.		1885.01.22	SC	CT.Hartford	Miss Foote has	CU-MARK	03127
Clemens, Samuel L.		1885.01.23	OLC	CT.Hartford	Send me word	Mo4	03144
Clemens, Samuel L.		1885.01.25	OLC	CT.Hartford	A bad dream	CU-MARK	03135
Clemens, Samuel L.		1885.01.26	OLC	CT.Hartford	Just one line	Mo4	03145
Clemens, Samuel L.		1885.01.29	OLC	CT.Hartford	Youth darling I	Mo4	08583
Clemens, Samuel L.		1885.01.31	OLC	CT.Hartford	Your telegram is	Mo4	03146

ADDRESSEE		DATE	WRITER	PLACE	CUE	SOURCE	NUMBER/NOTES
Clemens, Samuel L.	pm	1885.02.04	OLC	CT.Hartford	Only a few	Mo4	03152
Clemens, Samuel L.		1885.02.11	OLC	CT.Hartford	I am sorry	Mo4	03163
Clemens, Samuel L.		1885.02.16	OLC	CT.Hartford	Youth darling Clara	Mo4	03169
Clemens, Samuel L.		1885.02.20	OLC	CT.Hartford	The invitation from	Mo4	03175
Clemens, Samuel L.		1885.04.09	OLC	CT.Hartford	Life is not	Mo4	10660
Clemens, Samuel L.		1885.08.06	OLC	CT.Hartford	Your dispatch about	Mo4	03276
Clemens, Samuel L.		1885.12.01	SC	CT.Hartford	Mamma wanted me	CU-MARK	03322
Clemens, Samuel L.		1886.04.03	OLC	CT.Hartford	I have come	Mo4	03381
Clemens, Samuel L.		1886.05.05	OLC	CT.Hartford	Mary Foote and	Mo4	03398
Clemens, Samuel L.		1886.05.10	OLC	CT.Hartford	I rec'd your	Mo4	03399
Clemens, Samuel L.		1886.08.01	OLC	NY.Elmira	It is a	CU-MARK	03432
Clemens, Samuel L.		1886.10.27	OLC	CT.Hartford	I have nothing	CU-MARK	03476
Clemens, Samuel L.		1888.10.09	OLC	NY.New York	Old Sweetheart I	Mo4	03785
Clemens, Samuel L.	pm	1888.10.11	OLC	NY.New York	I wish I	Mo4	03789
Clemens, Samuel L.		1890.05.18	OLC	CT.Hartford	Shall I accept	CU-MARK	04048 telegram
Clemens, Samuel L.		1890.05.18	OLC	CT.Hartford	I was delighted	Mo4	08629
Clemens, Samuel L.		1890.05.20	OLC	CT.Hartford	I wish I	CU-MARK	04049
Clemens, Samuel L.		1890.05.22	OLC	CT.Hartford	We have a	Mo4	08632
Clemens, Samuel L.	pm	1890.11.27	OLC	NY.Elmira	We had a	Mo4	08630
Clemens, Samuel L.		1892.06.23	OLC	GE.Bad-Nauheim	I am going	Mo4	04301
Clemens, Samuel L.		1892.11.30	OLC	IT.Florence	To my dear	CU-MARK	04660 inscription
Clemens, Samuel L.		1893.03.26	OLC	IT.Florence	How I should	Mo4	04359
Clemens, Samuel L.		1893.04.02	OLC	IT.Venice	Youth Darling how	Mo4	04361
Clemens, Samuel L.		1893.04.09	OLC	IT.Venice	We have a	Mo4	04368
Clemens, Samuel L.		1893.04.12	OLC	IT.Venice	Your second dispatch	CU-MARK	04372
Clemens, Samuel L.	&	1893.04.14 1893.04.16	OLC	IT.Venice	The last Courant	CU-MARK	04373 misdated Apr 13
Clemens, Samuel L.		1893.04.19	OLC	IT.Florence	Five letters from	CU-MARK	04378

Clemens, Samuel L.		1893.04.22	OLC	IT.Florence	*	CU-MARK	10083 envelope only
Clemens, Samuel L.		1893.04.23	OLC	IT.Florence	Your letters rec'd	CU-MARK	04382
Clemens, Samuel L.		1893.04.24	OLC	IT.Florence	I have felt	Mo4	04385
Clemens, Samuel L.		1893.04.28	OLC	IT.Florence	I am spoiled	Mo4	04388
Clemens, Samuel L.		1893.04.30	OLC	IT.Florence	I am going	Mo4	04390
Clemens, Samuel L.		1893.08.**	OLC	Unknown	I am only	CU-MARK(tr)	04428
Clemens, Samuel L.		1893.09.12	OLC	GE.Franzensbad	Today we have	CU-MARK	04443
Clemens, Samuel L.		1893.11.14	OLC	FR.Paris	Jean the beloved	CU-MARK	04500
Clemens, Samuel L.		1893.12.17	OLC	FR.Paris	Your dispatch reached	CU-MARK	04531
Clemens, Samuel L.	pm	1894.07.13	OLC	FR.Paris	This afternoon Susy	Mo4	10489
Clemens, Samuel L.		1894.07.31	OLC	FR.Paris	We came back	CU-MARK	04768
Clemens, Samuel L.		1894.12.**	SC	FR.Paris	Thank you for	CU-MARK	04818
Clemens, Samuel L.		1896.05.19	OLC	AF.Durban	Please thank Mr.	CU-MARK	05048
Clemens, Samuel L.		1900.01.20	OLC	EN.Hindhead	It is a	CU-MARK	05751
Clemens, Samuel L.		1902.**.**	JC	Unknown	To the lover	CU-MARK	06213
Clemens, Samuel L.	bet &	1902.**.** 1903.**.**	OLC	NY.Riverdale	I am truly	293:250	08811
Clemens, Samuel L.	bet &	1902.**.** 1903.**.**	OLC	NY.Riverdale	Youth darling, have you	CU-MARK	08812
Clemens, Samuel L.		1903.08.05	OLC	NY.Elmira	Your delightful letter	CU-MARK	06718
Clemens, Samuel L.		1903.09.23	OLC	NY.Elmira	I was so	CU-MARK	06729
Clemens, Samuel L.		1904.**.**	OLC	Unknown	I feel so	CtHMTH	06780
Clemens, Samuel L.	bef	1904.10.19	CC	Unknown	immediately pay one	ViU	10770 fragment
Clemens, Samuel L.		1904.11.07	CC	Unknown	I feel like	CU-MARK(tr)	06947
Clemens, Samuel L.	o/a	1906.11.17	IVL	NY.New York	Mr. Megrue sent	CU-MARK	10963 on Megrue Nov 17
Clemens, Samuel L.		1906.11.25	IVL	CT.Hartford	I was unhappy	NNC	10964
Clemens, Samuel L.		1907.06.17	IVL	NY.New York	Everything goes well	CU-MARK	10977

ADDRESSEE		DATE	WRITER	PLACE	CUE	SOURCE	NUMBER/NOTES
Clemens, Samuel L.		1907.06.21	CC	NY.New York	Much worried remember	CU-MARK	07762 telegram
Clemens, Samuel L.		1907.06.24	IVL	NY.Tuxedo Park	How that is	CU-MARK	10978
Clemens, Samuel L.		1907.06.28	IVL	NY.New York	You don't know	CU-MARK	10981
Clemens, Samuel L.		1907.07.22	CC	MA.Boston	Welcome back am	CU-MARK	07787 telegram
Clemens, Samuel L.		1908.01.27	IVL	NY.New York	Many of your	CU-MARK	10982
Clemens, Samuel L.	pm	1908.01.31	IVL	NY.New York	*	CU-MARK	10983 envelope only
Clemens, Samuel L.		1908.08.14	CC	GE.Cronenberg	Cant I settle	CU-MARK	08085 telegram
Clemens, Samuel L.		1908.08.26	CC	GE.Cronenberg	No	CU-MARK	08095 telegram
Clemens, Samuel L.		1908.09.30	JC	SH.Pretoria	Delayed one day	CU-MARK	08114 telegram
Clemens, Samuel L.	ca	1908.10.01	JC	GE.Cuxhaven	Arrived. no bad	CU-MARK(tr)	08115 telegram
Clemens, Samuel L.		1909.03.05	JC	NJ.Montclair	You don't know	CU-MARK	08363
Clemens, Samuel L.		1909.04.**	CC	Unknown	Even if Miss	CU-MARK(tr)	08379
Clemens, Samuel L.	bet &	1909.06.01 1909.09.30	JC	CT.Redding	I am deserting	CU-MARK(tr)	08299
Clemens, Samuel L.		1909.06.03	IVL	NY.New York	I regret that	CU-MARK	10980
Clemens, Samuel L.		1909.07.09	CC	NY.New York	I am glad	CU-MARK	08434
Clemens, Samuel L.		1909.11.20	JC	CT.Redding	Nothing shall occur	CU-MARK	08497 telegram
Clemens, Samuel L.		1909.12.27	CC	GE.Wiesbaden	Just saw your	CU-MARK	08523 telegram
Clemens, Susy		1872.05.09	SLC	OH.Cleveland	Your grandmother	CtHMTH	00746
Clemens, Susy		1875.12.25	SLC	CT.Hartford	I have received	293:36	01290 date uncertain
Clemens, Susy		1877.07.16	SLC	NY.New York	Susie dear, you	Mo4	01451
Clemens, Susy		1877.07.19	SLC	NY.New York	Susie dear, Your	Mo4	01455
Clemens, Susy		1881.12.25	SLC	CT.Hartford	To that good-mannered	NN-B	10644 inscription
Clemens, Susy		1882.05.25	SLC	CT.Hartford	These volumes, (in	CCamarSJ	09121 inscription

Clemens, Susy		1884.11.23	SLC	NY.New York	Susy dear, I	CU-MARK	03035
Clemens, Susy		1884.12.05	SLC	NY.Utica	I have been	ViU(tr)	03046 other sources
Clemens, Susy		1884.12.14	SLC	MI.Grand Rapids	Vor zwei Tagen	CU-MARK	03059
Clemens, Susy	ca	1885.01.16	SLC	IL.Chicago	Susie dear, your	ViU(tr)	03095
Clemens, Susy		1885.01.23	SLC	MN.St. Paul	I am glad	ViU(tr)	03132
Clemens, Susy		1885.02.03	SLC	IL.Chicago	Mamma has sent	ViU(tr)	03151
Clemens, Susy		1885.02.08	SLC	IN.Indianapolis	When I get	ViU(tr)	03159
Clemens, Susy		1885.02.15	SLC	CN.Toronto	It was a	ViU(tr)	03168
Clemens, Susy		1889.07.16	SLC	CT.Hartford	Why, bless you	CU-MARK(tr)	03912
Clemens, Susy & Clemens, Clara L.		1891.06.28	SLC	FR.Aix-les-Bains	I love you	CU-MARK	04216
Clemens, Susy & Clemens, Clara L.		1891.06.29	SLC	FR.Aix-les-Bains	Mamma is a	CU-MARK	04217
Clemens, Susy & Clemens, Clara L.		1891.07.03	SLC & JC	FR.Aix-les-Bains	Day before yesterday	CU-MARK	04219
Clemens, Susy		1892.03.22	SLC & OLC	FR.Menton	I have been	CU-MARK	04276
Clemens, Susy		1893.05.07	SLC	NY.Elmira	Susy dear, about	CU-MARK(tr)	04397
Clemens, Susy		1893.11.06	SLC	NY.New York	I will drop	CU-MARK(tr)	04490
Clemens, Susy		1893.12.27	SLC	NY.New York	My Christmas dinner	CtHMTH(tr)	04540
Clemens, Susy		1894.08.08	SLC	NY.New York	Susie dear, I will	CU-MARK(tr)	04776
Clemens, Susy	to	1895.08.30 1895.08.31	OLC	SH.Warrimoo	We have land	CU-MARK(tr)	04957
Clemens, Susy		1895.10.20	OLC	AS.Ballarat	Last evening we	CU-MARK(tr)	04968
Clemens, Susy		1895.12.02	OLC	NZ.Palmerston N.	Here we are	CU-MARK(tr)	04979
Clemens, Susy		1896.02.07	SLC	II.Calcutta	Mamma is busy	CU-MARK(tr)	05018
Clemens, Will M.		****.**.**	OLC	NY.Riverdale	I thought my	ViU	09060
Clemens, Will M.		1879.11.18	SLC	CT.Hartford	Your letter received	296:11	01719 other sources
Clemens, Will M.		1881.01.16	SLC	CT.Hartford	How can I	296:12	01893 other sources

ADDRESSEE	DATE	WRITER	PLACE	CUE	SOURCE	NUMBER/NOTES
Clemens, Will M.	1882.01.**	SLC	Unknown	I haven't any	CtY(tr)	02139 on printed biography
Clemens, Will M.	1885.**.**	SLC	Unknown	You know my	296:136	03178
Clemens, Will M.	1900.06.06	SLC	EN.London	I am sorry	NN-B	08202
Clemens, Will M.	1902.02.16	OLC	NY.Riverdale	My husband says	NN-B	07095
Clement, Miss	1891.03.08	SLC	CT.Hartford	Yes, my name	ViU	04180
Clemons, Fanny	1900.06.13	SLC	EN.London	I hold myself	281:83-1	09510
Cleveland, E.S. & Bissell (Geo. P.) & Co.	1879.09.08	SLC	NY.Elmira	Please pay to	CtHMTH	09186
Cleveland, Esther	1892.11.03	SLC	IT.Florence	If you will	DLC	02398
Cleveland, Frances F.	****.**.**	SLC	Unknown	I am sorry	DLC(tr)	00051
Cleveland, Frances F.	1887.11.06	SLC	CT.Hartford	I do not	CU-MARK	03664
Cleveland, Frances F.	1888.03.22	SLC	DC.Washington	We cannot find	DLC	03710
Cleveland, Frances F.	1888.06.05	SLC	CT.Hartford	It is to	CU-MARK(dr)	03721
Cleveland, Frances F.	1908.06.25	SLC	CT.Redding	Your husband was	MoSW	08042
Cleveland, Grover	1885.09.23	SLC	CT.Hartford	Every now &	DLC	03290
Cleveland, Grover	1886.02.23	SLC	CT.Hartford	You not only	DLC	03371
Cleveland, Grover	1887.09.10	SLC	NY.Elmira	I have always	DLC	03648
Cleveland, Grover	1889.02.20	SLC	CT.Hartford	The book, & your	DLC	03865
Cleveland, Grover	1906.03.06	SLC	NY.New York	Your patriotic virtues	DLC	07365
Cleveland, Henry W.	o/a 1889.12.10	SLC per FGW	CT.Hartford	Please address the	CU-MARK(dr)	09089 on Cleveland Dec 10
Cleveland Orphan Asylum	1869.01.07	SLC	IL.Chicago	On several accounts	206:1869.01.12	00223
Cleveland, Ruth	1893.**.**	SLC	Unknown	I belong to	303:13	08673
Clinton, Margery H.	1907.12.02	SLC	NY.New York	I thank you	CU-MARK(ph)	07873
Clinton, Margery H.	1908.04.17	SLC	NY.New York	It was lovely	CU-MARK(ph)	07979
Clinton, Margery H.	1908.10.30	SLC	CT.Redding	Good, you're coming	CU-MARK(ph)	08150
Clinton, Margery H.	1909.02.09	SLC	CT.Redding	Ashcroft has just	CU-MARK(ph)	08343
Clinton, Margery H.	aft 1909.11.16	SLC	CT.Redding	Here's some more	CU-MARK(ph)	08491

Clover Club & Deacon, Charles R.		1884.01.03	SLC	CT.Hartford	I have unconsciously	CU-MARK(ph)	09948
Clover Club		1886.11.16	SLC	CT.Hartford	engagements already	116:1968.01.25	03481
Clover Club secretary.		1891.01.02	SLC per FGW	CT.Hartford	I have to	TxHU	04151
Coan, Titus M.	ca	1904.06.21	SLC	IT.Florence	For what you	NHi	09104 form letter
Cody, William F.		1885.07.14	SLC	NY.Elmira	I have now	252:1928.07.14	03259 other sources
Coe, Mai H.		1899.09.18	SLC	SE.Sanna	It was a	MFai	09243
Coe, Mai H.		1908.**.**	SLC	BE.Hamilton	Your father is	CtHMTH	07906
Coe, Mai H.		1908.06.**	SLC	Unknown	The above is	CtHMTH	08012 on "Endless chain Prayer"
Coe, Mai H.		1908.07.27	SLC	CT.Redding	A few days	CtHMTH	08061
Coe, Mai H.	o/a	1908.10.07	SLC	CT.Redding	Greeting and Salutation	CtHMTH	09217 form letter
Coe, Mai H. & Coe, William R.		1909.01.18	SLC	CT.Redding	It is lovely	CtHMTH	08316
Coe, Mai H. & Coe, William R.		1909.02.03	SLC	CT.Redding	It has arrived	CtHMTH	08339
Coe, Mai H.		1909.12.27	SLC	CT.Redding	You must not	CtHMTH	08524
Coe, William R.		****.12.24	SLC	NY.New York	I have sampled	418:1975.04.30	09409 other sources
Coe, William R.		1905.12.26	SLC	NY.New York	Thank you cordially	CtHMTH	07255
Coe, William R.		1908.12.25	SLC	CT.Redding	I have been	418:1975.04.30	10379
Coe, William R. & Coe, Mai H.		1909.01.18	SLC	CT.Redding	It is lovely	CtHMTH	08316
Coe, William R. & Coe, Mai H.		1909.02.03	SLC	CT.Redding	It has arrived	CtHMTH	08339
Coe, William R.		1909.06.16	SLC	CT.Redding	I was glad	CtHMTH	08421
Coe, William R.		1909.06.27	SLC	CT.Redding	Well, then, good-bye	CtHMTH	08428
Coggins, Paschal H.		1901.02.16	SLC	NY.New York	But I thank	CU-BANC	06000 typed
Colborne, John		1873.12.16	SLC per CWS	EN.London	I thank you	TxU	01008

ADDRESSEE	DATE	WRITER	PLACE	CUE	SOURCE	NUMBER/NOTES
Colcord, M.B.	1909.05.18	SLC	CT.Redding	You see, all	DFo	08397
Cole, Cornelius	1898.05.17	SLC & OLC	AU.Vienna	Yes, we know	CLU-S/C	05390
Cole, Cornelius	1898.05.18	OLC	AU.Vienna	I venture to	CLU-S/C	05391
Cole, George R.	1898.03.30	CC	AU.Vienna	Many thanks to	CLU-S/C	05360
Cole, George R.	1898.04.02	CC	AU.Vienna	I am sorry	CLU-S/C	05356
Cole, George R.	1898.04.07	CC	AU.Vienna	Dr. Freeland is	CLU-S/C	05347
Cole, George R.	1898.04.08	CC	AU.Vienna	I have just	CLU-S/C	05359
Cole, George R.	1898.04.12	CC	AU.Vienna	Will you come	CLU-S/C	05358
Cole, George R.	1898.04.14	CC	AU.Vienna	How stupid of	CLU-S/C	05357
Cole, George R.	pm 1898.05.11	CC	AU.Vienna	*	CLU-S/C	10943 envelope only
Cole, Mr.	1907.**.**	SLC	NY.New York	I feel sure	CU-MARK(tr)	07613 probably spurious
Coleman, Mrs.	****.**.**	SLC	Unknown	In bed, 9	157:1925.05.04	09870
Colfax, Schuyler	1869.10.09	SLC	NY.Elmira	I write now	MH-H	00362
Colfax, Schuyler	bet 1869.12.10 & 1869.12.11	SLC	NY.New York	Away at this	NSyU	00384
Collier, Robert & Bok, Edward W.	1903.07.21	SLC	NY.Elmira	Although I have	NN-B	11122 also to others
Collier, Robert	1908.01.**	SLC	Unknown	Will mama go	CU-MARK	07904 telegram
Collier, Robert	1909.04.24	SLC	CT.Redding	If in my	215	08388
Collier, Sarah S.	1906.02.21	SLC	NY.New York	Do you know	NN-B(tr)	07352
Collier's Weekly	1908.07.06	SLC	CT.Redding	Hon. Collier Weekly	CtY	08053
Collin, C.A.	ca 1883.07.01	SLC	NY.Elmira	1. Is it the	CU-MARK	06025
Collins, A. Chalkley	o/a 1904.07.19	SLC per IVL	MA.Lee	Mr. Clemens directs	CU-MARK(dr)	06889 on Collins July 19
Collins, Patrick A.	1897.01.26	SLC	EN.London	If there is	MChB	06209
Colt, Mrs.	1895.02.15	SLC	FR.Paris	It is not	CtHMTH	04844
Colt's Patent Fire-Arms	1872.07.12	SLC	CT.New Saybrook	A friend of	Ct	00768

Colwell, M. Worth	o/a	1905.06.26	SLC per IVL	NH.Dublin	refer to Miss	CU-MARK(dr)	07070 on Colwell June 26
Committee Salt Lake		1882.**.**	SLC	Unknown	The trade marks	125:161	00225 spurious
Cone, Robert B.		1901.12.20	SLC	NY.Riverdale	with the compliments	ViU	11094 inscription
Conley, Rose		****.**.**	SLC	Unknown	For Rose Conley	CU-MARK(ph)	10558 inscription
Connecticut Magazine		1902.12.11	SLC per IVL	NY.Riverdale	It is a	CU-MARK	06510
Conrad, Louise		1873.03.**	SLC	CT.Hartford	Recipe for making	CU-MARK	00878
Continental Hotel		1896.02.18	SLC	II.Calcutta	I am glad	CU-MARK(ph)	05024
Conway, Ellen D.		1873.06.25	SLC	EN.London	Pardon my dilatoriness	107:1925.04.16	00932 other sources
Conway, Ellen D.		1876.10.28	SLC	CT.Hartford	Just as we	NNC	01383
Conway, Ellen D.		1887.12.05	SLC	CT.Hartford	I couldn't, or	NNC	03674
Conway, Eustace		1876.08.14	SLC	NY.Elmira	I am very	CU-MARK(ph)	01358
Conway, Moncure D.		1872.09.22	SLC	EN.London	I have worried	NNC	00811
Conway, Moncure D.		1872.10.06	SLC	EN.London	It is with	NNC	00821
Conway, Moncure D.		1873.07.01	SLC	EN.London	It is too	NNC	00940
Conway, Moncure D.		1873.07.04	SLC	EN.London	Good--I have	ICN	00943
Conway, Moncure D.		1875.10.18	SLC	CT.Hartford	I don't know	NNC	01270
Conway, Moncure D.		1875.12.16	SLC	CT.Hartford	Good! Give us	CU-MARK(ph)	01287
Conway, Moncure D.		1876.01.01	SLC	CT.Hartford	Who will kindly	105:1941.01.22	09659 inscription; other sources
Conway, Moncure D.	pm	1876.01.05	SLC	CT.Hartford	All right. I've	105:1938.11.03	01295 other sources
Conway, Moncure D.		1876.02.26	SLC	CT.Hartford	Good! & many	NNC	01310
Conway, Moncure D.		1876.03.25	SLC	CT.Hartford	Got your telegram	NNC	01317
Conway, Moncure D.		1876.04.09	SLC	CT.Hartford	Got your letter	NNC	01320
Conway, Moncure D.		1876.04.16	SLC	CT.Hartford	Just as I	NNC	01323
Conway, Moncure D.		1876.05.05	SLC	CT.Hartford	Bliss says he	NNC	01332

ADDRESSEE	DATE	WRITER	PLACE	CUE	SOURCE	NUMBER/NOTES
Conway, Moncure D.	1876.05.27	SLC	CT.Hartford	I enclose postal	NNC	01336 fragment
Conway, Moncure D.	1876.07.04	SLC	NY.Elmira	I fear that	NNC	01347
Conway, Moncure D.	1876.07.24	SLC	NY.Elmira	My English copy	NNC	01351
Conway, Moncure D.	1876.08.01	SLC	NY.Elmira	Your last just	CU-MARK(ph)	01354
Conway, Moncure D.	1876.11.02	SLC	CT.Hartford	Belford Bros., Canadian	NNC	01386
Conway, Moncure D.	1876.12.13	SLC per FCH	CT.Hartford	It's a mistake	NNC	01394
Conway, Moncure D.	1876.12.29	SLC per FCH	CT.Hartford	Hart and I	NNC	01397 fragment
Conway, Moncure D.	ca 1877.01.01	SLC per FCH	CT.Hartford	the 3.10 for	NNC	01396 fragment
Conway, Moncure D.	1877.01.10	SLC per FCH	CT.Hartford	You did not	NNC	01400
Conway, Moncure D.	1877.08.06	SLC	NY.Elmira	I think, but	NNC	01466
Conway, Moncure D.	1877.11.08	SLC per FCH	CT.Hartford	In a letter	CU-MARK(tr)	01503
Conway, Moncure D.	1877.12.21	SLC	CT.Hartford	I've a letter	NNC	01515
Conway, Moncure D.	1878.01.21	SLC	CT.Hartford	All right. I	NNC	01525
Conway, Moncure D.	1878.04.11	SLC	NY.New York	I have a	CU-MARK	01555
Conway, Moncure D.	1878.06.02	SLC	GE.Heidelberg	In a thoughtless	NNC	01566
Conway, Moncure D.	1880.01.19	SLC	NY.Elmira	Yours & Harrisons's	NNC	01754
Conway, Moncure D.	1880.03.31	SLC	CT.Hartford	O, here's trouble	NNC	01778
Conway, Moncure D.	1880.04.20 to 1880.04.21	SLC	CT.Hartford	I started to I sent down	NNC NN-B	01787 Apr 20 to Chatto & Windus enc
Conway, Moncure D.	1880.05.01	SLC	CT.Hartford	I'm going to	NNC	01797
Conway, Moncure D.	1880.05.20	SLC	CT.Hartford	O, dear me	NNC	01808
Conway, Moncure D.	1880.08.17	SLC	NY.Elmira	Greeting & welcome	NNC	01824
Conway, Moncure D.	1880.10.08	SLC	CT.Hartford	Here we are	NNC	01838
Conway, Moncure D.	1881.01.03	SLC	CT.Hartford	Your head is	NNC	01887
Conway, Moncure D.	1882.02.05	SLC	CT.Hartford	Only a mere	NvU	02157
Conway, Moncure D.	1886.04.21	SLC	CT.Hartford	Thanks, a thousand	Mo2	02428

Conway, Moncure D.		1886.07.12	SLC	NY.Elmira	We are full	157:1910.11.28	09681
Conway, Moncure D.		1901.03.10	SLC	NY.New York	I have lost	NNC	06017
Conway, Moncure D.	ca	1904.06.21	SLC	IT.Florence	For what you	NNC	06845 form letter
Conway, Moncure D.	o/a	1905.12.06	SLC	NY.New York	To you, &	NNC	07234 form letter
Cook, Channing H.		1900.10.31	SLC	NY.New York	I discover no	ViU(tr)	10948 SLC tr
Cook, Channing H.		1900.11.19	SLC	NJ.Princeton	I have been	CU-MARK(ph)	09774
Cook, Channing H.		1901.02.04	SLC	NY.New York	Please send several	ViU	05988
Cook, Channing H.		1901.05.23	SLC	NY.New York	You were quite	CU-MARK(ph)	06062
Cooke, Addie M.	o/a	1890.03.31	SLC per FGW	CT.Hartford	Mr. C. would	CU-MARK(dr)	09084 on Cooke Mar 30
Cooke, John E.	o/b	1881.08.19	SLC	NY.Elmira	of some Betsy	DLC	02010 fragment
Cooke, Josephine S.		****.**.**	SLC	NY.Elmira	The author begs	229	10384 inscription
Cooke, Rose T.		1880.12.17	SLC	CT.Hartford	Good--I shall	CtHi	01875
Copeland, George		1906.09.07	SLC	NH.Dublin	It is one's	116:1942.09.24	09978 inscription
Corcoran, Mr.		****.**.**	SLC	DC.Washington	Pretty lonesome. Can't	NN-B	04564
Corelli, Marie		1907.06.24	SLC per RWA	EN.London	Mark Twain thanks	CU-MARK(dr)	07768
Corey, Susan		1889.12.25	SLC	CT.Hartford	With the compliments	CCamarSJ	10640 inscription
Cosgrave, Mrs. A.P.		1885.04.11	SLC	CT.Hartford	I thank you	ViU	03213
Cove, Robert B.		1901.12.20	SLC	NY.Riverdale	with the compliments	105:1938.03.03	09647 inscription
Covert, Nellie	o/a	1905.11.11	SLC per IVL	NY.New York	I knew of	CU-MARK(dr)	07203 on Covert Nov 11
Cowan, James		1879.12.09	SLC	CT.Hartford	I should be	TxU	01735 date uncertain
Cowan, John P.		1905.11.29	SLC	NY.New York	Health to you	Mo2(tr)	02574
Cowley, R.		1873.06.25	SLC	EN.London	I thank you	CU-MARK(tr)	00931

ADDRESSEE	DATE	WRITER	PLACE	CUE	SOURCE	NUMBER/NOTES
Cowley, R.	1873.06.25	SLC	EN.London	You are under	CU-MARK(tr)	00933
Cox, Frances A.	1883.04.06	SLC	CT.Hartford	If you will	CU-MARK(ph)	02367
Cox, Helen M.	1882.12.02	SLC	CT.Hartford	I have dictated	CU-MARK(ph)	02312
Cox, Mathew B.	1868.07.11	SLC	SH.Montana	How are you	CaNBFUA	02741
Cox, Mathew B.	1869.09.24	SLC	NY.Buffalo	who are bound	WU(tr)	10990
Cox, Samuel S.	1871.03.09	SLC	NY.Buffalo	Thanks for Knott's	Mo2	11006
Cox, Samuel S.	1874.02.04	SLC	CT.Hartford	Thanks for the	NN5	01046
Cox, Samuel S.	1875.02.08	SLC	CT.Hartford	If you want Petition	NN5 CU-MARK	01190 CU-MARK enc
Cox, Samuel S.	1887.07.09	SLC	NY.Elmira	If I had	NN5	03598
Crandall, M.H.	o/a 1905.07.31	SLC per IVL	NH.Dublin	Mr. Clemens directs	CU-MARK(dr)	07093 on Crandall July 31
Crane, C.D.	1887.01.20	SLC	CT.Hartford	I am just	CU-MARK(ph)	03516
Crane, C.D.	1887.01.24	SLC	CT.Hartford	Please leave out	305:1911.12.15	03374 other sources
Crane, Henry M.	1868.09.03	SLC	NY.Elmira	Your favor of	WU	02749
Crane, Henry M.	1868.10.07	SLC	CT.Hartford	If I have	ODa2	02740
Crane, Henry M.	1869.08.21	SLC	NY.Buffalo	I did hope	ViU	00338
Crane, Henry M.	1869.09.03	SLC	NY.Buffalo	I would do	Mo2	00345
Crane, Henry M.	1869.09.08	SLC	NY.Buffalo	I have already	ViU	00352
Crane, Henry M.	1869.09.21	SLC	NY.Buffalo	Now you have	ViU	00353
Crane, Susan L.	****.**.**	SLC	CT.Hartford	O dear, Sue	CU-MARK	08725
Crane, Susan L.	****.**.**	SLC & OLC	CT.Hartford	We are having	CU-MARK	08726
Crane, Susan L.	1869.03.09 & 1869.03.31	SLC	CT.Hartford & NY.Elmira	You must let	CU-MARK	00273
Crane, Susan L.	1870.02.12	OLC	NY.Buffalo	Who shall I	CtHMTH	02797 also to Jervis & Mrs. Jervis Langdon
Crane, Susan L.	aft 1870.02.25	SLC	NY.Buffalo	Sue, we are	153:409	00434
Crane, Susan L.	1870.04.16	SLC & OLC	NY.Buffalo	It seems as	CtHMTH	00454

Crane, Susan L.	ca	1870.11.18	SLC	NY.Buffalo	Two Views of	CU-MARK	08621 drawing & inscript.on
Crane, Susan L.		1871.03.12	SLC	NY.Buffalo	Clara is splendid	CU-MARK	00588
Crane, Susan L.		1871.03.14	SLC	NY.Buffalo	I hold Livy	CU-MARK	00589
Crane, Susan L.	ca	1872.11.02	SLC	EN.London	If you and	153:470	00826
Crane, Susan L.	ca	1873.01.**	OLC	CT.Hartford	Mr. Clemens seems	153:480	09500
Crane, Susan L.		1873.05.31	OLC	EN.London	Oh how I	CtHMTH	00921
Crane, Susan L.		1873.08.24	OLC	SK.Edinburgh	We leave Edinburgh	153:488	10595
Crane, Susan L.	aft	1873.10.06	OLC	EN.London	I enclose you	CU-MARK	00967 Brown Oct 6 enc
Crane, Susan L. & Crane, Theodore W.	ca	1874.09.24	SLC & OLC	CT.Hartford	We are perfectly	153:520	01262 also to Mrs. Jervis Langdon
Crane, Susan L. & Crane, Theodore W.		1874.11.**	SLC	CT.Hartford	Twichell came up	153:526	01283 to Cranes and/or Langdon
Crane, Susan L. & Crane, Theodore W.		1875.12.25	OLC	CT.Hartford	To The Cranes	166:19	09290 inscription
Crane, Susan L.		1877.04.23	SLC	CT.Hartford	On the 10th	CU-MARK	01415
Crane, Susan L.	o/a	1878.06.25	OLC	GE.Heidelberg	Sue dear, when	CU-MARK	09195 on Dahtweiner to OLC June 25
Crane, Susan L.	bet &	1878.11.18 1879.02.22	SLC & OLC	GE.Munich	six Germans in	CU-MARK	01609 fragment
Crane, Susan L.		1887.09.24	SLC	CT.Hartford	Sue you are	CU-MARK	03652
Crane, Susan L.		1888.03.12	SLC	CT.Hartford	Susie dear, Livy	CU-MARK	10315 misdated, see Apr
Crane, Susan L.		1888.04.12	SLC	CT.Hartford	Susie dear, Livy	CU-MARK	03708 misdated Mar
Crane, Susan L.		1888.04.28	SLC	CT.Hartford	Dear Aunt Sue	CtHMTH	03719
Crane, Susan L.	ca	1889.03.01	SLC	Unknown	Oh, come along	CU-MARK	03856
Crane, Susan L.		1889.04.15	SLC	CT.Hartford	Susie dear, I sent	CU-MARK	03884

ADDRESSEE	DATE	WRITER	PLACE	CUE	SOURCE	NUMBER/NOTES
Crane, Susan L.	1889.05.28	SLC	CT.Hartford	Susie dear, I	114:509	03896
Crane, Susan L.	1889.10.17	SLC	CT.Hartford	Put these in	CU-MARK	03953 mislabeled Elmira
Crane, Susan L.	1889.10.21	SLC	CT.Hartford	You dear Sue	CU-MARK	03954
Crane, Susan L.	1889.11.22	SLC	CT.Hartford	Susie dear, I never	CU-MARK	03974
Crane, Susan L.	1890.02.16	SLC	NY.New York	Susie dear, Livy	CU-MARK	04018
Crane, Susan L.	1890.12.08	SLC	CT.Hartford	Susie dear, Livy	CU-MARK	04118
Crane, Susan L.	1892.09.18	SLC	SW.Lucerne	Imagine how I	CU-MARK	02123
Crane, Susan L.	1892.09.30	SLC	IT.Florence	Dear Sue, Livy	CU-MARK	04662
Crane, Susan L.	1892.10.22	SLC & OLC	IT.Florence	We are getting	CU-MARK	02459
Crane, Susan L.	1893.03.19	SLC	IT.Florence	Susy dear, this	CtHMTH	04353
Crane, Susan L.	1893.04.07	SLC	NY.New York	Susy dear, I'm	CU-MARK	04366
Crane, Susan L.	1893.04.23	SLC	IL.Chicago	Susy dear, I could	CU-MARK	04381
Crane, Susan L.	1893.06.11	OLC	IT.Florence	I suppose this	CU-MARK	04414
Crane, Susan L.	1893.06.20	SLC	AU.Trent	Dear aunt Sue	CU-MARK	04418
Crane, Susan L.	1893.07.09	SLC	GE.Munich	The next time	CU-MARK	04423
Crane, Susan L.	1893.08.20	SLC	AU.Krankenheil	Sue, dear, we	CU-MARK	04438
Crane, Susan L.	1893.12.04	SLC	NY.New York	I can't deny	CU-MARK	04519
Crane, Susan L.	1894.06.25	SLC	FR.La Bourboule	Sue, dear, this	CU-MARK	04743
Crane, Susan L.	1895.09.05	OLC	SH.Warrimoo	This afternoon about	CU-MARK(tr)	04958
Crane, Susan L.	1895.11.03	OLC	SH.Mararva	People are good	ViU(tr)	04970
Crane, Susan L.	1895.11.24	OLC	NZ.Auckland	Just think--in	ViU(tr)	04976
Crane, Susan L.	1895.12.20 to 1895.12.26	OLC	AS.Sydney & AS.Melbourne	it is just	ViU(tr)	04983
Crane, Susan L.	1896.01.17 to 1896.01.24	OLC	SH.Oceana & II.Bombay	To-morrow about two	ViU(tr)	05012
Crane, Susan L.	1896.02.28	OLC	II.Agra	More than a	ViU(tr)	05025
Crane, Susan L.	1896.03.30	OLC	SH.Wardha	During the past	ViU(tr)	05034
Crane, Susan L.	1896.05.21	OLC	AF.Durban	The pine apples	ViU(tr)	05051
Crane, Susan L.	1896.06.03	OLC	AF.Durban	We sail for	ViU(tr)	05063

Crane, Susan L.	1896.06.16	OLC	AF.Port Eliz.	Your letter of	ViU(tr)	05074
Crane, Susan L.	1896.06.21	OLC	AF.Port Eliz.	Our plans seem	ViU(tr)	05079
Crane, Susan L.	1896.09.30	SLC	EN.London	Oh, oh, oh	CU-MARK	05121
Crane, Susan L.	1898.07.06	JC	AU.Kaltenleut.	the marked cottage	CU-MARK	05409
Crane, Susan L.	1899.12.22	SLC	EN.London	Susie, dear, Livy	CU-MARK	05723
Crane, Susan L.	1900.02.08	SLC	EN.London	The small pamphlet	CU-MARK	05758
Crane, Susan L.	1901.06.14	SLC	NY.New York	Susie dear, I don't	CU-MARK	06072
Crane, Susan L.	1901.08.29	SLC	NY.Saranac Lake	You have a	CU-MARK	06127
Crane, Susan L.	1901.10.**	SLC	NY.Riverdale	Stolen from Mrs.	CtHMTH	09366 inscription
Crane, Susan L.	1902.08.15	SLC	ME.York Harbor	Susie dear, Livy	CU-MARK	06407
Crane, Susan L.	1902.10.19	SLC	NY.Riverdale	I was immensely	CU-MARK	06469
Crane, Susan L.	1902.12.26	SLC	NY.Riverdale	Susie dear, I thank	CU-MARK	06529
Crane, Susan L.	1902.12.29	SLC	NY.Riverdale	Susie dear, two	CU-MARK	06533
Crane, Susan L.	1903.03.12	SLC	NY.Riverdale	Livy has just	CU-MARK	06597
Crane, Susan L.	1903.04.20	SLC	NY.Riverdale	I haven't seen	CU-MARK	06625
Crane, Susan L.	1903.05.05	SLC	NY.Riverdale	God is very	CU-MARK	06645
Crane, Susan L.	1903.06.25	SLC	NY.Riverdale	We are in	CU-MARK	06682
Crane, Susan L.	1904.02.15	SLC	IT.Florence	Susy dear, I have	CU-MARK	06795
Crane, Susan L.	1904.02.17	SLC	IT.Florence	Just a line	CU-MARK	06796
Crane, Susan L.	1904.03.08	SLC	IT.Florence	I find for	CU-MARK	06808
Crane, Susan L.	1904.05.20	SLC	IT.Florence	These are dismal	CU-MARK	06838
Crane, Susan L.	1904.06.06	SLC	IT.Florence	I have been	CU-MARK	06858
Crane, Susan L.	1904.07.03	SLC	NY.New York	Susy dear, will you	CU-MARK	06917
Crane, Susan L.	1904.08.22	SLC	MA.Lee	Susy dear, you	CU-MARK	06915
Crane, Susan L.	1904.09.09	SLC	NY.New York	Susy dear, the first	CU-MARK	06919
Crane, Susan L.	1904.10.23	SLC	NY.New York	I have been	CU-MARK	06936
Crane, Susan L.	1904.11.06	SLC	NY.New York	Aunt Sue, dear	CU-MARK	06943
Crane, Susan L.	1904.11.23	SLC	NY.New York	Jean will come	CtY	06955

ADDRESSEE		DATE	WRITER	PLACE	CUE	SOURCE	NUMBER/NOTES
Crane, Susan L.		1905.01.25	SLC	NY.New York	This is the	CU-MARK	06986
Crane, Susan L.	pm	1905.03.13	SLC	NY.New York	Sue dear, leg	CtHMTH	07016
Crane, Susan L.		1905.05.09	SLC	NY.New York	Susy dear, there	CU-MARK	07040
Crane, Susan L.		1905.05.10	SLC	NY.New York	Susy dear, it's over	CU-MARK	07041
Crane, Susan L.		1905.09.24	SLC	NH.Dublin	Susy dear, I have	114:777	07147
Crane, Susan L.		1908.08.12	SLC	CT.Redding	It was a	CU-MARK(tr)	08083
Crane, Theodore W.		****.08.10	SLC	Unknown	shall arrive at	CU-MARK	08724 telegram
Crane, Theodore W.		1870.04.22	SLC	NY.Buffalo	I enclose you	CtHMTH	00458 date uncertain
Crane, Theodore W. & Crane, Susan L.	ca	1874.09.24	SLC & OLC	CT.Hartford	We are perfectly	153:520	01262 also to Mrs. Jervis Langdon
Crane, Theodore W. & Crane, Susan L.		1874.11.**	SLC	CT.Hartford	Twichell came up	153:526	01283 to Cranes and/or Langdon
Crane, Theodore W. & Crane, Susan L.		1875.12.25	OLC	CT.Hartford	To The Cranes	166:19	09290 inscription
Crane, Theodore W.		1879.11.18	SLC	CT.Hartford	In Chicago I	NN-B	02536
Crane, Theodore W.		1887.09.19	SLC	CT.Hartford	Enclosed please find	CU-MARK	03650
Crane, Theodore W.		1888.09.30	SLC	CT.Hartford	The Twichells have	CU-MARK	03777
Crane, Theodore W.		1888.10.05	SLC	CT.Hartford	I am here	CU-MARK	03782
Crawford, John W.	o/a	1908.01.30	SLC per IVL	NY.New York	It is a	CU-MARK(tr)	07928 IVL tr
Creal, Henry W.		1867.05.20	SLC	NY.New York	I have received	WU	02779
Critic ed.		1889.05.08	SLC	CT.Hartford	One dramatic version	CU-MARK	03889 unsent
Crocker, Samuel R.		1872.12.**	SLC	CT.Hartford	The other charge	CtY	00836
Crockett, Samuel R.		1897.09.17	SLC	SW.Weggis	I know Cleg	ViU	05290
Croffert, William A.	ca	1908.02.16	SLC per IVL	NY.New York	You will see	DLC	07939
Crosby, Ernest H.		1902.01.11	SLC	NY.Riverdale	Make it 11	MiEM	06242

Crosby, Oscar T.	o/a	1907.05.22	SLC per IVL	NY.Tuxedo Park	I do not	CU-MARK(dr)	07724 on Crosby May 22
Crumrine, Boyd	o/a	1905.12.16	SLC per IVL	NY.New York	Mr. Clemens thinks	CU-MARK(dr)	07259
Cumming, George		1875.05.15	SLC	CT.Hartford	Your paragraph about	459:1875.05.22	11144
Curry, Abraham & Johnson, J. Neely		1866.11.01	SLC	NV.Virginia City	Been on sick	CU-MARK(tr)	00108 telegram; also to Howland
Curtis, George W.		1882.01.25	SLC	CT.Hartford	With the great	ODa2	09530 inscription
Curtis, Mrs. Jonathan		1897.04.23	OLC	EN.London	I hardly know	NjP	10695
Curts, Robert M.		1907.07.22	SLC	SH.Minnetonka	Truth is the	NhD	07788 inscription
Curzon, George N.		1907.06.19	SLC per RWA	EN.London	Mr. S.L. Clemens begs	CU-MARK(tr)	07749 RWA tr
Cutler, Mrs. W.K.		1864.05.23	SLC	NV.Virginia City	I address a	114:97	00080
Cutler, W.K.		1864.05.28	SLC	NV.Virginia City	To-day I have	CU-BANC	00083
Cutting, Mrs.		1907.09.20	SLC	NY.Tuxedo Park	S.L. Clemens	105:1950.11.27	09671 inscription
Cutting, Robert F.	o/a	1906.03.06	SLC per IVL	NY.New York	At present cannot	CU-MARK(dr)	07367 on Cutting Mar 6
D., U.		1879.11.05	SLC	CT.Hartford	I am sorry	ODa2	01706
Dacrow, Walter E.		1885.12.09	SLC	CT.Hartford	If anything in	CU-MARK(tr)	09069
Daggett, Rollin M.		1878.01.24	SLC	CT.Hartford	I am very	431:1878.02.03	01526
Daggett, Rollin M.		1880.05.01	SLC	CT.Hartford	I want to	CU-MARK	01798
Daggett, Rollin M.		1880.05.24	SLC	CT.Hartford	Here is the	CU-MARK	02811
Daggett, Rollin M.		1886.10.21	SLC	CT.Hartford	Thanks for your	CCamarSJ(tr)	03473
Dakin, Arthur H.		1902.02.05	SLC	NY.Riverdale	I should enjoy	CU-MARK(tr)	08875
Daly, Augustin		****.**.**	SLC	Unknown	Read at least	107:1900.03.19	09540 inscription
Daly, Augustin		1874.08.14	SLC	NY.Elmira	I will hope	MH-H	01116
Daly, Augustin		1874.10.29	SLC	CT.Hartford	Although I am	ViU	01140

ADDRESSEE	DATE	WRITER	PLACE	CUE	SOURCE	NUMBER/NOTES
Daly, Augustin	1876.05.04	SLC	CT.Hartford	One of these	MH-H	01330
Daly, Augustin	1877.08.03	SLC	NY.Elmira	Copy telegram which	DFo	01462
Daly, Augustin	1877.08.15	SLC	NY.New York	I can only	DFo	01471
Daly, Augustin	1884.02.17	SLC	CT.Hartford	I have been	ViU	02918
Daly, Augustin	ca 1884.09.23	SLC	NY.New York	Introducing Mr. Webster	MH-H	03079
Daly, Augustin	1887.03.15	SLC	CT.Hartford	Good. Count me	CU-MARK(ph)	03541
Daly, Augustin	1887.04.27	SLC	CT.Hartford	All right then	DFo	09246 telegram
Daly, Augustin	1888.01.03	SLC	CT.Hartford	Schon gut! I'll	MH-H	03695
Daly, Augustin	1888.04.05	SLC	CT.Hartford	If you will	DFo	03713 telegram
Daly, Augustin	aft 1888.10.01	SLC	NY.New York	I & the	MH-H	03795
Daly, Augustin	1888.10.06	SLC	CT.Hartford	Mrs. Clemens &	DFo	03784 telegram
Daly, Augustin	1888.11.15	SLC	CT.Hartford	Can you do	MH-H	03832
Daly, Augustin	1888.11.30	SLC	CT.Hartford	I have always	MH-H	03839
Daly, Augustin	1888.12.01	SLC	CT.Hartford	Company to arrive	MH-H	03798
Daly, Augustin	1888.12.29	SLC	CT.Hartford	Mrs. Clemens &	MH-H	03811
Daly, Augustin	1889.**.**	CC	CT.Hartford	How can I	DFo	03819
Daly, Augustin	1889.**.**	SLC	CT.Hartford	I am laid	MH-H	03842
Daly, Augustin	1889.**.**	SLC	CT.Hartford	We have to	MH-H	03843
Daly, Augustin	1889.03.13	SLC	CT.Hartford	The tribe is	MH-H	03872
Daly, Augustin	1889.04.05	SLC	CT.Hartford	I & Clara	ViU	03880
Daly, Augustin	1892.02.12	SLC	GE.Berlin	I would have	MH-H	04269
Daly, Augustin	1892.05.17	SLC	IT.Venice	Here is a	MH-H	04291
Daly, Augustin	1892.08.13	SLC	GE.Bad-Nauheim	I have your	CU-MARK(ph)	01728
Damon, Samuel C.	1866.07.19	SLC	HI.Honolulu	I return herewith	234:1866.08.01	00104
Dana, Charles A.	1883.07.19	SLC	NY.Elmira	All right, I'm	NNC	08857
Dana, Charles A.	1884.05.12	SLC	CT.Hartford	I am busy	CU-MARK	02978 per unknown amanuensis

Dana, Charles E.	****.**.**	SLC	Unknown	Work & Play	CU-MARK(tr)	09981 inscription
Darby, Frank B.	****.01.10	SLC	CT.Hartford	Many thanks for	NEIm2	09083
Darby, Frank B.	1887.11.08	SLC	CT.Hartford	Say--please send	NEIm2	09082
Darrall, Gertrude	1897.02.23	SLC	EN.London	These are very	C4	05179
Daulton, George	1903.07.21	SLC	NY.Elmira	I think the	CU-MARK(ph)	06706
Davies & Co.	1877.10.14	SLC	CT.Hartford	I remember having	CtHMTH	01495
Davis, Arthur K.	1909.04.29	SLC	CT.Redding	I am sorry	ViU	08392
Davis, Caleb F.	1882.07.08	SLC	CT.Hartford	I have been	IaK2	02233 typed
Davis, John	1887.04.19	SLC	Unknown	The above was	ViU	03564 on Loisette broadside
Dawes, Anna L.	1889.06.17	SLC	NY.Elmira	I thank you	MAnP	02805
Dawes, Henry L.	1885.09.23	SLC	CT.Hartford	I accept your	MAnP	02613
Dawson, Andrew H.	1880.01.24	SLC	CT.Hartford	I have the	CU-MARK	01755 fragment
Dawson, Minnie T.	1885.01.13	SLC	MO.Hannibal	Truly Yours	MoHM	09334 inscription
Dawson, Minnie T.	1902.05.30	SLC	MO.Hannibal	Truly Yours	MoHM	08880 inscription
Dawson, Minnie T.	1902.06.12	SLC	NY.Riverdale	I thank you	MoHM	06360
Dawson, Minnie T.	1902.12.06	SLC	NY.Riverdale	I thank you	MoHM	06501
Dawson, Samuel E.	1883.05.28	SLC	CN.Montreal	With this I	CaQMM	02391
Dawson, Samuel E.	1883.07.11	SLC	NY.Elmira	What a lucky	CaQMM	02304
Day, Alice H. & Day, Katherine S.	****.**.**	OLC	CT.Hartford	Susy & Clara	CtHSD	11119 for SC & CC
Day, Alice H. & Day, Katherine S.	****.**.**	SC & CC	CT.Hartford	Susy & Clara	CtHSD	10622 per OLC
Day, Alice H.	1866.12.25	OLC	NY.New York	I did not	CtHSD	10545
Day, Alice H.	1867.05.26	OLC	NY.Elmira	I have for	CtHSD	10543
Day, Alice H.	1867.06.07	OLC	NY.Elmira	Comfort em with	CtHSD	10542 fragment
Day, Alice H.	1867.06.17	OLC	NY.Elmira	I did not	CtHSD	00138

ADDRESSEE	DATE	WRITER	PLACE	CUE	SOURCE	NUMBER/NOTES
Day, Alice H.	1867.07.29	OLC	NY.Canandaigua	Your letter to	CtHSD	10541
Day, Alice H.	1867.10.04	OLC	NY.Elmira	I'm week today	CtHSD	00150
Day, Alice H.	1867.10.30	OLC	Unknown	Alice I love	CtHSD	10540
Day, Alice H.	1867.11.28	OLC	NY.Elmira	I rec'd your	CtHSD	00163
Day, Alice H.	1868.02.11	OLC	NY.Elmira	How many times	CtHSD	00193
Day, Alice H.	1868.03.08	OLC	NY.Elmira	Why in the	CtHSD	10539
Day, Alice H.	1868.04.22	OLC	NY.Elmira	I rec'd your	CtHSD	10538
Day, Alice H.	1868.08.08	OLC	NY.Elmira	Alice dear do	CtHSD	10537
Day, Alice H.	1868.09.29	OLC	NY.Elmira	It seems like	CtHSD	02754
Day, Alice H.	1868.11.05	OLC	NY.Elmira	Did you leave	CtHSD	10536
Day, Alice H.	1868.12.16	OLC	NY.Elmira	A year ago	CtHSD	10535
Day, Alice H.	1869.03.03	OLC	NY.Elmira	Do you suppose	CtHSD	00265
Day, Alice H.	1869.05.24	OLC	NY.Elmira	It is too	CtHSD	00308
Day, Alice H.	1869.11.01	OLC	NY.Elmira	Alice dear it	CtHSD	00370
Day, Alice H.	1870.01.14	OLC	NY.Elmira	I am going	CtHSD	00409
Day, Alice H.	1870.03.17	OLC	NY.Buffalo	I am mortified	CtHSD	00444
Day, Alice H.	1870.05.**	OLC	NY.Buffalo	To think that	CtHSD	00474
Day, Alice H.	1870.06.06	OLC	NY.Buffalo	Oh Alice the	CtHSD	00477
Day, Alice H.	1871.01.25	SLC & OLC	NY.Buffalo	You were so	CtHSD	00564
Day, Alice H.	1873.07.25	OLC	SK.Edinburgh	I was very	CtHSD	00776
Day, Alice H. & Day, John C.	1876.09.27	SLC	CT.Hartford	Mr. & Mrs.	CtHSD	01368
Day, Alice H.	1882.08.30	OLC	NY.Elmira	It is a	CtHSD	10530
Day, Alice H.	1884.01.07	OLC	CT.Hartford	Mr & Mrs	CtHSD	10529
Day, Alice H.	ca 1888.12.25	OLC	CT.Hartford	We are all	CtHSD	10603
Day, Alice H.	1890.04.11	OLC	CT.Hartford	We have been	CtHSD	10604
Day, Alice H.	1891.05.28	OLC	CT.Hartford	I have had	CtHSD	04211
Day, Alice H.	1892.03.07	OLC	FR.Menton	Your letter of	CtHSD	10526
Day, Alice H.	ca 1893.02.23	OLC	IT.Florence	I was so	CtHSD	10525

Day, Alice H.	1893.07.08	OLC	GE.Munich	I have not	CtHSD	10524
Day, Alice H.	1893.08.05	OLC	GE.Franzensbad	At last it	CtHSD	10523
Day, Alice H.	1893.08.27	OLC	GE.Franzensbad	Your letter followed	CtHSD	10522
Day, Alice H.	1893.09.09	OLC	GE.Franzensbad	Of course the	CtHSD	10521
Day, Alice H.	1893.10.10	OLC	GE.Hamburg	I am so	CtHSD	04472
Day, Alice H.	1894.02.04	OLC	FR.Paris	Thank you most	CtHSD	10520
Day, Alice H.	1894.04.01	OLC	FR.Paris	It is pleasant	CtHSD	10519
Day, Alice H.	1894.05.23	OLC	FR.Paris	Your welcome letter	CtHSD	10518
Day, Alice H.	1894.07.01	OLC	FR.La Bourboule	The address of	CtHSD	10599
Day, Alice H.	1894.10.07	OLC	FR.Rouen	Welcome back to	CtHSD	10516
Day, Alice H.	1894.10.16	SLC	FR.Rouen	Wish you all	CtHSD	04793 telegram
Day, Alice H.	1895.01.26	OLC	FR.Paris	I do so	CtHSD	10598
Day, Alice H.	1895.02.03	OLC	FR.Paris	Your letter of	CtHSD	10597
Day, Alice H.	1896.04.13	OLC	SH.Wardha	At Colombo I	CtHSD	05040
Day, Alice H.	1896.05.25	OLC	AF.Durban	You may be	CtHSD	10605
Day, Alice H.	1896.06.28	CC	AF.Cradock	This is to	CtHSD	10621
Day, Alice H. & Day, Katherine S.	aft 1896.08.18	CC	EN.London	It seems dreadful	CtHSD	10623
Day, Alice H.	1896.09.11	CC	EN.London	Mamma wants me	CtHSD	05108
Day, Alice H.	1896.10.22	OLC	EN.London	Ever since your	CtHSD	10606
Day, Alice H.	1901.08.18	OLC	NY.New York	I wish you	CtHSD	10607
Day, Edward	1903.03.21	SLC	NY.New York	No, it would	OC	06606
Day, John C. & Day, Alice H.	1876.09.27	SLC	CT.Hartford	Mr. & Mrs.	CtHSD	01368
Day, Katherine S. & Day, Alice H.	****.**.**	OLC	CT.Hartford	Susy & Clara	CtHSD	11119 for SC & CC
Day, Katherine S. & Day, Alice H.	****.**.**	SC & CC	CT.Hartford	Susy & Clara	CtHSD	10622 per OLC
Day, Katherine S.	1894.07.29	CC	SW.Fluelen	I was mighty	CtHSD	04765
Day, Katherine S. & Day, Alice H.	aft 1896.08.18	CC	EN.London	It seems dreadful	CtHSD	10623

ADDRESSEE		DATE	WRITER	PLACE	CUE	SOURCE	NUMBER/NOTES
Day, Katherine S.	pm	1900.12.21	CC	NY.New York	Can you come	CtHSD	10624
Day, Katherine S.	pm	1901.02.25	CC	NY.New York	On Wednesday March	CtHSD	10625
Day, Katherine S.		1901.11.**	CC	NY.Riverdale	Come in a	CtHSD	10626
Day, Katherine S.		1901.11.06	CC	NY.Riverdale	Don't forget the	CtHSD	10627
Day, Katherine S.	pm	1902.09.11	CC	ME.York Harbor	Long ago my	CtHSD	10628
Day, Katherine S.	pm	1903.02.02	CC	NY.Riverdale	Will you and	CtHSD	10629
Day, Katherine S.		1903.06.18	CC	NY.Riverdale	How lovely of	CtHSD	10630
Dayton, Charles W.		1890.03.12	SLC	NY.New York	Letters for "Mark	107:1918.03.13	09547
Dayton, Charles W.		1894.09.01	SLC	FR.Etretat	I am all	Mo2	04784
De Quille, Dan		*	*	*	*	*	10335 see Wright, William
De Winton, Francis		1883.05.28	SLC	CN.Ottawa	How simple &	ViU	11078 inscription
De Winton, Francis		1883.06.04	SLC	CT.Hartford	I very much	CU-MARK	01919
De Winton, Francis		1889.08.06	SLC	NY.Elmira	So it is	CU-MARK	03925
De Winton, Francis		1895.04.26	SLC	FR.Paris	Yesterday I signed	ViU	04872
Deacon, Charles R. & Clover Club		1884.01.03	SLC	CT.Hartford	I have unconsciously	CU-MARK(ph)	09948
Dean, Alletta F.		1902.01.29	SLC	NY.Riverdale	Don't you give	CU-MARK(tr)	06255
Dearborn, Harry W.		1907.05.13	SLC	NY.Tuxedo Park	As I have	CBev2	07718
Dearborn, Harry W.		1907.09.23	SLC	Unknown	Taking the pledge	122:1935.05.08	09254 inscription
Dearborn, Harry W.		1909.09.07	SLC	CT.Redding	My compulsion of	ViU	08448
Dennis, Fannie		1871.02.17	SLC	NY.Buffalo	To write an	CU-MARK(ph)	00578
Denslow, Ann W.		1899.**.**	SLC	Unknown	Father Goose has	207:1899.12.18	09081
Denslow, William W.	pm	1903.10.02	SLC	NY.Elmira	I wish I	Mo2	08886
Denver Post		1902.08.14	SLC	ME.York Harbor	Your telegram reached	317:1902.08.22	06406
Depew, Chauncey M.		1892.08.22	SLC	GE.Bad-Nauheim	I hold myself	DGW	01753
Depew, Chauncey M.	aft	1892.08.25	SLC	GE.Bad-Nauheim	P.S. Well, sir	CU-MARK	01882 enc in Sept 2 to Orion Clemens

Depew, Chauncey M.		1892.08.30	SLC	GE.Bad-Nauheim	I have sent	NN	01878
Depew, Chauncey M.		1899.02.02	SLC	AU.Vienna	Prince Lichnowsky is	NN	05541
Depew, Chauncey M.		1905.11.16	SLC per IVL	NY.New York	Having had some	DGW	07208 typed
Des Voeux, William		1900.04.06	SLC	Unknown	with the warm	ViU	10764 inscription
Deuel, Charles E.		1887.03.14	SLC	CT.Hartford	Won't you kindly	CU-MARK(tr)	03538
Devine, John T.		1901.01.22	SLC	NY.New York	Am very sorry	ViU(tr)	05978
Dickey, John M.		1902.11.19	SLC per IVL	NY.Riverdale	For the admiration	InU-Li	10827
Dickinson, Anna E.		1874.06.28	SLC	NY.Elmira	I've written the	DLC	01104
Dickinson, Anna E.	bet &	1874.07.07 1874.07.17	SLC	NY.Elmira	Make it 600	DLC	01106
Dickinson, Anna E.	ca	1874.08.01	SLC	NY.Elmira	I've written a	CU-MARK	03351 on John Brown July 18
Dickinson, Asa D.		1905.11.21	SLC	NY.New York	I am greatly	463:1935.11f	07215
Dickinson, Asa D.		1906.03.26	SLC per IVL	NY.New York	Be wise as	CU-MARK(tr)	07404 IVL tr; other sources
Dilke, Charles W. & Dilke, Katherine M.	bef	1873.06.09	SLC	EN.London	Mr. Clemens, called	Uk	03718 also to Field
Dilke, Katherine M. & Dilke, Charles W.	bef	1873.06.09	SLC	EN.London	Mr. Clemens, called	Uk	03718 also to Field
Dimmitt, Edward L.		1901.07.19	SLC	NY.Saranac Lake	By an error	114:708	06094
Ditson, Mrs.		1902.02.05	SLC	NY.Riverdale	We invariably feel	ViU	06268 inscription
Ditson, Mrs.		1906.03.05	SLC per IVL	NY.New York	I am glad to have	ODa2	11194
Dix, Eulabee		1908.01.23	SLC	NY.New York	On the whole	IU-R	09381 inscription
Dodd, Lyon & Tinsley		1907.07.30	SLC per RWA	Unknown	Dr. Clemens duly	CU-MARK(tr)	07797 RWA tr
Dodge, Mary M.		1880.11.19	SLC	CT.Hartford	My publisher contends	NN-B	02545
Dodge, Mary M.		1893.10.31	SLC	NY.New York	Land, we'd have	CCamarSJ	04479
Dodge, Mary M.		1894.01.21	SLC	NY.New York	I'm to be in Boston	ODa2	04676

ADDRESSEE	DATE	WRITER	PLACE	CUE	SOURCE	NUMBER/NOTES
Dodge, Mary M. & Clarke, William F.	1895.08.17	SLC	CN.Vancouver	This is to	Mo2	02405 to six editors
Dodge, Mary M.	1896.10.25	OLC	EN.London	How well I	NjBern2	09188
Dodge, Mary M.	1903.12.18	SLC	IT.Florence	Your dear &	ODa2	06770
Dolby, George	1889.12.16	SLC	CT.Hartford	I have written	NN-B	02704
Dole, Mr.	1903.01.10	SLC per IVL	NY.Riverdale	I thank you	CU-MARK(ph)	06553
Dolores	****.**.**	SLC	Unknown	When in doubt	CU-MARK(ph)	10477
Dombrowski	*	*	*	*	*	09514 see Underhill, Charles M.
Donaldson, Thomas	1885.08.06	SLC	NY.Elmira	$10 enclosed.)	NN-B	02620
Doubleday, Frank N.	1903.04.26	SLC per IVL	NY.Riverdale	Mr. Kellogg (was	CU-MARK(tr)	06631
Doubleday, Frank N.	1903.10.12 & 1903.10.13	SLC	NY.New York	The books came	114:746	06739
Doubleday, Frank N.	1904.11.**	SLC	NY.New York	I did not	114:760	06942
Doubleday, Frank N.	1906.05.23	SLC per IVL	NH.Dublin	The Gospel is	NN-B(tr)	07445
Doubleday, Frank N.	1906.05.25	SLC	NH.Dublin	Doubleday, please add	NN-B(tr)	02209
Doubleday, Frank N.	o/a 1906.08.15	SLC per IVL	NH.Dublin	will keep the	CU-MARK(dr)	07500 on Doubleday Aug 15
Doubleday, Neltje	1906.12.25	SLC	NY.New York	This book has	122:1939.05.02	09721 inscription
Douglas, William F.	1887.01.24	SLC	CT.Hartford	It was 1855	264:1929.10	03518
Downing, John B.	o/a 1881.08.18	SLC	NY.Elmira	And has it	114:496	02021
Downing, John B.	1899.02.26	SLC	AU.Vienna	No; it was	114:674	05550
Doyle, Arthur C.	1909.10.29	SLC per ABP	CT.Redding	Mr. Clemens, who	224:73	08478
Drake, Francis S.	1870.12.26	SLC	NY.Buffalo	I have received	NN-B	02790
Drake, John R.	1870.12.26	SLC	NY.Buffalo	I will with	CtY	02789
Drake, Mervyn	1884.10.09	SLC	CT.Hartford	Please to hurl	302:819	03005
Draper, Edith	1907.01.01	SLC	NY.New York	with the best	UkLi2	09208 inscription

Draper, Edith		1907.01.15	SLC	NY.New York	I will comply	UkLi2	07630
Du Cros, Louise	o/a	1904.05.04	OLC per IVL	IT.Florence	Miss Clemens has	CU-MARK(dr)	06828 on Du Cros to OLC May 4
Duff, Cara L.		1895.07.01	OLC	NY.Elmira	If Mr Clemens	NN7	04921
Dulany, Mr.		1902.06.17	SLC	NY.Riverdale	The views are	MoHM	08881
Duncan, William B.		1908.02.11	SLC	NY.New York	I am confined	CU-MARK(tr)	07935 SLC tr
Duneka, Frederick A.		****.**.**	SLC	Unknown	Miss Lyon sent	NN-B	01344
Duneka, Frederick A.		****.04.17	SLC	Unknown	I am still	IC3	01823
Duneka, Frederick A.	aft	1901.06.21	SLC	NY.Saranac Lake	It is my	221:217	09238
Duneka, Frederick A.		1901.09.12	SLC	NY.Saranac Lake	If you won't	NN-B	08218
Duneka, Frederick A.	bet &	1901.10.01 1902.02.22	SLC	NY.Riverdale	And yet again	CU-MARK(ph)	10576
Duneka, Frederick A.	o/a	1901.11.21	SLC	NY.Riverdale	Ever so many	105:1945.02.19	09652 on Harper Nov 21; other sources
Duneka, Frederick A.		1902.01.03	SLC	NY.Riverdale	Please send me	NN-B	08224
Duneka, Frederick A.		1902.01.18	SLC	Unknown	I haven't read	IC3	06248
Duneka, Frederick A.		1902.02.16	SLC	NY.Riverdale	Please send me	IC3	06279
Duneka, Frederick A.		1902.08.22	SLC	ME.York Harbor	I find your	CtRe	06410
Duneka, Frederick A.		1902.09.11	SLC	ME.York Harbor	When do you	NN-B	08228
Duneka, Frederick A.		1902.09.15	SLC	ME.York Harbor	My wife being	NN-B	08229
Duneka, Frederick A.		1902.09.19	SLC	ME.York Harbor	I am glad	IC3	06435
Duneka, Frederick A.		1902.10.06	SLC	ME.York Harbor	Oh, come, now	IC3	06454
Duneka, Frederick A.		1903.02.**	SLC	NY.Riverdale	This is a	ViU	06574
Duneka, Frederick A.		1903.04.26	SLC	NY.Riverdale	It is very	NSyU	06632
Duneka, Frederick A.		1903.04.27	SLC	NY.Riverdale	Yes, the collected	IC3	06634
Duneka, Frederick A.		1903.06.15	SLC	NY.Riverdale	I have just	C4	06678
Duneka, Frederick A.		1903.07.04	SLC	NY.Elmira	I am hatching	CU-MARK(ph)	06691
Duneka, Frederick A.		1903.10.21	SLC	NY.New York	Won't you send	IC3	06748

ADDRESSEE	DATE	WRITER	PLACE	CUE	SOURCE	NUMBER/NOTES
Duneka, Frederick A.	1903.12.30	SLC	IT.Florence	Happy Newyears to	MoSW	06773
Duneka, Frederick A.	1904.01.05	SLC	IT.Florence	I have finished	IC3	06782
Duneka, Frederick A.	1904.01.07	SLC	IT.Florence	Please send a	NN-B	08235
Duneka, Frederick A.	1904.01.08	SLC	IT.Florence	I see by	NN-B	08236
Duneka, Frederick A.	1904.02.08	SLC	IT.Florence	Yes I prefer	CU-MARK(ph)	06791
Duneka, Frederick A.	1904.02.17	SLC	IT.Florence	All right, put	NN-B	08238
Duneka, Frederick A.	1904.03.11	SLC per IVL	IT.Florence	Mr. Clemens has	CU-MARK(tr)	06809
Duneka, Frederick A.	1904.03.14	SLC per IVL	IT.Florence	Mr. Clemens wishes	CU-MARK(tr)	06810
Duneka, Frederick A.	1904.05.27	SLC	IT.Florence	I keep forgetting	IC3	06842
Duneka, Frederick A.	1904.12.03	SLC	NY.New York	It may interest	CU-MARK(ph)	02438
Duneka, Frederick A.	1905.06.16	SLC	NH.Dublin	I think your	CU-MARK	07064
Duneka, Frederick A.	ca 1905.06.24	SLC	NH.Dublin	I hear &	ViU	09660
Duneka, Frederick A.	1905.07.16	SLC	NH.Dublin	I wrote Eve's	NN-B	08240
Duneka, Frederick A.	1905.07.20	SLC	NH.Dublin	Good. Adam's Diary	NN-B	08241
Duneka, Frederick A.	1905.08.06	SLC per IVL	NH.Dublin	Mr. Clemens directs	CU-MARK(dr)	07102
Duneka, Frederick A.	1905.08.09	SLC per IVL	NH.Dublin	Mr. Clemens directs	CU-MARK(dr)	07105
Duneka, Frederick A.	1905.09.16	SLC	NH.Dublin	What's the new	IC3	07137
Duneka, Frederick A.	o/a 1905.09.19	SLC per IVL	NH.Dublin	Mr. Clemens will	CU-MARK(dr)	07140 on Duneka Sept 19
Duneka, Frederick A.	o/a 1905.09.26	SLC per IVL	NH.Dublin	Mr. Clemens only	CU-MARK(dr)	07148 on Duneka Sept 26
Duneka, Frederick A.	1905.09.30	SLC	NH.Dublin	I have written	CU-MARK(tr)	07155
Duneka, Frederick A.	1905.10.02	SLC	NH.Dublin	I have just	NN-B	08244
Duneka, Frederick A.	1905.10.09	SLC	NH.Dublin	As to the	114:781	07165 other sources
Duneka, Frederick A.	1905.10.09	SLC	NH.Dublin	Somebody came to	NNC	07170
Duneka, Frederick A.	1906.**.**	SLC	Unknown	It may interest	120:1934.06	09908 other sources

Duneka, Frederick A.	o/a 1906.02.17	SLC per IVL	NY.New York	Still of same	CU-MARK(dr)	07347 on Duneka Feb 17
Duneka, Frederick A.	1906.03.20	SLC	NY.New York	We all think	NN-B(tr)	08253
Duneka, Frederick A.	1906.06.04	SLC per IVL	NH.Dublin	I find that	NN7(tr)	07448
Duneka, Frederick A.	1906.10.31	SLC	MA.Boston	I was interrupted	NN-B	08270
Duneka, Frederick A.	1907.04.30	SLC	SH.Kanawha	Please send a	IC3	07699
Duneka, Frederick A.	o/a 1907.07.23	SLC per IVL	NY.Tuxedo Park	Not a newspaper	CU-MARK(dr)	07793 on Duneka July 23
Duneka, Frederick A.	1907.10.03 or 1907.10.10	SLC	NY.Tuxedo Park	Proofs sent to	NN-B	08276
Duneka, Frederick A.	1908.05.06	SLC per IVL	NY.New York	Mr. Clemens asks	CU-MARK(dr)	08007
Duneka, Frederick A.	1908.06.03	SLC	NY.New York	Ostler & I	NN-B	08015
Duneka, Frederick A.	1908.06.18	SLC	CT.Redding	I was just	NN-B	08282
Duneka, Frederick A.	o/a 1908.10.07	SLC	CT.Redding	Greeting and Salutation	205:1933.01.25	09778 form letter
Duneka, Frederick A.	1908.12.30	SLC	CT.Redding	I am perfectly	NN-B	08290
Duneka, Frederick A.	1909.04.12	SLC	CT.Redding	Page 31 of	IC3	08382
Duneka, Frederick A.	1909.06.30	SLC	CT.Redding	Why, they are	MoSW	08430
Duneka, Frederick A.	1909.10.27	SLC	CT.Redding	Bridal-token for	NNC	08476
Duneka, Frederick A.	1910.01.07	SLC	BE.Hamilton	Please get for	CAlb2	08536
Dunham, Laura	1883.06.**	SLC	CT.Hartford	from hers sincerely	105:1957.04.30	09461 inscription
Dunham, Laura	1889.12.19	OLC	CT.Hartford	I was delighted	CtHSD	03990
Dunham, Mr.	****.**.**	SLC	Unknown	Mrs. Clemens has	CtHSD	07643
Dunham, Mr.	1885.10.26	SLC	CT.Hartford	This is to	NjP	03296
Dunlap, O.E.	1888.06.19	SLC	CT.Hartford	I always hear of these	ODa2	11206
Dunne, Finley P.	1907.01.14	SLC per IVL	NY.New York	The bearer, Mr.	DLC	07627
Dunne, Finley P.	1909.11.30	JC	CT.Redding	Being secretary, since	CU-MARK(tr)	08502

ADDRESSEE	DATE	WRITER	PLACE	CUE	SOURCE	NUMBER/NOTES
Dunne, Peter F. & Howells, William D.	1907.02.06	SLC	NY.New York	The Human Race	Mo2	07644 also to Harvey
Duryee, George V.	1901.06.14	SLC	NY.New York	To my astonishment	187:58	09237 other sources
Duryee, George V. & Duryee, Mrs. George	1901.09.19	SLC	NY.Saranac Lake	Hail and farewell	187:58	09239
Duryee, Mrs. George & Duryee, George V.	1901.09.19	SLC	NY.Saranac Lake	Hail and farewell	187:58	09239
Dutcher, William	1907.03.21	JC	NY.Katonah	Please pardon my	NN	10745
Dutcher, William	1907.10.06	JC	NY.Katonah	I thought there	NN	10746
Dutcher, William	1907.10.16	JC	NY.Katonah	Thank you very	NN	07854
Dutcher, William	1908.05.18	JC	CT.Greenwich	I am very	NN	10747
Dutcher, William	1909.02.15	JC	NY.Babylon	I have just	NN	08348
Earnest, Frank B.	1879.12.18	SLC	CT.Hartford	I thank you	131:1880.01.02	01741 other sources
Eastwood, C. & Eastwood, Mrs. C.	1900.09.26	SLC	EN.London	with compliments of	260:1958.07.15	09270 inscription
Eastwood, Mrs. C. & Eastwood, C.	1900.09.26	SLC	EN.London	with compliments of	260:1958.07.15	09270 inscription
Eaton, C. Harry	1890.02.09	SLC per FGW	CT.Hartford	I have to	NEImC	08935
Eaton, Seymour	1905.03.28	SLC	NY.New York	May I ask	CU-MARK	07022
Eaton, Seymour	1906.01.08	SLC	NY.New York	I have rec'd	CU-MARK(tr)	07299
Eden, Robert	1878.09.**	SLC	Unknown	with the kindest	122:1936.01.29	09278 inscription
Edgar, William C.	1894.05.08	SLC	NY.New York	I have in	MnM	04732
Edmonds, J.E.	1907.09.27	SLC	NY.Tuxedo Park	I am often	418:1974.02.27	10377
Edwardes, H.S.	1897.05.22	SLC	EN.London	In the circumstances	297:106	05214
Edwards, A.M.	1880.12.08	SLC	CT.Hartford	I am very	CLU-S/C	01868
Edwards, Henry	1886.01.02	SLC	CT.Hartford	but--O hang	282:1901.11.21	09750
Edwards, Henry	1886.01.20	SLC	CT.Hartford	But dear me	MH-H	03359
Edwards, Henry	1886.04.09	SLC	CT.Hartford	But alas, I	157:1922.11.23	09751 other sources
Edwards, Henry	1887.02.23	SLC	CT.Hartford	I am downright	OMC	03531

Edwards, Henry		1888.02.23	SLC	CT.Hartford	When I say	IaMc	03705
Elder Manufacturing Co. & Miller & Bingham		1883.10.08	SLC	CT.Hartford	No, I am	CU-MARK(ph)	02849
Elder, Samuel J.		1905.06.21	SLC per IVL	NH.Dublin	I have read	ODa2	07067
Elderkin, John		1893.10.27	SLC	CT.Hartford	I am here	CU-MARK	04478
Elderkin, John		1893.12.06	SLC	NY.New York	I would dearly	ODa2	09955
Elderkin, John		1895.04.25	SLC	Unknown	I have been	317:1895.04.25	04871
Elliott & Fry		1897.05.22	SLC	EN.London	The one which	CU-MARK(tr)	05129 SLC tr
Elliott, Francis P.		1904.03.02	SLC per IVL	IT.Florence	Mr. Clemens directs	CU-MARK(dr)	06805
Ellis, D.B.		1889.**.**	SLC	Unknown	I should not	401:1889.08.23	04550
Ellsworth, William W.		****.**.**	SLC	Unknown	A fund? Raise	122:1936.12.09	03002
Ellsworth, William W.		1893.01.13	SLC	IT.Florence	It is the	230:223f	04325
Ellsworth, William W.	ca	1900.11.**	SLC	NY.New York	If you need	230:244	09345
Ellsworth, William W.		1900.11.02	SLC	NY.New York	All right--make	ViU	05894
Ellsworth, William W.		1901.10.15	SLC	NY.Riverdale	The project fascinated	ViU	06157
Ellsworth, William W.	o/a	1907.09.04	SLC per IVL	NY.Tuxedo Park	Looks as if	CU-MARK(dr)	07829 on Ellsworth Sept 4
Ely, Mary D.		****.**.**	SLC	Unknown	Yes, Tuesday evening	MiU-H	03136
Ely, Mary D.		****.02.20	SLC	Unknown	Enclosed I send	CAlb2	03105
Emerson, Ralph W. & Longfellow, Henry W.		1877.12.27	SLC	CT.Hartford	I come before	MH-H	01519 also to Oliver W. Holmes
Emma		****.**.**	SLC	NY.New York	I am very	ViU	04133
Enders, Harriet W.		1907.12.01	CC	NY.New York	It was sweet	CtHMTH	07875
Enders, Harriet W.	o/a	1908.10.07	SLC	CT.Redding	Greeting and Salutation	CtHMTH	11004 form letter
Enders, Harriet W.		1908.12.25	SLC	CT.Redding	It was lovely	CtHMTH	08188
Enders, Harriet W.		1909.02.16	IVL	CT.Redding	This to you	CtHMTH	10971
Enders, Harriet W.	bef	1909.10.06	SLC	Unknown	Mr. Samuel Clemens	CtHMTH	10591 form letter

ADDRESSEE	DATE	WRITER	PLACE	CUE	SOURCE	NUMBER/NOTES
Essais, Mr.	1867.09.24	SLC	SY.Jerusalem	Fix up the	CU-MARK	00149
Estes & Lauriat	1885.01.07	SLC	IN.Indianapolis	Your favor of	ViU	03103
Estes, Dana	1887.12.24	SLC	CT.Hartford	Both as author	410:9	03683
Etting, Frank M.	1876.02.23	SLC	CT.Hartford	I accept with	PHi	01309
Etting, Frank M.	1876.06.08	SLC	CT.Hartford	I have sketched	160:2.1.21	01339 other sources
Eustace, Jennie A.	1908.06.**	SLC	NY.New York	I wish to	131:1908.06.09	08019
Evans, Edward P.	****.**.**	SLC	Unknown	Mrs. Evans's kind	MiU	09112
Evans, Elizabeth	1900.12.18	SLC	NY.New York	It is a	ViU	05935
Ewing, Jeannie	pm 1889.04.10	SLC	CT.Hartford	*	CU-MARK(tr)	10302 envelope only
Ewing, John	****.**.**	SLC	Unknown	with kind regards	116:1980.05.15	09294 inscription
Eyre, Charles C.	1892.08.23	SLC	GE.Bad-Nauheim	My particular friend	NjP	01585 enc in Aug 23 to Hutton
Fagan, C.E.	1900.06.17	SLC	EN.London	I would gladly	CLU-S/C	05823
Fairbanks, Abel W.	1868.10.05	SLC	CT.Hartford	When I was	CSmH	02756
Fairbanks, Abel W. & Fairbanks, Mary M.	1869.08.14	SLC	NY.Buffalo	Before either your	CSmH	00332
Fairbanks, Charles M.	****.**.**	SLC	Unknown	With kindest regards	107:1914.04.02	09541 inscription
Fairbanks, Charles M.	1890.06.25	SLC	CT.Hartford	I skipped &	CSmH	04056
Fairbanks, Charles M. & Fairbanks, Mary P.	1899.07.31	SLC & OLC	SE.Sanna	The tidings that	298:279	05660 other sources
Fairbanks, Charles M. & Fairbanks, Pauline M.	1907.07.26	SLC per IVL	NY.Tuxedo Park	Mr. Clemens is	CtHMTH	05950
Fairbanks, Charles M.	1908.08.02	SLC	CT.Redding	Will you please	CtHMTH	05736
Fairbanks, Mary M.	1867.12.02	SLC	DC.Washington	It all came	ViU	00166
Fairbanks, Mary M.	1867.12.12	SLC	DC.Washington	Bless me how	CSmH	00172
Fairbanks, Mary M.	1868.01.24	SLC	CT.Hartford	Don't abuse me	CSmH	00183
Fairbanks, Mary M.	1868.01.30	SLC	Unknown	P.S.--I confess	CSmH	00186
Fairbanks, Mary M.	1868.02.09	SLC	DC.Washington	Glory, I have	CSmH	00191
Fairbanks, Mary M.	1868.02.20	SLC	DC.Washington	Your most welcome	CSmH	00196

Fairbanks, Mary M.		1868.03.10	SLC	NY.New York	A day or	CSmH	00200
Fairbanks, Mary M.		1868.03.18	SLC	SH.Henry Chaun.	We shall reach	CSmH	00202
Fairbanks, Mary M.	bet &	1868.04.** 1868.07.**	SLC	CA.San Francisco	The Prodigal in	CSmH	02737 fragment
Fairbanks, Mary M.	 &	1868.05.01 1868.05.05	SLC	NV.Virginia City & CA.San Francisco	I cannot go	CSmH	00204
Fairbanks, Mary M.		1868.05.12	SLC	CA.San Francisco	I beg pardon	298:27	02732
Fairbanks, Mary M.		1868.06.17	SLC	CA.San Francisco	I am back	CSmH	02735
Fairbanks, Mary M.		1868.07.05	SLC	CA.San Francisco	I lectured on	CSmH	02738
Fairbanks, Mary M.		1868.08.03	SLC	NY.New York	I wrote you	CSmH	02743
Fairbanks, Mary M.		1868.08.17	SLC	CT.Hartford	You didn't answer	CSmH	02745
Fairbanks, Mary M.		1868.09.24	SLC	MO.St. Louis	Yours of the	CU-MARK(tr)	02752
Fairbanks, Mary M.		1868.10.05	SLC	CT.Hartford	I have been	CSmH	02755
Fairbanks, Mary M.		1868.10.12	SLC	CT.Hartford	Yes, "how well	CSmH	02758
Fairbanks, Mary M.		1868.10.26	OLC	NY.Elmira	In looking at	CtHMTH	05843
Fairbanks, Mary M.		1868.10.31	SLC	NY.New York	Don't worry--I'm	CSmH	02761
Fairbanks, Mary M.	 &	1868.11.26 1868.11.27	SLC	NY.Elmira	It is my P.S.--Friday	NN-B CSmH	02767
Fairbanks, Mary M.		1868.12.12	SLC	NY.Norwich	It is noon	CSmH	02730
Fairbanks, Mary M.		1868.12.24	SLC	MI.Lansing	I shall arrive	CU-MARK(tr)	02777
Fairbanks, Mary M.		1869.01.06	SLC	IL.Rockford	Hoping to see	CSmH	00219
Fairbanks, Mary M.		1869.01.07	SLC	IL.Chicago	There you are	CSmH	00222
Fairbanks, Mary M.		1869.01.12	SLC	IL.El Paso	Enclosed are some	CSmH	00229
Fairbanks, Mary M.		1869.01.15	OLC	NY.Elmira	Your very welcome	CtHMTH	08626
Fairbanks, Mary M.		1869.02.05	SLC	NY.Elmira	Your blessing! It	CSmH	00246
Fairbanks, Mary M.		1869.02.13	SLC	OH.Ravenna	The lecture to-night	CSmH	00248
Fairbanks, Mary M.		1869.02.17	SLC	PA.Franklin	You are mistaken	CSmH	00258
Fairbanks, Mary M.		1869.02.17	SLC	PA.Titusville	It is all	CSmH	00257
Fairbanks, Mary M.		1869.02.27	SLC	NY.Lockport	I would have	CSmH	00261
Fairbanks, Mary M.		1869.03.13	SLC	CT.Hartford	What a time	CSmH	00276

ADDRESSEE	DATE	WRITER	PLACE	CUE	SOURCE	NUMBER/NOTES
Fairbanks, Mary M.	1869.03.24	SLC	NY.Elmira	Why in the	CSmH	00278
Fairbanks, Mary M.	1869.03.31 & 1869.04.01	SLC	NY.Elmira	Bless you I	CSmH	00280
Fairbanks, Mary M.	1869.04.12	SLC	NY.Elmira	One thing I	CSmH	00282
Fairbanks, Mary M.	1869.04.15	SLC	NY.Elmira	How much longer	CSmH	00284
Fairbanks, Mary M.	1869.05.10	SLC	CT.Hartford	I wrote you	CSmH	00296
Fairbanks, Mary M.	1869.06.04	SLC	NY.Elmira	I have been	CSmH	00313 fragment
Fairbanks, Mary M.	1869.07.04	SLC	NY.Elmira	I haven't got	CSmH	00324
Fairbanks, Mary M. & Fairbanks, Abel W.	1869.08.14	SLC	NY.Buffalo	Before either your	CSmH	00332
Fairbanks, Mary M.	1869.09.26 to 1869.09.27	SLC	NY.Buffalo	I'll love you	CSmH	00359
Fairbanks, Mary M.	1869.11.09	OLC	NY.Elmira	Your letter came	CtHMTH	05844
Fairbanks, Mary M.	1869.11.19	SLC	MA.Boston	Why mercy! were	CSmH	00373
Fairbanks, Mary M.	1870.01.06	SLC	NY.Amenia	You ought to	CSmH	00401
Fairbanks, Mary M.	1870.01.09	OLC	NY.Elmira	We have been	CtHMTH	05845
Fairbanks, Mary M.	1870.02.13	SLC & OLC	NY.Buffalo	Thank you for	CSmH	00426
Fairbanks, Mary M.	1870.03.22 to 1870.03.24	SLC & OLC	NY.Buffalo	Silence, Woman!	CSmH	00448
Fairbanks, Mary M.	1870.05.29	SLC	NY.Buffalo	Our plans for	CSmH	00472
Fairbanks, Mary M.	1870.06.25	SLC	NY.Elmira	We are summoned	CSmH	00482
Fairbanks, Mary M.	1870.09.02	SLC	NY.Buffalo	Up to where	CSmH	00500
Fairbanks, Mary M.	1870.10.13	SLC	NY.Buffalo	Your news is	CSmH	00512
Fairbanks, Mary M.	1870.11.05	SLC	NY.Buffalo	Livy is doing	CSmH	00525
Fairbanks, Mary M.	1870.11.19	SLC	NY.Buffalo	What the "Fat	CSmH	00538
Fairbanks, Mary M.	1870.12.17	SLC	NY.Buffalo	Mother dear, I am	CSmH	00551
Fairbanks, Mary M.	1871.01.26	SLC	NY.Buffalo	Tell Bone &	CSmH	00566 fragment
Fairbanks, Mary M.	1871.03.14	SLC	NY.Buffalo	If we haven't	CSmH	00590
Fairbanks, Mary M.	1871.04.18	SLC	NY.Elmira	Am just starting	CSmH	00604
Fairbanks, Mary M.	1871.04.26	SLC	NY.Elmira	My! how you	CSmH	00606

Fairbanks, Mary M.		1871.06.27	SLC & OLC	NY.Elmira	the first of	298:154	00625
Fairbanks, Mary M.		1871.06.29	SLC	NY.Elmira	It was hard	CSmH	00629
Fairbanks, Mary M.		1871.12.10	SLC	PA.Erie	Am writing a	CSmH	00688
Fairbanks, Mary M.		1872.02.13	SLC	CT.Hartford	At last I	CSmH	00725
Fairbanks, Mary M.		1872.03.**	SLC	CT.Hartford	There photographs are	CSmH	00728
Fairbanks, Mary M.		1872.08.11	SLC	CT.New Saybrook	What a brief	CSmH	00792
Fairbanks, Mary M.	pm	1872.09.25	OLC	CT.Hartford	away Mrs Orion	CtHMTH	05859 fragment
Fairbanks, Mary M.		1872.11.02	SLC	EN.London	Of course I	CSmH	00825
Fairbanks, Mary M.		1873.04.16	SLC	CT.Hartford	Laziness, obstructed by	CSmH	00900
Fairbanks, Mary M.		1873.07.06	SLC	EN.London	This is the	CSmH	00947
Fairbanks, Mary M.		1874.02.25	SLC	CT.Hartford	Now you talk	CSmH	01055
Fairbanks, Mary M.		1874.09.21	SLC	CT.Hartford	We are just	CSmH	01129
Fairbanks, Mary M.		1875.04.23	SLC	CT.Hartford	Bang away! I	CSmH	01222
Fairbanks, Mary M.		1876.02.13	SLC	CT.Hartford	I'm always writing	CSmH	01307
Fairbanks, Mary M.		1876.03.24	SLC	CT.Hartford	As soon as	CSmH	01316
Fairbanks, Mary M.		1876.06.03	SLC	CT.Hartford	I am very	CSmH	01338
Fairbanks, Mary M.		1876.08.04	SLC	NY.Elmira	Did you say	CSmH	01355
Fairbanks, Mary M.		1876.09.14	SLC	CT.Hartford	We just had	CSmH	01362
Fairbanks, Mary M.	&	1877.04.14 1877.04.17	SLC	CT.Hartford	This is prodigious	CSmH	01412
Fairbanks, Mary M.		1877.09.03	SLC	NY.Elmira	It is 16	CSmH	01477
Fairbanks, Mary M.		1877.10.31	SLC	CT.Hartford	No, it is	CSmH	01500
Fairbanks, Mary M.		1878.02.05	SLC	CT.Hartford	It was real	CSmH	01528
Fairbanks, Mary M.		1878.03.09	SLC	CT.Hartford	What a pity	CSmH	01542
Fairbanks, Mary M.		1879.03.06	SLC	FR.Paris	O, dear, dear	CSmH	01637
Fairbanks, Mary M.		1879.05.15	SLC	FR.Paris	O dear me	CSmH	01655
Fairbanks, Mary M.		1879.09.23	SLC	NY.Elmira	It is mighty	CSmH	01692
Fairbanks, Mary M.		1879.11.18	SLC	CT.Hartford	I'll be danged	CSmH	01731 date uncertain

ADDRESSEE	DATE	WRITER	PLACE	CUE	SOURCE	NUMBER/NOTES
Fairbanks, Mary M.	1879.12.21	SLC	CT.Hartford	I would be	CSmH	01743
Fairbanks, Mary M.	1880.02.06	SLC	CT.Hartford	It is a	CSmH	01758
Fairbanks, Mary M.	1881.01.24	SLC	CT.Hartford	P.S. (to the	CSmH	04130
Fairbanks, Mary M.	1881.03.05	SLC	CT.Hartford	I would certainly	CSmH	01923
Fairbanks, Mary M.	1881.05.**	SLC	CT.Hartford	I have just	CSmH	04131
Fairbanks, Mary M.	1881.09.18	SLC	NY.Elmira	I left here	CSmH	02036
Fairbanks, Mary M.	1881.12.20	SLC	CT.Hartford	With the love of	ODa2	11210 inscription
Fairbanks, Mary M.	1882.02.21	SLC	CT.Hartford	If Dan had	CSmH	02162 typed
Fairbanks, Mary M.	1883.05.07	SLC	CT.Hartford	No doubt I	CSmH	02384 typed
Fairbanks, Mary M.	1883.06.04	SLC	CT.Hartford	It was lovely	CSmH	01861
Fairbanks, Mary M.	1884.01.30	SLC	CT.Hartford	Only a line	CSmH	02901
Fairbanks, Mary M.	1885.03.31	SLC	CT.Hartford	with the love	NN-B	10794 inscription
Fairbanks, Mary M.	1886.11.16	SLC	CT.Hartford	The story isn't	CSmH	03480
Fairbanks, Mary M.	1887.01.24	SLC	CT.Hartford	Good--if Livy	CSmH	03519
Fairbanks, Mary M.	1887.03.22	SLC	CT.Hartford	It is a	CtHMTH	03547
Fairbanks, Mary M.	1887.11.16	SLC	CT.Hartford	We haven't made	CSmH	03668
Fairbanks, Mary M.	1887.11.25	SLC	CT.Hartford	I go from	CSmH	03671
Fairbanks, Mary M.	1888.12.30	SLC	CT.Hartford	I reckon you	CSmH	03813
Fairbanks, Mary M.	1889.09.13	SLC	NY.Elmira	Let me see	CSmH	03941
Fairbanks, Mary M.	1890.10.13	SLC	CT.Hartford	Yes indeed, you	CSmH	04101
Fairbanks, Mary M.	1891.05.29	SLC	CT.Hartford	I have not	CSmH	04213
Fairbanks, Mary M.	1893.01.18	SLC	IT.Florence	We are glad	CSmH	04327
Fairbanks, Mary M.	1893.05.08	SLC	NY.Elmira	I am all	CSmH	04399
Fairbanks, Mary M.	1893.11.10	SLC	NY.New York	O, dear me	CSmH	04498
Fairbanks, Mary M.	1894.04.22	SLC	NY.New York	Oh, I expect	CSmH	04725
Fairbanks, Mary M.	1894.07.16	SLC	NY.New York	I am sorry	CSmH	04755
Fairbanks, Mary M.	1895.02.09	SLC	FR.Paris	I mislaid your	CSmH	04841

Fairbanks, Mary M.		1896.12.28	OLC	EN.London	We are going	CtHMTH	05902
Fairbanks, Mary P.		1876.02.09	SLC	CT.Hartford	So you have	216:7	01306
Fairbanks, Mary P.		1877.08.06	SLC	NY.Elmira	Well, my darling	CSmH	01467
Fairbanks, Mary P.	ca	1881.04.16	SLC	CT.Hartford	Now Mollie dear	CU-MARK(ph)	09115
Fairbanks, Mary P. & Fairbanks, Charles M.		1899.07.31	SLC & OLC	SE.Sanna	The tidings that	298:279	05660 other sources
Fairbanks, Pauline M. & Fairbanks, Charles M.		1907.07.26	SLC per IVL	NY.Tuxedo Park	Mr. Clemens is	CtHMTH	05950
Fairchild, Charles S.		1882.06.20	SLC	CT.Hartford	Would I go	ODa2	03243 mislabeled Elmira
Fairchild, Charles S.		1882.09.22	SLC	CT.Hartford	Arrived last night	Mo2	02278
Fairchild, Charles S.		1902.08.13	SLC	ME.York Harbor	14 W. 10th	ODa2	06404
Fairchild, Charles S.		1903.03.02	SLC	NY.Riverdale	I have forgotten	ODa2	06590
Fairchild, Charles S.		1903.05.14	SLC	NY.Riverdale	Day before yesterday	ODa2	06659
Fairchild, Charles S. & Fairchild, Elisabeth	pm	1904.07.20	SLC	MA.Lee	For what you	ODa2	06891 form letter
Fairchild, Elisabeth		1881.10.06	SLC	CT.Hartford	No, indeed, poor	ODa2	02045
Fairchild, Elisabeth		1892.03.08	SLC	FR.Menton	You did not	ODa2	04273
Fairchild, Elisabeth & Fairchild, Charles S.	pm	1904.07.20	SLC	MA.Lee	For what you	ODa2	06891 form letter
Fairchild, Elisabeth		1909.12.26	SLC	CT.Redding	To all friends	ViU	08530 form letter
Fairchild, Lucius		1879.05.03	SLC	FR.Paris	O, dear, we	WHi	01652
Fairchild, Lucius		1879.06.14	SLC	FR.Paris	Enclosed please find	297:45f	01669
Fairchild, Lucius		1879.07.**	SLC	FR.Paris	Read this book	ViU	11072 inscription
Fairchild, Lucius		1880.04.28	SLC	CT.Hartford	For this long	297:47	01794 other sources
Fairchild, Lucius		1888.06.05	SLC	CT.Hartford	Although I can't	CU-MARK(ph)	10528
Fairchild, M.	o/a	1905.12.12	SLC per IVL	NY.New York	I realize, by	CU-MARK(dr)	07249 on Fairchild Dec 12
Fairchild, Mary		1888.10.01	SLC	CT.Hartford	I thank you	CU-MARK(ph)	03778

ADDRESSEE	DATE	WRITER	PLACE	CUE	SOURCE	NUMBER/NOTES
Fall, George L. & Redpath, James	1871.06.10	SLC	NY.Elmira	Without really intending	NHi	00614
Fall, George L.	1871.07.20	SLC	NY.Elmira	Redpath tells me	114:189	00638 other sources
Fall, George L. & Redpath, James	1871.10.11	SLC	CT.Hartford	The list is	WU(ph)	00659
Fall, George L. & Redpath, James	1871.12.08	SLC	NY.Buffalo	Notify all hands	ODa2	00687 telegram
Fall, George L. & Redpath, James	1872.01.13	SLC	PA.Pittsburgh	Enclosed please find	CCamarSJ	00717
Fall, George L. & Redpath, James	1872.02.26	SLC	CT.Hartford	Am not going	OrPR	00727 telegram
Fall, George L. & Redpath, James	1872.03.07	SLC	CT.Hartford	Fall does the	MH-H	00731
Farmers' Club	1870.12.26	SLC	NY.Buffalo	I thank you	114:180	02788
Farrar, Hilda	o/a 1905.03.27	SLC	NY.New York	Look at the	CU-MARK(dr)	07021 on Farrar Mar 27
Farrell, Eva L.	1899.11.12	SLC	EN.London	Except my daughter's	ODa2	05706
Feldman, Osip L.	1907.03.**	SLC	NY.New York	This bust is	RuL2	11124 inscription
Felicie	****.**.**	OLC	Unknown	Hoping this little	Mo2	09107 inscription
Fenn, George M.	1877.08.02	SLC	CT.Hartford	I would greatly	Mo2	02366 date & place uncertain
Fenn, Linus T.	aft 1881.01.08	SLC	CT.Hartford	But this charge	CU-MARK	09583 on Fenn Jan 8
Fenn, Linus T.	1887.07.05	SLC	NY.Elmira	*	CtHMTH	10077 envelope only
Fenton, Charles B.	1906.04.16	SLC	NY.New York	I remember you	CU-MARK(tr)	07434
Field, Kate	bef 1873.06.09	SLC	EN.London	Mr. Clemens, called	Uk	03703 also to Dilkes
Field, Kate	bef 1873.06.25	SLC	EN.London	I see that	MB	00920
Field, Kate	1886.03.08	SLC	CT.Hartford	Oh, dear me	446:448	03375
Field, Mary M.	1874.07.29	SLC	NY.Elmira	Your distress would	CU-MARK	01115
Field, Stephen J.	1868.01.09	SLC	DC.Washington	I wish you	CU-MARK	00177

Fields, Annie A.	1887.03.17	SLC	CT.Hartford	Of course I	C4	03543
Fields, Annie A.	1887.04.01	SLC	CT.Hartford	I reached home	CSmH	03553
Fields, Annie A.	1889.03.12	SLC	CT.Hartford	Mrs. Clemens has	CSmH	03871
Fields, Annie A.	1901.02.19	OLC	NY.New York	I cannot tell	CSmH	11092
Fields, James T.	1870.03.21	SLC	NY.Buffalo	Fields Osgood &	ViU	00446
Fields, James T.	1875.01.07	SLC	CT.Hartford	I send this	CSmH	01175 poem enc
Finlay, Francis D.	****.**.**	SLC	EN.London	It did just	CU-MARK(tr)	07646
Finlay, Francis D.	1874.01.12	SLC	EN.Liverpool	We had full	WU	01040
Finlay, Francis D.	1874.04.23	SLC	NY.Elmira	Consound it!	WU	01078
Finlay, Francis D.	1874.11.10	SLC	CT.Hartford	Now one of	WU	01146
Finlay, Francis D.	1887.05.17	SLC	CT.Hartford	Soldiers! My land	WU	03573
Finlay, Francis D.	1889.08.17	SLC	NY.Elmira	Through the carelessness	WU	03927
Finlay, Francis D.	1891.09.13	SLC	SW.Interlaken	We leave tomorrow	CU-MARK(tr)	04226
Finlay, Francis D.	1891.10.16	SLC	GE.Berlin	I am still	CU-MARK	04245
Finlay, Francis D.	1900.04.25	SLC	EN.London	Yes, sir, there	WU	05799
Finlay, Mary	1889.10.11	SLC	CT.Hartford	with the best	CU-MARK(tr)	09228 inscription
Firth, Frank J.	o/a 1905.07.06	SLC per IVL	NH.Dublin	Mr. Clemens directs	CU-MARK(dr)	07077 on Firth July 6
Fischer, Mr.	1901.12.17	SLC	NY.Riverdale	I am very	NcWsW	10793
Fischer, Mr.	1902.01.03	SLC	NY.Riverdale	My best thanks	CtY	06217
Fish, Williston	1900.09.12	SLC	EN.London	You make me	CU-MARK(ph)	09859
Fisher, Mrs. Herbert C.	1901.10.15	SLC per FGW	CT.Hartford	I thank you	TNJ	06158 form letter; FGW in Hartford
Fiske, Minnie M.	1905.09.18	SLC	NH.Dublin	I shall certainly	CU-MARK	07141
Fiske, Minnie M.	1905.09.30	SLC	NH.Dublin	I have just	CU-MARK	07154
Fiske, Minnie M.	1906.07.27	SLC	NH.Dublin	Oh, I thank	CU-MARK	07482
Fiske, Willard	1904.02.04	OLC	IT.Florence	I have never	CU-MARK	06789

ADDRESSEE		DATE	WRITER	PLACE	CUE	SOURCE	NUMBER/NOTES
Fiske, Willard		1904.06.16	SLC	IT.Florence	You have been	CU-MARK	06872
Fitch, Thomas	ca	1870.07.**	SLC	Unknown	Now try and	279:52	10553
Fitzgibbon, G.		1872.10.05	SLC	EN.London	I thank you	Mo2	00820
Fitzgibbon, G.		1873.06.12	SLC	EN.London	Thanks--many thanks	134:1930.01.31	00925 other sources
Fitzgibbon, G.		1873.06.19	SLC	EN.London	You must pardon	NN-B	00929
Fitzgibbon, G.		1873.11.28	SLC	EN.London	Thank you ever	Mo2	00990
Fitzgibbon, G.		1873.12.09	SLC	EN.London	We had such	MoSW	00995
Fitzgibbon, G.		1873.12.21	SLC	EN.London	I wish you	NN-B	01012
Fitzgibbon, G.		1873.12.30	SLC	EN.London	After all, I	NN-B	01020
Fitzgibbon, G.		1874.01.01	SLC	EN.London	Ever so many	Mo2	01027
Fitzgibbon, G.		1874.01.06	SLC	EN.London	Many thanks, my	Mo2	01035
Fitz-Simon, William		1908.06.05	SLC	NY.New York	Marriage--yes, it	114:811	08022
Flagg, Charles N.		1889.04.03	SLC	CT.Hartford	I thank you	TxAu2	10689
Flagg, Charles N.		1891.01.12	SLC	DC.Washington	Gilder reads	TxAu2	10691
Flagg, Charles N.		1891.01.31	SLC	CT.Hartford	Gilder's a jackass	TxAu2	10690
Flanagan, J. Woulfe		1897.01.19	SLC	EN.London	I find it	CU-MARK(tr)	05170 SLC tr
Flanagan, J. Woulfe		1897.01.20	SLC	EN.London	You compliment me	CU-MARK	05173 unsent
Fleck, C.L.		1883.02.06	SLC	CT.Hartford	I beg you	C4	02343
Fleming, Henry S.	o/a	1905.12.02	SLC per IVL	NY.New York	Should like it	CU-MARK(dr)	07228 on Fleming Dec 2
Flinn, John J.		1907.01.11	SLC per IVL	NY.New York	Eat, drink &	CU-MARK(dr)	07624 telegram dr on Flinn Jan 10
Flower, Charles E.		1873.07.14	SLC	EN.London	The more we	DFo	00952
Flower, Charles E.		1875.10.27	SLC	CT.Hartford	I am very	DFo	01276
Flower, Charles E.		1875.11.22	SLC	CT.Hartford	Since I received	CSmH	01282 unsent fragment
Foote, Cornelia W.		1887.12.02	SLC	CT.Hartford	Well, people &	CU-MARK(ph)	03672

Foote, Edward M.		1906.03.14	SLC	NY.New York	Indeed I should	CU-MARK(tr)	07384 SLC tr
Foote, Kate		1891.01.16	SLC	DC.Washington	Yours of day	C4	04160
Foote, Mary		****.**.**	CC	CT.Hartford	Why don't you	CtHMTH	10485
Foote, Mary		****.**.**	SC	CT.Hartford	Yes I know	CtHMTH	10507
Foote, Mary		****.10.13	SC	CT.Hartford	Clara's letter (although	CtHMTH	10509
Foote, Mary		****.10.27	SC	CT.Hartford	How I love	CtHMTH	10510
Foote, Mary		****.11.22	SC	CT.Hartford	I was very	CtHMTH	10508
Foote, Mary		1886.05.**	SC	CT.Hartford	1. She left me	CtHSD	03396
Foote, Mary		1886.05.**	SC	CT.Hartford	I can't possibly	CtHSD	03397
Foote, Mary		1886.05.15	SC	CT.Hartford	If you can	CtHSD	03400
Foote, Mary		1886.10.08	CC	CT.Hartford	Oh! Isn't it	CtHMTH	10483
Foote, Mary		1886.11.18	CC	CT.Hartford	I was very	CtHMTH	10484
Foote, Mary		1887.10.07	SC	CT.Hartford	Your dear letter	CtHMTH	10511
Foote, Mary		1890.10.18	SC	CT.Hartford	It is Saturday	CtHMTH	10506
Foote, Mary		1894.03.26	SLC	FR.Paris	As a rule	117:1968.08.14	04714
Forbes, H.F. Gordon		1899.09.15	SLC	SE.Sanna	I am taking	MoSW	05673
Forbes, H.F. Gordon		1899.10.01	SLC	EN.London	I am to	MoSW	05685
Forbes, H.F. Gordon		1899.11.10	SLC	EN.London	Events do seem	MoSW	05703
Ford, Eunice		1870.11.11	SLC	NY.Buffalo	I have waited	CtHMTH	00530
Ford, Eunice	o/b	1870.12.25	SLC	NY.Buffalo	With this I	CtHMTH	02787
Ford, Grace		1906.01.16	SLC per IVL	NY.New York	I dearly wish	CU-MARK(tr)	07311
Ford, Paul L.		1902.01.09	SLC	NY.Riverdale	As regards that	CU-MARK	06230 typed form letter
Forrest, Clarence F.		1900.12.20	SLC	NY.New York	I beg to	ViU	05936
Forsslund, Louise	o/a	1905.11.25	SLC per IVL	NY.New York	Must have been	CU-MARK(dr)	07218 on Forsslund Nov 25
Forster, Rudolph		1906.10.12	SLC	NH.Dublin	On that date	CU-MARK(dr)	07543

ADDRESSEE	DATE	WRITER	PLACE	CUE	SOURCE	NUMBER/NOTES
Fosdick, L.	o/a 1905.11.29	SLC per IVL	NY.New York	Before you engage	CU-MARK(dr)	07223 on Fosdick Nov 29
Foulke, William D. & Halford, E.W.	1888.10.03	SLC	CT.Hartford	For the sake	InU-Li	03780
Francis, David R.	1903.03.30	SLC	NY.New York	As regards the	131:1903.03.31	06610
Francis, David R.	1904.05.26	SLC	IT.Florence	It has been	114:756	06839
Franklin, Annie	bef 1878.03.01	SLC	CT.Hartford	Mrs. Clemens is	IaDaPM	01697
Franklin, William B.	1876.04.28	SLC	CT.Hartford	They say that	CU-MARK	01328 on H. Langdon Apr 27
Franklin, William B.	1877.05.12	SLC	CT.Hartford	We have 3	Ct	10581
Frazer, Clara & Frazer, Laura H.	1908.12.24	SLC	CT.Redding	The cup is	246:1935.03.06	09537
Frazer, Laura H.	bet 1870.01.01 & 1870.01.05	SLC	NY.Elmira	Mrs.--(married	246:1935.03.06	09533 on envelope
Frazer, Laura H.	1902.06.13	SLC	NY.New York	this remembrance of	246:1935.03.06	09534 inscription
Frazer, Laura H.	ca 1902.07.**	SLC	ME.York Harbor	I know that	246:1935.03.06	06382
Frazer, Laura H.	ca 1904.06.21	SLC	IT.Florence	For what you	246:1935.03.06	09535 form letter
Frazer, Laura H.	ca 1908.10.14	SLC	CT.Redding	with the love	246:1935.03.06	09536 inscription
Frazer, Laura H.	1908.11.04	SLC	CT.Redding	We enjoyed the	246:1935.03.06	08154
Frazer, Laura H. & Frazer, Clara	1908.12.24	SLC	CT.Redding	The cup is	246:1935.03.06	09537
Frazer, Laura H.	1909.02.**	SLC	CT.Redding	Who of this	246:1935.03.06	09538
Frechette, Louis	1881.12.25	SLC	CT.Hartford	with the high	105:1938.11.21	09651 inscription
Free Russia ed.	aft 1890.07.01	SLC	NY.Tannersville	I thank you	CU-MARK	04060
Freeman, Mary E.	1902.01.09	SLC	NY.Riverdale	As regards that	CU-MARK	06231 typed form letter
Freeman, Zoheth S.	1908.11.16	SLC	CT.Redding	I thank you	CU-MARK(ph)	08160
French, Alice	1902.01.09	SLC	NY.Riverdale	As regards that	CU-MARK	06232 typed form letter

French, William H. & Hoffman, Ogden	1866.12.06	SLC	CA.San Francisco	I cannot too	417:1866.12.08	02776 also to Low & Blasdel
Frisbie, Thomas S.	1897.10.25	SLC	AU.Vienna	The picture has	CU-MARK(ph)	05302
Frohman, Charles	1906.10.25	SLC	NY.New York	Will you do	CU-MARK	07555
Frohman, Daniel	1889.10.27	SLC	CT.Hartford	As the guest-season	DFo	03958
Frohman, Daniel	1890.02.02	SLC	NY.New York	Do not make	CCamarSJ	04010 unsent
Frohman, Daniel	1890.02.10	SLC	CT.Hartford	I have now	DFo	04014
Frohman, Daniel	1902.**.**	SLC	Unknown	My nephew, Jervis	CU-MARK(tr)	08659
Frohman, Daniel	1905.11.16	SLC per IVL	NY.New York	Thank you very	CU-MARK(dr)	07209
Frost, Lowell C.	1906.01.31	SLC	NY.New York	Your check has	NN-B(tr)	07322
Fuller, Frank	****.**.**	SLC	Unknown	If a man	CU-MARK(ph)	09079
Fuller, Frank	****.**.**	SLC	Unknown	Cut it off	WU(tr)	07756
Fuller, Frank	****.03.31	SLC	Unknown	A thousand thanks	157:1923.03.05	09871
Fuller, Frank	1867.06.01 & 1867.06.08	SLC	NY.New York	Please take charge	CtHMTH	00136
Fuller, Frank	1867.06.07	SLC	NY.New York	You are hereby	ViU	00135
Fuller, Frank	1867.08.07	SLC	IT.Naples	Don't make any	WU(tr)	00142
Fuller, Frank	1867.11.24	SLC	DC.Washington	Dog-gone it	NN5	00158
Fuller, Frank	1867.12.02	SLC	DC.Washington	I want you	PBL	00167
Fuller, Frank	1867.12.05	SLC	DC.Washington	You hit powerful	CtY	00170
Fuller, Frank	1867.12.13	SLC	DC.Washington	I believe I	NN5	00173
Fuller, Frank	1868.05.12	SLC	CA.San Francisco	I want to	105:1956.12.01	02782 other sources
Fuller, Frank	1868.08.15	SLC	CT.Hartford	You old fool	CLjC	02744
Fuller, Frank	1868.09.24	SLC	MO.St. Louis	Your six-line letter	CLjC	02753
Fuller, Frank	1870.04.26	SLC	NY.Buffalo	I was powerful	WU(tr)	00460
Fuller, Frank	1870.05.21	SLC	NY.Buffalo	You are the	CU-MARK(ph) ODa2	00466 ODa2 envelope
Fuller, Frank	1874.01.31	SLC	CT.Hartford	Bless us, Frank	MoSW	01041

ADDRESSEE	DATE	WRITER	PLACE	CUE	SOURCE	NUMBER/NOTES
Fuller, Frank	aft 1874.07.07	SLC	NY.Elmira	Just been to	CU-MARK	01107
Fuller, Frank	1874.09.06	SLC	NY.Elmira	His claim is	WU(tr)	01124
Fuller, Frank	1878.04.05	SLC	NY.New York	Give him any	MoSW	01552
Fuller, Frank	1878.08.20	SLC	SW.Lucerne	How are you	NN-B	02526
Fuller, Frank	1879.11.18	SLC	CT.Hartford	Read the enclosed	MoSW	01721
Fuller, Frank	1879.11.22	SLC	CT.Hartford	You did it	CLjC	01723
Fuller, Frank	1879.11.26	SLC	CT.Hartford	A hundred chances	NN5	01747
Fuller, Frank	1879.12.05	SLC	CT.Hartford	Come to my	CLjC	01733
Fuller, Frank	1879.12.19	SLC	CT.Hartford	I'm leaving the	CLjC	01742
Fuller, Frank	1880.02.24	SLC	CT.Hartford	Enclosed please find	CU-MARK	01762
Fuller, Frank	1880.04.22	SLC	CT.Hartford	I feel rich	WU(tr)	01791 other sources
Fuller, Frank	1880.10.02	SLC	CT.Hartford	Yes, that is	MoSW	01835
Fuller, Frank	1880.10.30	SLC	CT.Hartford	I have no	CLjC	01849 telegram
Fuller, Frank	1882.03.14	SLC	CT.Hartford	I was out	MiEM	03740 typed
Fuller, Frank	1882.07.05	SLC	CT.Hartford	We have scarlet	WU	02231 typed
Fuller, Frank	1884.10.18	SLC	CT.Hartford	I changed publishers	WU(tr)	03009
Fuller, Frank	1885.09.28	SLC	CT.Hartford	I want you	ViU	03291
Fuller, Frank	1885.11.11	SLC	CT.Hartford	Literary Life could	NN-B	02622
Fuller, Frank	1888.12.21	SLC	CT.Hartford	Bless you I've	WU(tr)	03805
Fuller, Frank	1888.12.29	SLC	CT.Hartford	Thank you ever	CU-MARK(ph)	03812
Fuller, Frank	1889.10.12	SLC	CT.Hartford	I am laid	WU(tr)	03951
Fuller, Frank	1889.10.16	SLC	CT.Hartford	Ah, I speculated	NN-B	02696
Fuller, Frank	1894.02.01	SLC	NY.New York	I'm in N.Y.	CtY	04683
Fuller, Frank	1894.02.18	SLC	NY.New York	I change my	CU-MARK(ph)	04694
Fuller, Frank	1894.03.06	SLC	NY.New York	I sail tomorrow	WU(tr)	04707
Fuller, Frank	1895.03.05	SLC	NY.New York	I am in	WU(tr)	04846
Fuller, Frank	1895.06.13	SLC	NY.Elmira	No, I am	ViU	04890

Fuller, Frank		1895.08.04	SLC	MT.Helena	Here's another	NN5	04938
Fuller, Frank		1897.03.26	SLC	EN.London	My friend Robert	Mo2	08844
Fuller, Frank		1897.05.01	SLC	EN.London	I was very	CU-MARK	05210
Fuller, Frank		1897.05.27	SLC	EN.London	Intimations have reached	WU(tr)	05216
Fuller, Frank		1897.06.02	SLC	EN.London	*	ViU	10102 envelope only
Fuller, Frank		1897.06.03	SLC	EN.London	If that project	WU(tr)	05223
Fuller, Frank		1897.07.02	SLC	EN.London	That plan of	WU(tr)	05248 other sources
Fuller, Frank	ca	1899.**.**	SLC	NY.New York	I change my	CSt	08912
Fuller, Frank	pm	1900.08.**	SLC	EN.London	*	ViU	10113 envelope only
Fuller, Frank		1900.08.12	SLC	EN.London	*	ViU 157:1924.11.06	09787 ViU envelope; 157 ghost text
Fuller, Frank		1901.06.18	SLC	NY.New York	Your book arrived	ViU	06073
Fuller, Frank		1901.11.16	SLC	NY.Riverdale	With the enfeebling	Mo2	08873
Fuller, Frank		1901.12.04	SLC	NY.Riverdale	It saddens me	WU(tr)	06181
Fuller, Frank		1906.02.10	SLC per IVL	NY.New York	I am so	CU-MARK(tr)	07336 IVL tr
Fuller, Frank		1906.03.20	SLC per IVL	Unknown	Mr. Clemens is	212:1945.05.12	09910
Fuller, John		1870.02.08	SLC	NY.Buffalo	In answer I	CtY	00421 form letter
Fuller, Mrs. Frank		****.**.**	SLC	NY.New York	I am sorry	MiEM	04134
Fuller, Mrs. Frank		1874.04.07	SLC	CT.Hartford	Since Frank left	MoSW	01071
Fuller, Mrs. Frank		1900.11.15	OLC	NY.New York	Thank you heartily	CLjC	05906
Fuller, W.O. Jr.		1901.01.26	SLC	NY.New York	Yes, the slippers	Mo2	05984
Fuller, W.O. Jr.		1903.02.04	SLC per IVL	NY.Riverdale	What in the	NmU	06576
Fulton, Helen		1907.04.06	SLC	NY.New York	with the respectful	C3	11098 inscription
Fulton, Robert L.		1905.05.24	SLC	NH.Dublin	I remember, as	C3	07048

ADDRESSEE	DATE	WRITER	PLACE	CUE	SOURCE	NUMBER/NOTES
Funk, Isaac	1902.07.16	SLC	ME.York Harbor	Maybe you let	DLC	11159
Gabrilowitsch, Clara C.	*	*	*	*	*	11126 see Clemens, Clara L.
Gabrilowitsch, Ossip	1908.12.24	SLC	CT.Redding	all good wishes	260:1958.07.15	09386 inscription; other sources
Gabrilowitsch, Ossip & Clemens, Clara L.	1910.03.12	SLC	BE.Hamilton	Clara dear, last	CU-MARK(tr)	08568
Gage, Lyman J.	1900.04.30	SLC	EN.London	The accompanying copy	CU-MARK	05802
Gage, Lyman J.	1900.09.27	SLC	EN.London	I have got	CU-MARK(ph)	05860
Garfield, James A.	ca 1880.11.26	SLC	CT.Hartford	If you meditate	MH-H(dr)	10776 enc in Nov 26 to Osgood
Garfield, James A.	1881.01.12	SLC	CT.Hartford	Several times since	ODa2	01891
Garland, Hamlin	1883.07.28	SLC	NY.Elmira	G'way, Leionidas! You	CLSU	02063
Garland, Hamlin	1889.03.23	SLC	CT.Hartford	I am heels	CLSU	03875
Garland, Hamlin	1905.05.20	SLC	NH.Dublin	The book has	CLSU	07047
Garland, Hamlin	1905.06.30	SLC	NH.Dublin	Yesterday I took	NNAL	07075
Garth, Douglas	1896.10.31	SLC	EN.London	I am writing	107:1925.03.03	00215
Garth, John	1882.07.03	SLC	CT.Hartford	Your letter of	114:422	02230
Garth, John	1890.05.01	SLC	CT.Hartford	I avoid all	122:1937.11.11	04045
Garth, Mr.	1896.10.09	SLC	EN.London	When the cold	NN-B	05242
Garth, Mrs.	1909.10.02	SLC	CT.Redding	Your letter left	TxU	08464
Garvan, Edward J.	o/a 1905.10.09	SLC per IVL	NH.Dublin	The last Mr.	CU-MARK(dr)	07166 on Garvan Oct 9
Gates, George A.	1901.01.21	SLC	NY.New York	That speech seems	ViU(tr)	05969
Gatts, Thomas F.	1903.05.30	SLC	NY.Riverdale	It is indeed	CU-MARK(dr)	06670
Gatts, Thomas F.	1903.06.08	SLC	NY.Riverdale	While I am	114:740	06674
Gay, Maria C.	1901.06.02	OLC	NY.New York	I came safely	CtHMTH	06067
Gay, Mrs. Julius	1889.12.25	SLC	CT.Hartford	with the compliments	105:1954.03.23	09432 inscription
Gebbie, George	bet 1880.07.14 & 1880.07.17	SLC	Unknown	I might possibly	CU-MARK(tr)	09202 telegram

Genard, Ernest A.	o/a	1906.03.08	SLC per IVL	NY.New York	I have taken	CU-MARK(dr)	07368 on Genard Mar 8
Geneseo Young Men		1869.02.18	SLC	PA.Franklin	unavoidably detained	236:1869.02.24	04736 telegram
Geneseo Young Men		1869.02.22	SLC	NY.Elmira	Advertize liberally and	236:1869.02.24	05164 probably telegram
Gerard, Henri		1871.05.05	SLC	NY.Elmira	I have hardly	228:123f	02456
Gerard, Mr.		1875.07.06	SLC	CT.Hartford	Our architect is	Mo2	01246 date uncertain
Gerhardt, Hattie J.		1881.02.22	SC	CT.Hartford	Will you please	CU-MARK(tr)	10955
Gerhardt, Hattie J. & Gerhardt, Karl	ca	1881.03.01	SLC	CT.Hartford	We want you	CU-MARK(tr)	10859
Gerhardt, Hattie J. & Gerhardt, Karl	to	1881.04.11 1881.04.19	SLC	CT.Hartford	Next time you P.S. The enclosed	NNWH ViU	01935
Gerhardt, Hattie J. & Gerhardt, Karl		1881.05.09	SLC	CT.Hartford	All right--try	MB	01952
Gerhardt, Hattie J. & Gerhardt, Karl		1881.06.26	SLC	CT.Branford	Your letter was	CU-MARK(ph)	01978
Gerhardt, Hattie J. & Gerhardt, Karl		1881.07.31	SLC	CT.Branford	Phew! it takes	MB	01991
Gerhardt, Hattie J.		1881.08.07	SLC & OLC	NY.Elmira	We enjoy so	NN-B	02552
Gerhardt, Hattie J. & Gerhardt, Karl		1881.08.31	SLC	NY.Elmira	The triumph in	C4	02019
Gerhardt, Hattie J. & Gerhardt, Karl		1881.10.09	SLC	CT.Hartford	I found it	MB	02049
Gerhardt, Hattie J. & Gerhardt, Karl		1881.11.07	SLC	CT.Hartford	It gives me	MB	02083
Gerhardt, Hattie J. & Gerhardt, Karl		1881.11.21	SLC	CT.Hartford	The medallion of	NN5	02094
Gerhardt, Hattie J. & Gerhardt, Karl		1882.02.24	SLC	CT.Hartford	When your letter	CCamarSJ	02165 typed
Gerhardt, Hattie J. & Gerhardt, Karl		1882.03.21	SLC	CT.Hartford	Don't you imagine	CCamarSJ	02177 typed
Gerhardt, Hattie J. & Gerhardt, Karl		1882.03.23	SLC	CT.Hartford	You see I	CCamarSJ	02179 typed

ADDRESSEE	DATE	WRITER	PLACE	CUE	SOURCE	NUMBER/NOTES
Gerhardt, Hattie J. & Gerhardt, Karl	1882.06.01	SLC	CT.Hartford	I have just	CCamarSJ	02210 typed
Gerhardt, Hattie J. & Gerhardt, Karl	o/a 1882.08.24	SLC	NY.Elmira	I turned this	NN5	02259 on St. Gaudens Aug 24
Gerhardt, Hattie J. & Gerhardt, Karl	1882.10.23	SLC	CT.Hartford	I started a	NN-B	02565 typed
Gerhardt, Hattie J. & Gerhardt, Karl	ca 1882.12.01	SLC	CT.Hartford	When you have	CU-MARK(dr)	02302
Gerhardt, Hattie J. & Gerhardt, Karl	1883.01.14	SLC	CT.Hartford	The prayers of	157:1924.11.10	09791
Gerhardt, Hattie J. & Gerhardt, Karl	1883.01.25 & 1883.02.06	SLC	CT.Hartford	I'm in a	CLjC	10134
Gerhardt, Hattie J. & Gerhardt, Karl	1883.03.26	SLC	CT.Hartford	We welcome the	CCamarSJ	02364 typed
Gerhardt, Hattie J. & Gerhardt, Karl	1883.05.01 & 1883.05.03	SLC	CT.Hartford	Mr. Fisk arrived	CCamarSJ	02380 typed
Gerhardt, Hattie J. & Gerhardt, Karl	1883.07.02	SLC	NY.Elmira	Just a line	MB	02300
Gerhardt, Hattie J. & Gerhardt, Karl	1883.08.01	SLC	NY.Elmira	I vastly like	Mo2	02818
Gerhardt, Hattie J. & Gerhardt, Karl	bet 1884.03.01 & 1884.05.31	SLC	CT.Hartford	Instead of sending	CU-MARK(tr)	02881
Gerhardt, Hattie J. & Gerhardt, Karl	1884.03.05	SLC	CT.Hartford	We are exceedingly	CCamarSJ	02926
Gerhardt, Hattie J. & Gerhardt, Karl	1884.05.04	SLC	CT.Hartford	I'm afraid we	CtY(tr)	02969
Gerhardt, Hattie J.	1885.05.30	SLC & OLC	CT.Hartford	I was so	NcWsW	03232
Gerhardt, Hattie J. & Gerhardt, Karl	1885.06.14	SLC	CT.Hartford	We arrive at	OC	09074
Gerhardt, Karl	****.**.**	SLC	CT.Hartford	Mrs. C. wrote	MoHM	08590 on envelope
Gerhardt, Karl	****.**.**	SLC	NY.Elmira	Call me at	CCC	00297
Gerhardt, Karl	****.08.21	SLC	Unknown	Yes, you must	MiD	04265
Gerhardt, Karl	****.09.11	SLC	Unknown	Let it wait	MiD	04135
Gerhardt, Karl & Gerhardt, Hattie J.	ca 1881.03.01	SLC	CT.Hartford	We want you	CU-MARK(tr)	10859

Gerhardt, Karl & Gerhardt, Hattie J.	to	1881.04.11 1881.04.19	SLC	CT.Hartford	Next time you P.S. The enclosed	NNWH ViU	01935
Gerhardt, Karl & Gerhardt, Hattie J.		1881.05.09	SLC	CT.Hartford	All right--try	MB	01952
Gerhardt, Karl		1881.05.30	SLC	CT.Hartford	*	MB	10064 envelope only
Gerhardt, Karl & Gerhardt, Hattie J.		1881.06.26	SLC	CT.Branford	Your letter was	CU-MARK(ph)	01978
Gerhardt, Karl	pm	1881.07.27	SLC	CT.Branford	*	NHC	10076 envelope only
Gerhardt, Karl & Gerhardt, Hattie J.		1881.07.31	SLC	CT.Branford	Phew! it takes	MB	01991
Gerhardt, Karl & Gerhardt, Hattie J.		1881.08.31	SLC	NY.Elmira	The triumph in	C4	02019
Gerhardt, Karl	pm	1881.09.02	SLC	NY.Elmira	*	Mo2	10065 envelope only
Gerhardt, Karl & Gerhardt, Hattie J.		1881.10.09	SLC	CT.Hartford	I found it	MB	02049
Gerhardt, Karl & Gerhardt, Hattie J.		1881.11.07	SLC	CT.Hartford	It gives me	MB	02083
Gerhardt, Karl & Gerhardt, Hattie J.		1881.11.21	SLC	CT.Hartford	The medallion of	NN5	02094
Gerhardt, Karl & Gerhardt, Hattie J.		1882.02.24	SLC	CT.Hartford	When your letter	CCamarSJ	02165 typed
Gerhardt, Karl & Gerhardt, Hattie J.		1882.03.21	SLC	CT.Hartford	Don't you imagine	CCamarSJ	02177 typed
Gerhardt, Karl & Gerhardt, Hattie J.		1882.03.23	SLC	CT.Hartford	You see I	CCamarSJ	02179 typed
Gerhardt, Karl & Gerhardt, Hattie J.		1882.06.01	SLC	CT.Hartford	I have just	CCamarSJ	02210 typed
Gerhardt, Karl & Gerhardt, Hattie J.	o/a	1882.08.24	SLC	NY.Elmira	I turned this	NN5	02259 on St. Gaudens Aug 24
Gerhardt, Karl	&	1882.09.30 1882.10.01	SLC	CT.Hartford	When we originally	MB	02282
Gerhardt, Karl & Gerhardt, Hattie J.		1882.10.23	SLC	CT.Hartford	I started a	NN-B	02565 typed
Gerhardt, Karl & Gerhardt, Hattie J.	ca	1882.12.01	SLC	CT.Hartford	When you have	CU-MARK(dr)	02302

ADDRESSEE	DATE	WRITER	PLACE	CUE	SOURCE	NUMBER/NOTES
Gerhardt, Karl & Gerhardt, Hattie J.	1883.01.14	SLC	CT.Hartford	The prayers of	157:1924.11.10	09791
Gerhardt, Karl & Gerhardt, Hattie J.	1883.01.25 & 1883.02.06	SLC	CT.Hartford	I'm in a	CLjC	10134
Gerhardt, Karl & Gerhardt, Hattie J.	1883.03.26	SLC	CT.Hartford	We welcome the	CCamarSJ	02364 typed
Gerhardt, Karl & Gerhardt, Hattie J.	1883.05.01 & 1883.05.03	SLC	CT.Hartford	Mr. Fisk arrived	CCamarSJ	02380 typed
Gerhardt, Karl	1883.05.07	SLC	CT.Hartford	Mrs. Clemens will	MiD	02379
Gerhardt, Karl & Gerhardt, Hattie J.	1883.07.02	SLC	NY.Elmira	Just a line	MB	02300
Gerhardt, Karl & Gerhardt, Hattie J.	1883.08.01	SLC	NY.Elmira	I vastly like	Mo2	02818
Gerhardt, Karl & Gerhardt, Hattie J.	bet 1884.03.01 & 1884.05.31	SLC	CT.Hartford	Instead of sending	CU-MARK(tr)	02881
Gerhardt, Karl & Gerhardt, Hattie J.	1884.03.05	SLC	CT.Hartford	We are exceedingly	CCamarSJ	02926
Gerhardt, Karl & Gerhardt, Hattie J.	1884.05.04	SLC	CT.Hartford	I'm afraid we	CtY(tr)	02969
Gerhardt, Karl	pm 1884.09.21	SLC	NY.Elmira	We think it	418:1982.04.28	00586
Gerhardt, Karl	1884.09.27	SLC	NY.New York	I may want	CCamarSJ	01319
Gerhardt, Karl	1884.09.28	SLC	CT.Hartford	I think your	MiD MB	01443 fragment; MB envelope
Gerhardt, Karl	o/a 1885.04.01	SLC	Unknown	City Hotel, 42nd	CU-MARK(dr)	03199 on Gerhardt Apr 1
Gerhardt, Karl	1885.04.10	SLC	PA.Philadelphia	Erastus Brainerd has	MB	03211
Gerhardt, Karl	bet 1885.06.01 & 1885.08.30	SLC	Unknown	P.S. Meanwhile comes	Mo2	02423
Gerhardt, Karl	1885.06.04	SLC	CT.Hartford	Mrs. Clemens is	NHi	03236
Gerhardt, Karl & Gerhardt, Hattie J.	1885.06.14	SLC	CT.Hartford	We arrive at	OC	09074
Gerhardt, Karl	1885.06.26	SLC	NY.Elmira	It is very	MB	03246
Gerhardt, Karl	1885.06.28	SLC	NY.Elmira	No, she could	NN-B	02618
Gerhardt, Karl	1885.07.05	SLC	NY.Elmira	Arrived last evening	CCamarSJ	03251
Gerhardt, Karl	1885.07.06	SLC	NY.Elmira	Show it to	CtY	03253

Gerhardt, Karl		1885.07.11	SLC	NY.Elmira	If it were	CtY	03258
Gerhardt, Karl		1885.07.18	SLC	NY.Elmira	And again, if	105:1939.04.04	03260
Gerhardt, Karl		1885.08.**	SLC	NY.Elmira	They think it	MB	03086 fragment
Gerhardt, Karl		1885.10.08	SLC	CT.Hartford	But you have	NN	03293
Gerhardt, Karl	&	1886.02.22 1886.02.23	SLC & OLC	CT.Hartford	Mr Clemens wishes	MB	03370
Gerhardt, Karl		1886.07.15	SLC	NY.Elmira	If that committee	MB	03420
Gerhardt, Karl		1889.10.16	SLC	CT.Hartford	I want to	MB	03952
Gerhardt, Karl		1889.12.02	SLC	CT.Hartford	my type-setter offer	116:1942.09.10	09174
Gerhardt, Karl		1895.07.06	SLC	NY.Elmira	Land, I wish	MB	04927
Gerken, Irene		1908.02.29	SLC	BE.Hamilton	with the affectionate	NN-B	10802 inscription
Gessford, J.G.		1904.07.30	SLC per IVL	MA.Lee	In returning the	ViAl2	06907
Gessford, J.G.		1904.08.07	SLC per IVL	MA.Lee	I asked you	ViAl2	06910
Gibbon, John		1875.03.01	SLC	CT.Hartford	I thank you	MdHi	01202
Gibson, A.K.	pm	1903.10.02	SLC	NY.Elmira	None but the	CSmH	10693
Gibson, Jay H.		1886.07.12	SLC	NY.Elmira	I have been	CLjC	10671
Gibson, Mr.		1905.06.08	SLC	NH.Dublin	If you should	CAlb2	07059
Gibson, Mrs.		****.**.**	SLC	Unknown	Truly Yours	205:1937.06.09	09809 inscription
Gilbert, Arthur E.		1898.02.06	SLC	AU.Vienna	No, I have	NN	05343
Gilbert, Arthur E.		1898.02.12	SLC	AU.Vienna	Yes, large bowl	NN	05349
Gilbert, Arthur E.		1898.04.15	SLC	AU.Vienna	It is the	NN	05376
Gilbert, Elizabeth W.		1901.06.19	SLC	NY.New York	It is a	DLC	06075
Gilbert, Josiah H.		1884.02.25	SLC	CT.Hartford	Yes you can	CU-MARK(ph)	10563
Gilbert, O.A.F. & Rice, Henry F.		1866.11.01	SLC	NV.Virginia City	Your kind and	431:1866.11.04	02775 also to Blasdel & Helm

ADDRESSEE	DATE	WRITER	PLACE	CUE	SOURCE	NUMBER/NOTES
Gilder, Jeannette L.	1881.12.12	SLC	CT.Hartford	The newspaper custom	CU-MARK(tr)	02113 SLC tr misaddressed Mr. Gilder
Gilder, Jeannette L.	1885.12.15	SLC	CT.Hartford	I have just	NhD	03330
Gilder, Jeannette L.	1887.05.14	SLC	CT.Hartford	We shall spend	CU-MARK	03572
Gilder, Jeannette L.	1905.11.**	SLC	Unknown	Two months ago	CU-MARK(dr)	07192
Gilder, Joseph B.	o/a 1907.04.10	SLC per IVL	NY.New York	I am under	CU-MARK(dr)	07687 on Gilder Apr 10
Gilder, Joseph B.	1909.11.19	SLC	CT.Branchville	I am very	NN	08496 telegram
Gilder, Richard W.	****.**.**	SLC	Unknown	I can't--though	NN	04304
Gilder, Richard W.	****.05.19	SLC	Unknown	I've told him	NN	05053
Gilder, Richard W.	****.09.28	SLC	CT.Hartford	I can't do	107:1929.01.31	09559
Gilder, Richard W.	****.12.17	SLC	Unknown	But wont you	107:1921.03.04	09548
Gilder, Richard W.	1887.02.03	SLC	CT.Hartford	Say--please send	120:1930.09	09893
Gilder, Richard W.	1887.03.17	SLC	CT.Hartford	Please send me	C4	03542
Gilder, Richard W.	1887.03.28	SLC	CT.Hartford	First appeared in	ViU	03552
Gilder, Richard W.	1887.05.21	SLC	Unknown	I have this	NSyU	03576
Gilder, Richard W.	1887.08.08	SLC	NY.Elmira	Oh, I didn't	SzG2	09192
Gilder, Richard W.	1887.09.21	SLC	CT.Hartford	Consound you, I	107:1928.05.07	09557
Gilder, Richard W.	1887.09.28	SLC	CT.Hartford	Thanks, very much	CtY	03654
Gilder, Richard W.	1887.11.06	SLC	CT.Hartford	Exhibit A says	105:1958.04.28	09700 other sources
Gilder, Richard W.	ca 1887.11.16	SLC	CT.Hartford	It doesn't seem	ViU	10871
Gilder, Richard W.	1888.03.04	SLC	CT.Hartford	I am trying	DLC	11150
Gilder, Richard W.	1888.03.11	SLC	NY.New York	I'm ashamed to	NN	03707
Gilder, Richard W. & Johnson, Robert U.	1888.08.12	SLC	NY.Elmira	I'll tell you	NN-B	02684 also to Buel
Gilder, Richard W.	1888.08.24	SLC	NY.Elmira	If you still	NNAL	03753
Gilder, Richard W.	1889.02.21	SLC	CT.Hartford	Thank you ever	NN	03866
Gilder, Richard W.	1889.05.16	SLC	CT.Hartford	S.E. Moffett is	NN	03893

Gilder, Richard W.	1889.05.30	SLC	Unknown	All right; I'll	TxU	03897
Gilder, Richard W.	1889.08.17	SLC	NY.Elmira	The title as	InU-Li	10829 telegram
Gilder, Richard W.	1889.10.05	SLC	CT.Hartford	Fellowcroft Club, 32	NN	03945
Gilder, Richard W.	bef 1890.12.16	SLC	CT.Hartford	C.N. Flagg, descendent	111:189	08624
Gilder, Richard W.	1891.04.16	SLC	CT.Hartford	Here is Mr.	107:1926.03.03	04190
Gilder, Richard W.	1892.10.19	SLC	IT.Florence	a noble &	157:1928.12.03	09229
Gilder, Richard W.	bef 1892.10.19	SLC	IT.Florence	And now I come to	ODa2	11179 fragment
Gilder, Richard W.	1893.03.20	SLC	IT.Florence	If you know	161:13.408	04355
Gilder, Richard W.	1893.11.06	SLC	NY.New York	You do not	ViU	04491
Gilder, Richard W. & Johnson, Robert U.	1895.08.17	SLC	CN.Vancouver	This is to	Mo2	02462 to six editors
Gilder, Richard W.	1896.03.12	SLC	II.Jaipur	Colonel Jacob has	219:1896.04.25	05031
Gilder, Richard W.	1897.01.13	SLC	AU.Vienna	Yours of Dec.	CLU-S/C	10309 misdated, see 1898
Gilder, Richard W.	1898.01.13	SLC	AU.Vienna	Yours of Dec.	CLU-S/C	05167 misdated 1897
Gilder, Richard W.	1898.04.02	SLC	AU.Vienna	I am mailing	CtY	05373
Gilder, Richard W.	1898.04.29	SLC	AU.Vienna	All right, measure	NNPM	05381
Gilder, Richard W.	1898.05.07	SLC	AU.Kaltenleut.	If I want	CtY(ph)	05386
Gilder, Richard W.	1898.11.06 & 1896.11.13	SLC	AU.Vienna	I have been	CtY	05459
Gilder, Richard W.	1898.12.28	SLC	AU.Vienna	I don't know	107:1927.01.05	10090 other sources
Gilder, Richard W.	1899.01.06	SLC	AU.Vienna	I learn, through	CU-MARK(ph)	05534
Gilder, Richard W.	1899.02.02	SLC	AU.Vienna	Prince Lichnowsky is	NN	05542
Gilder, Richard W.	1899.02.25	SLC	AU.Vienna	I have abandoned	CtY	05548
Gilder, Richard W.	1899.03.14	SLC	AU.Vienna	What is it	NN	05562
Gilder, Richard W.	1899.05.15	SLC	AU.Vienna	Why hang it	120:1934.10	09903 other sources
Gilder, Richard W.	1899.06.02	SLC	EN.London	It was not	107:1921.03.04	05629

ADDRESSEE	DATE	WRITER	PLACE	CUE	SOURCE	NUMBER/NOTES
Gilder, Richard W.	1899.07.23	SLC	SE.Sanna	All right, &	CtY(ph)	05657
Gilder, Richard W.	1899.08.22	SLC	SE.Sanna	We have been	CtY(ph)	05663
Gilder, Richard W.	1899.10.**	SLC	EN.London	Can't you send	TxU	05682
Gilder, Richard W.	1899.10.16	SLC	EN.London	This is to	NN	05690
Gilder, Richard W.	1900.07.06	SLC	EN.Willesden	Not able to	InU-Li	10830 telegram
Gilder, Richard W.	1900.07.08	SLC	EN.London	If you only	449:f	05833
Gilder, Richard W.	1900.07.31	SLC	EN.London	It said all	107:1921.03.04	05841
Gilder, Richard W.	1900.10.**	OLC	NY.New York	Enclosed please find	CU-MARK(ph)	05875
Gilder, Richard W.	1900.11.30	SLC	NY.New York	I am laid	NN	05923
Gilder, Richard W.	ca 1900.12.11	SLC	NY.New York	I can't. If	NN	05929
Gilder, Richard W.	1900.12.18	SLC	NY.New York	Yes, $1500 is	Mo2	11011
Gilder, Richard W.	1902.06.20	OLC	NY.Riverdale	Just a line	CU-MARK(tr)	06370
Gilder, Richard W.	1902.12.10	SLC per IVL	NY.Riverdale	Mr. Clemens who	NN	06508
Gilder, Richard W. & Alden, Henry M.	1903.07.21	SLC	NY.Elmira	Although I have	NN-B	08234 also to others
Gilder, Richard W.	1903.08.01	SLC	NY.Elmira	The enclosed is	NN	06717 Moffett July 30 enc
Gilder, Richard W.	1904.05.12 & 1904.05.13	SLC	IT.Florence	A friend of	CU-MARK(ph)	06835
Gilder, Richard W.	1904.05.27	SLC	IT.Florence	Here are samples	CU-MARK(ph)	06841
Gilder, Richard W.	1904.06.07	SLC	IT.Florence	I have been	CU-MARK(ph)	06862 to Gilder family
Gilder, Richard W.	1904.06.08	SLC	IT.Florence	Gilder we want	CU-MARK(ph)	06863 telegram
Gilder, Richard W.	1905.06.01	SLC per IVL	NH.Dublin	Mr. Clemens wishes	NN	07054
Gilder, Richard W.	1905.08.15	SLC	CT.Norfolk	I can say	NN	07110
Gilder, Richard W.	1905.11.03	SLC	MA.Boston	Your question just	NN	07194 telegram
Gill, Everett	1902.06.01	SLC	MO.Hannibal	I find it	DLC	06349

Gill, Watson		1894.12.09	OLC per SLC	FR.Paris	Mr. Colby has	NN7(tr)	04822 on Gill to Rogers bef Dec 9
Gill, William F.		1875.05.31	SLC	CT.Hartford	I see you	ViU	01237
Gill, William F.		1875.06.08	SLC	CT.Hartford	It is perhaps	MH-H(tr)	01241 SLC tr
Gillette, William H.		1903.10.22	SLC	NY.New York	Thank you for	CtHSD	06751
Gillis, James N.		1870.01.26	SLC	NY.Elmira	I remember that	CCamarSJ(ph)	00416
Gillis, James N.		1871.07.02	SLC	NY.Elmira	I am here	CCamarSJ(ph)	00631
Gillis, Steve		1907.06.07	SLC	NY.New York	with the unabated	Mo2	09260 inscription
Gillis, William R.	ca	1866.02.**	SLC	CA.San Francisco	I am leaving	237:75	00095
Gillis, William R.		1902.05.16	SLC	NY.Riverdale	It isn't your	CU-MARK	06337
Gilman, Arthur		1883.01.08	SLC	CT.Hartford	If total unfitness	ViU	02332
Gilman, Mr.		1879.09.15	SLC	NY.Elmira	I haven't any	ViU	01689
Gilsey, Henry		1894.08.07	SLC	NY.New York	I am very	NN5	04774
Gleason, Rachel B.		1874.09.12	SLC	NY.New York	It was a	NElmHi	01127
Globe ed.		1873.04.**	SLC	CT.Hartford	I don't know	239:1873.05	00894
Gluck, James F.		1885.11.12	SLC	CT.Hartford	I will comply	CCamarSJ	03305
Glyn, Elinor		1908.01.24	SLC	NY.New York	It reads pretty	CtY(tr)	07929
Godfrey, Sarah H.		1901.01.21	SLC	NY.New York	The "Alonzo Child"	ViU(tr)	05970
Godwin, Harold		1897.12.10	SLC	AU.Vienna	Of the creditors	CU-MARK(tr)	05318 SLC tr
Goepp, Philip H.		1902.05.23	SLC	NY.Riverdale	Your kind letter	CU-MARK(ph)	06344
Goldburg, Jesse J.	o/a	1905.08.30	SLC per IVL	NH.Dublin	If agent is	CU-MARK(dr)	07120 on Goldburg Aug 30
Good, Dr.		1894.06.25	SLC	FR.La Bourboule	We are located	C4	04746
Goodell, Abner C.		1900.12.31	SLC	NY.New York	I think you	CU-MARK(ph)	05942
Goodkind, Milt	ca	1907.05.05	SLC	NY.New York	Latitude 43 degrees	131:1907.05.05	07714 telegram
Goodkind, Mr.	o/a	1905.12.06	SLC	NY.New York	To you, &	Mo2	08890 form letter

ADDRESSEE		DATE	WRITER	PLACE	CUE	SOURCE	NUMBER/NOTES
Goodman, Joseph T.		1867.10.24	SLC	SP.Cadiz	Between you and	431:1867.12.01	00153
Goodman, Joseph T.		1889.10.07	SLC	CT.Hartford	I had a	CtY	03948
Goodman, Joseph T.		1889.11.16	SLC	CT.Hartford	I have just	CU-MARK	03968
Goodman, Joseph T.		1889.11.17	SLC	CT.Hartford	Close no bargain	CU-MARK	03969 telegram
Goodman, Joseph T.		1889.11.19	SLC	CT.Hartford	I shall be	CtY	03970
Goodman, Joseph T.		1889.11.29	SLC	CT.Hartford	Things are getting	114:521	03980
Goodman, Joseph T.		1889.12.04	SLC	CT.Hartford	As I am	CtY	03982
Goodman, Joseph T.		1890.03.31	SLC	CT.Hartford	If you were	114:530	04033
Goodman, Joseph T.		1890.04.16	SLC	CT.Hartford	Take the earliest	CU-MARK	04039 telegram
Goodman, Joseph T.		1890.04.18	SLC	CT.Hartford	Your letter &	CtY	04041
Goodman, Joseph T.	ca	1890.04.25	SLC	CT.Hartford	Your letter made	CU-MARK	08608
Goodman, Joseph T.		1890.06.23	SLC	CT.Hartford	I have been	CtY	04053
Goodman, Joseph T.		1890.10.23	SLC	CT.Hartford	Of course I	CtY	04105
Goodman, Joseph T.		1891.02.24	SLC	CT.Hartford	Think of this	NN-B	04573
Goodman, Joseph T.		1891.04.**	SLC	CT.Hartford	Well, it's all	ViU	04186
Goodman, Joseph T.		1902.05.16	SLC	NY.Riverdale	No--you don't	CU-MARK	06335
Goodman, Joseph T.		1902.06.13	SLC	NY.Riverdale	I am lost	114:721	06364
Goodman, Joseph T.		1903.10.09	SLC	NY.New York	The cutting has	CU-MARK CAIb2	06738 CAIb2 envelope
Goodman, Joseph T.		1906.04.16	SLC	NY.New York	I thank you	CU-MARK CAIb2	07430 CAIb2 envelope
Goodman, Joseph T.		1908.07.30	SLC	CT.Redding	I have authorized	C4(tr)	08064
Goodman, Joseph T.	ca	1910.04.01	SLC	Unknown	Come on and	428:1910.04.23	10707
Goodman (J.T.) & Co.		1864.02.29	SLC	NV.Virginia City	Please pay Orion	CU-MARK	00075
Goodrich-Freer, Adela		1900.01.11	SLC	EN.London	Now I think	ViU CLU-S/C	05745 CLU-S/C envelope
Goodrich-Freer, Adela		1900.05.11	SLC	EN.London	Indeed we shall	ViU	05805
Goodridge, Miss		1895.05.01	SLC	FR.Paris	Luck has departed	ViU	04290
Goodwin, Mr.		1889.11.08	SLC	CT.Hartford	If I had	CCC	03961

Goodwin, Mrs.		1902.12.06	SLC per IVL	NY.Riverdale	As I am	CtHMTH	06502
Gordon, John C.		1900.07.28	SLC	EN.London	We all join	UkE2	05839
Gordon, Laing		1904.02.27	SLC	IT.Florence	You will remember	CU-MARK	06801
Gordon, Mrs. William & Gordon, William P.		1906.01.24	SLC	NY.New York	I have just	WaCheh2	07316
Gordon, William P. & Gordon, Mrs. William		1906.01.24	SLC	NY.New York	I have just	WaCheh2	07316
Gorky, Maxim & Willard, J.F.		1906.04.13	SLC	NY.New York	Mr. Willard, the	CU-MARK	07429
Gosse, Edmund W.		1899.07.06	SLC	EN.London	Training for the	CU-MARK(tr)	05651
Gottlieb, J. Adelphi	o/a	1906.11.10	SLC per IVL	NY.New York	I thank the	CU-MARK(dr)	07566
Gould, L.M. & Gould, S.C.		1886.12.06	SLC per FGW	CT.Hartford	Please discontinue	CU-MARK	10752 on Goulds Dec 1
Gould, S.C. & Gould, L.M.		1886.12.06	SLC per FGW	CT.Hartford	Please discontinue	CU-MARK	10752 on Goulds Dec 1
Gourlie, John H.		1869.09.07	SLC	NY.Buffalo	With pleasure	CtHMTH	10500 inscription
Graham, Malcolm		1908.05.25	SLC	NY.New York	Yes, it is my shell	ODa2	10463
Graham, Margaret S.		1904.04.12	SLC	IT.Florence	It is a	CLjC	06822
Graham, Mrs. John		1905.12.**	SLC	NY.New York	Perhaps Mrs. John	110:1970.12.10	10374 inscription
Grant, Butler		1903.05.08	SLC	NY.Riverdale	Happy Birthday	462:47	11161 inscription; possibly spurious
Grant, David C.	o/a	1905.10.09	SLC per IVL	NH.Dublin	I ratify &	CU-MARK(dr)	07168 on Grant Oct 9
Grant, Frederick D.		1906.03.**	SLC	NY.Babylon	I shall be	CU-MARK(tr)	08248 telegram; SLC tr
Grant, Frederick D.		1906.03.**	SLC	NY.New York	I mean the	CU-MARK(tr)	08247 SLC tr
Grant, Frederick D.		1906.03.**	SLC	NY.New York	Because I stopped	CU-MARK(tr)	07359 telegram; SLC tr

ADDRESSEE	DATE	WRITER	PLACE	CUE	SOURCE	NUMBER/NOTES
Grant, Julia D.	1886.02.03	SLC	CT.Hartford	I expected to	ICarbS	03365
Grant, Percy S.	1906.12.25	SLC	NY.New York	Do not cast	NN-B	08272 inscription
Grant, Robert	1902.01.09	SLC	NY.Riverdale	As regards that	CU-MARK	06233 typed form letter
Grant, Ulysses S.	1881.03.15	SLC	CT.Hartford	This letter is	OKentU	01927
Grant, Ulysses S.	o/a 1885.04.01	SLC	Unknown	I hope you	CU-MARK(dr)	03201 on Gerhardt Apr 1
Grant, Ulysses S.	1885.04.30	SLC	NY.New York	This is an	NPV	03221
Grant, Ulysses S.	1885.07.04	SLC	NY.Elmira	I got back	CLjC	10672
Grant, Ulysses S. Jr.	1885.**.**	SLC	Unknown	from S.L. Clemens	105:1945.01.23	09427 inscription
Grant, Ulysses S. Jr.	1885.**.**	SLC	Unknown	from the Author	105:1954.03.23	09434 inscription; other sources
Grant, Ulysses S. Jr.	1885.11.**	SLC	Unknown	from the Author	ViU	09433 inscription; other sources
Grant, Ulysses S. Jr.	1906.03.09	SLC per IVL	NY.New York	I prize your	CU-MARK(tr)	07369 IVL tr
Grasmere, David L.	1882.09.14	SLC	NY.Elmira	Your letter has	ViU	02267
Gratz, Simon	1872.12.16	SLC	CT.Hartford	I regret that	PHi	00845
Gray, Edmund	1882.07.31	SLC	NY.Elmira	Hang it, no	CU-MARK(ph)	02242
Greeley, Horace	1871.08.17	SLC	CT.Hartford	I am here	NN	00645
Green, Charles P.	1886.12.26	SLC	CT.Hartford	The book arrived	MH-H	03503
Green, Colonel	1900.09.01	SLC	EN.London	I thank you	CU-MARK(ph)	05861
Green, G.G.	1890.03.19	SLC per FGW	CT.Hartford	In reply to	CU-MARK(tr)	09097 FGW tr & SLC dr; misdated Mar 18
Greenall, John	1906.04.06	SLC per IVL	NY.New York	How things do	Mo2	08891
Greene, Belle C.	1887.01.17	SLC	CT.Hartford	In my judgment	CU-MARK(tr)	03512
Greene, Henry C.	ca 1905.02.27	SLC per IVL	NY.New York	Mr. S.L. Clemens	CU-MARK	08729

Greene, Henry C.	o/a	1905.07.28	SLC per IVL	NH.Dublin	Mr. Clemens wishes	CU-MARK(dr)	07091 on Greene July 28
Greenslet, Ferris	aft	1907.03.26	SLC per IVL	NY.New York	We were a	CSmH	07678
Gregory, Augusta	pm	1903.03.09	SLC	NY.Riverdale	I have been	CU-MARK 144:400	06589 CU-MARK envelope
Gregory, Augusta		1904.02.16	SLC	IT.Florence	I wish to	CU-MARK(ph)	09403
Gregory, Augusta		1907.07.08	SLC	EN.London	I thank you	418:1982.12.15	09401
Gresham, Walter Q.		1893.04.06	SLC	NY.New York	It is not	NNU-F	04549
Greville, Frances E.		1907.10.12	SLC	EN.London	with the warm	CU-MARK(ph)	10555 inscription
Grieg, William		1898.02.28	SLC per OLC	AU.Vienna	Thank you very	CU-MARK	05355
Grieg, William S.		1905.12.19	SLC per IVL	NY.New York	I have forgotten	CU-MARK(dr)	07258 on Grieg Dec 16
Griffin, George		1880.09.11	SLC	NY.Elmira	Show this telegram	CtHMTH	01830 telegram
Gripenberg, Alexandra		1888.09.15	SLC	NY.Elmira	The "Century" folk	FiH2	03764
Gripenberg, Alexandra		1888.12.27	SLC	CT.Hartford	I have been	FiH2	03808
Griswold, George		1870.03.07	SLC	NY.Buffalo	some friends have	107:1916.05.11	00441 date uncertain
Griswold, George		1907.02.28	SLC per IVL	NY.New York	Mr. Clemens directs	CU-MARK(dr)	07669
Griswold, Mr.		1900.12.20	SLC	NY.New York	I shall be	DLC(tr)	05937
Griswold, Mr.		1902.11.07	SLC	NY.Riverdale	I shall be	FSp2	08814
Grocco, Pietro		1904.02.07	SLC	IT.Florence	We find that	CU-MARK(dr)	06790 another dr per JC in Italian
Gross, Frank & Gross, Mrs. Frank		****.**.**	SLC	Unknown	*	CAlb2	10179 envelope only
Gross, Mrs. Frank & Gross, Frank		****.**.**	SLC	Unknown	*	CAlb2	10179 envelope only
Gross, William H.		1887.01.20	SLC	CT.Hartford	All right, friend	ViU	03515

ADDRESSEE	DATE	WRITER	PLACE	CUE	SOURCE	NUMBER/NOTES
Gross, William H.	1887.07.21	SLC	NY.Elmira	Whatinthehell	130:1982.11.08	09193
Grossman, Edwina B.	*	*	*	*	*	11165 see Booth, Edwina
Grube, Gustave	****.**.**	SLC per OLC	Unknown	I regret that	As2	09045
Guilford, Mrs. L.T.	1909.01.28	SLC per MLH	CT.Redding	X and to	CtHMTH CU-MARK(tr)	08328 CtHMTH dr
Guinness, Bridget & Guinness, Mr.	bef 1909.02.18	SLC & CC	NY.New York	Miss Clara Clemens	CU-MARK	08351
Guinness, Mr. & Guinness, Bridget	bef 1909.02.18	SLC & CC	NY.New York	Miss Clara Clemens	CU-MARK	08351
Gulick, Thomas L.	1891.01.08	SLC	CT.Hartford	I cannot thank	MWA	04155
Gummere, Mr.	1906.01.31	SLC per IVL	NY.New York	I thank you	MH-H	07321
Gwynn, Mr.	1875.06.21	SLC	CT.Hartford	Will you come	WvU	03801 date uncertain
Haddon, Frederick W.	1874.05.10	SLC	NY.Elmira	Your letter has	AuMS	10692
Haddon, Frederick W.	1895.11.14	SLC	NZ.Christchurch	I will hear	AuMS	04973
Haldane, Mrs. James A.	1899.03.22	OLC	EN.London	I too was	UkENL	05566
Hale, Edward E.	1899.11.01	SLC	EN.London	I thank you	PU	05698
Hale, Edward E.	1905.03.28	SLC	NY.New York	Howells has sent	PU	07023
Hale, Edward E.	o/a 1905.04.11	SLC per IVL	NY.New York	Mr. Clemens directs	CU-MARK(dr)	07028 on Hale Apr 8
Hale, Edward E.	1906.04.10	SLC per IVL	NY.New York	I had already	PU	07418
Hales, Ernest C.	1905.03.06	SLC	NY.New York	I thank you	297:104	07013
Halford, E.W. & Foulke, William D.	1888.10.03	SLC	CT.Hartford	For the sake	InU-Li	03780
Hall, Blakely	1891.04.03	SLC	CT.Hartford	My great trouble	CU-MARK	04188
Hall, Frederick J.	****.**.**	SLC	NY.New York	I have not	NN-B	08982
Hall, Frederick J.	****.**.**	SLC	Unknown	It would be	165:1963.04.05	09657
Hall, Frederick J.	****.**.**	SLC	Unknown	I will be	CU-MARK(ph)	08981
Hall, Frederick J.	****.**.**	SLC	Unknown	Send him a	Mo2	08505
Hall, Frederick J.	****.**.**	SLC	Unknown	Been to Bunce's	NN-B	08980

Hall, Frederick J.		****.**.**	SLC	Unknown	Get them on	NN-B	08979
Hall, Frederick J.		****.**.**	SLC	Unknown	Please send $175	NN-B	08978
Hall, Frederick J.		****.**.**	SLC	Unknown	Please send this	NN-B	05229
Hall, Frederick J.		****.**.**	SLC	Unknown	I forgot. Whitford is	ODa2	11205
Hall, Frederick J.		****.10.24	SLC	Unknown	Remind me to	NN-B	08977
Hall, Frederick J.		1885.10.05	SLC	CT.Hartford	You have in	NIC	03292
Hall, Frederick J.		1886.07.12	SLC	NY.Elmira	That sounds like	NN-B	02636
Hall, Frederick J.		1886.07.14	SLC	NY.Elmira	Mr. Howells has	ViU	03416
Hall, Frederick J.		1886.07.16	SLC	NY.Elmira	No, I don't	NN-B	02637
Hall, Frederick J.		1886.07.21	SLC	NY.Elmira	I find that	NN-B	02639
Hall, Frederick J.		1886.08.06	SLC	Unknown	Read the enclosed I did not	NN-B ViU	02640 ViU enc
Hall, Frederick J.		1886.08.17	SLC	NY.Elmira	It is good	NN-B	02641
Hall, Frederick J.		1886.08.19	SLC	NY.Elmira	1. I want	NN-B	02642
Hall, Frederick J.		1886.08.25	SLC	NY.Elmira	Won't you please	NPV	03444
Hall, Frederick J.		1886.08.28	SLC	NY.Elmira	I am very	NN-B	02643
Hall, Frederick J.		1886.09.03	SLC	NY.Elmira	Of course I	CU-MARK(ph)	03451
Hall, Frederick J.		1886.09.04	SLC	NY.Elmira	I think we	NN-B	02644
Hall, Frederick J.		1886.09.11	SLC	NY.Elmira	Answer him thus	NN-B	02645
Hall, Frederick J.		1886.09.30	SLC	CT.Hartford	Please send me	NN-B	02646
Hall, Frederick J.	o/a	1887.06.21	SLC	Unknown	give him the	226:49	03586 on Van Zandt June 21
Hall, Frederick J.		1887.07.09	SLC	NY.Elmira	Yes, we do	NPV	03597
Hall, Frederick J.		1887.07.12	SLC	NY.Elmira	If your prospectus	NN-B	02664
Hall, Frederick J.		1887.07.15	SLC	NY.Elmira	No, if the	NN-B	02665
Hall, Frederick J. & Webster, Charles L.		1887.08.15	SLC	NY.Elmira	Thank you very	NN-B	02668
Hall, Frederick J.		1887.09.02	SLC	NY.Elmira	Consider the propriety	NN-B	02673
Hall, Frederick J. & Webster, Charles L.		1887.09.05	SLC	Unknown	You need to	NN-B	02672

ADDRESSEE	DATE	WRITER	PLACE	CUE	SOURCE	NUMBER/NOTES
Hall, Frederick J.	1887.09.08	SLC	NY.Elmira	I think it	NN-B	02674
Hall, Frederick J.	o/a 1887.09.26	SLC	CT.Hartford	I am quite	CU-MARK	03655 on Webster Sept 26
Hall, Frederick J.	1888.05.07	SLC	CT.Hartford	The proposed book	NN-B	02682
Hall, Frederick J.	1888.11.12	SLC	CT.Hartford	I approve, all	NN-B	02686
Hall, Frederick J.	1888.11.12	SLC	CT.Hartford	Mr. Wright has	ViU	03831
Hall, Frederick J.	1889.01.11	SLC	CT.Hartford	The substitution of	VtMiM	03850
Hall, Frederick J.	1889.07.02	SLC	NY.Elmira	The first article	CU-MARK	03906
Hall, Frederick J.	1889.07.24	SLC	NY.Elmira	Upon reflection--this	DLC	03916
Hall, Frederick J.	1889.08.20	SLC	NY.Elmira	You are perfectly	ViU	03929
Hall, Frederick J.	1889.09.05	SLC	NY.Elmira	I made the	NN-B	02694
Hall, Frederick J.	1889.11.24	SLC	CT.Hartford	I send you	CU-MARK	03978
Hall, Frederick J.	1890.04.19	SLC	CT.Hartford	Mr. Whitmore has	NN-B	04552
Hall, Frederick J.	1890.04.21	SLC	CT.Hartford	I think well	212:1948.04.24	10445
Hall, Frederick J.	1890.06.30	SLC	CT.Hartford	The letter accounts	NN-B	04553
Hall, Frederick J.	1890.09.03	SLC	NY.Tannersville	The price of	NN-B	04554
Hall, Frederick J.	1890.10.15	SLC	CT.Hartford	Just as you	NN-B	04557
Hall, Frederick J.	1890.10.23	SLC	CT.Hartford	Come up next	NN-B	04559
Hall, Frederick J.	1890.11.11	SLC	CT.Hartford	Mrs. Clemens lends	CU-MARK	04113
Hall, Frederick J.	1890.11.30	SLC	CT.Hartford	I couldn't reach	NN-B	04561
Hall, Frederick J.	1890.12.11	SLC	CT.Hartford	Come up at	NvU	04003 telegram
Hall, Frederick J.	1890.12.13	SLC	NY.New York	Got belated, or	NN-B	04562
Hall, Frederick J.	1890.12.15	SLC	CT.Hartford	That Innocents Abroad	NN-B	04563
Hall, Frederick J.	1890.12.27	SLC	CT.Hartford	I don't believe	ViU	04121
Hall, Frederick J.	1891.02.03	SLC	CT.Hartford	It's an excellent	NN-B	04565
Hall, Frederick J.	1891.02.13	SLC	CT.Hartford	What does the	NN-B	04566
Hall, Frederick J.	1891.02.13	SLC	CT.Hartford	Yes, wait till	NN-B	04567
Hall, Frederick J.	1891.02.14	SLC	CT.Hartford	The mailing clerk	NN-B	04568
Hall, Frederick J.	1891.02.15	SLC	CT.Hartford	This is from	NN-B	04569

Hall, Frederick J.	1891.02.17	SLC	CT.Hartford	It is all	NN-B	04570
Hall, Frederick J.	1891.02.22	SLC	CT.Hartford	When you get	NN-B	04571
Hall, Frederick J.	1891.02.27	SLC	CT.Hartford	Within please find	NN-B	04574
Hall, Frederick J.	1891.03.10	SLC	CT.Hartford	The dummy is	NN-B	04576
Hall, Frederick J.	1891.03.12	SLC	CT.Hartford	Good. Shall look	NN-B	04577
Hall, Frederick J.	1891.03.29	SLC	CT.Hartford	How many subscriptions	NN-B	04578
Hall, Frederick J.	1891.04.03	SLC	CT.Hartford	The game is	NN-B	04580
Hall, Frederick J.	1891.04.04	SLC	CT.Hartford	All your news	NN-B	04582
Hall, Frederick J.	1891.04.09	SLC	CT.Hartford	If I tried	NN-B	04583
Hall, Frederick J.	1891.04.14	SLC	CT.Hartford	Privately--keep it	NN-B	04584
Hall, Frederick J.	1891.05.02	SLC	CT.Hartford	Bok wants to	CU-MARK(tr)	04202 telegram
Hall, Frederick J.	1891.05.04	SLC	CT.Hartford	I don't think	NN-B	04585
Hall, Frederick J.	1891.05.13	SLC	CT.Hartford	All right, accept	NN-B	04586
Hall, Frederick J.	1891.05.13	SLC	CT.Hartford	Don't begin to	NN-B	04587
Hall, Frederick J.	1891.05.20	SLC	CT.Hartford	Please see Laffan	NN-B	04589
Hall, Frederick J.	1891.06.12	SLC per FGW	CT.Hartford	Your favor of	CU-MARK(tr)	08616 FGW tr
Hall, Frederick J.	1891.06.17	SLC	FR.Paris	A cablegram informs	NN-B	04590
Hall, Frederick J.	1891.07.10	SLC	FR.Aix-les-Bains	Please see Johnson	NN-B	04591
Hall, Frederick J.	1891.07.26	SLC	FR.Aix-les-Bains	Yes, the statement	NN-B	04592
Hall, Frederick J.	1891.08.07	SLC	GE.Bayreuth	If I remember	NN-B	04593
Hall, Frederick J.	1891.08.24	SLC	GE.Marienbad	I am mailing	NN-B	04594
Hall, Frederick J.	1891.09.15	SLC	SW.Geneva	We arrived here	NN-B	04595
Hall, Frederick J.	1891.10.16	SLC	GE.Berlin	This is the	NN-B	04597
Hall, Frederick J.	1891.10.20	SLC	GE.Berlin	I want to	NN-B	04598
Hall, Frederick J.	1891.10.27	SLC	GE.Berlin	Mighty glad to	CSmH	04247
Hall, Frederick J.	1891.10.28	SLC	GE.Frankfurt	Can't buy Struwwelpeter	CSmH	04248
Hall, Frederick J.	1891.11.07	SLC	GE.Berlin	I made a	NN-B	04599

ADDRESSEE	DATE	WRITER	PLACE	CUE	SOURCE	NUMBER/NOTES
Hall, Frederick J.	1891.11.08 & 1891.11.09	SLC	GE.Berlin	All I ever	NN-B	04600
Hall, Frederick J.	1891.11.19	SLC	GE.Berlin	If you think	NN-B	04601
Hall, Frederick J.	1891.11.20	SLC	GE.Berlin	I think I	Mo2	04254
Hall, Frederick J.	1891.11.22	SLC	GE.Berlin	I am returning	NN-B	04602
Hall, Frederick J.	1891.11.27	SLC	GE.Berlin	That kind of	NN-B	04603
Hall, Frederick J.	1891.12.01	SLC	GE.Berlin	The enclosed is	NN-B	04604
Hall, Frederick J.	1891.12.16	OLC	GE.Berlin	My brother writes me	ODa2	11193
Hall, Frederick J.	1891.12.22	SLC	GE.Berlin	I corrected both	NN-B	04605
Hall, Frederick J.	1891.12.26	SLC	GE.Berlin	Happy New-Year	ViU	10837
Hall, Frederick J.	1892.01.06	SLC	GE.Ilsenburg	I enclose check	NN-B	04606
Hall, Frederick J.	1892.01.21	OLC	GE.Berlin	Your letter written	IC3	04266
Hall, Frederick J.	1892.01.25	SLC	GE.Berlin	Mrs. Clemens was	NN-B	04608
Hall, Frederick J.	1892.02.02	SLC	GE.Berlin	You are going	NN-B	04609
Hall, Frederick J.	1892.02.05	SLC	GE.Berlin	The game-board	NN-B	04610
Hall, Frederick J.	1892.02.12	SLC	GE.Berlin	Daly wants to	CU-MARK(tr)	04270
Hall, Frederick J.	1892.03.08	SLC	FR.Menton	The fatalest objection	NN-B	04612
Hall, Frederick J.	1892.03.08	SLC	FR.Menton	Please preserve this	ViU	04274 on McClure Mar 2
Hall, Frederick J.	1892.04.04	SLC	IT.Rome	Howells and I	NN-B	04611
Hall, Frederick J.	1892.04.24	SLC	IT.Rome	I enclose the	NN-B	04613
Hall, Frederick J.	1892.05.22	SLC	IT.Venice	Yours of May	NN-B	04614
Hall, Frederick J.	1892.06.11	SLC	GE.Bad-Nauheim	If this arrives	NN-B	04297
Hall, Frederick J.	1892.07.22	SLC	GE.Bad-Nauheim	Yours of July	NN-B	04615
Hall, Frederick J.	1892.07.24	SLC	GE.Bad-Nauheim	I have not	NN-B	04616
Hall, Frederick J.	1892.08.04	SLC	GE.Bad-Nauheim	Land, you hadn't	IC3	10333 misdated, see Sept 4-5
Hall, Frederick J.	1892.08.09	SLC	Unknown	But if he	212:1943.06.19	09896
Hall, Frederick J.	1892.08.10	SLC	GE.Bad-Nauheim	I have dropped (The foregoing	TxFTC NN-B	04617

Hall, Frederick J.	1892.08.23	SLC	GE.Bad-Nauheim	I will itemize	NN-B	04618
Hall, Frederick J.	1892.09.04 & 1892.09.05	SLC	GE.Bad-Nauheim	Land, you hadn't P.S. Sept 5	IC3 NN-B	04653 misdated Aug
Hall, Frederick J.	1892.09.05	SLC	IT.Florence	The August statement	NN-B	10316 misdated, see Oct
Hall, Frederick J.	1892.09.18	SLC	SW.Lucerne	I left a	NN-B	04620
Hall, Frederick J.	1892.09.23	SLC	IT.Florence	Yours of Sept.	212:1948.04.24	02224 other sources
Hall, Frederick J.	1892.09.29	SLC	IT.Florence	Hereafter you may	107:1925.03.03	01191
Hall, Frederick J.	1892.10.05	SLC	IT.Florence	The August statement	NN-B	04619 misdated Sept
Hall, Frederick J.	1892.10.13	SLC	IT.Florence	I am sending	NN-B	04622
Hall, Frederick J.	1892.10.31	SLC	IT.Florence	Yours of the	CU-MARK(tr)	08927
Hall, Frederick J.	1892.11.24	SLC	IT.Florence	Yours of Nov.	NN-B 212:1954.12.01	04624 212 envelope
Hall, Frederick J.	1892.12.02	SLC	IT.Florence	My registered cable	CU-MARK(ph)	00786
Hall, Frederick J.	1892.12.07	SLC	IT.Florence	If the $500	CU-MARK	02411
Hall, Frederick J.	1892.12.12	SLC	IT.Florence	November check received	NN-B	04626
Hall, Frederick J.	1892.12.26	SLC	IT.Florence	Carey is right	ViU	04314
Hall, Frederick J.	1892.12.28	SLC	IT.Florence	I am proposing	NN-B	04627
Hall, Frederick J.	1893.01.01	SLC	IT.Florence	Yours of Dec.	CLjC	04318
Hall, Frederick J.	1893.01.24	SLC	IT.Florence	I sent the	NN-B	04628
Hall, Frederick J.	1893.01.28	SLC	IT.Florence	Here it is	NN-B	04630
Hall, Frederick J.	1893.01.28	SLC	IT.Florence	I want to	NN-B	04629
Hall, Frederick J.	1893.02.03	SLC	IT.Florence	Won't you carry	NN-B	04631
Hall, Frederick J.	1893.02.05	SLC	IT.Florence	Check for 102.8.4	NN-B	04632
Hall, Frederick J.	1893.02.25	SLC	IT.Florence	Land, I seem	NN-B	04633
Hall, Frederick J.	1893.03.02	SLC	IT.Florence	The check for	NN-B	04634
Hall, Frederick J.	1893.03.08	SLC	IT.Florence	Very good, we	NN-B	04636
Hall, Frederick J.	1893.03.13	SLC	IT.Florence	I am busy	NN-B	04637
Hall, Frederick J.	1893.03.23	OLC	IT.Florence	I send you	CAlb2	04357

ADDRESSEE	DATE	WRITER	PLACE	CUE	SOURCE	NUMBER/NOTES
Hall, Frederick J.	1893.04.23	OLC	IT.Florence	Thank you for	CAlb2	04383
Hall, Frederick J.	1893.04.30	OLC	IT.Florence	Will you please	CAlb2	04391
Hall, Frederick J.	1893.05.05	SLC	NY.Elmira	I enclose endorsed	NN-B	04395
Hall, Frederick J.	1893.05.08	SLC	NY.Elmira	I suspect that	NN-B	04640
Hall, Frederick J.	1893.05.13	OLC	IT.Florence	Thank you most	CAlb2	04404
Hall, Frederick J.	1893.05.30	SLC	IT.Florence	You were to	114:583	04408
Hall, Frederick J.	1893.06.02	SLC	IT.Florence	The $500 monthly	NN-B	04643
Hall, Frederick J.	1893.06.03	SLC	IT.Florence	Whatever money comes	219:1948.10.02	04410 other sources
Hall, Frederick J.	1893.06.03	SLC	IT.Florence	The enclosed is	NN-B	04644
Hall, Frederick J.	1893.06.26	SLC	GE.Munich	We have reached	NN-B	04645
Hall, Frederick J.	1893.06.28	OLC	GE.Munich	Your letter to	CAlb2	04419
Hall, Frederick J.	ca 1893.07.**	SLC	Unknown	Why not sell	173:1941.12.02	09182
Hall, Frederick J.	1893.07.03	SLC	GE.Munich	You make a	NN-B	04646
Hall, Frederick J.	1893.07.08	SLC	GE.Munich	No, I suppose I am sincerely	TxU 114:588	04422
Hall, Frederick J.	1893.07.18 & 1893.07.22	SLC	AU.Krankenheil	Doubtless Mr. Walker	NN-B	04647
Hall, Frederick J.	1893.07.19	SLC	AU.Krankenheil	Thanks, many thanks	ViU	04424
Hall, Frederick J.	1893.07.26	SLC	AU.Krankenheil	If you could	NN-B	01633
Hall, Frederick J.	1893.07.30	SLC	AU.Krankenheil	This time "Pudd'nhead	TxFTC	04427
Hall, Frederick J.	1893.08.06	SLC	AU.Krankenheil	I am very	NN-B	04648
Hall, Frederick J.	1893.08.09	SLC	AU.Krankenheil	Won't you have	NN-B	04649
Hall, Frederick J.	1893.08.14 & 1893.08.16	SLC	AU.Krankenheil	I have thought I am very	CU-MARK NN-B	04437
Hall, Frederick J.	1893.09.16	SLC	NY.New York	Tell my brother	ODa2	04451
Hall, Frederick J.	o/a 1893.10.24	SLC	NY.New York	Don't wait for	CoAur2	08983 on Langdon Oct 24
Hall, Frederick J.	bet 1893.11.** & 1893.12.**	SLC	NY.New York	July 26, I	438:64	04658
Hall, Frederick J.	1894.01.06	SLC	NY.New York	I think I	NN-B	04906
Hall, Frederick J.	1894.01.14	SLC	NY.New York	I told Whitmore	NN-B	04907

Hall, Frederick J.		1894.01.14	SLC	Unknown	from his friend	226:30	09855 inscription
Hall, Frederick J.		1894.03.31	SLC	FR.Paris	Lord Dufferin, the	CtY	04715
Hall, Frederick J.		1894.05.08	SLC	NY.New York	Will you speak	TxHU	04729
Hall, Frederick J.		1894.06.01	SLC	FR.Paris	Mrs. Clemens &	ViU	04737
Hall, Miss A.		1893.06.14	SLC & OLC	IT.Florence	Mrs. Clemens was	Mo2	08837
Hall, W.T.		1906.03.19	SLC	NY.New York	I thank you	NN-B(tr)	07394
Halley, Albert R.	o/a	1905.12.25	SLC per IVL	NY.New York	Have always declined	CU-MARK(dr)	07271 on Halley Dec 25
Halstead, Murat		1893.10.20	SLC	NY.New York	That's the kind	Mo2	08838
Hamersley, William T.		****.**.**	SLC	Unknown	I am generally	CtHMTH	07537
Hamersley, William T.		1889.08.31	SLC	NY.Elmira	You didn't holler	CU-MARK(tr)	03934 SLC tr
Hamersley, William T.		1889.09.01	SLC	NY.Elmira	He drove up	CU-MARK(tr)	03936 telegram; SLC tr
Hamersley, William T.		1890.07.11	SLC	NY.Tannersville	When I fulfilled	CU-MARK(tr)	04062
Hamersley, William T.		1891.05.19	SLC	CT.Hartford	I enclose the	CU-MARK(tr)	04207 SLC tr
Hamilton, William A.		1910.04.05	CC	GE.Wiesbaden	Sailing home Saturday	CU-MARK	08578 telegram
Hammond, Natalie		1896.05.19	SLC	AF.Johannesburg	Your kind letter	CU-MARK	05049 telegram; enc in May 19 to OLC
Hamon, Louis or Cheiro		1895.**.**	SLC	Unknown	Cheiro has exposed	244:133	09120 inscription
Hampden-Cook, E.	o/a	1905.09.08	SLC per IVL	NH.Dublin	Messrs. C & W.	CU-MARK(dr)	07133 on Hampden-Cook Sept 8
Hampton, Crittenden		1907.05.27	SLC	NY.Tuxedo Park	I dictated a	CSoM	10493
Handy, Mr.		1885.12.29	SLC	CT.Hartford	I very much	CtY	03348
Haney, Jesse		1870.11.14	SLC	NY.Buffalo	Can't meddle with	CtHSD	00534
Hannibal Courier-Post	pm	1907.12.03	SLC	NY.New York	Next spring it	MoHM	07881

ADDRESSEE	DATE	WRITER	PLACE	CUE	SOURCE	NUMBER/NOTES
Hannibal Merchants	o/a 1905.02.15	SLC per IVL	NY.New York	No objection to	CU-MARK(dr)	07000 on Merchants Feb 15
Hanson, Joseph M.	o/a 1906.07.25	SLC per IVL	NH.Dublin	Grant Marsh incident	CU-MARK(dr)	07475 on Hanson July 9
Hantz, F.R.	o/a 1905.08.03	SLC per IVL	NH.Dublin	Mr. Clemens directs	CU-MARK(dr)	07100 on Hantz Aug 3
Hapgood, Emily B.	bef 1905.04.29	SLC per IVL	Unknown	Mr. Clemens wishes	CU-MARK(dr)	07036
Hapgood, Mrs.	1894.06.**	SLC	Unknown	with the kindest	CU-MARK(ph)	09295 inscription
Hapgood, Norman	****.**.**	SLC	NY.New York	It is honest	InU-Li	10825
Hapgood, Norman	****.**.**	SLC	NY.New York	I am so	TNJ	05340
Hapgood, Norman	o/a 1905.06.05	SLC per IVL	NH.Dublin	Mr. Clemens says	CU-MARK(dr)	07052 on Hapgood June 5
Hapgood, Norman	ca 1905.09.**	SLC	NH.Dublin	The more I	M3	07123
Hapgood, Norman	o/a 1907.02.02	SLC per IVL	NY.New York	unspeakably glad its	CU-MARK(dr)	07640 on Hapgood Feb 2
Hardenbrook, William T.	o/a 1905.11.08	SLC per IVL	NY.New York	Mr. Clemens does	CU-MARK(dr)	07198 on Hardenbrook Nov 8
Hardenbrook, William T.	o/a 1905.11.16	SLC per IVL	NY.New York	Mr. Clemens never	CU-MARK(dr)	07213 on Hardenbrook Nov 16
Hardy, Mr.	1894.02.03	SLC	NY.New York	I believe it	CU-BANC	04687
Harlon, Elizabeth K.	o/a 1907.05.22	SLC per IVL	NY.Tuxedo Park	They have applied	CU-MARK(dr)	07726 on Harlon May 22
Harmsworth, Mary M.	1908.11.21	SLC	Unknown	with the compliments	122:1931.04.29	09385 inscription; other sources
Harnum, Albert	1893.08.09	SLC	AU.Krankenheil	Mrs. Clemens &	CU-MARK(ph)	04433
Harper & Brothers	1898.11.02	SLC	AU.Vienna	Rogers has Hadleyburg	CU-MARK(tr)	05419 telegram; SLC tr
Harper & Brothers	1899.10.01	SLC	EN.London	Yes, I think	CtY(tr)	11064 SLC tr

Harper & Brothers		1900.01.23	SLC	EN.London	I have no	CBev2	09394 on Weitz to Harper Jan 8
Harper & Brothers	pm	1900.08.**	SLC	EN.London	*	CU-MARK	10112 envelope only
Harper & Brothers	pm	1901.01.19	SLC	NY.New York	*	266:136	10115 envelope only
Harper & Brothers		1903.01.27	SLC per IVL	NY.Riverdale	I can't tell	CU-MARK(tr)	06572 IVL tr
Harper & Brothers		1903.03.13	SLC	NY.Riverdale	Concerning the copyright	CU-MARK(tr)	06598 SLC tr
Harper & Brothers		1903.10.23	SLC & OLC	NY.New York	You are hereby	ViU(tr)	06752
Harper & Brothers	o/a	1903.12.01	SLC	IT.Florence	Make all payments	CU-MARK(dr)	06763 telegram; dr on Harper Dec 1
Harper & Brothers		1904.**.**	SLC	Unknown	Please send me	NRU	06925
Harper & Brothers		1905.**.**	SLC	Unknown	Please Correct bad	CU-MARK	06969
Harper & Brothers	o/a	1905.01.29	SLC	NY.New York	Read proofs of	CU-MARK(dr)	06990 on Harper Jan 29
Harper & Brothers		1905.06.07	SLC	NH.Dublin	Please hand to	CU-MARK	07058
Harper & Brothers		1905.09.29	SLC per IVL	NH.Dublin	Mr. S.L. Clemens	CU-MARK(dr)	07152
Harper & Brothers		1905.10.09	SLC	NH.Dublin	It is probably	CU-MARK(ph)	07169
Harper & Brothers	o/a	1906.03.29	SLC per IVL	NY.New York	In Buffalo began	CU-MARK(dr)	07406 on Harper Mar 29
Harper & Brothers	o/a	1906.06.13	SLC per IVL	NH.Dublin	If that person	CU-MARK(dr)	07456 on Harper June 13
Harper & Brothers	o/a	1906.08.17	SLC per IVL	NH.Dublin	Mr. Clemens thinks	CU-MARK(dr)	07501 on Harper Aug 17
Harper & Brothers	o/a	1906.12.28	SLC per IVL	NY.New York	Tell him I	CU-MARK(dr)	07602 on Harper Dec 28
Harper & Brothers		1907.**.**	SLC	Unknown	Please send the	CU-MARK(dr)	07614

ADDRESSEE	DATE	WRITER	PLACE	CUE	SOURCE	NUMBER/NOTES
Harper & Brothers	o/a 1907.04.02	SLC	NY.New York	have accepted one	CU-MARK(dr)	07684 on Harper Apr 2
Harper & Brothers	1907.04.12	SLC	NY.New York	Yes, I am	NNC CU-MARK(dr)	02690 NNC tr
Harper & Brothers	o/a 1907.05.29	SLC per IVL	NY.Tuxedo Park	If the London	CU-MARK(dr)	07736 on Harper May 29
Harper & Brothers	1909.11.03	SLC	CT.Redding	Beasley's Xmas Party	151:1909.12.18	11108
Harper, J. Henry	1894.08.03	SLC	NY.Lawrence	It is human	CU-MARK(ph)	09221 inscription
Harper, J. Henry	1894.09.11	SLC	FR.Etretat	The M.S. arrived	ViU	04786
Harper, J. Henry	1895.04.23	SLC	FR.Paris	If Mr. Rogers	WU(tr)	04869
Harper, J. Henry	1895.08.17	SLC	CN.Vancouver	I hope you	248:575	04946
Harper, J. Henry	1895.08.21	SLC	CN.Vancouver	My wife is	248:576	04956
Harper, J. Henry	1895.10.28	SLC	AS.Melbourne	The Clemens family	NN-B	05001
Harper, J. Henry	1896.08.05	SLC	EN.Southampton	I find that	NN-B	05238
Harper, J. Henry	1896.08.07	SLC	EN.Guildford	Yes, I find	CLjC	05105
Harper, J. Henry	1896.10.07	SLC	EN.London	In these days	CU-MARK(ph)	05125
Harper, J. Henry	1896.10.27	SLC	EN.London	If anybody asks	CU-MARK(ph)	05136
Harper, J. Henry	1896.10.29	SLC	EN.London	It occurs to	134:1924.04.23	09956
Harper, J. Henry	1896.12.05	SLC	EN.London	You lately mentioned	ODa2	09957
Harper, J. Henry	1898.02.08	SLC	AU.Vienna	I have always	IU-R	05345
Harper, J. Henry	1898.08.29	SLC	AU.Kaltenleut.	Dear Mr. Harper	CU-MARK	05427 unsent & unfinished
Harper, J. Henry	1898.08.30	SLC	AU.Kaltenleut.	O dear, dear	InU-Li	05429
Harper, J. Henry	1899.12.21	SLC	EN.London	I return the	Mo2	05720
Harper's Weekly ed. & Lloyd's Weekly ed.	1902.11.15	SLC	NY.Riverdale	I am approaching	CU-MARK	06489
Harper's Weekly ed.	1905.07.11	SLC	NY.New York	I was not	151:1905.08.12	07080
Harper's Weekly ed.	1905.10.03	SLC	NH.Dublin	In his article	RPB-JH	07160
Harper's Weekly ed.	1905.10.18	SLC	NH.Dublin	Equal laws for	151:1905.11.04	07182
Harper's Weekly ed.	1905.12.24	SLC	NY.New York	Scarcely had Watchman	151:1906.01.13	07269

Harriet	1876.06.14	SLC	CT.Hartford	I am a	ViU	01342
Harriott, F.C.	1902.12.04	SLC	NY.Riverdale	I have letters	CU-MARK(tr)	06497 IVL tr
Harriott, F.C.	1902.12.17	SLC	NY.Riverdale	We learn from	CU-MARK(tr)	06521 SLC tr
Harris, Elmer B.	o/a 1905.06.01	SLC per IVL	NH.Dublin	It was very	CU-MARK(dr)	07057 on Harris June 1
Harris, Joel C.	1881.08.10	SLC	NY.Elmira	You can argue	GEU	01997
Harris, Joel C.	1881.12.12	SLC	CT.Hartford	I was very	GEU	02114
Harris, Joel C.	1882.04.02	SLC	CT.Hartford	Jo Twichell brought	GEU	02194
Harris, Joel C.	1882.09.05	SLC	NY.Elmira	No, I'm not	GEU	02264
Harris, Joel C.	1885.11.29	SLC	CT.Hartford	I thank you	GEU	03319
Harris, Joel C. & Warner, Charles D.	1885.11.29	SLC	CT.Hartford	It was the	CLU-S/C	02420 also to Holmes & Stockton
Harrison, Burton	1900.12.15	SLC	NY.New York	I should enjoy	DLC	05933
Harrison, Katherine I.	1895.04.15	SLC	FR.Paris	Won't you please	122:1936.12.09	04868 on Alden Apr 3
Harrison, Katherine I.	1897.05.26	SLC	EN.London	Will you keep	282:1915.03.03	09744
Harrison, Katherine I.	1899.12.21 & 1899.12.22	SLC	EN.London	The "World" wants	NN7	05722
Harrison, Katherine I.	1900.01.08	SLC	EN.London	I feel quite	CU-MARK	05742
Harrison, Katherine I.	1901.05.01	SLC	NY.New York	Mr. Rogers approves	KyU	06048
Harrison, Katherine I.	1902.04.26	SLC	NY.Riverdale	Please place $5,000	CLjC	06330
Harrison, Katherine I.	1902.08.29	SLC	ME.York Harbor	The check for	CBev2	09395
Harrison, Katherine I.	1903.01.12	SLC	NY.Riverdale	I keep forgetting	CU-MARK	06554
Harrison, Katherine I.	1903.01.16	SLC	NY.Riverdale	The Plasmon Co	CAlb2	06563
Harrison, Katherine I.	1904.03.01	IVL	IT.Florence	Mr. Clemens has been	ODa2	11215
Harrison, Katherine I.	1904.11.17	SLC	NY.New York	Please place 3,500	CU-MARK	08664
Harrison, Katherine I.	1904.11.22	SLC	NY.New York	This Aeolian bill	CU-MARK(ph)	06952
Harrison, Katherine I.	1905.06.13	SLC per IVL	NH.Dublin	Mr. Clemens directs	CU-MARK	07062

ADDRESSEE	DATE	WRITER	PLACE	CUE	SOURCE	NUMBER/NOTES
Harrison, Katherine I.	1905.07.12	SLC per IVL	NH.Dublin	Mr. Clemens directs	CU-MARK	07081
Harrison, Katherine I.	1905.08.15	SLC per IVL	NH.Dublin	Mr. Clemens directs	CU-MARK	07109
Harrison, Katherine I.	1905.10.02	SLC per IVL	NH.Dublin	Mr. Clemens directs	CU-MARK	07157
Harrison, Katherine I.	o/a 1906.01.16	SLC per IVL	NY.New York	Miss Lyon wrote	CU-MARK(dr)	07313 on Harrison Jan 16
Harrison, Mrs. Burton	1902.01.09	SLC	NY.Riverdale	As regards that	CU-MARK	06234 typed form letter
Harrison, William P.	1901.**.**	SLC	Unknown	All right, it's	110:1970.06.04	05945
Hart, I.F.	1874.01.10	OLC	CT.Hartford	Mr Clemens is	CU-MARK	01038
Hart, John S.	****.**.**	SLC	CT.Hartford	For convenience sake	NIC	05522
Hart, Jules	1901.12.16	SLC	NY.Riverdale	When politics enter	WU(ph)	06190 misdated Dec 17
Hart, Jules	1901.12.17	SLC	NY.Riverdale	If you use	WU(ph)	06191
Hart, Jules	1901.12.26	SLC	NY.Riverdale	I realize that	TxU	06197
Hart, Miss	1901.11.20	SLC	NY.Riverdale	I am very	Mo2	08874 inscription
Hart, Rabie	o/a 1905.12.06	SLC	NY.New York	To you, &	CU-MARK(tr)	07240 form letter
Harte, Bret	1867.05.01	SLC	NY.New York	I take my	CtY	00128
Hartford Art Society	1885.06.01	SLC	CT.Hartford	I accept your	117:1885.06.02	03235
Hartford city	bef 1874.04.23	SLC	CT.Hartford	Why is it	CtHMTH	01075 enc in May 8 to Perkins
Hartford city	1888.10.14	SLC	CT.Hartford	The following is	CCamarSJ	08825
Hartford Courant	1875.09.13	SLC	RI.Newport	Please change my	TxU	01259
Hartford Courant	1875.10.19	SLC	CT.Hartford	Please mail to	C4	01271
Hartford Courant ed.	1873.03.30	SLC	CT.Hartford	About noon yesterday	117:1873.03.31	00893
Hartford Courant ed.	1874.04.13	SLC	CT.Hartford	I find the	NNPM	01077
Hartford Courant ed.	bef 1875.09.29	SLC	CT.Hartford	I have been	117:1875.09.29	01265

Hartford Courant ed.	bet &	1875.10.19 1875.10.25	SLC	CT.Hartford	I lately published	117:1875.10.25	01272
Hartford Courant ed.		1877.09.19	SLC	CT.Hartford	The above appeared	117:1877.09.20	01481
Hartford Courant ed.		1879.02.02	SLC	GE.Munich	In a delayed	CU-MARK	09111
Hartford Courant ed.		1879.11.22	SLC	CT.Hartford	Editor Atlantic The new postal	CtHSD 117:1879.11.25	01725 Ct deposit at CtHSD
Hartford Courant ed.	ca	1879.12.08	SLC	Unknown	A day or	117:1879.12.09	02807 other sources
Hartford Courant ed.	ca	1879.12.08	SLC	Unknown	If you will	117:1879.12.09	02808
Hartford Courant ed.	bet &	1880.09.20 1880.09.24	SLC	CT.Hartford	You are aware	CU-MARK	01748
Hartford Courant ed.		1884.07.18	SLC	NY.Elmira	It would seem	CtHMTH	01540
Hartford Evening Post		1873.01.28	SLC	CT.Hartford	With the present	251:1873.01.28	00869
Hartford Flag Committee		1879.09.08	SLC	NY.Elmira	Out of the	117:1879.09.11	01685
Hartford gas company	ca	1888.07.18	SLC	NY.Elmira	There are but	CU-MARK(dr)	03741
Hartford Post ed.		1874.11.03	SLC	CT.Hartford	I have been	CU-MARK	01144
Harvey, Dorothy		1908.10.30	SLC	CT.Redding	Dear Dorothy, you	CU-MARK(tr)	08149
Harvey, George B.		****.**.**	SLC	Unknown	If you &	107:1927.11.22	09628
Harvey, George B.		****.02.22	SLC	Unknown	I asked my nephew	ODa2	09982
Harvey, George B.		1900.04.12	SLC	EN.London	Enclosed is a	MH-H	05791
Harvey, George B.		1900.04.14	SLC	EN.London	There shall be	134:1924.04.23	09965
Harvey, George B.		1900.11.20	SLC	NY.New York	If the rush	MH-H	05914
Harvey, George B.		1900.11.26	SLC	NY.New York	The terms proposed	CU-MARK(ph)	05921
Harvey, George B.		1901.05.04	SLC	NY.New York	I think that	CtY	06052 typed
Harvey, George B.		1901.10.09	SLC	NY.Riverdale	If you are	NN-B	08219
Harvey, George B.		1902.02.26	SLC	NY.Riverdale	From a competent	CU-MARK(tr)	06284 SLC tr
Harvey, George B.		1902.03.08	SLC	NY.Riverdale	I told Bliss	CtY(tr)	06292 SLC tr
Harvey, George B.		1903.01.12	SLC per IVL	NY.Riverdale	I shall want	CtY	06556

ADDRESSEE	DATE	WRITER	PLACE	CUE	SOURCE	NUMBER/NOTES
Harvey, George B. & McClure, Samuel S.	1903.07.21	SLC	NY.Elmira	Although I have	NN-B	11120 also to others
Harvey, George B.	1903.11.26	SLC	IT.Florence	Will you or	NNC	06760
Harvey, George B.	1903.12.28	SLC	IT.Florence	If Wood is	CU-MARK	06772
Harvey, George B.	1904.**.**	SLC	Unknown	The Government of	268:80	08588
Harvey, George B.	1904.03.05 & 1904.03.06	SLC	IT.Florence	Won't you run	MH-H	06806
Harvey, George B.	1905.01.24	SLC	NY.New York	No, this is	CU-MARK(dr)	06983 telegram; other sources
Harvey, George B.	o/a 1905.07.22	SLC per IVL	NH.Dublin	Mr. Clemens has	CU-MARK(dr)	07089 on Harvey July 22
Harvey, George B.	1905.07.30	SLC	NH.Dublin	I have corrected	WU	07098
Harvey, George B.	1905.08.21	SLC	CT.Norfolk	I am publishing	268:81	07094
Harvey, George B.	1905.08.31	SLC	NH.Dublin	Wait a while	MH-H	07122
Harvey, George B.	1905.09.05	SLC	NH.Dublin	I am still	CU-MARK	07129
Harvey, George B.	1905.09.05	SLC	NH.Dublin	I cannot come	CU-MARK	07130 telegram
Harvey, George B.	1905.09.21	SLC	NH.Dublin	All right, bang	MH-H	08243
Harvey, George B.	1905.10.12	SLC	NH.Dublin	Yes, I see	MH-H	07173
Harvey, George B.	1905.12.24	SLC	NY.New York	O Harvey the	MH-H	07270
Harvey, George B.	1906.02.15	SLC	NY.New York	I greet your	MH-H	07345
Harvey, George B.	o/a 1906.07.25	SLC per IVL	NH.Dublin	Mr. Clemens agrees	CU-MARK(dr)	07480 on Harvey July 24
Harvey, George B.	o/a 1906.09.11	SLC per IVL	NH.Dublin	Let the tale	CU-MARK(dr) InU-Li	07520 telegram; InU-Li tr
Harvey, George B.	1907.02.06	SLC	NY.New York	The Human Race	Mo2	05004 also to Howells & Dunne
Harvey, George B.	1907.10.05	SLC	NY.Tuxedo Park	The Pilgrim invitation	ODa2	07847
Harvey, George B.	1908.07.30	SLC	CT.Redding	I do not	C4(tr)	08065
Harvey, George B.	1908.08.10	SLC	CT.Redding	To-day I have	MH-H	08079

Harvey, George B.		1909.03.08	SLC	CT.Redding	I suppose the	151:1909.03.27	08367
Harvey, George B.		1909.08.12	SLC	CT.Redding	It was lovely	MH-H	08443
Hatch, Elizabeth		1909.10.23	SLC	CT.Redding	All sorts of	Mo2	08904
Hathaway, George H. & Pond, James B.		1879.11.25	SLC	CT.Hartford	Sent you a	NN-B	10797
Hatton, Joseph		1890.11.15	SLC	CT.Hartford	Yes, the Berringer	NEImC	04114
Hawk, William		1904.11.22	SLC	NY.New York	I thank you	CU-MARK(ph)	06954
Hawkes, W.L.		1903.04.23	SLC	NY.Riverdale	I have just	CU-MARK	06629
Hawley, Joseph R.		1869.02.15	SLC	OH.Ravenna	Your letter of	CtHi	00253
Hawthorne, Julian		1882.12.12	SLC	CT.Hartford	Osgood & I	107:1924.03.10	09459
Hawthorne, Julian		1885.12.18	SLC	CT.Hartford	Am I too	NN	03336
Hay, John M.		1873.01.12	SLC	CT.Hartford	Bliss is going	OClWHi	00856
Hay, John M.		1899.02.02	SLC	AU.Vienna	Prince Lichnowsky is	DLC	05540
Hay, John M.		1899.03.11	SLC	AU.Vienna	I thank you	DLC	05560
Hay, John M.		1899.03.11	SLC	AU.Vienna	I forgot to	ViU	09028
Hay, John M.		1899.05.04	SLC	AU.Vienna	This is only	DLC	05586
Hay, John M.		1900.02.27	SLC	EN.London	No, if I	DLC	05764
Hay, John M.		1901.06.28	SLC	NY.Saranac Lake	Out of a	RPB-JH	06080
Hay, John M.		1903.03.11	SLC	NY.Riverdale	The next time	DLC	06596
Hay, John M.	ca	1904.06.21	SLC	IT.Florence	For what you	DLC	06850 form letter
Hay, John M.		1905.**.**	SLC	Unknown	I never hear	CU-MARK	06976
Hay, William E.		1877.01.01	SLC & OLC	Unknown	A Merry Christmas	PSt	09286 inscription
Hayes, Rutherford B.		1877.09.20	SLC	CT.Hartford	The Jonas Smith	DNA CU-MARK(dr)	01483 DNA SLC tr enc in Sept 20 to Sherman
Hayes, Rutherford B.		1882.04.10	SLC	CT.Hartford	An odd thing	OFH	02198
Haynes & Simmons	o/a	1880.07.01	SLC	CT.Hartford	You have made	CU-MARK	09219 on Haynes & Simmons bill July 1

ADDRESSEE	DATE	WRITER	PLACE	CUE	SOURCE	NUMBER/NOTES
Hayward, Florence	1896.10.29	SLC	EN.London	Our wound is	MoHi	05139
Hayward, Florence	1897.01.29	SLC	EN.London	I am still	MoHi	05174
Hayward, Florence	1897.07.03	SLC	EN.London	Perhaps I could	MoHi	05255
Hayward, Florence	1897.07.06	OLC	EN.London	I don't know	MoHi	05247
Hayward, Florence	1901.07.06	SLC	NY.Saranac Lake	It was made	MoHi	06085
Hazlett, Charles A.	1907.07.25	SLC per IVL	NY.Tuxedo Park	Mr. Clemens directs	CU-MARK	07803
Healy, George P.	1879.03.25	SLC	FR.Paris	We were very	NN-B	02530
Heller, H.E.	o/a 1905.09.16	SLC per IVL	NH.Dublin	Idea is very	CU-MARK(dr)	07135 on Heller Sept 18
Helm, Alfred & Blasdel, Henry G.	1866.11.01	SLC	NV.Virginia City	Your kind and	431:1866.11.04	00109 also to Gilbert & Rice
Helm, W.H.	1900.08.23	SLC	EN.London	They have arrived	CU-MARK	05857
Helm, W.H.	1900.09.17	SLC	EN.London	I am ever	ViU	05863
Helm, W.H.	o/a 1907.05.12	SLC per IVL	NY.Tuxedo Park	Mr. Clemens gone	CU-MARK(dr)	07717 on Helm May 12
Helmer, George J.	o/a 1906.12.31	SLC per IVL	NY.New York	Have read his	CU-MARK(dr)	07601
Helmer, George J.	o/a 1907.02.23	SLC per IVL	NY.New York	Did for the	CU-MARK(dr)	07661 on Helmer Feb 23
Henderson, Archibald	1908.10.03	SLC per RWA	CT.Redding	Couldn't you come	NmA2	08120
Henderson, Archibald	1908.10.19	SLC per RWA	CT.Redding	Your letter of	NmA2	08139 typed
Henderson, Archibald	1909.01.14	SLC per IVL	CT.Redding	I gave your	NmA2	08313
Henderson, Archibald	1909.02.**	IVL	CT.Redding	I've just read	NmA2	08338
Henderson, Archibald	1909.02.13	SLC per RWA	CT.Redding	Miss Lyon has	NmA2	08347
Henderson, Archibald	1909.02.16	SLC per RWA	CT.Redding	Mr. Clemens' comment	NmA2	08350
Henderson, Archibald	1909.02.21	SLC per RWA	CT.Redding	We spell it	NmA2	08353

Henderson, Archibald	1909.04.10	SLC per IVL	CT.Redding	Mr. Clemens saw	NmA2	08380
Henderson, Archibald	1909.09.09	SLC per ABP	CT.Redding	I have presented	NmA2	08449
Henderson, Archibald	1909.09.20	SLC per ABP	CT.Redding	I have your	NmA2	08455
Henderson, Archibald	1909.10.18	SLC per ABP	CT.Redding	This is a	NmA2	08471
Henderson, Archibald	1909.11.15	SLC per ABP	CT.Redding	Your article in	NmA2	08492
Henniker-Heaton, J.	1908.10.01	SLC	CT.Redding	At midnight to-night	CU-MARK(tr)	08117
Henniker-Heaton, J.	1909.01.18	SLC	CT.Redding	I do hope	114:827	08314
Henslowe, Leonard	bet 1907.05.11 & 1907.06.06	SLC	NY.Tuxedo Park	I am shut	187:38f	08815
Hesse, Fanny C.	1880.05.21	SLC	CT.Hartford	Don't know yr	CU-MARK	01091
Hewins, Caroline M.	1884.10.13	SLC	CT.Hartford	Will Miss Hewins	CtH	03006
Hewins, Mr.	1883.04.10	SLC	CT.Hartford	Never mind about	CtHMTH	02369 typed
Hickman, Joseph G.	1881.07.24	SLC	CT.Branford	Your letter arrived	306:1881.08.12	01989
Higbie, Calvin H.	1886.12.16	SLC	CT.Hartford	Lord, it's good	129:1920.09.11	03498
Higbie, Calvin H.	1906.03.26	SLC per IVL	NY.New York	I went down	CU-MARK(tr)	07403 IVL tr; other sources
Higbie, Calvin H.	1906.04.12	SLC per IVL	NY.New York	Yes, his manuscript	129:1920.09.11	07426
Higbie, Calvin H.	1906.08.**	SLC	NH.Dublin	I have read	CU-MARK(tr)	07494
Higgins, I.N.	1868.09.**	SLC	Unknown	With best wishes	ViU	10494 inscription
Higgins, Miss	1902.01.28	SLC	CT.Hartford	One's sins are	VtMiM	06254
Higginson, Mary P.	1907.04.06	SLC	NY.New York	with the warm	ViU	09419 inscription
Higginson, Thomas W.	****.**.**	SLC	Unknown	O, dear the	452	10468
Higginson, Thomas W.	1905.03.26	SLC	NY.New York	I early learned	114:771	07020
Hill, Herbert E.	****.11.15	SLC	CT.Hartford	No, it would	CLjC	09455
Hill, Herbert E.	1880.11.03	SLC	CT.Hartford	I suppose the	ODa2	09943

ADDRESSEE	DATE	WRITER	PLACE	CUE	SOURCE	NUMBER/NOTES
Hill, Herbert E.	1886.**.**	SLC	CT.Hartford	I shall be	165:1962.11.02	09772
Hill, William	1905.09.01	SLC per IVL	NH.Dublin	Mr. Clemens is	CU-MARK(tr)	07124 IVL tr
Hillern, Mrs. von	1893.08.**	SLC	AU.Krankenheil	from one who	CU-MARK(ph)	09301 inscription
Hillhouse, Mansfield L.	o/a 1906.01.10	SLC per IVL	NY.New York	I desire to	CU-MARK(dr)	08776 on Hillhouse Jan 10
Himes, George H.	1886.01.17	SLC	CT.Hartford	I am not	MoPeS	03356
Hinds, Minnie N.	o/a 1906.11.26	SLC per IVL	NY.New York	Thank her very	CU-MARK(dr)	07569 on Hinds Nov 13
Hine, Charles C.	1870.02.10	SLC	NY.Buffalo	You make out	CU-MARK	00424
Hingston, Edward P.	1867.01.15	SLC	NY.New York	I have been	PBL	00118
Hobby, Josephine S.	1906.10.20	SLC	NY.New York	Let us save	CtH	10548 inscription
Hobby, Josephine S.	1907.09.15	SLC	NY.Tuxedo Park	Truth is the	CtH	10549 inscription
Hobby, Josephine S.	pm 1910.01.07	SLC per ABP	CT.Redding	To all friends	CtH	10547 form letter
Hoffman, Ogden & French, William H.	1866.12.06	SLC	CA.San Francisco	I cannot too	417:1866.12.08	02776 also to Low & Blasdel
Hogue, Mr.	1892.10.14	SLC	IT.Florence	The rest of	ViU	00636
Hogue, Mr.	ca 1900.**.**	SLC	Unknown	On Albumen get	CU-MARK	08731
Holcombe, Return I.	1883.09.04	SLC	NY.Elmira	I haven't the	MnHi	02833
Holcombe, Return I.	1883.09.17	SLC	CT.Hartford	I know of	MnHi	02836
Holden, E.R.	1882.07.16	SLC	NY.Elmira	I & my	CSmH	02236
Holden, Mr.	1904.10.**	SLC	NY.New York	with the compliments	105:1938.03.03	09646 inscription
Holland, Josiah G.	1875.04.29	SLC	CT.Hartford	I thank you	CoU	01266
Holland, Josiah G.	1881.09.05	SLC	NY.Elmira	I shall not	CCC	02028
Hollister, Joseph W.	1903.03.20	SLC	NY.New York	Indeed, yes, it	CU-MARK(tr)	06605
Holmes, Oliver W.	1869.09.30	SLC	NY.Buffalo	If I can	DLC	00360

Holmes, Oliver W.		1877.12.27	SLC	CT.Hartford	I come before	MH-H	01184 also to Emerson & Longfellow
Holmes, Oliver W. & Stockton, Frank R.		1885.11.29	SLC	CT.Hartford	It was the	CLU-S/C	03318 also to Warner & Harris
Holmes, Phoebe	o/a	1906.01.29	SLC per IVL	NY.New York	Matter of no	CU-MARK(dr)	07319 on Holmes Jan 29
Holt, Adele D.		1907.05.03	SLC	NY.New York	I thank the	297:155	07712
Holt, Winifred	o/a	1905.08.07	SLC per IVL	NH.Dublin	Wrote her a	CU-MARK(dr)	07103 on Holt Aug 7
Holt, Winifred	o/a	1906.01.15	SLC per IVL	NY.New York	Shall hope Mr.	CU-MARK(dr)	07310 on Holt Jan 15
Holt, Winifred	o/a	1907.01.07	SLC per IVL	NY.New York	Can't go	CU-MARK(dr)	07622 on Holt Jan 5
Hood, Tom & Routledge & Sons		1873.03.10	SLC	CT.Hartford	The Jubliee Singers	407:14	00886 other sources
Hooker, Alice		*	*	*	*	*	10303 see Day, Alice H.
Hooker, Isabella B.		1867.04.07	OLC	NY.Elmira	I have been	CtHSD	09124
Hooker, Isabella B.		1884.05.27	SLC	CT.Hartford	Mrs. Clemens & I	CtHSD	10482
Hookway, Amelia D.		1908.10.**	SLC	CT.Redding	Although I am	CU-MARK	08096
Hooper, Lucy		1882.01.21	SLC	CT.Hartford	The young lady	ViU	02151 enc in Jan 21 to Orion Clemens
Hooper, Robert M.		1879.05.12	SLC	FR.Paris	A previous engagement	MoSW	08942
Hopkinson, Charles		****.**.**	SLC	Unknown	from one of	305:1909.05.17	09757 inscription
Horne, Mr.		1895.06.19	SLC	NY.Elmira	I find it	ViU	04894
Horner, Afsa		1899.07.01	SLC	EN.London	Always be good	CU-MARK(ph)	09362 inscription
Horner, John		1906.01.12	SLC per IVL	NY.New York	I find the	CU-MARK(dr)	07306

ADDRESSEE	DATE	WRITER	PLACE	CUE	SOURCE	NUMBER/NOTES
Hosford, W.B.	o/a 1905.12.07	SLC per IVL	NY.New York	left the River	CU-MARK(dr)	07243 on Hosford Dec 7
Hosmer, Hezekiah L.	1870.09.15	SLC	NY.Buffalo	Four or five	MtHi	00506
Houghton (H.O.) & Co.	1875.01.05	SLC	CT.Hartford	Please send Atlantic	MH-H	01173
Houghton (H.O.) & Co.	1875.01.06	SLC	CT.Hartford	Many thanks for	MH-H	01174
Houghton (H.O.) & Co.	1875.02.12	SLC	CT.Hartford	I like the	MH-H	01192
Houghton (H.O.) & Co.	1875.10.28	SLC	CT.Hartford	Pray accept my	ViU	01278
House, Edward H.	1880.08.31 & 1880.09.01	SLC	NY.Elmira	Tell David I	173:1939.10.24	01828
House, Edward H.	1880.10.06	SLC	CT.Hartford	All right, you	ViU	01836
House, Edward H.	1880.11.09	SLC	CT.Hartford	I'm ever so	ViU	02851
House, Edward H.	1881.02.04	SLC	CT.Hartford	I like the	ViU	01905
House, Edward H.	1881.02.19	SLC	CT.Hartford	Consound it, what	ViU	01910
House, Edward H.	1881.10.04	SLC	CT.Hartford	We have all	ViU	02043
House, Edward H.	1881.10.08	SLC	CT.Hartford	Why, hang it	ViU	02048
House, Edward H.	1881.10.21	SLC	CT.Hartford	I am mighty	ViU	02057
House, Edward H.	1881.10.24	SLC	CT.Hartford	I am under	ViU	02059
House, Edward H.	1881.10.26	SLC	CT.Hartford	By George I'm	ViU	02069
House, Edward H.	1881.11.16	SLC	CT.Hartford	We are still	ViU	02088
House, Edward H.	1881.11.21	SLC	CT.Hartford	When I was	ViU	02095
House, Edward H.	1881.12.27	SLC	CT.Hartford	All right, my	ViU	02126
House, Edward H.	1882.02.23	SLC	CT.Hartford	Coto's shawl will	ViU	02164 typed
House, Edward H.	1882.12.02	SLC	CT.Hartford	I have been	ViU	02313 typed
House, Edward H.	1883.10.01	SLC	CT.Hartford	How odd it	ViU	02844
House, Edward H.	1883.11.12	SLC	CT.Hartford	This is a	ViU	02855 typed
House, Edward H.	1884.01.14	SLC	CT.Hartford	To our minds	ViU	02889
House, Edward H.	1884.02.27	SLC	CT.Hartford	Thanks for the	ViU	02923
House, Edward H.	1884.05.23	SLC	CT.Hartford	But your darned	ViU	02983

House, Edward H.	1884.10.31	SLC	CT.Hartford	What in the	ViU	03015
House, Edward H.	1885.05.13	SLC per JR	CT.Hartford	We are infinitely	ViU	03227
House, Edward H.	1885.07.21	SLC	NY.Elmira	Yes, you got	ViU	03263
House, Edward H.	1885.12.19	SLC	CT.Hartford	We've got the	173:1939.10.24	03338
House, Edward H.	1886.05.26	SLC	CT.Hartford	As soon as	ViU	03402
House, Edward H.	1886.06.05	SLC	CT.Hartford	Koto is gone	ViU	03405
House, Edward H.	1886.07.16	SLC	NY.Elmira	Only a line	ViU	03422
House, Edward H.	1886.07.26	SLC	NY.Elmira	I have come	ViU	03427
House, Edward H.	1886.08.11	SLC	NY.Elmira	No, it isn't	ViU	03437
House, Edward H.	1886.08.14	SC	NY.Elmira	Thank you so	ViU	03438
House, Edward H.	1886.08.24	SC	NY.Elmira	Indeed your letter	ViU	03443
House, Edward H.	1886.10.08	SLC	CT.Hartford	I am coming	ViU	03466
House, Edward H.	1886.10.18	SLC	CT.Hartford	O yes, there	ViU	03470
House, Edward H.	1886.11.26	SLC	CT.Hartford	This is heavy	ViU	03484
House, Edward H.	1886.12.17	SLC	CT.Hartford	We burnt one	ViU	03499
House, Edward H.	1886.12.26	SLC	CT.Hartford	I've ordered a	ViU	03502
House, Edward H.	1887.05.05	SLC	CT.Hartford	B'gosh you couldn't	ViU	03567
House, Edward H.	1887.05.07	SLC	CT.Hartford	All right--ship	ViU	03568
House, Edward H.	1887.06.29	CC	NY.Elmira	Ich war soh	ViU	03581
House, Edward H.	1887.07.05	SC	NY.Elmira	Thank you so	ViU	03591
House, Edward H.	1887.07.14	CC	NY.Elmira	You do not	ViU	03604
House, Edward H.	1887.07.17	SC	NY.Elmira	Your second letter	ViU	03606
House, Edward H.	1887.07.24	CC	NY.Elmira	I was of	ViU	03610
House, Edward H.	1887.07.24	OLC	NY.Elmira	I am glad	ViU	03609
House, Edward H.	1887.08.09	CC	NY.Elmira	I was delighted	ViU	03620
House, Edward H.	1887.08.19	SC	NY.Elmira	We also, have	ViU	03630
House, Edward H.	1887.08.19	SC	NY.Elmira	Your letter was	ViU	03631
House, Edward H.	1887.09.07	SC	NY.Elmira	This is my	ViU	03644

ADDRESSEE	DATE	WRITER	PLACE	CUE	SOURCE	NUMBER/NOTES
House, Edward H.	1888.07.09	OLC	NY.Elmira	I spent part	ViU	03729
House, Edward H.	1888.07.19	CC	NY.Elmira	I have every	ViU	03743
House, Edward H.	1888.10.14	OLC	CT.Hartford	Certainly you are	ViU	03790
House, Edward H.	1888.12.09	OLC	CT.Hartford	The book which	ViU	03803
House, Edward H.	1889.01.13	OLC	CT.Hartford	I was so	ViU	03852
House, Edward H.	1889.02.26	SLC	CT.Hartford	I gather the	131:1890.01.27	03867
House, Edward H.	1889.03.19	SLC	CT.Hartford	I was not	ViU	03873
House, Koto	1881.02.12	SLC	CT.Hartford	With kindest regards	ViU	10346 inscription
House, Koto	1882.01.02	SLC	CT.Hartford	with the affectionate	ViU	09648 inscription
Howard, A.D.	o/a 1906.02.14	SLC per IVL	NY.New York	I believe the	CU-MARK(dr)	07341 on Howard Feb 14
Howard, John R. & King, Horatio C.	1869.03.13	SLC	CT.Hartford	Yours of Feb.	PCarlD	11118
Howard, Oliver O.	1901.01.08	SLC	NY.New York	I'm venturing to	MeB	05961
Howard, Oliver O.	1901.02.07	SLC	NY.New York	My wife and	NjN	05991
Howard, Oliver O.	1901.02.13	SLC	NY.New York	You are a	MeB	05993
Howard, Oliver O.	1909.01.12	SLC	CT.Redding	You pay me	CU-MARK	08312
Howard, W.L.	1901.05.02	SLC	NY.New York	I thank you	MoCoJ	06051
Howe, Edgar W.	1884.02.13	SLC	CT.Hartford	I am glad	CU-MARK	02916
Howe, Edgar W.	1884.03.28	SLC	CT.Hartford	Care of the	CU-MARK	02941
Howe, Edgar W.	1884.04.20	SLC	CT.Hartford	Been visiting, a	TxU	02961
Howe, M.A. DeWolfe	1901.03.18	SLC	NY.New York	I remember our	MH-H	06020
Howell, Mr. S.	1890.03.24	SLC	CT.Hartford	Our Satan is	122:1934.05.09	04031
Howells, Corinne	1884.11.03	SLC	CT.Hartford	Yes, I think	CU-MARK(tr)	03018
Howells, Elinor M. & Howells, William D.	bet 1875.01.26 & 1875.02.10	SLC	CT.Hartford	Mrs. Clemens is	NN-B	02485
Howells, Elinor M.	1875.04.23	OLC	CT.Hartford	Don't dream for	MH-H	01223
Howells, Elinor M.	1877.**.**	SLC	CT.Hartford	I beg to	MH-H	10846 inscription

Howells, Elinor M. & Howells, William D.		1878.02.26	SLC	CT.Hartford	Imagined my Mrs. Clemens	NN-B MH-H	02522
Howells, Elinor M.		1880.08.17	SLC	NY.Elmira	O hang my	MH-H	01825
Howells, Elinor M.		1881.02.28	OLC	Unknown	I am so	MH-H	01918
Howells, Elinor M.		1881.11.25	SLC	CT.Hartford	How you startle	MH-H	02099
Howells, Elinor M.		1889.11.14	SLC	CT.Hartford	It was a	MH-H	03966
Howells, Elinor M.		1889.12.13	SLC	CT.Hartford	I write for	MH-H	03986
Howells, Elinor M.		1909.08.07	SLC	CT.Redding	Clara thinks that	MH-H	08441
Howells, John M.		1908.07.03	SLC	CT.Redding	You have set	DLC(ph)	08899
Howells, Mildred		****.06.06	SLC	Unknown	It is all	MH-H	06299
Howells, Mildred		1900.03.02	SLC & CC	EN.London	Mrs. Clemens has	MH-H	05766
Howells, William D.		****.**.**	SLC	NY.New York	I've waited an	MH-H	03822
Howells, William D.		****.**.**	SLC	Unknown	That man seems	258:16	09496
Howells, William D.		****.**.**	SLC	Unknown	Introducing Mrs.	CSmH	06027
Howells, William D.		****.**.**	SLC	Unknown	I have just	MH-H	10879
Howells, William D.		****.**.**	SLC	Unknown	P.S. Later. My	MH-H(tr)	10778
Howells, William D.		****.**.**	SLC	Unknown	You have answered	MH-H	08964
Howells, William D.	pm	****.06.29	SLC	NY.Elmira	*	ViU	10182 envelope only
Howells, William D.	pm	****.09.17	SLC	Unknown	*	NIC	10183 envelope only
Howells, William D.		****.12.31	SLC	Unknown	No, I answered	MH-H	08965
Howells, William D.		1872.01.07	SLC	OH.Wooster	Please telegraph the	MH-H	00707 telegram
Howells, William D.		1872.03.18	SLC	NY.Elmira	We are very	MH-H	00732
Howells, William D.	bet &	1872.05.20 1872.06.10	SLC	NY.Elmira or CT.Hartford	Since penning the	193:229	00754
Howells, William D.		1872.06.15	SLC	CT.Hartford	Could you tell	NN-B	00756
Howells, William D.		1873.03.13	SLC	CT.Hartford	This is from	ViU	00887
Howells, William D.		1874.02.27	SLC	CT.Hartford	I am in	OFH	01058

ADDRESSEE	DATE	WRITER	PLACE	CUE	SOURCE	NUMBER/NOTES
Howells, William D.	1874.03.03	SLC	CT.Hartford	All right come	MH-H	01059 telegram
Howells, William D.	1874.03.04	SLC	CT.Hartford	We ought to	MH-H	01061 telegram
Howells, William D.	1874.03.20	SLC	CT.Hartford	You or Aldrich	NN-B	02468
Howells, William D.	1874.05.10	SLC	NY.Elmira	I am so	MH-H	01088
Howells, William D.	1874.06.21	SLC	NY.Elmira	I am not	MH-H	01102
Howells, William D.	1874.07.15	SLC	NY.Elmira	Consound my cats	ViU	10847 misdated, see July 25
Howells, William D.	1874.07.25	SLC	NY.Elmira	Consound my cats	ViU	01110 misdated July 15
Howells, William D.	1874.08.22	SLC	NY.Elmira	I have just	NN-B	02472
Howells, William D.	1874.09.02	SLC	NY.Elmira	Your telegram just	NN-B	02473
Howells, William D.	1874.09.20	SLC	CT.Hartford	All right, my	NN-B	02474
Howells, William D.	1874.10.24	SLC	CT.Hartford	I have delayed	NN-B	02475
Howells, William D.	1874.10.24	SLC	CT.Hartford	I shall not	NN-B	02476
Howells, William D.	1874.10.29	SLC	CT.Hartford	All right--I'll	CU-MARK(ph)	01141
Howells, William D.	1874.11.13	SLC	MA.Webster	We arrive by	CtY	01167
Howells, William D.	1874.11.16	SLC	MA.Boston	You observe I	NN-B	02477 addressed to OLC in jest
Howells, William D.	1874.11.17	SLC	CT.Hartford	We must apologize	MH-H	01154
Howells, William D.	bet 1874.11.17 & 1874.11.19	SLC	CT.Hartford	Cut it, scarify	NN-B	02478
Howells, William D.	1874.11.25	SLC	CT.Hartford	Your amendment was	MH-H	01155
Howells, William D.	1874.12.02	SLC	CT.Hartford	Mrs. Clemens is	MH-H	01159
Howells, William D.	1874.12.03	SLC	CT.Hartford	Let us change	101:1917.05f	01160
Howells, William D.	1874.12.06	OLC	CT.Hartford	Very many thanks	MH-H	01161
Howells, William D.	1874.12.08	SLC	CT.Hartford	It isn't the	NN-B	05257
Howells, William D.	1874.12.09	SLC	CT.Hartford	I want to	NN-B	02480 typed
Howells, William D.	1874.12.11	SLC	CT.Hartford	Mrs. Clemens is	MH-H	01164

Howells, William D.	1874.12.13	SLC	CT.Hartford	I want you	NN-B	02481
Howells, William D.	1874.12.14	SLC	CT.Hartford	Mrs. Clemens received	MH-H	01165 typed
Howells, William D.	1874.12.18	SLC	CT.Hartford	I left No.	NN-B	02482
Howells, William D.	1874.12.21	SLC	CT.Hartford	Oh, come, now	TxDaM-P	01098
Howells, William D.	1875.01.12	SLC	CT.Hartford	We mustn't give	MH-H	01178
Howells, William D.	1875.01.15	SLC	CT.Hartford	I am very	MH-H	01180
Howells, William D.	1875.01.26	SLC	CT.Hartford	When Mrs. Clemens P.S.--Look here	NN-B MH-H	02483
Howells, William D. & Howells, Elinor M.	bet 1875.01.26 & 1875.02.10	SLC	CT.Hartford	Mrs. Clemens is	NN-B	02485
Howells, William D.	1875.02.10	SLC	CT.Hartford	Your praises of	NN-B	02487
Howells, William D.	1875.02.20	SLC	CT.Hartford	After all, I	MH-H	01195
Howells, William D.	1875.03.01	SLC	CT.Hartford	Now you shall	NN-B	02488
Howells, William D.	1875.03.02 or 1875.03.09	SLC	CT.Hartford	Howells, didn't I	MH-H	01203 on Twichell n.d.
Howells, William D.	1875.03.16	SLC	CT.Hartford	Well, all that	MH-H	01208
Howells, William D.	1875.04.23	SLC	CT.Hartford	I've got Mrs.	NN-B	02489
Howells, William D.	1875.04.24	SLC	CT.Hartford	An actor named	NN-B	02490
Howells, William D.	1875.04.25 or 1875.04.26	SLC	CT.Hartford	Good for Fawcett	MH-H	01225
Howells, William D.	1875.05.07	SLC	CT.Hartford	I'm glad to	MH-H	01230 fragment
Howells, William D.	1875.05.12	SLC	CT.Hartford	All right, I'll	MH-H	01232
Howells, William D.	1875.05.22	SLC	CT.Hartford	I have scratched	MH-H	01235
Howells, William D.	1875.06.07	SLC	CT.Hartford	By all means	MH-H	01239
Howells, William D.	1875.06.21	SLC	CT.Hartford	O, the visit	MH-H	01242
Howells, William D.	1875.06.25	SLC	CT.Hartford	I told Patrick	NN-B	02491
Howells, William D.	1875.07.05	SLC	CT.Hartford	I have finished	NN-B	01247
Howells, William D.	1875.07.13	SLC	CT.Hartford	Just as soon	NN-B	02492
Howells, William D.	1875.09.14	SLC	CT.Hartford	I question if	MH-H	01261

ADDRESSEE	DATE	WRITER	PLACE	CUE	SOURCE	NUMBER/NOTES
Howells, William D.	1875.09.18	SLC	CT.Hartford	My plan is Whereas	NN-B MH-H	02493 MH-H enc
Howells, William D.	1875.09.22 & 1875.09.27	SLC	CT.Hartford	I'm not going	MH-H	01263
Howells, William D.	1875.10.04	SLC	CT.Hartford	We had a	MH-H	10307 misdated, see Nov
Howells, William D.	1875.10.19	SLC	CT.Hartford	That is a	NN-B	02495
Howells, William D.	1875.10.27	SLC	CT.Hartford	Say boss, do	MH-H	01277
Howells, William D.	1875.11.04	SLC	CT.Hartford	We had a	MH-H	02494 misdated Oct
Howells, William D.	1875.11.23	SLC	CT.Hartford	Herewith is the	NN-B	02496
Howells, William D.	1876.01.01	SLC	CT.Hartford	Howells, I would	CU-MARK(ph)	00849
Howells, William D.	1876.01.10 or 1876.01.11	SLC	CT.Hartford	Indeed we haven't	NN-B	02497
Howells, William D.	1876.01.18	SLC	CT.Hartford	Thanks, & ever	NN-B	02498
Howells, William D.	1876.03.13	SLC	CT.Hartford	Here is the	MH-H	01329
Howells, William D.	1876.04.03	SLC	CT.Hartford	It is a	NN-B	02499
Howells, William D.	1876.04.22	SLC	CT.Hartford	You'll see per	NN-B	02500
Howells, William D.	1876.04.26	SLC	CT.Hartford	Thanks for the	NN-B	02501
Howells, William D.	1876.05.01	SLC	MD.Baltimore	Found I was	NN-B	10855 misdated, see 1877
Howells, William D.	1876.05.04	SLC	CT.Hartford	I shall reach	NN-B	02502
Howells, William D.	1876.05.12 & 1876.05.14	SLC	CT.Hartford	We have just	MH-H	01333
Howells, William D.	1876.08.09	SLC	NY.Elmira	You better give	NN-B	02503
Howells, William D.	1876.08.23	SLC	NY.Elmira	I am glad	NN-B	02504
Howells, William D.	1876.09.14	SLC	CT.Hartford	Yes, the collection	NN-B	02505
Howells, William D.	1876.09.21	SLC	CT.Hartford	Look here, Howells	MH-H	01367
Howells, William D.	1876.10.11	SLC	CT.Hartford	I don't believe	NN-B	02508
Howells, William D.	1876.10.12	SLC	CT.Hartford	I see where	MH-H	01375
Howells, William D.	1876.11.08	SLC	CT.Hartford	I love to	MH-H	01387 telegram

Howells, William D.		1876.11.09	SLC	CT.Hartford	Praise God from	MH-H	01388 telegram
Howells, William D.		1876.11.26	SLC	CT.Hartford	All gone to	MH-H	01389
Howells, William D.	pm	1876.12.05	SLC	CT.Hartford	If there is	MH-H	01392
Howells, William D.		1877.02.22	SLC	CT.Hartford	Here's a shout	OFH	01533
Howells, William D.		1877.02.26	SLC	CT.Hartford	Good! I'll be	MH-H	01311
Howells, William D.		1877.03.23	SLC	CT.Hartford	Been reading Out	MH-H	01185 date uncertain
Howells, William D.		1877.04.19	SLC	CT.Hartford	Many thanks. I	MH-H	01413
Howells, William D.		1877.04.27	SLC	MD.Baltimore	I am needed	MH-H	01419
Howells, William D.		1877.05.01	SLC	MD.Baltimore	Found I was	NN-B	01422 misdated 1876
Howells, William D.		1877.05.05	SLC	CT.Hartford	Here is as	CU-MARK	01425 on Orion Clemens May 2
Howells, William D.		1877.05.29	SLC	CT.Hartford	Confound you, Joe	NN-B	02509
Howells, William D.		1877.06.06	SLC	CT.Hartford	No sir, I	MH-H	01439
Howells, William D.		1877.06.14	SLC	NY.Elmira	Good for you	MH-H	01441
Howells, William D.		1877.06.21	SLC	CT.Hartford	Never mind about	CU-MARK(ph)	11173
Howells, William D.		1877.06.21	SLC	NY.Elmira	Three or four	CU-MARK(ph)	01066
Howells, William D.		1877.06.27	SLC	NY.Elmira	If you should	NN-B	02510
Howells, William D.	&	1877.07.04 1877.07.06	SLC	NY.Elmira	It is splendid P.S.--2 days	NN-B MH-H	02511
Howells, William D.		1877.07.11	SLC	NY.Elmira	It's finished.	NN-B	02512
Howells, William D.		1877.08.03	SLC	NY.Elmira	I have mailed	NN-B	02513
Howells, William D.	&	1877.08.25 1877.08.27	SLC	NY.Elmira	I thought	NN-B	02515
Howells, William D.		1877.08.29	SLC	NY.Elmira	Just got your	NN-B	02516
Howells, William D.		1877.09.19	SLC	CT.Hartford	All right--shan't	NN-B	02517
Howells, William D.		1877.10.15	SLC	CT.Hartford	I am entirely	MH-H	01496
Howells, William D.		1877.11.01	SLC	CT.Hartford	I don't know	MH-H	01501
Howells, William D.		1877.12.23	SLC	CT.Hartford	My sense of	NN-B	02520

ADDRESSEE	DATE	WRITER	PLACE	CUE	SOURCE	NUMBER/NOTES
Howells, William D.	1877.12.28	SLC	CT.Hartford	Your letter was	NN-B	02521
Howells, William D.	1878.01.04	SLC	CT.Hartford	The play is	MH-H	01522
Howells, William D. & Howells, Elinor M.	1878.02.26	SLC	CT.Hartford	Imagined my Mrs. Clemens	NN-B MH-H	02522
Howells, William D.	1878.03.15	SLC	CT.Hartford	If you print	MH-H	01543
Howells, William D.	1878.03.23	SLC	CT.Hartford	No, we won't	MH-H	01548
Howells, William D.	1878.05.04	SLC	GE.Frankfurt	I only propose	NN-B	02523
Howells, William D.	1878.05.26	SLC	GE.Heidelberg	are divinely located	NN-B	02524
Howells, William D.	1878.06.27	SLC	GE.Heidelberg	What do the	MH-H	01573
Howells, William D.	1878.09.27	SLC	IT.Venice	Have I offended	MH-H	01597
Howells, William D.	1878.11.17	SLC	GE.Munich	We arrived here	NN-B	02527
Howells, William D.	1879.01.21	SLC	GE.Munich	It's no use	NN-B	02528
Howells, William D.	1879.01.30	SLC	GE.Munich	It took a	MH-H	01625
Howells, William D.	1879.02.02	SLC	GE.Munich	I thought I	MH-H	01626
Howells, William D.	1879.02.09	SLC	GE.Munich	I have just	NN-B	02529 dr of Feb 9 letter enc
Howells, William D.	1879.04.15	SLC	FR.Paris	Have just got	MH-H	01568
Howells, William D.	1879.09.08	SLC	NY.Elmira	Are you dead	MH-H	01687
Howells, William D.	1879.09.15	SLC	NY.Elmira	When & where	NN-B	02534
Howells, William D.	ca 1879.10.01	SLC	NY.Elmira	If you should	MH-H	01695
Howells, William D.	1879.10.09	SLC	NY.Elmira	Your letter brought	NN-B	02535
Howells, William D.	1879.10.27	SLC	CT.Hartford	Will I come	MH-H	01700
Howells, William D.	1879.11.17	SLC	CT.Hartford	Just got home	MH-H	01718
Howells, William D.	1879.11.23	SLC	CT.Hartford	My book is	MH-H	01724 date uncertain
Howells, William D.	1879.11.27	SLC	CT.Hartford	Warner & I	MH-H	01727 date uncertain
Howells, William D.	1879.11.28	SLC	CT.Hartford	If anybody talks	NN-B	02537 date uncertain
Howells, William D.	1879.12.09	SLC	CT.Hartford	Am very much	MH-H	01736
Howells, William D.	1879.12.10	SLC	CT.Hartford	Will you please	MH-H	01738

Howells, William D.		1880.01.08	SLC	CT.Hartford	Am waiting for	NN-B	02538
Howells, William D.		1880.01.24	SLC	NY.Elmira	Say--are you	MH-H	01756
Howells, William D.		1880.03.05	SLC	CT.Hartford	I reckon you	MH-H	01767
Howells, William D.		1880.03.11	SLC	CT.Hartford	Many thanks--I	NN-B	02539
Howells, William D.		1880.03.24	SLC	CT.Hartford	Your & Mrs.	MH-H	01774
Howells, William D.		1880.04.01	OLC	CT.Hartford	We do thank	MH-H	01780
Howells, William D.		1880.04.01	SLC	CT.Hartford	That is perfectly	MH-H	01779
Howells, William D.	o/a	1880.04.11	SLC	CT.Hartford	If you've got	MH-H	01784 on Lewis Apr 11
Howells, William D.		1880.04.19	SLC	CT.Hartford	I have just	MH-H	01785
Howells, William D.		1880.04.22	SLC	CT.Hartford	I have scribbled	MH-H	01790
Howells, William D.		1880.04.23	SLC	CT.Hartford	If you want	MH-H	01793
Howells, William D.		1880.04.29	SLC	CT.Hartford	I return the	MH-H	01795
Howells, William D.	&	1880.05.06 1880.05.07	SLC	CT.Hartford	There you stick	NN-B	02542
Howells, William D.		1880.05.18	SLC	CT.Hartford	I know you	MH-H	01806
Howells, William D.		1880.06.09	SLC	CT.Hartford	Some time ago	MH-H	02812
Howells, William D.		1880.06.09	SLC	CT.Hartford	Well, old practical	NN-B	02543
Howells, William D.		1880.06.10	SLC	CT.Hartford	I think that	MH-H	10857 Orion Clemens essay enc
Howells, William D.		1880.06.15	SLC	CT.Hartford	The family are	MH-H	01812
Howells, William D.		1880.07.26	SLC	NY.Elmira	I have been	MH-H	01819
Howells, William D.		1880.08.01	SLC	NY.Elmira	Say--Howells, dear	MH-H	01820
Howells, William D.		1880.08.09	SLC	NY.Elmira	The box came	MH-H	01821
Howells, William D.		1880.09.03	SLC	NY.Elmira	Like enough, you	MH-H	01829
Howells, William D.		1880.10.13	SLC	CT.Hartford	I expect to	MH-H	01840
Howells, William D.		1880.10.15	SLC	MA.Boston	I will bet	MH-H	01842 telegram
Howells, William D.		1880.10.19	SLC	CT.Hartford	Read the letter	MH-H	01843
Howells, William D.		1880.10.24	SLC	CT.Hartford	Here's a letter	NN-B	02544

ADDRESSEE	DATE	WRITER	PLACE	CUE	SOURCE	NUMBER/NOTES
Howells, William D.	1880.10.28	SLC	CT.Hartford	Receive a lesson	MH-H	01848
Howells, William D.	1880.10.30	SLC	CT.Hartford	Will the proposed	MH-H	01850
Howells, William D.	1880.12.24	SLC	CT.Hartford	I was prodigiously	NN-B	02546
Howells, William D.	1881.01.14	SLC	CT.Hartford	Here is Gebbie's	MH-H	01892
Howells, William D.	1881.02.04	SLC	CT.Hartford	Don't you remember	MH-H	01906
Howells, William D.	1881.02.15	SLC	CT.Hartford	I'm not going	MH-H	01908
Howells, William D.	1881.02.21	SLC	CT.Hartford	Well, here is	NN-B	02549
Howells, William D.	1881.02.27	SLC	CT.Hartford	I go to	NN-B	02550
Howells, William D.	1881.03.03	SLC	CT.Hartford	Did you get	MH-H	01921
Howells, William D.	1881.03.04	SLC	CT.Hartford	1. Read the	MH-H	01922
Howells, William D.	1881.04.19	SLC	CT.Hartford	Good idea! That	MH-H	01937
Howells, William D.	1881.08.12	SLC	NY.Elmira	Say--I am	MH-H	02001
Howells, William D.	1881.08.18	SLC	NY.Elmira	Your news about	MH-H	02009
Howells, William D.	1881.09.03	SLC	NY.Elmira	What I call	MH-H	02023
Howells, William D.	1881.09.05	SLC	NY.Elmira	Osgood says something	MH-H	02027
Howells, William D.	1881.10.15	SLC	CT.Hartford	Slash away, with	MH-H	02053
Howells, William D.	1881.10.26	SLC	CT.Hartford	I am delighted	NN-B	02553
Howells, William D.	1881.12.16	SLC	CT.Hartford	It was a	NN-B	02557
Howells, William D.	1882.01.18	SLC	CT.Hartford	I haven't written	MH-H	02150
Howells, William D.	1882.01.28	SLC	CT.Hartford	Nobody knows, better	NN-B	02560
Howells, William D.	1882.03.14	SLC	CT.Hartford	That hotel bill	MH-H	02172 typed
Howells, William D.	1882.03.14	SLC	CT.Hartford	The mail has	MH-H	09215
Howells, William D.	1882.03.23	SLC	CT.Hartford	What would you	MH-H	02178 typed
Howells, William D.	1882.03.27	SLC	CT.Hartford	I can imagine	MH-H	02180 typed
Howells, William D.	1882.04.16	SLC	CT.Hartford	O dear! I	MH-H	02200 typed
Howells, William D.	1882.06.16	SLC	CT.Hartford	I have enveloped	MH-H	02220
Howells, William D.	1882.06.20	SLC	CT.Hartford	After infinite labor	MH-H	02221 typed

Howells, William D.		1882.06.22	SLC	CT.Hartford	I am in people's all the	NN-B MH-H	02564
Howells, William D.		1882.07.24	SLC	NY.Elmira	Many thanks for	MH-H	02239
Howells, William D.		1882.10.03	SLC	CT.Hartford	I do not	NN-B	02567 typed
Howells, William D.		1882.11.04	SLC	CT.Hartford	Yes, it would	NN-B	02568 typed
Howells, William D.		1883.02.05	SLC	CT.Hartford	I haven't any	CU-MARK	02342 SC and CC lists enc
Howells, William D.		1883.03.01	SLC	CT.Hartford	We got ourselves	NN-B	02569 typed
Howells, William D.		1883.05.18	SLC	CT.Hartford	I have just	MH-H	02388 typed
Howells, William D.		1883.07.20	SLC	NY.Elmira	We are desparately	NN-B	02571
Howells, William D.		1883.08.22	SLC	NY.Elmira	How odd it	NN-B	02572
Howells, William D.		1883.09.20	SLC	CT.Hartford	While Madam stops	MH-H	02839
Howells, William D.		1883.10.15	SLC	CT.Hartford	Your letter must	MH-H	02852
Howells, William D.	o/a	1883.10.16	SLC	CT.Hartford	Twichell and I	CSmH	08612 typed
Howells, William D.		1883.11.04	SLC	CT.Hartford	I telegraphed last	MH-H	02854
Howells, William D.		1883.11.19	SLC	CT.Hartford	Please do come	MH-H	02857 telegram
Howells, William D.		1883.11.21	SLC	CT.Hartford	Good--& all	MH-H	02858 typed
Howells, William D.		1883.12.20	SLC	CT.Hartford	I couldn't telegraph	MH-H	02870
Howells, William D.		1884.01.07	SLC	CT.Hartford	O my goodn's	NN-B	02573
Howells, William D.		1884.01.18	SLC	CT.Hartford	This is admirable	MH-H	02892
Howells, William D.		1884.01.20	SLC	CT.Hartford	So Webster has	MH-H	02894
Howells, William D.		1884.02.02	SLC	CT.Hartford	I have just	NN-B	02576
Howells, William D.		1884.02.09	SLC	CT.Hartford	If you still	MH-H	02914
Howells, William D.		1884.02.13	SLC	CT.Hartford	When Mallory tackled	MH-H	02917
Howells, William D.		1884.02.18	SLC	CT.Hartford	You will not	MH-H	02919
Howells, William D.		1884.02.26	SLC	CT.Hartford	Ah, what the	MH-H	02922

ADDRESSEE	DATE	WRITER	PLACE	CUE	SOURCE	NUMBER/NOTES
Howells, William D.	1884.03.05	SLC	CT.Hartford	At last I've	MH-H	02933
Howells, William D.	1884.03.13	SLC	CT.Hartford	I have been	MH-H	02935
Howells, William D.	1884.03.15	SLC	CT.Hartford	Mallory is still	MH-H	02936 telegram
Howells, William D.	1884.04.**	SLC	CT.Hartford	Webster has been	134:1930.10.16	02946 telegram
Howells, William D.	1884.04.08	SLC	CT.Hartford	It took my	NN-B	02578
Howells, William D.	1884.05.06	SLC	CT.Hartford	Well, then, some	MH-H	02971
Howells, William D.	1884.05.12	SLC	CT.Hartford	I am powerful	MH-H	02977
Howells, William D.	1884.05.24	SLC	CT.Hartford	Good land, have	MH-H(tr)	02986
Howells, William D.	1884.06.01	SLC	CT.Hartford	How much does	MH-H	02989
Howells, William D.	1884.06.28	SLC	NY.Elmira	Aforetime, I would	MH-H	02998
Howells, William D.	1884.07.15	SLC	NY.Elmira	I meant to	MH-H	01529
Howells, William D.	1884.08.07	SLC	NY.Elmira	I have no	MH-H	01537
Howells, William D.	1884.08.31	SLC	NY.Elmira	Thank you ever	NN-B	02586
Howells, William D.	1884.09.07	SLC	NY.Elmira	My whole interest	MH-H	01434
Howells, William D.	1884.09.15	SLC	NY.Elmira	Well, isn't the	MH-H	01331
Howells, William D.	1884.09.17	SLC	NY.Elmira	Before I forget	NN-B	02588
Howells, William D.	1884.09.17	SLC	NY.Elmira	Somehow I can't	NN-B	02587
Howells, William D.	1884.10.17	SLC	CT.Hartford	Yes, give Osgood	MH-H	03008
Howells, William D.	1884.10.20	SLC	CT.Hartford	Please send me	MH-H	03010
Howells, William D.	1885.02.27	SLC	PA.Philadelphia	To-night in Baltimore	NN-B	02605
Howells, William D.	o/a 1885.03.12	SLC	CT.Hartford	Who is this	CU-MARK	03188 on Howland Mar 12
Howells, William D.	1885.03.26	SLC	CT.Hartford	We did have	MH-H	03197
Howells, William D.	1885.05.05	SLC	CT.Hartford	Heiliger Gott! but	NN-B	02610
Howells, William D.	1885.06.05	SLC	CT.Hartford	I read the	MH-H	03239
Howells, William D.	1885.07.21	SLC	NY.Elmira	You are really	NN-B	02619
Howells, William D.	ca 1885.07.23	SLC	Unknown	still watch that	MH-H	03264 fragment
Howells, William D.	1885.10.18	SLC	CT.Hartford	I reckon it	NN-B	02621

Howells, William D.	1885.12.02	SLC	NY.New York	I told Webster	NN-B	02623
Howells, William D.	1885.12.07	SLC	CT.Hartford	There ain't any	MH-H	03325
Howells, William D.	1885.12.16	SLC	CT.Hartford	No, don't keep	MH-H	03332
Howells, William D.	o/a 1885.12.20	SLC	CT.Hartford	It is all	CU-MARK	03340 on Clark Dec 20
Howells, William D.	1885.12.26	SLC	CT.Hartford	Good--we claim	MH-H	03343
Howells, William D.	1886.01.03	SLC	CT.Hartford	The date set	NN-B	02627
Howells, William D.	1886.03.19	SLC	CT.Hartford	Good! Choose your	MH-H	03377
Howells, William D.	1886.04.12	SLC	CT.Hartford	Good--it's all	MH-H	03383
Howells, William D.	1886.05.03	SLC	CT.Hartford	My notion that	MH-H	03388
Howells, William D.	1886.05.08	SC	CT.Hartford	Recd no dispatch	CU-MARK	03392 telegram
Howells, William D.	1886.05.13 to 1886.05.17	SLC	CT.Hartford	No, no sir	MH-H	03395
Howells, William D.	1886.05.19	SLC	CT.Hartford	Go 'long with	NN-B	02635
Howells, William D.	1886.06.04	SLC	CT.Hartford	I reckon it	MH-H	03404
Howells, William D.	1886.07.15	SLC	NY.Elmira	I am immensely	MH-H	03417
Howells, William D.	1886.10.19	SLC	CT.Hartford	This is to	Mo2	08940
Howells, William D.	1886.12.12	SLC	CT.Hartford	I understand your	MH-H	03496
Howells, William D.	1887.02.04	SLC	CT.Hartford	That is the	MH-H	03523
Howells, William D.	1887.02.12	SLC	CT.Hartford	The American Claimant	MH-H	03526
Howells, William D.	1887.02.15	SLC	CT.Hartford	I was in	NN-B	02655
Howells, William D.	1887.04.25	SLC	CT.Hartford	Been laid up	MH-H	03634 misdated Aug
Howells, William D.	1887.05.09	SLC	CT.Hartford	You spoke of	MH-H	03569
Howells, William D.	1887.08.22	SLC	NY.Elmira	I have my	NN-B	02670
Howells, William D.	1887.08.25	SLC	CT.Hartford	Been laid up	MH-H	09483 misdated, see Apr
Howells, William D.	1888.03.31	SLC	CT.Hartford	Here is that	MH-H	03712
Howells, William D.	1889.07.13	SLC	CT.Hartford	I came on	NN-B	02691

ADDRESSEE	DATE	WRITER	PLACE	CUE	SOURCE	NUMBER/NOTES
Howells, William D.	1889.07.24	SLC	NY.Elmira	I, too, was	NN-B	02692
Howells, William D.	1889.08.05	SLC	NY.Elmira	Mrs. Clemens will	MH-H	03924
Howells, William D.	1889.08.21	SLC	NY.Elmira	They'll be along	MH-H	03931
Howells, William D.	1889.08.24	SLC	NY.Elmira	If you should	NN-B	02693
Howells, William D.	1889.09.22	SLC	CT.Hartford	It is immensely	NN-B	02695
Howells, William D.	1889.10.21	SLC	CT.Hartford	I'm afraid we	MH-H	03955
Howells, William D.	1889.10.28	SLC	CT.Hartford	Don't be afraid	MH-H	03959
Howells, William D.	1889.11.22	SLC	CT.Hartford	These are immense	MH-H	03973
Howells, William D.	1889.12.23	SLC	CT.Hartford	The magazine came	NN-B	02706
Howells, William D.	1890.01.31	SLC	CT.Hartford	This seems to	MH-H	04007
Howells, William D.	1890.02.11	SLC	CT.Hartford	All right--I've	MH-H	04016
Howells, William D.	1890.04.01	SLC	CT.Hartford	It will be	MH-H	04036
Howells, William D.	1890.11.27	SLC	CT.Hartford	Your words of	MH-H	04115
Howells, William D.	1891.02.10	SLC	CT.Hartford	I am very	MH-H	04169
Howells, William D.	1891.02.24	SLC	CT.Hartford	Mrs. Clemens has	NN-B	04572
Howells, William D.	1891.02.28	SLC	CT.Hartford	Won't you drop	NN-B	04575
Howells, William D.	1891.04.04	SLC	CT.Hartford	I'm ashamed. It	NN-B	04581
Howells, William D.	1891.05.20	SLC	CT.Hartford	For her health's	NN-B	04588
Howells, William D.	1893.04.11	SLC	NY.New York	What a pity	MH-H	04371
Howells, William D.	1893.05.12	SLC	NY.New York	I am so	NN-B	04641
Howells, William D.	1893.11.14	SLC	NY.New York	Land, I wish	MH-H	04503
Howells, William D.	1893.11.17	SLC	NY.New York	This will cause	MH-H	04504
Howells, William D.	1893.11.30	SLC	NY.New York	I am to	MH-H	04513
Howells, William D.	1893.12.15	SLC	NY.New York	Say--tell me	MH-H	04528
Howells, William D.	1894.09.14	SLC	FR.Etretat	I have heard	CSmH	04788
Howells, William D.	1895.08.17	SLC	CN.Vancouver	This is my	MH-H	04947
Howells, William D.	1896.08.05	SLC	EN.Southampton	Certainly your White	MH-H	05091
Howells, William D.	1896.09.24	SLC	EN.London	Yes, you two	MH-H	05116
Howells, William D.	1897.02.23	SLC	EN.London	I find your	NN-B	05505

Howells, William D.		1898.01.22	SLC	AU.Vienna	Look at those	MH-H	05337
Howells, William D.		1898.08.16	SLC	AU.Kaltenleut.	Your letter came	NN-B	05492
Howells, William D.		1898.08.30	SLC	AU.Kaltenleut.	This morning I	MH-H	05428
Howells, William D.	&	1898.12.30 1899.01.03	SLC	AU.Vienna	I begin with I forgot to	NN-B MH-H	05499
Howells, William D.		1899.04.02	SLC	AU.Vienna	I am waiting	NN-B	05601
Howells, William D.	to	1899.05.12 1899.05.13	SLC	AU.Vienna	When Bliss engaged	NN-B	05607
Howells, William D.		1899.07.03	SLC	EN.London	Of course go	NN-B	05616
Howells, William D.		1899.09.26	SLC	SE.Sanna	Just a line	NN-B	05621
Howells, William D.		1899.10.19	SLC	EN.London	My, it's a	NN-B	05624
Howells, William D.	&	1900.01.25 1900.01.26	SLC	EN.London	Yes, the short	NN-B	08197
Howells, William D.		1900.05.27	SLC	EN.London	I can't venture	MH-H	05809
Howells, William D.	ca	1900.08.01	SLC	EN.London	I read the	MH-H	10779
Howells, William D.		1901.05.**	SLC	NY.New York	Won't you come	MH-H	06066
Howells, William D.		1901.05.27	SLC	NY.New York	Old Clemens his	MH-H	06064
Howells, William D.		1901.11.21	SLC	NY.Riverdale	Yours has arrived Read this	MH-H CU-MARK	06175 CU-MARK enc
Howells, William D.		1902.01.03	SLC	NY.Riverdale	Yes--take it	MH-H	06218
Howells, William D.		1902.01.08	SLC	NY.Riverdale	Oh, great Scott	MH-H	06226
Howells, William D.		1902.01.12	SLC	NY.Riverdale	Say--Howells, don't	MH-H	06243
Howells, William D.		1902.01.18	SLC	NY.Riverdale	This has been	MH-H(tr)	10780
Howells, William D.		1902.07.29	SLC	ME.York Harbor	if there is	MH-H	06393 on envelope
Howells, William D.	or	1902.09.23 1902.09.24	SLC	ME.York Harbor	I go on	MH-H	06438
Howells, William D.		1902.10.03	SLC	ME.York Harbor	It is a	MH-H	06452
Howells, William D.		1902.10.11	SLC	ME.York Harbor	Say--stay where	MH-H	06459
Howells, William D.		1902.10.21	SLC	NY.Riverdale	Yes, keep the	NAlf	06471
Howells, William D.		1902.11.13	SLC	NY.Riverdale	I am glad	NNPM(tr)	10884

ADDRESSEE	DATE	WRITER	PLACE	CUE	SOURCE	NUMBER/NOTES
Howells, William D.	1902.11.28	SLC	NY.New York	Done by Truly	NAIf	09200 engraved inscription
Howells, William D.	1902.12.24	SLC	NY.Riverdale	I'll be there	MH-H	06525
Howells, William D.	1902.12.26	SLC	NY.Riverdale	I have not	MH-H	06530
Howells, William D.	1902.12.27 & 1902.12.28	SLC	NY.Riverdale	Suppose you send	MH-H	06532
Howells, William D.	1903.02.09	SLC per IVL	NY.Riverdale	I don't hear	NN	06579
Howells, William D.	1903.02.13	SLC	NY.Riverdale	I am infinitely	MH-H	06581
Howells, William D.	1903.04.14	SLC	NY.Riverdale	I shall do	MH-H	06621 unfinished
Howells, William D.	1903.04.29	SLC	NY.Riverdale	B'gosh, I suppose	MH-H	06640
Howells, William D.	1903.05.07	SLC	NY.Riverdale	Set-fire, you	CU-MARK	06649
Howells, William D.	1903.07.25	SLC	NY.Elmira	O, hellfire! as	MH-H	06708
Howells, William D.	1903.12.04	SLC	IT.Florence	The Xmas No.	MH-H	06767
Howells, William D.	1904.01.16	SLC	IT.Florence	I've struck it	MH-H	06786
Howells, William D.	1904.03.14	SLC	IT.Florence	Yes, I sat	NN-B	08237
Howells, William D.	1904.06.06	SLC	IT.Florence	Last night at	MH-H	06859
Howells, William D.	1904.06.12	SLC	IT.Florence	We have to	MH-H	06868
Howells, William D.	1906.02.25	SLC	NY.New York	Miss Lyon brought	MH-H	07355
Howells, William D.	1906.04.10	SLC	NY.New York	It is lovely	MH-H	07424
Howells, William D.	1906.06.07	SLC	NH.Dublin	Please don't burden	CU-MARK(dr)	05068 telegram
Howells, William D.	1906.06.17	SLC	NH.Dublin	It was wrong	NN-B	08262
Howells, William D.	1906.06.26	SLC	NY.New York	It is lovely	NN-B	08263
Howells, William D.	1906.08.03	SLC	NH.Dublin	I am very	MH-H	07487
Howells, William D.	1906.08.25	SLC	NH.Dublin	If it were	NN-B(tr)	02244
Howells, William D.	1906.08.29	SLC	NH.Dublin	If it were	MH-H	07508
Howells, William D.	1907.01.01	SLC	NY.New York	Appy New Year	MH-H	07611 inscription
Howells, William D. & Dunne, Peter F.	1907.02.06	SLC	NY.New York	The Human Race	Mo2	07644 also to Harvey

Howells, William D.		1907.10.04	SLC	NY.Tuxedo Park	Howells it is	CtY	07845
Howells, William D.		1908.01.22	SLC	NY.New York	I find that	MH-H	07925
Howells, William D.		1908.07.22	SLC	CT.Redding	Thank you once	MH-H	08057
Howells, William D.		1908.08.12	SLC	CT.Redding	Won't you &	NN-B	08284
Howells, William D.		1908.09.24	SLC	CT.Redding	Oh I reckon	MH-H	08111
Howells, William D.		1908.10.26	SLC	CT.Redding	Oh, I say	NAlf	08145
Howells, William D.		1908.11.23	SLC	CT.Redding	There'll be a	MH-H	08161
Howells, William D.		1909.01.18	SLC	CT.Redding	I have to	IU-R	08315
Howells, William D.		1909.03.13	SLC	CT.Redding	Bring the letters	MH-H	08372
Howells, William D.		1909.04.17	SLC	CT.Redding	When I wrote My pen has	MH-H NN-B	08292
Howells, William D.		1909.11.07	SLC	CT.Redding	This week being	MH-H	08484
Howland, Louise A. & Howland, Robert M.		1870.03.06	SLC	NY.Buffalo	I have had	CU-MARK	00440
Howland, Louise A. & Howland, Robert M.		1871.04.06	SLC	NY.Elmira	We were very	CU-MARK	00600
Howland, Louise A. & Howland, Robert M.	ca	1877.09.03	SLC & OLC	NY.Elmira	We were delighted	CU-MARK	04656
Howland, Louise A.		1883.01.23	SLC	CT.Hartford	Luckily the scare	CU-MARK	02339
Howland, Louise A.		1883.02.13	OLC	NY.New York	We were so	CU-MARK	02345
Howland, Louise A.		1890.01.31	SLC	CT.Hartford	I was deeply	CU-MARK	04009
Howland, Louise A.	pm	1905.12.19	SLC	NY.New York	To you, &	CU-MARK	07265 form letter
Howland, Robert M.		1866.10.29	SLC	NV.Virginia City	I have just	NvHi	00107
Howland, Robert M.		1866.11.01	SLC	NV.Virginia City	Been on sick	CU-MARK(tr)	00062 telegram; also to Curry & Johnson
Howland, Robert M. & Howland, Louise A.		1870.03.06	SLC	NY.Buffalo	I have had	CU-MARK	00440
Howland, Robert M.		1870.06.**	SLC	NY.Buffalo	In memory of	CU-MARK	00476
Howland, Robert M. & Howland, Louise A.		1871.04.06	SLC	NY.Elmira	We were very	CU-MARK	00600
Howland, Robert M.		1871.11.20	OLC	CT.Hartford	Your letter of	CU-MARK	00677

ADDRESSEE	DATE	WRITER	PLACE	CUE	SOURCE	NUMBER/NOTES
Howland, Robert M. & Howland, Louise A.	ca 1877.09.03	SLC & OLC	NY.Elmira	We were delighted	CU-MARK	04656
Howland, Robert M.	1879.10.27	SLC	CT.Hartford	They are the	CU-MARK(ph)	07428
Howland, Robert M.	1879.12.14	SLC	CT.Hartford	Thanks for the	CU-MARK	02810
Howland, Robert M.	1879.12.29	SLC	CT.Hartford	If your engagements	CU-MARK	04128
Howland, Robert M.	1880.05.02	SLC	CT.Hartford	With the affectionate	CU-MARK	09310 inscription
Howland, Robert M.	1888.01.15	SLC	CT.Hartford	A thing has	CU-MARK	03700
Hoyt (Wm. H.) & Co.	1903.10.20	SLC	NY.New York	In my absence	ViU(tr)	06745
Hubbard & Farmer	1882.08.04	SLC	NY.Elmira	Sell out I.B.&W	CU-MARK(tr)	10479 telegram
Hubbard, Elbert	1906.11.**	SLC	NY.New York	Truth is the	105:1938.02.25	09642 inscription
Hubbard, H.P.	1885.02.18	SLC	CT.Hartford	Your kind invitation	404:1885.02.26	03172
Hubbard, L.P.	1881.11.16	SLC	CT.Hartford	Having already accepted	317:1881.12.23	02089
Hubbard, Mary N.	1901.01.13	SLC	NY.New York	I remember the	MoHM	05964
Hudson, Laura K.	1906.01.12	SLC per IVL	NY.New York	I am forever	CU-MARK(tr)	07307
Hughes, Fred	o/a 1907.01.05	SLC per IVL	NY.New York	Had no acquaintance	CU-MARK(dr)	07621 on Hughes Jan 5
Hullah, Annette	1898.10.22	SLC	AU.Vienna	from her best	CU-MARK(ph)	05454 inscription
Hullah, Annette	1899.03.23	SLC	AU.Vienna	You think I	CU-MARK(ph)	05568
Hullah, Annette	1899.04.18	SLC	AU.Vienna	I know you	CU-MARK(ph)	05578
Hunt, Leigh	bet 1906.10.13 & 1906.10.23	SLC	NH.Dublin	I am ailing	CU-MARK(dr)	07547 telegram
Hurst, John F.	1897.10.08	SLC	AU.Vienna	Thank you ever	CtHMTH	05296
Hutchings, C. Edwin	1902.06.12	SLC	NY.Riverdale	I ought to	297:110	06361
Hutchings, Mrs.	1902.11.14	SLC	NY.Riverdale	I suspect--as	297:25	06487
Hutchins, Mr.	1890.02.11	SLC	CT.Hartford	Well, I wish	176:75	04017
Hutchins, Stilson	****.**.**	SLC	Unknown	By the kindness	CU-MARK	09125
Hutton, Eleanor V.	****.12.29	SLC	Unknown	Thank you ever	261:421	06368
Hutton, Eleanor V.	1884.03.07	SLC	CT.Hartford	Mr. Irving will	NjP	02934

Hutton, Eleanor V.		1894.06.19	SLC	FR.Paris	This is only	NjP	04741
Hutton, Eleanor V.		1895.03.09	SLC	NY.New York	I've got your	NjP	04848
Hutton, Eleanor V.		1896.11.26	SLC	EN.London	I thank you	NjP	05149
Hutton, Eleanor V. & Hutton, Laurence		1896.12.22	SLC	EN.London	I am powerful	NjP	05156
Hutton, Eleanor V.		1901.01.01	SLC	NY.New York	No, my idea	NjP	05957
Hutton, Eleanor V.		1902.09.04	SLC	ME.York Harbor	Didn't I answer	NjP	06426
Hutton, Eleanor V.		1902.11.06	SLC	NY.Riverdale	I think it	NjP	06483
Hutton, Eleanor V. & Hutton, Laurence		1903.07.02	SLC	NY.Elmira	You leave tomorrow	NjP	06688
Hutton, Eleanor V.		1903.12.03	SLC	IT.Florence	I thank you	NjP	06765
Hutton, Laurence		****.**.**	SLC	NY.New York	In the meantime	NjP	08989
Hutton, Laurence		****.**.**	SLC	NY.New York	Twichell is here	NjP	03692
Hutton, Laurence		****.**.**	SLC	Unknown	Thank you, &	NjP	08990
Hutton, Laurence	pm	****.02.22	SLC	CT.Hartford	*	NjP	10244 envelope only
Hutton, Laurence	pm	****.09.29	SLC	CT.Hartford	*	NjP	10243 envelope only
Hutton, Laurence	pm	****.11.25	SLC	CT.Hartford	*	NjP	10245 envelope only
Hutton, Laurence		1883.04.22	SLC	CT.Hartford	I have long	NjP	02373
Hutton, Laurence		1883.12.20	SLC	CT.Hartford	I enclose a	NjP	02871
Hutton, Laurence		1884.**.**	SLC	CT.Hartford	This telegram came	NjP	02999
Hutton, Laurence		1884.02.04	SLC	CT.Hartford	Warner was in	NjP	02905
Hutton, Laurence		1884.02.12	SLC	CT.Hartford	You see what	NjP	02915
Hutton, Laurence		1884.02.19	SLC	CT.Hartford	I'm not able	NjP	02921
Hutton, Laurence		1884.04.30	SLC	NY.New York	This space reserved	451:29	09330 inscription
Hutton, Laurence	pm	1884.12.19	SLC	CT.Hartford	*	NjP	10242 envelope only
Hutton, Laurence		1884.12.22	SLC	CT.Hartford	I mustn't venture	NjP	03065
Hutton, Laurence		1885.**.**	SLC	CT.Hartford	Indeed I wish	NjP	03094

ADDRESSEE	DATE	WRITER	PLACE	CUE	SOURCE	NUMBER/NOTES
Hutton, Laurence	1885.12.07	SLC	CT.Hartford	This family meets	WU(ph)	03326
Hutton, Laurence & Laffan, William M.	1886.02.25	SLC & OLC	CT.Hartford	Lawrence Barrett is	MH-H NjP	03372 to Huttons & Laffans; NjP envelope
Hutton, Laurence	1887.09.22	SLC	CT.Hartford	But you ought	NjP	03651
Hutton, Laurence	1887.11.24	SLC	CT.Hartford	I am just	NjP	03670
Hutton, Laurence	1890.07.05	SLC	NY.Tannersville	The Last Meeting	219:1904.11	09894 poem inscription
Hutton, Laurence	1890.11.05	SLC	CT.Hartford	I thank you	NjP	04111
Hutton, Laurence	1891.02.03	SLC	CT.Hartford	Accept my very	CU-MARK(tr)	04166
Hutton, Laurence	1892.08.12	SLC	GE.Bad-Nauheim	But what are	NjP	01720
Hutton, Laurence	1892.08.23	SLC	GE.Bad-Nauheim	The hotel New	NjP	01786 Aug 23 to Eyre enc
Hutton, Laurence	1892.09.05	SLC	GE.Bad-Nauheim	Verily 'tis well	NjP	02070
Hutton, Laurence	1892.09.28	SLC	IT.Florence	I have just	NjP	02382
Hutton, Laurence	1892.10.21	SLC	IT.Florence	La vostra belle	NjP	04661
Hutton, Laurence	1892.10.30	SLC	IT.Florence	Postscript. Respectfully	NjP	08925 inscription
Hutton, Laurence	1892.12.15	SLC	IT.Florence	I said to	NjP	04308
Hutton, Laurence	1893.01.02	SLC	IT.Florence	By gracious I	NjP	04321
Hutton, Laurence	1893.02.05	SLC	IT.Florence	Poem: You thought	NjP	04337
Hutton, Laurence	1893.03.16	SLC	IT.Florence	I hope you	NjP	04351
Hutton, Laurence	1893.09.13	SLC	NY.New York	It's Clara who	NjP	04449
Hutton, Laurence	1894.07.26	SLC	NY.New York	It's Jean's birth-day	NjP	04762
Hutton, Laurence	1895.03.22	SLC	NY.New York	O, I am	NjP	04853
Hutton, Laurence	1895.12.24	SLC	SH.Oceana	This is to introduce	AuSN-M	11220 enc in Dec 24 to Windeyer
Hutton, Laurence	1896.09.06	SLC	EN.Guildford	No, dear Laurence	NjP	05104
Hutton, Laurence	1896.10.05	SLC	EN.London	I shall take	NjP	05123
Hutton, Laurence & Hutton, Eleanor V.	1896.12.22	SLC	EN.London	I am powerful	NjP	05156

Hutton, Laurence	1898.02.20	SLC	AU.Vienna	Two months ago	NjP	05352
Hutton, Laurence	1898.05.13	SLC	AU.Vienna	The book has	CU-MARK(tr)	05389
Hutton, Laurence	1898.10.20	SLC	AU.Vienna	This is to	NjP	05453
Hutton, Laurence	1899.03.12	SLC	AU.Vienna	I do certainly	NjP	05561
Hutton, Laurence	1899.07.13	SLC	SE.Sanna	So you sail	NjP	05654
Hutton, Laurence	1899.09.18	SLC	SE.Sanna	The enclosed comes	NjP	05679
Hutton, Laurence	1900.01.01	SLC	EN.London	To encourage you	NjP	05740
Hutton, Laurence	1900.10.31	SLC	NY.New York	Mrs. Clemens says	NjP	05890
Hutton, Laurence	1900.11.05	SLC	NY.New York	Prosperity and happiness	451:129	09268 inscription
Hutton, Laurence	1900.11.05	SLC	Unknown	reverence and love	451:129	09267 inscription
Hutton, Laurence	1900.11.07	SLC	NY.New York	We are gradually	NjP	05899
Hutton, Laurence	1900.11.21	SLC	NY.New York	Dear Laurence dam	NjP	05916
Hutton, Laurence	1900.11.25	OLC	NY.New York	By some misfortune	NjP	05919
Hutton, Laurence	1900.12.03	SLC	NY.New York	Won't you please	NjP	05925 per unknown amanuensis
Hutton, Laurence	1901.04.15	SLC	NY.New York	I am glad	NjP	06037 typed
Hutton, Laurence	1901.05.08	SLC	NY.New York	I am coming	NjP	06054
Hutton, Laurence	1902.02.27	SLC	NY.Riverdale	If you would	NjP	06285
Hutton, Laurence	1902.03.02	SLC	NY.Riverdale	A navy-blue suit	NjP	06289
Hutton, Laurence	1902.10.16	SLC	NY.Riverdale	Yes, if you	NjP	06463
Hutton, Laurence	1902.12.20	SLC per IVL	NY.Riverdale	I don't lecture	NjP	06523
Hutton, Laurence	1903.03.18	SLC	NY.Riverdale	Mr. Rogers has	NjP	06600
Hutton, Laurence	1903.03.19	SLC	NY.New York	A very few	NjP	06602 group letter
Hutton, Laurence & Hutton, Eleanor V.	1903.07.02	SLC	NY.Elmira	You leave tomorrow	NjP	06688
Hutton, Laurence	1903.10.02	SLC	NY.Elmira	Yours from Thusis	NjP	06734
Iles, George	1884.08.24	SLC	NY.Elmira	I am on	CaQMM	01461

ADDRESSEE	DATE	WRITER	PLACE	CUE	SOURCE	NUMBER/NOTES
Iles, George	1884.09.08	SLC	NY.Elmira	You have my	ViU	01359
Iles, George	1884.11.24	SLC	DC.Washington	Alas, it's no	CaQMM	03039
Iles, George	1885.02.12	SLC	MI.Detroit	I am so	DCos	03164
Iles, George	1885.04.27	SLC	CT.Hartford	I had already	ViU	03220
Iles, George	1887.01.24	SLC	CT.Hartford	I'm returning those	DLC	03517
Iles, George	1900.10.28	SLC	NY.New York	I thank you	CaQMM	05889
Iles, George	1902.05.26	SLC	NY.Riverdale	Yesterday I read	MoHi	06346
Iles, George	1902.06.13	SLC	NY.Riverdale	I hand you	NBu Mo2	06365 Mo2 envelope
Iles, George	1903.01.19	SLC per IVL	NY.Riverdale	Mr. Clemens wishes	CaQMMO	00546
Iles, George	o/a 1905.09.19	SLC per IVL	NH.Dublin	We return to	CU-MARK(dr)	07142 on Iles Sept 19
Iles, George	1907.02.20	SLC	NY.New York	Goldwin Smith	CU-MARK	07654
Ingersoll (R.H.) & Bro.	1901.05.21	SLC	NY.New York	Please send me	CU-MARK(ph)	06060
Ingersoll, Robert G.	1879.12.09	SLC	CT.Hartford	If you have	CU-MARK(tr)	01737
Ingersoll, Robert G.	1879.12.14	SLC	CT.Hartford	Thank you most	DLC(tr)	01740
Ingersoll, Robert G.	1881.08.10	SLC	NY.Elmira	Your letter &	CU-MARK(tr)	01998
Ingram, Mr.	o/a 1905.12.06	SLC	NY.New York	To you, &	CU-MARK(ph)	07232 form letter
Irving, Henry	1885.03.14	SLC	NY.New York	for your high	250:1980.06	08606 form letter
Irving, Henry	1893.11.13	SLC	NY.New York	Will you dine	ViU	04499 group letter
Irwin, John	o/a 1905.12.17	SLC per IVL	NY.New York	Haven't any idea	CU-MARK(dr)	07261 on Irwin Dec 17
Irwin, Wallace	1909.03.08	SLC	CT.Redding	The aged &	CU-BANC	00540
Italian Ambassador	1903.07.21	SLC	NY.Elmira	I am most	CU-MARK(dr)	06705
Jack	1882.06.23	SLC	CT.Hartford	The twins arrived	NN4	02225
Jackson, Alice D.	*	*	*	*	*	10602 see Day, Alice H.

Jacob, Swinton		1897.01.**	SLC	EN.London	Now if I	CtHMTH	09348 inscription
Jacobs, Ward		1903.06.11	SLC	NY.Riverdale	Simplified, the facts	CU-MARK	06675
Jacobs, Ward & Bliss, Frank E.		1903.06.25	SLC	NY.Riverdale	I forgot one	CtHi	06684
Jacobs, Ward		1903.07.04	SLC	NY.Elmira	Frank Bliss's letter	CtHi	06690
Jacobs, William W.		1908.10.28	SLC	CT.Redding	It has a	114:823	08148
James		1896.01.13	CC	SH.Oceana	It is a	ViU(tr)	05013
James, George W.	o/a	1906.01.13	SLC per IVL	NY.New York	Mr. Mighels is	CU-MARK(dr)	07309 on James Jan 13
James, Thomas L.		1910.01.30	SLC	BE.Hamilton	Please send me	312:1910.05.02	08550
James, Thomas L.		1910.02.15	SLC	BE.Hamilton	The parcel of	ODa2	08557
James, T.N.	o/a	1906.02.26	SLC per IVL	NY.New York	My contract with	CU-MARK(dr)	07358 on James Feb 26
James, William		1900.04.17	SLC	EN.London	Mrs. Clemens &	MH-H	05792
James, William		1900.04.23	SLC	EN.London	Indeed you are	MH-H	05796
Janney, Mary		****.05.04	SLC	NY.Elmira	It took me	Mo2	08531
Japp, John		1907.06.19	SLC per RWA	EN.London	Mr. Clemens directs	CU-MARK(tr)	07750 RWA tr
Japp, John		1907.06.21	SLC per RWA	EN.London	I have great	CU-MARK(tr)	07764 RWA tr
Japp, John		1907.06.22	SLC per RWA	EN.London	Mr. Clemens directs	CU-MARK(tr)	07765
Jenkins, Elizabeth E.		1886.10.02	SLC	CT.Hartford	The wall by	CtHSD	08836
Jenkins, Elizabeth E.		1886.10.20	SLC	CT.Hartford	Land of Goshen	CtHSD	03472
Jenkins, Margaret		1905.05.19	SLC per IVL	NH.Dublin	Mr. Clemens directs	CU-MARK(tr)	07045 IVL tr
Jenks, Tudor S.	o/a	1906.07.25	SLC per IVL	NH.Dublin	In the conditions	CU-MARK(dr)	07472 on Jenks July 3
Jennings, Annie B.		1891.03.22	SLC	CT.Hartford	Old & lame	CU-MARK(tr)	04184
Jennings, Louis J.		1875.04.26	SLC	CT.Hartford	Will you print	DFo	01226
Jesse, Richard H.		1902.04.14	SLC	NY.Riverdale	The distinguished honor	MoCoJ	06322

ADDRESSEE	DATE	WRITER	PLACE	CUE	SOURCE	NUMBER/NOTES
Jessup, Miss	****.**.**	SLC	Unknown	Directions. To be	ViU	11101 inscription
Jewett, Sarah O.	1887.03.14	SLC	CT.Hartford	Alas! I dine	CU-MARK(ph)	03540
Jewett, Sarah O.	1887.03.17	SLC	CT.Hartford	I think we	MeWC	08910
Jewett, Sarah O.	1902.01.09	SLC	NY.Riverdale	As regards that	CU-MARK	06235 typed form letter
Johnson, Alvin J.	1872.02.03	SLC	CT.Hartford	Domestic duties deny	450:67	00724
Johnson, Charlotte	*	*	*	*	*	11140 see Teller, Charlotte
Johnson, H.O.	1882.10.27	SLC	CT.Hartford	In answer to	CU-MARK	02297 typed
Johnson, J. Neely & Curry, Abraham	1866.11.01	SLC	NV.Virginia City	Been on sick	CU-MARK(tr)	00108 telegram; also to Howland
Johnson, Joseph Jr.	ca 1901.10.20	SLC	NY.New York	I forgot to	CSmH	06162
Johnson, Parish B.	1884.05.06	SLC	CT.Hartford	I remember when	CSmH	02970
Johnson, Robert U.	****.**.**	SLC	Unknown	I hope engagements	CU-MARK(ph)	08994
Johnson, Robert U.	1885.03.18	SLC	CT.Hartford	I'll have to	Mo2	03191
Johnson, Robert U.	1885.07.06	SLC	NY.Elmira	I'm glad to	C4	03252
Johnson, Robert U.	1885.07.28	SLC	NY.Elmira	I'm trying to	CU-MARK(tr)	03268
Johnson, Robert U.	1885.08.15	SLC	NY.Elmira	I did what	Mo2	02424
Johnson, Robert U.	1885.09.08	SLC	NY.Elmira	Mrs. Clemens has	CU-MARK(tr)	03285
Johnson, Robert U.	1887.10.31	SLC	CT.Hartford	All right, &	ViU	03663
Johnson, Robert U. & Gilder, Richard W.	1888.08.12	SLC	NY.Elmira	I'll tell you	NN-B	02684 also to Buel
Johnson, Robert U.	1888.09.06	SLC	NY.Elmira	O, hang it	NN	03757
Johnson, Robert U.	1889.08.03	SLC	NY.Elmira	Beard is the	ViU	03921
Johnson, Robert U.	1889.08.16	SLC	NY.Elmira	I see Gilder's	InU-Li	10828 telegram
Johnson, Robert U.	1891.07.10	SLC	FR.Aix-les-Bains	Hail, & howdy	Mo2	04220
Johnson, Robert U.	1894.05.30	SLC	FR.Paris	Yours in a	107:1925.02.24	09551 other sources

Johnson, Robert U.		1895.05.30	SLC	NY.Elmira	I am in	ViU	04882
Johnson, Robert U.		1895.07.05	SLC	NY.Elmira	I am still	NSyU	04926
Johnson, Robert U. & Gilder, Richard W.		1895.08.17	SLC	CN.Vancouver	This is to	Mo2	02462 to six editors
Johnson, Robert U.	pm	1900.11.11	SLC	NY.New York	You'd much better	CLU-S/C	05901
Johnson, Robert U.		1901.03.31	SLC	NY.New York	It is fine	ViU	06030
Johnson, Robert U.		1901.10.11	SLC	NY.Riverdale	I have been	NN-B	08220
Johnson, Robert U.		1902.04.14	SLC	NY.Riverdale	There's nothing in	ViU	06323
Johnson, Robert U.		1903.10.21	SLC	NY.New York	In boxing &	NN-B	06747
Johnson, Robert U.		1903.10.21	SLC	NY.New York	I'll be sure	ViU	06749
Johnson, Robert U.		1904.12.10	SLC	NY.New York	I beg to	NNAL	06958
Johnson, Robert U.		1905.04.07	SLC per IVL	NY.New York	Mr. Clemens wishes	NNAL	07027
Johnson, Robert U.		1905.04.28	SLC	NY.New York	I shall be	NNAL	07034
Johnson, Robert U.		1905.05.03	SLC	NY.New York	No, I've named	NNAL	07039
Johnson, Robert U.		1905.09.29	SLC per IVL	NH.Dublin	Mr. Clemens directs	NNAL	07153
Johnson, Robert U.		1905.12.19	SLC per IVL	NY.New York	Mr. Clemens directs	NNAL	07266
Johnson, Robert U.		1906.12.02	SLC	NY.New York	Mouldy 71 thanks	ViU	07581
Johnson, Robert U.		1907.05.31	SLC per IVL	NY.Tuxedo Park	Mr. Clemens asks	NNAL	07737
Johnson, Robert U.		1909.06.05	SLC	CT.Redding	I had just	ViU	08416
Johnston, C.H.		1909.03.22	SLC	CT.Redding	Messages like yours	116:1957.05.02	08375
Johnston, John H.		1902.03.07	SLC	NY.Riverdale	I thank you	116:1957.05.02	09972
Johnston, Richard M.		1887.04.05	SLC	CT.Hartford	It would not	MdBE	03556
Johnston, Richard M.		1888.11.09	SLC	CT.Hartford	We hear that	MdBE	03830
Johnston, Richard M.		1889.01.04	SLC	CT.Hartford	Thank you ever	MdBE	03846
Johnston, Richard M.		1889.01.09	SLC	CT.Hartford	Private. I shall	MdBE	03848
Johnston, Richard M.		1889.01.11	SLC	CT.Hartford	Thanks, a thousand	MdBE	03851
Johnston, Richard M.		1889.07.12	SLC	CT.Hartford	I tell you	MdBE	03910

ADDRESSEE	DATE	WRITER	PLACE	CUE	SOURCE	NUMBER/NOTES
Joline, Adrian H.	1902.11.28	SLC	NY.New York	Done by Truly	157:1914.12.15	09874 engraved inscription
Jones, David M.	1906.12.27	SLC	NY.New York	It is a	AuBrU	07579
Jones, Florence D.	1907.05.27	SLC	NY.Tuxedo Park	I have read	CtY	07732
Jones, Francis A.	o/a 1905.12.20	SLC per IVL	NY.New York	Any forenoon at	CU-MARK(dr)	07267
Jones, John P.	1891.01.20	SLC	CT.Hartford	The main items	CU-MARK(dr)	04162
Jones, John P.	ca 1891.02.**	SLC	Unknown	For a whole	CU-MARK(dr)	04164
Jones, John P.	1891.02.09	SLC	CT.Hartford	In the pressure	CU-MARK(tr)	04168 SLC tr
Jones, John P.	1891.02.13	SLC	CT.Hartford	If you had	CU-MARK(tr)	04172 SLC tr
Jones, Mr.	1879.11.07	SLC	CT.Hartford	All right, my	CtY	01710
Jordan, Elizabeth	****.**.**	SLC	CT.Redding	I wrote the	NN	08195
Jordan, Elizabeth	1905.03.10	SLC	NY.New York	Once I could	NN	07015
Jordan, Elizabeth	o/a 1906.05.29	SLC per IVL	NH.Dublin	Mr. Clemens is	CU-MARK(tr)	07600
Jordan, Elizabeth	1906.07.06	SLC	NY.New York	I am here	NN	07473
Jordan, Elizabeth	1906.07.30	SLC per IVL	NH.Dublin	Mr. Clemens requests	NN	07484
Jordan, Elizabeth	1906.08.04	SLC	NH.Dublin	I was hoping	148:259	07488
Jordan, Elizabeth	o/a 1906.11.23	SLC per IVL	NY.New York	Thank Mrs. Frances	CU-MARK(dr)	07572 on Jordan Nov 23
Jordan, Elizabeth	1908.12.04	SLC	CT.Redding	Indeed & 'deed	CU-MARK(ph)	08169
Jordan, Elizabeth	ca 1909.01.01	SLC	CT.Redding	Nothing in Dr.	NN	08194
Jordan, Elizabeth	1909.06.26	SLC	CT.Redding	I have with	NN	08427
Jordan, Elizabeth	o/a 1909.06.26	SLC	CT.Redding	Wir hatten sollen	CU-MARK(dr)	08424 on Jordan June 23
Jordan, Mary A.	1889.06.29	SLC	NY.Elmira	Mrs. Clemens desires	MNS	08913
Judd, Albert Francis	1870.12.20	SLC	NY.Buffalo	Your letter made	CU-MARK(ph)	02784
Katie	1897.12.25	SLC	AU.Vienna	To our seventeen-year	CU-MARK(tr)	09352 inscription

Kauffman, Reginald W.	o/a	1906.03.13	SLC per IVL	NY.New York	Mr. Clemens wrote	CU-MARK(dr)	07380 on Kauffman Mar 13
Keene, Francis B.		1904.05.29	SLC	IT.Florence	I am very	CU-MARK(ph)	06843
Keep, Robert P.		****.01.10	SLC	Unknown	I thank you	CtFP	07752
Keily, Mary		1880.02.21	SLC	CT.Hartford	Well, Mary, my	192:1880.03.25	10652
Keller, George H.		1900.11.25	SLC	NY.New York	I am hopelessly	CtHSD	05920
Keller, Helen		1903.03.17	SLC	NY.Riverdale	I must steal	NNAF	06599
Keller, Helen		1904.07.26	SLC	MA.Lee	Your letter of	NNAF	06904
Keller, Helen	o/a	1905.12.06	SLC	NY.New York	To you, &	NNAF	10680 form letter
Keller, Helen		1906.12.23	SLC	NY.New York	O, thank you	NNAF	07595
Keller, Helen		1908.11.14	SLC	CT.Redding	The book has	NNPM	08159 deposit
Keller, Helen		1908.11.22	SLC per IVL	CT.Redding	Mr. Clemens asks	NNAF	10683
Keller, Helen	ca	1909.01.01	SLC	CT.Redding	I command you	273:52	09507
Keller, Helen	ca	1909.01.01	SLC	CT.Redding	Recommended by the	NNAF	10684 inscription
Keller, Helen	ca	1909.01.08	SLC	CT.Redding	Greeting and Salutation	NNAF	10681 form letter
Keller, Helen		1909.06.29	SLC	CT.Redding	In that booklet	NNAF	08429
Keller, Helen		1910.01.26	SLC	BE.Hamilton	To all friends	NNAF	10688 form letter
Keller, Mary M.		1890.09.12	SLC	NY.Tannersville	I thank you	CtHSD	04095
Kelley, William D.		1891.04.03	SLC per FGW	CT.Hartford	In reply to	CU-MARK(tr)	04189 FGW tr
Kellogg & Co.	o/a	1905.06.29	CC per IVL	NH.Dublin	Kindly return this	CU-MARK(dr)	07074 on Lincoln Bank to CC June 29
Kelsey, Carl	o/a	1907.04.01	SLC per IVL	NY.New York	My membership would	CU-MARK(dr)	07683 on Kelsey Apr 1
Kennedy, Anthony		1888.**.**	SLC	Unknown	I applaud the	263:40.560	09429

ADDRESSEE	DATE	WRITER	PLACE	CUE	SOURCE	NUMBER/NOTES
Kennedy, Daniel E.	o/a 1905.10.02	SLC per IVL	NH.Dublin	Mr. Clemens has	CU-MARK(dr)	07158 on Kennedy Oct 2
Kennedy, William S.	****.**.**	SLC	Unknown	Of course I	231:219	10738
Kenney, C.S.	1905.04.09	SLC	NY.New York	I thank you	CU-MARK	07030
Kester, Paul	1900.03.24	SLC	EN.London	I should like	NN	05782
Kester, Paul	1900.03.25	SLC	EN.London	P.S. March 25.	NN	05784
Kester, Paul	pm 1902.06.19	SLC	NY.Bronx	*	NN	10168 envelope only
Kester, Paul	ca 1902.06.24	SLC	ME.York Harbor	By an oral	NN	06380
Kester, Paul	1902.07.27	SLC	ME.York Harbor	I will refer	NN	06390
Kester, Paul	pm 1903.02.10	SLC per IVL	NY.New York	*	NN	10169 envelope only
Kester, Paul	1903.02.14	SLC per IVL	NY.Riverdale	Mr. Clemens who	NN	06582
Kester, Paul	1903.02.26	SLC per IVL	NY.Riverdale	Mr. Clemens wishes	NN	06586
Kester, Paul	1903.03.09	SLC	NY.Riverdale	I shall express	NN	06593
Kester, Paul	1905.09.18	SLC per IVL	NH.Dublin	Mr. Clemens is	NN	07139
Kester, Paul	pm 1910.01.17	SLC per ABP	CT.Redding	To all friends	NN	08543 form letter
Kiefer, Daniel	1906.**.**	SLC per IVL	Unknown	I should be	CU-MARK(dr)	07289
Kimball, James N.	1884.01.04	SLC	CT.Hartford	Yes, you are	Mo2	02886
Kimball, James N.	1890.12.08	SLC per FGW	CT.Hartford	In response to	CU-MARK(tr)	10580 on Kimball Dec 6
Kimball, W.C. & Kimball, W.W.	1866.04.26	SLC	HI.Maui	Don't you think	ODa2	00098
Kimball, W.W. & Kimball, W.C.	1866.04.26	SLC	HI.Maui	Don't you think	ODa2	00098
King, C.A.	1870.07.22	SLC	NY.Elmira	I can't possibly	MWC	00491
King, Grace E.	****.**.**	CC	Unknown	It seems as	LU-Ar	03818
King, Grace E.	****.**.**	OLC	Unknown	I am a	LU-Ar	08955
King, Grace E.	****.**.**	SC	CT.Hartford	I thought it	LU-Ar	04146

King, Grace E.		1887.12.28	CC	CT.Hartford	We were so	LU-Ar	03686
King, Grace E.		1888.01.01	SC	CT.Hartford	Clara and I	LU-Ar	03689
King, Grace E.		1888.04.29	CC	CT.Hartford	I don't want	LU-Ar	03720
King, Grace E.	&	1888.06.17 1888.08.07	OLC	CT.Hartford & NY.Elmira	Mr Clemens and	LU-Ar	03724
King, Grace E.		1888.07.29	CC	NY.Elmira	I don't think	LU-Ar	03744
King, Grace E.		1888.08.**	CC	NY.Elmira	You can't realize	LU-Ar	03746
King, Grace E.		1888.08.26	SC	NY.Elmira	We are all	LU-Ar	03754
King, Grace E.		1888.09.12	SLC	NY.Elmira	The handless fore-arm	LU-Ar	03760
King, Grace E.		1888.10.25	SLC	NY.New York	This is to	LU-Ar	03794
King, Grace E.		1888.11.16	SLC	CT.Hartford	I do suppose	LU-Ar	03833
King, Grace E.		1888.12.04	SLC & OLC	CT.Hartford	I can not	LU-Ar	03799
King, Grace E.	pm	1888.12.06	SC	CT.Hartford	How I miss	LU-Ar	04145
King, Grace E.		1888.12.22	CC	CT.Hartford	Perhaps you have	LU-Ar	04144
King, Grace E.		1889.**.**	SC	CT.Hartford	Mamma's eyes are	LU-Ar	04143
King, Grace E.		1889.02.03	CC	CT.Hartford	I was so	LU-Ar	03857
King, Grace E.		1889.02.10	JC	Unknown	I thank you	LU-Ar	03862
King, Grace E.	or	1889.03.07 1889.03.08	CC	CT.Hartford	I have not	LU-Ar	03870
King, Grace E.		1889.03.24	OLC	CT.Hartford	I desparately want	LU-Ar	03877
King, Grace E.		1889.04.**	SC	CT.Hartford	It is lovely	LU-Ar	03878
King, Grace E.		1889.12.**	OLC	EN.London	I can not	LU-Ar	05729
King, Grace E.		1890.02.25	OLC	CT.Hartford	How I wish	LU-Ar	04021
King, Grace E.		1890.09.10	OLC	NY.Tannersville	You will see	LU-Ar	04093
King, Grace E.		1891.01.14	OLC	CT.Hartford	How I wish	LU-Ar	04159
King, Grace E.		1891.05.28	OLC	CT.Hartford	What a shame	LU-Ar	04212
King, Grace E.		1891.08.23	OLC	GE.Marienbad	I want so	LU-Ar	04224
King, Grace E.		1892.05.20	OLC	IT.Venice	Do come and	LU-Ar	04209
King, Grace E.	ca	1892.06.01	OLC	Unknown	We go the	LU-Ar	04292

ADDRESSEE	DATE	WRITER	PLACE	CUE	SOURCE	NUMBER/NOTES
King, Grace E.	1892.07.01	OLC	GE.Bad-Nauheim	I thought of	LU-Ar	01558
King, Grace E.	1892.08.30	OLC	GE.Bad-Nauheim	Your letter has	LU-Ar	01880
King, Grace E.	1892.09.05	OLC	GE.Bad-Nauheim	Glorious! Grace dear	LU-Ar	02071
King, Grace E.	1892.11.10	SLC	IT.Florence	is requested to	NN-B	09303 inscription
King, Grace E.	ca 1893.01.**	JC	IT.Florence	There has been	LU-Ar	08956
King, Grace E.	1893.06.14	OLC	IT.Florence	It is a	LU-Ar	04417
King, Grace E.	1893.11.05	OLC	FR.Paris	Here we are	LU-Ar	04489
King, Grace E.	1894.04.30	SLC	NY.New York	Oh, it isn't	LU-Ar	04727
King, Grace E.	1894.05.16 & 1894.06.03	OLC	FR.Paris	I was greatly	LU-Ar	04733
King, Grace E.	ca 1894.06.16	OLC	FR.Paris	surely full enough	LU-Ar	08665 fragment
King, Grace E.	1897.03.09	OLC	EN.London	Your last note	LU-Ar	05185
King, Grace E.	1897.06.27	OLC	EN.London	Your letter has	LU-Ar	05235
King, Grace E.	1900.**.**	OLC	EN.London	What a wonderful	LU-Ar	05728
King, Grace E.	1901.02.15 & 1901.02.24	OLC	NY.New York	This is the	LU-Ar	05999
King, Grace E.	1903.06.22	CC	NY.Riverdale	Your letter to	LU-Ar	06375
King, Grace E.	ca 1904.06.21	SLC	IT.Florence	For what you	LU-Ar	06846 form letter
King, Grace E.	1909.12.26	SLC	CT.Redding	To all friends	LU-Ar	06962 form letter
King, Helen M.	o/a 1907.02.18	SLC per IVL	NY.New York	Wrote the book	CU-MARK(dr)	07652 on King Feb 18
King, Horatio C. & Howard, John R.	1869.03.13	SLC	CT.Hartford	Yours of Feb.	PCarlD	11118
King, Horatio C.	1889.05.12	SLC	CT.Hartford	I wish I	424:82	03890
Kingsley, Charles	1874.02.13	SLC	CT.Hartford	Won't you kindly	ViU	01048
Kinney, Henry N.	****.03.22	SLC	CT.Hartford	I suffered all	C4	00468
Kinney, John C.	****.05.15	SLC	Unknown	Ah, if I	Ct	10550
Kinney, John C.	1881.10.25	SLC	Unknown	I'm mighty glad	Dn	09114
Kinney, John C.	1885.12.15	SLC	CT.Hartford	Thank you very	Ct	03333

Kinney, John C.	or	1887.01.30 1887.02.06	SLC	CT.Hartford	Here is the	ViU	08917
Kinney, John C.		1888.10.16	SLC	CT.Hartford	Certainly. That covers	CtHMTH	10592
Kinney, John C.		1888.10.16	SLC	CT.Hartford	I would very	CtHMTH	03792
Kinney, John C.		1889.06.03	SLC	CT.Hartford	I would very	NSyU	03899
Kinney, John C.		1889.09.28	SLC	CT.Hartford	Thou knowest I	Ct	03943
Kinney, Mrs. John		1886.02.13	SLC	CT.Hartford	I have sworn	Ct	10551
Kinsey, Joseph		1895.11.21	OLC	NZ.Auckland	It seems a	NzW2	04974
Kinsey, Joseph		1895.12.12	CC	NZ.Wellington	My Mother has	NzW2	04981
Kinsey, Joseph		1895.12.12	SLC	NZ.Wellington	The books came	NzW2	04980
Kinsey, Joseph		1895.12.13	OLC	NZ.Wellington	(O dear me!	NzW2	04982
Kinsey, Sarah G.		1895.11.23	SLC	NZ.Auckland	I look back	NzW2	04975
Kipling, Rudyard		1895.08.16	SLC	CN.Vancouver	It is reported	114:629	04945
Kipling, Rudyard		1899.03.07	SLC	AU.Vienna	I tender my	Uk5	05557 telegram
Kipling, Rudyard		1901.05.23	SLC	NY.New York	I was hoping	Uk5	06063
Kirby, Edmund B.		1901.01.22	SLC	NY.New York	I cannot deny	ViU(tr)	05979
Kirby, Thomas B.	ca	1879.12.08	SLC	Unknown	When you shall	117:1879.12.09	02806 other sources
Kirk, S.J.		1889.**.**	SLC	Unknown	with compts. of	ViU	09643 inscription; other sources
Kirkland, Henry R.		1907.07.11	SLC	EN.Liverpool	Very very sorry	ViU	11097 telegram
Kirlicks, John A.		1907.05.15	SLC	NY.New York	It is a	150:1910.04.24f	07723
Kitton, Frederic G.		1886.11.08	SLC	CT.Hartford	I would be	NN-B	03558
Klaw & Erlanger		1902.07.27	SLC	ME.York Harbor	I want to	Mo2	06391
Kloieda, Edmund		1898.10.19	SLC	AU.Vienna	I am sorry	ViU	05451
Knabe (Wm.) & Co.	o/a	1905.12.18	SLC per IVL	NY.New York	Entirely in sympathy	CU-MARK(dr)	07262 on Knabe Dec 18

ADDRESSEE	DATE	WRITER	PLACE	CUE	SOURCE	NUMBER/NOTES
Knickerbocker Pub.	o/a 1905.09.20	SLC per IVL	NH.Dublin	If you ask	CU-MARK(dr)	07143 on Knickerbocker Sept 20
Knickerbocker Pub.	o/a 1906.12.13	SLC per IVL	NY.New York	Can come see	CU-MARK(dr)	07593 on Knickerbocker Dec 13
Knickerbocker Trust Co.	1908.01.17	SLC	NY.New York	The time is	Mo2 CU-MARK(tr)	08895 Mo2 dr
Knickerbocker Trust Co.	ca 1908.01.17	SLC	NY.New York	I expect nothing	CU-MARK(tr) NN-B	07915 NN-B dr
Knickerbocker Trust Co.	ca 1908.01.17	SLC	Unknown	I am in	Mo2	08896
Knight, William	1899.06.24	SLC	EN.London	Your invitation is	NNPM	05642
Knight, William H.	1885.11.28	SLC	CT.Hartford	I thank you	CU-MARK(ph)	03317
Knowlton, G.W.	1894.08.11	SLC	CT.Hartford	You run us	CtHMTH	04780
Knox, Mr.	****.**.**	SLC	NY.New York	to see Col.	107:1925.03.03	09631
Knox, Thomas W.	1873.09.10	SLC	EN.London	God bless your	IGK	04137
Knox, William M.	1888.01.16	SLC	CT.Hartford	Keep the contract	Mo2	02436
Koerner, Anna	1891.06.04	SLC	CT.Hartford	from the author	122:1936.04.22	09720 inscription
Koerner, Marie	1889.01.01	JC	CT.Hartford	One that loves	122:1936.04.22	09718 inscription
Koerner, Marie	1889.03.29	SLC	CT.Hartford	You leave a	122:1936.04.22	09717 inscription
Koerner, Marie	1889.04.04	SLC	CT.Hartford	Truly yours	122:1936.04.22	09719 inscription
Krantz Hotel	1899.06.**	SLC	EN.London	Ask Cook when	NN-B	05611 telegram
Krause, Mr.	bet 1899.10.** & 1900.07.**	SLC	EN.London	It is too	CU-MARK(ph)	05727
Krause, Mrs. R. Howard & Krause, R. Howard	1898.02.11	SLC	AU.Vienna	with the kindest	CtHMTH	09353 inscription
Krause, R. Howard & Krause, Mrs. R. Howard	1898.02.11	SLC	AU.Vienna	with the kindest	CtHMTH	09353 inscription
Kreisler, Mr.	****.**.**	SLC	Unknown	with the compliments	CU-MARK	09991 inscription
Krueger, Mr.	1883.07.22	SLC	NY.Elmira	I enclose it	NIC	01749

Laffan, William M.	o/a	1880.02.18	SLC	CT.Hartford	Who is this	CU-MARK	06202 on Barrett Feb 18
Laffan, William M. & Hutton, Laurence		1886.02.25	SLC & OLC	CT.Hartford	Lawrence Barrett is	MH-H NjP	03372 to Huttons & Laffans; NjP envelope
Laffan, William M.		1888.09.28	SLC	CT.Hartford	Burglars out of	CU-MARK	03776
Laffan, William M.		1902.11.28	SLC	NY.New York	Done by Truly	NN-B	09407 engraved inscription
Laird, James L.		1864.05.21	SLC	NV.Virginia City	I wrote you	431:1864.05.24	02773
Laird, James L.		1864.05.21	SLC	NV.Virginia City	In your paper	431:1864.05.24	00079
Laird, James L.		1864.05.21	SLC	NV.Virginia City	Your reply to	431:1864.05.24	02774
Lampton, William J.		1901.03.**	SLC	NY.New York	Will you allow	169:1901.03.23	06011
Lancaster, Charles		1897.07.07	SLC	EN.London	with best wishes	NSyU	09349 inscription
Lancaster, Charles		1907.06.19	SLC per RWA	EN.London	Mr. Clemens has	CU-MARK(tr)	07751 RWA tr
Lane, Emma		1888.03.06	SLC	CT.Hartford	with the kind	116:1958.04.17	09953 inscription
Lane, Joseph		1888.12.20	SLC	CT.Hartford	with the regards	NN-B	10813 inscription
Lang, Andrew	ca	1890.**.**	SLC	Unknown	They vote, but	CU-MARK	03823 fragment
Lang, Andrew		1891.05.04	SLC	CT.Hartford	It is a	CU-MARK(ph)	04203
Lang, Andrew		1907.08.21	SLC per IVL	NY.Tuxedo Park	See note at	CU-MARK(tr)	07817 IVL tr
Lang, Andrew		1908.04.25	SLC	NY.New York	I haven't seen	114:810	07984
Langdon, Andrew		1900.11.02	SLC	NY.New York	It is a	CU-MARK	05895
Langdon, Andrew		1901.01.21	SLC	NY.New York	We were sorry	ViU(tr)	05971
Langdon, Charles family & Langdon, Charles J.	pm	1910.01.07	SLC per ABP	CT.Redding	To all friends	CtHMTH	08521 form letter
Langdon, Charles J.		****.**.**	SLC	Unknown	Put the statement	102:11	09241
Langdon, Charles J.	ca	1868.08.24	SLC	Unknown	Train stops every	102:5	02746 telegram

ADDRESSEE	DATE	WRITER	PLACE	CUE	SOURCE	NUMBER/NOTES
Langdon, Charles J.	1870.11.14	SLC	NY.Buffalo	We are well	CU-MARK	00535
Langdon, Charles J.	1870.11.20	SLC	NY.Buffalo	We thank you	CtHMTH	00541
Langdon, Charles J.	1873.09.20	OLC	EN.London	I rec'd today	CU-MARK(ph)	00802
Langdon, Charles J.	ca 1874.11.27	SLC & OLC	CT.Hartford	Your exquisite gift	CtHMTH	01156
Langdon, Charles J.	1875.01.27	SLC	CT.Hartford	Congratulations from all	102:3	01186 telegram; other sources
Langdon, Charles J.	1875.03.19	SLC	CT.Hartford	Livy, after reading	114:251	01211 other sources
Langdon, Charles J.	1878.07.21	OLC	GE.Heidelberg	I was so	CtHMTH	01578
Langdon, Charles J.	1879.03.09	OLC	FR.Paris	We were exceedingly	CtHMTH	01638
Langdon, Charles J.	1879.06.**	OLC	Unknown	I rec'd today	CtHMTH	01618
Langdon, Charles J.	1879.06.17	SLC	FR.Paris	Why can't you	CtHMTH	01673
Langdon, Charles J.	1883.01.15	SLC	CT.Hartford	You are hereby	CtHMTH	02260 on printed notice
Langdon, Charles J.	1883.04.24	SLC & OLC	CT.Hartford	Your loving letter	CtHMTH	02375
Langdon, Charles J.	1885.05.17	SLC	CT.Hartford	Can I see	CU-MARK	10699 telegram
Langdon, Charles J.	1887.07.25	OLC per SLC	NY.Elmira	Your remittance to	CU-MARK	03614 on form letter
Langdon, Charles J.	o/a 1888.01.31	SLC	CT.Hartford	Return it to	CU-MARK	03699 on Peale Jan 31
Langdon, Charles J.	1892.08.07	SLC	GE.Bad-Nauheim	We had to	CtHMTH	01660
Langdon, Charles J.	1896.09.13	SLC	EN.London	This is Sunday	CtHMTH	05109
Langdon, Charles J.	1898.04.24	OLC	AU.Vienna	What a terrible	CtHMTH	05378
Langdon, Charles J.	1902.09.11	SLC	ME.York Harbor	Livy is very	CU-MARK	06431
Langdon, Charles J.	1902.12.26	SLC	NY.Riverdale	The check arrived	CtHMTH	06531
Langdon, Charles J.	1904.02.14	SLC	IT.Florence	Your letter to	CtHMTH	06794
Langdon, Charles J.	1904.05.27	SLC	IT.Florence	Livy thanks you	CtHMTH	06840
Langdon, Charles J.	1904.06.06	SLC	IT.Florence	She passed peacefully	CtHMTH	06860 telegram

Langdon, Charles J.		1904.06.08	SLC	IT.Florence	The ruined household	CtHMTH	06864 telegram
Langdon, Charles J.		1904.06.08	SLC	IT.Florence	Thirty years ago	CtHMTH	06865
Langdon, Charles J.		1904.06.13	SLC	IT.Florence	Poor Livy's last	CtHMTH	06869
Langdon, Charles J.		1904.06.19	SLC	IT.Florence	I am a	CtHMTH	06875
Langdon, Charles J.		1904.06.26	SLC	IT.Rome	Jean, Katy &	CtHMTH	06881
Langdon, Charles J.		1904.07.25	SLC	MA.Lee	As to that	CtHMTH	06901
Langdon, Charles J.		1904.10.13	SLC	NY.New York	Will you attend	CU-MARK	06929
Langdon, Charles J.		1906.04.04	SLC	NY.New York	Answer me this	CtHMTH	07412
Langdon, Charles J.	o/a	1906.05.23	SLC per IVL	NH.Dublin	The letters which	NN-B(dr)	10675 on Langdon May 23
Langdon, Charles J.		1908.02.11	SLC	NY.New York	There is good	CtHMTH	07934
Langdon, Charles J.		1908.12.12	SLC	CT.Redding	This is to	CtHMTH	08180
Langdon, Charles J.	ca	1909.01.18	IVL per MLH	CT.Redding	Miss L asks	CtHMTH(dr)	08331 for SLC
Langdon, Charles J. & Langdon, Charles family	pm	1910.01.07	SLC per ABP	CT.Redding	To all friends	CtHMTH	08521 form letter
Langdon, Eleanor S.		1902.09.27	SLC & OLC	ME.York Harbor	Now that you	CU-MARK	08663
Langdon, Ida		1885.12.28	SLC	CT.Hartford	I thank you	CU-MARK	03195 also to Jervis & Julia O. Langdon
Langdon, Ida		1893.05.11	SLC	NY.New York	I came through	CtHMTH	04401
Langdon, Ida		1901.03.31	SLC	NY.New York	It is very	CU-MARK	06031
Langdon, Ida		1901.09.26	JC	NY.New York	in remembrance of	CU-MARK	11093 inscription
Langdon, Ida		1901.12.24	SLC	NY.Riverdale	sh! Ida dear	CtHMTH	06195
Langdon, Ida		1902.08.28	SLC	ME.York Harbor	It is lovely	CtHMTH	06418
Langdon, Ida		1902.09.27	SLC	ME.York Harbor	Livy & I	CU-MARK	06446
Langdon, Ida		1910.03.17	CC	MC.Monte Carlo	I came across	CtHSD	10633
Langdon (J.) & Co.	pm	1878.10.09	SLC	IT.Venice	*	CtHMTH	10063 envelope only

ADDRESSEE	DATE	WRITER	PLACE	CUE	SOURCE	NUMBER/NOTES
Langdon (J.) & Co.	1879.06.05	SLC	FR.Paris	I drew 200	ViU	01663
Langdon, Jervis & Langdon, Mrs. Jervis	****.**.**	SLC	Unknown	tell Charley we	CtHMTH	08958 fragment
Langdon, Jervis	1868.12.02	SLC	NY.New York	I wish I	CtHMTH	02772
Langdon, Jervis	1868.12.29	SLC	OH.Cleveland	I wrote to	Mo4	00212
Langdon, Jervis & Langdon, Mrs. Jervis	1870.02.09	SLC & OLC	NY.Buffalo	Livy has gone	CtHMTH	00423
Langdon, Jervis & Langdon, Mrs. Jervis	1870.02.12	OLC	NY.Buffalo	Who shall I	CtHMTH	00425 also to Susan Crane
Langdon, Jervis	1870.02.26	SLC & OLC	NY.Buffalo	Your note came	CtHMTH	00433
Langdon, Jervis & Langdon, Mrs. Jervis	1870.03.02	OLC	NY.Buffalo	Dear Father or	CtHMTH	00436
Langdon, Jervis	1870.03.02 to 1870.03.03	SLC & OLC	NY.Buffalo	Got your dispatch	CtHMTH	00437
Langdon, Jervis & Langdon, Mrs. Jervis	1870.03.27	SLC & OLC	NY.Buffalo	It is snowing	CtHMTH	00450
Langdon, Jervis & Langdon, Mrs. Jervis	1870.04.01	SLC & OLC	NY.Buffalo	I can use	CU-MARK(tr)	00452
Langdon, Jervis & Langdon, Mrs. Jervis	1870.04.16 to 1870.04.17	SLC & OLC	NY.Buffalo	Day before yesterday	CtHMTH	00455
Langdon, Jervis	1870.05.13	SLC & OLC	NY.Buffalo	There is no	CtHMTH	00464
Langdon, Jervis	1870.05.22	SLC	NY.Buffalo	For several days	CtHMTH	00469
Langdon, Jervis & Langdon, Mrs. Jervis	1870.06.19	SLC	NY.Buffalo	We are all	CU-MARK	00480
Langdon, Jervis II	1883.12.19	SLC	CT.Hartford	I hope you	CtHMTH	02867
Langdon, Jervis II	1885.03.21	SLC	NY.New York	with the love	CtHMTH	09183 inscription
Langdon, Jervis II & Langdon, Julia O.	1885.12.28	SLC	CT.Hartford	I thank you	CU-MARK	03346 also to Ida Langdon
Langdon, Julia L.	*	*	*	*	*	11132 see Barber, Julia L.
Langdon, Julia O. & Langdon, Jervis II	1885.12.28	SLC	CT.Hartford	I thank you	CU-MARK	03346 also to Ida Langdon

Langdon, Julia O.	1889.11.10	SLC	CT.Hartford	Thank you ever	CU-MARK	03964
Langdon, Julia O.	1904.08.18	SLC	NY.Great Neck	Julia dear, I	CU-MARK	06913
Langdon, Julia O.	1908.01.16	SLC	NY.New York	Julie dear, it is	CU-MARK(tr)	07916
Langdon, Julia O.	1908.01.17	SLC	NY.New York	Julie dear, I wrote	CU-MARK(tr)	07918
Langdon, Julia O.	1910.01.20	CC	GE.Berlin	I hope that	CU-MARK	08542
Langdon, Julia O.	1910.01.23	CC	Unknown	Although I send	CU-MARK	08545
Langdon, Julia O.	1910.02.21	SLC	BE.Hamilton	Julie dear, bless	CU-MARK	08560
Langdon, Mrs. Jervis	****.**.**	OLC	CT.Hartford	My trip home	CtHMTH	08962
Langdon, Mrs. Jervis	****.**.**	SLC	CT.Hartford	Livy has been	102:8	03820
Langdon, Mrs. Jervis & Langdon, Jervis	****.**.**	SLC	Unknown	tell Charley we	CtHMTH	08958 fragment
Langdon, Mrs. Jervis	****.12.25	SLC & OLC	Unknown	Merry Christmas to	CtHMTH	10588
Langdon, Mrs. Jervis	1869.02.13	SLC	OH.Ravenna	It is not	CU-MARK	00249
Langdon, Mrs. Jervis	1869.06.23	SLC	NY.New York	It is 7.30	NPV	00319
Langdon, Mrs. Jervis	1870.02.06	OLC	NY.Buffalo	It is a	CtHMTH	00419
Langdon, Mrs. Jervis & Langdon, Jervis	1870.02.09	SLC & OLC	NY.Buffalo	Livy has gone	CtHMTH	00423
Langdon, Mrs. Jervis & Langdon, Jervis	1870.02.12	OLC	NY.Buffalo	Who shall I	CtHMTH	00425 also to Susan Crane
Langdon, Mrs. Jervis	1870.02.16	OLC	NY.Buffalo	I have had	CtHMTH	00427
Langdon, Mrs. Jervis	1870.02.20	OLC	NY.Buffalo	Mr Clemens and I	CtHMTH	00429
Langdon, Mrs. Jervis	1870.02.20	SLC & OLC	NY.Buffalo	I thank you	CtHMTH	00430
Langdon, Mrs. Jervis & Langdon, Jervis	1870.03.02	OLC	NY.Buffalo	Dear Father or	CtHMTH	00436
Langdon, Mrs. Jervis & Langdon, Jervis	1870.03.27	SLC & OLC	NY.Buffalo	It is snowing	CtHMTH	00450
Langdon, Mrs. Jervis & Langdon, Jervis	1870.04.01	SLC & OLC	NY.Buffalo	I can use	CU-MARK(tr)	00452
Langdon, Mrs. Jervis & Langdon, Jervis	1870.04.16 to 1870.04.17	SLC & OLC	NY.Buffalo	Day before yesterday	CtHMTH	00455

ADDRESSEE	DATE	WRITER	PLACE	CUE	SOURCE	NUMBER/NOTES
Langdon, Mrs. Jervis & Langdon, Jervis	1870.06.19	SLC	NY.Buffalo	We are all	CU-MARK	00480
Langdon, Mrs. Jervis	1870.11.07	SLC	NY.Buffalo	Langdon Clemens was	CtHMTH	00526 telegram
Langdon, Mrs. Jervis	1870.11.19	SLC	NY.Buffalo	Thank you ever	CtHMTH	00539
Langdon, Mrs. Jervis	1872.12.03	SLC	CT.Hartford	We have not	CtHMTH	00838
Langdon, Mrs. Jervis	1873.01.19	OLC	CT.Hartford	It is too	CtHMTH	00859
Langdon, Mrs. Jervis	ca 1873.03.**	SLC & OLC	CT.Hartford	Why don't we	CtHMTH	00879
Langdon, Mrs. Jervis	1873.05.17	SLC & OLC	SH.Batavia	Mrs. Fairbanks has	CtHMTH	00916
Langdon, Mrs. Jervis	1873.05.23 & 1873.05.26	OLC	SH.Batavia	Here it is	CtHMTH	00918 date uncertain
Langdon, Mrs. Jervis	1873.07.**	OLC	EN.London	I am just	CtHMTH	00938
Langdon, Mrs. Jervis	1873.07.05	OLC	EN.London	I feel just	CtHMTH	00761
Langdon, Mrs. Jervis	bet 1873.07.17 & 1873.07.25	SLC	EN.York	For the present	114:207	00955
Langdon, Mrs. Jervis	1873.08.02 & 1873.08.06	SLC & OLC	SK.Edinburgh	I have been	CtHMTH	00959
Langdon, Mrs. Jervis	1873.08.10 to 1873.08.15	OLC	SK.Edinburgh	I wrote the	CtHMTH	00790
Langdon, Mrs. Jervis	1873.08.31 & 1873.09.02	OLC	IR.Belfast	Here it is	CtHMTH	00801
Langdon, Mrs. Jervis	1873.09.21	OLC	EN.London	This note paper	CtHMTH	00804
Langdon, Mrs. Jervis	1873.09.25 & 1873.09.28	OLC	EN.London	I want to	CtHMTH	00964
Langdon, Mrs. Jervis	1873.10.12	SLC	EN.London	No indeedy, mother	CtHMTH	00973
Langdon, Mrs. Jervis	ca 1874.09.24	SLC & OLC	CT.Hartford	We are perfectly	153:520	01133 also to Cranes
Langdon, Mrs. Jervis	1874.11.**	SLC	CT.Hartford	Twichell came up	153:526	01143 to Langdon and/or Cranes
Langdon, Mrs. Jervis	1875.03.14	SLC & OLC	CT.Hartford	Clara's beautiful silver	CtHMTH	01207
Langdon, Mrs. Jervis	1875.03.21	OLC	CT.Hartford	I wish you	CtHMTH	01213
Langdon, Mrs. Jervis	1875.05.09	OLC	CT.Hartford	Mr Clemens is	CtHMTH	01231

Langdon, Mrs. Jervis		1875.12.22	SLC	CT.Hartford	I have been	CtHMTH	01288
Langdon, Mrs. Jervis	&	1877.02.02 1877.02.04	SLC & OLC	CT.Hartford	Your lovely it is the	CtHMTH CU-MARK	01405
Langdon, Mrs. Jervis		1877.05.06	OLC	CT.Hartford	Mr Clemens &	CtHMTH	01427
Langdon, Mrs. Jervis		1877.12.05	SLC	CT.Hartford	We are getting	CtHMTH	01509
Langdon, Mrs. Jervis		1877.12.25	SLC	CT.Hartford	Mother dear, the Satsuma	CU-MARK	01517
Langdon, Mrs. Jervis	&	1877.12.26 1877.12.30	OLC	CT.Hartford	Mother dear, or	CtHMTH	01518
Langdon, Mrs. Jervis		1878.04.20	SLC	SH.Holsatia	Mother dear, having	CtHMTH	01556 on printed menu
Langdon, Mrs. Jervis		1878.04.26	OLC	GE.Hamburg	Here we are	CtHMTH	01557
Langdon, Mrs. Jervis	&	1878.05.07 1878.05.12	OLC	GE.Heidelberg	We are now	CtHMTH	01559
Langdon, Mrs. Jervis		1878.05.12	SC per OLC	GE.Heidelberg	We have rided	CtHMTH	01561
Langdon, Mrs. Jervis		1878.05.26	OLC	GE.Heidelberg	How I wish	CtHMTH	01564
Langdon, Mrs. Jervis		1878.06.09	OLC	GE.Heidelberg	Clara has gone	CtHMTH	01569
Langdon, Mrs. Jervis	ca	1878.06.10	CC per OLC	GE.Heidelberg	I got a	CtHMTH	01565
Langdon, Mrs. Jervis	&	1878.08.04 1878.08.05	OLC	GE.Baden Baden	Mr. Twichell came	CtHMTH	01582
Langdon, Mrs. Jervis		1878.08.18	OLC	SW.Lucerne	It is a	CtHMTH	01584
Langdon, Mrs. Jervis	&	1878.09.01 1878.09.02	OLC & SC	SW.Ouchy	Here it is	CtHMTH	01593
Langdon, Mrs. Jervis		1878.09.13	SLC	SW.Geneva	Mother dear, Livy	CtHMTH	01595
Langdon, Mrs. Jervis		1878.09.15	OLC	FR.Chambery	Here we are	CtHMTH	01596
Langdon, Mrs. Jervis	to	1878.09.29 1878.09.30	CC	IT.Venice	Here we are	CtHMTH	10594 also by OLC & SC
Langdon, Mrs. Jervis	to	1878.09.29 1878.09.30	OLC & SC	IT.Venice	Here we are	CtHMTH	01598 also by CC
Langdon, Mrs. Jervis		1878.10.13	OLC	IT.Venice	It is evening	CtHMTH	01600
Langdon, Mrs. Jervis	&	1878.10.21 1878.10.27	OLC	IT.Florence	We are enjoying	CtHMTH	01602

ADDRESSEE	DATE	WRITER	PLACE	CUE	SOURCE	NUMBER/NOTES
Langdon, Mrs. Jervis	1878.11.10	OLC	IT.Rome	I am afraid	CtHMTH	01605
Langdon, Mrs. Jervis	1878.11.20 & 1878.11.25	OLC	GE.Munich	All last evening	CtHMTH	01607
Langdon, Mrs. Jervis	1878.12.02	SLC	GE.Munich	Mother dear, I thank	CtHMTH	01611
Langdon, Mrs. Jervis	1878.12.07	SC	GE.Munich	We have a	CtHMTH	02213 also by SLC & OLC
Langdon, Mrs. Jervis	1878.12.07	SLC & OLC	GE.Munich	We have a	CtHMTH	01612 also by SC
Langdon, Mrs. Jervis	1878.12.11	OLC	GE.Munich	The letter with	CtHMTH	01613
Langdon, Mrs. Jervis	1878.12.22	OLC	GE.Munich	Your letter for	CtHMTH	01616
Langdon, Mrs. Jervis	aft 1878.12.25	SLC	GE.Munich	Mother dear, I want	CtHMTH	01617
Langdon, Mrs. Jervis	1879.**.**	OLC	Unknown	picture that I	CtHMTH	01619 fragment
Langdon, Mrs. Jervis	1879.01.01 & 1879.01.05	OLC	GE.Munich	I am just	CtHMTH	01620
Langdon, Mrs. Jervis	1879.01.19	SLC & OLC	GE.Munich	It is evening things go on	CtHMTH CU-MARK	01621
Langdon, Mrs. Jervis	1879.02.02	OLC	GE.Munich	I do hope	CtHMTH	01627
Langdon, Mrs. Jervis	1879.02.16	OLC	GE.Munich	Friday morning as	CtHMTH	01634
Langdon, Mrs. Jervis	1879.02.23	SLC	GE.Munich	It has been	CtHMTH	01635
Langdon, Mrs. Jervis	ca 1879.03.**	SC	FR.Paris	Today I have	CtHMTH	01641
Langdon, Mrs. Jervis	1879.03.02	OLC	FR.Paris	You will see	CtHMTH	01636
Langdon, Mrs. Jervis	1879.03.16	OLC	FR.Paris	Clara is seated	CU-MARK(tr)	01640
Langdon, Mrs. Jervis	1879.03.30	SC	FR.Paris	Mother dear, it is	CtHMTH	01645 also from SLC & OLC
Langdon, Mrs. Jervis	1879.03.30	SLC & OLC	FR.Paris	Mother dear, it is	CtHMTH	01646 also from SC
Langdon, Mrs. Jervis	1879.04.13	OLC	FR.Paris	It is a	CtHMTH	01647
Langdon, Mrs. Jervis	1879.04.28	OLC	FR.Paris	I think you	CtHMTH	01651 Lilly Millet to OLC Mar 31 enc
Langdon, Mrs. Jervis	1879.05.13 & 1879.05.16	OLC	FR.Paris	Think of its	CtHMTH	01579

Langdon, Mrs. Jervis		1879.05.25	OLC	FR.Paris	It is a	CtHMTH CU-MARK(tr)	01657 CtHMTH envelope
Langdon, Mrs. Jervis		1879.06.**	OLC	FR.Paris	I so want	CtHMTH	01674
Langdon, Mrs. Jervis		1879.07.06	OLC	FR.Paris	If all goes	CtHMTH	01676
Langdon, Mrs. Jervis		1879.07.20	OLC	EN.London	Doesn't that address	CtHMTH	01677
Langdon, Mrs. Jervis		1879.08.03	OLC	EN.Oxford	We arrived here	CtHMTH	01679
Langdon, Mrs. Jervis		1879.08.17	OLC	EN.London	I feel as	CU-MARK(tr)	01680
Langdon, Mrs. Jervis	ca	1879.11.01	OLC	CT.Hartford	It is too	CtHMTH	01705
Langdon, Mrs. Jervis		1879.11.16	OLC	CT.Hartford	I am so	CtHMTH	01717
Langdon, Mrs. Jervis		1879.11.30	OLC	CT.Hartford	How could you	CtHMTH	01730
Langdon, Mrs. Jervis		1879.12.08	OLC	CT.Hartford	I did not	CtHMTH	02809
Langdon, Mrs. Jervis		1880.03.28	OLC	CT.Hartford	Mr. Clemens is	CtHMTH	01776
Langdon, Mrs. Jervis		1880.08.19	SLC & JC	NY.Elmira	I arrived pretty	CtHMTH	01826
Langdon, Mrs. Jervis		1880.12.25	SLC	CT.Hartford	Mother dear, your	CU-MARK	01881
Langdon, Mrs. Jervis		1881.01.09	SLC	CT.Hartford	Well--let's draw	CU-MARK	01889
Langdon, Mrs. Jervis		1883.08.19	SLC	NY.Elmira	Mother dear, it	CtHMTH	02824
Langdon, Mrs. Jervis		1886.10.19	SLC	CT.Hartford	Now, mother dear	CtHMTH	03471
Langdon, Mrs. Jervis		1886.10.21	SLC	CT.Hartford	Mother dear, we	CtHMTH	03474
Langdon, Mrs. Jervis		1887.**.**	OLC	CT.Hartford	A line shall	CtHMTH	03579
Langdon, Mrs. Jervis		1887.01.13	OLC	CT.Hartford	How could you	CtHMTH	03508
Langdon, Mrs. Jervis		1888.04.19	SLC	CT.Hartford	Mother dear, your letter	CtHMTH	03716
Langdon, Mrs. Jervis		1888.08.19	SLC & OLC	NY.Elmira	With love to	CtHMTH	03751
Langdon, Mrs. Jervis		1888.11.19	OLC	CT.Hartford	It has seemed	CtHMTH	03834
Langdon, Mrs. Jervis		1888.11.30	OLC	CT.Hartford	I thank you	CtHMTH	03840
Langdon, Mrs. Jervis		1888.12.01	SLC	CT.Hartford	Mother dear, thank	CU-MARK	03797
Langdon, Mrs. Jervis		1888.12.06	SLC	CT.Hartford	Yes, indeed, mother	CtHMTH	03802
Langdon, Mrs. Jervis	&	1888.12.14 1888.12.19	SLC & OLC	CT.Hartford	I have been	CtHMTH	03804

ADDRESSEE	DATE	WRITER	PLACE	CUE	SOURCE	NUMBER/NOTES
Langdon, Mrs. Jervis	1888.12.30	JC	CT.Hartford	I thank you	CtHMTH	03814
Langdon, Mrs. Jervis	1889.02.10	OLC	CT.Hartford	We are pining	CtHMTH	03861
Langdon, Mrs. Jervis	1889.03.24	OLC	CT.Hartford	It is a	CtHMTH	03876
Langdon, Mrs. Jervis	1889.04.17	SLC	CT.Hartford	Mother dear, Livy	CtHMTH	03885
Langdon, Mrs. Jervis	1889.10.07	SLC	CT.Hartford	Mother dear, Livy	CtHMTH	03947
Langdon, Mrs. Jervis	1889.11.09	SLC	CT.Hartford	Mother dear, I suppose	CtHMTH	03963
Langdon, Mrs. Jervis	1889.12.18	SLC	CT.Hartford	Mother dear, we had	CtHMTH	03988
Langdon, Mrs. Jervis	1889.12.22	SLC	CT.Hartford	Mother dear, Livy	CtHMTH	03992
Langdon, Mrs. Jervis	aft 1889.12.25	CC	CT.Hartford	I thank you	CtHMTH	03996
Langdon, Mrs. Jervis	1889.12.27	SLC & OLC	CT.Hartford	Mother dear, accept	CtHMTH	03994
Langdon, Mrs. Jervis	1890.02.02	OLC	CT.Hartford	Until I wrote	CtHMTH	04011
Langdon, Mrs. Jervis	1890.03.10	OLC	CT.Hartford	It was so	CtHMTH	04024
Langdon, Mrs. Jervis	1890.04.06	SC	CT.Hartford	I have written	CtHMTH	04037
Langdon, Mrs. Jervis	1890.04.20	OLC	CT.Hartford	How I wish	CtHMTH	04042
Langdon, Mrs. Jervis	1890.05.07	OLC	CT.Hartford	Here we are	CU-MARK(tr)	04046
Langdon, Mrs. Jervis	1890.06.14	CC	CT.Hartford	Please pardon my	CtHMTH	04052
Langdon, Mrs. Jervis	aft 1890.07.01	JC	NY.Tannersville	I am ever	CtHMTH	04059
Langdon, Mrs. Jervis	aft 1890.07.01	SC	NY.Tannersville	I am so	CtHMTH	04057
Langdon, Mrs. Jervis	1890.08.19	SLC & OLC	NY.Elmira	on this her	CtHMTH	04082 inscription
Langdon, Mrs. Jervis	1890.08.24	JC	NY.Tannersville	It is a	CtHMTH	04085
Langdon, Mrs. Jervis	1890.08.24	OLC	NY.Tannersville	I hope this	CtHMTH	04084
Langdon, Mrs. Jervis	1890.09.15	OLC	NY.Tannersville	The cold wave	CtHMTH	04096
Langdon, Mrs. Jervis	1890.10.20	SC	PA.Bryn Mawr	I am writing	CtHMTH	04104
Langdon, Mrs. Jervis	1890.10.26	OLC	CT.Hartford	The sun has	CtHMTH	04107
Langdon, Mrs. Jervis	1890.11.03	OLC	CT.Hartford	We have a	CtHMTH	04109
Langdon, Mrs. Jervis	1890.11.08	OLC	CT.Hartford	Thank you so	CtHMTH	04112
Langdon, Olivia Lewis	*	*	*	*	*	11138 see Langdon, Mrs. Jervis

Langdon, Olivia Louise		*	*	*	*	*	10311 see Clemens, Olivia L.
Langen, Albert		1907.09.01	SLC	NY.Tuxedo Park	In namen Gotter	NoOU	07828
Lanigan, Miss		1890.08.06	SLC	NY.Tannersville	Mrs. Clemens thanks	CtHMTH	04074
Lankford, Livius		1909.05.26	SLC	CT.Redding	A discharged secretary	NmR2	08921
Lanningham, Irene Van		1899.07.15	SLC	SE.Sanna	I add my	CU-MARK(ph)	08615 on Bliss to Lanningham June 14
Lant, John A.		1871.09.28	SLC	NY.Buffalo	Thank you kindly	MoSW	00655
Lark, Charles T.		1910.04.06	SLC	BE.Hamilton	I have told	114:843	08579
Larkin, John	o/a	1905.01.28	SLC per IVL	NY.New York	Mr. Clemens would	CU-MARK(dr)	06988 on Larkin Jan 28
Larkin, John		1905.05.31	SLC per IVL	NH.Dublin	Mr. Clemens directs	CU-MARK	07050
Larkin, John		1905.06.17	SLC per IVL	NH.Dublin	Mr. Clemens directs	CU-MARK	07065
Larkin, John		1905.11.15	SLC per IVL	NY.New York	Mr. Clemens directs	CU-MARK(tr)	07206
Larkin, John	o/a	1907.04.10	SLC per IVL	NY.New York	Thank them ever	CU-MARK(dr)	07688 on Larkin Apr 10
Larkin, John	ca	1909.01.18	SLC per MLH	CT.Redding	X sending this	CtHMTH(dr)	08320
Larned, Josephus N.		1873.03.22	SLC	CT.Hartford	I thank you	NBuHi	00889 form letter
Larned, Josephus N.		1900.11.01	SLC	NY.New York	Indeed I have	NN-B	08209
Lascelles, Frank C.		1907.12.14	SLC	Unknown	Best wishes for	CU-MARK(dr)	07890 telegram
Lascelles, Frank C.		1909.01.19	SLC per IVL	CT.Redding	Mr. Clemens asks	NN5	08336
Lathrop, George P.		1884.04.14	SLC	CT.Hartford	Nothing in the	MB	02952
Lathrop, George P.		1889.07.12	SLC	CT.Hartford	I will send	CU-MARK(ph)	11168
Lathrop, Rose H.		1901.10.19	SLC	NY.Riverdale	I wish I	297:170	06161

ADDRESSEE	DATE	WRITER	PLACE	CUE	SOURCE	NUMBER/NOTES
Lauder, George B.	o/a 1905.11.06	SLC per IVL	NY.New York	You fooled me	CU-MARK(dr)	07197
Lauderbach, Edward	1906.05.05	SLC	Unknown	It is not	CU-MARK(ph)	09344 inscription
Laura	****.**.**	SLC	Unknown	with the love	205:1934.06.20	09816 inscription
Laura	****.**.**	SLC	Unknown	Laura dear, it	TxU	09240
Lawrence, Frank R.	o/a 1905.12.19	SLC per IVL	NY.New York	Certainly use my	CU-MARK(dr)	07263 on Lawrence Dec 19
Lawrence, Herbert M.	1881.05.09	SLC	CT.Hartford	What is earliest	CtHMTH	01951 telegram
Lawrence, Herbert M.	bet 1881.08.31 & 1881.09.04	SLC per CLW	NY.New York	What is earliest	NPV(dr)	09236 telegram
Lawrence, Mrs.	1901.03.23	SLC	NY.New York	with the best	406:1979.05.17	09969 inscription
Lawton, Mary	****.**.**	SLC	Unknown	I am very	212:1945.05.12	09928
Lawton, Miss	ca 1902.05.18	SLC	NY.Riverdale	The matter of	165:1954.04.23	09761
Le Row, Caroline B.	o/a 1887.04.13	SLC	CT.Hartford	Please return this	CU-MARK	03560 on Cornish Apr 13
Le Row, Caroline B.	1888.11.04	SLC	CT.Hartford	It makes me	NN5	03827
Leary, Daniel D.	1867.08.26	SLC	RU.Yalta	Whereas we the	CU-MARK(tr)	09123 group letter
Leary, Katie	1898.03.02	SLC	AU.Vienna	keep in mind	WRI2	10953 inscription
Leary, Katie	1904.04.**	SLC	IT.Florence	Truly Yours	110:1971.12.09	10372 inscription
Leary, Katie	1904.11.27	SLC	NY.New York	who has been	CU-MARK(tr)	10645 inscription
Leary, Katie	1906.09.26	SLC	Unknown	It is your	WRI2	10954 inscription
Leary, Katie	1906.12.25	SLC	NY.New York	with the affectionate	122:1934.02.15	09248 inscription
Leary, Katie	1907.01.**	SLC	NY.New York	Let us save	CU-MARK(tr)	10887 inscription
Leary, Katie	1910.02.20	SLC	BE.Hamilton	I enclose page	CU-MARK(tr)	08559

Leary, Warren		1900.12.25	SLC	NY.New York	with the kindest	WRI3	10642 inscription
Leathers, Jesse M.		1875.10.05	SLC	CT.Hartford	I have heard	CU-MARK(tr)	01267
Lee, Ambrose	o/a	1905.10.18	SLC per IVL	NH.Dublin	Mr. Clemens thanks	CU-MARK(dr)	07180 on Lee Oct 18
Lee, Henry		1872.10.04	SLC &	EN.London	One o'clock to-morrow	CU-MARK(ph)	00818
Lee, Henry		1872.10.19	SLC	EN.London	From his friend	NN-B	10800 inscription
Lee, Henry		1872.10.25	SLC	EN.London	Can't. I am	ViU	00824
Lee, Henry		1872.11.05	SLC	EN.London	Cable telegram from	CU-MARK(ph)	11069
Lee, Henry		1873.**.**	SLC	EN.London	All right, my	120:1938.10	09891
Lee, Henry	pm	1873.06.02	SLC	EN.London	Long life to	ViU	00922
Lee, Henry	to	1873.06.13 1873.06.14	SLC	EN.London	It was just	CtHSD	00924
Lee, Henry		1873.07.05	SLC	EN.London	must leave again	105:1954.11.24	00944
Lee, Henry	pm	1873.07.14	SLC	EN.London	*	CU-MARK(tr)	10291 envelope only
Lee, Henry		1873.09.10	SLC	EN.London	We called yesterday	ViU	00961
Lee, Henry	pm	1873.09.26	SLC	EN.London	No--don't write	CCamarSJ	00965
Lee, Henry		1873.10.07	SLC	EN.London	I begin Monday	CU-MARK	00968
Lee, Henry		1873.10.08	SLC	EN.London	Am writing to P.S. I have	MoSW ViU	00970
Lee, Henry		1873.11.22	SLC per CWS	EN.London	I am afraid	ViU	00986
Lee, Henry		1873.12.09	SLC	EN.London	I like Hingston	CU-MARK(ph)	00996
Lee, Henry		1874.01.**	SLC	EN.London	with the warmest	105:1968.04.02	09693 inscription
Lee, Mr.		1899.09.18	SLC	SE.Sanna	I have written	CU-MARK	05680
Lee, Mr.		1900.12.**	SLC	NY.New York	No, it's lovely	308:163	05924
Lee, Sidney		1907.06.18	SLC per RWA	EN.London	Mr. Clemens is	CU-MARK(tr)	07745 RWA tr
Leggett, Mortimer D.		1871.10.06	SLC	CT.Hartford	In response to	DNA	00656
Leigh, Major		1909.04.10	SLC per IVL	CT.Redding	This is what	CU-MARK(ph)	08381

ADDRESSEE	DATE	WRITER	PLACE	CUE	SOURCE	NUMBER/NOTES
Leigh, Sarah	1909.01.31	SLC	CT.Redding	with the kindest	105:1956.12.11	09472 inscription
Leighton, Stella B.	o/a 1907.03.02	SLC per IVL	NY.New York	The Clemens to	CU-MARK(dr)	07668 on Leighton Mar 2
Lentz, W.H.	bef 1881.10.08	SLC	Unknown	Therefore observe you	124:123	09393
Lentz, W.H.	1881.11.22	SLC	CT.Hartford	I have received	123:1897.83	02096
Leslie, Elsie L.	****.**.**	SLC	Unknown	This book is	105:1957.05.21	09504 inscription
Leslie, Elsie L.	1889.01.03	SLC	Unknown	with the kindest	105:1957.05.21	09498 inscription; other sources
Leslie, Elsie L.	1889.01.03	SLC	Unknown	This is the	CU-MARK(ph)	03845 inscription
Leslie, Elsie L.	1889.10.05	SLC	CT.Hartford	The way of	NNPM	03946
Leslie, Elsie L.	1890.02.02	SLC	NY.New York	from her friend	105:1957.05.21	09505 inscription
Leslie, Elsie L.	1890.05.15	OLC	CT.Hartford	I wonder if	NNPM	10702
Leslie, Elsie L.	1893.12.25	SLC	NY.New York	Hel-lo!--is it	NNPM	04538
Leslie, Elsie L.	pm 1904.07.21	SLC	MA.Lee	For what you	TxU	06899 form letter
Levetus, Amelia S.	1898.03.15	SLC	AU.Vienna	I am sorry	110:1966.11.03	05364
Levetus, Amelia S.	1898.05.**	SLC	Unknown	with compliments of	110:1966.11.03	10360 inscription
Levy, Edwina L.	1906.03.10	SLC	NY.New York	O, dear me	ViU	07377
Levy, Helen F.	1900.07.27	SLC	EN.London	The signature in	NNPM	08685
Lewenhaupt, Claes	1887.10.21	SLC	CT.Hartford	Mrs. Clemens &	Sw2	03660
Lewis, Charles E.	1886.12.04	SLC per FGW	CT.Hartford	Your favor of	CU-MARK(tr)	10751
Lewis, Dudley P.	o/a 1905.08.14	SLC per IVL	Unknown	Hope that at	CU-MARK(dr)	07108 on Lewis Aug 14
Lewis, Harriet	1869.01.10	SLC	IL.Galesburg	No, that is	CtY	00226
Lewis, Harriet	1873.12.25	SLC	Unknown	A Merry Christmas	116:1979.12.20	09940 inscription; other sources

Lewis, Harriet	1877.12.25	SLC	Unknown	Merry Christmas, 1877	441:1927.07.19	10339 inscription
Lewis, John T.	1877.08.24	SLC	NY.Elmira	from Mark Twain	CtHMTH	09282 inscription
Libby, Norman	o/a 1909.03.10	SLC per IVL	CT.Redding	never departed from	CU-MARK(dr)	08369 on Libby Mar 10
Lindau, Rudolf	****.**.**	SLC	Unknown	Yes, time is	ViU	08961
Lindau, Rudolf	1891.**.**	SLC	GE.Berlin	I am delighted	ViU	08960
Lindau, Rudolf	1891.12.11	SLC	GE.Berlin	The dinner was	ViU	04259
Lindau, Rudolf	1891.12.24	SLC	GE.Berlin	I sieze the	ViU	04264
Lindau, Rudolf	1898.03.30	SLC	AU.Vienna	At last the	ViU	05372
Lindau, Rudolf	1898.12.14	SLC	AU.Kaltenleut.	Our scheme is	ViU	05480
Lindau, Rudolf	1901.04.24	SLC	NY.New York	This family were	ViU	06042 typed
Littleton, Mrs.	aft 1908.10.08	SLC per IVL	CT.Redding	You dear Mrs.	CU-MARK(tr)	08129
Littleton, Mrs.	1908.12.06	SLC	CT.Redding	Thank you for	CU-MARK(tr)	08171
Littlewood, Kate S.	1898.08.05	SLC	AU.Kaltenleut.	Oh yes indeed	CLjC	08818
Liverpool Lord Mayor	1907.05.06	SLC	NY.New York	I thank your	CU-MARK	07713 telegram
Llangattoch, Georgiana	1907.07.08	SLC	EN.London	with the homage	168:329	10734 inscription
Lloyd's Weekly ed. & Harper's Weekly ed.	1902.11.15	SLC	NY.Riverdale	I am approaching	CU-MARK	06489
Locke, Franklin D.	1870.08.24	SLC	NY.Buffalo	By authority of	CU-MARK(ph)	00432 date uncertain
Locker, Arthur	1872.09.17	SLC	EN.London	I believe the	NElmC	00808
Lockwood, Ingersoll	1887.02.21	SLC	CT.Hartford	Upon reflection, I	CSmH	03532 unsent
Lockwood, Thomas D.	1882.12.30	SLC	CT.Hartford	None but pirated	CU-MARK(ph)	02316 typed
Logan, James	1907.02.02	SLC	NY.New York	I owe you	CU-MARK	07639
London Daily Telegraph	1872.11.08	SLC	EN.London	With your kind	ViU	00830
London Evening Post ed.	1873.06.25	SLC	EN.London	In your issue	C4	00934

ADDRESSEE	DATE	WRITER	PLACE	CUE	SOURCE	NUMBER/NOTES
London Lord Mayor	1897.02.02	SLC	EN.London	Mr. S.L. Clemens	MH-H	05175
London Lord Mayor	1907.07.12	SLC per RWA	EN.London	I shall to-morrow	CU-MARK(tr)	07785
London Morning Post ed.	1873.12.10	SLC	EN.London	Now that my	288:1873.12.11	00997
London Postmaster	1897.07.16	SLC	EN.London	Please send mail	CtHMTH	05263
London Standard ed.	1873.10.07	SLC	EN.London	In view of	289:1873.10.09	00969
London Times	1872.11.05	SLC	EN.London	With your kind	457:1872.11.07	11068
London Times ed.	bet 1900.07.02 & 1900.09.30	SLC	EN.London	It has often	CU-MARK	08734
Longfellow, Henry W.	1877.06.04	SLC	CT.Hartford	I beg your	Mo2	01438
Longfellow, Henry W. & Emerson, Ralph W.	1877.12.27	SLC	CT.Hartford	I come before	MH-H	01519 also to Oliver W. Holmes
Longfellow, Julia D.	o/a 1906.01.20	SLC per IVL	NY.New York	Look upon it	CU-MARK(dr)	07314 on Longfellow Jan 20
Loomis, Edward E.	1904.07.15	SLC	NY.New York	If I may	CU-MARK	06885
Loomis, Edward E.	1910.01.07	SLC	BE.Hamilton	I have just	CU-MARK	08535
Loomis, Julia L.	*	*	*	*	*	11133 see Langdon, Julia O.
Lorberg, H.A.	o/a 1905.12.16	SLC per IVL	NY.New York	Have no photos	CU-MARK(dr)	07260 on Lorberg Dec 16
Lorch, Paula	bet 1905.12.29 & 1905.12.31	SLC per IVL	NY.New York	I am happy	NN-B(tr)	07281
Lord, Chester S.	1900.**.**	SLC	NY.New York	I hold his	308:202	08963
Lord, Chester S.	1900.03.09	SLC	EN.London	I accept that	CLjC	05772
Lord, Chester S.	1901.12.31	SLC	NY.Riverdale	I wish I	CU-MARK(ph)	06201
Lord, Chester S.	1902.06.10	SLC	NY.Riverdale	I shall be	ODa2	06358
Lorne, marquis of	1883.05.19	SLC	CT.Hartford	I make a	CU-MARK(dr)	02389 on Dawson May 19
Lorne, marquis of	1883.05.19	SLC	Unknown	I make limitless	CU-MARK(dr)	04069 on Lorne May 19

Lotos Club	o/a	1907.12.24	SLC per IVL	NY.New York	I was not	CU-MARK(dr)	07894 on Lotos Club Dec 24
Louisville Courier-J.		1874.10.09	SLC	CT.Hartford	Mr. Owen S.	290:1874.10.16	01136
Lounsbury, Mr.		1909.03.06	SLC	CT.Redding	Mr. Clemens, who	CU-MARK(tr)	08365
Lounsbury, Thomas R.		1900.11.20	SLC	NY.New York	I wish I	CtY	05915
Lounsbury, Thomas R.		1902.04.10	SLC	NY.Riverdale	Yes--it is	CtY	06320
Lounsbury, Thomas R.		1904.07.21	SLC	MA.Lee	I know you	CtY	06896
Low, Anne W. & Low, Seth		1904.07.25	SLC	MA.Lee	We are hurt	NNC	06902
Low, Frederick F. & Blasdel, Henry G.		1866.12.06	SLC	CA.San Francisco	I cannot too	417:1866.12.08	00115 also to French & Hoffman
Low, Seth & Low, Anne W.		1904.07.25	SLC	MA.Lee	We are hurt	NNC	06902
Low, Seth	o/a	1905.12.06	SLC	NY.New York	To you, &	NNC	07233 form letter
Lubbock, John		1907.06.19	SLC per RWA	EN.London	Mr. Clemens was	CU-MARK(tr)	07747 RWA tr
Lucas, Annie E.		1881.01.31	SLC	CT.Hartford	Will I be	297:36	01899
Lucas, E. Duncan	pm	1899.11.11	SLC	EN.London	I've forgotten, now	NNC	05704
Lucas, Edward V.		1908.07.20	SLC	CT.Redding	My permission to	CU-MARK(tr)	08056
Lucy, Henry W.		1902.**.**	SLC	Unknown	The enclosed is	151:1902.11.15	06214
Lucy, Henry W.		1903.10.04	SLC	NY.Elmira	Your letter went	291:222	06735
Lukens, H. Clay		1880.11.09	SLC	CT.Hartford	I should like	444:23	01852
Lukens, H. Clay		1880.12.06	SLC	CT.Hartford	I should be	320:54	01865
Lumley, Arthur		1900.10.16	SLC	NY.New York	Gen. Bunker means	NN-B	08207
Lummis, Edward W.		1886.05.17	SLC	CT.Hartford	If I too	CU-MARK(ph)	10561
Lutz, Robert		1899.02.27	SLC	AU.Vienna	I want to	MB	05551
Lutz, Robert		1899.04.03	SLC	AU.Vienna	I am sending	MB	05574
Lutz, Robert		1899.07.14	SLC	SE.Sanna	This is the	MB	05655
Lutz, Robert		1907.05.27	SLC per IVL	NY.Tuxedo Park	At the end	CU-MARK(dr)	07719 on Lutz May 13

ADDRESSEE	DATE	WRITER	PLACE	CUE	SOURCE	NUMBER/NOTES
Lutzow, Countess	1899.03.02	SLC	AU.Vienna	With salutations &	C7	11087 inscription
Lynch, Jerome	o/a 1908.02.13	SLC per IVL	NY.New York	Mr. Clemens is	CU-MARK(dr)	07937 on Lynch Feb 13
Lyon, Isabel V.	****.**.**	SLC	Unknown	Why aren't Italian	PP	04218
Lyon, Isabel V.	1903.06.04	JC	NY.Riverdale	with much love	CU-MARK(tr)	10755 inscription
Lyon, Isabel V.	aft 1904.03.01	OLC	IT.Florence	Yes, I remember	CU-MARK	06803
Lyon, Isabel V.	aft 1904.07.20	SLC	MA.Lee	Send $15	CU-MARK(dr)	06893 on Romeike July 20
Lyon, Isabel V.	1904.08.17	SLC	NY.New York	Please make entry	ViU	06912
Lyon, Isabel V.	1904.10.07	SLC per RWA	NY.New York	Please fill up	NPV	10888
Lyon, Isabel V.	1904.10.12	SLC	NY.New York	Henceworth address all	CU-MARK	06926
Lyon, Isabel V.	o/a 1904.10.13	SLC	NY.New York	Miss Lyon, please tell	CU-MARK	06927 on Miller Oct 13
Lyon, Isabel V.	o/a 1904.10.13	SLC	NY.New York	Miss Lyon, please	CU-MARK	06928 on Ward to Gilder Oct 13
Lyon, Isabel V.	1904.10.18	SLC	NY.New York	*	CU-MARK	09495 envelope only
Lyon, Isabel V. & Clemens, Jean	pm 1904.10.18	SLC	NY.New York	All right, Jean	NRU	06931 on envelope
Lyon, Isabel V.	o/a 1904.10.18	SLC	NY.New York	Here is Madame	CU-MARK	06932 on Freese Oct 18
Lyon, Isabel V.	o/a 1904.12.15	SLC	NY.New York	No, add $15	CU-MARK	06959 on Brownell to IVL Dec 15
Lyon, Isabel V.	1905.**.**	SLC	Unknown	Checks received &	CU-MARK	06973
Lyon, Isabel V.	1905.04.12	JC	NY.New York	with the kindest	ODa2	10754 inscription
Lyon, Isabel V.	o/a 1905.04.27	SLC	NY.New York	Ask Mr H	CU-MARK	07029 on Hale to Howells Apr 8
Lyon, Isabel V.	pm 1905.05.12	SLC	NY.New York	*	CU-MARK(tr)	10760 envelope only

Lyon, Isabel V.		1905.08.15	SLC	CT.Norfolk	Next week or	NN-B	08242
Lyon, Isabel V.		1905.08.16	SLC	CT.Norfolk	I go to	CU-MARK	07115
Lyon, Isabel V.	&	1905.08.20 1905.08.21	SLC	CT.Norfolk	You will have	CU-MARK	07112 on Larkin Aug 17
Lyon, Isabel V.	o/a	1905.08.23	SLC	NH.Dublin	Please send him	CU-MARK(ph)	07116 on Knickerbocker Aug 23
Lyon, Isabel V.	ca	1905.08.31	SLC	NH.Dublin	Miss Lyon, you	CU-MARK	07111 on Ashcroft Aug 18
Lyon, Isabel V.	o/a	1905.10.06	SLC	NH.Dublin	Stir Mr. Chamberlaine	CU-MARK(dr)	07162 on Goyder Oct 6
Lyon, Isabel V.	o/a	1905.10.14	SLC	NH.Dublin	Send $25	CU-MARK	07176 on Jerome Oct 14
Lyon, Isabel V.		1905.10.25	SLC	MA.Boston	Please write him	CU-MARK	07186 on Hittchison Oct 25
Lyon, Isabel V.		1905.10.25	SLC	MA.Boston	Yes, deposit $200	ViU	07187
Lyon, Isabel V.	o/a	1905.11.11	SLC	NY.New York	Send $5	CU-MARK	07204 on Parker Nov 11
Lyon, Isabel V.	o/a	1905.12.08	SLC	NY.New York	We will sign	CU-MARK(dr)	07244
Lyon, Isabel V.	o/a	1905.12.11	SLC	NY.New York	Answer c/o	CU-MARK	07200 on Rosenthal Dec 11
Lyon, Isabel V.	o/a	1905.12.14	SLC	NY.New York	Decline it	CU-MARK(dr)	07254 on Weston Dec 14
Lyon, Isabel V.	bef	1906.01.01	SLC	NY.New York	Decline it	CU-MARK	07297 on Lord ca Jan 1
Lyon, Isabel V.		1906.01.13	SLC	NY.New York	Ask Larkin to	InU-Li	10823
Lyon, Isabel V.	o/a	1906.01.23	SLC	NY.New York	Decline	CU-MARK	07315 on Rule Jan 23
Lyon, Isabel V.	o/a	1906.02.17	SLC	NY.New York	We ought to	CU-MARK	07348 on Roosevelt Feb 17

ADDRESSEE	DATE	WRITER	PLACE	CUE	SOURCE	NUMBER/NOTES
Lyon, Isabel V.	o/a 1906.03.12	SLC	NY.New York	Telegraph "yes"	CU-MARK	07379 on Henschel Mar 12
Lyon, Isabel V.	1906.03.14	SLC	NY.New York	If I am	InU-Li	10822
Lyon, Isabel V.	1906.05.04	SLC	NY.New York	Send it Monday	CU-MARK	10966
Lyon, Isabel V.	pm 1906.05.23	JC	NY.New York	*	CU-MARK	10151 envelope only
Lyon, Isabel V.	1906.07.**	SLC	NY.New York	I did not	NSyU	11110 on July to Teller
Lyon, Isabel V.	1906.07.10	SLC	NY.New York	I enclose copy	CU-MARK	07478
Lyon, Isabel V.	1906.07.10	SLC	NY.New York	About ten last	NN5	07476
Lyon, Isabel V.	1906.07.16	SLC	NY.New York	I have just	NPV	10889
Lyon, Isabel V.	o/a 1906.08.24	SLC	NH.Dublin	Tell him apparently	CU-MARK	07503 on Doubleday Aug 24
Lyon, Isabel V.	o/a 1906.09.07	SLC	NH.Dublin	Tell him I	NNC	08813
Lyon, Isabel V.	o/a 1906.09.11	SLC	NH.Dublin	Preserve this	CU-MARK	10960 on Harvey Sept 11
Lyon, Isabel V.	o/a 1906.09.14	SLC	NH.Dublin	Miss Lyon, tell	CtY	07523 on Twichell Sept 14
Lyon, Isabel V.	1906.09.20	SLC	NY.New York	Clara & I	InU-Li CU-MARK(tr)	07527 CU-MARK(tr) envelope
Lyon, Isabel V.	o/a 1906.09.20	SLC	NH.Dublin	Thank him for	CU-MARK	07526 on Bigelow Sept 20
Lyon, Isabel V.	o/a 1906.10.27	SLC	NY.New York	Tell her I	CU-MARK	10961
Lyon, Isabel V.	o/a 1907.01.01	SLC	Unknown	Can't do it	CU-MARK	07619 on Keen Jan 1
Lyon, Isabel V.	1907.02.**	SLC	NY.New York	with affectionate best	NN-B	09273 inscription
Lyon, Isabel V.	o/a 1907.04.05	SLC	NY.New York	Thank him for	CU-MARK	07686 on Beard Apr 5
Lyon, Isabel V.	1907.04.29	SLC	VA.Fort Monroe	Delayed indefinitely by	CU-MARK	07698 telegram

Lyon, Isabel V.	o/a 1907.05.05	SLC	NY.New York	Return it, with	CU-MARK	07715 on Callaghan May 5
Lyon, Isabel V.	o/a 1907.09.30	SLC	NY.Tuxedo Park	Please never correct	InU-Li	10819 on RWA to IVL Sept 30
Lyon, Isabel V.	1908.**.**	CC	NY.New York	Many times I	CU-MARK	07902
Lyon, Isabel V.	1908.**.**	SLC	Unknown	S.L. Clemens	116:1970.06.11	09980 inscription
Lyon, Isabel V.	1908.02.26	JC	CT.Greenwich	It's raining cats	CU-MARK	07949
Lyon, Isabel V.	1908.02.27	CC	NY.Auburn	I hope that	CU-MARK	07950
Lyon, Isabel V.	1908.06.24	CC	NY.New York	What a shame	CU-MARK	08040
Lyon, Isabel V.	1908.08.01	JC	MA.Gloucester	I have had	CU-MARK	08070
Lyon, Isabel V.	1908.08.04	JC	MA.Gloucester	I looked for	CU-MARK	08074
Lyon, Isabel V.	1908.08.05	JC	MA.Gloucester	Dr. Peterson yesterday	CU-MARK	08075
Lyon, Isabel V.	1908.09.18	JC	MA.Gloucester	Couldn't get room	CU-MARK	08107 telegram
Lyon, Isabel V.	1908.09.22	JC	NY.New York	Saturday the grain	CU-MARK	08110
Lyon, Isabel V.	1908.10.08	JC	SH.Postdampfers	In my bank-book	CU-MARK	08130
Lyon, Isabel V.	1908.10.10	JC	GE.Hamburg	*	CU-MARK	10163 envelope only
Lyon, Isabel V.	1908.10.19	JC	GE.Berlin	This is just	CU-MARK	08138
Lyon, Isabel V.	1908.10.20	JC	GE.Berlin	I haste &	CU-MARK	08140
Lyon, Isabel V.	1908.10.27	JC	GE.Berlin	Yesterday, just after	CU-MARK	08147
Lyon, Isabel V.	1908.12.11	JC	GE.Berlin	I am sending	CU-MARK	08178
Lyon, Isabel V.	1909.05.29	SLC	CT.Redding	I desire to	CU-MARK(tr)	08407
MacAlister, John Y.	1897.03.02	SLC	EN.London	I thank you	ViU	05181
MacAlister, John Y.	1897.03.30	OLC	EN.London	Thank you most	ViU	05195
MacAlister, John Y.	1897.04.06	OLC	EN.London	How can I	ViU	05198
MacAlister, John Y.	1897.04.06	SLC	EN.London	Ah, but I	ViU	05197
MacAlister, John Y.	1897.04.14	SLC	EN.London	I finished my	NN-B	05507
MacAlister, John Y.	1897.05.08	SLC	EN.London	Yes, I will	ViU	05211

ADDRESSEE	DATE	WRITER	PLACE	CUE	SOURCE	NUMBER/NOTES
MacAlister, John Y.	1897.05.26	SLC	EN.London	*	ViU	10103 envelope only
MacAlister, John Y.	1897.06.02	SLC	EN.London	Good--I'm ready	ViU	05221
MacAlister, John Y.	1897.06.13 to 1897.06.14	SLC	EN.London	I am afraid	ViU	05227
MacAlister, John Y.	1897.07.08	SLC per OLC	EN.London	I write for	ViU	05256
MacAlister, John Y.	1897.07.17	SLC	EN.London	Mrs. C. & I	ViU	05264
MacAlister, John Y.	1897.07.20	SLC	SW.Weggis	Yes indeed, I	ViU	05265
MacAlister, John Y.	1897.09.07	SLC	SW.Weggis	I do not	ViU	05285
MacAlister, John Y.	1898.03.12	SLC	AU.Vienna	The correspondent of	ViU	05362
MacAlister, John Y.	1898.09.14	SLC	AU.Kaltenleut.	I mustn't venture	CU-MARK	05433
MacAlister, John Y.	1899.05.22	SLC	AU.Vienna	I thank you	CU-MARK	05593
MacAlister, John Y.	1899.06.02	SLC	EN.London	Yes, I'm for	CU-MARK(ph)	05630
MacAlister, John Y.	1899.06.03	SLC	EN.London	Good--make the	CU-MARK	05631
MacAlister, John Y.	1899.10.04	SLC	EN.London	Nein, mein Herr	ViU	05686
MacAlister, John Y.	1899.11.17	OLC	EN.London	Thank you heartily	ViU	05708
MacAlister, John Y.	1899.11.24	SLC	EN.London	Assist me. In	ViU	05714
MacAlister, John Y.	1899.12.01	SLC	EN.London	Thank you ever	ViU	05715
MacAlister, John Y. & MacAlister, Mrs. John	ca 1899.12.25	OLC	EN.London	Wishing them a	ViU	05725
MacAlister, John Y.	1900.03.07	SLC	EN.London	I had it	ViU	05770
MacAlister, John Y.	1900.03.08	SLC	EN.London	I enclose the	ViU	05771
MacAlister, John Y.	1900.03.09	SLC	EN.London	Do not be	ViU	05773
MacAlister, John Y.	1900.03.10	SLC	EN.London	I will ask	ViU	05774
MacAlister, John Y.	1900.03.17	SLC	EN.London	The Harpers are	ViU	05777
MacAlister, John Y.	1900.03.23	SLC	EN.London	I notice only	PP3	05780
MacAlister, John Y.	pm 1900.03.23	SLC	EN.London	I do not	ViU	05781
MacAlister, John Y.	1900.03.24	SLC	EN.London	Can't I have	ViU	09426
MacAlister, John Y.	1900.04.02	SLC	EN.London	I have received	ViU	10766
MacAlister, John Y.	1900.06.10	OLC	EN.London	more about the	ViU	10768 fragment

MacAlister, John Y.	1900.06.11	SLC	EN.London	Thanks to you	ViU	05819
MacAlister, John Y.	1900.06.20	OLC	Unknown	Thank you &	ViU	10767
MacAlister, John Y.	1900.06.29	SLC	EN.London	I quite agree	ViU	05827 on MacAlister June 28
MacAlister, John Y.	1900.07.01	SLC	EN.London	I can't go	ViU	05829
MacAlister, John Y.	1900.07.05	SLC	EN.London	Oh, it's too	ViU	05831
MacAlister, John Y.	1900.08.01	SLC	EN.London	Within a day	ViU	05846
MacAlister, John Y.	1900.08.17	SLC	EN.London	I don't know	ViU	05852
MacAlister, John Y.	1900.08.18	SLC	EN.London	This is our	ViU	05854
MacAlister, John Y.	1900.09.19	SLC	EN.London	I should like	ViU	05865
MacAlister, John Y.	1900.09.24	SLC	EN.London	It is too	ViU	05867
MacAlister, John Y.	1900.09.26	SLC	EN.London	Please represent me	ViU	05870
MacAlister, John Y.	1900.09.27	SLC	EN.London	It is too	ViU	05871
MacAlister, John Y.	1900.09.28	SLC	EN.London	Please look at	CU-MARK(ph)	05873
MacAlister, John Y.	bef 1900.10.01	SLC	EN.London	I meant to	ODa2	05874
MacAlister, John Y.	1900.10.06	OLC	SH.Minnehaha	I expected to	ViU	10769
MacAlister, John Y.	1900.10.16	SLC	SH.Minnehaha	We have had	ViU	05877
MacAlister, John Y.	1900.10.27	SLC	NY.New York	I wrote you	ViU	05887
MacAlister, John Y.	1900.10.31	SLC	NY.New York	This following is	ViU	05891
MacAlister, John Y.	1900.12.05	SLC	NY.New York	The General postoffice	ViU	05927
MacAlister, John Y.	1900.12.31	SLC	NY.New York	Yours of ten	ViU	05943
MacAlister, John Y.	1901.03.24	SLC	NY.New York	I am giving	ViU	06024
MacAlister, John Y.	1901.04.24	SLC	NY.New York	I do immensely	ViU	06043 typed
MacAlister, John Y.	1901.08.27	SLC	NY.Saranac Lake	Drop that mental	ViU	06121
MacAlister, John Y.	1901.10.**	SLC	NY.Riverdale	with the very	107:1928.01.04	09556 inscription
MacAlister, John Y.	1902.03.17	SLC	FL.Palm Beach	In your letter	ViU	06304
MacAlister, John Y.	1902.09.06	SLC	ME.York Harbor	None of which	ViU	06427
MacAlister, John Y.	1902.09.23	SLC	ME.York Harbor	Pigeon-hole the	ViU	06439

ADDRESSEE	DATE	WRITER	PLACE	CUE	SOURCE	NUMBER/NOTES
MacAlister, John Y.	1902.10.18	SLC	NY.Riverdale	Mrs. Clemens is	ViU	06466
MacAlister, John Y.	1903.04.07 & 1903.05.08	SLC	NY.Riverdale	Yours arrived last	ViU	06617
MacAlister, John Y.	1903.04.07	SLC	NY.Riverdale	Received of J.Y.	ViU	06616
MacAlister, John Y.	1903.10.22	SLC	NY.New York	Substantially, we are	ViU	06750
MacAlister, John Y.	1903.11.17	SLC	IT.Florence	It's a jolly	ViU	06759
MacAlister, John Y.	1903.12.01	SLC	IT.Florence	Only 2 days	ViU	06764
MacAlister, John Y.	1904.03.21	SLC	IT.Florence	I hope you	NN	06811
MacAlister, John Y.	1904.03.25	SLC	IT.Florence	I had not	ViU	06817
MacAlister, John Y.	1904.04.07	SLC	IT.Florence	Your very delightful	ViU	06821
MacAlister, John Y.	1904.04.12	SLC	IT.Florence	Hoping this will	TxU	06824
MacAlister, John Y.	1904.04.25	SLC	IT.Florence	We had an	ViU	06825
MacAlister, John Y.	pm 1904.06.17	SLC	IT.Florence	Clara slowly recovering	ViU	06873 telegram
MacAlister, John Y.	pm 1904.06.22	SLC	IT.Florence	For what you	ViU	06877 form letter
MacAlister, John Y.	1904.10.27	SLC	NY.New York	I am profoundly	ViU	06938
MacAlister, John Y.	1904.11.09	SLC	NY.New York	I must live	ViU	06948
MacAlister, John Y.	1904.11.22	SLC	NY.New York	I have thought	MiD	06953
MacAlister, John Y.	1905.02.20	SLC	NY.New York	I wish I	ViU	07005
MacAlister, John Y.	1905.07.16	SLC	NH.Dublin	I am so	ViU	07085
MacAlister, John Y.	1905.10.17	SLC	NH.Dublin	All our people	CU-MARK	07178
MacAlister, John Y.	1905.10.19	SLC	NH.Dublin	It was most	ViU	07183 CC & Leary letters enc
MacAlister, John Y.	o/a 1905.12.06	SLC	NY.New York	To you, &	ViU	07236 form letter
MacAlister, John Y.	1906.01.16	SLC	NY.New York	Ashcroft is on	ViU	07312
MacAlister, John Y.	1906.11.29	SLC	NY.New York	It was good	ViU	07577
MacAlister, John Y.	1907.02.21	SLC	NY.New York	This has been	NN-B	07658
MacAlister, John Y.	1907.06.20	SLC per RWA	EN.London	Mr. Clemens directs	CU-MARK	07760

MacAlister, John Y.		1907.07.30	SLC per RWA	NY.Tuxedo Park	Miss Lyon had	CU-MARK(tr)	07798 RWA tr
MacAlister, Mrs. John & MacAlister, John Y.	ca	1899.12.25	OLC	EN.London	Wishing them a	ViU	05725
MacAlister, Mrs. John		1900.07.07	SLC	EN.London	Punctuality is the	ODa2	09364 inscription
MacArthur, James		1900.05.26	SLC	EN.London	Very many thanks	NN-B	08201
MacArthur, James	o/a	1904.12.16	SLC per IVL	NY.New York	Mr. Clemens is	CU-MARK(dr)	06960 on MacArthur Dec 16
Macdonald, A.P.	bef	1907.06.30	SLC	Unknown	I have found	314:1907.06.30	09172
MacDonald, E.H.	o/a	1907.02.13	SLC per IVL	NY.New York	I remember the	CU-MARK(dr)	07648 on MacDonald Feb 13
MacDonald, G.		****.**.**	SLC	Unknown	With kindest regards	105:1951.05.21	09672 inscription
MacDonald, George		1882.09.19	SLC	NY.Elmira	I'll send you	299:458	02270
MacDonald, George		1883.03.09	SLC	CT.Hartford	I do most	CU-MARK	02356
MacElhinney, Mark G.		1907.04.16	SLC per IVL	NY.New York	Thank him for	CU-MARK(dr)	07685 on MacElhinney Apr 3
MacHugh, A.		1905.11.**	SLC	Unknown	Yes, both publicly	CU-MARK(dr)	07190
MacKenzie, Robert S.		1874.09.23	SLC	CT.Hartford	Thank you very	PHi	01130
Mackey, Robert K.		1904.06.**	SLC	IT.Florence	For what you	CU-MARK(ph)	06778 form letter
Mackey, Robert K.		1905.12.22	SLC per IVL	NY.New York	Mr. Clemens directs	MH-H	10841
Mackey, Robert K.		1905.12.23	SLC per IVL	NY.New York	Mr. Clemens wishes	MH-H	10839
Mackey, Robert K.		1906.03.07	SLC per IVL	NY.New York	Mr. Clemens was	MH-H	10840
MacMillan, Helen		1907.06.19	SLC per RWA	EN.London	Mr. Clemens directs	CU-MARK(tr)	07753 RWA tr
MacVeagh, Wayne		1896.09.27	SLC	EN.London	The solacing word	PHi	05118
MacVeagh, Wayne		1897.07.27	SLC	SW.Weggis	We are thus	CU-MARK(tr)	05272
MacVeagh, Wayne		1897.08.22	SLC	SW.Weggis	All this time	CU-MARK	05280

ADDRESSEE	DATE	WRITER	PLACE	CUE	SOURCE	NUMBER/NOTES
Macy, Anne S.	1905.01.19	JC	NY.New York	As Father is	NNAF	10678
Macy, Anne S.	ca 1909.01.08	SLC	CT.Redding	Greeting and Salutation	NNAF	10682 form letter
Macy, Anne S.	1909.01.11	SLC	CT.Redding	with warm regard	NNAF	09387 ins
Macy, John A.	1909.02.25	SLC	CT.Redding	Thank you for	NNAF(tr)	10685
Macy, John A.	1909.03.27	SLC	CT.Redding	Alas! I can't	NNAF(tr)	10686
Macy, John A.	1909.04.08	SLC	CT.Redding	I emptied into	NNAF(tr)	10687
Magnetic Rock Spring Co	1883.08.01	SLC	NY.Elmira	I find the	214:1883.08.11	02817
Major, Charles	1901.01.04	SLC	NY.New York	We are in	InLP	05958
Malashkina, Elizaveta	1902.08.01	SLC	ME.York Harbor	I sent your	RuM2	10664
Mallory Brothers	1883.09.19	SLC	CT.Hartford	You have a	CU-MARK	02838
Mallory, H.	1892.07.01	SLC	CT.Hartford	I concluded I	CU-MARK	01563
Malone, John	1898.11.16	SLC	AU.Vienna	It was good	CU-MARK	05468
Maloy, Daniel	1883.06.04	OLC	CT.Hartford	Presented to	CtHMTH	09696 inscription
Mann, William D.	1906.01.03	SLC	NY.New York	I supposed its	CU-MARK(dr)	07298
Manning, William	1899.07.05	SLC	EN.London	I thank you	TxU	05648
Mantz, Mary E.	*	*	*	*	*	10848 see Moffett, Mary E.
Marbury, Elisabeth	1901.12.03	SLC	NY.Riverdale	Yes, in the	CU-MARK(tr)	06179 SLC tr
Marbury, Elisabeth	1902.01.06	SLC	NY.Riverdale	The situation is	CU-MARK(tr)	06222 SLC tr
Marbury, Elisabeth	1902.02.10	SLC	NY.Riverdale	The reason I	ViU	06274
Marbury, Elisabeth	1902.05.13	SLC	NY.Riverdale	Above letter is	CU-MARK	06333 on Weekes May 7
Marbury, Elisabeth	o/a 1906.02.06	SLC per IVL	NY.New York	Satisfactory	CU-MARK(dr)	07331 on Marbury Feb 6
Margery	1907.01.01	SLC	Unknown	Happy New Year	CU-MARK(tr)	07606 inscription
Marshall, Oscar	1885.03.21	SLC	NY.New York	with the compliments	InU-Li	09337 inscription

Martin, Edward S.		1882.12.16	SLC	CT.Hartford	I sometimes write	MH-H	10842 typed
Martin, Hellen	ca	1908.04.17	SLC	NY.New York	I miss you	CU-MARK(tr)	07978
Martin, Mr.	ca	1900.**.**	SLC	EN.London	I am dreadfully	NNU-F	05730
Martin, Mr.		1907.08.05	SLC	NY.Tuxedo Park	Taking the pledge	MoSW	09257 inscription
Marvin, James		****.**.**	SLC	Unknown	I hereby certify	159:4.4	11148
Mary		****.**.**	SLC	Unknown	The whispering child	Mo2	10531 inscription
Mary		1889.05.31	SLC	CT.Hartford	I thank you	PBL	03898
Mary		1907.12.09	JC	NY.Katonah	For three days	DSI	07885
Mary		1909.02.14	SLC	CT.Redding	You will refrain	111:369	09388 inscription
Mason, Mr.		1893.02.25	SLC	IT.Florence	Thanks for your	IaDmE	04343
Mason, Mr.		1904.07.23	SLC	MA.Lee	Will you place	CU-MARK	06900
Mason, Wallace E.		1901.02.18	SLC	NY.New York	I thank you	MLeoHi	10732 form letter
Massett, Stephen		1869.09.02	SLC	NY.Buffalo	Got it--thank	Mo2	00218
Massett, Stephen		1881.01.31	SLC	CT.Hartford	Glad to hear	ViU	01900
Massett, Stephen		1881.10.07	SLC	CT.Hartford	Am sorry, but	CU-MARK(ph)	02047
Massett, Stephen		1881.10.10	SLC	CT.Hartford	All right, my	CaQMM	02050
Massiglia, Frances R.		1903.11.12	SLC	IT.Florence	I wish to	CU-MARK(tr)	06757 SLC tr
Matthews, Brander & Wilson, Francis		****.**.**	SLC	Unknown	He did	185	04426 telegram
Matthews, Brander		1885.03.31	SLC	NY.New York	Most sincere thanks	NNC	03200
Matthews, Brander		1885.12.08	SLC	CT.Hartford	My land, I	NNC	03328
Matthews, Brander		1898.07.26	SLC	AU.Kaltenleut.	I am ever	NNC	05414
Matthews, Brander		1900.07.11	SLC	EN.London	My souls, I'm	NNC	08824
Matthews, Brander		1900.07.25	SLC	EN.London	Are you still	NNC	05838
Matthews, Brander		1900.08.14	SLC	EN.London	We-uns are	NNC	05850
Matthews, Brander		1900.11.02	SLC	NY.New York	Land, I wish	NNC	05896

ADDRESSEE		DATE	WRITER	PLACE	CUE	SOURCE	NUMBER/NOTES
Matthews, Brander		1900.11.06	SLC	NY.New York	Dang it, I'm	NNC	05897
Matthews, Brander		1901.**.**	SLC	NY.New York	You tempt me	NNC	05947
Matthews, Brander		1901.02.21	SLC	NY.New York	I thank you	NNC	06008
Matthews, Brander		1902.01.07	SLC	NY.Riverdale	There's not a	NNC	06223
Matthews, Brander		1903.05.04	SLC	NY.Riverdale	I haven't been	NNC	06644
Matthews, Brander		1903.05.08	SLC	NY.Riverdale	I'm still in	NNC	06651
Matthews, Brander	ca	1904.06.21	SLC	IT.Florence	For what you	NNC	07587 form letter
Matthews, Brander		1905.05.23	SLC	NH.Dublin	You have my	NNC	07038
Matthews, Brander		1906.06.24	SLC	NH.Dublin	I thank you	NNC	07467
Matthews, Brander		1906.10.03	SLC	NH.Dublin	Certainly you can	NNC	07536
Matthews, Brander	o/a	1907.03.01	SLC per IVL	NY.New York	wont go to	CU-MARK(dr)	07667 on Matthews Jan 30
Matthews, Brander		1908.**.**	SLC	NY.New York	Would I like	NNC	07907
Maxwell, Mr.		1897.04.10	SLC	EN.London	What do I	CU-MARK	05200
McAleer, Patrick		1905.03.06	JC	NY.New York	I hadn't the	CU-MARK(tr)	08669
McCall, Samuel W.	o/a	1905.11.06	SLC per IVL	NY.New York	If I would	CU-MARK(dr)	07196 on McCall Nov 6
McCloud, Richard		1876.03.16	SLC	CT.Hartford	I am very	117:1876.03.18	01313
McClure, Phillips Co.	o/a	1906.11.26	SLC per IVL	NY.New York	Send me her	CU-MARK(dr)	07573 on Co. Nov 23
McClure, Robert		1900.08.24	SLC	EN.London	with the kindest	NN-B	10806 inscription
McClure, Samuel S.		1892.02.26	SLC	GE.Berlin	I have a	UPB	10864
McClure, Samuel S.		1897.08.07	SLC	SW.Lucerne	No, there are	CU-MARK(ph)	11086
McClure, Samuel S.	ca	1900.02.01	SLC	EN.London	Let us not	CU-MARK(dr)	08735
McClure, Samuel S. & Harvey, George B.		1903.07.21	SLC	NY.Elmira	Although I have	NN-B	11120 also to others
McClure, Samuel S.	o/a	1906.06.08	SLC per IVL	NH.Dublin	It may be	CU-MARK(dr)	07452 on McClure June 8

McClure, Samuel S.	o/a	1906.06.13	SLC per IVL	NH.Dublin	Mr. Clemens suggests	CU-MARK(dr)	07455 on McClure June 13
McClure's Magazine ed.		****.**.**	SLC per IVL	Unknown	Mr. Clemens directs	CU-MARK(dr)	09801
McComb, John		1867.06.08	SLC	NY.New York	D--n it I	C4	00137
McComb, John		1869.06.01	SLC	NY.Elmira	I got your	MoSW	00310
McComb, John	ca	1870.02.06	SLC	NY.Buffalo	I have read	417:1870.02.14	00420 addressee uncertain
McCook, General		1903.01.20	SLC	NY.Riverdale	Greeting & salutation	DLC	06569
McCook, John J.		1888.07.15	SLC	NY.Elmira	That paper is	CtHMTH	03733
McCook, John J.		1889.11.08	SLC	CT.Hartford	You must look	CtHSD	03962
McCook, John J.		1890.04.08	SLC	CT.Hartford	I will forward	CtHMTH	04038
McCook, Mrs.		1903.02.18	SLC	NY.Riverdale	Jean has told	DLC	06583
McCoy, Effie		1901.09.08	SLC	NY.Saranac Lake	Satan. Very Truly	CBev2	09396
McCrackan, W.D.		1902.12.05	SLC	NY.Riverdale	I am glad	CU-MARK(tr)	06498 other sources
McCrackan, W.D.		1902.12.15	SLC	NY.Riverdale	I thank you	CU-MARK(ph)	06515
McCrackan, W.D.		1902.12.17	SLC	NY.Riverdale	Have you begun	CU-MARK(ph)	06522
McCrackan, W.D.		1903.01.01	SLC	NY.Riverdale	I wish you	CU-MARK(ph)	06544
McCrary, George W.		1877.02.27	SLC	CT.Hartford	I beg you	OFH	09190
McDonald, Louisa		1873.09.29	SLC	EN.London	We concluded to	ViU	00966
McElroy, M.	o/a	1906.02.13	SLC per IVL	NY.New York	meeting will take	CU-MARK(dr)	07340 on McElroy Feb 13
McJilton, Mr.		1875.09.13	SLC	CT.Hartford	I have examined my	ODa2	11183
McKelway, St. Clair		1905.04.30	SLC	NY.New York	Your innumerable friends	114:771	07037
McKinney, Owen S.		1874.10.13	SLC	CT.Hartford	The woman is	CU-MARK	01138
McKinstry, Willard		1871.01.28	SLC	NY.Buffalo	I thank you	ViU	00569
McLean, Sarah P.		1881.12.12	SLC	CT.Hartford	I am just	ViU	02115
McPherson, John A.		1877.05.29	SLC	CT.Hartford	Mark Twain was	417:1877.06.09	01436 date uncertain

ADDRESSEE	DATE	WRITER	PLACE	CUE	SOURCE	NUMBER/NOTES
McQuiston, Laura F.	1901.03.26	SLC	NY.New York	You have my	Mo2	08868
McQuiston, Laura F.	1901.03.28	SLC	NY.New York	She came yesterday	Mo2	08869
McQuiston, Laura F.	1901.03.31	SLC	NY.New York	I am afraid	Mo2	08870
McQuiston, Laura F.	1901.04.01	SLC	NY.New York	I judge that	Mo2	08871
McQuiston, Laura F.	1901.04.11	SLC	NY.New York	I shall lose	NN5	06033
Medberry, James K.	1869.11.20	SLC	MA.Boston	You must excuse	300:f	00375
Medill, S.J.	****.10.02	SLC	Unknown	I yield	NIC	04482 inscription
Megrue, Roi C.	1905.08.05	SLC	NH.Dublin	I have your	CU-MARK(dr)	07101 on Megrue Aug 3
Megrue, Roi C.	o/a 1906.05.19	SLC per IVL	Unknown	From your favor	CU-MARK(dr)	07443 on Megrue May 19
Megrue, Roi C.	o/a 1906.11.17	SLC per IVL	NY.New York	Mr. Timory can	CU-MARK(dr)	07570 on Megrue Nov 17
Merkle, Frederick B.	1901.02.16	SLC	NY.New York	Always do right	CU-MARK(ph)	09399 inscription
Merriam (G.&C.) Co.	1891.03.07	SLC	CT.Hartford	A Dictionary is	CtY	04178
Merriam (G.&C.) Co.	1901.07.26	SLC	NY.Saranac Lake	To me also	CtY	06096
Merrill, Ernestine L.	o/a 1906.08.27	SLC per IVL	NH.Dublin	Add an aphorism	CU-MARK(dr)	07506 on Merrill Aug 27
Merrill, George S.	1877.02.08	SLC per FCH	CT.Hartford	I am very	ViW	04140
Merritt, John C.	1877.02.22	SLC	CT.Hartford	I have ordered	CU-MARK(tr)	01407 check enc
Metcalf, Lorettus S.	1888.04.13	SLC	CT.Hartford	When I left	ODa2	03714
Meyer, Miss	1901.10.25	SLC	NY.Riverdale	I stumbled by	CU-MARK(ph)	10476
Meyers, Mr.	****.**.**	SLC	Unknown	Very good--Sunday	Mo2	08539
Miale, Nicholas	1904.05.18	SLC per IVL	IT.Florence	Your kind letter	CU-MARK(dr)	06836 on Miale May 17
Miller & Bingham & Elder Manufacturing Co.	1883.10.08	SLC	CT.Hartford	No, I am	CU-MARK(ph)	02849

Miller, Hugh G.	1906.03.**	SLC	NY.New York	I cannot say	CU-MARK(tr)	07360 telegram; SLC tr
Miller, Joaquin	1873.06.11	SLC	EN.London	I am exceedingly	ViU	00923
Miller, Joaquin	1873.07.01 to 1873.07.02	SLC	EN.London	I meant to	ViU	00941
Miller, Joaquin	1873.07.05	SLC	EN.London	Indeed I would	Uk2	00945
Miller, Mr.	****.**.**	SLC	Unknown	This is the	NN-B	09876 inscription
Miller, Mr.	1902.06.17	SLC	NY.Riverdale	I saw that	MoHM	06367
Millet, Elizabeth M.	****.**.**	SLC	Unknown	Mrs. Lilly Millett	212:1943.12.11	09529 inscription
Millet, Francis D.	1877.03.**	SC	CT.Hartford	Bay and I	ViU(tr)	01401
Millet, Francis D.	1877.08.07	SLC	NY.Elmira	Your letter was	MH-H	01468
Millicent Lib. patrons	1893.12.25	SLC	NY.New York	Greeting and Salutation	MFai	04537 inscription
Millicent Lib. patrons	1894.02.02	SLC	Unknown	To the young	MFai	09226 inscription
Millicent Lib. Sec.	1893.12.10	SLC	NY.New York	I have allowed	MFai	04524
Millicent Library	1894.02.22	SLC	MA.Fairhaven	I am glad	MFai	04696
Mills, Abraham G.	1889.03.23	SLC	CT.Hartford	It could not	NN	10740
Mills, Abraham G.	1889.03.27	SLC	CT.Hartford	In answer to	NN	10741
Mills, Abraham G.	1889.04.04	SLC	CT.Hartford	All right--I	NN	10742
Mills, Abraham G.	1889.04.15	SLC	CT.Hartford	I thank you	NN	10743
Milly, Miss	1883.09.12	SLC	NY.Elmira	With the best	NcWsW	09328 inscription
Minor, W.	1885.06.17	SLC	CT.Hartford	I believe if	CU-MARK	03241
Missouri Hist. Soc.	aft 1902.12.01	SLC per IVL	NY.Riverdale	I thank you	MoHi	06535
Missouri University	1902.10.20	SLC	NY.Riverdale	I go to	MoU	10875 telegram
Mitchell, Percy	1897.06.24	SLC	EN.London	Here is the	CU-MARK(tr)	08635
Mochim, Maxim A.	1903.04.10	SLC	NY.Riverdale	with kindest greetings	RuL2	11125 inscription

ADDRESSEE	DATE	WRITER	PLACE	CUE	SOURCE	NUMBER/NOTES
Moffett, Anita	1906.12.**	SLC	Unknown	with affectionate Xmas	ODa2	11187 inscription
Moffett, Annie	*	*	*	*	*	10317 see Webster, Annie M.
Moffett, Mary M.	pm 1887.03.14	OLC	CT.Hartford	We all here	CU-MARK	03537
Moffett, Mary M.	ca 1887.03.22	SLC & OLC	CT.Hartford	With hearty	CU-MARK	08740 inscription
Moffett, Mary M. & Moffett, Samuel E.	aft 1889.12.25	SC	CT.Hartford	The basket is	CU-MARK	03752
Moffett, Mary M. & Moffett, Samuel E.	1890.01.30	OLC	CT.Hartford	I cannot tell	CU-MARK	04008
Moffett, Mary M. & Moffett, Samuel E.	ca 1904.06.21	SLC	IT.Florence	For what you	NPV	06847 form letter
Moffett, Mary M.	1908.08.02	SLC	CT.Redding	The family deeply	CU-MARK(dr)	08072 telegram
Moffett, Mary M.	1908.08.15	CC	GE.Cronenberg	This is a	CU-MARK	08088
Moffett, Pamela A.	****.**.**	OLC	CT.Hartford	I am going	CU-MARK	04493
Moffett, Pamela A.	****.**.**	SLC	CT.Hartford	wasn't that train	NPV	10880 fragment
Moffett, Pamela A.	****.**.**	SLC	CT.Hartford	We came home	NPV	10893 fragment
Moffett, Pamela A.	****.**.**	SLC	Unknown	*	CU-MARK	10295 envelope only
Moffett, Pamela A.	****.02.14	SLC	Unknown	I snatch a	NPV	00575
Moffett, Pamela A.	****.08.24	SLC	Unknown	I overlooked that	CU-MARK	08595
Moffett, Pamela A.	1853.09.**	SLC	NY.New York	From the gallery	114:21	02713
Moffett, Pamela A.	1853.10.08	SLC	NY.New York	I have not	CU-MARK	00001
Moffett, Pamela A.	1853.12.05	SLC	PA.Philadelphia	I have already	NPV	00005
Moffett, Pamela A. & Clemens, Jane L.	1856.06.10	SLC	IA.Keokuk	I have nothing	NPV	00011
Moffett, Pamela A.	1859.03.09 & 1859.03.11	SLC	LA.New Orleans	beginning of Lent	CU-MARK	00019 fragment
Moffett, Pamela A. & Clemens, Jane L.	1861.09.19 to 1861.09.24	SLC	NV.Carson City	The level ranks	114:56	00029
Moffett, Pamela A. & Clemens, Jane L.	1861.10.25	SLC	NV.Carson City	I have just	NPV	00030

Moffett, Pamela A. & Clemens, Jane L.	1862.02.08 to 1862.02.09	SLC	NV.Carson City	By George, Pamela	NPV	00036
Moffett, Pamela A.	1862.08.15	SLC	NV.Esmeralda	I mailed a	114:85	00058
Moffett, Pamela A. & Clemens, Jane L.	1863.02.16	SLC	NV.Virginia City	I suppose I	NPV	00061
Moffett, Pamela A. & Clemens, Jane L.	1863.04.11 to 1863.04.12	SLC	NV.Virginia City	It is very of great, dark	NPV CU-MARK	00063
Moffett, Pamela A. & Clemens, Jane L.	1863.05.**	SLC	CA.San Francisco	No 1--$20	CU-MARK	00065
Moffett, Pamela A. & Clemens, Jane L.	1863.06.01	SLC	CA.San Francisco	The Unreliable &	NPV	00066
Moffett, Pamela A. & Clemens, Jane L.	1863.06.04	SLC	CA.San Francisco	My visit to	CU-MARK	00067
Moffett, Pamela A. & Clemens, Jane L.	1863.07.18	SLC	NV.Virginia City	Ma, you are	CU-MARK	00069
Moffett, Pamela A. & Clemens, Jane L.	1863.08.05	SLC	NV.Virginia City	I got burned	CU-MARK	00070
Moffett, Pamela A. & Clemens, Jane L.	1863.08.19	SLC	NV.Steamboat Sp.	Ma, you have	NPV	00071
Moffett, Pamela A. & Clemens, Jane L.	1864.01.10	SLC	NV.Carson City	2 P.M. Sunday	CU-MARK	00073
Moffett, Pamela A.	1864.03.18	SLC	NV.Virginia City	I will not of much consequence	CU-MARK NPV	00076
Moffett, Pamela A. & Clemens, Jane L.	1864.05.16	SLC	NV.Virginia City	I had rather	CU-MARK(tr)	00077
Moffett, Pamela A. & Clemens, Jane L.	1864.09.25	SLC	CA.San Francisco	You can see	NPV	00087
Moffett, Pamela A. & Clemens, Jane L.	1866.01.20	SLC	CA.San Francisco	Ma's last letter	CU-MARK	00094
Moffett, Pamela A. & Clemens, Jane L.	1866.03.05	SLC	CA.San Francisco	I start to	NPV	00096
Moffett, Pamela A. & Clemens, Jane L.	1866.04.03	SLC	HI.Honolulu	I have been	NPV	00097
Moffett, Pamela A. & Clemens, Jane L.	1866.05.04	SLC	HI.Maui	11 o'clock at	NPV	00099
Moffett, Pamela A. & Clemens, Jane L.	1866.06.21	SLC	HI.Honolulu	I expect I	NPV	00102

ADDRESSEE	DATE	WRITER	PLACE	CUE	SOURCE	NUMBER/NOTES
Moffett, Pamela A. & Clemens, Jane L.	1866.06.27	SLC	HI.Honolulu	I enjoy being	NPV	00103
Moffett, Pamela A. & Clemens, Jane L.	1866.07.30 to 1866.08.20	SLC	SH.Smyrniote & CA.San Francisco	I write, now	NPV	00105
Moffett, Pamela A. & Clemens, Jane L.	1868.01.08	SLC	DC.Washington	And so the	NPV	00175
Moffett, Pamela A. & Clemens, Jane L.	1868.01.09	SLC	DC.Washington	That infernal lecture	NPV	00176
Moffett, Pamela A. & Clemens, Jane L.	1868.01.24	SLC	CT.Hartford	This is a	NPV	00182
Moffett, Pamela A. & Clemens, Jane L.	1868.02.06	SLC	DC.Washington	For two months	NPV	00190
Moffett, Pamela A.	ca 1868.12.01	SLC	NY.New York	Rondout & Newark	Mo4	02771 fragment
Moffett, Pamela A.	1868.12.24	SLC	MI.Lansing	I have nothing	NPV	00209
Moffett, Pamela A.	1869.01.14	SLC	IA.Davenport	I lectured here	NPV	00233
Moffett, Pamela A.	bet 1869.04.08 & 1869.04.11	SLC	NY.Elmira	I wrote yesterday	Mo4	00289
Moffett, Pamela A.	1869.06.23	SLC	NY.New York	We have all	CU-MARK	00320
Moffett, Pamela A. & Clemens, Jane L.	1869.06.26	SLC	NY.Elmira	I shipped my	CU-MARK	00322
Moffett, Pamela A.	1869.08.20 to 1869.08.21	SLC	NY.Buffalo	I have only liking & the	NPV Mo4	00336
Moffett, Pamela A.	1869.11.09	SLC	MA.Boston	Three or four	114:167	00371
Moffett, Pamela A.	1869.12.17	SLC	MA.Boston	Yours of 10th	CU-MARK	00390
Moffett, Pamela A.	1870.01.14	SLC	NY.Utica	Am in a	NPV	00412 misdated Jan 15
Moffett, Pamela A.	1870.06.12	SLC & OLC	NY.Buffalo	We were snatched	NPV	00479
Moffett, Pamela A. & Clemens, Jane L.	1870.06.25	SLC	NY.Elmira	We were called	NPV	00481
Moffett, Pamela A. & Clemens, Jane L.	1870.07.27	SLC	NY.Elmira	Mr Langdon is	NPV	00492
Moffett, Pamela A.	1870.08.06	SLC	NY.Elmira	Father died this	NPV	00495 telegram
Moffett, Pamela A.	ca 1870.08.15	SLC	NY.Buffalo	I will come	NPV	00497

Moffett, Pamela A.	1870.08.31	SLC	NY.Buffalo	I know I	NPV	00498
Moffett, Pamela A.	1871.02.03	OLC	NY.Buffalo	Mr Clemens has	NPV	00572
Moffett, Pamela A. & Clemens, Jane L.	1872.11.06	SLC	EN.London	I have been	NPV	00829
Moffett, Pamela A. & Clemens, Jane L.	1872.11.26	SLC	CT.Hartford	Very glad to	NPV	00835 on Mollie Clemens Nov 26
Moffett, Pamela A.	1873.01.22	SLC	CT.Hartford	Ma & Annie	CU-MARK	00861
Moffett, Pamela A. & Clemens, Jane L.	1873.06.15	OLC	EN.London	We are so	NPV	00926
Moffett, Pamela A. & Clemens, Jane L.	1873.07.**	OLC	EN.London	We have not	NPV	00939
Moffett, Pamela A. & Clemens, Jane L.	1873.08.15	OLC	SK.Edinburgh	Your letter was	NPV	00793
Moffett, Pamela A. & Clemens, Jane L.	1874.08.15	SLC	NY.Elmira	I came away	114:220	01117
Moffett, Pamela A.	bet 1874.08.16 & 1874.08.30	SLC	NY.Elmira	I keep forgetting	CU-MARK	01118
Moffett, Pamela A. & Clemens, Jane L.	1875.04.25	SLC	CT.Hartford	We want to	CU-MARK	01224 date uncertain
Moffett, Pamela A.	1875.06.28	SLC	CT.Hartford	Livy has been	CU-MARK	01244 fragment
Moffett, Pamela A.	1875.07.23	SLC	CT.Hartford	I was only	NPV	01253
Moffett, Pamela A.	1875.08.16	SLC	RI.Newport	We send hearty	CU-MARK	01256
Moffett, Pamela A.	1877.01.19	SLC per FCH	CT.Hartford	I have found	CU-MARK	02801
Moffett, Pamela A.	1877.02.27	SLC	CT.Hartford	I think Livy	ViU	01409
Moffett, Pamela A. & Clemens, Jane L.	1878.04.07	SLC	NY.Elmira	I have told	NPV 114:325	01553
Moffett, Pamela A. & Clemens, Jane L.	1878.07.01	SLC	GE.Heidelberg	The letter came	CU-MARK(tr)	01575
Moffett, Pamela A. & Clemens, Jane L.	1878.08.20	SLC	SW.Lucerne	We came into	CU-MARK	01587
Moffett, Pamela A. & Clemens, Jane L.	1878.12.01	SLC	GE.Munich	I broke the	CU-MARK	01610

ADDRESSEE	DATE	WRITER	PLACE	CUE	SOURCE	NUMBER/NOTES
Moffett, Pamela A. & Clemens, Jane L.	bet 1879.02.14 & 1879.02.27	SLC	GE.Munich	that finest character	CU-MARK(tr)	09211
Moffett, Pamela A.	ca 1879.03.26	SLC	FR.Paris	By a letter	CU-MARK(tr)	09212
Moffett, Pamela A. & Clemens, Jane L.	1879.05.29	SLC	FR.Paris	I have just	NPV	01661
Moffett, Pamela A.	1879.09.15	SLC	NY.Elmira	I have no	NPV	01690
Moffett, Pamela A.	1879.11.18	SLC	CT.Hartford	I am such	NPV	01722
Moffett, Pamela A.	1879.11.30	SLC	CT.Hartford	You must thank	NPV	01729
Moffett, Pamela A.	1880.01.25	SLC	NY.Elmira	Our plan is	NPV	01757
Moffett, Pamela A.	1880.02.28	SLC	CT.Hartford	Have written Orion	NPV	01765
Moffett, Pamela A.	1880.03.08 or 1880.03.15	SLC	Unknown	Check for 25	CU-MARK	04129
Moffett, Pamela A. & Clemens, Jane L.	1880.04.11	SLC	CT.Hartford	We leave for	NPV	01783
Moffett, Pamela A. & Clemens, Jane L.	1880.04.21	SLC	CT.Hartford	I don't know	NPV	01789
Moffett, Pamela A. & Clemens, Jane L.	1880.05.14	SLC	CT.Hartford	My advice to	NPV	01804
Moffett, Pamela A.	1880.07.23	SLC	NY.Elmira	I cannot conceive	NPV	01818
Moffett, Pamela A.	1880.12.08	SLC	CT.Hartford	Sam tells me	NPV	01869
Moffett, Pamela A.	1880.12.11	SLC	CT.Hartford	Won't you take	CU-MARK	01870
Moffett, Pamela A.	1880.12.24	SLC	CT.Hartford	They were exactly	NPV	01879
Moffett, Pamela A.	1881.01.10	SLC	CT.Hartford	The books which	CU-MARK	01890
Moffett, Pamela A.	1881.02.03	SLC	CT.Hartford	Send the enclosed	CU-MARK	01903 Chamberlaine Feb 1 enc
Moffett, Pamela A.	1881.02.04	SLC	CT.Hartford	Ella Lampton doesn't	NPV	01189
Moffett, Pamela A.	bet 1881.02.17 & 1881.03.16	SLC	Unknown	O, dear, don't	CU-MARK(tr)	09523
Moffett, Pamela A.	ca 1881.03.01	SLC	CT.Hartford	If the Howards	CU-MARK(tr)	09497
Moffett, Pamela A.	1881.03.16	SLC	CT.Hartford	To-day we bought	NPV	01928
Moffett, Pamela A. & Clemens, Jane L.	1881.05.02	SLC	CT.Hartford	I believe there	NPV	01946
Moffett, Pamela A.	1881.12.20	SLC	CT.Hartford	Merry Christmas to	NPV	02121

Moffett, Pamela A.		1882.10.21	SLC	CT.Hartford	Autographs are a	CU-MARK	02293 typed
Moffett, Pamela A.		1882.12.02	SLC	CT.Hartford	I have sent	NPV	02311 typed
Moffett, Pamela A. & Moffett, Samuel E.		1883.12.19	SLC	CT.Hartford	Merry Xmas to	CU-MARK	02868
Moffett, Pamela A.		1885.**.**	SLC	Unknown	I have sent	NPV	03093
Moffett, Pamela A.		1885.04.15	SLC	CT.Hartford	The Chronicle	NPV	03219
Moffett, Pamela A.		1885.06.12	SLC	CT.Hartford	Ma has sent	NPV	03240
Moffett, Pamela A.		1885.06.28	SLC	NY.Elmira	It is dreadful	CU-MARK	03247
Moffett, Pamela A.		1886.12.03	SLC	CT.Hartford	Livy is hoping It wasn't that	CU-MARK ViU	03489
Moffett, Pamela A.	pm	1887.01.02	CC	CT.Hartford	Will you please	CU-MARK	03485
Moffett, Pamela A.		1887.01.14	SLC	CT.Hartford	As per request	CU-MARK	03509
Moffett, Pamela A.		1887.04.02	SLC	CT.Hartford	This Mrs. Boardman	NPV	03391
Moffett, Pamela A.		1887.07.12	SLC	NY.Elmira	I had no	NPV	03602
Moffett, Pamela A.		1887.09.27	SLC	CT.Hartford	I think Sam	CU-MARK	03653
Moffett, Pamela A.		1887.12.18	SLC	CT.Hartford	Will you take	114:494	03679
Moffett, Pamela A.		1888.09.15	SLC	NY.Elmira	I have ordered	NPV	03763
Moffett, Pamela A.		1889.01.27	OLC	CT.Hartford	I have been	NPV	03855
Moffett, Pamela A.		1889.07.01	SLC	NY.Elmira	Orion's suggestion	CU-MARK	03905
Moffett, Pamela A.		1889.10.09	SLC	CT.Hartford	Your postal card	NPV	03950
Moffett, Pamela A.	ca	1890.01.27	OLC	CT.Hartford	It is a	CU-MARK	03997
Moffett, Pamela A.	pm	1890.03.13	SLC	CT.Hartford	*	CU-MARK	09478 envelope only
Moffett, Pamela A.		1890.05.13	SLC	CT.Hartford	Indeed my character	NPV	04047
Moffett, Pamela A.		1890.10.12	SLC	CT.Hartford	I am very	CU-MARK	04100
Moffett, Pamela A.		1891.06.03	SLC	CT.Hartford	I am very	NPV	04215
Moffett, Pamela A.		1892.03.21	SLC	FR.Menton	Your letter has	NPV	04275
Moffett, Pamela A.		1893.02.05	SLC	IT.Florence	Orion writes me	NPV	04336
Moffett, Pamela A.		1893.04.26	SLC	NY.New York	Orion does not	CU-MARK	04387

ADDRESSEE		DATE	WRITER	PLACE	CUE	SOURCE	NUMBER/NOTES
Moffett, Pamela A. & Webster, Annie M.		1893.09.21	SLC	NY.New York	Yes, I saw	NPV	04458
Moffett, Pamela A.		1894.02.25	SLC	NY.New York	By the power	CU-MARK	04698
Moffett, Pamela A.	pm	1894.05.08	SLC	NY.New York	I write a	CU-MARK	04731
Moffett, Pamela A.		1894.06.25	SLC	FR.La Bourboule	Mr. Hall's letter	CU-MARK	04744
Moffett, Pamela A.		1895.07.14	SLC	NY.Elmira	I have not	CU-MARK(tr)	04931
Moffett, Pamela A.		1895.09.**	OLC	AS.Melbourne	I received a	CU-MARK(tr)	09170 inscription
Moffett, Pamela A.		1896.02.**	CC	Unknown	as no Christian	ViU(tr)	05015 fragment
Moffett, Pamela A.		1896.11.**	SLC	EN.London	*	CU-MARK	10124 envelope only
Moffett, Pamela A.		1897.01.07	SLC	EN.London	Orion says you	CU-MARK	05166
Moffett, Pamela A.		1897.03.28	SLC	EN.London	I have asked	NPV	05193
Moffett, Pamela A.		1900.04.25	SLC	EN.London	We have moved	CU-MARK	05800
Moffett, Pamela A.		1900.12.30	SLC	NY.New York	Many thanks for	CU-MARK	05941 on Montgomery Dec 26
Moffett, Pamela A.		1904.07.21	SLC	MA.Lee	For what you	NPV	06897 form letter
Moffett, Samuel E.		****.**.**	CC	CT.Hartford	I thank you	CU-MARK	08737
Moffett, Samuel E.		****.**.**	CC	NY.Riverdale	We are all	CU-MARK	08686
Moffett, Samuel E.		****.**.**	CC	Unknown	My father wants	ViU	04497
Moffett, Samuel E.		****.**.**	OLC	NY.Riverdale	Yes, it is	CU-MARK	08689
Moffett, Samuel E.		****.**.**	OLC	Unknown	I have mislaid	CU-MARK	08714
Moffett, Samuel E.		****.**.**	OLC	Unknown	We were so	CU-MARK	04483
Moffett, Samuel E.		****.**.**	SC	CT.Hartford	Thank you so	ViU	09035
Moffett, Samuel E.		****.**.**	SLC	Unknown	I don't seem	CU-MARK	04492
Moffett, Samuel E.		****.01.16	CC	Unknown	Please excuse the	CU-MARK	08736
Moffett, Samuel E. & Webster, Annie M.	ca	1866.11.**	SLC	Unknown	will all come	NPV	00111 fragment
Moffett, Samuel E.		1867.10.**	SLC	SH.Quaker City	From his Uncle	CtHMTH	00154
Moffett, Samuel E.		1879.02.03	OLC	GE.Munich	I had a	CU-MARK	01628

Moffett, Samuel E.		1879.03.09	OLC	FR.Paris	We arrived safely	CU-MARK	01639
Moffett, Samuel E.	pm	1879.05.14	SLC	FR.Paris	Don't tell anybody	CU-MARK	01654 date uncertain
Moffett, Samuel E.		1879.07.22	OLC	EN.London	I was glad	CU-MARK	01678
Moffett, Samuel E.		1879.12.26	SLC	CT.Hartford	It is funny	CU-MARK	01744
Moffett, Samuel E.		1880.03.11	SLC	CT.Hartford	I enclose a	CU-MARK	01769
Moffett, Samuel E.		1882.08.13	OLC	NY.Elmira	Your uncle Sam	CU-MARK	02251
Moffett, Samuel E. & Moffett, Pamela A.		1883.12.19	SLC	CT.Hartford	Merry Xmas to	CU-MARK	02868
Moffett, Samuel E.		1885.07.21	SLC	NY.Elmira	I confess it	CU-MARK	03262
Moffett, Samuel E.		1887.01.15	JC per SLC	CT.Hartford	I liked those	CU-MARK	03511
Moffett, Samuel E.		1887.03.22	SLC	CT.Hartford	Your aunt Livy	CU-MARK	03548
Moffett, Samuel E.		1888.03.30	SLC	CT.Hartford	All right. If	CU-MARK	03711
Moffett, Samuel E.		1889.04.20	SLC	CT.Hartford	Your aunt Livy	CU-MARK	03886
Moffett, Samuel E.		1889.05.16	SLC	CT.Hartford	Good--we shall	CU-MARK	03891
Moffett, Samuel E.		1889.11.16	SLC	CT.Hartford	Please find out	CU-MARK	03967
Moffett, Samuel E.		1889.11.28	SLC	CT.Hartford	I herewith enclose	CU-MARK	03979
Moffett, Samuel E. & Moffett, Mary M.	aft	1889.12.25	SC	CT.Hartford	The basket is	CU-MARK	03752
Moffett, Samuel E. & Moffett, Mary M.		1890.01.30	OLC	CT.Hartford	I cannot tell	CU-MARK	04008
Moffett, Samuel E.		1890.12.**	JC	CT.Hartford	I am very	CU-MARK	03738
Moffett, Samuel E.	pm	1893.10.26	SLC	CT.Hartford	*	CU-MARK	10094 envelope only
Moffett, Samuel E.		1895.04.09	SLC	FR.Paris	I found the	CU-MARK	04864
Moffett, Samuel E.		1895.06.11	SLC	NY.Elmira	I am thoroughly	CU-MARK	04888
Moffett, Samuel E.	&	1895.08.14 1895.08.15	SLC	CN.Vancouver	Here it is	CU-MARK CAlb2	04943 CAlb2 envelope
Moffett, Samuel E.		1895.08.17	CC	CN.Vancouver	We are so	CU-MARK	04948
Moffett, Samuel E.		1895.08.17	SLC	CN.Vancouver	I can't remember	CU-MARK	04949
Moffett, Samuel E.		1895.08.20	OLC	CN.Vancouver	I send you	CU-MARK	04954

ADDRESSEE	DATE	WRITER	PLACE	CUE	SOURCE	NUMBER/NOTES
Moffett, Samuel E.	1895.11.10	SLC	NZ.Timaru	If I resolve	CU-MARK	04971
Moffett, Samuel E.	1895.11.12	CC	NZ.Omaru	Your book has	CU-MARK	04972
Moffett, Samuel E.	1895.12.30	SLC	AS.Adelaide	This is just	CU-MARK	04986
Moffett, Samuel E.	1896.04.07	CC	SH.Wardha	Thank you ever	CU-MARK	05037
Moffett, Samuel E.	1896.05.27	SLC	AF.Johannesburg	Yours of April	CU-MARK	05058
Moffett, Samuel E.	1896.06.23	SLC	AF.Port Eliz.	When Mr. Hearst's	CU-MARK	05081
Moffett, Samuel E.	1897.07.07	SLC	EN.London	We have given	CU-MARK	05254
Moffett, Samuel E.	1897.11.28	SLC	AU.Vienna	I was half	CU-MARK	05317
Moffett, Samuel E.	1898.01.06	OLC	AU.Vienna	Ever since your	CU-MARK	05331
Moffett, Samuel E.	1898.01.11	SLC per OLC	AU.Vienna	Your uncle wants	CU-MARK	05334
Moffett, Samuel E.	1898.01.14	OLC	AU.Vienna	One important thing	ViU	05330
Moffett, Samuel E.	1899.04.25	SLC	AU.Vienna	Your letter, with	CU-MARK	05583
Moffett, Samuel E.	1899.05.13	SLC	AU.Vienna	Won't you answer	CU-MARK	05592 on Hollister & Norman Apr 29
Moffett, Samuel E.	1899.07.14	SLC	SE.Sanna	This biographical sketch	CU-MARK	05656
Moffett, Samuel E.	1899.09.15	SLC	SE.Sanna	As I remember	CU-MARK	05674
Moffett, Samuel E.	1900.04.23	SLC	EN.London	I reveal to	ViU	05797
Moffett, Samuel E.	1900.05.17 & 1900.05.19	SLC	EN.London	Your preliminary letter	CU-MARK	05807
Moffett, Samuel E.	1900.07.01	SLC	EN.London	This is a	CU-MARK	05830
Moffett, Samuel E.	1900.07.28	SLC	EN.London	I perceive that	CU-MARK	05840
Moffett, Samuel E.	1900.09.27	SLC	EN.London	The uncertainties seem	CU-MARK	08823
Moffett, Samuel E.	1900.11.15	OLC	NY.New York	I have stupidly	CU-MARK	05907
Moffett, Samuel E.	pm 1900.11.27	CC	NY.New York	I am sorry	CU-MARK	06204
Moffett, Samuel E.	o/a 1901.01.09	SLC	NY.New York	You answer him	ViU	05962 on Robinson Jan 9
Moffett, Samuel E.	1901.02.14	SLC	NY.New York	Sam, for God's	CU-MARK	05997 on Montgomery Feb 14
Moffett, Samuel E.	1901.02.19	SLC	NY.New York	Please atten to	CU-MARK	06005

Moffett, Samuel E.	o/a	1901.02.20	SLC	NY.New York	Please tell him	CU-MARK	06007 on Cochran Feb 20
Moffett, Samuel E.	o/a	1901.03.06	SLC	Unknown	Doubleday said he	CU-MARK	09199 on Page Mar 6
Moffett, Samuel E.		1901.03.26	SLC	NY.New York	Dr. Helmer Thinks	CU-MARK	06028 typed
Moffett, Samuel E.		1901.07.07	OLC	NY.Saranac Lake	Your uncle Sam	CU-MARK	06086
Moffett, Samuel E.		1901.07.17	OLC	NY.Saranac Lake	I do wish	CU-MARK	06089
Moffett, Samuel E.		1901.07.28	OLC	NY.Saranac Lake	We hear from	CU-MARK	06097
Moffett, Samuel E.		1901.09.11	SLC	NY.Saranac Lake	Your article in	CU-MARK	06135
Moffett, Samuel E.		1901.09.17	OLC	NY.Saranac Lake	Your letter to	NPV	06138
Moffett, Samuel E.		1902.01.23	OLC	NY.Elmira	Your Uncle Sam	NPV	06252
Moffett, Samuel E.		1902.01.31	SLC	NY.Riverdale	You can call	CU-MARK	06261
Moffett, Samuel E.		1902.08.11	SLC	ME.York Harbor	Your aunt Livy	CU-MARK	06403
Moffett, Samuel E.		1902.08.22	SLC	ME.York Harbor	Much better. Doing	CU-MARK	06411
Moffett, Samuel E.		1902.08.26	SLC	ME.York Harbor	No, I don't	CU-MARK	06415
Moffett, Samuel E.		1902.10.24	SLC	NY.Riverdale	I am just	NN-B	08231
Moffett, Samuel E. & Moffett, Mary M.	ca	1904.06.21	SLC	IT.Florence	For what you	NPV	06847 form letter
Moffett, Samuel E.		1904.08.06	SLC	MA.Lee	Yes, Clara has	CU-MARK	06909
Moffett, Samuel E.	pm	1907.02.08	SLC	NY.New York	*	CU-MARK	10159 envelope only
Moffett, Samuel E.		1907.09.09	SLC per IVL	NY.Tuxedo Park	Mr. Clemens asks	CU-MARK	07831
Moffett, William A.		1858.06.15	SLC	TN.Memphis	Henry's recovery is	CU-MARK	00015 telegram
Moffett, William A.		1858.06.21	SLC	TN.Memphis	Henry Died this	CU-MARK	00017 telegram
Monahan, Michael		1905.01.28	SLC	NY.New York	It is strong	NNC	06989
Monahan, Michael		1905.02.04	SLC	NY.New York	I thank cordially	NIC	06992
Monday Afternoon Club		****.12.31	SLC & OLC	CT.Hartford	Mr. & Mrs.	CtHMTH	04621

ADDRESSEE	DATE	WRITER	PLACE	CUE	SOURCE	NUMBER/NOTES
Monday Evening Club	bef 1880.04.05	SLC	CT.Hartford	On the Decay	110:1965.12.14	10343 form letter
Moore, I.P.	o/a 1907.02.15	SLC per IVL	NY.New York	My branch of	CU-MARK(dr)	07650 on Moore Feb 15
Moore, J. Howard	1907.02.02	SLC	NY.New York	The book has	114:804	07641
Moore, J. Murray	1874.01.09	SLC per CWS	EN.Liverpool	I expect to	CU-MARK(ph)	01036
Moore, John T.	1859.07.06	SLC	TN.Memphis	I have made	285:1883.07.18	02714
Moore, Robert H.	1886.12.03	SLC	CT.Hartford	The weather--consider	IaU	03490
Morel, Edmund D.	1904.10.15 & 1904.10.16	SLC	NY.New York	I received Lord	UkL2	06930
Morel, Edmund D.	aft 1906.01.08	SLC	NY.New York	The map, etc.	UkL2	07300
Morgan, George H.	1882.12.16	SLC	CT.Hartford	I believe all	CU-MARK(ph)	02319 typed
Morgan, John P.	****.**.**	SLC	NY.Riverdale	Please send $100	CU-MARK	08702
Morgan, John P.	1909.09.15	SLC	CT.Redding	Your letter of	NNPM	08452
Morrison, George A.	1901.11.28	SLC per OLC	NY.Riverdale	Mr. Clemens asks	NHi	09106
Morse, Mr.	1894.09.01	SLC	FR.Etretat	How does that	418:1964.05.25	05010
Mortimer, F.W.	1900.03.13	SLC	EN.London	Miss Penfold was	CU-MARK	05776
Morton, J. Sterling	1893.04.06	SLC	NY.New York	Your petitioner, Mark	161:13.409	04364
Moscovitz, Mr.	1893.12.31	SLC	NY.New York	Thank you most	NElmC	04547
Mott, Mrs. Jordan	1904.04.12	SLC	IT.Florence	Ah, if we could!	ODa2	11196
Mouland, John E.	1872.11.23	SLC	SH.Batavia	You have brought	ViU	00834
Mouland, John E.	1872.12.03	SLC	CT.Hartford	You must run	ViU	00839
Mouland, John E.	1873.01.22	SLC	CT.Hartford	I am just	ViU	00862
Mouland, John E.	1873.04.29	SLC	CT.Hartford	The bearer is	CU-MARK(tr)	00910
Moulton, Louise C.	1872.06.18	SLC	CT.Hartford	(I will explain	DLC	00757
Moulton, Louise C.	1874.02.13	SLC	CT.Hartford	I am very	DLC	01049
Moulton, Louise C.	1874.10.14	SLC	CT.Hartford	I have just	DLC	01139
Moulton, Louise C.	1875.01.08	SLC	CT.Hartford	I have been	DLC	01176

Moulton, Louise C.		1905.11.**	SLC	Unknown	Mr. Clemens will	DLC	07189 form letter
Mullen, Barbara		1901.05.20	SLC	NY.New York	I wish I	271:1952.03.29	06058
Mullen, Barbara		1901.05.30	SLC	NY.New York	I wish to	271:1952.03.29	06065
Mullen, Barbara		1902.05.30	SLC	MO.Hannibal	I wish to	271:1952.03.29	06350
Mullen, Barbara		1902.12.12	SLC	NY.Riverdale	It is touching	271:1952.03.29	06514
Mullen, Barbara	pm	1905.11.17	SLC	NY.New York	I have not	271:1952.03.29	07211
Mullen, Barbara		1906.06.14	SLC per IVL	NH.Dublin	Don't you mind	CU-MARK(dr)	07458 other sources
Munro, David A.		****.**.**	SLC	Unknown	*	301:241	10180 envelope only
Munro, David A.		****.**.**	SLC	Unknown	Many thanks for	NjMoHP	04713
Munro, David A.		1902.03.09	SLC	NY.Riverdale	To-morrow I shall	134:1924.04.23	09975 other sources
Munro, David A.	ca	1902.04.01	SLC	NY.Riverdale	Do get the	MA	06207
Munro, David A.		1902.11.20	SLC	NY.Riverdale	Mr. Franklin's count	122:1934.04.04	06491
Munro, David A.		1902.12.06	SLC per IVL	NY.Riverdale	Mr. McCracken proposes	CU-MARK(tr)	06503
Munro, David A. or North American Review	bef	1903.01.12	SLC	NY.Riverdale	Private. If McCrackan	CU-MARK	08692
Munro, David A.		1903.01.19	SLC per IVL	NY.Riverdale	Please bear in	NcD	06568
Munro, David A.		1903.06.14	SLC	NY.Riverdale	McCrackan has been	134:1931.04.09	06677
Munro, David A.		1905.**.**	SLC	NY.New York	This is for	157:1928.02.23	09863
Munro, David A.		1905.02.08	SLC	NY.New York	Thank you ever	NN-B	06995
Munro, David A.		1905.08.05	CC	NY.New York	My father has	WU	07099
Munro, David A.	aft	1906.12.10	SLC	NY.New York	Make page twelve-twenty	CU-MARK(dr)	07589
Munro, John	aft	1879.12.20	SLC	Unknown	My twins (born	CU-MARK(tr)	01745
Murphy O'Mulligan Club		1880.**.**	SLC	Unknown	We know there	CU-MARK(tr)	10862
Murray, Katy		1907.04.06	SLC	NY.New York	On the whole	C4	09262 inscription
Murray, Katy		1907.09.01	SLC	NY.Tuxedo Park	The main difference	C4	09255 inscription

ADDRESSEE	DATE	WRITER	PLACE	CUE	SOURCE	NUMBER/NOTES
Murray, Mrs. T. Douglas	1900.06.07	SLC	EN.London	Jean drifted into	UkOxU	05818
Murray, Mrs. T. Douglas	1900.08.14	SLC	EN.London	Mrs. Clemens has	NN5	05851
Murray, T. Douglas	bet 1899.08.** & 1899.09.**	SLC	SE.Sanna	How lucky that	155:1936.03.24	05668
Murray, T. Douglas	1899.08.25	SLC	SE.Sanna	Yours (undated) has	CU-MARK(tr)	05666
Murray, T. Douglas	1899.08.29	SLC	SE.Sanna	Stop--I may	CU-MARK(tr)	05556 other sources
Murray, T. Douglas	1899.09.03	SLC	SE.Sanna	Yes, it does	CU-MARK(tr)	05670
Murray, T. Douglas	1899.09.15	SLC	SE.Sanna	There is something	205:1937.02.18	09812
Murray, T. Douglas	1900.01.31	SLC	EN.London	I enclose the	CU-MARK	05755
Murray, T. Douglas	1900.05.02	SLC	EN.London	I think I	NN-B	08198
Murray, T. Douglas	1900.08.27	SLC	EN.London	I am afraid	CU-MARK(ph)	05858
Murray, T. Douglas	1900.08.27	SLC	EN.London	I will not	CU-MARK(tr)	06193 SLC tr
Murray, Thomas H.	1880.05.13	SLC	CT.Hartford	I remember you	CU-MARK	01803
Muscatine Journal	1853.12.04	SLC	PA.Philadelphia	There is very	158:1853.12.16	00004
Muscatine Journal	1853.12.24	SLC	PA.Philadelphia	The weather last	158:1854.01.06	00006
Muscatine Journal	1854.02.17 to 1854.02.18	SLC	DC.Washington	When I came	158:1854.03.24	00007
Muscatine Tri-Weekly J.	1855.02.16	SLC	MO.St. Louis	Whether it is	310:1855.02.28	00008
Muscatine Tri-Weekly J.	1855.02.24	SLC	MO.St. Louis	An arrangement has	310:1855.03.09	09994
Muscatine Tri-Weekly J.	1855.03.01	SLC	MO.St. Louis	Yesterday afternoon	310:1855.03.12	09995
Muscatine Tri-Weekly J.	1855.03.05	SLC	MO.St. Louis	Business on the	310:1855.03.14	00009
Muscatine Weekly J.	1854.02.03	SLC	PA.Philadelphia	The Consolidation Bill	158:1854.02.17	09400
Nansen, Eva H.	1899.01.13	SLC	AU.Vienna	I thank you	NoOU	05536
Nash, Mary	*	*	*	*	*	10873 see Hubbard, Mary N.
Nast, Thomas	****.**.**	SLC	Unknown	With the best	NN-B	09763 inscription
Nast, Thomas	1871.04.04	SLC	NY.Elmira	I like that	ViU	00599
Nast, Thomas	ca 1871.04.24	SLC	NY.Elmira	Take any sketch	305:1907.02.06	00605

Nast, Thomas	1872.06.**	SLC	Unknown	With warm regards	157:1911.11.28	09799 inscription
Nast, Thomas	1872.12.10	SLC	CT.Hartford	As the best	NjP	00843
Nast, Thomas	1872.12.17	SLC	CT.Hartford	The Almanac has	321:263	00846
Nast, Thomas	1877.11.12	SLC	CT.Hartford	I did not	NN-B	02518
Nast, Thomas	1884.12.04	SLC	NY.Syracuse	All these days	OCIW	03047
National Academy A&L	1905.11.10	SLC per IVL	NY.New York	I desire to	CU-MARK(ph)	09722
Natkin, Gertrude	****.**.**	SLC per IVL	Unknown	And to say	CU-MARK(tr)	08968 fragment
Natkin, Gertrude	1905.12.28	SLC	NY.New York	It was very	CU-MARK	07278
Natkin, Gertrude	1906.01.01	SLC	NY.New York	Don't forget, dear	CU-MARK	07296
Natkin, Gertrude	1906.02.03	SLC	NY.New York	Now then, dear	CU-MARK	07325
Natkin, Gertrude	1906.02.08	SLC	NY.New York	Aren't you the	CU-MARK	07332
Natkin, Gertrude	1906.02.14	SLC	NY.New York	It was a	CU-MARK	07342
Natkin, Gertrude	1906.02.20	SLC	NY.New York	Isn't it odd	CU-MARK	07351
Natkin, Gertrude	1906.03.02	SLC	NY.New York	Marjorie dear, Mr.	CU-MARK	07361
Natkin, Gertrude	1906.03.04 to 1906.03.09	SLC	NY.New York	But you were	CU-MARK	07375
Natkin, Gertrude	1906.03.13	SLC	NY.New York	One unto you	CU-MARK	07381
Natkin, Gertrude	1906.03.16	SLC	NY.New York	And thereto--this	CU-MARK	07389
Natkin, Gertrude	1906.03.18	SLC	NY.New York	Aren't you dear	CU-MARK	07393
Natkin, Gertrude	1906.03.24	SLC	NY.New York	Are you listening	CU-MARK	07401
Natkin, Gertrude	1906.04.03	SLC per IVL	NY.New York	Mr. Clemens has	CU-MARK	07411
Natkin, Gertrude	1906.04.08	SLC	NY.New York	You are the	CU-MARK	07421
Natkin, Gertrude	1906.04.19	SLC	NY.New York	Please admit these	CU-MARK	07432
Natkin, Gertrude	1906.04.27	SLC	NY.New York	Those lovely flowers	CU-MARK	07436
Natkin, Gertrude	1906.05.10	SLC	NY.New York	Hail & Aufwiedersehen	CU-MARK	07439
Natkin, Gertrude	1906.05.13	SLC	NY.New York	with the love	418:1972.11.28	10464 inscription

ADDRESSEE	DATE	WRITER	PLACE	CUE	SOURCE	NUMBER/NOTES
Natkin, Gertrude	1906.11.30	SLC	NY.New York	The same to	CU-MARK	07578 telegram
Natkin, Gertrude	1906.12.**	SLC	NY.New York	Wish you same	CU-MARK(tr)	07585
Natkin, Gertrude	1906.12.31	SLC	NY.New York	A happy New	CU-MARK	07603
Natkin, Gertrude	1907.01.**	SLC	NY.New York	The same to	CU-MARK	07608
Natkin, Gertrude	1908.12.31	SLC	CT.Redding	It is the	CU-MARK	08193
Nelson, Henry L.	1889.10.23	SLC	CT.Hartford	Great Scott, what	NN-B	02697
Nelson, Henry L.	1895.02.12	SLC	FR.Paris	Oh, but I	C4	04842
Nesbit, Edward P.	1895.10.13	SLC	AS.Adelaide	I am grateful	CU-MARK(ph)	10252
Nettie	1885.08.27	SLC	Unknown	Anybody can tell	Mo2	09340 inscription
New England Phono. Co.	1891.04.10	SLC per FGW	CT.Hartford	Mr. Clemens wired	CU-MARK	08619
New England Society	****.11.07	SLC	NY.New York	To respond to	157:1911.01.12	09800 other sources
New York Even. Post ed.	1908.08.25	SLC	CT.Redding	If you had	CU-MARK(tr)	08091
New York Evening Post	1876.07.22	SLC	NY.Elmira	Now when there	CU-MARK(tr)	01350
New York Evening Post	1880.09.14	SLC	NY.Elmira	I have just	119:1880.09.16	01833
New York governor	1909.**.**	SLC	CT.Redding	We your petitioners	CU-MARK(dr)	08301
New York Graphic ed.	1873.04.17	SLC	CT.Hartford	Your note is	313:1873.04.22	00901
New York Herald	bef 1887.12.15	SLC	CT.Hartford	At this time	314:1887.12.15	03677
New York Independent or Ward, William H.	****.05.03	SLC	CT.Hartford	Although I have	CU-MARK(tr)	07672
New York Journal	bef 1910.03.03	SLC	BE.Hamilton	Not ill enough	315:1910.03.03	09474
New York Medical School	o/a 1907.04.17	SLC per IVL	NY.New York	It is not	CU-MARK(dr)	07694 on Medical School n.d.
New York Press Club	1869.06.01	SLC	NY.Elmira	I thank you	ViU	00312
New York Sheriff's Jury	ca 1901.02.15	SLC	NY.New York	I will not	317:1901.02.15	05998
New York Sun ed.	1885.**.**	SLC	Unknown	I find the	NPV	03087
New York Sun ed.	1885.07.27	SLC	NY.Elmira	The newspaper atmosphere	114:456	03267
New York Times ed.	1874.10.09	SLC	CT.Hartford	In this morning's	131:1874.10.12	01137
New York Times ed.	1875.04.26	SLC	CT.Hartford	I have just	131:1875.04.29	01227

New York Times ed.	1909.03.29	JC	NJ.Montclair	Is it possible	CU-MARK(tr)	08378
New York Tribune ed.	*	*	*	*	*	10325 see also Reid, Whitelaw
New York Tribune ed.	1870.12.29	SLC	NY.Buffalo	John H. Surratt's	317:1871.01.04	10334 misdated, see Dec 31
New York Tribune ed.	1870.12.31	SLC	NY.Buffalo	John H. Surratt's	317:1871.01.04	02792 misdated Dec 29
New York Tribune ed.	1871.04.29	SLC	NY.Elmira	I believe in	317:1871.05.03	00608
New York Tribune ed.	1872.12.05	SLC	CT.Hartford	This Missouri case	317:1872.12.07	00841
New York Tribune ed.	1873.01.03	SLC	CT.Hartford	When you do	317:1873.01.06	00850 other sources
New York Tribune ed.	1873.01.06	SLC	CT.Hartford	Having explained who	317:1873.01.09	00854 other sources
New York Tribune ed.	1873.01.25	SLC	CT.Hartford	Some people do	317:1873.01.27	00867
New York Tribune ed.	1873.01.30	SLC	CT.Hartford	Can you send	NN	00870
New York Tribune ed.	1873.03.07	SLC	CT.Hartford	Please send 2	NN	00885
New York Tribune ed.	1873.04.08	SLC	CT.Hartford	When the Mississippi	317:1873.04.11	00898
New York Tribune ed.	1901.02.13	SLC	NY.New York	This is Rev.	CU-MARK(tr)	05994
New York Tribune ed.	1901.02.18	SLC	NY.New York	Several of your	CU-MARK(tr)	06004 SLC tr
New York Tribune ed.	bef 1905.11.04	SLC	Unknown	I expect to	317:1905.11.04	07195
New York World ed.	1877.02.14 & 1877.02.16	SLC	CT.Hartford	I see by	319:1877.02.18	01406
New York World ed.	1877.02.22	SLC	CT.Hartford	If you should	319:1877.02.25	01408
New York World ed.	1877.07.31	SLC	NY.New York	Will the night	CLSU	03779
New York World ed.	1907.11.**	SLC	Unknown	You ask me	ViU(tr)	07860
Newall, Arthur	o/a 1905.01.24	SLC per IVL	NY.New York	Mr. Clemens still	CU-MARK(dr)	06985 on Newall Jan 24
Newbegin, R.G.	1901.06.01	SLC	NY.New York	I shall be	107:1924.11.24	09450
Newcomb, Ethel	1909.12.24	SLC	CT.Redding	I thank you	CU-MARK(tr)	08514 telegram

ADDRESSEE	DATE	WRITER	PLACE	CUE	SOURCE	NUMBER/NOTES
Newman, Ethel	1897.04.23	SLC	EN.London	I thank you	CU-MARK(ph)	05206
Newton, Mr.	1894.01.01	SLC	Unknown	It would not	CU-MARK	04666
Nichols, Frank A.	aft 1885.03.18	SLC	CT.Hartford	I am in	CU-MARK	03179
Nichols, Miss C.A.	****.**.**	SLC	Unknown	Miss Nichols, please	ViU	08969
Nichols, Miss C.A.	pm 1898.01.27	SLC	AU.Vienna	Yes, do it	NN-B	05486
Niles, S.J.	o/a 1906.06.19	SLC per IVL	NH.Dublin	Nobody but the	CU-MARK(dr)	07461 on Niles June 19
Noel, Lillie T.	1906.03.10	SLC	NY.New York	The standard of	NN-B(tr)	07374
Nolde de, Baroness	1904.05.03	SLC per IVL	IT.Florence	Mr. Clemens wishes	CU-MARK	06826
Nolen, J.H.	o/a 1905.12.26	SLC per IVL	NY.New York	Thanks, value much	CU-MARK(dr)	07273 on Nolen Dec 26
Norris, Charles G.	1908.09.17	SLC	CT.Redding	Some day, I	NN-B	08285
North American Phono.	1888.07.30	SLC	NY.Elmira	I ordered two	CU-MARK(tr)	10907 enc in July 30 to FGW
North American Review	1902.10.30	SLC	NY.Riverdale	I have mailed	CU-MARK(ph)	10578
North American Review or Munro, David A.	bef 1903.01.12	SLC	NY.Riverdale	Private. If McCrackan	CU-MARK	08692
North, E.D.	1900.11.**	SLC	NY.New York	E.D. North, Esq	105:1953.10.27	09665 inscription
Northcliffe, Lady	*	*	*	*	*	11167 see Harnsworth, Mary M.
Norton, Charles E.	ca 1880.07.**	SLC	NY.Elmira	I should certainly	111:156	04370
Norton, Charles E.	1881.07.24	SLC	CT.Branford	Yes indeed, I	CU-MARK	01988
Norton, Charles E.	1881.08.23	SLC	NY.Elmira	I have been	111:369 CU-MARK	02012 other sources; CU-MARK envelope
Norton, Charles E.	1881.08.30	SLC	NY.Elmira	It is most	MH-H	02018
Norton, Charles E.	1884.08.06	SLC	NY.Elmira	Mrs. Clemens came	CU-MARK	01482
Norton, O.W.	1906.10.12	SLC per IVL	NH.Dublin	I am just	CU-MARK(tr)	07535

Nowell, Kate R.	1905.02.26	SLC	NY.New York	Indeed the portrait	CU-MARK(tr)	07008
Noyes, Edward F.	1879.03.18	SLC	FR.Paris	Conway tells me	CSmH	01642
Noyes, Edward F.	1881.02.26	SLC	CT.Hartford	Will you do	MiD	01916
Noyes, Miss	1882.02.23	SLC	CT.Hartford	It is a	CU-MARK	02163
Nunnally, Cora W.	1907.07.12	SLC	EN.London	with warm regards	CSmH	10696 inscription
Nunnally, Frances	1907.**.**	SLC per IVL	Unknown	I hope note	NPV(dr)	10909
Nunnally, Frances	1907.07.07	SLC	EN.London	Itinerary. (Subject to	CSmH	07780
Nunnally, Frances	1907.07.09	SLC	EN.London	the title of	CSmH	10698 inscription
Nunnally, Frances	1907.07.12	SLC	EN.London	with the affectionate	CSmH	10697 inscription
Nunnally, Frances	1907.08.03	SLC	NY.Tuxedo Park	Dear Francesca, if	CSmH	07806
Nunnally, Frances	1907.08.18	SLC	NY.Tuxedo Park	I am very	CSmH	09126
Nunnally, Frances	1907.09.25	SLC	NY.New York	I have just	CSmH	07774
Nunnally, Frances	1907.10.04	SLC	NY.Tuxedo Park	Thank you very	CSmH	07844
Nunnally, Frances	1907.10.28	SLC	NY.New York	Now, dear Francesca	CSmH	07858
Nunnally, Frances	1907.11.18	SLC	NY.New York	Francesca dear, I am	CSmH	07864
Nunnally, Frances	1907.11.27	SLC	NY.New York	I hope your	CSmH	07869 telegram
Nunnally, Frances	1907.12.20	SLC	NY.New York	I suppose you	CSmH	07888
Nunnally, Frances	1907.12.29	SLC	NY.New York	Ah, you dear	CSmH	07898
Nunnally, Frances	1908.01.15	SLC	NY.New York	Where are you	CSmH	07913
Nunnally, Frances	1908.01.21	SLC	NY.New York	I wish you	CSmH	07922
Nunnally, Frances	1908.02.08	SLC	NY.New York	Francesca dear, I	CSmH	07932
Nunnally, Frances	1908.02.24	SLC	BE.Hamilton	I got your	CSmH	07948
Nunnally, Frances	1908.03.10	SLC	BE.Hamilton	Yes, you dear	CSmH	07958
Nunnally, Frances	1908.03.14 & 1908.03.16	SLC	BE.Hamilton	I was very	CSmH	07961
Nunnally, Frances	1908.03.24	SLC	BE.Hamilton	Francesca dear, this	CSmH	07964
Nunnally, Frances	1908.03.31	SLC	BE.Hamilton	Your letter has	CSmH	07968

ADDRESSEE	DATE	WRITER	PLACE	CUE	SOURCE	NUMBER/NOTES
Nunnally, Frances	1908.05.01	SLC	NY.New York	The way you	CSmH	07990
Nunnally, Frances	1908.06.03	SLC	NY.New York	Franscesca dear, I am	CSmH	08016
Nunnally, Frances	1908.06.06	SLC	NY.New York	You are a	CSmH	08023
Nunnally, Frances	1908.06.20	SLC	CT.Redding	You dear little	CSmH	08038
Nunnally, Frances	1908.07.29	SLC	CT.Redding	Your letter arrived	CSmH	08063
Nunnally, Frances	1908.09.18	SLC	CT.Redding	Francesca dear, you	CSmH	08103
Nunnally, Frances	1908.10.10 & 1908.10.12	SLC	CT.Redding	I have had	CSmH	08133
Nunnally, Frances	1908.10.24 & 1908.10.31	SLC	CT.Redding	Yes, keep the	CSmH	08144
Nunnally, Frances	1908.11.01	SLC	CT.Redding	Francesca dear, don't	NN-B	08287
Nunnally, Frances	1908.12.09	SLC	CT.Redding	They will celebrate	CSmH	08174
Nunnally, Frances	1908.12.29	SLC	CT.Redding	Go it, dear	CSmH	08196
Nunnally, Frances	1909.02.09	SLC	CT.Redding	You dear Francesca	CSmH	08344
Nunnally, Frances	1909.02.17	SLC	CT.Redding	Oh, you sweet	CSmH	08356
Nunnally, Frances	1909.03.28	SLC	CT.Redding	Dearheart, where are	CSmH	08377
Nunnally, Frances	1909.04.29	SLC	CT.Redding	Snowing hard. No	CSmH	08393
Nunnally, Frances	1909.05.18	SLC	CT.Redding	Certainly, you dear	CSmH	08399
Nunnally, Frances	1909.06.07	SLC	CT.Redding	Yes, indeed, you	CSmH	08419
Nunnally, Frances	1909.06.18	SLC	CT.Redding	Well, no, you	CSmH	08422
Nunnally, Frances	pm 1909.07.15	SLC	CT.Redding	I can answer	CSmH	08413
Nunnally, Frances	1909.08.27	SLC	CT.Redding	Yes, I got	CSmH	08445
Nunnally, Frances	1909.09.27	SLC	CT.Redding	Francesca dear, you are	CSmH	08460
Nunnally, Frances	1909.12.14	SLC	BE.Hamilton	Francesca dear, I	CSmH	08510
Nunnally, Frances	ca 1909.12.17	SLC	BE.Hamilton	Love & Merry	CSmH	07895
Nye, Edgar W. (Bill) & Riley, James W.	1889.03.04	SLC	CT.Hartford	The St. Botolph	NN-B	02688
Nye, Edgar W. (Bill)	1890.04.17	SLC	CT.Hartford	I am just	326:286	04040
Nye, Fred	o/a 1906.01.12	SLC per IVL	NY.New York	I think it	CU-MARK(dr)	07305 on Nye Jan 12
Obersteiner, Heinrich	1897.10.05	SLC	AU.Vienna	I enclose a	NN5	05294

O'Connor, T.P.	o/a	1907.06.20	SLC	EN.London	Yes, I will	CU-MARK(dr)	07761 on O'Connor June 20
O'Connor, T.P.		1909.10.26	SLC	CT.Redding	I am living	CU-MARK	08475 typed
Oddie, Claire		1907.01.17	SLC	NY.New York	I was born	CU-MARK(tr)	07629
Ogden, Augusta	ca	1909.01.01	SLC	CT.Redding	It is a	IC3	08304
Ogden, Augusta		1909.09.22	SLC	CT.Redding	It is very	IC3	08458
Ogden, Augusta		1909.10.13	SLC	CT.Redding	Indeed yes! Greenwich	IC3	08467
Ogden, Augusta		1909.10.19	SLC	CT.Redding	Good--I shall	IC3	08472
Ogden, Augusta		1909.10.30	SLC	CT.Redding	It was shabby	IC3	08480
Ogle, Pelham		1885.11.15	SLC	CT.Hartford	Your kind note	NN	03308
Ohio Society		1901.03.**	SLC	NY.New York	I have at	274:341	06012
O'Lanus, Corry		*	*	*	*	*	10304 see Stanton, John
Oldroyd, Osborn H.		1874.02.17	SLC	CT.Hartford	Certainly I will	ICU	01050
Olds, Nathaniel S.		1902.04.21	SLC	NY.Riverdale	Between you and	MiD	06326
Omaha-World Herald		1902.08.23	SLC	ME.York Harbor	Your telegram has	131:1902.09.06	06414
O'Neil, Ellen & O'Neil, John	ca	****.12.25	JC	Unknown	the best of	CtHSD	10634
O'Neil, Ellen		1892.05.30	OLC	IT.Como	I wish I	CtHSD	10613
O'Neil, Ellen		1898.02.27	OLC	AU.Vienna	I was glad	CtHSD	10614
O'Neil, Ellen		1898.04.21	OLC	AU.Vienna	I was glad	CtHSD	10615
O'Neil, Ellen	pm	1901.09.13	OLC	NY.New York	I failed to	CtHSD	10618
O'Neil, Ellen		1901.12.23	OLC	NY.Riverdale	think, and then	CtHSD	10620 fragment
O'Neil, Ellen		1904.07.16	SLC	NY.New York	Of all the	ViU	06886
O'Neil, John & O'Neil, Ellen	ca	****.12.25	JC	Unknown	the best of	CtHSD	10634
O'Neil, John	pm	1900.10.27	OLC	NY.New York	*	CtHSD	10616 envelope only
O'Neil, John	pm	1901.02.13	OLC	NY.New York	Will you send	CtHSD	10617

ADDRESSEE	DATE	WRITER	PLACE	CUE	SOURCE	NUMBER/NOTES
O'Neil, John	pm 1901.11.29	OLC	NY.Riverdale	Will you send	CtHSD	10619
Onteora Club ladies	1890.09.27	SLC	CT.Hartford	The "Mort de	Mo2	08936
Oppenheimer Institute	1905.11.**	SLC	NY.New York	I beg to	CU-MARK(dr)	07191
Orcutt, Mrs. William & Orcutt, William D.	1904.06.03 or 1904.06.04	SLC	IT.Florence	They are superb	145:172f	06855
Orcutt, William D. & Orcutt, Mrs. William	1904.06.03 or 1904.06.04	SLC	IT.Florence	They are superb	145:172f	06855
Ordway, Edward W.	1901.02.03	SLC	NY.New York	I myself have	NN	05987
Ordway, Edward W.	1901.05.01	SLC	NY.New York	I am very	NN	06049
Ordway, Edward W.	1902.01.14	SLC	NY.Riverdale	I only want	NN	06244
Ordway, Edward W.	1902.11.02	SLC	NY.Riverdale	Although I cannot	NN	06480
Ordway, Edward W.	1905.01.**	SLC per IVL	Unknown	Mr. Clemens directs	CU-MARK	06979
Ordway, Edward W.	1905.01.13	SLC	NY.New York	Yes, I shall	NN	06982
Orr, Charles	1906.07.30	SLC	NH.Dublin	I cannot thank	NjP	07486
Osborn, Lucretia T.	1903.01.19	SLC	NY.Riverdale	The grace &	116:1975.10.16	09973
Osborne, Duffield	1906.01.31	SLC	NY.New York	The recommendation to	CU-MARK(tr)	07320
Osborne, Duffield	o/a 1906.03.17	SLC per IVL	NY.New York	Yes certainly--use	CU-MARK(dr)	07391 on Osborne Mar 17
Osgood, James R.	****.**.**	SLC	Unknown	You better go	175:1894.11.28	09878
Osgood, James R.	****.**.**	SLC	Unknown	Ask Howells if	MH-H	08970
Osgood, James R.	****.03.13	SLC	Unknown	I've accepted Hutton's	NjP	08973
Osgood, James R.	****.05.28	SLC	CT.Hartford	I think Mr.	175:1898.03.31	09867
Osgood, James R.	bet 1872.03.24 & 1872.04.07	SLC	NY.Elmira	Indeed I would	NjP	00739
Osgood, James R.	ca 1873.07.**	SLC	EN.London	Enclosed is a	415:53	00937
Osgood, James R.	1875.01.13	SLC	CT.Hartford	Indeed I wish	MH-H	01179
Osgood, James R.	1875.02.12	SLC	CT.Hartford	Concerning that	MH-H	01193
Osgood, James R.	1875.07.13	SLC	CT.Hartford	Do you see	MH-H	01249
Osgood, James R.	1875.07.20	SLC	CT.Hartford	It seems a	CtY	01251
Osgood, James R.	1875.07.23	SLC	CT.Hartford	A Card My idea is	MH-H CU-MARK(tr)	01254

Osgood, James R.		1875.08.16	SLC	RI.Newport	You see, per	MH-H	01257
Osgood, James R.		1876.01.17	SLC	CT.Hartford	Yes, hand the	MH-H	01298
Osgood, James R.		1876.01.25	SLC	CT.Hartford	Yes I would	MH-H	01302
Osgood, James R.		1880.10.19	SLC	CT.Hartford	Am very much	402:C	10668 other sources
Osgood, James R.		1880.11.17	SLC	CT.Hartford	You just look	297:17	01854 other sources
Osgood, James R.		1880.11.26	SLC	CT.Hartford	Seems to me	MH-H	01856 ca Nov 26 to Garfield enc
Osgood, James R.		1880.12.13	SLC	CT.Hartford	I don't like	CU-MARK(ph)	01871
Osgood, James R.		1880.12.16	SLC	CT.Hartford	I am mighty	CU-MARK(ph)	01873
Osgood, James R.		1881.01.21	SLC	CT.Hartford	I enclose note	105:1941.12.10	01894 other sources
Osgood, James R.	ca	1881.01.23	SLC	CT.Hartford	That concern is	MH-H	01895
Osgood, James R.		1881.02.01	SLC	CT.Hartford	Here is what	CAlb2	01901
Osgood, James R.		1881.02.12	SLC	CT.Hartford	Mrs. Clemens will	MH-H	01907
Osgood, James R.		1881.03.07	SLC	CT.Hartford	First & foremost	MH-H	01924
Osgood, James R.	bet &	1881.03.09 1881.03.10	SLC	CT.Hartford	It is rumored	MH-H	01925
Osgood, James R.		1881.03.26	SLC	CT.Hartford	Now before you	MH-H	01931
Osgood, James R.		1881.03.30	SLC	CT.Hartford	Yes, must have	NN-B	02551
Osgood, James R.		1881.05.07	SLC	CT.Hartford	If the matter	CCC	01949
Osgood, James R.		1881.05.16	SLC	CT.Hartford	Many thanks for	212:1948.04.24	10435
Osgood, James R.		1881.05.30	SLC	CT.Hartford	I signed the	CU-MARK	01961
Osgood, James R.		1881.06.03	SLC	CT.Hartford	I have ciphered	IU-R	01968
Osgood, James R.		1881.08.22	SLC	NY.Elmira	All right--but	MH-H	02011
Osgood, James R.		1881.08.23	SLC	NY.Elmira	My Dear Osgood	418:1974.11.19	02013
Osgood, James R.		1881.10.02	SLC	CT.Hartford	Have just arrived	ViU	02041
Osgood, James R.		1881.10.10	SLC	CT.Hartford	Forgot to say	107:1925.04.16	09637
Osgood, James R.		1881.10.19	SLC	CT.Hartford	I have filled	TxU	02056
Osgood, James R.		1881.10.21	SLC	CT.Hartford	Ned House calls	CtY	02058

ADDRESSEE	DATE	WRITER	PLACE	CUE	SOURCE	NUMBER/NOTES
Osgood, James R.	1881.10.24	SLC	CT.Hartford	Here is an	CU-MARK	02060
Osgood, James R.	1881.10.24	SLC	CT.Hartford	I am going	CU-MARK(ph)	02061
Osgood, James R.	1881.10.25	SLC	CT.Hartford	Wouldn't it answer	CU-MARK	02064
Osgood, James R.	1881.10.27	SLC	CT.Hartford	If the North	134:1916.11.03	09947
Osgood, James R.	1881.10.27	SLC	CT.Hartford	I'm setting up	CU-MARK(ph)	02074
Osgood, James R.	1881.10.28	SLC	CT.Hartford	How would it	NN-B	02555
Osgood, James R.	1881.10.31	SLC	CT.Hartford	O, I see	PU	02078
Osgood, James R.	1881.11.01	SLC	Unknown	I forgot. Howells's	MH-H	02079
Osgood, James R.	1881.11.02	SLC	CT.Hartford	Shall come per	CU-MARK	11171 telegram; unsent
Osgood, James R.	1881.11.02	SLC	CT.Hartford	Please preserve these	CU-MARK	02081 dr letters enc
Osgood, James R.	o/a 1881.11.05	SLC	Unknown	I told Webster	CU-MARK	09346 on Langdon Nov 5
Osgood, James R.	1881.11.28	SLC	CN.Montreal	Have just returned	MH-H	02104
Osgood, James R.	1881.12.08	SLC	CN.Montreal	Here is the	MoSW	02112
Osgood, James R.	1881.12.12	SLC	CT.Hartford	Will you send	NhD	02116
Osgood, James R.	1881.12.29	SLC	CT.Hartford	I enclose a	NN-B	02559
Osgood, James R.	1881.12.31	SLC	CT.Hartford	Never mind. Crane	MH-H	02130
Osgood, James R.	1882.01.04	SLC	CT.Hartford	India-paper books	ViU	02142
Osgood, James R.	1882.01.07	SLC	CT.Hartford	Glad to hear	MH-H	02145
Osgood, James R.	1882.01.25	SLC	CT.Hartford	If you &	CU-MARK	02154
Osgood, James R.	1882.02.12	SLC	CT.Hartford	I didn't know	MH-H	02159
Osgood, James R.	bef 1882.03.02	SLC	CT.Hartford	won't let howells	CU-MARK(tr)	10437 telegram
Osgood, James R.	1882.03.04	SLC	CT.Hartford	I's gwyne to	NN-B	02561
Osgood, James R.	1882.03.25	SLC	Unknown	Good; you stop	FG2	09117
Osgood, James R.	bef 1882.04.01	SLC	NY.New York	Submit this to	MH-H	02183
Osgood, James R.	1882.04.07	SLC	CT.Hartford	1. I have	MH-H	02197
Osgood, James R.	1882.04.14	SLC	CT.Hartford	All right, call	ViU	02135

Osgood, James R.	ca	1882.04.15	SLC	Unknown	You need to	CU-MARK	01541 on Slote Apr 15
Osgood, James R.		1882.05.12	SLC	CT.Hartford	Old man, you	CU-MARK(tr)	09209
Osgood, James R.		1882.06.03	SLC	CT.Hartford	Have written to	NN-B	02562
Osgood, James R.		1882.06.11	SLC	CT.Hartford	I wish you	CU-MARK(ph)	08975
Osgood, James R.		1882.07.19	SLC	NY.Elmira	Won't you please	CtY	02238
Osgood, James R.		1882.09.15	SLC	NY.Elmira	Am mailing you	282:1910.02.15	09749
Osgood, James R.		1882.09.18	SLC	NY.Elmira	Welcome home! I	CU-MARK(tr)	02269
Osgood, James R.		1882.10.18	SLC	CT.Hartford	I am sending	ViU	02292
Osgood, James R.		1882.12.29	SLC	CT.Hartford	I shipped all	NNPM	02320
Osgood, James R.		1883.01.15	SLC	CT.Hartford	Old man, you	CtY	02334
Osgood, James R.		1883.01.21	SLC	CT.Hartford	I have read	CU-MARK(ph)	01632
Osgood, James R.	aft	1883.01.21	SLC	CT.Hartford	Knock this picture	121:138f	08820
Osgood, James R.		1883.02.02	SLC	Unknown	that chapter which	282:1910.02.15	09748
Osgood, James R.		1883.04.06	SLC	CT.Hartford	Cable read Parson	CLjC	02803
Osgood, James R.		1883.04.17	SLC	CT.Hartford	Nevertheless I am	MH-H	02372
Osgood, James R.		1883.09.01	SLC	NY.Elmira	Welcome home, &	WE	04139
Osgood, James R.		1883.12.21	SLC	CT.Hartford	No, I shall	MH-H	02872
Osgood, James R.		1884.01.**	SLC	Unknown	I expected to	NPV	10905
Osgood, James R.		1884.01.17	SLC	CT.Hartford	I have thought	MH-H	02890
Osgood, James R.		1884.03.20	SLC	CT.Hartford	I received the	MH-H	02937
Osgood, James R.		1884.05.24	SLC	CT.Hartford	The left-over sketches	NjP	02985
Osgood, James R.		1890.03.20	SLC	CT.Hartford	What is the	MH-H	04030
Osgood (J.R.) & Co.		1880.11.28	SLC	CT.Hartford	Please send me	260:1958.07.15	01859
Osgood (J.R.) & Co.		1881.05.23	SLC	CT.Hartford	Enclosed please find	ViU	01959
Osgood (J.R.) & Co.		1881.06.16	SLC	CT.Branford	Please find enclosed	ViU	01972
Osgood (J.R.) & Co.		1881.07.02	SLC	CT.Branford	Hold on--hold	CtY	01980
Osgood (J.R.) & Co.	ca	1881.08.06	SLC	NY.Elmira	From Charles Dudley	Mo2	09234 on Warner July 31

ADDRESSEE	DATE	WRITER	PLACE	CUE	SOURCE	NUMBER/NOTES
Osgood (J.R.) & Co.	1881.10.15	SLC	CT.Hartford	Dam the dam	CSmH	02054
Osgood (J.R.) & Co.	1881.10.21	SLC	Unknown	Please send me	CU-MARK	08618
Osgood (J.R.) & Co.	1881.12.28	SLC	CT.Hartford	Sylvester Baxter, of	MH-H	02128
Osgood (J.R.) & Co.	1883.01.06	SLC	CT.Hartford	Yes, make two	ViU	02331
Osler, William	1909.09.21	SLC	CT.Redding	I wish I	IAurC	08456
Otremba, F.N.	1908.11.30	SLC per IVL	CT.Redding	The mantel is	WU(ph)	08163
Overshiner, E.B.	o/a 1907.01.03	SLC per IVL	NY.New York	Should like to	CU-MARK(dr)	07620 on Overshiner Jan 3
Owsley, Elizabeth	*	*	*	*	*	10872 see Hatch, Elizabeth
Packard, Silas S.	1869.06.01	SLC	NY.Elmira	Can't come--enclose	ViU	00311 date uncertain
Packard, Silas S.	1869.09.21	SLC	NY.Buffalo	Taint any use	328:1885.04	00356 date uncertain
Packard's Short-Hand	****.**.**	SLC	Unknown	No; I only	328:1885.01	08997
Paderewski, Helena G.	1907.12.09	SLC	NY.New York	I am glad	105:1960.11.29	09702 inscription
Paderewski, Ignace J.	1908.01.**	SLC per IVL	NY.New York	My excuse for	CU-MARK	07903
Pae, David	o/a 1906.01.26	SLC per IVL	NY.New York	not familiar enough	CU-MARK(dr)	07317 on Pae Jan 26
Page, Miss	aft 1892.05.01	SLC	IT.Florence	I am the	Mo2	08941
Page, Miss	aft 1892.05.01	SLC	IT.Florence	Mrs. Clemens had	Mo2	02452
Page, Miss	1892.11.08	SLC	IT.Florence	I wish to	Mo2	02401
Page, Walter H. & Walker, John B.	1903.07.21	SLC	NY.Elmira	Although I have	NN-B	11121 also to others
Paige, James W.	1886.08.16	SLC	NY.Elmira	At last I	CtHMTH	03439
Paige, James W.	1886.11.13	SLC	CT.Hartford	On what date	CU-MARK	10753 on Schuckers Nov 12
Paige, James W.	1890.12.24	SLC	CT.Hartford	From what I	CU-MARK	04120
Paige, James W.	1890.12.31	SLC	CT.Hartford	I think, myself	CU-MARK(tr)	04122 SLC tr

Paige, James W.		1890.12.31	SLC per FGW	CT.Hartford	Mr Clemens desires	CU-MARK	04123
Paige, James W.		1891.01.03	SLC per FGW	CT.Hartford	I have received	CU-MARK(tr)	04152 FGW tr
Paige, James W.		1891.01.04	SLC	CT.Hartford	I am glad	CU-MARK(tr)	04154 SLC tr
Paige, James W.		1891.02.10	SLC	CT.Hartford	I had already	CU-MARK(tr)	04170 SLC tr
Paige, James W.		1891.03.19	SLC	CT.Hartford	Yours is at	ViU(tr)	04182
Paine, Albert B.		****.**.**	SLC	Unknown	with kindest regards	ViU	11102 inscription
Paine, Albert B.	o/a	1908.10.07	SLC	CT.Redding	Greeting and Salutation	122:1937.11.11	10515 form letter
Paine, Albert B.		1909.**.**	SLC	BE.Hamilton	I want Helen	NN2	08302
Paine, Albert B.		1910.01.11	SLC	BE.Hamilton	There was a	114:837	08537
Paine, Albert B.	o/a	1910.01.20	SLC	BE.Hamilton	Paine, write her	CStoC	09412 on Miller Jan 20
Paine, Albert B.		1910.01.21	SLC	BE.Hamilton	Thanks for your	114:838	08544
Paine, Albert B.		1910.01.24	SLC	BE.Hamilton	Can you get	CU-MARK(ph)	08546
Paine, Albert B.		1910.01.26	SLC	BE.Hamilton	in a desperate	COMC	08549
Paine, Albert B.		1910.02.03	SLC	BE.Hamilton	I've got some	120:1940.12	10733
Paine, Albert B.	&	1910.02.05 1910.02.07	SLC	BE.Hamilton	Your preliminary report	WU(tr)	08555
Paine, Albert B.		1910.02.14	SLC	BE.Hamilton	Don't you think	WU	08556
Paine, Albert B.	ca	1910.03.30	SLC	BE.Hamilton	We must look	114:841	08576
Paine, Albert B.	ca	1910.04.01	SLC	BE.Hamilton	I have been	114:842	08577
Paine, Albert B.		1910.04.21	SLC	CT.Redding	bring me my	CU-MARK	08582
Paine, Louise		1908.09.30	SLC	CT.Redding	I was very	CtRe	08112
Paine, Louise		1908.11.04	SLC	CT.Redding	I don't expect	414:1958.06.19	08151
Pall Mall Gazette ed.		1889.01.28	SLC	CT.Hartford	But you do	400:1889.02.16	09086
Palmer, Charles T.		1882.10.03	SLC	CT.Hartford	All the questions	CU-BANC	02284 typed
Palmer, Courtlandt		1886.01.20	SLC	CT.Hartford	Nein! I thought	NNAL	03357

ADDRESSEE	DATE	WRITER	PLACE	CUE	SOURCE	NUMBER/NOTES
Palmer, C.S.	o/a 1906.09.26	SLC	NH.Dublin	Pressure of work	ViU(dr)	07530 on Palmer Sept 26
Palmer, Frederick	o/a 1907.02.06	SLC per IVL	NY.New York	If you will	CU-MARK(dr)	08822 on Palmer Feb 6
Parish, Emma	1874.08.29	SLC	NY.Elmira	My mother has	100:1933.07.10f	01121
Parish, Emma	1874.09.20	SLC	CT.Hartford	I got your	100:1933.07.10	01126 other sources
Parish, Emma	1874.11.**	SLC	CT.Hartford	Susie? Susie resembles	CU-MARK(tr)	01142 addressee uncertain
Parish, Emma	1874.11.10	SLC	CT.Hartford	Bless you, don't	CU-MARK(tr)	01147
Parker, Dr.	1886.12.06	SLC	CT.Hartford	Will you dine	ViU	03492
Parker, Edwin P.	1880.05.15	SLC	CT.Hartford	Being taken suddenly	ViU	01805
Parker, Edwin P.	o/a 1880.12.22	SLC	CT.Hartford	I wish you	ViU	01876
Parker, Edwin P.	1880.12.24	SLC	CT.Hartford	I thank you	NN-B	02547
Parker, Edwin P.	1881.12.20	SLC	CT.Hartford	With the warmest	NN-B	10807 inscription
Parker, Edwin P.	1883.04.** or 1883.04.**	SLC	CT.Hartford	With kindest regards of	ODa2	11190 inscription
Parker, Edwin P.	1898.08.02	SLC	AU.Kaltenleut.	Motto to chew	ODa2	05418 inscription
Parker, Edwin P.	1903.10.14	SLC	NY.New York	When I read	ViU	06743
Parker, Louis N.	1907.06.18	SLC	EN.London	Twice I saw	CU-MARK(tr)	07746 telegram
Parker, Mr.	1893.12.31	SLC	NY.New York	I comply with	ODa2	09077
Parkhurst, Clinton	1883.01.25	SLC	CT.Hartford	No, if my	IaHi	09242
Parkhurst, L.E.	1889.12.20	SLC	CT.Hartford	I should not	CtY	03991
Parkhurst, W.E.	1885.04.07	SLC	CT.Hartford	W.E. Parkhurst	462:47	11163 inscription
Parsloe, Charles T.	1877.05.07	SLC	CT.Hartford	I am on	131:1877.05.08	01428 telegram
Parsons, Floyd & Archer, Sally	****.**.**	SLC	Unknown	Yes, I received	CU-MARK	08744
Parsons, Francis	1883.06.13	SC & CC	CT.Hartford	Susy & Clara	CtHMTH	09326

Parsons, Frank		1901.05.06	SLC per FAR	NY.New York	I wish I	CtY	09119 typed per unknown amanuensis
Parsons, George		1907.07.29	SLC	NY.Tuxedo Park	I thank you	InU-Li	07794
Parvin, Theodore S.		1890.03.18	SLC per FGW	CT.Hartford	In reply to	IaCrM	00594
Patterson, Ada	o/a	1906.03.14	SLC per IVL	NY.New York	Mr. Clemens couldn't	CU-MARK(dr)	07385 on Patterson Mar 14
Patterson, Mabel L.		1908.10.02	SLC	CT.Redding	The contents of	114:821	08119
Paxson, Katherine L.	aft	1904.11.23	SLC	NY.New York	I seem to	461:1907.01.28	11149
Peabody, Frederick W.		1902.12.05	SLC	NY.Riverdale	Have you a	CU-MARK(ph)	10635
Peabody, Frederick W.		1902.12.05	SLC	NY.Riverdale	Yes, I think	CU-MARK(ph)	06499
Peabody, Frederick W.		1902.12.15	SLC	NY.Riverdale	I shall take	CU-MARK(ph)	06516
Peabody, Frederick W.		1903.01.10	SLC	NY.Riverdale	But aren't you	CU-MARK(ph)	10636
Peabody, Frederick W.		1903.01.14	SLC	NY.Riverdale	I am very	CU-MARK(ph)	06559
Peabody, Frederick W.		1903.04.04	SLC	NY.Riverdale	That is a	CU-MARK(ph)	06613
Peabody, Josephine P.	ca	1905.12.25	SLC	Unknown	To you, &	Mo2	11013 form letter
Pearmain, S.B.	ca	1906.12.15	SLC per IVL	NY.New York	Mr. Clemens has	CU-MARK(dr)	07584
Pears, Muriel M.		1901.12.04	SLC	NY.Riverdale	Continue to keep	CtY	06182
Pears, Muriel M.		1902.**.**	SLC	Unknown	P.S. Did you	CU-MARK	06208
Pears, Muriel M.		1902.01.21	CC	NY.Riverdale	You, knowing Time	CtY	06251
Pears, Muriel M.		1902.02.14	SLC	NY.Riverdale	Impale it on	CtY	06276 on printed card
Pears, Muriel M.		1902.06.21	SLC	NY.Riverdale	You were to	CtY	06372
Pears, Muriel M.		1902.10.13	SLC	ME.York Harbor	You being the	CtY	06460
Pears, Muriel M.		1902.12.15	SLC	NY.Riverdale	There isn't going	CtY	06517
Pears, Muriel M.		1903.01.14	SLC	NY.Riverdale	Clara is a	CtY	06560
Pears, Muriel M.		1903.10.17	SLC	NY.New York	It isn't that	CtY	06744
Pears, Muriel M.		1904.01.04	SLC	IT.Florence	I cannot say	CtY	06781

ADDRESSEE		DATE	WRITER	PLACE	CUE	SOURCE	NUMBER/NOTES
Pears, Muriel M.		1904.05.09	SLC	IT.Florence	It's a long	CtY	06831
Pears, Muriel M.	ca	1904.06.21	SLC	IT.Florence	For what you	CtY	06848 form letter
Pears, Muriel M.		1904.10.23	SLC	NY.New York	That will (presently)	TxU	06935
Pears, Muriel M.		1905.02.18	SLC	NY.New York	It was delightful	CtY	07002
Pears, Muriel M.		1905.03.13	SLC	NY.New York	This is indeed	CtY	07017
Pears, Muriel M.		1905.07.26	SLC	NH.Dublin	With great pleasure	CtY	07090
Pears, Muriel M.		1905.10.11	SLC	NH.Dublin	When my letter	CtY	07172
Pears, Muriel M.		1908.06.29	CC	EN.London	We are leaving	CtY	08043
Pearson, T. Gilbert	o/a	1906.03.20	SLC per IVL	NY.New York	Letters should be	CU-MARK(dr)	07397 on Pearson Mar 20
Pease, Lucius C.		1895.08.21	SLC	CN.Victoria	Good enough. You	128:1983.07	10869 telegram
Peck, E.B.		1882.02.11	SLC	CT.Hartford	If I might	TxU	02158
Peltier, P.D.		1879.10.14	SLC	NY.Elmira	Please receive my	Mo2	01699
Pemberton-Hinks, Mrs.		****.**.**	SLC	NY.New York	a most piratical-looking	155:1966.07.13	10466 inscription
Pendleton, Louis		1888.08.04	SLC	NY.Elmira	I found your	114:497	03747
Pennsylvania Hist.Soc.		1885.12.08	SLC	CT.Hartford	Mr. SL Clemens begs	PHi	03327
Perkins, Charles E.		****.09.29	SLC	Unknown	Your notice of	CtHMTH	07545
Perkins, Charles E.		1872.05.08	SLC	NY.Elmira	I have received	CtHMTH	00745
Perkins, Charles E.		1874.05.08	SLC	NY.Elmira	Of course the	CtHMTH	01085 Apr 23 to Hartford city enc
Perkins, Charles E.	bet &	1875.06.01 1875.07.31	SLC	CT.Hartford	P.S. Hadn't we	CtHMTH	01382
Perkins, Charles E.		1876.10.05	SLC	CT.Hartford	If I thought	CtHMTH	01370
Perkins, Charles E.		1876.10.16	SLC	CT.Hartford	Will you let	CtHMTH	01376
Perkins, Charles E.		1876.10.20	SLC	CT.Hartford	Received the Philadephia	CtHMTH	01378
Perkins, Charles E.		1876.12.11	SLC	CT.Hartford	Raymond still waits	CtHMTH	01393
Perkins, Charles E.		1876.12.20	SLC	CT.Hartford	Shall go to	CtHMTH	01395

Perkins, Charles E.	pm	1877.01.22	SLC	CT.Hartford	Have you sent	CtHMTH	01402 date uncertain
Perkins, Charles E.		1877.04.26	SLC	MD.Baltimore	Please tell Bergen	CtHMTH	01417
Perkins, Charles E.	bet &	1877.05.04 1877.05.16	SLC	CT.Hartford	You perceive, Mr.	CtHMTH	01423
Perkins, Charles E.		1877.05.15	SLC	CT.Hartford	Please drop Harte	CtHMTH	01432
Perkins, Charles E.		1877.06.12	SLC	NY.Elmira	Enclosed is the	CtHMTH	01440
Perkins, Charles E.		1877.07.04	SLC	NY.Elmira	I have learned	CtHMTH	01445
Perkins, Charles E.		1877.07.07	SLC	NY.Elmira	I am astounded	CtHMTH CU-MARK	01448 CU-MARK enc
Perkins, Charles E.		1877.07.07	SLC	NY.Elmira	Telegraph me Bergens	CtHMTH	01447 telegram
Perkins, Charles E.		1877.08.03	SLC	NY.Elmira	Just back from	CtHMTH	01463
Perkins, Charles E.		1877.08.03	SLC	NY.Elmira	Mine & Bret	CtHMTH	01464
Perkins, Charles E.	pm	1877.08.11	SLC	NY.Elmira	Apply to Chas.	CtHMTH	01469
Perkins, Charles E.	o/a	1877.08.17	SLC	NY.Elmira	Mr. Perkins, do	CtHMTH	01472 on Bissell & Co. bill Aug 17
Perkins, Charles E.		1877.09.20	SLC	CT.Hartford	Mr. Perkins, please	CtHMTH	01485
Perkins, Charles E.		1877.09.21	SLC	CT.Hartford	I have told	CtHMTH	01486
Perkins, Charles E.		1877.09.24	SLC	CT.Hartford	Edwards wrote, a	CtHMTH	01488
Perkins, Charles E.	ca	1877.10.01	SLC	CT.Hartford	The Routledges wrote	CtHMTH	01489 on Dore Sept 21
Perkins, Charles E.	pm	1877.10.04	SLC	CT.Hartford	Please re-mail that	CtHMTH	01491
Perkins, Charles E.	o/a	1877.10.05	SLC	CT.Hartford	The agreement was	CtHMTH	01492
Perkins, Charles E.		1877.10.14	SLC	CT.Hartford	If you approve	CtHMTH	01494
Perkins, Charles E.		1877.10.18	SLC	CT.Hartford	Send this or	CtHMTH	01497
Perkins, Charles E.	o/a	1877.10.19	SLC	CT.Hartford	I suppose they	CtHMTH	03233 on Davies Oct 19
Perkins, Charles E.		1877.12.28	SLC	CT.Hartford	Nothing from Bergen	CtHMTH	01521
Perkins, Charles E.	ca	1879.07.**	SLC	Unknown	Just pile in	CtHMTH	09843 fragment

ADDRESSEE	DATE	WRITER	PLACE	CUE	SOURCE	NUMBER/NOTES
Perkins, Charles E.	1879.09.09	SLC	NY.Elmira	Keep the key	CtHMTH	01688
Perkins, Charles E.	1879.11.07	SLC	CT.Hartford	Please examine this	CU-MARK	01711 contract enc
Perkins, Charles E.	1880.09.13	SLC	NY.Elmira	I invested $4,500	CtHMTH	01831 on Bissell Sept 13
Perkins, Charles E.	1880.09.23	SLC	CT.Hartford	I found your	CtHMTH	08623
Perkins, Charles E.	1880.10.25	SLC	CT.Hartford	Hereafter, please	CtHMTH	01846
Perkins, Charles E.	1881.02.03	SLC	CT.Hartford	Please cast your	CtHMTH	01904
Perkins, Charles E.	1881.02.25	SLC	CT.Hartford	Have you Mills's	CtHMTH	01915
Perkins, Charles E.	1881.07.02	SLC	CT.Branford	I thought that	CtHMTH	01981
Perkins, Charles E.	1881.12.12	SLC	CT.Hartford	Will you put	CtHMTH	01739
Perkins, Charles E.	1882.09.02	SLC	NY.Elmira	Please put in	CtHMTH	02262
Perkins, Charles E.	1882.09.06	SLC	NY.Elmira	Will you please	CtHMTH	02265
Perkins, Lucy A.	****.**.**	SLC	CT.Hartford	Livy's abed yet	ODa2	11180
Perkins, Miss	1880.04.30	SLC	CT.Hartford	Yes, it is	CtY	01796
Perkins, Mrs. Charles	*	*	*	*	*	11209 see Perkins, Lucy A.
Perry, Bliss	1902.10.14	SLC	NY.Riverdale	It is quite	MH-H	06462
Perry, Bliss	1903.01.12	SLC per IVL	NY.Riverdale	We feel alike	MH-H	06555
Perry, Delle W.	o/a 1907.02.20	SLC per IVL	NY.New York	To be likened	CU-MARK(dr)	07655 on Perry Feb 20
Pew, Marlen E.	o/a 1905.09.28	SLC per IVL	NH.Dublin	Mr. Clemens will	CU-MARK(dr)	07151 on Pew Sept 28
Pfaff, Harriet L.	*	*	*	*	*	10306 see Lewis, Harriet
Phelps, Marian	1893.02.14	SLC	IT.Florence	The purpose of	CSmH	04339
Phelps, William L.	1901.04.24	SLC	NY.New York	I was not	CtY	06044 typed
Phelps, William L.	1909.12.13	JC	CT.Redding	Father is in	CtY	08509
Phelps, William L.	1910.03.12	SLC	BE.Hamilton	I thank you	MoHM	08571

Phelps, William W.	1891.10.**	SLC	Unknown	I shall be	CSmH	04239
Phelps, William W.	bet 1891.10.** & 1891.12.**	SLC	GE.Berlin	We accept with	CSmH	04249
Phelps, William W.	1892.08.05	SLC	GE.Bad-Nauheim	If you had	CSmH	01649
Phelps, William W.	1892.09.24	SLC	IT.Florence	There is a	CSmH	02295
Phelps, William W.	1893.01.02	SLC	IT.Florence	But don't you	CSmH	04319
Phelps, William W.	1893.05.29	SLC	IT.Florence	Hail & farewell	CSmH	04407
Phelps, W.J.	1907.08.05	SLC	NY.Tuxedo Park	a conversation with	CU-MARK(tr)	07808 on Phelps July 30
Philippi, Louis	1875.12.25	SLC	Unknown	Louis Phillippi from	441:1927.07.19	10344 inscription
Phillips, Horatio G.	1861.10.29	SLC	NV.Carson City	Bob showed me	TxU	00032
Phillips, Mary E.	1901.02.14	SLC	NY.New York	I am so	MB	05996
Phillips, Mary E.	1901.02.16	SLC	NY.New York	The book is	MB	06002 typed
Phillips, Mary E.	1901.04.14	SLC	NY.New York	As a rule	MB(tr)	06036
Phillips, Mary E.	1904.08.08	SLC	MA.Lee	For what you	MB	06911 form letter
Phillpotts, Eden	1907.06.21	SLC	EN.London	First the lovely	CU-MARK(ph)	09402
Phillpotts, Eden	1908.01.01	SLC per IVL	NY.New York	There above I	CU-MARK(tr)	07901 IVL tr
Phillpotts, Eden	1908.02.12	SLC per IVL	NY.New York	Indeed there is	ViU	07936
Phillpotts, Eden	1908.04.26	SLC	NY.New York	The Human Boy	ViU	07985
Piatt, Donn	1871.03.27	SLC	NY.Elmira	If my letter	178:1947.09	00596
Picard, Helene	****.**.**	SLC	Unknown	I was thinking	278:1912.02	08998
Picard, Helene	1902.02.22	SLC	NY.Riverdale	If you will	114:717	06282 other sources
Picard, Helene	1902.04.21	SLC	NY.Riverdale	You have been	278:1912.02	06327
Picard, Helene	1902.10.13	SLC	ME.York Harbor	I am very	278:1912.02	06461
Picard, Helene	1902.12.15	SLC	NY.Riverdale	There isn't going	278:1912.02	06518
Picard, Helene	1903.01.14	SLC	NY.Riverdale	I am remiss	278:1912.02	06561

ADDRESSEE	DATE	WRITER	PLACE	CUE	SOURCE	NUMBER/NOTES
Picard, Helene	1903.07.11	SLC	NY.Elmira	I thank you	278:1912.02	06697
Picard, Helene	1904.01.05	SLC	IT.Florence	We have been	278:1912.02	06783
Picard, Helene	1904.03.21	SLC	IT.Florence	I am up	278:1912.02	06813
Picard, Helene	aft 1905.12.06	SLC	NY.New York	To you, &	278:1912.02	07241 form letter
Picard, Helene	1909.08.26	SLC	CT.Redding	It is a	CU-MARK	08444
Piepel, Marion	o/a 1907.10.19	SLC	NY.Tuxedo Park	Mr. Clemens is	CU-MARK(dr)	07857
Pierce, Henry L.	1884.10.22	SLC	CT.Hartford	You know, as	CU-MARK	03011
Pilgrims President	1908.11.05	SLC	CT.Redding	I am sorry	InU-Li(dr)	08156 telegram
Pitt, L.A.	****.**.**	SLC	Unknown	Will you return	277:15	08245
Pixley, Seymour & Sears, G.A.	1864.01.23	SLC	NV.Carson City	Certainly. If the	201	00074
Plasmon Co.	1902.04.10	SLC	NY.Riverdale	Has Mr. Butters	CU-MARK(ph)	06321
Plasmon Co.	1902.04.25	SLC	NY.Riverdale	I'm due at	TxU	06329
Plasmon Co.	1903.04.07	SLC	NY.Riverdale	Please transfer to	ViU	06619
Plasmon Co.	1905.01.**	SLC	Unknown	The only needful	CU-MARK	06977 typed
Plasmon Co.	1907.12.12	SLC per IVL	NY.New York	I hereby tender	CU-MARK(dr)	07874
Players Club members	1896.11.24	SLC	EN.London	O, thank you	317:1896.12.31	05158
Players Club members & Reid, Robert	1904.11.11	SLC	NY.New York	Surely those lovely	NNWH	06950
Players Club secretary	1895.08.04	SLC	MT.Helena	I desire to	WU(tr)	04939
Polar Star Lodge	1860.12.26	SLC	MO.St. Louis	The subscriber residing	IaCrM(tr)	10665
Pond, James B.	****.**.**	CC	NY.Riverdale	My mother is	NN-B	07363
Pond, James B.	****.**.**	CC	NY.Riverdale	You couldn't have	NN-B	07335
Pond, James B.	****.**.**	OLC	Unknown	I am going	NN-B	07329
Pond, James B.	****.**.**	SLC	CT.Hartford	Blame it, we	NN-B	08954
Pond, James B.	****.**.**	SLC	NY.New York	I wish I	Mo2	08553
Pond, James B.	****.**.**	SLC	NY.New York	I am hampered	NN-B	04551
Pond, James B.	****.**.**	SLC	NY.New York	Read the enclosure	NN-B	08683

Pond, James B.		****.**.**	SLC	Unknown	Say! Some time	408:227	08745
Pond, James B.		****.**.**	SLC	Unknown	1. Please send	NN-B	08945
Pond, James B.		****.**.**	SLC	Unknown	I shall be	NN-B	08948
Pond, James B.		****.**.**	SLC	Unknown	Lead us not	NN-B	08774
Pond, James B.		****.**.**	SLC	Unknown	No, don't use	NN-B	08124
Pond, James B.		****.**.**	SLC	Unknown	No--if you'd	NN-B	08952
Pond, James B.		****.**.**	SLC	Unknown	Now how you	NN-B	08944
Pond, James B.		****.**.**	SLC	Unknown	Oh, dear, I	NN-B	08949
Pond, James B.		****.**.**	SLC	Unknown	Oh dear me	NN-B	08951
Pond, James B.		****.**.**	SLC	Unknown	Won't you please	NN-B	08946
Pond, James B.		****.01.02	SLC	CT.Hartford	No, Pond, I	NN-B	06991
Pond, James B.		****.02.17	SLC	Unknown	Spell of sickness	NN-B	06580
Pond, James B.		****.03.09	SLC	Unknown	I wish I	NN-B	06442
Pond, James B.		****.10.26	SLC	Unknown	Can't	NN-B	07293
Pond, James B.		****.11.17	SLC	CT.Hartford	Be sure to	NN-B	07623
Pond, James B.		1876.09.27	SLC	CT.Hartford	My lawyer has	NN-B	02506
Pond, James B.		1876.10.11	SLC	CT.Hartford	I seem to	NN-B	02507
Pond, James B.	pm	1879.11.24	SLC	CT.Hartford	My Dear Boy	MNS	04013
Pond, James B. & Hathaway, George H.		1879.11.25	SLC	CT.Hartford	Sent you a	NN-B	10797
Pond, James B.		1883.02.15	SLC	CT.Hartford	Cable leaves for	LNT	10708 telegram
Pond, James B.		1883.03.09	SLC	CT.Hartford	Postscript to todays	LNT	10709 telegram
Pond, James B.		1884.01.28	SLC	CT.Hartford	Cables doctor sent	LNT	10713 telegram
Pond, James B.		1884.01.28	SLC	CT.Hartford	Has Mr. Pond	LNT	10715 telegram
Pond, James B.		1884.01.28	SLC	CT.Hartford	Mr. Cable is	LNT	10714 telegram
Pond, James B.		1884.01.30	SLC	CT.Hartford	Cable better but	LNT	10716 telegram

ADDRESSEE	DATE	WRITER	PLACE	CUE	SOURCE	NUMBER/NOTES
Pond, James B.	1884.01.30	SLC	CT.Hartford	Cable requests me	LNT	10717 telegram
Pond, James B.	1884.02.02	SLC	CT.Hartford	He had a	LNT	10718 tel
Pond, James B.	1884.02.03	SLC	CT.Hartford	He is in	LNT	02904
Pond, James B.	1884.02.04	SLC	CT.Hartford	He is very	LNT	10719 telegram
Pond, James B.	1884.02.05	OLC	CT.Hartford	Mr Cable is	LNT	10721 telegram
Pond, James B.	1884.02.06	SLC	CT.Hartford	Medicines are about	LNT	10722 telegram
Pond, James B.	1884.02.12	SLC	CT.Hartford	Cable dresses and	LNT	10723 telegram
Pond, James B.	o/a 1884.02.26	SLC	CT.Hartford	The last I	NN-B	02577 on Fairchild Feb 26
Pond, James B.	1884.05.15	SLC	CT.Hartford	Roswell got up	NN-B	02979
Pond, James B.	1884.07.03	SLC	NY.Elmira	I promised, the	NN-B	02580
Pond, James B.	1884.07.08	SLC	NY.Elmira	O damnation, I	NN-B	02581
Pond, James B.	1884.07.10	SLC	NY.Elmira	Yes, offer Cable	LNT	10724
Pond, James B.	1884.07.15	SLC	NY.Elmira	All right. Webster	NN-B	02582
Pond, James B.	1884.07.16	SLC	NY.Elmira	Oh, dang it	NN-B	08909
Pond, James B.	1884.07.27	SLC	NY.Elmira	Something I forgot	NN-B	02584
Pond, James B.	1884.07.28	SLC	NY.Elmira	Yes, we want	NN-B	02585
Pond, James B.	1884.09.01	SLC	NY.Elmira	This fambly will	CU-MARK(ph)	01446
Pond, James B.	1884.09.20	SLC	NY.Elmira	I & the	NN-B	02590
Pond, James B.	1884.09.26	SLC	CT.Hartford	Cable didn't come	NN-B	02591
Pond, James B.	1884.10.**	SLC	CT.Hartford	Please send Mrs.	NN-B	02592
Pond, James B.	1884.10.02	SLC	CT.Hartford	Come up &	NN-B	02593
Pond, James B.	1884.10.11	SLC	CT.Hartford	You bet you	NN-B	02594
Pond, James B.	1884.10.15	SLC	CT.Hartford	No sir--can't	NN-B	02595
Pond, James B.	1884.10.22	SLC	CT.Hartford	I have selected	NN-B	02596
Pond, James B.	1884.10.24	SLC	CT.Hartford	Hold on, I	NN-B	02597

Pond, James B.	aft	1884.10.27	SLC	CT.Hartford	Letter rec'd last	NN-B	02598
Pond, James B.		1884.10.28	SLC	CT.Hartford	It is now	NN-B	03012
Pond, James B.		1884.10.31	SLC	CT.Hartford	All right, shall	NN-B	02599
Pond, James B.		1884.11.11	SLC	MA.Boston	Enclosed are programs	NN-B	03023
Pond, James B.		1884.11.15	SLC	MA.Boston	Louder advertising is	NN-B	03025
Pond, James B.		1884.11.16	SLC	CT.Hartford	Your program for	NN-B	02600
Pond, James B.		1884.12.22	SLC	CT.Hartford	You were right	NN-B	02601
Pond, James B.		1885.**.**	SLC	Unknown	Mrs. Clemens invites	NN-B	02607
Pond, James B.		1885.02.02	OLC	CT.Hartford	We could hardly	NN-B	05525
Pond, James B.		1885.02.03	SLC	IL.Chicago	No, I don't	NN-B	02604
Pond, James B.		1885.03.14	SLC	CT.Hartford	My boy, you	NN-B	02606
Pond, James B.		1885.04.15	SLC	CT.Hartford	I hasten to	NN-B	02609
Pond, James B.	bef	1885.04.15	SLC	CT.Hartford	Please send Redpath	NN-B	02608
Pond, James B.		1885.05.16	SLC	CT.Hartford	We are offered	NN-B	02611
Pond, James B.		1885.05.17	SLC	CT.Hartford	Please send me	NN-B	02612
Pond, James B.		1885.06.03	SLC	CT.Hartford	Damn it, we	NN-B	02614
Pond, James B.		1885.06.17	SLC	CT.Hartford	Many, many thanks	NN-B	02615
Pond, James B.		1885.06.18	SLC	NY.New York	I am ever	NN-B	02617
Pond, James B.		1885.12.08	SLC	CT.Hartford	I haven't a	NN-B	02624
Pond, James B.		1885.12.28	SLC	CT.Hartford	Goway!--you &	NN-B	02626
Pond, James B.		1886.01.04	SLC	CT.Hartford	Here's the program	NN-B	02628
Pond, James B.		1886.01.10	SLC	CT.Hartford	O, come now	NN-B	02629
Pond, James B.		1886.01.15	SLC	CT.Hartford	Chamberlaine's letter	NN-B	02631
Pond, James B.		1886.01.20	SLC	Unknown	Come--Chamberlain is	NN-B	02632
Pond, James B.		1886.05.03	SLC	CT.Hartford	Projects connected with	NN-B	02634
Pond, James B.		1886.05.10	OLC	CT.Hartford	Mr Clemens has	NN-B	05103
Pond, James B.		1886.11.13	SLC	CT.Hartford	Come--you are	NN-B	02649
Pond, James B.		1886.11.18	SLC	CT.Hartford	If I were	NN-B	02650
Pond, James B.		1886.11.30	SLC	CT.Hartford	We have for	NN-B	02652

ADDRESSEE	DATE	WRITER	PLACE	CUE	SOURCE	NUMBER/NOTES
Pond, James B.	1886.12.03	SLC	CT.Hartford	Of course I'll	NN-B	02653
Pond, James B.	1887.04.25	SLC	CT.Hartford	I think we	NN-B	02659
Pond, James B.	1887.05.10	SLC	CT.Hartford	O, b'gosh I	CU-MARK(ph)	03570
Pond, James B.	1887.12.30	SLC	CT.Hartford	You know the	NN-B	02681
Pond, James B.	1888.11.30	SLC	CT.Hartford	She can't read	NN-B	02687
Pond, James B.	1889.07.02	SLC	NY.Elmira	It is too	NN-B	02689
Pond, James B.	1890.10.13	SLC	CT.Hartford	I'm coming down	NN-B	04556
Pond, James B.	1890.10.17	SLC	CT.Hartford	There are two	NN-B	04558
Pond, James B.	1890.11.29	SLC	CT.Hartford	I thank you	NN-B	04560
Pond, James B.	1891.03.31	SLC	CT.Hartford	Knox hasn't written	Mo2	02449
Pond, James B.	1893.11.14	SLC	NY.New York	Mrs. S.L. Clemens	NN-B	04654
Pond, James B.	1894.**.**	SLC	NY.New York	But alas, the	NN-B	08953
Pond, James B.	1894.**.**	SLC	NY.New York	Oh, I'm just	NN-B	08817
Pond, James B.	1894.04.20	SLC	NY.New York	Thank you a	NN-B	04910
Pond, James B.	1895.05.01	SLC	FR.Paris	Thanks for the	NN-B	04991
Pond, James B.	1895.05.24	SLC	NY.Elmira	Come, old man	NN-B	04992
Pond, James B.	1895.06.09	SLC	NY.Elmira	If we can	NN-B	04993
Pond, James B.	1895.06.11	SLC	NY.Elmira	If you've got	NN-B	04994
Pond, James B.	1895.06.13	SLC	NY.Elmira	The first good	NN-B	04995
Pond, James B.	1895.06.17	SLC	NY.Elmira	It's a good	NN-B	04996
Pond, James B.	1895.06.19	SLC	NY.Elmira	Yes, it's a	NN-B	04997
Pond, James B.	bef 1895.06.19	SLC	NY.Elmira	The other two	NN-B	04884 fragment
Pond, James B.	1895.07.01	SLC	NY.Elmira	This is my	NN-B	04999
Pond, James B.	1895.07.02	SLC	NY.Elmira	As I have	NN-B	05000
Pond, James B.	1895.07.21	SLC	MI.Mackinac	This is too	403:1895.07.31	04934
Pond, James B.	ca 1895.08.15	SLC	Unknown	Here ends one	408:220	09512 inscription
Pond, James B.	1895.08.22	SLC	CN.Victoria	Sincerely his'n	Ii2	10749 inscription

Pond, James B.	1895.08.22	SLC	CN.Victoria	from his friend	ViU	11082 inscription
Pond, James B.	1895.11.30	SLC	NZ.Napier	No; fifty lectures	NN-B	05003
Pond, James B.	1896.08.10	SLC	EN.Southampton	We are busy	NN-B	05239
Pond, James B.	1897.07.**	SLC	EN.London	I am findable	NN-B	05516
Pond, James B.	1897.07.06	SLC	EN.London	Make it 9	NN-B	05515 telegram
Pond, James B.	1897.07.08	SLC	EN.London	No, it isn't	NN-B	08947
Pond, James B.	1897.07.20	SLC	SW.Weggis	I am very	NN-B	05266
Pond, James B.	1897.09.17	SLC	SW.Weggis	It is a	NN-B	05289
Pond, James B.	1898.02.21	CC	AU.Vienna	Thanks for your	CtHMTH	05353
Pond, James B.	1898.03.15	SLC	AU.Vienna	Thank you for	NN-B	05488
Pond, James B.	1898.06.17	SLC	AU.Kaltenleut.	My, it's a	408:227	05401
Pond, James B.	1898.10.07	SLC	AU.Kaltenleut.	Whenever you see	NN-B	05495 mislabeled Vienna
Pond, James B.	1898.11.06	SLC	AU.Vienna	Rice knows mighty	NN-B	05498
Pond, James B.	1899.03.**	CC	AU.Baden	I want to	NN-B	06771
Pond, James B.	1899.04.04	SLC	AU.Vienna	No--I don't	NN-B	05603
Pond, James B.	1899.09.26	SLC	SE.Sanna	I am glad	NN-B	05622
Pond, James B.	1899.10.19	SLC	EN.London	Those are very	NN-B	05625
Pond, James B.	1899.10.31	SLC	EN.London	No, no, write	NN-B	05626
Pond, James B.	1900.07.01	SLC	EN.London	I didn't see	NN-B	08203
Pond, James B.	1900.08.12	SLC	EN.London	No, sir, the	NN-B	08204
Pond, James B.	1900.09.14	SLC	EN.London	This being a	NN-B	08205
Pond, James B.	1900.10.04	SLC	EN.London	I don't doubt	NN-B	08206
Pond, James B.	1900.10.31	SLC	NY.New York	We can't go	NN-B	08208
Pond, James B.	1900.11.13	SLC	NY.New York	The pamphlet is	NN-B	08210
Pond, James B.	1900.12.03	SLC	NY.New York	I find your	NN-B	08211
Pond, James B.	1900.12.29	SLC	NY.Elmira	We are on	NN-B	08212
Pond, James B.	1901.01.21	SLC	NY.New York	Won't you please	ViU(tr)	05972

ADDRESSEE	DATE	WRITER	PLACE	CUE	SOURCE	NUMBER/NOTES
Pond, James B.	1901.04.24	SLC	NY.New York	Some day, but	NN-B	08215
Pond, James B.	1901.05.20	SLC	NY.New York	Your book is	NN-B	08216 typed
Pond, James B.	ca 1901.09.**	SLC	NY.Saranac Lake	You "may" be	NN-B	08213
Pond, James B.	1901.09.12	SLC	NY.Saranac Lake	Yes, by all	NN-B	08217
Pond, James B.	1902.07.04	SLC	ME.York Harbor	Your belated pad	NN-B	08226
Pond, James B.	1902.10.30	SLC	NY.Riverdale	I would strain	NN-B	06476
Pond, James B.	1902.12.04	SLC per IVL	NY.Riverdale	You are making	NN-B	08233
Pond, James B.	1906.03.31	SLC per IVL	NY.New York	Mr. Clemens requests	NN-B	10987
Pond, Martha G.	1895.08.05	SLC	MT.Helena	with the warm	ViU	11083 inscription
Pond, Martha G.	bet 1896.10.** & 1897.07.11	CC	EN.London	I am sorry	CtHSD	08585
Pond, Martha G.	1904.07.21	IVL	MA.Lee	Miss Clemens wishes	NN-B	07144
Pond, Ozias W.	1885.01.01	SLC	OH.Cincinnati	Happy New Year's	NN-B	09333 inscription
Pond, Ozias W.	1885.02.03	SLC & GWC	Unknown	Now wit you	CU-MARK(tr)	03639 GWC tr enc in Feb 4 to OLC
Porter, Charles E.	1881.11.07	SLC	CT.Hartford	Mail this to	MB	10429 on Nov 7 to Gerhardts
Porter, George	bef 1905.07.19	SLC per IVL	NH.Dublin	Mr. Clemens has	CU-MARK(dr)	07088
Porter, Mr.	1903.**.**	SLC	Unknown	Words are futile	CU-MARK(dr)	06538
Porter, Robert P.	aft 1909.01.19	IVL per MLH	CT.Redding	Miss L asks	CtHMTH(dr)	08330 for SLC
Portsmouth, Countess of	*	*	*	*	*	11141 see Wallop, Beatrice M.
Portsmouth, Earl of	*	*	*	*	*	11141 see Wallop, Newton

Postmaster	1867.04.27	SLC	Unknown	Per Steamer--d--n	CU-BANC	05724 on envelope to Stoddard Apr 27
Pottenger, J.H.	1868.03.25	SLC	Unknown	This Mallet is	IaCrM	10666 inscription
Potter, Edward T.	1874.05.08	SLC	NY.Elmira	Mrs. Clemens says	CtHSD	01086 addressee uncertain
Powell, Lyman P.	1907.05.27	SLC	NY.Tuxedo Park	Oh dear, no	CU-MARK(ph)	07734
Powers, L.M.	****.**.**	SLC	Unknown	Apparently it stands	305:1911.04.04	09725 inscription
Powers, L.M.	****.**.**	SLC	Unknown	I do not	305:1911.04.04	09728 inscription
Powers, L.M.	****.**.**	SLC	Unknown	It is a	305:1911.04.04	09735 inscription
Powers, L.M.	****.**.**	SLC	Unknown	It is genuine	305:1911.04.04	09727 inscription
Powers, L.M.	****.**.**	SLC	Unknown	No	305:1911.04.04	09731 inscription
Powers, L.M.	****.**.**	SLC	Unknown	Only a very	305:1911.04.04	09723 inscription; other sources
Powers, L.M.	****.**.**	SLC	Unknown	Partially I was	305:1911.04.04	09734 inscription; other sources
Powers, L.M.	****.**.**	SLC	Unknown	Pirated edition, I	305:1911.04.04	09730 inscription
Powers, L.M.	****.**.**	SLC	Unknown	Same date	305:1911.04.04	09729 inscription
Powers, L.M.	****.**.**	SLC	Unknown	Weiss nicht	305:1911.04.04	09732 inscription
Powers, L.M.	****.**.**	SLC	Unknown	Yes indeed	305:1911.04.04	09726 inscription
Powers, L.M.	****.**.**	SLC	Unknown	Yes, it is	305:1911.04.04	09733 inscription
Powers, L.M.	****.**.**	SLC	Unknown	Yes	305:1911.04.04	09736 inscription
Powers, L.M.	****.**.**	SLC	Unknown	Yes--one or	305:1911.04.04	09724 inscription

ADDRESSEE	DATE	WRITER	PLACE	CUE	SOURCE	NUMBER/NOTES
Powers, L.M.	****.**.**	SLC	Unknown	John Paul never	CU-MARK	09626 inscription
Powers, L.M.	1902.02.19	SLC	NY.Riverdale	You make it	PPiU	06281
Powers, L.M.	1902.02.24	SLC	NY.Riverdale	Thank you very	NSyU	06283
Powers, L.M.	1905.11.09	SLC per IVL	NY.New York	I should accept	TxU	07202
Powers, L.M.	o/a 1908.12.23	SLC	CT.Redding	Published without my	CU-MARK(dr)	08177 on Powers Dec 10
Prang (L.) & Co.	1871.02.09	SLC	NY.Buffalo	The chromo came	MoKHC	00573
Pratt & Whitney Co.	o/a 1887.08.11	SLC	NY.Elmira	Your esteemed favor	CU-MARK(dr)	03621
Pratt, Francis A.	1890.**.**	SLC	Unknown	I went to	CU-MARK(tr)	04141 SLC tr
Prehn, Captain	1907.07.30	SLC per RWA	NY.Tuxedo Park	Mark Twain duly	CU-MARK(tr)	07799 RWA tr
Press Club of Chicago	****.04.20	SLC	Unknown	I have reformed	305:1911.11.20	09869
Press Club of Chicago	1880.12.29	SLC	CT.Hartford	I have been	409:24	01884
Prime, William C.	1886.01.31	SLC	NY.New York	In the interest	DLC	03985
Proctor, I. Goldsmith	aft 1904.05.06	SLC per IVL	IT.Florence	Mr. Clemens wishes	CU-MARK(dr)	06830
Prondfit, E.B.	1905.10.03	SLC per IVL	NH.Dublin	Mr. Clemens directs	CU-MARK(dr)	08671
Pryor, James W.	1901.01.22	SLC	NY.New York	I thank you	ViU(tr)	05980
Pugh, T.B.	****.12.21	SLC	CT.Hartford	It is too	C4	00413
Pugh, T.B.	1870.11.14	SLC	NY.Buffalo	I have had	CU-MARK(ph)	00536
Pugh, T.B.	1872.09.23	SLC	EN.London	I snatch a	PHi	00812
Pugh, T.B.	1873.01.20	SLC	CT.Hartford	It will be	PHi	00860
Pugh, T.B.	1873.07.27	SLC	SK.Edinburgh	I have got	CtY	00957
Pulitzer, Joseph	1907.09.01	SLC	NY.Tuxedo Park	I suppose your	NN-B(tr)	07825
Putman, Helen R.	1888.11.30	SLC	CT.Hartford	Between guests &	NPV	03841
Putnam, George H.	1878.03.16	SLC	CT.Hartford	I have received	CtY	01544
Putnam, George H.	1878.03.26	SLC	CT.Hartford	Yes, I shall	ODa2	01550 addressee uncertain

Putnam, Herbert	1905.11.21	SLC	NY.New York	I shall be	DLC	07216
Putnam, Irving	1889.01.26	SLC	CT.Hartford	I thank you	NWhp2	03854
Putzel, Charles	o/a 1906.03.08	SLC per IVL	NY.New York	I intended to	TxU(tr)	07370 IVL tr
Quick, Dorothy	1907.07.**	SLC	NY.Tuxedo Park	Dorothy dear, will	CU-MARK	07775
Quick, Dorothy	bet 1907.07.** & 1907.08.**	SLC	NY.Tuxedo Park	Dorothy dear, I am	CU-MARK	08816
Quick, Dorothy	1907.07.31	SLC	NY.Tuxedo Park	Letter for you	CU-MARK	07801 telegram
Quick, Dorothy	1907.08.05	SLC	Unknown	Consider the proportions	NEh	09256 inscription
Quick, Dorothy	1907.08.09	SLC	NY.Tuxedo Park	Dorothy dear, one	CU-MARK	07811
Quick, Dorothy	1907.08.11 & 1907.08.15	SLC	NY.Tuxedo Park	This isn't a	CU-MARK	07812
Quick, Dorothy	1907.08.17 to 1907.08.22	SLC	NY.Tuxedo Park	Do you know	CU-MARK	07816
Quick, Dorothy	1907.08.26 & 1907.08.27	SLC	NY.Tuxedo Park	At last you	CU-MARK	07819
Quick, Dorothy	1907.08.31	SLC per IVL	NY.Tuxedo Park	I wanted to	CU-MARK	07822
Quick, Dorothy	1907.09.**	SLC	NY.Tuxedo Park	You have written	CU-MARK(tr)	07827
Quick, Dorothy	1907.09.01	SLC	NY.Tuxedo Park	I tried to	CU-MARK	08275 telegram
Quick, Dorothy	1907.09.01	SLC	NY.Tuxedo Park	Truly Yours	NN-B	10795 inscription
Quick, Dorothy	1907.09.02	SLC per IVL	NY.Tuxedo Park	Mr. Clemens has	CU-MARK	10967
Quick, Dorothy	1907.09.08	SLC	NY.Tuxedo Park	Consider well the	CU-MARK	07832 inscription
Quick, Dorothy	1907.09.12 to 1907.09.14	SLC	NY.Tuxedo Park	Dorothy dear, you	CU-MARK	07834
Quick, Dorothy	1907.09.13	SLC	NY.Tuxedo Park	Affectionately S.L.	CU-MARK	11096 inscription
Quick, Dorothy	1907.09.19	IVL	NY.Tuxedo Park	This is just	CU-MARK	07835
Quick, Dorothy	1907.09.26	SLC	NY.Tuxedo Park	Dorothy dear, I hear	CU-MARK	07838

ADDRESSEE	DATE	WRITER	PLACE	CUE	SOURCE	NUMBER/NOTES
Quick, Dorothy	1907.10.02 & 1907.10.03	SLC	NY.Tuxedo Park	It is a	CU-MARK	07841
Quick, Dorothy	1907.10.07	IVL	NY.Tuxedo Park	Two days ago	CU-MARK	07848
Quick, Dorothy	1907.10.19	SLC	NY.Tuxedo Park	Dorothy dear, it	CU-MARK	08680
Quick, Dorothy	1907.11.18	SLC	NY.New York	Why you sweet	CU-MARK	07865
Quick, Dorothy	1907.12.**	SLC	NY.New York	Merry Christmas and	CU-MARK	07876
Quick, Dorothy	1907.12.29	SLC	NY.New York	Happy New Year	CU-MARK	07897
Quick, Dorothy	1908.01.13	SLC	NY.New York	You are just	CU-MARK	07912
Quick, Dorothy	1908.01.17	SLC	NY.New York	O you dear	CU-MARK	07917
Quick, Dorothy	1908.01.18	SLC	NY.New York	You are ill	CU-MARK	07919 telegram
Quick, Dorothy	pm 1908.01.21	SLC	NY.New York	Dorothy dear, tell	CU-MARK	07924
Quick, Dorothy	1908.02.20	SLC	NY.New York	I got your	CU-MARK(tr)	07941
Quick, Dorothy	1908.02.23	CC	NY.New York	I received a	CU-MARK	07946
Quick, Dorothy	1908.03.10	SLC	BE.Hamilton	Dorothy dear, I am	CU-MARK	07957
Quick, Dorothy	1908.03.12 to 1908.03.16	SLC	BE.Hamilton	My poor little	CU-MARK	07960
Quick, Dorothy	1908.03.28	SLC	BE.Hamilton	The weather is	CU-MARK	07965
Quick, Dorothy	1908.03.31	SLC	BE.Hamilton	You dear little	CU-MARK	07967
Quick, Dorothy	1908.04.16	SLC	NY.New York	Friday--Saturday--Sunday	CU-MARK	07977
Quick, Dorothy	pm 1908.04.24	SLC	NY.New York	I miss you	CU-MARK	07983
Quick, Dorothy	1908.04.28	SLC	NY.New York	Oh, you dear	CU-MARK	07987
Quick, Dorothy	1908.05.04	SLC	NY.New York	You are just	CU-MARK	07991
Quick, Dorothy	1908.05.08	SLC	NY.New York	Your letter came	CU-MARK	07993
Quick, Dorothy	1908.05.09	SLC	NY.New York	I hope the	CU-MARK	07995
Quick, Dorothy	pm 1908.05.12	SLC	NY.New York	You dear little	CU-MARK	07997
Quick, Dorothy	1908.06.02	SLC	NY.New York	You dear little	CU-MARK	08013
Quick, Dorothy	1908.06.07	SLC	NY.New York	You dear little	CU-MARK	08024
Quick, Dorothy	1908.06.14	SLC	NY.New York	I am so	CU-MARK	08027
Quick, Dorothy	1908.06.19	SLC	CT.Redding	Oh, this will	CU-MARK	08034
Quick, Dorothy	1908.06.28	SLC	CT.Redding	Dorothy dear, bring	CU-MARK	08011

Quick, Dorothy		1908.06.29	SLC per ABP	MA.Boston	Mr Clemens asks	CU-MARK	08047
Quick, Dorothy		1908.06.29	SLC	MA.Boston	Have written you	CU-MARK	08044 telegram
Quick, Dorothy		1908.07.02	SLC	CT.Redding	You dear Dorothy	CU-MARK	08050
Quick, Dorothy		1908.07.26	SLC	CT.Redding	Dorothy dear, I miss	CU-MARK	08060
Quick, Dorothy	pm	1908.08.10	SLC	CT.Redding	Dorothy dear I have	CU-MARK	08080
Quick, Dorothy		1908.08.12	SLC	CT.Redding	Dorothy dear, I wrote	CU-MARK	08082
Quick, Dorothy		1908.09.03	SLC	CT.Redding	Dorothy dear, I have	CU-MARK	08100
Quick, Dorothy		1908.09.18	SLC	CT.Redding	Dorothy dear, the post	CU-MARK	08105
Quick, Dorothy		1908.10.07	SLC	CT.Redding	How are you	CU-MARK	08125
Quick, Dorothy		1908.11.05	SLC	CT.Redding	Dear heart, I	CU-MARK	08155
Quick, Dorothy		1908.12.10	SLC	CT.Redding	I am sorry	CU-MARK	08175
Quick, Dorothy		1908.12.10	SLC	NY.New York	I am sorry	CU-MARK	08176
Quick, Dorothy		1909.01.01	SLC	CT.Redding	Happy New Year	CtHMTH	08746 inscription
Quick, Dorothy		1909.01.02	SLC	CT.Redding	It is a	CU-MARK	08305
Quick, Dorothy		1909.03.03	SLC	CT.Redding	Well, dear, so	CU-MARK	08360
Quick, Dorothy	&	1909.03.05 1909.03.31	SLC	CT.Redding	L. If you could	CU-MARK	08364
Quick, Dorothy		1909.05.26	SLC	CT.Redding	Well, you dear	CU-MARK	08401
Quick, Dorothy		1909.06.04	SLC	CT.Redding	Dorothy Dear, it is	CU-MARK	08414
Quick, Dorothy		1909.07.11	SLC	CT.Redding	Dorothy dear, I've been	CU-MARK	08433
Quick, Dorothy		1909.09.10	SLC	CT.Redding	I am glad	CU-MARK	08450
Quick, Dorothy		1909.11.18	SLC	CT.Redding	Dorothy dear, I haven't	CU-MARK	08494
Quick, Dorothy	o/a	1909.12.21	SLC	CT.Redding	Merry Xmas to	CU-MARK	08503
Quick, Dorothy		1910.03.13	SLC	BE.Hamilton	Dorothy dear, I am	CU-MARK	08572
Quick, Dorothy		1910.04.21	SLC per ABP	CT.Redding	May I be	CU-MARK	08580 typed
Quick, E. Gertrude		1907.08.01	SLC per IVL	NY.Tuxedo Park	Mr. Clemens is	CU-MARK	07805

ADDRESSEE	DATE	WRITER	PLACE	CUE	SOURCE	NUMBER/NOTES
Quick, E. Gertrude	1907.08.09	SLC	NY.Tuxedo Park	This is to	CU-MARK	07807 misdated Aug 5
Quick, E. Gertrude	1907.08.15	SLC	NY.Tuxedo Park	It gives me	CU-MARK	07813
Quick, E. Gertrude	1907.09.01 & 1907.09.02	IVL	NY.Tuxedo Park	Will you give	CU-MARK	07826
Quick, E. Gertrude	1907.10.08	IVL	NY.Tuxedo Park	I am sorry	CU-MARK	07850
Quick, E. Gertrude	1907.12.13	SLC	NY.New York	Thank you so	CU-MARK	07889
Quick, E. Gertrude	1910.01.17	SLC per ABP	CT.Redding	Mr. Clemens sailed	CU-MARK(tr)	08540
Raif	****.**.**	SLC	Unknown	Inform Miss Lyon	CU-MARK	09762 telegram
Ramsay, Frances A.	1907.**.**	SLC	NY.New York	Please come tomorrow	NHor2	10791
Ramsay, Frances A.	1907.03.**	SLC	NY.New York	If you could	NHor2	02804
Ramsay, Frances A.	1907.03.14	SLC	NY.New York	Accumulation of letters	NHor2	02798
Ramsay, Frances A.	ca 1907.06.11	SLC	NY.New York	Please come tomorrow	NHor2	05948
Ramsdell, Hiram J.	1869.11.23	SLC	MA.Boston	Confound it, I	110:1964.05.21	00376
Randall, Reverend	1908.01.03	SLC	NY.New York	We ought never	116:1942.09.24	09935 inscription; other sources
Ransom, William L.	1887.08.22	SLC	NY.Elmira	I desire to	CtLHi	03632
Rathbone, Frederick	1907.07.30	SLC per RWA	NY.Tuxedo Park	I have your	CU-MARK(tr)	07800 RWA tr
Rathbone, Harriet A.	1909.12.29	SLC	CT.Redding	I know of	NElmC	08528
Rathbun, Julius G.	****.**.**	SLC	CT.Hartford	*	ODa2	11203 envelope only
Rawcliffe, Henry	1906.12.25	SLC	NY.New York	It is easy	105:1954.02.23	09663 inscription
Raymond, John T.	1875.01.11	SLC	CT.Hartford	I am aware	117:1875.01.13	01177
Raymond, John T.	o/a 1875.05.12	SLC	CT.Hartford	Can lend you	CtHMTH(tr)	01233 telegram; SLC tr
Raymond, John T.	o/a 1875.05.13	SLC	CT.Hartford	sent Raymond $1500	CtHMTH(tr)	01234 SLC tr
Raymond, John T.	1876.10.27	SLC	CT.Hartford	I supposed we	CtHMTH(tr)	01381
Raymond, John T.	1878.03.16	SLC per CEP	CT.Hartford	I hereby nominate	CtHMTH	01545

Reade, A. Arthur	1882.03.14	SLC	CT.Hartford	I have not	430:120	02173
Reasoner, A.	1885.12.01	SLC	NY.New York	with the kindest	ODa2	10348 inscription
Red Cross Committee	bef 1908.12.28	SLC	CT.Redding	In paying new	319:1908.12.28	09171 other sources
Redding Court	1908.11.06	SLC	CT.Redding	This is to	NN-B	08288
Redpath, James	****.05.07	SLC	CT.Hartford	All right, old	MiU-H	07763
Redpath, James	1869.04.20	SLC	NY.Elmira	Nasby and I	305:1906.05.14	00287
Redpath, James	1869.05.10	SLC	CT.Hartford	I have been the New England	CU-MARK(tr) CtY	00298 other sources
Redpath, James	1869.07.09	SLC	NY.Elmira	I failed to	CAlb2(tr)	00325
Redpath, James	1869.08.14	SLC	NY.Buffalo	I feel compelled	305:1906.05.14	00386
Redpath, James	1869.12.04	SLC	NY.New York	Yes I did I will	ODa2	02445 telegram
Redpath, James	1869.12.06	SLC	NY.New York	I talked with	ViU	00383
Redpath, James	1869.12.13	SLC	Unknown	About twice a	305:1906.05.14	00385
Redpath, James	1870.**.** or 1871.**.**	SLC	Unknown	When I think	175:1900.01.22	09998
Redpath, James	1870.01.08	SLC	NY.Albany or NY.Troy	Cahoes was another	ViU	00405
Redpath, James	1870.03.22	SLC	NY.Buffalo	I am not	114:172	00447 other sources
Redpath, James	1870.05.10	SLC	NY.Elmira	I guess I	114:172	00463
Redpath, James	1870.05.21	SLC	NY.Buffalo	I mislaid the	163:1900.08.27	00467 other sources
Redpath, James	1870.07.**	SLC	NY.Buffalo	I find in	292:3	00485
Redpath, James	1870.10.04	SLC	NY.Fredonia	If Mr. Prang	MH-H	00510
Redpath, James	1870.10.09	SLC	NY.Buffalo	Have had a	CU-MARK(ph)	10496
Redpath, James	1870.11.08	SLC	NY.Buffalo	A son was	319:1870.11.11	00528
Redpath, James	1870.11.12	SLC	NY.Buffalo	That was all	MH-H	00532
Redpath, James	1870.12.03	SLC	NY.Buffalo	Joe Larned, (my	WU	00549
Redpath, James	1871.01.22	SLC	NY.Buffalo	I left the	NN-B	00561
Redpath, James	1871.01.30	SLC	NY.Buffalo	I may talk	MH-H	00570

ADDRESSEE	DATE	WRITER	PLACE	CUE	SOURCE	NUMBER/NOTES
Redpath, James	1871.02.22	SLC	NY.Buffalo	In haste--	MH-H	00580
Redpath, James & Fall, George L.	1871.06.10	SLC	NY.Elmira	Without really intending	NHi	00614
Redpath, James	1871.06.12	SLC	NY.Elmira	Begin my tour	MH-H	00616
Redpath, James	1871.06.15	SLC	NY.Elmira	1. Bully for	257:172	00617
Redpath, James	1871.06.27	SLC	NY.Elmira	Don't be in	CU-MARK(ph)	00621
Redpath, James	1871.06.27	SLC	NY.Elmira	Wrote another lecture	CU-MARK(ph)	00623
Redpath, James	1871.06.28	SLC	NY.Elmira	1. Yes, "where	MH-H	00627
Redpath, James	1871.06.28	SLC	NY.Elmira	You are making	MH-H	00626
Redpath, James	bet 1871.07.05 & 1871.07.08	SLC	NY.Elmira	You seem to	TxU	00632
Redpath, James	1871.07.10	SLC	NY.Elmira	P.S.--The title	GMar2	09938
Redpath, James	1871.07.10	SLC	NY.Elmira	A more careful	IC3	00635
Redpath, James	1871.07.10	SLC	NY.Elmira	Excuse my delay	ViU	00634
Redpath, James	1871.07.14	SLC	NY.Elmira	Don't lecture me	163:1900.08.28	00637
Redpath, James	1871.07.19	SLC	NY.Elmira	I'll speak in	CU-MARK(ph)	10497
Redpath, James	1871.08.08	SLC	CT.Hartford	I am different	IC	00642
Redpath, James	1871.09.15	SLC	NY.Elmira	We don't want	NN-B	02457
Redpath, James	1871.09.22	SLC	NY.Buffalo	The Young Men's	CU-MARK(ph)	10498
Redpath, James	1871.09.26	SLC	NY.Buffalo	We have thought	114:191	00654
Redpath, James	1871.10.09	SLC	CT.Hartford	Send along the	Mo2	00657
Redpath, James & Fall, George L.	1871.10.11	SLC	CT.Hartford	The list is	WU(ph)	00659
Redpath, James	1871.10.24	SLC	DC.Washington	I have come	CU-MARK(ph)	00666
Redpath, James	ca 1871.12.08	SLC	Unknown	I like this	157:1903.12.14	09706 other sources
Redpath, James & Fall, George L.	1871.12.08	SLC	NY.Buffalo	Notify all hands	ODa2	00687 telegram
Redpath, James	1871.12.11	SLC	OH.Toledo	My new lecture	MH-H	00689
Redpath, James	1872.01.02	SLC	IN.Logansport	Had a splendid	114:193	00701 other sources
Redpath, James	1872.01.07	SLC	OH.Wooster	Paterson wails. Weeps	CU-MARK(ph)	00710

Redpath, James & Fall, George L.	1872.01.13	SLC	PA.Pittsburgh	Enclosed please find	CCamarSJ	00717
Redpath, James	1872.01.17	SLC	PA.Milton	No, I can't	IaU	00719
Redpath, James	1872.01.26	SLC	CT.Hartford	Oh, no, they	107:1924.11.24	00721
Redpath, James	1872.01.27	SLC	CT.Hartford	1. Say no	MH-H	00722
Redpath, James	1872.02.13	SLC	CT.Hartford	If you could	282:1905.02.14	00726 other sources
Redpath, James & Fall, George L.	1872.02.26	SLC	CT.Hartford	Am not going	OrPR	00727 telegram
Redpath, James	1872.03.03	SLC	CT.Hartford	I have seen	ViU	00729
Redpath, James & Fall, George L.	1872.03.07	SLC	CT.Hartford	Fall does the	MH-H	00731
Redpath, James	1872.04.20	SLC	NY.Elmira	Warrington's article was	ViU	00742
Redpath, James	1872.05.15	SLC	NY.Elmira	Thank you with	MB	00748
Redpath, James	1872.07.18	SLC	CT.New Saybrook	It is pleasant	NN-B	00769
Redpath, James	1872.11.03	SLC	EN.London	Good for Andrews	CU-MARK(tr)	00828 other sources
Redpath, James	1873.01.17	SLC	CT.Hartford	$1000 wouldn't pay	122:1929.10.30	09230 other sources
Redpath, James	1873.01.24	SLC	CT.Hartford	I am already	NN	00864
Redpath, James	1873.05.12	SLC	NY.Elmira	We sail from	159:5.1.19	00914
Redpath, James	1873.12.17	SLC	EN.London	I shall go	NHi	01009
Redpath, James	1873.12.21	SLC per CWS	EN.London	How would it	ViU	01013
Redpath, James	1873.12.31	SLC	EN.London	Shall sail in	MiD	01023
Redpath, James	bet 1874.01.26 & 1874.02.01	SLC	CT.Hartford	I said to	153:502	05995
Redpath, James	1874.02.01	SLC	CT.Hartford	Sitting in church	WU(ph)	01043
Redpath, James	1874.02.13	SLC	CT.Hartford	I'm going to	CtY	02450
Redpath, James	1874.02.23	SLC	CT.Hartford	Wrote you a	ODa2	01053
Redpath, James	1874.02.28	SLC	CT.Hartford	Please secure me	CRc2	01057
Redpath, James	1874.03.03	SLC	CT.Hartford	Why don't you	ODa2	01060 telegram

ADDRESSEE	DATE	WRITER	PLACE	CUE	SOURCE	NUMBER/NOTES
Redpath, James	1874.03.13	SLC	CT.Hartford	Oh thunder & lightning	ODa2	08722 telegram
Redpath, James	1874.04.10	SLC	CT.Hartford	I will try	107:1925.04.16	01076
Redpath, James	1874.04.11	SLC	CT.Hartford	How would it	107:1924.11.24	05322 other sources
Redpath, James	bef 1874.10.01	SLC	CT.Hartford	Your offer of	117:1874.10.01	01135
Redpath, James	1874.11.09	SLC	CT.Hartford	Rev. J.H. Twichell	191:1874.11.12	01145
Redpath, James	1874.11.13	SLC	MA.Webster	We have made	191:1874.11.14	01151 telegram
Redpath, James	1874.11.29	SLC	CT.Hartford	Can't lecture this	ViU	01157
Redpath, James	1874.12.28	SLC	CT.Hartford	No, thanks my	TxU	01170 typed
Redpath, James	1875.09.22	SLC	CT.Hartford	I perceive that	MH-H	01264
Redpath, James	1876.03.17	SLC	CT.Hartford	I want to	CU-MARK	01314
Redpath, James	1886.09.27	SLC	CT.Hartford	Neither of us	178:1947.09	03460
Reed, Susan P.	1902.12.07	SLC	NY.Riverdale	There is none	CU-MARK	06505
Reeves, George W.	1903.07.30	SLC	NY.Elmira	I return the	CU-MARK(ph)	06713
Reeves, George W.	1903.10.20	SLC	NY.New York	I sail on	ViU(tr)	06746
Reich, Lorenz	1882.12.02	SLC	CT.Hartford	When doctors disagree	NHi	09103
Reid, Charles D.	1906.01.**	SLC	NY.New York	Truth is the most	ODa2	11186 inscription
Reid, Robert	1901.01.21	SLC	NY.New York	I reached home	CU-MARK(ph)	10573
Reid, Robert & Players Club members	1904.11.11	SLC	NY.New York	Surely those lovely	NNWH	06950
Reid, Robert	1905.11.28	SLC	NY.New York	I am just	ViU	07220
Reid, Robert	1906.04.30	SLC	NY.New York	I keep thinking	NN-B(tr)	07437
Reid, Whitelaw	*	*	*	*	*	10332 see also New York Tribune ed.
Reid, Whitelaw	1869.06.15	SLC	NY.New York	I am exceedingly	DLC	00317
Reid, Whitelaw	1869.06.26	SLC	NY.Elmira	I got your	DLC	00323
Reid, Whitelaw	1869.08.15	SLC	NY.Buffalo	To-day my new	DLC	00334
Reid, Whitelaw	1869.09.07	SLC	NY.Buffalo	I was away	DLC	00350

Reid, Whitelaw	1870.11.08	SLC	NY.Buffalo	As per my	DLC	00529
Reid, Whitelaw	1870.12.26	SLC	NY.Buffalo	I would like	DLC	02791
Reid, Whitelaw	1870.12.31	SLC	NY.Buffalo	They are bound	DLC	02793
Reid, Whitelaw	1871.02.22	SLC	NY.Buffalo	I thank you	DLC	00581
Reid, Whitelaw	1871.04.29	SLC	NY.Elmira	I have written	DLC	00607
Reid, Whitelaw	1871.06.27	SLC	NY.Elmira	Thank you for	DLC	00624
Reid, Whitelaw	1873.01.03	SLC	CT.Hartford	Will write the	DLC	00851 telegram
Reid, Whitelaw	1873.01.03	SLC	CT.Hartford	The Lord knows	DLC	00852
Reid, Whitelaw	1873.01.06	SLC	CT.Hartford	Have mailed second	DLC	00853 telegram
Reid, Whitelaw	1873.01.13 & 1873.01.17	SLC	CT.Hartford	Your check for	DLC	00857
Reid, Whitelaw	1873.01.25	SLC	CT.Hartford	Warner was by	DLC	00865
Reid, Whitelaw	1873.02.01	SLC	CT.Hartford	Andrews and I	DLC	00871 telegram
Reid, Whitelaw	1873.02.18	SLC	CT.Hartford	Can you put	DLC	00874
Reid, Whitelaw	1873.03.07	SLC	CT.Hartford	Hang it, I	DLC	00883
Reid, Whitelaw	1873.03.07	SLC	CT.Hartford	Leave it out	DLC	00882 telegram
Reid, Whitelaw	1873.03.07	SLC	CT.Hartford	Leave out the	NN	00884
Reid, Whitelaw	1873.03.28	SLC	CT.Hartford	Cheque for $15	DLC	00892
Reid, Whitelaw	1873.04.09	SLC	CT.Hartford	Thanks for check	DLC	00899 Apr 8 to New York Tribune enc
Reid, Whitelaw	1873.04.18	SLC	CT.Hartford	How's that, for	DLC	00902 book notice enc
Reid, Whitelaw	1873.04.20	SLC	CT.Hartford	My Dear Reid	DLC	00903
Reid, Whitelaw	1873.04.22	SLC	CT.Hartford	Cheque received for	DLC	00905 clipping enc
Reid, Whitelaw	1873.04.22	SLC	CT.Hartford	Now that notice	DLC	00906
Reid, Whitelaw	1873.04.22	SLC	CT.Hartford	Warner hasn't finished	DLC	00907

ADDRESSEE	DATE	WRITER	PLACE	CUE	SOURCE	NUMBER/NOTES
Reid, Whitelaw	1882.01.**	SLC	CT.Hartford	Your note of	CU-MARK	02140
Reid, Whitelaw	1907.05.**	SLC	NY.Tuxedo Park	The dates are	217:380	07703
Reid, Whitelaw	1907.05.03	SLC	NY.New York	I sail in	CU-MARK	00147 telegram
Reid, Whitelaw	1907.05.03	SLC	NY.New York	Recognition by Oxford	DLC	07710
Reid, Whitelaw	1907.05.03	SLC	NY.New York	I will come	ViU CU-MARK(dr)	07709 telegram; ViU dr
Reid, Whitelaw	1907.05.15	SLC	NY.New York	Letter received. Many	CU-MARK	07721 telegram
Reimer, Friedrich	1890.10.13	SLC	CT.Hartford	I am ever	Mo2	08938
Remington (E.) & Sons	1875.03.19	SLC	CT.Hartford	Please do not	151:1905.03.18	01212 other sources
Remington, Frederic	1902.02.08	SLC	NY.Riverdale	In my time	NOg2	06272
Remington, Frederic	1906.02.01	SLC	NY.New York	The book is	NOg2	07324
Renwick, James A.	1908.07.06	SLC per RWA	CT.Redding	Mr Clemens directs	CU-MARK(dr)	08052
Reuter, Grace	1900.04.28	SLC	EN.London	I think it	CU-MARK	05801
Reynolds, Cuyler	****.**.**	SLC	Unknown	To be good	448:1934.11.22	09932 inscription
Reynolds, F.S.	1895.05.**	SLC	FR.Paris	with the compliments	ViU	11084 inscription
Reynolds, H.M.	1872.**.**	SLC	Unknown	I only make	CU-MARK	10651 inscription; deposit
Rhodes, John D.	pm 1905.12.15	SLC	NY.New York	To you, &	PP4	10729 form letter
Rice, Alice H.	o/a 1904.08.06	SLC	Unknown	I am glad	146:76f	06908
Rice, Clarence C.	1888.07.04	SLC	NY.Elmira	with the kindest regards	ODa2	11191 inscription
Rice, Henry F. & Gilbert, O.A.F.	1866.11.01	SLC	NV.Virginia City	Your kind and	431:1866.11.04	02775 also to Blasdel & Helm
Rice, Julia B.	1907.12.10	SLC	NY.New York	I am with	CU-MARK(dr)	07886
Rice, Julia B.	1908.02.20	SLC	Unknown	I have an	232:39.564f	07943
Rice, Thorndike	1885.01.03	SLC	OH.Cincinnati	Haven't time to	NN-B	02602

Rice, Thorndike	1885.01.07	SLC	IN.Indianapolis	I am seeking	CU-MARK	10704 telegram
Richards	1907.06.19	SLC	EN.London	To friend Richards	179:95	09225 inscription
Richards, P.	1907.06.14	SLC	SH.Minneapolis	Taking the pledge	453:16	09259 inscription
Richardson, Abby S.	1890.02.19	SLC	CT.Hartford	If I seem	CU-MARK	04019
Riddle, James T.	****.09.30	SLC	CT.Hartford	I should be	NbO	08999
Rideing, William H.	1894.02.**	SLC	NY.New York	I got your	PBL	04681
Rideing, William H.	1894.03.11	SLC	SH.New York	I have written	233:1932.05.20	09936
Ridgway, William H.	1905.12.31	SLC	NY.New York	None genuine without	NN-B(tr)	07283 inscription
Riggs, Kate D.	*	*	*	*	*	10329 see Wiggin, Kate D.
Riley	****.**.**	SLC	Unknown	Well, done, good	107:1924.03.10	09453 inscription
Riley, James W. & Nye, Edgar W. (Bill)	1889.03.04	SLC	CT.Hartford	The St. Botolph	NN-B	02688
Riley, James W.	1890.12.29	SLC	CT.Hartford	Thanks, a thousand	InU-Li	10831
Riley, James W.	1891.02.02	SLC	CT.Hartford	It's a darling	InU-Li	04165
Riley, James W.	1898.01.16	SLC	AU.Vienna	By gracious, old	InU-Li	10832
Riley, James W.	1903.07.27	SLC	NY.Elmira	The delightful book	InU-Li	10833
Riley, John H.	1870.12.02	SLC	NY.Buffalo	Your letter has	CU-MARK(tr) NN-B	00547
Riley, John H.	1871.03.03	SLC	NY.Buffalo	Your letters have	NN-B	00582
Riley, John H.	1871.03.27	SLC	NY.Elmira	My wife has	CtY	00597
Riley, John H.	1871.10.09	SLC	CT.Hartford	It isn't me	NN-B	02458
Riley, John H.	1872.01.04	SLC	OH.Dayton	Heaven prosper the	NN-B	00706
Riley, John H.	1872.03.27	SLC	NY.Elmira	I don't really	ViU	00740
River Record eds.	1880.08.09	SLC	NY.Elmira	I read the	118:1880.08.09	09210
RoBards, John L.	1876.04.17	SLC	CT.Hartford	Long, long ago	MoHM	01324
RoBards, John L.	1876.06.10	SLC	CT.Hartford	I thank you	MoHM	01341

ADDRESSEE	DATE	WRITER	PLACE	CUE	SOURCE	NUMBER/NOTES
RoBards, John L.	1882.06.10	SLC	CT.Hartford	Don't worry about	MoHM	02217 typed
RoBards, John L.	1882.08.02	SLC	NY.Elmira	What promise? I	MoHM	02248
RoBards, John L.	1902.06.03	SLC	MO.Hannibal	My dear old	MoHM	06354
RoBards, John L.	1908.06.07	SLC	NY.New York	If the graves	MoHM	08025
Robert	1903.01.21	SLC	NY.Riverdale	Simplified, the case	CU-MARK	06570
Robert	1908.02.20	JC	CT.Greenwich	I saw Mr.	DSI	07942
Robert	1908.04.09	JC	CT.Greenwich	I meant to	DSI	07971
Roberts, Charles G.	1902.01.09	SLC	NY.Riverdale	As regards that	CU-MARK	06236 typed form letter
Roberts, Helen	1909.11.08	SLC	CT.Redding	I am not	CU-MARK	08485
Roberts, Mr.	1910.01.**	SLC	BE.Hamilton	You were so	CU-MARK(tr)	08533
Robins, Miss	1904.03.25	SLC	IT.Florence	I thank you	CU-MARK	06816
Robinson, Eliza N.	****.**.**	SLC	CT.Hartford	I can't tell	CtY	11056
Robinson, Eliza N.	1898.01.28	OLC	AU.Vienna	Thank you so	CtY	05219
Robinson, Henry C.	1875.02.20	SLC	CT.Hartford	I accede to	117:1875.02.23	01153 also to Sprague & Sill
Robinson, Henry C.	1892.03.28	SLC	IT.Rome	Accept the offer	CU-MARK(tr)	04280 telegram; SLC tr
Robinson, Henry C.	1892.03.29	SLC	IT.Rome	No, it is	CU-MARK(tr)	02381 telegram; SLC tr
Robinson, Henry C.	1892.04.01	SLC	IT.Rome	Keep me posted	CU-MARK(tr)	04281 telegram; SLC tr
Robinson, Henry C.	1892.04.05	SLC	IT.Rome	Do they offer	CU-MARK(tr)	04282 telegram; SLC tr
Robinson, Henry C.	1892.04.18	SLC	IT.Rome	See letter March	CU-MARK(tr)	04283 telegram; SLC tr
Robinson, Henry C.	1892.11.13	SLC	IT.Florence	We have received	CtY	11049
Robinson, Henry C.	1893.07.20	SLC	AU.Krankenheil	Apparently we can	CtY	11050

Robinson, Henry C.		1894.04.20	SLC	NY.New York	Thank you cordially	CtH2	04722
Robinson, Henry C.		1894.07.23	SLC	NY.New York	I have been	CtY	11051
Robinson, Henry C.		1894.11.29	SLC	FR.Paris	We got the	CtY	11053
Robinson, Henry C.		1895.12.24	SLC	SH.Oceana	This is to make you	AuSN-M	11219 enc in Dec 24 to Windeyer
Robinson, Henry C.		1896.07.04	SLC	AF.Capetown	Salutation & best	CtY	11052
Robinson, Henry C.		1896.09.28	SLC	EN.London	It is as	CtY	05120
Robinson, Henry C.		1896.11.08	SLC	EN.London	It was a	CtY	11054
Robinson, Henry C.		1897.01.13	SLC	AU.Vienna	It was good	CtY	11055 misdated, see 1898
Robinson, Henry C.		1898.01.13	SLC	AU.Vienna	It was good	CtY	11123 misdated 1897
Robinson, Lucius		1900.02.16	SLC	EN.London	Your cablegram gave	CtY	05759
Robinson, Mazie S.		1901.06.05	SLC	NY.New York	I have tried	CtHSD	09793 telegram
Robinson, Mr.		1901.04.11	SLC	NY.New York	Mrs. Clemens has	CU-MARK(tr)	06034
Robson, Eleanor		1907.01.**	SLC	Unknown	I feel that	131:1907.01.30	07638
Roche, James J.		1905.04.11	SLC	NY.New York	We are all	RPB-JH(tr)	07031
Rockefeller, William		1906.03.20	SLC	NY.New York	I am very	NN-B(tr)	07395
Rogers, Emilie R.		****.**.**	SLC	NY.New York	*	CU-MARK(tr)	10200 envelope only
Rogers, Emilie R.	pm	****.06.15	SLC	NY.New York	*	CU-MARK(tr)	10198 envelope only
Rogers, Emilie R.		1896.11.26	SLC	EN.London	Experience has convinced	MFai	05150
Rogers, Emilie R. & Rogers, Henry H.		1896.12.18	SLC	EN.London	This is a	MFai	05153
Rogers, Emilie R.		1896.12.22	SLC	EN.London	It is superb	MFai	05157
Rogers, Emilie R.		1900.10.31	SLC	NY.New York	Mrs. Clemens took	MFai	05892
Rogers, Emilie R.		1900.11.06	SLC	NY.New York	Mrs. Clemens sends	MFai	05898
Rogers, Emilie R.		1900.11.13	SLC	NY.New York	I am coming	MFai	05905
Rogers, Emilie R.		1901.01.22	SLC	NY.New York	Oh, thank you	MFai	05981

ADDRESSEE	DATE	WRITER	PLACE	CUE	SOURCE	NUMBER/NOTES
Rogers, Emilie R.	1901.04.11	SLC	NY.New York	I am bedridden	CU-MARK	08668 on Reed Apr 6
Rogers, Emilie R.	1901.04.16	SLC	NY.New York	Mrs. Clemens thanks	MFai	06039
Rogers, Emilie R.	1902.12.25	SLC	NY.Riverdale	It is lovely	MFai	06528
Rogers, Emilie R.	1903.01.02	SLC	NY.Riverdale	I hasten to	MFai	06546
Rogers, Emilie R.	1903.02.01	SLC	NY.Riverdale	Mrs. Clemens's delight	MFai	06575
Rogers, Emilie R.	1903.02.06	SLC	NY.Riverdale	Yes, dear Mrs.	MFai	06578
Rogers, Emilie R.	1903.04.20	SLC	NY.Riverdale	Your kind letter	MFai	06627
Rogers, Emilie R.	1903.04.28	SLC	NY.Riverdale	Thank you for	MFai	06637
Rogers, Emilie R.	1903.07.30	OLC	NY.Elmira	It was four	MFai	06714
Rogers, Emilie R.	1903.10.22	OLC	NY.New York	What a delicious	MFai	06753
Rogers, Emilie R.	1904.07.26	SLC	MA.Lee	Your kind word	MFai	06905
Rogers, Emilie R.	1905.**.**	SLC	NH.Dublin	*	CU-MARK(tr)	10202 envelope only
Rogers, Emilie R.	1905.08.** or 1906.08.**	SLC	NH.Dublin	*	CU-MARK(tr)	10199 envelope only
Rogers, Emilie R.	1905.12.07	SLC	NY.New York	I walked out	MFai	02176
Rogers, Emilie R.	1906.07.**	SLC	NY.New York	In packing my	MFai	07470
Rogers, Emilie R.	1906.08.27	SLC	NH.Dublin	I brought away	CU-MARK(tr)	07514
Rogers, Emilie R.	1906.09.11	SLC	NH.Dublin	*	CU-MARK(tr)	10203 envelope only
Rogers, Emilie R.	1906.10.24	SLC	NY.New York	Dear Mrs. Rogers, it	MFai	07554
Rogers, Emilie R.	1906.11.05	SLC	NY.New York	The billiard table	MFai	07561
Rogers, Emilie R.	1906.12.08	SLC	DC.Washington	Oh, Dear me	MFai	07588
Rogers, Emilie R.	1906.12.22	SLC	NY.New York	I thank you	MFai	07596
Rogers, Emilie R.	1907.03.04	SLC	NY.New York	In packing my	NN-B(tr)	02254
Rogers, Emilie R.	1907.08.18	SLC	NY.Tuxedo Park	Then it is	MFai	07814
Rogers, Emilie R.	1907.08.27	SLC per IVL	NY.Tuxedo Park	Mr. Clemens would	NN7	07820
Rogers, Emilie R.	1907.11.01	SLC	NY.New York	*	CU-MARK(tr)	10201 envelope only
Rogers, Emilie R.	1907.12.02	SLC	NY.New York	It helps to	MFai	07879

Rogers, Emilie R. & Rogers, Henry H.	1908.02.**	SLC & CC	NY.New York	Miss Clara Clemens	CU-MARK	07930
Rogers, Emilie R.	1908.03.02	SLC	BE.Hamilton	He is getting	MFai	07953
Rogers, Emilie R.	1908.08.06	SLC	CT.Redding	Yes, it is	NN7	08076
Rogers, Emilie R.	1908.10.07	SLC	CT.Redding	The letter was	MFai	08128
Rogers, Emilie R.	1908.10.12	SLC	CT.Redding	Yes, I was	MFai	08137
Rogers, Emilie R.	1908.10.24	SLC	CT.Redding	Thank you very	MFai	08142
Rogers, Emilie R.	1908.11.23	SLC	CT.Redding	I'm a-coming just	MFai	08162
Rogers, Emilie R.	1909.05.02	SLC	CT.Redding	I shall arrive	MFai	08395
Rogers, Emilie R.	1909.12.24	SLC	CT.Redding	I thank you	CU-MARK(tr)	08515 telegram
Rogers, Harry & Rogers, Mary B.	1907.05.**	SLC	NY.Tuxedo Park	The pleasure of	NNC	07682
Rogers, Henry H.	****.**.**	SLC per IVL	Unknown	Mr. Clemens is	C4(dr)	09018 telegram
Rogers, Henry H.	****.**.**	SLC	Unknown	I used to	CtHMTH	10487
Rogers, Henry H.	****.**.**	SLC	Unknown	I think I	CU-MARK(tr)	09017
Rogers, Henry H.	1893.12.13	SLC	NY.New York	I can't feel	CU-MARK	04526
Rogers, Henry H.	1893.12.20	SLC	NY.New York	All right--I	Mo2	03918
Rogers, Henry H.	1893.12.20	SLC	NY.New York	The medicines were	Mo2	04534
Rogers, Henry H.	aft 1893.12.29	SLC	NY.New York	Mr. C.B. Knevals	CU-MARK	04546
Rogers, Henry H.	1893.12.30	SLC	NY.New York	If Newton accepts	MFai	04544
Rogers, Henry H.	1894.01.01	SLC	NY.New York	I did want	CU-MARK	04665
Rogers, Henry H.	1894.01.01	SLC	NY.New York	This is the	CU-MARK	08645 on dr of Jan 1 to Newton
Rogers, Henry H.	1894.01.03	SLC	NY.New York	Caleb & Ward	NN7	04667
Rogers, Henry H.	1894.01.27	SLC	NY.New York	I'll be there	CU-MARK	08647
Rogers, Henry H.	1894.02.14	OLC	FR.Paris	I am going	NN7	02716
Rogers, Henry H.	1894.03.04	SLC	NY.New York	Please deliver to	CAlb2	04704
Rogers, Henry H.	1894.03.04	SLC	NY.New York	The enclosed note	NN7	04703 OLC to Rogers Feb 14 enc

ADDRESSEE	DATE	WRITER	PLACE	CUE	SOURCE	NUMBER/NOTES
Rogers, Henry H.	1894.03.04	SLC	NY.New York	Please deliver to	NN-B	04908
Rogers, Henry H.	1894.03.08	SLC	SH.New York	How would this	NN7	04709
Rogers, Henry H.	1894.03.19	SLC	FR.Paris	I am always	NN7	04711
Rogers, Henry H.	1894.03.22	SLC	FR.Paris	I've had a	CU-MARK	04712
Rogers, Henry H.	1894.03.26	SLC	FR.Paris	In answer to	CU-MARK	08648
Rogers, Henry H.	1894.03.30	SLC	FR.Paris	We have been	CU-MARK	08649
Rogers, Henry H.	1894.05.08	SLC	NY.New York	Enjoy your trip	CU-MARK	08650
Rogers, Henry H.	1894.05.16	SLC	SH.New York	It was ever	CU-MARK	04734
Rogers, Henry H.	1894.05.22	SLC	FR.Paris	Mrs. Duff &	NN7	04735
Rogers, Henry H.	1894.05.25	SLC	FR.Paris	Those children of	CU-MARK	08651
Rogers, Henry H.	1894.05.31	SLC	FR.Paris	Miss Harrison's letter	NN-B	04911
Rogers, Henry H.	1894.06.16	SLC	FR.Paris	The dismal work	NN7	04738
Rogers, Henry H.	1894.06.25	SLC	FR.La Bourboule	As the cablegram	CU-MARK	04745
Rogers, Henry H.	1894.06.29	SLC	FR.La Bourboule	Unavoidably detained	CtHMTH	04749 telegram
Rogers, Henry H.	1894.06.29	SLC	FR.La Bourboule	This family is	CU-MARK	04748
Rogers, Henry H.	1894.08.25	SLC	FR.Etretat	I find the	NN-B	04913
Rogers, Henry H.	1894.09.02 to 1894.09.03	SLC	FR.Etretat	The facts are	CU-MARK	04785
Rogers, Henry H.	1894.09.09	SLC	FR.Etretat	I drove the	NN-B	04914
Rogers, Henry H.	1894.09.14	SLC	FR.Etretat	I am very	CU-MARK	04789
Rogers, Henry H.	1894.09.16	SLC	FR.Etretat	Oh, that's all	CU-MARK	04790
Rogers, Henry H.	1894.09.16	SLC	FR.Etretat	This is to	Mo2	09291
Rogers, Henry H.	1894.09.24	SLC	FR.Etretat	There isn't anything	NN7	04791
Rogers, Henry H.	1894.09.30	SLC	FR.Etretat	As your letter	CU-MARK	04792
Rogers, Henry H.	1894.10.05	SLC	FR.Rouen	We are stalled	CU-MARK	04795
Rogers, Henry H.	1894.10.07	SLC	FR.Rouen	Yours of the	NN-B	04915
Rogers, Henry H.	1894.10.11	SLC	FR.Rouen	I have your	CU-MARK	04796
Rogers, Henry H.	1894.10.13	SLC	FR.Rouen	Yours of the	CU-MARK	04799
Rogers, Henry H.	1894.10.19	SLC	FR.Rouen	Gill makes a	NN7	04800

Rogers, Henry H.	1894.10.28	SLC	FR.Rouen	It seems to	NN7	04803
Rogers, Henry H.	1894.11.02	SLC	FR.Paris	The doctor delayed	NN7	04805
Rogers, Henry H.	1894.11.06	SLC	FR.Paris	It isn't a	CU-MARK	04807
Rogers, Henry H.	1894.11.07	SLC	FR.Paris	Just as long	NN7	04808
Rogers, Henry H.	1894.11.11	SLC	FR.Paris	I wonder if	NN7	04809
Rogers, Henry H.	1894.11.15	SLC	FR.Paris	I have been	CU-MARK	04810
Rogers, Henry H.	1894.11.21	SLC	FR.Paris	It seems an	NN7	04812
Rogers, Henry H.	1894.11.28	SLC	FR.Paris	I am out	NN7	04814
Rogers, Henry H.	1894.11.29 to 1894.11.30	SLC	FR.Paris	Your letter, written	CU-MARK	04815
Rogers, Henry H.	1894.12.07	SLC	FR.Paris	I haven't any	CU-MARK	04819
Rogers, Henry H.	1894.12.09	SLC	FR.Paris	Yours of Nov.	CU-MARK	04821
Rogers, Henry H.	1894.12.16	SLC	FR.Paris	I started the	CU-MARK	04825
Rogers, Henry H.	1894.12.21	SLC	FR.Paris	Can you delay	CtHMTH	04826 telegram
Rogers, Henry H.	1894.12.22	SLC	FR.Paris	I seemed to	NN-B	04916
Rogers, Henry H.	1894.12.27	SLC	FR.Paris	Notwithstanding your	NN-B	04917
Rogers, Henry H.	1895.01.02	SLC	Unknown	Yours of Dec.	CU-MARK	04829
Rogers, Henry H.	1895.01.03	SLC	FR.Paris	All night I	CU-MARK	04830
Rogers, Henry H.	1895.01.08	SLC	FR.Paris	As usual, Whitmore	CU-MARK	04833
Rogers, Henry H.	1895.01.21	SLC	FR.Paris	Yours of the	NN7	04836
Rogers, Henry H.	1895.01.23	SLC	FR.Paris	After I wrote	NN-B	04987
Rogers, Henry H.	1895.01.29	SLC	FR.Paris	Your felicitous &	NN-B	04988
Rogers, Henry H.	1895.02.03	SLC	FR.Paris	Yesterday was our	NN7	04839
Rogers, Henry H.	1895.02.08 & 1895.02.09	SLC	FR.Paris	Yours of Jan. P.S. I didn't	CU-MARK CU-MARK(tr)	04840
Rogers, Henry H.	1895.02.12	SLC	FR.Paris	More Mental Telegraphy	NN7	04843
Rogers, Henry H.	1895.03.28	OLC	FR.Paris	Please pay Mr	NN7	04856
Rogers, Henry H.	1895.04.03	SLC	SH.Paris	Mrs. Rice &	NN7	04859
Rogers, Henry H.	1895.04.03	SLC	SH.Paris	We are approaching	NN7	04860

ADDRESSEE	DATE	WRITER	PLACE	CUE	SOURCE	NUMBER/NOTES
Rogers, Henry H.	1895.04.07	SLC	FR.Paris	Now I am	NN7	04862
Rogers, Henry H.	1895.04.09	SLC & OLC	FR.Paris	Please pay to	NN7	04865
Rogers, Henry H.	1895.04.14	SLC	FR.Paris	Yours of the	CU-MARK	04866
Rogers, Henry H.	1895.04.28	SLC	FR.Paris	Within the last	NN7	04873
Rogers, Henry H.	1895.04.29	SLC	FR.Paris	I have been	NN-B	04990
Rogers, Henry H.	1895.05.01	SLC	FR.Paris	This is very	CU-MARK	04874
Rogers, Henry H.	1895.05.15	OLC	SH.New York	Please honor Mr.	NN7	04877
Rogers, Henry H.	1895.05.26	SLC	NY.Elmira	It seems plain	CU-MARK	04879
Rogers, Henry H.	1895.06.04	SLC	NY.Elmira	Well, I am	CU-MARK	04886
Rogers, Henry H.	1895.06.11	SLC	NY.Elmira	Bliss is plucking	CU-MARK	04889
Rogers, Henry H.	1895.06.15	SLC	NY.Elmira	Since writing a	NN7	04891
Rogers, Henry H.	1895.06.19	SLC	NY.Elmira	Will you please	NN-B	04998
Rogers, Henry H.	1895.06.22	SLC	NY.Elmira	I have made	CU-MARK	04895
Rogers, Henry H.	1895.06.22	SLC	NY.Elmira	Mr. Colby thinks	NN7	02718
Rogers, Henry H.	1895.06.25 to 1895.06.26	SLC	NY.Elmira	Good--I hope	NN7	04898
Rogers, Henry H.	1895.06.26	SLC	NY.Elmira	How exasperating it	CtHMTH	04903
Rogers, Henry H.	1895.06.27	OLC	NY.Elmira	I have been	NN7	04904
Rogers, Henry H.	1895.06.29	SLC	NY.Elmira	No, indeedy, it	NN7	02717
Rogers, Henry H.	1895.06.30	SLC	NY.Elmira	In case Mr.	NN7	04905
Rogers, Henry H.	1895.07.01	OLC	NY.Elmira	I feel as	NN7	04922
Rogers, Henry H.	1895.07.05	SLC	NY.Elmira	Mrs. Clemens was	NN7	04925
Rogers, Henry H.	1895.07.06	SLC & OLC	NY.Elmira	It is of	NN7	04892
Rogers, Henry H.	1895.07.08	SLC	NY.Elmira	A telephone message	CU-MARK	04928
Rogers, Henry H.	1895.07.14	SLC	NY.Elmira	You will feel	CU-MARK	04930
Rogers, Henry H.	1895.07.16	SLC	OH.Cleveland	We both thank	NN7	04932
Rogers, Henry H.	1895.07.20 to 1895.07.22	SLC	MI.Mackinac	Your telegram saying	CU-MARK NN7	04933
Rogers, Henry H.	1895.07.24	SLC	MN.Minneapolis	I have Mr.	NN7	04935

Rogers, Henry H.	1895.07.29	SLC	MN.Crookston	We got your	CU-MARK	04936
Rogers, Henry H.	1895.08.07	SLC	WA.Spokane	Certainly no objection	CtHMTH	04940 telegram
Rogers, Henry H.	1895.08.15	SLC	CN.Vancouver	Steamer does not	CtHMTH	04944 telegram
Rogers, Henry H.	1895.08.17	OLC	CN.Vancouver	I very readily	ViU	04952
Rogers, Henry H.	1895.08.17	SLC & OLC	CN.Vancouver	Days ago my	NN7	04951
Rogers, Henry H.	1895.08.17	SLC	CN.Vancouver	I wish you'd	NN7	04950
Rogers, Henry H.	1895.08.19	SLC	CN.Vancouver	It was always	NN7	04953
Rogers, Henry H.	1895.08.22	SLC	CN.Victoria	It is midnight	ODa2	11201
Rogers, Henry H.	1895.08.30	SLC	SH.Warrimoo	In a couple of hours	ODa2	11199
Rogers, Henry H.	1895.09.13 to 1895.09.15	SLC	SH.Warrimoo	I think it	NN7	04959
Rogers, Henry H.	1895.09.25	SLC	AS.Sydney	I perceive that	NN7	04965
Rogers, Henry H.	1895.11.10	SLC	NZ.Timaru	This is a P.S. to the	ODa2	11200
Rogers, Henry H.	1895.12.12	SLC	NZ.Wellington	I imagine that if I	ODa2	11202
Rogers, Henry H.	1896.01.01	SLC	SH.Oceana	There is nothing	NN7	05009
Rogers, Henry H.	1896.01.12	SLC	SH.Oceana	I am shut	NN7	05011
Rogers, Henry H.	1896.02.05	SLC	II.Benares	I was delighted	NN7	05016 mislabeled Bombay
Rogers, Henry H.	1896.02.08	SLC	II.Calcutta	Yours of Dec.	NN7	05020
Rogers, Henry H.	1896.02.17	SLC	II.Calcutta	Yours of Jan.	NN7	05023
Rogers, Henry H.	1896.03.06	SLC	II.Jaipur	Whether Harper gets	NN7	05026
Rogers, Henry H.	1896.03.15	SLC	II.Jaipur	Your cable has	NN7	05033
Rogers, Henry H.	1896.04.02	SLC	SH.Wardha	I didn't quite	NN7	05035
Rogers, Henry H.	1896.04.24	SLC	MU.Curepipe	We have been	CtHMTH	05041
Rogers, Henry H.	1896.05.08	SLC	AF.Durban	We reached here	NN7	05043
Rogers, Henry H.	1896.05.26	SLC	AF.Pretoria	It is intensely	CtHMTH	05056
Rogers, Henry H.	1896.06.06	SLC	AF.Queenstown	I find myself	CtHMTH	05066

ADDRESSEE	DATE	WRITER	PLACE	CUE	SOURCE	NUMBER/NOTES
Rogers, Henry H.	1896.06.11	OLC	AF.Port Eliz.	Harpers dramatic share	ViU	05072 telegram
Rogers, Henry H.	1896.06.18	SLC	AF.Port Eliz.	Your very long	MFai	05076
Rogers, Henry H.	1896.06.19	SLC	AF.Port Eliz.	Mrs. Clemens wrote	CtHMTH	05078
Rogers, Henry H.	1896.06.22	SLC	AF.Port Eliz.	I don't know	MFai	05080
Rogers, Henry H.	1896.07.22	SLC	SH.Norman	I think we	CtHMTH	05087
Rogers, Henry H.	1896.07.31	SLC	EN.Southampton	We are just	CtHMTH	05088
Rogers, Henry H.	1896.08.12	SLC	EN.Guildford	Land, but the	CtHMTH	05093
Rogers, Henry H.	1896.08.14	SLC	EN.Guildford	We have been	NN7	05094
Rogers, Henry H.	1896.09.10	SLC	EN.Guildford	I have just	NN7	05107
Rogers, Henry H.	1896.09.20	SLC	EN.London	I gathered the	NN7	05114
Rogers, Henry H.	1896.09.27	SLC	EN.London	I was glad	NN7	05119
Rogers, Henry H.	1896.10.06	SLC	EN.London	The proposed	NN7	05124
Rogers, Henry H.	1896.10.13	SLC	EN.London	I enclose answer	NN7	05128
Rogers, Henry H.	1896.10.20	SLC	EN.London	Yours of Oct.	NN7	05133
Rogers, Henry H.	1896.11.01	SLC	EN.London	My goodness, have	NN7	05141
Rogers, Henry H.	1896.11.06	SLC	EN.London	I am very	MFai	05142
Rogers, Henry H.	ca 1896.11.10	SLC	EN.London	The contracts clear	CU-MARK	08653
Rogers, Henry H.	1896.11.24	SLC	EN.London	In two of	NN7	05148
Rogers, Henry H. & Rogers, Emilie R.	1896.12.18	SLC	EN.London	This is a	MFai	05153
Rogers, Henry H.	1897.01.04	SLC	EN.London	Yours of Dec.	NN7	05165
Rogers, Henry H.	1897.01.15	SLC	EN.London	We like the	NN7	05168
Rogers, Henry H.	1897.01.19	SLC	EN.London	As soon as	NN7	05172
Rogers, Henry H.	1897.02.02	SLC	EN.London	The moment the	NN7	05176
Rogers, Henry H.	1897.02.08	SLC	EN.London	Well, I've had	NN7	05178
Rogers, Henry H.	1897.02.26	SLC	EN.London	I am grown	NN7	05180
Rogers, Henry H.	1897.03.05	SLC	EN.London	The cable "Signed"	NN7	05183
Rogers, Henry H.	1897.03.19	SLC	EN.London	I have just	NN7	05188
Rogers, Henry H.	1897.03.26	SLC	EN.London	Damnation! That cable	NN7	05192

Rogers, Henry H.	1897.04.08	SLC	EN.London	I signed the	NN7	05199
Rogers, Henry H.	1897.04.14	SLC	EN.London	This is to	CtHMTH	05202
Rogers, Henry H.	1897.04.14	SLC	EN.London	I finished the	NN7	05203
Rogers, Henry H.	1897.04.16	SLC	EN.London	I wrote Frank	NN7	05204
Rogers, Henry H.	1897.04.26 to 1897.04.28	SLC	EN.London	Yours enclosing Bliss's	NN7	05207
Rogers, Henry H.	1897.05.18	SLC	EN.London	I am unspeakably	NN7	05212
Rogers, Henry H.	1897.06.03	SLC	EN.London	Your order to	NN7	05224
Rogers, Henry H.	1897.06.16	SLC	EN.London	Your cablegram came	NN7	04684
Rogers, Henry H.	1897.06.23	SLC	EN.London	I wrote the	NN7	05231
Rogers, Henry H.	1897.06.25	SLC	EN.London	Mrs. Clemens was	NN7	05233
Rogers, Henry H.	1897.07.07	SLC	EN.London	Chatto was about	NN7	05253
Rogers, Henry H.	1897.07.12	SLC	EN.London	We broke up	NN7	05261
Rogers, Henry H.	1897.07.23	SLC	SW.Weggis	In case all	CU-MARK(ph)	05268
Rogers, Henry H.	1897.08.06	SLC	SW.Weggis	Yours of July	NN7	05277
Rogers, Henry H.	1897.08.13	SLC	SW.Weggis	Miss Harrison's note	CU-MARK(ph)	05278
Rogers, Henry H.	1897.09.13	SLC	SW.Weggis	Your letter has	NN7	05288
Rogers, Henry H.	1897.09.18	SLC	SW.Weggis	The Swiss vacation	NN7	05291
Rogers, Henry H.	1897.10.08	SLC	AU.Vienna	We have been	NN7	05295
Rogers, Henry H.	1897.11.10 & 1897.11.11	SLC	AU.Vienna	I throw up	NN7	05312
Rogers, Henry H.	1897.11.17	SLC & OLC	AU.Vienna	Please divide pro	NN7	05313
Rogers, Henry H.	1897.12.16	SLC	AU.Vienna	We are delighted	NN7	05324
Rogers, Henry H.	1897.12.21	SLC	AU.Vienna	Yes, you are	NN7	05325
Rogers, Henry H.	1897.12.29	SLC	AU.Vienna	Yours of the	NN7	05329
Rogers, Henry H.	1898.01.20	SLC	AU.Vienna	Yours of the	NN7	05336
Rogers, Henry H.	1898.02.05 & 1898.02.06	SLC	AU.Vienna	Yours of Jan.	NN7	05342
Rogers, Henry H.	1898.02.07	SLC	AU.Vienna	Please accept for	NN7	05344
Rogers, Henry H.	1898.03.07	SLC	AU.Vienna	The copies of	NN7	05361

ADDRESSEE	DATE	WRITER	PLACE	CUE	SOURCE	NUMBER/NOTES
Rogers, Henry H.	1898.03.15	SLC	AU.Vienna	Indeed I do	NN7	05363
Rogers, Henry H.	1898.03.17 & 1898.03.20	SLC	AU.Vienna	I've landed a	NN7	05365
Rogers, Henry H.	1898.03.22	SLC	AU.Vienna	To-day I am	NN7	05366
Rogers, Henry H.	1898.03.23	SLC	AU.Vienna	I was present	NN7	05367
Rogers, Henry H.	1898.03.24	SLC	AU.Vienna	(I feel like	NN7	05368
Rogers, Henry H.	1898.04.12	SLC	AU.Vienna	A week or	NN7	05375
Rogers, Henry H.	1898.04.21	SLC	AU.Vienna	You have furnished	NN7	05377
Rogers, Henry H.	1898.04.29	SLC	AU.Vienna	We are securing	NN7	05379
Rogers, Henry H.	1898.05.13	SLC	AU.Vienna	They find it	NN7	05387
Rogers, Henry H.	1898.05.31	SLC	AU.Kaltenleut.	I am very	NN7	05397
Rogers, Henry H.	1898.06.10	OLC	AU.Kaltenleut.	I hereby formally	NN7	05399
Rogers, Henry H.	1898.06.10	SLC	AU.Kaltenleut.	I will enclose	NN7	05398
Rogers, Henry H.	1898.07.10	SLC	AU.Kaltenleut.	At a first	NN7	05411
Rogers, Henry H.	1898.07.26	SLC	AU.Kaltenleut.	A couple of	NN7	05416
Rogers, Henry H.	1898.08.03	SLC	AU.Kaltenleut.	I must stop	NN7	05420
Rogers, Henry H.	1898.08.19	SLC	AU.Ischl	We are in	NN7	05422
Rogers, Henry H.	1898.08.28	SLC	AU.Kaltenleut.	A dozen days	NN7	05426
Rogers, Henry H.	1898.09.14	SLC	AU.Kaltenleut.	Are you home	NN7	05434
Rogers, Henry H.	1898.09.21	SLC	AU.Kaltenleut.	I am finishing	NN7	05436
Rogers, Henry H.	1898.09.26	SLC	AU.Kaltenleut.	In something short	NN7	05438
Rogers, Henry H.	1898.10.01	SLC	AU.Kaltenleut.	I am a	NN7	05440
Rogers, Henry H.	1898.10.18	SLC	AU.Vienna	I am undergoing	NN7	05450
Rogers, Henry H.	1898.11.02	SLC	AU.Vienna	That is immense	CU-MARK	05457
Rogers, Henry H.	1898.11.06 to 1898.11.07	SLC	AU.Vienna	The other day	NN7	05461
Rogers, Henry H.	1898.11.12	SLC	AU.Vienna	Your welcome cable	NN7	05466
Rogers, Henry H.	1898.11.17	SLC	AU.Vienna	Oh, dear me	NN7	05469
Rogers, Henry H.	1898.12.08 to 1898.12.13	SLC	AU.Vienna	It is 12	NN7	05476 fragment

Rogers, Henry H.		1898.12.27	SLC	AU.Vienna	Accept two thousand	NN7	05484 telegram
Rogers, Henry H.		1898.12.27	SLC	AU.Vienna	Yours of the	NN7	05483
Rogers, Henry H.		1899.01.03	SLC	AU.Vienna	Follow your judgement	CU-MARK(tr)	05475 telegram; SLC tr
Rogers, Henry H.		1899.01.03	SLC	AU.Vienna	Yours of Dec.	NN7	05532
Rogers, Henry H.		1899.01.21	SLC	AU.Vienna	Splendid bird, set	CU-MARK(tr)	05061 telegram; SLC tr
Rogers, Henry H.		1899.01.24	SLC	AU.Vienna	I am gradually	NN7	05538
Rogers, Henry H.		1899.02.02	SLC	AU.Vienna	Now that I	CU-MARK	05543
Rogers, Henry H.		1899.02.19	SLC	AU.Vienna	Why, it is	NN7	05547
Rogers, Henry H.		1899.03.14	SLC	AU.Vienna	Unberufen--keep her	NN7	05563
Rogers, Henry H.		1899.04.18	SLC	AU.Vienna	All right, I	NN7	05579
Rogers, Henry H.		1899.05.10	SLC	AU.Vienna	Those removes are	NN7	05590
Rogers, Henry H.		1899.06.06	SLC	EN.Broadstairs	I am very	NN7	05634
Rogers, Henry H.		1899.06.25	SLC	EN.London	I judge the	NN7	05644
Rogers, Henry H.		1899.07.03	SLC	EN.London	I have been	NN7	05646
Rogers, Henry H.		1899.08.03	SLC	SE.Sanna	Yours of July	NN7	05662
Rogers, Henry H.		1899.08.22	SLC	SE.Sanna	I have looked	NN7	05664
Rogers, Henry H.		1899.09.03	SLC	SE.Sanna	I wonder what	NN7	05671
Rogers, Henry H.	pm	1899.09.27	SLC	SE.Sanna	Won't you please	NN	05681
Rogers, Henry H.		1899.10.04	SLC	EN.London	Yours of Sept.	NN7	05687
Rogers, Henry H.		1899.11.09	SLC	EN.London	My temper is	NN7	05701
Rogers, Henry H.		1899.11.17	SLC	EN.London	We have a	NN7	05707
Rogers, Henry H.		1899.11.20	SLC	EN.London	I know that	CU-MARK	05712
Rogers, Henry H.		1899.12.07	SLC	EN.London	If I remember	NN7	05717
Rogers, Henry H.		1899.12.11	SLC	EN.London	I didn't really	NN7	05718
Rogers, Henry H.		1899.12.26	SLC	EN.London	If you approve	NN7	05726
Rogers, Henry H.		1900.01.08	SLC	EN.London	It was splendid	NN7	05743

ADDRESSEE	DATE	WRITER	PLACE	CUE	SOURCE	NUMBER/NOTES
Rogers, Henry H.	1900.01.13	SLC	EN.London	S.S. McClure	CU-MARK	05747
Rogers, Henry H.	1900.02.05	SLC	EN.London	I mark it	NN7	05757
Rogers, Henry H.	1900.02.27 to 1900.03.04	SLC	EN.London	No, somehow I	NN7	05765
Rogers, Henry H.	1900.03.11	SLC	EN.London	In bank here	NN7	05775
Rogers, Henry H.	1900.03.25	SLC	EN.London	Another job for	CU-MARK	05783
Rogers, Henry H.	1900.04.08 to 1900.04.09	SLC	EN.London	McClure wrote, some	NN7	05790
Rogers, Henry H.	1900.04.20	SLC	EN.London	By a letter	NN7	05794
Rogers, Henry H.	1900.05.17	SLC	EN.London	Program re-organized	NN7	05808
Rogers, Henry H.	1900.06.13	SLC	EN.London	Well, you have	NN7	05821
Rogers, Henry H.	1900.07.31	SLC	EN.London	It is too	NN7	05842
Rogers, Henry H.	1900.08.17	SLC	EN.London	Before leaving London	CU-MARK	05853
Rogers, Henry H.	1900.08.20	SLC	EN.London	And now if	NN7	05856
Rogers, Henry H.	1900.11.16	SLC	NY.New York	Please look these	ViU	05910 on Gillette Nov 15
Rogers, Henry H.	1900.11.21	SLC	NY.New York	I find a	CtHMTH	05917
Rogers, Henry H.	pm 1901.01.21	SLC	NY.New York	I shall be	CU-MARK	05968
Rogers, Henry H.	o/a 1901.03.09	SLC	NY.New York	Whitmore thinks as	ViU	06016 on Whitmore Mar 9
Rogers, Henry H.	1901.06.03	SLC	NY.New York	These have come	ViU	06069
Rogers, Henry H.	1901.06.14	SLC	NY.New York	Helmer allows us	Mo2	08872 on Leon June 1
Rogers, Henry H.	1901.06.19	SLC	NY.New York	I don't know	CU-MARK	06076
Rogers, Henry H.	1901.06.28	SLC	NY.Saranac Lake	We are sweating	CU-MARK	06081
Rogers, Henry H.	1901.07.05	SLC	NY.Saranac Lake	How would Ex-President	CU-MARK(ph)	06084
Rogers, Henry H.	1901.07.09	SLC	NY.Saranac Lake	Your telegram hasn't	CU-MARK	08641
Rogers, Henry H.	1901.07.17	SLC	NY.Saranac Lake	Judge Howland can't	CU-MARK	06092
Rogers, Henry H.	1901.07.31	SLC	NY.Saranac Lake	I shall be	105:1959.04.28	06102 on Sloane July 29
Rogers, Henry H.	1901.08.23	SLC	NY.Saranac Lake	I am just	CU-MARK	06117

Rogers, Henry H.	1901.08.29 to 1901.09.06	SLC	NY.Saranac Lake	I carried off	CU-MARK	08657
Rogers, Henry H.	o/a 1901.09.06	SLC	NY.Saranac Lake	From Twichell. Needn't	CU-MARK	06129 on Twichell Sept 5
Rogers, Henry H.	1901.09.07	SLC	NY.Saranac Lake	I have finished	CU-MARK	06130
Rogers, Henry H.	1901.09.12	SLC	NY.Saranac Lake	How can you	NN7	06136
Rogers, Henry H.	1901.09.18	SLC	NY.Saranac Lake	We are packed	CU-MARK	06139
Rogers, Henry H.	1901.09.25	SLC	NY.Elmira	The trouble with	CU-MARK	06141
Rogers, Henry H.	1901.09.26	SLC	NY.New York	Langdon hopes to	CU-MARK	06143
Rogers, Henry H.	1901.09.29	SLC	NY.New York	I shall try	NN7	06145 on Twichell Sept 27
Rogers, Henry H.	1901.11.21	SLC	NY.New York	The Baker letter	CU-MARK	08658
Rogers, Henry H.	1901.12.12	SLC	NY.Riverdale	For 20 years	CU-MARK	06188 on Flandrau Dec 5
Rogers, Henry H.	1901.12.12	SLC	NY.Riverdale	I found a	CU-MARK	06187
Rogers, Henry H.	1901.12.21	SLC	NY.Riverdale	Wally, Bliss was	CU-MARK	06194
Rogers, Henry H.	1901.12.27	SLC	NY.Riverdale	Ah, the luck	NN7	06198
Rogers, Henry H.	1902.01.02	SLC	NY.Riverdale	Tacacci, of McClure's	NN7	06216
Rogers, Henry H.	1902.01.31	SLC	NY.Riverdale	Enclosed is the	CU-MARK	06262
Rogers, Henry H.	1902.02.07	SLC	NY.Riverdale	Very many thanks	NN7	06271
Rogers, Henry H.	1902.03.08	SLC	NY.Riverdale	Can't get away	CU-MARK(dr)	08660 telegram
Rogers, Henry H.	1902.03.18	SLC	FL.Miami	Nassau: That's the	CU-MARK	06312 misdated Mar 28
Rogers, Henry H.	1902.03.28	SLC	FL.Miami	Nassau: That's the	CU-MARK	10883 misdated, see Mar 18
Rogers, Henry H.	1902.04.14	SLC	NY.Riverdale	Mrs. Clemens bought	NN7	06324
Rogers, Henry H.	o/a 1902.04.17	SLC	Unknown	This is well	NN7	06325 on tr of Reed to Rogers Apr 17

ADDRESSEE	DATE	WRITER	PLACE	CUE	SOURCE	NUMBER/NOTES
Rogers, Henry H.	1902.05.16	SLC	NY.Riverdale	Great Scott!--why	CtHMTH	06338
Rogers, Henry H.	1902.05.17	SLC	NY.Riverdale	I believe the	NN7	06339 Reed to Cooper May 17 enc
Rogers, Henry H.	1902.05.26	SLC	NY.Riverdale	I leave tomorrow	CU-MARK	06347
Rogers, Henry H.	1902.06.27	SLC	ME.York Harbor	Housed and at	CtHMTH	06377 telegram
Rogers, Henry H.	1902.07.07	SLC	ME.York Harbor	It was a	NN7	06385
Rogers, Henry H.	1902.07.11	SLC	ME.York Harbor	I know what	NN7	06386
Rogers, Henry H.	1902.07.28	SLC	ME.York Harbor	I'm enclosing the	NN7	06392
Rogers, Henry H.	1902.08.02	SLC	ME.York Harbor	I can't tell	CU-MARK	06398 on Whitmore Aug 1
Rogers, Henry H.	1902.08.03	SLC	ME.York Harbor	I am mailing	CU-MARK	06399
Rogers, Henry H.	1902.08.07	SLC	ME.York Harbor	Your letter entirely	CU-MARK	06401
Rogers, Henry H.	1902.08.13	SLC	ME.York Harbor	Matters reached a	NN7	06405
Rogers, Henry H.	1902.08.21	SLC	ME.York Harbor	As soon as	NN7	06408
Rogers, Henry H.	1902.08.22	SLC	ME.York Harbor	The air bed	NN7	06412
Rogers, Henry H.	1902.08.27	SLC	ME.York Harbor	We are scheming	NN7	06417
Rogers, Henry H.	1902.08.28 & 1902.08.29	SLC	ME.York Harbor	To-day I've struck	NN7	06420
Rogers, Henry H.	1902.08.28	SLC	ME.York Harbor	Thank you without	CtHMTH	06419 telegram
Rogers, Henry H.	1902.09.01	SLC	ME.York Harbor	It is lovely	NN7	06424
Rogers, Henry H.	1902.09.03	SLC	ME.York Harbor	Mrs. Clemens began	NN7	06425
Rogers, Henry H.	1902.09.11	SLC	ME.York Harbor	Mrs. Clemens said	NN7	06432
Rogers, Henry H.	1902.09.18 & 1902.09.19	SLC	ME.York Harbor	Confound it, the	NN7	06434
Rogers, Henry H.	1902.09.20	SLC	ME.York Harbor	It was pretty	NN7	06436
Rogers, Henry H.	1902.09.23	SLC	ME.York Harbor	We have been	NN7	06440
Rogers, Henry H.	1902.09.24	SLC	ME.York Harbor	Your letter is	NN7	06441
Rogers, Henry H.	1902.09.26	SLC	ME.York Harbor	Mrs. Clemens has	NN7	06444
Rogers, Henry H.	1902.10.11	SLC	ME.York Harbor	We expect to	NN7	06458

Rogers, Henry H.		1902.12.25	SLC	NY.Riverdale	I am right	CU-MARK	06527
Rogers, Henry H.	ca	1903.01.01	SLC	NY.Riverdale	Here is what	CtHMTH	08625 on Harvey Dec 31
Rogers, Henry H.	aft	1903.01.02	SLC	NY.Riverdale	Party here name	ViU	06547
Rogers, Henry H.		1903.02.21	SLC	NY.Riverdale	I am nearly	157:1923.11.21	09775 other sources
Rogers, Henry H.		1903.02.28	SLC	NY.Riverdale	Consound it, Clara	NN7	06588
Rogers, Henry H.		1903.03.13	SLC	NY.New York	I gather that	CU-MARK	08642
Rogers, Henry H.		1903.04.07	SLC	NY.Riverdale	By George, if	NN7	06618
Rogers, Henry H.		1903.04.20	SLC	NY.Riverdale	This is dreadful	CU-MARK	06626
Rogers, Henry H.		1903.05.11	SLC	NY.Riverdale	It's fine, that	NN7	06656
Rogers, Henry H.		1903.05.20	SLC	NY.Riverdale	I believe it	CU-MARK	06664
Rogers, Henry H.		1903.06.04	SLC	CT.Hartford	I destroyed it	NN7	06673
Rogers, Henry H.		1903.06.25	SLC	NY.Riverdale	Frank Bliss &	ViU	06683
Rogers, Henry H.	ca	1903.09.10	SLC	NY.New York	I'm accepting. When	IC3	09708 on Stone Sept 8
Rogers, Henry H.		1903.09.14	SLC	NY.Elmira	Your telegram from	CU-MARK	08643
Rogers, Henry H.		1903.09.18	SLC	NY.Elmira	I am ashamed	NN7	06725
Rogers, Henry H.	&	1903.11.12 1903.11.15	SLC	IT.Florence	The fact is	NN7	06758
Rogers, Henry H.		1903.11.28	SLC	IT.Florence	Yes, I am	NN7	06761
Rogers, Henry H.	&	1903.12.16 1903.12.18	SLC	IT.Florence	I am not	NN7	06768
Rogers, Henry H.		1903.12.30	SLC	IT.Florence	I am very	NN7	06775
Rogers, Henry H.		1904.01.25	SLC	IT.Florence	Mrs. Clemens says	NN7	06787
Rogers, Henry H.	&	1904.02.25 1904.02.26	SLC	IT.Florence	I wish you	NN7	06798
Rogers, Henry H.	&	1904.03.21 1904.03.22	SLC	IT.Florence	I have been	NN7	06814
Rogers, Henry H.		1904.04.12	SLC	IT.Florence	Clara made a	NN7	06823
Rogers, Henry H.		1904.05.09	SLC	IT.Florence	I wish I	NN7	06832

ADDRESSEE	DATE	WRITER	PLACE	CUE	SOURCE	NUMBER/NOTES
Rogers, Henry H.	1904.06.06	SLC	IT.Florence	You have received	NN7	06861
Rogers, Henry H.	1904.06.08	SLC	IT.Florence	I am very	NN7	06866
Rogers, Henry H.	1904.06.13	SLC	IT.Florence	The "Prince Oscar"	NN7	06870
Rogers, Henry H.	1904.08.18	SLC	NY.Great Neck	I have been	NN7	06914
Rogers, Henry H.	ca 1904.09.15	SLC	NY.Elmira	Could you have	NN7	06922
Rogers, Henry H.	1904.09.24	SLC	NY.Elmira	We shall reach	NN7	06923
Rogers, Henry H.	1905.04.21	SLC	NY.New York	I was going	NN7	07032
Rogers, Henry H.	1905.06.19	SLC	NH.Dublin	Why, I must	NN7	07066
Rogers, Henry H.	1905.06.28	SLC	NH.Dublin	This is a	NN7	07072
Rogers, Henry H.	1905.07.09	SLC	NH.Dublin	If the news	NN7	07079
Rogers, Henry H.	1905.07.13	SLC	NH.Dublin	That check comes	NN7	07083
Rogers, Henry H.	1905.07.26 & 1905.07.27	SLC	NH.Dublin	I ought to	CU-MARK	08670
Rogers, Henry H.	1905.08.07	SLC	NH.Dublin	I am keeping	NN7	07104
Rogers, Henry H.	1905.08.14	SLC	CT.Norfolk	I am stranded	CU-MARK	07107
Rogers, Henry H.	1905.08.21	SLC	CT.Norfolk	I am going	NN7	07114
Rogers, Henry H.	1905.09.07	SLC	NH.Dublin	I want to	CtHMTH	07132
Rogers, Henry H.	1905.09.16	SLC	NH.Dublin	Read & destroy	NN7	07138
Rogers, Henry H.	ca 1905.09.22	SLC	NH.Dublin	I have just	NN7	07145
Rogers, Henry H.	1905.10.05	SLC	NH.Dublin	At 3 p.m.	NN7	07161
Rogers, Henry H.	1905.10.20	SLC	NH.Dublin	I suppose you	NN7	07185
Rogers, Henry H.	1905.12.30	SLC per IVL	NY.New York	I had already	CU-MARK	07280
Rogers, Henry H.	1906.04.09	SLC	NY.New York	When you come	NN7	07423
Rogers, Henry H.	1906.04.30	SLC per IVL	NY.New York	Mr. Clemens directs	CU-MARK	08675
Rogers, Henry H.	1906.05.18	SLC	NH.Dublin	I am lying	NN7	07441
Rogers, Henry H.	1906.06.06	SLC	NH.Dublin	Yes still am	CtHMTH	07450 telegram
Rogers, Henry H.	1906.06.06	SLC	NH.Dublin	I've been sending	NN7	07449
Rogers, Henry H.	1906.06.13	SLC per IVL	NH.Dublin	Please get my	CtHMTH	07457

Rogers, Henry H.	1906.06.17	SLC	NH.Dublin	Certainly I retain	NN7	07460
Rogers, Henry H.	1906.08.**	SLC	NH.Dublin	I'm accepting	122:1934.04.04	09015 on invitation
Rogers, Henry H.	1906.08.05	SLC	NH.Dublin	Upon second thought	NN-B(tr)	07493 Aug 5 to Twichell enc
Rogers, Henry H.	1906.09.03	SLC	NH.Dublin	God be thanked	CU-MARK(tr)	08265 telegram
Rogers, Henry H.	aft 1906.09.03	SLC	NH.Dublin	Do not send	CU-MARK(dr)	10959 telegram
Rogers, Henry H.	aft 1906.09.03	SLC	NH.Dublin	Family prostrate	CU-MARK(dr)	10958 telegram
Rogers, Henry H.	aft 1906.09.03	SLC	NH.Dublin	He was all	CU-MARK(dr)	11109 telegram
Rogers, Henry H.	aft 1906.09.03	SLC	NH.Dublin	I am afraid	CU-MARK(dr)	07525 four telegrams
Rogers, Henry H.	1907.01.01	SLC	NY.New York	After you were	NN7	07617
Rogers, Henry H.	1907.05.29	SLC	NY.Tuxedo Park	Why hang it	CU-MARK(ph)	07735
Rogers, Henry H.	1907.07.29	SLC	NY.Tuxedo Park	I am in	CtHMTH	07792
Rogers, Henry H.	1907.09.01	SLC	NY.Tuxedo Park	In my dream	IEN	07824
Rogers, Henry H.	1907.09.20	SLC	NY.Tuxedo Park	I hope you	NN7	07836
Rogers, Henry H.	1907.09.26	SLC	NY.Tuxedo Park	This is my	NN7	07839
Rogers, Henry H.	1907.10.03	SLC per IVL	NY.Tuxedo Park	Very much disappointed	CU-MARK(dr)	08679
Rogers, Henry H.	1907.10.04	SLC	NY.Tuxedo Park	Didn't Mary promise	NN7	07846
Rogers, Henry H.	1907.10.08	SLC	NY.Tuxedo Park	I'm coming up	NN7	07851
Rogers, Henry H. & Rogers, Emilie R.	1908.02.**	SLC & CC	NY.New York	Miss Clara Clemens	CU-MARK	07930
Rogers, Henry H.	1908.06.26	SLC	CT.Redding	Will you &	NN7	08041
Rogers, Henry H.	1908.12.19	SLC	CT.Redding	That trip would	NN7	08185
Rogers, Henry H.	1909.02.25	SLC	CT.Redding	I love you	CU-MARK(tr)	08354
Rogers, Henry H.	1909.03.04	SLC	CT.Redding	I think it	MFai	08362
Rogers, Henry H.	1909.04.26	SLC	CT.Redding	I will spend	CtHMTH	08391 telegram

ADDRESSEE	DATE	WRITER	PLACE	CUE	SOURCE	NUMBER/NOTES
Rogers, Henry H.	1909.05.04	SLC	CT.Redding	The check-books &	NN7	08396
Rogers, Henry H.	1909.05.09	SLC	CT.Redding	Lounsbury says the	CU-MARK	08677
Rogers, Mary B.	1900.10.25	SLC	NY.New York	I feel a	NNC	05884
Rogers, Mary B.	1906.**.**	SLC	Unknown	What was it	NNC	02402
Rogers, Mary B.	1906.07.04	SLC	MA.Fairhaven	with the compliments	CtHMTH	09251 inscription
Rogers, Mary B.	1906.08.04	SLC	NH.Dublin	You are a	NNC	07490
Rogers, Mary B.	1906.08.14	SLC	NH.Dublin	Ho, you miraculous	NNC	07499
Rogers, Mary B.	1906.08.25 to 1906.08.28	SLC	NH.Dublin	Now this can't	NNC	07504
Rogers, Mary B.	1906.08.28	SLC	NH.Dublin	Oh, don't mind	NNC	07509
Rogers, Mary B.	o/a 1906.08.31	SLC	NH.Dublin	Come, Mariechen, isn't	CU-MARK	07512 on Gilbert Aug 31
Rogers, Mary B.	1906.09.06	SLC	NH.Dublin	Oh, dont mind	NN-B(tr)	07518
Rogers, Mary B.	o/a 1906.09.07	SLC	NH.Dublin	You see, dear	NNC	07522 on Harvey Sept 7
Rogers, Mary B.	1906.09.21 to 1906.09.23	SLC	NY.New York	At 3 p.m.	NNC	07528
Rogers, Mary B.	o/a 1906.09.30	SLC	NH.Dublin	Mary, I'm sending	CU-MARK	07532 on Aldrich Sept 30
Rogers, Mary B.	1906.10.12 to 1906.10.17	SLC	NH.Dublin	It isn't right	NNC	07544
Rogers, Mary B.	1906.10.13	SLC	NH.Dublin	You hope you	NN-B(tr)	02246
Rogers, Mary B.	1906.10.16	SLC	NH.Dublin	Dear Pal, there	NNC	02377
Rogers, Mary B.	1906.10.22	SLC	NY.New York	I went Sabbath-breaking	NNC	07553
Rogers, Mary B.	1906.10.25	SLC	NY.New York	Mariechen dear, it must	NNC	02390
Rogers, Mary B.	o/a 1906.10.27	SLC	NY.New York	You have seen	CU-MARK	07557 on Stockbridge Oct 27
Rogers, Mary B.	1906.11.02	SLC	NY.New York	Can it be	NNC	07560
Rogers, Mary B.	1906.11.07	SLC	NY.New York	Dear pal, there	NNC	07562
Rogers, Mary B.	1906.11.08	SLC	NY.New York	P.S. My dear	NN-B(tr)	07564

Rogers, Mary B.	1906.11.19	SLC	NY.New York	Hang it!	NNC	07571
Rogers, Mary B.	1906.11.25	SLC	NY.New York	I was dictating	NNC	07575 on IVL Nov 25
Rogers, Mary B.	1906.11.26	SLC	NY.New York	Dear Pal, you have	NNC	07576
Rogers, Mary B.	1906.12.26	SLC	NY.New York	Mariechen dear, the	NNC	07598
Rogers, Mary B.	1907.05.**	SLC	NY.New York	O dear me	NNC	02418
Rogers, Mary B. & Rogers, Harry	1907.05.**	SLC	NY.Tuxedo Park	The pleasure of	NNC	07682
Rogers, Mary B.	ca 1907.10.**	SLC	NY.New York	Butter wanted	NNC	02431
Rogers, Mary B.	bef 1907.10.07	SLC	NY.New York	Read this &	NNC	02589
Rogers, Mary B.	1907.10.11	SLC	NY.Tuxedo Park	Mariechen dear, Flower	NNC	07852
Rogers, Mary B.	1907.11.21 & 1907.11.29	SLC	NY.New York	Well, dear, you	NNC	07867
Rogers, Mary B.	1908.02.07	SLC	NY.New York	Tuesday Feb. 11	NNC	02415
Rogers, Mary B.	1908.06.15	SLC	NY.New York	Mariechen dear, it is	NNC	08030
Rogers, Mary B.	1908.06.19	SLC	CT.Redding	I looked in	NNC	08033
Rogers, Mary B.	1908.08.**	SLC	CT.Redding	Why, bless your	NNC	08068
Rogers, Mary B.	1908.08.17	SLC	CT.Redding	Where are you	NNC	08069
Rogers, Mary B.	1909.03.08 to 1909.03.09	SLC	CT.Redding	Mariechen dear, I	NNC	08368
Rogers, Mary B.	1909.12.29	SLC	CT.Redding	You are your	NNC	08529
Rogers, Mary B.	1910.02.21	SLC	BE.Hamilton	You dear Mariechen	NNC	08562
Rogers Peet Clothing	1890.08.15	SLC	NY.Tannersville	I am away	256:1943.10	09064
Rohr, Lorenz	1884.05.12	SLC	CT.Hartford	The translators all	CU-MARK(ph)	02975
Rollins, Philip A.	1881.12.31	SLC	CT.Hartford	I haven't seen	NjP	10694
Roosevelt, Edith K.	1905.11.28	SLC	NY.New York	I did not	CU-MARK(tr)	07221 SLC tr
Roosevelt, Theodore	1901.12.24	SLC	NY.Riverdale	Not Duncan himself	DLC	06196
Roosevelt, Theodore	1902.08.11	SLC	ME.York Harbor	There above, you	NN-B	08227
Root, Oren Jr.	1906.05.05	SLC	NY.New York	My daughters are	CU-MARK(ph)	08892
Root, Oren Jr.	1906.05.13	SLC	NY.New York	I thank you	CU-MARK(ph)	08893

ADDRESSEE	DATE	WRITER	PLACE	CUE	SOURCE	NUMBER/NOTES
Roseboult, Charles J.	1891.01.19	SLC	CT.Hartford	Please do not	CU-MARK	04161
Ross, Janet D.	1892.08.09	SLC	GE.Bad-Nauheim	It will not	416:321	01681
Ross, Janet D.	1893.03.20	SLC	IT.Florence	It was my	416:324	04356
Ross, Janet D.	1893.04.14	SLC	IL.Chicago	I asked Secretary	416:331	04375
Rothmann, Laura	1897.09.30	SLC	AU.Vienna	We are greatly	127	11063
Routledge & Sons & Hood, Tom	1873.03.10	SLC	CT.Hartford	The Jubliee Singers	407:14	00886 other sources
Routledge, Robert A.	1873.12.12	SLC per CWS	EN.London	All right, any	UkL5	01003
Row, Mr.	1905.11.14	SLC per IVL	NY.New York	That alleged portrait	CU-MARK	07207
Royal Humane Society	1872.11.20	SLC	SH.Batavia	The Batavia sailed	189:1872.11.26	00833 other sources
Royal Society	1900.06.14	SLC	EN.London	Mr. & Mrs.	CU-MARK	05822
Roycrofters	1903.06.**	SLC per IVL	NY.Riverdale	Mr. Clemens regrets	CtHMTH	10590
Ruffner, Ann V.	1856.05.07	SLC	MO.Hannibal	Good-bye, good-bye	246:1935.03.06	11213 poem inscription
Russ, H.Q.	1898.10.03	SLC	AU.Kaltenleut.	Your letter has	NNC	05441 mislabeled Vienna
Russell, Edward	1907.07.12	SLC	EN.London	I was deeply	122:1936.12.09	07772
Russell, H.F.	1899.06.24	SLC	EN.London	If you mean	NN5	05643
Russell, Horace	1882.11.16	SLC	CT.Hartford	I struck a	CU-MARK(tr)	02306
Russell, Horace	1882.12.12	SLC	CT.Hartford	Woodford wrote me	ViU	02314
Russell, R.H.	bet 1899.06.01 & 1899.06.03	SLC	EN.London	Many thanks. Wednesday	CRc2	07741
Russell, Thomas W.	1884.10.14 & 1884.10.16	SLC	CT.Hartford	I am obliged	CtHMTH	03007
Russian, Wanda M.	o/a 1906.04.05	SLC per IVL	NY.New York	I don't know	CU-MARK(dr)	07415 on Russian Apr 5
Rutherford, David	o/a 1909.08.19	SLC	CT.Redding	I advised nothing	CU-MARK(dr)	08439 on Rutherford Aug 19

S., E.		1899.08.07	SLC	SE.Sanna	Nearly all of	RuM3	09363 inscription
S., Miss	ca	1909.01.18	SLC per MLH	CT.Redding	X and thank	CtHMTH(dr)	08318
Sacramento Union		1866.08.13	SLC	CA.San Francisco	Arrived in Smyrniote	N5(dr)	10676 telegram
Sadler, Mr.		1895.10.16	SLC	AS.Adelaide	I thank you	CU-MARK(ph)	10956
Sag, Mrs.		1905.**.**	SLC per IVL	NH.Dublin	Mr. Clemens wishes	CU-MARK	06970
Sage, Dean		1875.04.22	SLC	CT.Hartford	I should have	NN5	01221
Sage, Dean		1885.03.28	SLC	CT.Hartford	with the warmest	ViU	09338 inscription
Sage, Dean		1890.02.05	SLC	CT.Hartford	I saw House	ODa2	04012
Sage, Sarah A.		1885.08.31	SLC	NY.Elmira	I find my	CU-MARK(tr)	03284
Sage, Sarah A.		1889.10.06	SLC	CT.Hartford	Mrs. Clemens begs	Mo2	02443
Samatsinhji, Kumar S.		1896.02.05	SLC	II.Benares	It would be	CU-MARK(tr)	05017
San Francisco Alta ed.	ca	1867.03.02	SLC	Unknown	Send me $1,200	154:333	10992 telegram
San Francisco Alta ed.		1872.12.03	SLC	CT.Hartford	Certain gentlemen here	MH-H	00837
Sanborn, John W.		1878.01.24	SLC	CT.Hartford	Sh! Don't say	419:8	10421
Sanborn, John W.		1879.10.01	SLC	NY.Elmira	I have read	419:9	10422
Sanborn, John W.		1881.11.11	SLC	CT.Hartford	I am very	419:10	10423
Sanborn, John W.		1882.03.03	SLC	CT.Hartford	I wish you	419:12	10424
Sanborn, Miss		****.**.**	SLC	NY.New York	Oh,--nation, it's	NcWsW	09001
Sandifer, Mr.		****.**.**	SLC	Unknown	Yrs Truly	CU-MARK	11105 inscription
Saturday Morning Club		1878.03.25	SLC & OLC	CT.Hartford	For Mrs. Clemens	CtHMTH	01549
Saturday Morning Club		1880.06.**	SLC	CT.Hartford	The Clemenses accept	CtHSD	10480
Saunders, Louise B.		1904.09.03	SLC	NY.New York	I am grateful	NCH	06916
Saunders, Louise B.		1906.10.16	SLC	NH.Dublin	Your moving letter	NCH	07548
Saunders, Xantippe		1876.10.19	SLC	CT.Hartford	Your letter arrived	T	01377
Savitar ed.		1906.03.03	SLC	NY.New York	The Savitar has	MoU	10874

ADDRESSEE	DATE	WRITER	PLACE	CUE	SOURCE	NUMBER/NOTES
Sayles, Eleanor	*	*	*	*	*	11142 see Langdon, Eleanor S.
Scarano, R.	o/a 1906.03.29	SLC per IVL	NY.New York	Cornell possesses almost	CU-MARK(dr)	07407 on Scarano Mar 29
Schaykovsky, Nikolai	*	*	*	*	*	11216 see Chaikovsky, Nikolai V.
Schlesinger, Sigmund	1898.02.01	SLC	AU.Vienna	Gut! Also werde	Mo2	05338
Schlesinger, Sigmund	1898.05.20	SLC	AU.Vienna	We go to	NRU	00228
Schlesinger, Sigmund	1898.05.30	SLC	AU.Kaltenleut.	Certainly! Take another	NHC	05396
Schlesinger, Sigmund	1898.07.28	SLC	AU.Kaltenleut.	A manuscript written	NRU	00295
Schlesinger, Sigmund	1898.10.20	SLC	AU.Vienna	November 1. Schon	MiD	05452
Schlesinger, Sigmund	1899.01.01	SLC	AU.Vienna	If you can	CU-MARK(tr)	05455 telegram; SLC tr
Schmitt, Marguerite	1908.09.24	SLC	CT.Redding	with the high	ODa2	09384 inscription
Schmitt, Marguerite	bet 1909.01.** & 1909.02.**	JC	Unknown	seule de ta	NmA2	08300 fragment
Schmitt, Marguerite	1909.09.30	JC	CT.Redding	Je n'ai pas	NmA2	08462
Schmitt, Marguerite	1909.10.19	JC	CT.Redding	Nou, Bout, je	NmA2	08473
Schmitt, Marguerite	1909.11.07	JC	CT.Redding	Croyais-tu que	NmA2	08483
Schmitt, Marguerite	1909.11.20	JC	CT.Redding	Je suis si	NmA2	08498
Schmitt, Marguerite	1909.12.19	JC	CT.Redding	Quel jour t'es	NmA2	08512
Schmitt, Marguerite	1909.12.21	JC	CT.Redding	Que c'est facile	NmA2	08513
Schmitt, Marguerite	ca 1909.12.26	SLC	CT.Redding	To all friends	CU-MARK(tr)	08518 form letter
Schonstadt, A.	1902.01.30	SLC	NY.Riverdale	I have no	CtHSD	10584
Schulz, Laura	1902.02.04	OLC	NY.Riverdale	I have just	CtHMTH	06267
Schurz, Carl family	o/a 1906.05.14	SLC per IVL	NY.New York	I beg the	CU-MARK(dr)	07440
Scott, Albert J.	1879.10.27	SLC	CT.Hartford	1. Began to	ICN	01701

Scott, Daisy	pm	1905.12.28	SLC	NY.New York	Mark Twain	ODa2	11222 inscription
Scott, Frank H.		1895.06.18	SLC	NY.Elmira	I am at	NN-B(tr)	10796 SLC tr
Scribner's Sons		****.11.17	SLC	CT.Hartford	I sent a	NjBern2	09187
Scroll & Key Society		1868.11.18	SLC	OH.Cleveland	Allow me the	CtY	02764
Scudder, Horace E.		1891.07.21	SLC	FR.Aix-les-Bains	It is very	MH-H	04222
Scully, C.D.		1876.03.20	SLC	CT.Hartford	I mislaid your	PPiHi	01773
Searbright, Frank T.	o/a	1907.04.12	SLC per IVL	NY.New York	Never make another	CU-MARK(dr)	07693 on Searbright Apr 12
Sears, G.A. & Pixley, Seymour		1864.01.23	SLC	NV.Carson City	Certainly. If the	201	00074
Sears, O.B.		1902.07.16	SLC	ME.York Harbor	I wish I	MoHM	06388
Seaver, David W.		1909.10.29	SLC	CT.Redding	I remember your	NN-B	08294
Seaver, David W.		1909.11.30	JC	CT.Redding	Father is in	NN-B	07290
Seaver, William A.		****.**.**	SLC	CT.Hartford	I would have	WU	07707
Seaver, William A.		1874.05.01	SLC	NY.Elmira	If you can't	WU	01081
Seaver, William A.		1874.05.20	SLC	NY.Elmira	That is the	WU	01090
Seaver, William A.		1874.09.25	SLC	CT.Hartford	Am now answering	WU	01100
Seaver, William A.		1875.02.26	SLC	CT.Hartford	Yes sir! You	WU	01198
Seaver, William A.		1875.03.06	SLC	CT.Hartford	We did the	WU	01204
Seaver, William A.		1875.12.**	SLC	CT.Hartford	To the aged	105:1968.05.14	09687 inscription
Seaver, William A.		1875.12.05	SLC	CT.Hartford	Why, you old	WU	01286
Seaver, William A.		1876.09.16	SLC	CT.Hartford	My Dear Boy	WU	01365
Seaver, William A.		1876.10.04	SLC	CT.Hartford	I can't, old	CU-MARK(tr)	01372
Seaver, William A.		1878.06.28	SLC	GE.Heidelberg	There be humorists	CLjC	01574
Seaver, William A.		1880.12.29	SLC	CT.Hartford	Yes, old Man	CU-MARK(tr)	01885
Seaver, William A.		1894.07.31	SLC	CT.Hartford	Some of my	NN-B	10803 inscription

ADDRESSEE	DATE	WRITER	PLACE	CUE	SOURCE	NUMBER/NOTES
Selkirk, George A.	ca 1869.11.20	SLC	MA.Boston	Give him a	CU-MARK	10552 on George Nov 9
Senour, Caro S.	****.**.**	SLC	AU.Vienna	What you have	120:1942.07	09918
Sergeant, Lewis	1873.06.25	SLC	EN.London	I shall be	CU-MARK(tr)	00935
Severance, Emily A.	1867.12.24	SLC	DC.Washington	Your letter came	156:218	02780 other sources
Severance, Emily A.	1869.10.27	SLC	NY.Elmira	I thank you	CU-MARK(tr)	00364 other sources
Severy, Melvin L.	o/a 1906.02.05	SLC per IVL	NY.New York	All documents can	CU-MARK(dr)	07330
Severy, Melvin L.	o/a 1906.08.10	SLC per IVL	NH.Dublin	I am quite	CU-MARK(dr)	07498 on Severy Aug 10
Seward, Theodore F.	1875.03.08	SLC	CT.Hartford	I am expecting	190:1875.03.13	01205
Seward, Theodore F.	aft 1887.08.09	SLC	NY.Elmira	I judge the	CU-MARK	02666
Seward, Theodore F.	aft 1887.08.15	SLC	Unknown	Come--come--take	CU-MARK	03623
Seymour, George S.	1901.04.23	SLC	NY.New York	Here you have	IGK	06041
Sharp, R. Farquborson	1897.09.03	SLC	SW.Weggis	I have made	ViU	05286
Sharples, Jenny	1883.01.15	SLC	CT.Hartford	The birth-day is	CU-MARK(tr)	02335
Sharples, Jenny	1883.05.01	SLC	CT.Hartford	The dainty marvel	NN-B	02570
Shattuck, L.E.	1906.02.15	SLC per IVL	NY.New York	I believe that	CtHMTH	07344
Shaw, George B.	1907.07.04	SLC	EN.London	Between you &	ViU	07777
Shaw, Henry W.	1870.05.16	SLC	NY.Buffalo	Dear Josh	CU-MARK	09804 unsent
Shaw, Henry W.	1873.03.**	SLC	CT.Hartford	I think a	318:1873.07.14	00877
Sheldon, Isaac E.	1871.04.06	SLC	NY.Elmira	I am glad	CU-MARK	00601
Sheridan, Philip H.	1884.12.26	SLC	CT.Hartford	I beg to	NPV	03071
Sherman, John	1877.09.20	SLC	CT.Hartford	I have the	DNA	01484 tr of Sept 20 to Hayes enc
Sherman, John	1877.09.22	SLC	CT.Hartford	I am very	DNA	01487
Sherman, William T.	1885.09.19	SLC	CT.Hartford	Indeed I will	DLC	01606

Sherman, William T.	&	1885.10.05 1885.10.06	SLC	CT.Hartford	You tempt me	DLC	04126
Sherman, William T.		1885.10.12	SLC	CT.Hartford	I think you	DLC	03859
Sherman, William T.		1885.12.15	SLC	CT.Hartford	This is the	DLC	03977
Sherry, Margaret		1904.02.07	SLC	IT.Florence	We relieved those	Mo2	08888
Sherry, Margaret		1904.04.05	SLC	IT.Florence	Mrs. Clemens thanks	Mo2	08889
Sherry, Margaret		1904.07.16	SLC	NY.New York	Your lovely flowers	297:103	06887
Shields, Henry J.	o/a	1905.06.22	SLC per IVL	NH.Dublin	article was written	CU-MARK(dr)	07068 on Shields June 22
Shillaber, Benjamin P.		1870.05.28	SLC	NY.Buffalo	Yourself & daughter	IU-R	00470
Shinn, Milicent		1882.10.27	SLC	CT.Hartford	Delegated work is	CU-MARK	02296 typed
Shinn, Milicent		1884.02.06	SLC	CT.Hartford	P.S. Private	CU-MARK	02908
Shipman, Arthur L.		1887.04.01	SLC	CT.Hartford	*	ViU	03554 envelope only
Shipman, Ernest		1902.01.14	SLC	NY.Riverdale	Mr Clemens instructs	CU-MARK(dr)	06245
Shipman, Mary C.		****.**.**	SLC & OLC	Unknown	I constitute myself	CtHMTH	09113
Shipman, Mary C.	bef	1878.03.01	SLC	CT.Hartford	I have got	ViU	01539
Shipman, Mary C.		1893.08.11	SLC & OLC	AU.Krankenheil	I was so	ViU	04434
Shubert, Lee & Shubert, Sam S.	o/a	1905.12.13	SLC per IVL	NY.New York	Send someone down	CU-MARK(dr)	07252 on Shuberts Dec 13
Shubert, Sam S. & Shubert, Lee	o/a	1905.12.13	SLC per IVL	NY.New York	Send someone down	CU-MARK(dr)	07252 on Shuberts Dec 13
Siebert, Wilbur H.		1902.12.05	SLC	NY.Riverdale	I think it	CU-MARK(ph)	09058
Silk, A.	o/a	1904.11.09	SLC per IVL	NY.New York	I thank you	CU-MARK(dr)	06946 on Silk Nov 6
Sill, George G. & Sprague, Joseph H.		1875.02.20	SLC	CT.Hartford	I accede to	117:1875.02.23	01196 also to Robinson
Sill, Louise M.	pm	1902.12.11	SLC	NY.Riverdale	This is Obituary	CU-MARK	06511 on Stickley Dec 9

ADDRESSEE	DATE	WRITER	PLACE	CUE	SOURCE	NUMBER/NOTES
Sill, Mrs.	pm 1902.12.26	SLC	NY.New York	*	ODa2	11175 envelope only
Silvers, L. Fred	1902.07.31	SLC	ME.York Harbor	It does indeed	CU-MARK(tr)	06395
Simboli, Rafforele	1904.06.14	IVL	IT.Florence	You will understand	CU-MARK(dr)	06871 on Simboli June 14
Simon, Miss	1880.06.19	SLC	NY.Elmira	Your note has	CU-MARK	01815
Simons, Michael L.	1873.01.27 to 1873.01.28	SLC	CT.Hartford	I regret the	NN-B	00868
Sinnett, Percy F.	1881.07.24	SLC	CT.Hartford	I thought I	162:1881.10.15	09442 other sources
Sinsheimer, Madelaine	1905.02.15	SLC	NY.New York	Your good &	CU-MARK(ph)	09191
Skinner, Mr.	****.05.23	SLC	NY.New York	I thank you	CU-MARK(ph)	09002
Skinner, Otis	1906.05.07	SLC	NY.New York	So you have	CCamarSJ	07438
Skrine, Francis H.	1897.01.19	SLC	EN.London	We were very	NWhp2	05171
Skrine, Francis H.	1897.08.22	SLC	SW.Weggis	It is my	ViU	05281
Skrine, Francis H.	pm 1897.09.10	SLC	SW.Weggis	The cigars have	ViU	05284
Skrine, Francis H.	1897.11.03	SLC	AU.Vienna	This is good	ViU	05306
Skrine, Francis H.	1899.03.09	SLC	AU.Vienna	If we were	ViU	05558
Skrine, Francis H.	1899.05.24	SLC	AU.Vienna	It is lovely	CU-MARK(ph)	05595
Skrine, Francis H.	1899.07.01	SLC	EN.London	Alas, we shall	CU-MARK(ph)	10569
Skrine, Francis H.	1899.07.05	SLC	EN.London	It is exceedingly	CaQMM	05649
Skrine, Francis H.	1899.09.15	SLC	SE.Sanna	It's a darling	CtY	05676
Skrine, Francis H.	1901.07.29	SLC	NY.Saranac Lake	The pleasure is	CU-MARK	06099
Skrine, Francis H.	1902.01.07	SLC	NY.Riverdale	Although the Sir	UkENL	06224
Skrine, Francis H.	1902.02.05 to 1902.02.13	SLC	NY.Riverdale	I read to	454:1978.06	06270 other sources
Skrine, Francis H.	1903.12.17	SLC	IT.Florence	It is a	WU	06769
Skrine, Helen	1897.06.18	SLC	EN.London	Then with you	CLU-S/C	05230
Sladen, Douglas B.	1899.06.10	SLC	EN.London	Thank you, I	UkL4	09110
Sladen, Douglas B.	1899.06.11	SLC	EN.London	Did I tell	UkL4	09109
Sladen, Douglas B.	1899.07.07	SLC	EN.London	I have been	ViU	05652

Sladen, Douglas B.	pm	1899.10.30	SLC	EN.London	Of course I	UkL4	09108
Slote, Daniel		****.**.**	SLC	Unknown	*	CU-MARK	09477 envelope only
Slote, Daniel		1867.08.07	SLC	IT.Naples	Bier bot. 3	TxU	00143
Slote, Daniel		1870.06.27	SLC	NY.Elmira	Charley has been	CtHMTH	00484
Slote, Daniel	ca	1876.09.**	SLC	Unknown	I have invented	460	11146 other sources
Slote, Daniel		1879.09.04	SLC	NY.Elmira	I was lucky	155:1963.11.11	10434
Slote, Daniel		1880.06.29	SLC	NY.Elmira	Yours received--so	NPV	01817
Slote, Daniel		1880.12.16	SLC	CT.Hartford	I am very	NPV	01872
Slote, Daniel		1881.01.26	SLC	CT.Hartford	Am very sorry	NPV	01898
Slote, Daniel	&	1881.02.19 1881.02.21	SLC	CT.Hartford	I want that	NPV	01911
Slote, Daniel		1881.02.24	SLC	MA.Boston	The plate is	NPV	01914
Slote, Daniel		1881.03.16	SLC	CT.Hartford	Those handsome	NPV	01929
Slote, Daniel		1881.03.31	SLC	CT.Hartford	In offering $100	MoHi	01933
Slote, Daniel		1881.03.31	SLC	CT.Hartford	Let the wages	NPV	01934
Slote, Woodman & Co.		1878.02.10	SLC	CT.Hartford	I hereby certify	460	11147
Smedley, Will L.		1903.05.30	SLC per IVL	NY.Riverdale	I thank you	N4	10782
Smedley, Will L.		1903.08.29	SLC	NY.New York	I thank you	N4	10783
Smedley, Will L.		1903.09.03	SLC	NY.Elmira	The picture has	N4	10784
Smedley, Will L.	pm	1905.12.01	SLC	NY.New York	To you, &	N4	10781 form letter
Smith, Benjamin E.	o/a	1903.02.27	SLC	NY.Riverdale	It has never	CtNh2	06587 on Smith Feb 27
Smith, Benjamin E.		1906.08.06	SLC per IVL	NH.Dublin	I am authority	CtNh2	07491
Smith, Charles S.	o/a	1906.12.24	SLC per IVL	NY.New York	I am quite	CU-MARK(tr)	07597
Smith, Elizabeth W.		1860.01.26	SLC	MO.St. Louis	Ma has not	C4	00021
Smith, Ellen T.		1871.08.30	SLC	NY.Elmira	I wish your	I2	00648

ADDRESSEE	DATE	WRITER	PLACE	CUE	SOURCE	NUMBER/NOTES
Smith, George G.	1903.12.21	SLC	IT.Florence	Thursday is our	MoFu2	10730
Smith, George W.	1888.09.12	SLC	NY.Elmira	we have been	178:1947.09	03761
Smith, George W.	1888.11.06	SLC	CT.Hartford	Here is some	NGH	03829
Smith, J. Wylie	1909.08.07	SLC	CT.Redding	My view of	CU-MARK	08440
Smith, Jim	1885.02.18 to 1885.02.20	SLC	CN.Montreal	We thank you	151:1906.03.24	04078
Smith, Judson	1901.03.10	SLC	NY.New York	If Dr. Ament	CU-MARK	06018
Smith, Kingsland	1883.07.28	SLC	NY.Elmira	I haven't seen	ViU	02075
Smith, Kingsland	1885.01.23	SLC	MN.St. Paul	I shan't be	178:1950.05	09118
Smith, Kingsland	1900.04.05	SLC	EN.London	Ah, but I	107:1925.03.03	09633
Smith, Mr.	1873.07.11	SLC	EN.London	We should be	CU-MARK(tr)	00949
Smith, Mr.	1890.03.27	OLC	CT.Hartford	You will I	CU-MARK	04032
Smith, Mrs. A.W.	1902.01.27	SLC per FGW	CT.Hartford	*	M2	10105 envelope only
Smith, Mrs. Ira L.	1901.01.**	SLC	NY.New York	The Library of	ViU(tr)	05955
Smith, Mrs. Samuel E.	1901.01.01	SLC	NY.New York	This is a	NBron2	05956
Smith, Roswell	1884.05.06	SLC	CT.Hartford	I hunted up	422:1982.05.15	04199
Smith, Roswell	1885.03.09	SLC	CT.Hartford	All right--I've	VtMiM	03186
Smith, T. Max	1889.11.**	CC	CT.Hartford	If it is	CtHMTH	03960
Smith, William	1886.10.18	SLC	CT.Hartford	I hold myself	CU-MARK(ph)	03462
Smith, William	1886.12.15	SLC	CT.Hartford	Now we shall see!	ODa2	11176
Smith, William	1887.02.03 & 1887.02.04	SLC	CT.Hartford	We are delighted	ODa2	03522
Smith, William	1887.12.05	SLC	CT.Hartford	I've read it	CU-MARK(tr)	03673
Smith, William	1891.04.28	SLC	CT.Hartford	It is our	CU-MARK(tr)	04198
Society Psychical Res.	1884.10.04	SLC	CT.Hartford	I should be	269:1884.10	03004
Solomons, Miss	1898.12.28	SLC	AU.Vienna	I tried to	CU-MARK	05485
Somerville, Edith A.	1886.07.15	SLC	NY.Elmira	As I am	MH-H	03421
Sonnichsen, Albert	1901.03.18	SLC	NY.New York	I thank you	IC3	06021 typed
Spalding, Mr.	****.**.**	SLC	Unknown	The big envelops	NN-B	09003

Spalding, Mr.		1896.10.02	SLC	Unknown	No, we'll not	157:1925.11.30	09786
Spalding, Mr.		1897.11.20	SLC	AU.Vienna	I want to	CtY	05315
Spalding, Mr.		1900.09.02	SLC	EN.London	with the kindest	CtHMTH	09271 inscription
Spalding, Mrs. Percy & Spalding, Percy	ca	1904.06.21	SLC	IT.Florence	For what you	ViU	06849 form letter
Spalding, Percy		1897.06.22	SLC	EN.London	For goodness Sake	NN-B	05514 telegram
Spalding, Percy		1899.05.03	SLC	AU.Vienna	Enclosed please find	ViU	05585
Spalding, Percy		1899.05.10	SLC	AU.Vienna	The telegram came	ViU	05591
Spalding, Percy		1899.05.24	SLC	AU.Vienna	Thank you ever	ViU	05596
Spalding, Percy		1899.06.01	OLC	EN.London	On returning to	NN-B	06797
Spalding, Percy		1899.06.07	SLC	EN.Broadstairs	Will you look	NN-B	05612
Spalding, Percy		1899.07.06	SLC	EN.London	The enclosed Combination	NN-B	05617
Spalding, Percy		1899.07.23	OLC	SE.Sanna	Thank you so	NN-B	06819
Spalding, Percy		1899.10.16	SLC	EN.London	Upon my return	ViU	05691
Spalding, Percy		1899.10.17	SLC	EN.London	Cannot lunch till	NN-B	05623 telegram
Spalding, Percy		1899.11.03	OLC	EN.London	Thank you heartily	NN-B	07051
Spalding, Percy		1900.10.01	SLC	EN.London	all the family	105:1958.04.28	09699
Spalding, Percy		1902.12.15	SLC	NY.Riverdale	I am preparing	ViU	06519
Spalding, Percy & Spalding, Mrs. Percy	ca	1904.06.21	SLC	IT.Florence	For what you	ViU	06849 form letter
Spaulding, Clara L.		1880.04.**	SLC	CT.Hartford	To Clara L	157:1923.01.24	09776 inscription
Spaulding, Clara L.		1881.12.20	SLC	CT.Hartford	With more than	157:1923.01.24	09777 inscription
Spaulding, Clara L.		1886.08.20	SLC	NY.Elmira	Many will give	CU-MARK(ph)	03442
Spaulding, Clara L.		1886.09.01	SLC	NY.Elmira	As an all	CU-MARK(ph)	03447
Spaulding, Clara L.		1889.09.29	SLC	CT.Hartford	Yes, you can	CU-MARK(ph)	03944
Spaulding, Clara L.		1895.07.02	SLC	NY.Elmira	Livy says it	CU-MARK(ph)	04924
Spectator ed.		1872.09.20	SLC	EN.London	I only venture	426:1872.09.21	00809

ADDRESSEE	DATE	WRITER	PLACE	CUE	SOURCE	NUMBER/NOTES
Spitzka, Edward A.	o/a 1907.04.10	SLC per IVL	NY.New York	Well I read	CU-MARK(dr)	07689 on Spitzka Apr 10
Spofford, Ainsworth R.	aft 1870.09.16	SLC	NY.Buffalo	Mr. Spofford, could	DLC	00507
Spofford, Ainsworth R.	1873.04.21	SLC	CT.Hartford	Enclosed please find	DLC	00904
Spofford, Ainsworth R.	1874.03.19	SLC	CT.Hartford	I am going	CSmH	01065
Spofford, Ainsworth R.	1874.05.07	SLC	NY.Elmira	I enclose design	DLC	01084
Spofford, Ainsworth R.	1874.05.21	SLC	NY.Elmira	I lately copyrighted	DLC	01092
Spofford, Ainsworth R.	1875.02.16	SLC	CT.Hartford	Will you be	DLC	01194
Spofford, Ainsworth R.	1876.10.23	SLC	CT.Hartford	I enclose printed	DLC	02467
Spofford, Ainsworth R.	1879.09.26	SLC	NY.Elmira	I desire to	DLC	01693
Spofford, Ainsworth R.	1880.03.11	SLC	CT.Hartford	I beg leave	DLC	01770
Spofford, Ainsworth R.	1884.02.28	SLC	CT.Hartford	I desire to	DLC	02924
Spofford, Ainsworth R.	1896.08.11	SLC	EN.London	I desire to	Mo2	08841
Spofford, Ainsworth R.	1897.01.30	SLC	EN.London	I hereby make	NN-B	05502
Spofford, Ainsworth R.	1897.05.19 to 1897.07.12	SLC	EN.London	I as author	DLC	05218 other sources
Sprague, Joseph H. & Sill, George G.	1875.02.20	SLC	CT.Hartford	I accede to	117:1875.02.23	01196 also to Robinson
Sprague, Mr.	1909.10.18	SLC	CT.Redding	That fine are	CU-MARK(tr)	10491
Spring, Mrs.	1898.11.06	SLC	AU.Vienna	I am very	CU-MARK	05462
Springfield Repub. ed.	1881.12.18	SLC	CT.Hartford	If you will	131:1881.12.25	02119 other sources
Spurgeon, Frian	1897.04.27	SLC	EN.London	Yes, I changed	ViU	05209
St. Andrew's Society	ca 1901.11.**	SLC	NY.Riverdale	Mr. SL. Clemens	NHi	09105
St. Elizabeth Guild	1904.11.08	SLC	NY.New York	from a friend	NN-B	10801 inscription
St. Louis Republic ed.	1907.**.**	SLC	Unknown	May my namesake	CU-MARK(tr)	09865
Stanchfield, Clara L.	*	*	*	*	*	10314 see Spaulding, Clara
Stanchfield, John B.	1904.01.29	SLC	IT.Florence	Your letter came	CU-MARK	06788

Stanchfield, John B.	o/a	1905.03.04	SLC per IVL	NY.New York	Mr. Clemens does	CU-MARK(tr)	07012 on Stanchfield Mar 4
Stancliff, J.W.	bet &	1875.10.25 1875.11.17	SLC	CT.Hartford	The illuminations are	117:1875.11.17	01275
Standen, Robert F.		1906.02.24	SLC per IVL	NY.New York	It is quite	CU-MARK(dr)	07343 on Standen Feb 14-24
Standring, George		1886.08.25	SLC	NY.Elmira	I very much	CU-MARK(ph)	03445
Standring, George		1905.12.31	SLC	NY.New York	Dear Standring it	NN-B(tr)	07282
Stanley, Dorothy T.		1904.05.11	SLC	IT.Florence	I have lost	CU-MARK	06833
Stanley, Henry M.		1886.11.18	SLC	CT.Hartford	You needn't write	NN-B	02651
Stanley, Henry M.		1889.03.22	SLC	CT.Hartford	Hope you will	TxU(tr)	03874 telegram; SLC tr
Stanley, Henry M.		1889.06.18	SLC	Unknown	Goodness only knows	TxU(tr)	03902
Stanley, Robert N.		1901.01.21	SLC	NY.New York	You do not	CtHSD	05973 typed
Stanton, John		1867.05.14	SLC	NY.New York	I am to	CU-MARK	00129
Stanton, John		1867.05.20	SLC	NY.New York	I am one	CU-MARK	00131
Stanton, Theodore M.		1898.05.26	SLC	AU.Kaltenleut.	I thank you	NjR	05395
Stanton, Theodore M.		1901.10.**	SLC	NY.Riverdale	I will remain	NjR	06150
Stanton, Theodore M.		1901.10.13	OLC	NY.Riverdale	I was more	NjR	06154
Stanton, Theodore M.		1901.12.09	SLC	NY.Riverdale	Many thanks for	NjR	06186
Stanton, Theodore M.		1902.01.10	SLC	NY.Riverdale	So far--good	NjR	06241
Stanton, Theodore M.		1902.10.01	SLC	ME.York Harbor	Welcome home! Mrs.	NjR	06451
Stanton, Theodore M.		1902.10.18	SLC	NY.Riverdale	Any time, now	NjR	06467
Stanton, Theodore M.		1903.01.14	SLC per IVL	NY.Riverdale	I recall the	NjR	06562
Stanton, Theodore M.	ca	1904.06.21	SLC	IT.Florence	For what you	NjR	06851 form letter
Staples, Kate		1886.10.08	SLC	CT.Hartford	Yes, the truth	NN-B	02647
Starbird, Nathaniel W.		1877.12.20	SLC	CT.Hartford	Please send to	CU-MARK	01514
Starkey, Jennie		1902.10.07	SLC	ME.York Harbor	It was Bill	462:47	09521

ADDRESSEE	DATE	WRITER	PLACE	CUE	SOURCE	NUMBER/NOTES
Starr, Moses A.	1905.02.26	SLC per IVL	NY.New York	I have been	CU-MARK	06994
Starr, Moses A.	o/a 1906.03.22	SLC per IVL	NY.New York	I am most	CU-MARK(dr)	07398 on Starr Mar 21
Starr, W.J.	o/a 1908.10.07	SLC	CT.Redding	Greeting and Salutation	CtY	10790 form letter
Stead, William T.	1890.03.17	SLC	CT.Hartford	I am a	132:63f	04025
Stead, William T.	1890.06.24	SLC	CT.Hartford	May I wish	CU-MARK(tr)	04054
Stead, William T.	1894.11.30	SLC	FR.Paris	As I understand	ViU	04817
Stead, William T.	1899.01.09	SLC	AU.Vienna	Peace by compulsion	114:672	10946
Stead, William T.	1899.01.09	SLC	AU.Vienna	The Czar is	114:672	05535
Stead, William T.	1901.01.21	SLC	NY.New York	I am afraid	ViU(tr)	05974
Stebbins, C.L.	o/a 1905.04.06	SLC per IVL	NY.New York	Impossible for Mr.	CU-MARK(dr)	07026 on Stebbins Apr 6
Stedman, Arthur	1892.12.08	SLC	IT.Florence	Your kind note	NN-B	04625
Stedman, Arthur	1906.07.10	SLC	NY.New York	You know it	284:11	10462
Stedman, Edmund C.	1883.01.10	SLC	CT.Hartford	Twelve days hence	PBL	02333
Stedman, Edmund C.	1883.01.22	SLC	CT.Hartford	with the kindest	157:1911.01.12	09797 inscription
Stedman, Edmund C.	1883.02.06	SLC	CT.Hartford	I have been	PBL	02344
Stedman, Edmund C.	1885.01.15	SLC	IA.Keokuk	Take from any	NN-B	02603
Stedman, Edmund C.	1888.11.02	SLC	NY.New York	I am disappointed	NNC	03825
Stedman, Edmund C.	1889.05.18	SLC	CT.Hartford	I shall be	CtY	03894
Stedman, Edmund C.	1889.07.11	SLC	CT.Hartford	I am as	134:1912.04.19	09934 other sources
Stedman, Edmund C.	1889.12.10	SLC	CT.Hartford	It was ever	107:1914.01.20	09421 inscription; other sources
Stedman, Edmund C.	1896.10.16	SLC	EN.London	Do not show	NNC	05130
Stedman, Edmund C.	1900.11.07	SLC	NY.New York	The invitation is	InU-Li	10834
Stedman, Edmund C.	1900.11.15	SLC	NY.New York	That's all right	NhD	05908
Stedman, Edmund C.	1900.12.12	SLC	NY.New York	It is most	NNC(tr)	05930

Stedman, Edmund C.		1901.10.08	SLC	NY.Riverdale	Mr. Dodge gave	ViU	06153
Stedman, Edmund C.	bef	1903.06.25	SLC	NY.Riverdale	On behalf of	429:474	09532 group letter
Stedman, Edmund C.		1904.12.21	SLC per IVL	NY.New York	Mr. Clemens wishes	NNAL	06961
Steele, E.L.G.		****.09.18	SLC	CT.Hartford	I would be	ViU	08099
Stein, Louis E.		1898.03.15	SLC	AU.Vienna	I am sorry	103:1910.05.01	10785
Stephen		1897.04.27	SLC	EN.London	It was pleasant	105:1938.11.21	05160
Stephens, E.W.	ca	1890.06.10	SLC	CT.Hartford	I have been	133	10444
Stephens, Mrs. E.W.		1902.06.12	SLC	NY.Riverdale	I beg to	CU-MARK(tr)	06362
Stepniak, Sergei M.		1891.04.23	SLC	CT.Hartford	The words which	RuM2	06149
Stepniak, Sergei M.		1891.05.**	SLC	CT.Hartford	Yrs Truly	RuM2	09213 inscription
Sterling, C.F.		1871.01.24	SLC	NY.Buffalo	It isn't any	ViU	00563
Sterling-Maxwell, W.		1873.06.28	SLC	EN.London	Your note apprising	UkG2	09201
Stern, Ike		1901.01.21	SLC	NY.New York	I desire to	ViU(tr)	05975
Stevens, Ashton		1907.01.**	SLC	Unknown	Taking the pledge	CU-MARK(tr)	09263 inscription
Stevens, Elizabeth S.		1879.06.12	SLC	FR.Paris	The following is	DLC	01667
Stevens, Jenny		*	*	*	*	*	11131 see Boardman, Jenny S.
Stevens, John H.		1901.08.28	SLC	NY.Saranac Lake	If Brooklyn were	CU-MARK	06124
Stevenson, Robert L.		****.**.**	SLC	Unknown	Truly yours	175:1902.04.25	09879 inscription
Stevenson, Robert L.		1888.04.15	SLC	CT.Hartford	How fortunate!--I	CLjC	03715
Stewart, William M.		1907.08.09	SLC per IVL	NY.Tuxedo Park	Since Mr. Clemens's	CU-MARK	07810
Stiattesi, Raffaello		1905.02.19	SLC per IVL	NY.New York	It was most	CU-MARK(tr)	07004 IVL tr
Stickey, Miss		1906.03.10	SLC	NY.New York	This note from	CU-MARK(ph)	07376
Still, Andrew T.		1900.02.23	SLC	EN.London	By argument of	Mo3	05762
Stillson, Jerome B.		1874.03.23	SLC	CT.Hartford	I have written	NN-B	02469

ADDRESSEE	DATE	WRITER	PLACE	CUE	SOURCE	NUMBER/NOTES
Stillson, Jerome B.	1874.04.09	SLC	CT.Hartford	Will you please	111:174	01073 other sources
Stillson, Jerome B.	1874.04.13	SLC	CT.Hartford	large number of	107:1924.11.24	09451
Stillson, Jerome B.	1874.09.18	SLC	NY.New York	Been wanting to	ViU	01125 telegram
Stillson, Jerome B.	1875.01.19	SLC	CT.Hartford	This morning's Tribune	159:15.3.1	01182
Stillson, Jerome B.	1875.01.25	SLC	CT.Hartford	Will you please	159:15.3.1	01183
Stillson, Jerome B.	1876.01.19	SLC	CT.Hartford	I comply with	Mo2	01301 date uncertain
Stockbridge, Anne W.	1906.10.04	SLC	NH.Dublin	Yes, I should	NN-B(tr)	02245
Stockbridge, Henry	1901.04.24	SLC	NY.New York	I thank you	ViU	06045 typed
Stockton, Frank R. & Holmes, Oliver W.	1885.11.29	SLC	CT.Hartford	It was the	CLU-S/C	03318 also to Warner & Harris
Stockton, Frank R.	1902.01.09	SLC	NY.Riverdale	As regards that	CU-MARK	06237 typed form letter
Stoddard, Charles W.	1867.**.**	SLC	Unknown	Every now and	CSmH	00125
Stoddard, Charles W.	1867.04.23	SLC	NY.New York	You see I	CU-MARK	00124
Stoddard, Charles W.	1867.04.27	SLC	Unknown	*	CU-BANC	10084 envelope only
Stoddard, Charles W.	1869.08.25	SLC	NY.Buffalo	I have written	233:1936.03.23	00340
Stoddard, Charles W.	bet 1870.01.01 & 1870.01.05	SLC	NY.Elmira	Tell me--what	ViU	08584 on envelope
Stoddard, Charles W.	1873.10.19	SLC	EN.London	I am leaving	CU-MARK	00976
Stoddard, Charles W.	1874.01.09	SLC	EN.Liverpool	We've done with	NN-B	01037
Stoddard, Charles W.	1875.02.01	SLC	CT.Hartford	All right about	MB	01187
Stoddard, Charles W.	1875.03.17	SLC	CT.Hartford	Yrs rec'd last	ODa2	01210
Stoddard, Charles W.	1876.09.20	SLC	CT.Hartford	We have returned	OFH	01366
Stoddard, Charles W.	1876.11.01	SLC	CT.Hartford	That man's cheek	198:1960.10.01	01385 addressee uncertain
Stoddard, Charles W.	1877.**.**	SLC	Unknown	from S.L. Clemens	111:250	10337 inscription

Stoddard, Charles W.		1877.**.**	SLC	Unknown	from his friend	InU-Li	09289 inscription
Stoddard, Charles W.		1877.10.**	SLC	Unknown	from his friend	157:1924.11.10	09765 inscription
Stoddard, Charles W.		1877.10.**	SLC	Unknown	from S.L. Clemens	157:1924.11.10	09764 inscription
Stoddard, Charles W.		1877.10.**	SLC	Unknown	from S.L. Clemens	NN-B	09281 inscription
Stoddard, Charles W.		1877.10.22	SLC	CT.Hartford	My wife has	CCamarSJ	01490
Stoddard, Charles W.		1878.03.20	SLC	CT.Hartford	Bong voig to	MB	01546
Stoddard, Charles W.		1880.06.17	SLC	NY.Elmira	Now what the	MoSW	01813
Stoddard, Charles W.		1881.10.26	SLC	CT.Hartford	A Parthian arrow	NN-B	02554
Stoddard, Charles W.		1881.12.20	SLC	CT.Hartford	With the love	107:1914.01.20	09316 inscription
Stoddard, Charles W.		1885.06.01	SLC	CT.Hartford	I have read	InNd	03234
Stoddard, Charles W.		1886.03.16	SLC	CT.Hartford	It is your	CCC	03376
Stoddard, Charles W.		1891.10.**	SLC	Unknown	from his oldest	CU-BANC(tr)	09306 inscription
Stoddard, Charles W.		1898.11.06	SLC	AU.Vienna	I've almost forgotten	CSmH(tr)	05460 other sources
Stoddard, Charles W.		1902.12.15	SLC	NY.Riverdale	Yours received. I	CSt	06520
Stoddard, Charles W.	pm	1904.07.28	SLC	MA.Lee	For what you	ViU	06883 form letter
Stoddard, Henry L.		1902.11.28	SLC	NY.New York	Done by Truly	ODa2(ph)	11218 engraved inscription
Stoker, Bram		****.10.23	SLC	Unknown	Receive Miss Lawton	212:1945.05.12	09929
Stoker, Bram		1887.11.19	SLC	NY.New York	We have to	NN-B	02679
Stoker, Bram		1891.03.29	SLC	CT.Hartford	Do you know	NN-B	04579
Stoker, Bram		1893.12.06	SLC	NY.New York	Thank you ever	CaQMM	04521
Stoker, Bram		1894.**.**	SLC	Unknown	Pudd'nhead Wilson's	ViU	11081 inscription
Stoker, Bram		1894.02.13	SLC	NY.New York	I am glad	Mo2	02461
Stoker, Bram	bef	1894.02.13	SLC	NY.New York	Now it's all	Mo2	08839

ADDRESSEE	DATE	WRITER	PLACE	CUE	SOURCE	NUMBER/NOTES
Stoker, Bram	1894.03.03	SLC	NY.New York	Many thanks for	CU-MARK	07515
Stoker, Bram	1896.11.02	SLC	EN.London	As you may	NN-B	05243
Stoker, Bram	1896.12.17	CC	EN.London	It was lovely	UkLe2	05086
Stoker, Bram	1897.05.06	SLC	EN.London	I am getting	Mo2	08846
Stoker, Bram	1898.09.25	SLC	AU.Kaltenleut.	Mr. Bowyer-Lane	CU-MARK(ph)	05437
Stoker, Bram	1899.06.17	OLC	EN.London	Thank you so	UkLe2	05640
Stoker, Bram	1899.06.28	SLC per CC	EN.London	I am writing	UkLe2	05645
Stoker, Bram	1900.08.24	SLC	EN.London	from his friend	NN-B	09275 inscription
Stoker, Bram	1902.04.01	OLC	NY.Riverdale	Thank you most	UkLe2	06314
Stoker, Bram	pm 1904.06.22	SLC	IT.Florence	For what you	CU-MARK(ph)	06853 form letter
Stoker, Bram	1908.05.13	SLC	NY.New York	This is George	TxU	07996
Stoker, Bram	1909.12.26	SLC	CT.Redding	To all friends	NN-B	08295 form letter
Stokes, Helen L.	1901.11.01	SLC	NY.Riverdale	It is too	CtY	08609
Stone, George F.	****.**.**	SLC	Unknown	We are glad	CtHMTH	10587
Stone, Melville E.	1880.04.03	SLC	CT.Hartford	Mr. Wakeman has	ICN	01781
Stone, Melville E.	1904.09.11	SLC	NY.New York	It is so	ICN	06921
Stone, Melville E.	1906.09.**	SLC	NH.Dublin	I will make	CU-MARK(dr)	07516 telegram
Stone, Melville E.	1906.09.**	SLC	Unknown	Give me second	InU-Li(dr)	10878 telegram
Stone, Melville E.	1908.02.**	SLC & CC	NY.New York	Miss Clara Clemens	ICN	07931
Stone, Melville E.	1908.09.**	SLC	CT.Redding	No. I can	InU-Li(dr)	08097 telegram
Stone, Melville E.	1909.09.14	SLC	CT.Redding	I have been	CU-MARK	08451
Stone, Melville E.	1909.09.30	SLC	CT.Redding	This is a	ICN	08461
Storer, Bellamy	1905.05.16	SLC	NY.New York	I beg that	CU-MARK	07043
Stormfield guests	1909.03.13	SLC	CT.Redding	To Get Hot	NN3	09389
Stotts, Susan B.	1860.08.11	SLC	IL.Cairo	Confound me if	NPV	00024

Strafford, Lady	*	*	*	*	*	11143 see Byng, Emily G.
Strang, David	1902.05.**	SLC per HHR	NY.Riverdale	My son-in-law	CU-MARK(tr)	08661
Strauss, Adele H.	1899.06.06	SLC	EN.Broadstairs	I am deeply	As2	05635
Strauss, Johann	1899.05.25	SLC	AU.Vienna	The card came	As2	05597
Street, Miss	1874.12.01	SLC	CT.Hartford	I remember your	ViU	01158
Strong, William E.	1879.10.28	SLC	CT.Hartford	I have been	CU-MARK	01702
Strong, William E.	1879.11.06	SLC	CT.Hartford	I accept, with	CU-MARK(tr)	01708
Sturgis, Dorothy	1908.02.**	SLC	NY.New York	Good-night, dear	NNC	07905
Sturgis, Dorothy	1908.04.12	SLC	Unknown	The Major is	NNC	07972
Sturgis, Dorothy	1908.04.13	SLC	NY.New York	Good-night, dear	NNC	07973
Sturgis, Dorothy	1908.04.19	SLC	NY.New York	Yes, indeed, dear	NNC	07981
Sturgis, Dorothy	aft 1908.04.19	SLC	NY.New York	I thank you	NNC	07982
Sturgis, Dorothy	1908.05.09	SLC	NY.New York	Why, bless your	NNC	07994
Sturgis, Dorothy	1908.05.15	SLC	NY.New York	Yours of day	NNC	08000
Sturgis, Dorothy	1908.05.24	SLC	NY.New York	Indeed I would	NNC	08008
Sturgis, Dorothy	1908.06.02	SLC	NY.New York	I am just	NNC	08014
Sturgis, Dorothy	1908.06.07	SLC	NY.New York	The Directors of	NNC	08026
Sturgis, Dorothy	1908.06.14	SLC	NY.New York	Charles Rann Kennedy	NNC	08029
Sturgis, Dorothy	1908.07.**	SLC	CT.Redding	Dear Dorothy, I was	NNC	08048
Sturgis, Dorothy	1908.08.03	SLC	CT.Redding	Good! Then you	NNC	08073
Sturgis, Dorothy	1908.08.15	SLC	CT.Redding	Good! you will	NNC	08087
Sturgis, Dorothy	1908.09.30	SLC	CT.Redding	You dear delightful	NNC	08113
Sturgis, Dorothy	1908.10.27	SLC	CT.Redding	Dear Annieanlouise, when	NNC	08146
Sturgis, Dorothy	1908.12.06	SLC	CT.Redding	A week ago	NNC	08170
Sturgis, Dorothy	1908.12.26	SLC	CT.Redding	All the 12	NNC	08189
Sturgis, Dorothy	1909.01.31	SLC	CT.Redding	I have been	NNC	08337
Sturgis, Dorothy	1909.03.03	SLC	CT.Redding	Of course I	NNC	08361

ADDRESSEE	DATE	WRITER	PLACE	CUE	SOURCE	NUMBER/NOTES
Success Magazine ed.	1906.10.12	SLC	NH.Dublin	There must have	NN-B(tr)	02274
Sulamith, Miss	1910.03.21	SLC	BE.Hamilton	I think it	114:841	08573
Sullivan, Anne	*	*	*	*	*	10679 see Macy, Anne S.
Sullivan, George E.	o/a 1907.02.18	SLC per IVL	NY.New York	Should like to	CU-MARK(dr)	07653 on Sullivan Feb 18
Sullivan, Mr.	1899.11.08	SLC	EN.London	It is an	Mo2	08943
Sunderland, Philip N.	ca 1908.10.07	SLC	CT.Redding	Greeting and Salutation	113:1982	10861 form letter
Sunderland, Philip N.	1908.12.26	SLC per IVL	CT.Redding	But you did	414:1958.06.19	08191
Sutphen, Van T.	1902.11.28	SLC	NY.New York	Done by Truly	NN-B	09406 engraved inscription
Sutro, Adolph H.	1871.07.24	SLC	NY.Elmira	Give me your	CLSU	00640
Sutro, Adolph H.	1871.08.19	SLC	CT.Hartford	Got your letter	CAlb2	00647
Sutro, Adolph H.	1871.08.24	SLC	CT.Hartford	When do you	NhD	03649 telegram
Sutro, Adolph H.	1871.08.25	SLC	CT.Hartford	All right will	NhD	02815 telegram
Sutro, Adolph H.	1871.08.29	SLC	CT.Hartford	How long will	NvHi	10728 telegram
Sutro, Adolph H.	1872.06.11	SLC	CT.Hartford	Yes, I know	ODa2	00755
Suttner, Bertha von	1898.02.17	SLC	AU.Vienna	It is going	MoHi	05351
Suttner, Bertha von	1899.03.27	SLC	HU.Budapest	It is with	MoHi	05569
Suttner, Bertha von	1899.05.07	SLC	EN.London	It is ever	CtY(dr)	05588 SLC tr
Suverkrop, Euphemia A.	1898.04.11	SLC	AU.Vienna	Months ago, either	110:1966.01.31	10336
Swain, Gertrude	1902.10.16	SLC	NY.Riverdale	I would rather	ODa2	06464
Swigart, B. Frank	1906.02.01	SLC per IVL	NY.New York	Mr. Clemens sent	CU-MARK(dr)	07318 on Swigart Jan 26
Swigart, B. Frank	1906.02.01	SLC	NY.New York	Let us save	CU-MARK(tr)	10940 inscription
Swisshelm, Jane G.	ca 1880.12.**	SLC	Unknown	I thank you	CU-MARK(tr)	08607

Swords, J.F.	1887.02.15	SLC per FGW	CT.Hartford	Your favor of	CU-MARK(tr)	10761
Sykes, E.S.	1877.11.09	SLC	CT.Hartford	Mr. Burton's note	CU-MARK	01504
Taft, C.	****.**.**	SLC	Unknown	all the day	CtHMTH	10481 fragment
Taft, Charles E.	1885.05.15	SLC	CT.Hartford	I shall probably	CU-MARK(ph)	07711
Taft, Cincinnatis A.	1884.06.07 or 1884.06.14	SLC	CT.Hartford	Mrs. Clemens &	CtHMTH	02991
Taft, Ellen T.	1882.07.**	SLC	CT.Hartford	This is the	CtHMTH	09321 inscription
Taft, Ellen T.	1882.12.12	SLC	CT.Hartford	Do I understand	CtHMTH	02315 inscription
Taft, Ellen T.	1883.08.14	SLC	NY.Elmira	I must not	CtHMTH	02821
Taft, Ellen T.	ca 1884.07.**	SLC	NY.Elmira	grown sacred to	CtHMTH	03000 fragment
Taft, Ellen T.	1884.07.10	SLC	NY.Elmira	You did not	CtHMTH	08928
Taft, Ellen T.	1900.05.06	OLC	EN.London	We have acc'd	CU-MARK(ph)	05803
Tapley, D.J.	1887.04.18	SLC per FGW	CT.Hartford	I am requested	CU-MARK(tr)	11115 FGW tr
Tapley, J.F.	1887.01.25	SLC	CT.Hartford	I cannot remember	305:1910.12.06	09639
Tapley, K.C.	o/a 1890.01.14	SLC per FGW	CT.Hartford	Slote & Co	CU-MARK(dr)	09090 on Tapley Jan 13
Tarkington, Booth	1902.01.09	SLC	NY.Riverdale	As regards that	CU-MARK	06238 typed form letter
Tatlock, Mr.	1899.**.**	SLC	EN.London	We were very	ViU	05528
Tatlock, Mr.	1900.08.20	SLC	EN.London	Thank you for	CU-MARK(tr)	09205
Tauchnitz, Christian B.	1876.09.14	SLC	CT.Hartford	I met my	106:59f	01364
Tauchnitz, Christian B.	1879.05.25	SLC	FR.Paris	I am glad	327:125	01659
Tauchnitz, Christian B.	1880.10.07	SLC	CT.Hartford	This is to	327:125	01837
Tauchnitz, Christian B.	1883.03.01	SLC	CT.Hartford	The Jumping Frog	327:125	02352
Tauchnitz, Christian B.	1900.12.07	SLC	NY.New York	Indeed I will	327:126	05928
Taxen-Worm, A.	1909.08.12	SLC	CT.Redding	If the Herald	CU-MARK	08442

ADDRESSEE	DATE	WRITER	PLACE	CUE	SOURCE	NUMBER/NOTES
Taylor, Annie E	1856.05.21 & 1856.05.25	SLC	IA.Keokuk	Well, Annie, I	270:1926.03.21	00010
Taylor, Annie E	1857.06.01	SLC	LA.New Orleans	I am not	270:1926.03.21	00013 other sources
Taylor, Bayard	1877.01.24	SLC	CT.Hartford	Good--we shall P.S. I meant	CtY NIC	01403
Taylor, Bayard	1878.02.28	SLC	CT.Hartford	Your appointment was	NIC	01538
Taylor, Bayard	1878.05.07	SLC	GE.Heidelberg	Wir werden hier	NIC	01560
Taylor, Bayard	1878.06.10	SLC	GE.Heidelberg	Don't know whether	NIC	01570
Taylor, Bayard	1878.09.08	SLC	SW.Geneva	I have learned	NIC	01594
Taylor, Bayard	1878.12.14	SLC	GE.Munich	When we were	NIC	01614
Taylor, Charles H.	1889.03.02	SLC	CT.Hartford	Our bottom reason	Mo2	11015
Taylor, Charles H.	1889.10.25	SLC	CT.Hartford	I desire to	MWA	03957
Taylor, Charles H.	1901.10.01	SLC	NY.Riverdale	This is to	MWA	06151
Taylor, Douglas	1887.12.24	SLC	CT.Hartford	I am sorry	IsJJNL	03682
Taylor, Douglas	1889.10.21	SLC	CT.Hartford	I have been	NN5	03956
Taylor, Howard P.	1891.01.29	SLC	CT.Hartford	Been away. I	CU-MARK	04163 telegram
Taylor, Howard P.	1891.03.09	SLC per FGW	CT.Hartford	In reply to	CU-MARK(tr)	04181 FGW tr
Taylor, Howard P.	1891.04.27	SLC	CT.Hartford	I approve of	CU-MARK(tr)	04197 telegram
Taylor, Howard P.	1891.04.30	SLC per FGW	CT.Hartford	Mr. Clemens desires	CU-MARK(tr)	04200 FGW tr
Taylor, Tom	1873.12.29	SLC per CWS	EN.London	I went to	ODa2	01019
Taylor, Tom	1874.01.05	SLC	EN.London	I called the	159:14.1.8	01034
Teall, F.A.	1881.04.22	SLC	CT.Hartford	The sketch is	ViU	01938
Telephone Co.	****.**.**	SLC	Unknown	This marvelous	ODa2	07770 fragment
Telephone Operators	1909.01.04	SLC	CT.Redding	I have received	ViU	08310
Teller, Charlotte	****.**.**	SLC	Unknown	Tell him I	107:1927.11.22	09629
Teller, Charlotte	1906.**.**	SLC	NH.Dublin	I shall be	NN-B	03690
Teller, Charlotte	1906.**.**	SLC	NY.New York	Dear Charlotte, Mr.	NN-B	03549

Teller, Charlotte		1906.**.**	SLC	NY.New York	I have come	NN-B	03349
Teller, Charlotte		1906.**.**	SLC	NY.New York	It is fine	NN-B	03737
Teller, Charlotte		1906.**.**	SLC	NY.New York	Please send me	NN-B	03425
Teller, Charlotte		1906.**.**	SLC	Unknown	No, it was	433:10	10757
Teller, Charlotte		1906.**.**	SLC	Unknown	*	CU-MARK	10157 envelope only
Teller, Charlotte	ca	1906.**.**	SLC	NH.Dublin	Dear Charlotte, I	NN-B	03618
Teller, Charlotte	ca	1906.**.**	SLC	NH.Dublin	You are discouraged	NN-B	03595
Teller, Charlotte	ca	1906.**.**	SLC	NY.New York	I am getting	NN-B	08250
Teller, Charlotte	ca	1906.**.**	SLC	NY.New York	I have your	NN-B	08256
Teller, Charlotte	ca	1906.**.**	SLC	NY.New York	It is fine	NN-B	03521
Teller, Charlotte		1906.04.13	SLC	NY.New York	Now then, dear	NN-B	08254
Teller, Charlotte	&	1906.04.20 1906.04.21	SLC	NY.New York	It was a	NN-B	08255
Teller, Charlotte	bef	1906.05.18	SLC	NY.New York	It is bronchitis	NN-B	08257
Teller, Charlotte	o/a	1906.05.23	SLC	NH.Dublin	Charlotte, the only	NN-B	08258 on Langdon May 23
Teller, Charlotte		1906.06.**	SLC	NH.Dublin	Charlotte, (I tried	NN-B	08259
Teller, Charlotte		1906.06.10	SLC	NH.Dublin	Let me congratulate	NN-B	08260
Teller, Charlotte		1906.06.16	SLC	NH.Dublin	I am sending	NN-B	08261 fragment
Teller, Charlotte		1906.07.**	SLC	NH.Dublin	Monday. I keep	433:21	10759
Teller, Charlotte		1906.07.**	SLC	NY.New York	That Mr. Mansfield	NSyU	07469 unsent
Teller, Charlotte		1906.07.31	SLC	NH.Dublin	Dear Charlotte, you are	NN-B	08264
Teller, Charlotte		1906.08.27	SLC	NH.Dublin	Well, Charlotte dear	NN-B	08266
Teller, Charlotte		1906.10.03	SLC	NH.Dublin	Dear Charlotte, I got	NN-B	08267
Teller, Charlotte		1906.10.09	SLC	NH.Dublin	Dear Charlotte, I	NN-B	08268
Teller, Charlotte		1907.08.22	SLC	NY.Tuxedo Park	I am very	CU-MARK(tr)	07823 SLC tr
Teller, Charlotte		1909.07.**	SLC	CT.Redding	Your news is	NN-B	08293

ADDRESSEE		DATE	WRITER	PLACE	CUE	SOURCE	NUMBER/NOTES
Tenney, Mrs. Arthur J.	o/a	1907.04.24	SLC per IVL	NY.New York	Thanks for photo	CU-MARK(dr)	07695 on Tenney Apr 22
Tennyson, Alfred		1873.12.15	SLC	EN.London	You have better	ODa2	01006
Terry, Ellen	ca	1906.04.05	SLC	NY.New York	Age has not	CU-MARK(tr)	07417 telegram
Tesla, Nikola		1894.03.04	SLC	NY.New York	If I can	YuB2	04706
Tesla, Nikola		1894.03.09	SLC	NY.New York	I am desperately	YuB2	04710
Tesla, Nikola		1898.11.17	SLC	AU.Vienna	Have you Austrian	YuB2	05471
Thaxton, Nannie S.		1909.12.06	JC	CT.Redding	Father is in	TxU	08508
Thayer, Abbott H.		1901.07.17	SLC	NY.Saranac Lake	Indeed we should	MH-H	06093
Thayer, Abbott H.	o/a	1905.02.25	SLC per IVL	NY.New York	Too ill to	CU-MARK(dr)	07007
Thayer, Abbott H.		1905.02.27	SLC per IVL	NY.New York	Mr. Clemens directs	CU-MARK	07009
Thayer, Abbott H.		1905.02.28	SLC	NY.New York	I shall no	CCamarSJ	07011
Thayer, Emma B.		*	*	*	*	*	11130 see Beach, Emeline B.
Thayer, Mrs.		****.06.05	SLC	NY.New York	It is a	ViU	09005
Thomas, C.W.		1890.01.13	SLC	CT.Hartford	Yes, you are	CSjU	03998
Thompson, Charles E.		1887.03.21	SLC	CT.Hartford	I will report	CU-MARK(tr)	03546
Thompson, M. Jeff		1874.03.28	SLC	CT.Hartford	I don't wonder	428:1874.04.28	11170
Thoreson, Valdemar		1908.12.09	SLC per IVL	CT.Redding	Mr. Clemens directs	131:1910.02.06	08173
Thornburgh, Mrs.		1887.02.05	SLC	CT.Hartford	No indeed, you	ViU	03524
Thursby, Miss		1905.**.**	SLC	Unknown	Of course you	CU-MARK	06968
Ticknor, Benjamin H.		****.**.**	SLC	Unknown	He didn't come	121:145	03858
Ticknor, Benjamin H.		1881.08.01	SLC	CT.Branford	We go hence	CtY	01992
Ticknor, Benjamin H.		1881.08.11	SLC	NY.Elmira	I reckon I	CtY	02000
Ticknor, Benjamin H.		1881.08.14	SLC	NY.Elmira	I'll suggest one	CtY	02006
Ticknor, Benjamin H.		1881.08.15	SLC	CT.Hartford	Yes that is	121:132f	02007
Ticknor, Benjamin H.	bet &	1881.08.16 1881.08.22	SLC	NY.Elmira	If the printers	121:139	02133

Ticknor, Benjamin H.		1881.09.09	SLC	NY.Elmira	I didn't think	CtY	02032
Ticknor, Benjamin H.	aft	1883.01.21	SLC	CT.Hartford	Make these various	NN	02329
Ticknor, Benjamin H.		1883.03.14	SLC	CT.Hartford	I telegraphed you	DLC	11153 typed
Ticknor, Benjamin H.		1885.11.12	SLC	CT.Hartford	Osgood had the	CtY	03306
Tiffany & Co.	bet &	1880.09.01 1880.09.17	SLC	CT.Hartford	Please return the	CU-MARK	09220 on Tiffany bill Sept 1
Tiffany, Louis C.		1881.09.19	SLC	NY.Elmira	Where can I	NPV	02416 enc in Sept 19 to Tiffany
Tiffany, Louis C.	aft	1882.05.24	SLC	CT.Hartford	I have been	276:20	02211
Tilden-Hendricks	ca	1876.08.01	SLC	NY.Elmira	You have asked	153:581	05983
Tiliston, Merrill	o/a	1905.12.03	SLC per IVL	NY.New York	Mr. Clemens would	CU-MARK(dr)	07229 on Tilliston Dec 3
Toncray, Alex C.		1906.03.08	SLC	NY.New York	It is plain	NN-B(tr)	07371
Toole, John L.		1873.12.10	SLC per CWS	EN.London	I would gladly	MH-H	00998
Toole, John L.		1875.01.16	SLC	CT.Hartford	I was going	MH-H	01181
Torbert, G.L.		1869.01.12	SLC	IL.El Paso	I have heard	CU-MARK	00230 on Morris Jan 4
Tower, Mr.		****.**.**	OLC	Unknown	As I fear	ViU	03989
Towner, Ausburn		1869.09.17	SLC	NY.Elmira	With more than	CU-MARK	08697
Townsend, Edward W.		1902.11.28	SLC	NY.New York	Done by Truly	122:1936.01.29	10370 inscription; other sources
Townsend, George A.		1880.**.**	SLC	CT.Hartford	I read it	CtY(tr)	08598
Townsend, Malcolm		1867.04.22	SLC	NY.New York	I don't know	NN-B	02444
Townsend, Mr.		1901.01.04	SLC	NY.New York	I am better	CU-MARK(tr)	05959
Tracy, Gilbert A.		1901.03.04	SLC	NY.New York	Although you, in	NjHi	02802 typed
Trask, Mary C.		1901.12.30	SLC	NY.Riverdale	It is sixteen	NN-B	08222
Tremain, John F.		1906.03.07	SLC per IVL	NY.New York	I desire to	NEImHi	07366

ADDRESSEE		DATE	WRITER	PLACE	CUE	SOURCE	NUMBER/NOTES
Tremain, John F.	o/a	1906.03.15	SLC per IVL	NY.New York	Mr. Clemens doesn't	CU-MARK(dr)	07388 on Tremain Mar 15
Trent, Hilary		1903.04.26	SLC	NY.Riverdale	Naturally I have	CU-MARK(ph)	06633
Trist, Sydney G.		1899.05.26	SLC	AU.Vienna	I believe I	CU-MARK(ph)	05598
Tri-State Old Settlers		1887.06.20	SLC	CT.Hartford	Frankness, candor	CU-MARK(tr)	03585
Trout, Grace W.		1887.04.07	SLC	CT.Hartford	It is an	NN-B	03555
Trowbridge, Clara		1881.12.20	SLC	CT.Hartford	Your note is	NN-B	02558
Trumbull, Annie E.		****.**.**	SLC	CT.Hartford	Dank' am Besten	CtY	10998
Trumbull, Annie E.		****.**.**	SLC	CT.Hartford	Mit heilerem Sinne	CtY	11037
Trumbull, Annie E.	ca	1872.12.27	SLC	CT.Hartford	Dear Miss Trumbull (Oh	CtY	10997
Trumbull, Annie E.		1877.**.**	OLC	Unknown	I hope you	CtHSD	09056
Trumbull, Annie E.		1885.11.04	SLC	NY.New York	Das Alter hat	CtY	11018
Trumbull, Annie E.		1890.04.28	SLC	CT.Hartford	All right, May	CtY	11019
Trumbull, Annie E.		1891.01.11	SLC	CT.Hartford	Oh, Great Scott	CtY	11021
Trumbull, Annie E.		1891.05.31	SLC	CT.Hartford	It certainly was	CtY	11020
Trumbull, Annie E.		1892.01.09	SLC	GE.Ilsenburg	Mrs. Clemens &	CtY	11022
Trumbull, Annie E.		1892.03.08	SLC & OLC	FR.Menton	In the Club	CtY	11023
Trumbull, Annie E.		1893.04.23	SLC	NY.New York	I'll tell you	CtY	11024
Trumbull, Annie E.		1893.04.26	SLC	NY.New York	Oh don't you	CtY	11025
Trumbull, Annie E.		1893.05.07	SLC	NY.New York	Ich habe vor	CtY	11027
Trumbull, Annie E.		1893.05.16	SLC	SH.Kaiser Wilh.	I do not	CtY	11030
Trumbull, Annie E.		1893.12.06	SLC	NY.New York	If Providence lets	CtY	11029
Trumbull, Annie E.		1893.12.14	SLC	NY.New York	I am miserably	CtY	11028
Trumbull, Annie E.		1893.12.17	SLC	NY.New York	Charley Warner has	CtY	11026
Trumbull, Annie E.		1894.01.14	SLC	NY.New York	It was the	CtY	11031
Trumbull, Annie E.		1894.01.25	OLC	FR.Paris	Letters just rec'd	CtY	10999
Trumbull, Annie E.		1895.01.18	OLC	FR.Paris	of the fact	CtY	11035 fragment
Trumbull, Annie E.	ca	1895.08.19	OLC	CN.Vancouver	we never finished	CtY	11036 fragment

Trumbull, Annie E.		1896.07.04	SLC	AF.Capetown	Mir ist als	CtY	11032
Trumbull, Annie E.		1903.06.16	SLC	NY.Riverdale	Livy instructs me	CtY	11033
Trumbull, Annie E.		1903.07.20	OLC	NY.Elmira	It is a	CtY	11034
Trumbull, Annie E.		1905.12.09	SLC	NY.New York	To you, &	CtHMTH	07245 form letter
Trumbull, James H.		1873.02.15	SLC	CT.Hartford	I shall be	CtHi	00873
Trumbull, James H.	ca	1876.06.20	SLC	CT.Hartford or NY.Elmira	I think I'll	CtHi	05077 on Etting June 18
Trumbull, James H.		1881.02.01	SLC	CT.Hartford	I'm safe in	CtHi	01902
Trumbull, Sarah A.	ca	1883.12.26	OLC	CT.Hartford	I cannot help	CtY	11038
Trumbull, Sarah A.		1891.05.31	OLC	CT.Hartford	This is my	CtY	11039
Trumbull, Sarah A.		1892.07.18	SLC	GE.Bad-Nauheim	I wish to	CtY	11017
Trumbull, Sarah A.		1902.05.19	OLC	NY.Riverdale	I want to	CtY	11040
Tucker, Howard		1867.04.11	SLC	MO.St. Louis	I hasten to	IaK	00121
Tuckerman, Mr.		****.**.**	SLC	CT.Hartford	I tried to	ViU	04148
Tuohy, James M.		1898.11.02	SLC	AU.Vienna	For several months	CCamarSJ	05458
Tuohy, James M.		1898.11.08	SLC	AU.Vienna	If you find	CCamarSJ	05463
Tuohy, James M.		1898.11.10	SLC	AU.Vienna	I made a	CCamarSJ	05465
Tuohy, James M.		1898.12.09	SLC	AU.Vienna	No, that isn't	ViU	05477
Tuohy, James M.		1899.03.03	SLC	AU.Vienna	I am very	CCamarSJ	05554
Tuohy, James M.		1899.03.22	SLC	AU.Vienna	You may not	CCamarSJ	05567
Tuohy, James M.		1899.10.30	SLC	EN.London	It is finished	CCamarSJ	05697
Tuohy, James M.		1899.11.04	SLC	EN.London	Enclosed please find	CCamarSJ	05699
Tuohy, James M.		1899.12.19	SLC	EN.London	I forgot. I	CCamarSJ	05719
Tuohy, James M.		1900.**.**	SLC	Unknown	But you know	110:1964.10.08	10365
Turner, Ethel S.		1895.09.24	SLC	AS.Sydney	I have stolen	AuSN-M	04964
Turner, W.A.		1872.11.03	SLC	EN.London	My time is	Mo2	00827
Tuthill, Richard S.	aft	1879.11.25	SLC	CT.Hartford	What we can	CU-MARK(tr)	09194
Tuthill, Richard S.		1885.08.11	SLC	NY.Elmira	I would give	OCHP	03278

ADDRESSEE	DATE	WRITER	PLACE	CUE	SOURCE	NUMBER/NOTES
Twe, Dihdwo	1905.12.11	SLC per IVL	NY.New York	Mr. Clemens directs	CU-MARK(dr)	07247
Twe, Dihdwo	o/a 1905.12.15	SLC per IVL	NY.New York	Would suggest that	CU-MARK(dr)	07257 on Twe Dec 15
Twe, Dihdwo	o/a 1906.02.08	SLC per IVL	NY.New York	Mr. Clemens will	CU-MARK(dr)	07333 on Twe Feb 8
Twe, Dihdwo	1906.10.23	SLC per IVL	NY.New York	I know Mr.	NN-B(tr)	08269
Twichell, Harmony C. & Twichell, Joseph H.	1869.10.31	OLC	NY.Elmira	Mr Clemens left	CtY	00369
Twichell, Harmony C. & Twichell, Joseph H.	1870.11.12	SLC	NY.Buffalo	I came into	CtY	00533
Twichell, Harmony C. & Twichell, Joseph H.	1874.06.11	SLC	NY.Elmira	The baby is	CtY	01097
Twichell, Harmony C. & Twichell, Joseph H.	1885.12.24	SLC	CT.Hartford	Livy & I	CtY	03342
Twichell, Harmony C.	1909.10.01	CC	Unknown	Would you mind	CtHSD	10632
Twichell, Harmony C. & Twichell, Joseph H.	1909.12.27	SLC	CT.Redding	Do not come	CtY	08525
Twichell (Jos.) family & Twichell, Joseph H.	1868.11.18	SLC	OH.Cleveland	Congratulate me, my	CtY	02765
Twichell (Jos.) family & Twichell, Joseph H.	1869.01.23	SLC	OH.Cleveland	Hurrah!--because you	Mo4	00240
Twichell (Jos.) family & Twichell, Joseph H.	1869.02.14	SLC	OH.Ravenna	I greet you	Mo4	00252
Twichell, Joseph H.	****.**.**	SLC	Unknown	In a Gentleman's	CtY	09020
Twichell, Joseph H.	****.**.**	SLC	Unknown	Oh, this infernal	CU-MARK(tr)	09021
Twichell, Joseph H. & Twichell (Jos.) family	1868.11.18	SLC	OH.Cleveland	Congratulate me, my	CtY	02765
Twichell, Joseph H.	1868.11.28	SLC	NY.New York	Sound the loud	ViU	02769
Twichell, Joseph H.	1868.12.12	SLC	NY.Norwich	Hip-hip-Hurrah	Mo4	02729
Twichell, Joseph H.	1869.01.01	SLC	OH.Cleveland	While they get	Mo4	00216
Twichell, Joseph H. & Twichell (Jos.) family	1869.01.23	SLC	OH.Cleveland	Hurrah!--because you	Mo4	00240
Twichell, Joseph H. & Twichell (Jos.) family	1869.02.14	SLC	OH.Ravenna	I greet you	Mo4	00252

Twichell, Joseph H. & Twichell, Harmony C.		1869.10.31	OLC	NY.Elmira	Mr Clemens left	CtY	00369
Twichell, Joseph H.		1869.12.28	SLC	NY.New York	I hasten to	CtY	00395
Twichell, Joseph H.		1870.01.**	SLC	NY.Elmira	I have invited	295:108	02796
Twichell, Joseph H. & Twichell, Harmony C.		1870.11.12	SLC	NY.Buffalo	I came into	CtY	00533
Twichell, Joseph H.		1870.12.19	SLC	NY.Buffalo	All is well	CtY	02783
Twichell, Joseph H.		1871.01.03	SLC	NY.Buffalo	I tell you	NN5	00554
Twichell, Joseph H.	aft	1872.12.20	SLC	CT.Hartford	I wrote a	CtY	00848
Twichell, Joseph H.		1873.06.29	SLC & OLC	EN.London	I consider myself	CtY	00936
Twichell, Joseph H.		1874.01.05	SLC	EN.London	I knew you	114:210	01032
Twichell, Joseph H. & Warner, Lilly G.		1874.04.14	SLC	CT.Hartford	Borrowed of the	297:35	11145
Twichell, Joseph H. & Twichell, Harmony C.		1874.06.11	SLC	NY.Elmira	The baby is	CtY	01097
Twichell, Joseph H.	bet &	1874.07.28 1874.08.05	SLC	NY.Elmira	Stop our postman	CtY	01113
Twichell, Joseph H.	o/b	1875.12.30	SLC	CT.Hartford	Religious Conundrum	CtY	01291
Twichell, Joseph H.		1877.06.27	SLC	NY.Elmira	Your letter came	CtY	01444
Twichell, Joseph H.		1878.04.10	SLC	NY.Elmira	Goodbye, Joe dear	CtY	01554
Twichell, Joseph H.		1878.09.09	SLC	SW.Geneva	It is actually	CtY	02800
Twichell, Joseph H.		1878.11.03	SLC	IT.Rome	I am disgusted	CtY	01603
Twichell, Joseph H. & Warner, Susan L.		1878.11.20	SLC	GE.Munich	By George but	CtY	01608
Twichell, Joseph H.		1879.01.23	SLC	GE.Munich	I've got to	CtY	01624
Twichell, Joseph H.		1879.01.26	SLC	GE.Munich	Your delicious letter	114:347	01577 other sources
Twichell, Joseph H.		1879.02.24	SLC	GE.Munich	It was a	114:357	01292
Twichell, Joseph H.		1879.06.10	SLC	FR.Paris	I ought to	CtY	01666
Twichell, Joseph H.		1879.10.02	SLC	NY.Elmira	George retains his	CtY	01696
Twichell, Joseph H.		1880.03.16	SLC	CT.Hartford	Just imagine it	CtY	01771

ADDRESSEE	DATE	WRITER	PLACE	CUE	SOURCE	NUMBER/NOTES
Twichell, Joseph H.	1880.03.24	SLC	CT.Hartford	Remail this to	CU-MARK	09197 on Howells Mar 22
Twichell, Joseph H.	1880.08.29	SLC	NY.Elmira	Concerning Jean Clemens	114:383	01827
Twichell, Joseph H.	1880.10.14	SLC	MA.Boston	I want you	CtY	01841 telegram
Twichell, Joseph H.	1881.02.15 or 1881.02.16	SLC	CT.Hartford	All right, I'll	CU-MARK	01909 on Warner Feb 15
Twichell, Joseph H.	bet 1882.02.12 & 1882.02.23	SLC	Unknown	The Holbrooks always	CtY	02132
Twichell, Joseph H.	1882.09.19	SLC	NY.Elmira	I honestly meant	CtY	02271
Twichell, Joseph H.	1883.07.20	SLC	NY.Elmira	For the time	117:1883.07.24	09080
Twichell, Joseph H.	1884.08.24	SLC	Unknown	That portrait by	122:1934.04.04	09949 on St. Gaudens bef Aug 24
Twichell, Joseph H.	1884.09.16	SLC	NY.Elmira	On the contrary	CtY	01327
Twichell, Joseph H. & Twichell, Harmony C.	1885.12.24	SLC	CT.Hartford	Livy & I	CtY	03342
Twichell, Joseph H.	1886.**.**	SLC	CT.Hartford	Livy sent me	CtY	03321
Twichell, Joseph H.	o/a 1886.12.22	SLC	CT.Hartford	It is fine	CU-MARK	10075 on Twichell pm Dec 22
Twichell, Joseph H.	1887.03.14	SLC	CT.Hartford	It is a	CtY	03539
Twichell, Joseph H.	1888.06.28	SLC	NY.Elmira	How they waste	CtY	03726
Twichell, Joseph H.	1889.01.25	SLC	CT.Hartford	It is a	CtY	03853
Twichell, Joseph H.	o/a 1890.02.21	SLC	CT.Hartford	Ys Ever	CU-MARK	10777 on Webster Feb 21
Twichell, Joseph H.	1891.10.01	SLC	FR.Nimes	I have been	CtY	04241
Twichell, Joseph H.	1892.04.25	SLC	IT.Rome	Your delightful letter	CtY	04285
Twichell, Joseph H.	1893.06.09	SLC	IT.Florence	The sea voyage	CtY	04412
Twichell, Joseph H.	1893.10.09	SLC	NY.New York	I am likely	MWA	04471
Twichell, Joseph H.	1893.11.20	SLC	NY.New York	It is delicious	CtY(tr)	04508
Twichell, Joseph H.	1894.04.12	SLC	SH.New York	I am on	CU-MARK(tr)	04716
Twichell, Joseph H.	1895.11.29	SLC	NZ.Napier	Your welcome letter	CtY	04977

Twichell, Joseph H.	1896.05.24	SLC	AF.Pretoria	Harper for May	114:631	05054
Twichell, Joseph H.	1896.09.27	SLC	EN.London	Through Livy and Katy	114:635	05117
Twichell, Joseph H.	1897.01.19	SLC	EN.London	Do I want	CtY	05169
Twichell, Joseph H.	1897.04.10	SLC	EN.London	Mrs. Plunkett's letter	CtY	05201
Twichell, Joseph H.	1897.07.08	SLC	EN.London	Susy Crane &	CtY	05258
Twichell, Joseph H.	1897.07.31	SLC	SW.Weggis	In this came	CtY	05275
Twichell, Joseph H.	1897.08.22	SLC	SW.Weggis	Livy made a	114:645	05279
Twichell, Joseph H.	1897.10.23	SLC	AU.Vienna	We are gradually	114:646	05301
Twichell, Joseph H.	1897.11.19	SLC	AU.Vienna	Above is our	CtY	05314
Twichell, Joseph H.	1897.12.10	SLC	AU.Vienna	Pond sends me	CtY	05319
Twichell, Joseph H.	1898.02.03	SLC	AU.Vienna	There's that letter	114:657	05339
Twichell, Joseph H.	bef 1898.05.26	SLC	Unknown	Have you read	CU-MARK(tr)	05394
Twichell, Joseph H.	1898.06.17	SLC	AU.Kaltenleut.	You are living	114:663	05400
Twichell, Joseph H.	1898.09.13	SLC	AU.Kaltenleut.	You are mistaken	114:666	05432
Twichell, Joseph H.	1898.12.02	SLC	AU.Vienna	I will not	CtHT-W	05473
Twichell, Joseph H.	1899.01.03	SLC	AU.Vienna	Your letter has	CtY	05533
Twichell, Joseph H.	1899.04.**	SLC	AU.Vienna	other, full of	CU-MARK(tr)	05577 fragment
Twichell, Joseph H.	1899.05.**	SLC	AU.Vienna	I reckon the	CtY	05599
Twichell, Joseph H.	1899.06.11	SLC	EN.London	We arrived last	CtY	05637
Twichell, Joseph H.	1899.07.03	SLC	EN.London	Only a line	CtY	05647
Twichell, Joseph H.	1899.09.06	SLC	SE.Sanna	I've no business	CtY	05672
Twichell, Joseph H.	1899.11.21	SLC	EN.London	The enclosed is	CtY	05713
Twichell, Joseph H.	1900.01.01	SLC	EN.London	Who is Miss	CU-MARK	05741
Twichell, Joseph H.	1900.01.08	SLC	EN.London	Mental Telegraphy has	114:689	05744
Twichell, Joseph H.	1900.01.27	SLC	EN.London	Apparently we are	114:694	05753
Twichell, Joseph H.	1900.03.04	SLC	EN.London	Henry Robinson's death	CtHT-W	05769
Twichell, Joseph H.	1900.06.22	SLC	EN.London	I attended a	CtY	05825
Twichell, Joseph H.	1900.08.12	SLC	EN.London	The Sages &	CtY	05849

ADDRESSEE	DATE	WRITER	PLACE	CUE	SOURCE	NUMBER/NOTES
Twichell, Joseph H.	1900.08.18	SLC	EN.London	No, it was	CtY	05855
Twichell, Joseph H.	1901.01.23	SLC	NY.New York	Certainly. I used	CtY	05982
Twichell, Joseph H.	1901.01.29	SLC	NY.New York	I'm not expecting	114:704	05985
Twichell, Joseph H.	1901.04.24	SLC	NY.New York	Yes, it was	CtY(tr)	06046
Twichell, Joseph H.	1901.06.**	SLC	NY.New York	Well, it is	CtY	06068
Twichell, Joseph H.	1901.07.28	SLC	NY.Saranac Lake	As you say	CtY	06098
Twichell, Joseph H.	1901.08.28	SLC	NY.Saranac Lake	Just a word	NPV	06125
Twichell, Joseph H.	1901.09.08	SLC	NY.Saranac Lake	Ah me, I	CtY	06132
Twichell, Joseph H.	1901.09.10	SLC	NY.Saranac Lake	It is another	114:713	06134
Twichell, Joseph H.	1901.09.29	SLC	NY.New York	It looks now	CtY	06146
Twichell, Joseph H.	1902.01.04	SLC	NY.Riverdale	It is a	CtY	06220
Twichell, Joseph H.	1902.01.18	SLC	NY.Riverdale	Can't go to	RPB-JH	06249
Twichell, Joseph H.	1902.02.**	SLC	NY.Riverdale	After compliments. From	114:719	06264
Twichell, Joseph H.	1902.09.**	SLC	ME.York Harbor	Verey was not	CtY	06423
Twichell, Joseph H.	1902.09.30	SLC	ME.York Harbor	We think the	CtY	06448
Twichell, Joseph H.	1902.10.**	SLC	ME.York Harbor	We shall try	CtY	06450 on Allbut Sept 29
Twichell, Joseph H.	1902.10.31	SLC	NY.Riverdale	It is ten	114:728	06477
Twichell, Joseph H.	1902.12.31 & 1903.01.01	SLC	NY.Riverdale	It is 10	CtY	06534
Twichell, Joseph H.	1903.01.03 & 1903.01.04	SLC	NY.Riverdale	Joe, this is	CtY	06548 on Bowen Jan 2
Twichell, Joseph H.	1903.01.28	SLC	NY.Riverdale	P.S. Livy had	CtY	06573
Twichell, Joseph H.	1903.04.04	SLC	NY.Riverdale	Livy does really	MoKiU	06614
Twichell, Joseph H.	1903.07.21	SLC	NY.Elmira	That love-letter	CtY	06704
Twichell, Joseph H.	1903.09.01	SLC	NY.Elmira	Livy sends bushels	CtY	06722
Twichell, Joseph H.	1903.10.09	SLC	NY.New York	Yours of yesterday	CtY	06737
Twichell, Joseph H.	1904.01.07 & 1904.01.10	SLC	IT.Florence	I have had	114:748	06784
Twichell, Joseph H.	1904.05.11	SLC	IT.Florence	Yours has this	114:752	06834
Twichell, Joseph H.	1904.06.08	SLC	IT.Florence	We were eager	CtY	06867

Twichell, Joseph H.	1904.06.18	SLC	IT.Florence	It is 13	CU-MARK	06874
Twichell, Joseph H.	1904.07.28	SLC	MA.Lee	How life &	CtY	06906
Twichell, Joseph H.	1904.10.23	SLC	NY.New York	After I got	CtY	06934
Twichell, Joseph H.	1904.10.28	SLC	NY.New York	It is good	CtY	06940
Twichell, Joseph H.	1904.11.04	SLC	NY.New York	Oh, Dear! get	CtY	06945
Twichell, Joseph H.	1905.02.16	SLC	NY.New York	I knew I	CtY	07001
Twichell, Joseph H.	1905.03.14	SLC	NY.New York	I have a	114:767	07018
Twichell, Joseph H.	1905.04.23	SLC	NY.New York	I have just	CtHT-W	07033
Twichell, Joseph H.	1905.06.01	SLC	NH.Dublin	Certainly, give Osborn	WU(tr)	07055
Twichell, Joseph H.	1905.06.24	SLC	NH.Dublin	When I was	CtY	07069
Twichell, Joseph H.	1905.07.13	SLC	NH.Dublin	I want you	CtY	07082
Twichell, Joseph H.	1906.02.26	SLC per IVL	NY.New York	Shall reach Hartford	TxU(tr)	07356 telegram; IVL tr
Twichell, Joseph H.	1906.08.05	SLC	NH.Dublin	Certainly archaeology	NN-B(tr)	07492 enc in Aug 5 to Rogers
Twichell, Joseph H.	1906.09.14	SLC	NH.Dublin	It's all right	CtY	07524
Twichell, Joseph H.	1907.01.26	SLC	NY.New York	All the periodicals	CtY	07636
Twichell, Joseph H.	1908.**.**	SLC	Unknown	I am glad	VtMiM	07900
Twichell, Joseph H.	1908.01.21	SLC	NY.New York	Miss Lyon told	CU-MARK	07923 deposit
Twichell, Joseph H.	1909.04.19	SLC	CT.Redding	Joe dear, I think	CU-MARK	08386
Twichell, Joseph H.	1909.06.14	JC	CT.Redding	Your sweet letter	CtHSD	10610
Twichell, Joseph H.	1909.06.23	SLC	CT.Redding	I have escaped	CtY	08425
Twichell, Joseph H.	1909.09.19	SLC	CT.Redding	Nine days ago	CtY	08454
Twichell, Joseph H.	1909.09.26	CC	CT.Redding	Can you keep	CtHSD	10631
Twichell, Joseph H.	1909.10.17	JC	CT.Redding	As Father didn't	CtHSD	10611
Twichell, Joseph H.	1909.11.27	JC	CT.Redding	Father left a	CtHSD	10612
Twichell, Joseph H. & Twichell, Harmony C.	1909.12.27	SLC	CT.Redding	Do not come	CtY	08525
Tyler, Mr.	1878.07.30	SLC	GE.Baden Baden	The rheumatism staid	VtMiM	01580

ADDRESSEE	DATE	WRITER	PLACE	CUE	SOURCE	NUMBER/NOTES
Tyson, A.H.	1902.12.05	SLC	NY.Riverdale	Yours is a	297:108	06500
Underhill, Charles M.	1872.08.06	SLC	CT.New Saybrook	My next payment	NN-B	08840
Underhill, Charles M.	1886.07.17	SLC	NY.Elmira	I am glad	NN-B	02638
Underhill, Charles M.	1889.12.10	SLC	CT.Hartford	Don't forget that	NN-B	10799 inscription
Underhill, Charles M.	1893.04.14	SLC	IL.Chicago	I have worked	N6	04374
Underhill, Charles M.	1902.10.27	SLC	NY.Riverdale	It isn't much	NN-B	08232
Underhill, Irving S.	1893.04.06	SLC	NY.New York	I should not	NN-B	04639
Underhill, Irving S.	1900.05.23	SLC	EN.London	It is straight	NN-B	08199
Underhill, Irving S.	1901.01.01	SLC	NY.New York	No, the Adam	NN-B	08214
Underhill, Irving S.	o/a 1901.01.31	SLC	Unknown	Will you call	122:1936.01.29	04316 on Lanier Jan 31
Underhill, Irving S.	1902.01.03	SLC	NY.Riverdale	Ah, but they	NN-B	08225
Underwood, John C.	1875.10.07	SLC	CT.Hartford	The person I	CU-MARK	01269
Underwood, Mr.	1901.07.21	SLC	NY.Saranac Lake	I have tried	107:1924.11.24	09452 other sources
United Cigar Stores Co.	o/a 1905.10.13	SLC per IVL	NH.Dublin	Mr. Clemens would	CU-MARK(dr)	07174 on Co. Oct 13
United States Treasury	1902.10.13	SLC	NY.Riverdale	Prices for the	NN-B(dr)	08230 other sources
United States Treasury	1904.07.16	SLC	NY.New York	I desire to	CU-MARK	06888
Unknown	****.**.**	CC	Unknown	You slipped away	CU-MARK	08704
Unknown	****.**.**	SLC per IVL	Unknown	I thank you	CU-MARK	08716
Unknown	****.**.**	SLC per IVL	Unknown	Mr. Clemens directs	CU-MARK	08715
Unknown	****.**.**	SLC per IVL	Unknown	Mr. Clemens has	CU-MARK	08708
Unknown	****.**.**	SLC	CT.Hartford	I don't know	202:4	09065
Unknown	****.**.**	SLC	CT.Hartford	Billards postponed to	CU-MARK	08705
Unknown	****.**.**	SLC	CT.Hartford	have it overcome	CU-MARK	08732 fragment
Unknown	****.**.**	SLC	CT.Hartford	beyond the year's end	ODa2	11184 fragment

Unknown	****.**.**	SLC	FR.Paris	Replying to your	159:3.1.17	10812
Unknown	****.**.**	SLC	IT.Florence	Thursdays is	210:1979.10.24	09962
Unknown	****.**.**	SLC	NY.Buffalo	Experience has not	CU-MARK(dr)	00593 form letter
Unknown	****.**.**	SLC	NY.Elmira	If that big	CtY	08132
Unknown	****.**.**	SLC	NY.Elmira	Livy wants Sue	CU-MARK	08711
Unknown	****.**.**	SLC	NY.Elmira	will find me	NN	09046 fragment
Unknown	****.**.**	SLC	NY.New York	O, no, bless	134:1918.01.16	09961
Unknown	****.**.**	SLC	NY.New York	the pictures are	227:1931	09922
Unknown	****.**.**	SLC	NY.New York	I am dead	441:1923.06.07	10396
Unknown	****.**.**	SLC	NY.New York	If I were	ViU	09029
Unknown	****.**.**	SLC	NY.Riverdale	No, I wouldn't	CU-MARK(tr)	06104
Unknown	****.**.**	SLC	NY.Riverdale	The bearer is	ViU	09034
Unknown	****.**.**	SLC	Unknown	Speech? If anybody	105:1957.03.05	09695
Unknown	****.**.**	SLC	Unknown	Took when his	105:1968.05.21	09688 inscription
Unknown	****.**.**	SLC	Unknown	Call at the	107:1925.05.04	09553
Unknown	****.**.**	SLC	Unknown	Send this to	107:1926.04.01	09570 on de Batz n.d.
Unknown	****.**.**	SLC	Unknown	Why weren't Italian	107:1927.11.22	09627
Unknown	****.**.**	SLC	Unknown	I would gladly	111:174	10858
Unknown	****.**.**	SLC	Unknown	I don't suppose	116:1942.10.01	09988 on envelope
Unknown	****.**.**	SLC	Unknown	Say they ought	116:1943.04.02	09963
Unknown	****.**.**	SLC	Unknown	Inasmuch as I	122:1936.12.09	09919
Unknown	****.**.**	SLC	Unknown	I'd like you	157:1908.03.06	09847
Unknown	****.**.**	SLC	Unknown	I give it	157:1911.01.12	09887
Unknown	****.**.**	SLC	Unknown	Can't come down	157:1915.01.08	09889
Unknown	****.**.**	SLC	Unknown	My wife asked	157:1923.12.17	09881
Unknown	****.**.**	SLC	Unknown	O, d--ear! (It's	157:1924.11.10	09882

ADDRESSEE	DATE	WRITER	PLACE	CUE	SOURCE	NUMBER/NOTES
Unknown	****.**.**	SLC	Unknown	the border will	173:1940.03.26	09927
Unknown	****.**.**	SLC	Unknown	Could you quietly	175:1902.01.24	09883
Unknown	****.**.**	SLC	Unknown	I am rested	177:16	09342
Unknown	****.**.**	SLC	Unknown	I am greatly	178:1975	09351
Unknown	****.**.**	SLC	Unknown	With pleasure, over	212:1949.03.12	09923 inscription
Unknown	****.**.**	SLC	Unknown	After filling the	212:1956.02.01	09925
Unknown	****.**.**	SLC	Unknown	Where the hell's	235:142	09397
Unknown	****.**.**	SLC	Unknown	Many thanks for	280:77	09066
Unknown	****.**.**	SLC	Unknown	Truth is the	324:1931.10.15	09244 inscription
Unknown	****.**.**	SLC	Unknown	I delayed because	C4	07692
Unknown	****.**.**	SLC	Unknown	Sample of post-card	C4	05380
Unknown	****.**.**	SLC	Unknown	that humiliating office	CCamarSJ	09051 fragment
Unknown	****.**.**	SLC	Unknown	This is a	CSmH	09372 inscription
Unknown	****.**.**	SLC	Unknown	Be happy, dear	CtHMTH	09048
Unknown	****.**.**	SLC	Unknown	with the love	CtHMTH	09184 inscription
Unknown	****.**.**	SLC	Unknown	If I had	CtHMTH	10589
Unknown	****.**.**	SLC	Unknown	It is a	CtHMTH	10653
Unknown	****.**.**	SLC	Unknown	But it was	CtHSD	10583
Unknown	****.**.**	SLC	Unknown	splendid is the	CtNc2	08200
Unknown	****.**.**	SLC	Unknown	200 cards	CtY	11041
Unknown	****.**.**	SLC	Unknown	Ah, but time	CtY	11042 inscription
Unknown	****.**.**	SLC	Unknown	I think it	CtY	11043
Unknown	****.**.**	SLC	Unknown	Answer Howells	CU-MARK	08707
Unknown	****.**.**	SLC	Unknown	Best compliments to	CU-MARK	08712
Unknown	****.**.**	SLC	Unknown	Bet Cal & Sac	CU-MARK	08696 on envelope

Unknown	****.**.**	SLC	Unknown	It is a	CU-MARK	08693 form letter
Unknown	****.**.**	SLC	Unknown	No, Sir, I	CU-MARK	02880 fragment
Unknown	****.**.**	SLC	Unknown	Form for declining	CU-MARK	08695
Unknown	****.**.**	SLC	Unknown	I thank you	CU-MARK	08701
Unknown	****.**.**	SLC	Unknown	If he had	CU-MARK	08709
Unknown	****.**.**	SLC	Unknown	Mrs. Clemens would	CU-MARK	08706
Unknown	****.**.**	SLC	Unknown	I thank you	CU-MARK(ph)	09078 form letter
Unknown	****.**.**	SLC	Unknown	I thought it	CU-MARK(ph)	10571
Unknown	****.**.**	SLC	Unknown	Some points that	CU-MARK	08699
Unknown	****.**.**	SLC	Unknown	truly yours	CU-MARK(tr)	09272 inscription
Unknown	****.**.**	SLC	Unknown	I have seen	CU-MARK(tr)	09052
Unknown	****.**.**	SLC	Unknown	I thank you	DLC	05526
Unknown	****.**.**	SLC	Unknown	This Thursday evening	MdBE	09039
Unknown	****.**.**	SLC	Unknown	I'm ashamed to	MH-H	09049
Unknown	****.**.**	SLC	Unknown	A Sentiment (which	Mo2	09277 inscription
Unknown	****.**.**	SLC	Unknown	With lots of	Mo2	10533
Unknown	****.**.**	SLC	Unknown	Dr. Rice is	NjP	09025
Unknown	****.**.**	SLC	Unknown	before the middle	NN-B	09042 fragment
Unknown	****.**.**	SLC	Unknown	I've had a	NN-B	09043
Unknown	****.**.**	SLC	Unknown	Mrs. Clemens wishes	NN-B	05627
Unknown	****.**.**	SLC	Unknown	P.S. If you	NPV	09054
Unknown	****.**.**	SLC	Unknown	3 Souveniers James	ODa2	11174
Unknown	****.**.**	SLC	Unknown	Jean is just over a	ODa2	11182 fragment
Unknown	****.**.**	SLC	Unknown	Tell the truth or	ODa2	11177 inscription

ADDRESSEE	DATE	WRITER	PLACE	CUE	SOURCE	NUMBER/NOTES
Unknown	****.**.**	SLC	Unknown	Private & confidential	ODa2	11178 on envelope
Unknown	****.**.**	SLC	Unknown	Well Mr. Anthony	TxU	08020
Unknown	****.**.**	SLC	Unknown	Read & corrected	ViU	11106 inscription
Unknown	****.**.**	SLC	Unknown	Yours has moved	ViU	11103 inscription
Unknown	****.**.**	SLC	Unknown	P.S. This should	ViU	09031
Unknown	****.**.**	SLC	Unknown	The necessary money	WaPS	07288
Unknown	****.01.01	SLC	Unknown	Happy New Year	CU-MARK	08691 inscription
Unknown	****.01.23	SLC	Unknown	This being merely	116:1943.05.14	09986
Unknown	****.01.24	SLC	CT.Hartford	Please send me	C4	00475
Unknown	****.02.09	SLC	CT.Hartford	Will you please	WaPS	09024
Unknown	****.02.14	SLC	MA.Boston	The only Valentine	164:1984.02.12	10775
Unknown	****.03.24	SLC	Unknown	Here is the	NNWH	09047
Unknown	****.04.08	SLC	CT.Hartford	I've ordered the	CU-MARK(ph)	10562
Unknown	****.04.09	SLC	CT.Hartford	I do not	107:1925.04.16	09641 other sources
Unknown	****.04.18	SLC	NY.Elmira	The speech on	Mo2	11014
Unknown	****.04.24	SLC	CT.Hartford	we desire to	105:1954.12.07	09466
Unknown	****.04.24	SLC	CT.Hartford	The invitations have	ViU	09032
Unknown	****.04.25	SLC	CT.Hartford	any N.Y. book store	105:1971.02.02	09691
Unknown	****.05.06	SLC	Unknown	They are very	Mo2	08279
Unknown	****.05.30	SLC	Unknown	For my sake	Mo2	08283
Unknown	****.06.08	SLC	CT.Hartford	Please ship the	MdHi	08157
Unknown	****.06.24	SLC	CT.Hartford	Mr. S.L. Clemens	116:1950.02.02	09987
Unknown	****.07.02	SLC	NY.Elmira	Thank you, old	WU(tr)	09053
Unknown	****.07.27	SLC	NY.Elmira	I have no	PYHi	09023
Unknown	****.08.18	SLC	NY.Elmira	I thank you	ViU	09036
Unknown	****.09.01	SLC	NY.Elmira	I am sorry	IaCrM	09041
Unknown	****.11.10	SLC	CT.Hartford	I just missed	Mo2	07425

Unknown	****.11.12	SLC	Unknown	With warm friendly	227:1931	09921 inscription
Unknown	****.11.12	SLC	Unknown	Sent you a	CU-MARK	08698
Unknown	****.11.15	SLC	CT.Hartford	That sketch exists	PP2	09224
Unknown	****.12.18	SLC	CT.Hartford	I never heard	CU-MARK(ph)	10663
Unknown	1867.05.09	SLC	NY.New York	With compliments of	MoHM	10643 inscription
Unknown	1867.05.29	SLC	NY.New York	Yrs. Twain &	412:1937.05.25	09996 inscription
Unknown	1869.08.10	SLC	Unknown	much matter worthy	418:1975.04.30	09997
Unknown	1869.09.06	SLC	NY.Buffalo	With assurances of	122:1936.01.29	09820 inscription
Unknown	1869.10.07	SLC	NY.Elmira	Well I like	CU-MARK	00361
Unknown	1869.10.29	SLC	PA.Pittsburgh	Saml. L. Clemens	CU-MARK(ph)	10495 inscription
Unknown	1869.10.31	SLC	PA.Pittsburgh	Yrs Truly	InU-Li	10818 inscription
Unknown	1869.12.**	SLC	Unknown	With pleasure	NvU	10674 inscription
Unknown	1870.03.01	SLC	NY.Buffalo	In answer. I	163:1900.08.27	00435 form letter
Unknown	1870.03.16	SLC	Unknown	I am far	305:1906.11.12	09756
Unknown	1870.05.28	SLC	NY.Buffalo	Hapsburgh's Minister	324:1930.12.05	00471
Unknown	1870.07.04	SLC	NY.Buffalo	Excuse delay--which	CAlb2	02799 date uncertain
Unknown	1871.**.**	SLC	Unknown	It isn't egotism	308:183	09298 inscription
Unknown	1871.02.13	SLC	NY.Buffalo	In answer I	ICU	00574 form letter
Unknown	1871.03.**	SLC	NY.Buffalo	Yrs Truly	111:250	09937 inscription
Unknown	1871.05.14	SLC	Unknown	Harper & Bros.	CtY	09296 inscription
Unknown	1871.11.20	SLC	CT.Hartford	from place to	157:1914.01.26	09850
Unknown	1872.03.19	SLC	NY.Elmira	Born, in Elmira	PBL	00735

ADDRESSEE	DATE	WRITER	PLACE	CUE	SOURCE	NUMBER/NOTES
Unknown	1873.**.**	SLC	Unknown	Truly Yours	CU-MARK(ph)	11070 inscription
Unknown	1873.01.12	SLC per OLC	CT.Hartford	I thank you	CCamarSJ	00855 form letter
Unknown	1873.04.**	SLC	CT.Hartford	Original M.S. of	MH-H	10821 inscription
Unknown	1873.04.**	SLC	CT.Hartford	Will this do	NN-B	00895 inscription
Unknown	1873.04.07	SLC	CT.Hartford	Enclosed is page	MA	00897
Unknown	1873.07.11	SLC	EN.London	Will Tuesday evening	CU-MARK(tr)	00950
Unknown	1873.07.31	SLC	SK.Edinburgh	I am afraid	MHi	00958
Unknown	1873.10.11	SLC	EN.London	I thank you	Mo2	00971
Unknown	1873.10.22	SLC	SH.Batavia	Thanks for the	CU-MARK	00977
Unknown	1873.12.08	SLC per CWS	EN.London	Thanks for the	Uk6	09207
Unknown	aft 1874.03.05	SLC	CT.Hartford	In reply I	CU-MARK	01062 form letter
Unknown	1874.03.23	SLC	CT.Hartford	Please send me	PHi	01067
Unknown	1874.06.24	SLC	NY.Elmira	Mark Twain was	ViU	01103
Unknown	1874.09.25	SLC	CT.Hartford	I hasten to	OrPR	01134
Unknown	1874.12.05	SLC	CT.Hartford	The article never	CU-MARK(ph)	09848
Unknown	1875.02.**	SLC	Unknown	Yours Truly Saml	212:1949.03.12	09892 inscription
Unknown	1875.04.11	SLC	CT.Hartford	I publish only	MeHi	00518 date uncertain
Unknown	1875.07.06	SLC	CT.Hartford	Who can I	134:1932.05.17	01248
Unknown	1875.07.19	SLC	CT.Hartford	I send copies	105:1963.12.03	09485 other sources
Unknown	1875.10.05	SLC	CT.Hartford	I beg to	MoSW	01268
Unknown	1875.12.**	SLC	NY.New York	Charity covers a	NNWH	10433 inscription
Unknown	1876.01.**	SLC	CT.Hartford	I repent me	ViU	10772 inscription
Unknown	1876.01.01	SLC	Unknown	New Year's Card	CU-MARK	09288 form letter

Unknown	1876.04.04	SLC	CT.Hartford	I am sorry	InFwLW	09203
Unknown	1876.06.09	SLC	CT.Hartford	Please instruct &	NPV	01340
Unknown	1876.10.**	SLC	CT.Hartford	Very Truly Yours	CtHSD	10582 inscription
Unknown	bef 1876.10.02	SLC	CT.Hartford	We like men	117:1876.10.02	01371 place uncertain
Unknown	1876.10.19	SLC	CT.Hartford	The book has	436:1934.02.27	10345
Unknown	1876.10.25	SLC	CT.Hartford	Yes, I am	118:1876.11.05	01379 other sources
Unknown	1876.11.30	SLC	CT.Hartford	Truly Yours	107:1924.11.24	09448 inscription; other sources
Unknown	1877.**.**	SLC	CT.Hartford	I have the	NPV	01399 form letter
Unknown	ca 1877.05.**	SLC	Unknown	Mr. Clemens has	CU-MARK	08684 form letter
Unknown	1877.07.**	SLC	Unknown	Always acknowledge a	CU-MARK	09284 inscription
Unknown	1877.08.**	SLC	Unknown	Leaving a blank	PBL	09283 inscription
Unknown	1877.12.01	SLC	Unknown	The great question	108:118f	09279 inscription
Unknown	1877.12.11	SLC per FCH	CT.Hartford	A fraudulent concern	CU-MARK	08617
Unknown	1878.11.03	SLC	IT.Rome	Will you do	Mo2	01604
Unknown	1879.01.**	SLC	GE.Munich	I have no	111:250	10341
Unknown	1879.09.**	SLC	NY.Elmira	Yrs Truly	NPV	10850 inscription
Unknown	1879.10.**	SLC	Unknown	The man of	116:1971.03.18	09746 inscription
Unknown	1879.11.26	SLC	CT.Hartford	I am in	305:1909.12.03	09849
Unknown	1880.**.**	SLC	Unknown	A Sentiment which	CU-MARK(tr)	08710
Unknown	1880.03.08	SLC	CT.Hartford	Ys truly	255:130	10342 inscription
Unknown	1880.03.14	SLC	CT.Hartford	When a distressed	CtY	09309 inscription

ADDRESSEE	DATE	WRITER	PLACE	CUE	SOURCE	NUMBER/NOTES
Unknown	1880.05.**	SLC	Unknown	Ys Truly	Mo2	11007 inscription
Unknown	1880.05.20	SLC	CT.Hartford	Yr Truly	ODa2	11214 inscription
Unknown	1880.06.**	SLC	Unknown	Ys Truly	CtY	11048 inscription
Unknown	1880.11.**	SLC	Unknown	None genuine without	MWA	09311 inscription
Unknown	aft 1880.11.02	SLC	CT.Hartford	I would not	116:1947.01.23	09179
Unknown	1880.11.20	SLC	IT.Florence	None genuine without	462:47	09944 inscription
Unknown	1880.12.**	SLC	CT.Hartford	Ys Truly	InU-Li	10817 inscription
Unknown	1880.12.**	SLC	Unknown	Cat Asleep. From	C4	01862 inscription
Unknown	o/a 1880.12.09	SLC	CT.Hartford	would be a	CU-MARK	09062 on Perkins Dec 9
Unknown	1880.12.16	SLC	Unknown	Truly Yours	MiU	10701 inscription
Unknown	1881.01.**	SLC	CT.Hartford	Yrs Truly	PHC	10849 inscription
Unknown	aft 1881.01.01	SLC	Unknown	This is as	CU-MARK(ph)	09232 on printed biography
Unknown	1881.01.24	SLC	CT.Hartford	Total Abstinence is	OFH	09312 inscription
Unknown	1881.02.26	SLC	CT.Hartford	To any U.S.	107:1925.04.16	01822
Unknown	1881.03.**	SLC	Unknown	Yr Truly	CU-MARK(ph)	10559 inscription
Unknown	1881.03.05	SLC	CT.Hartford	Yours Sincerely	111:169	09313 inscription
Unknown	1881.03.05	SLC	Unknown	Please send me	Mo2	11008
Unknown	1881.04.15	SLC	CT.Hartford	Thanks. It is	CU-MARK(tr)	02358 SLC tr
Unknown	1881.05.**	SLC	Unknown	Part of which	CtY	09314 inscription
Unknown	1881.05.31	SLC	CT.Hartford	I know you	CU-MARK(tr)	01964 SLC tr

Unknown		1881.07.05	SLC	CT.Branford	P.S. But never	NjP	01982 inscription
Unknown		1881.09.19	SLC	NY.Elmira	I can decide	CtY	02040
Unknown		1881.10.25	SLC	CT.Hartford	Your letter is	CU-MARK(tr)	02065
Unknown	aft	1881.10.30	SLC	CT.Hartford	In reply I	NPV	01694 form letter
Unknown		1881.12.23	SLC	CT.Hartford	Never put off	Mo2	11009 inscription
Unknown		1882.01.02	SLC	CT.Hartford	Yours truly	173:1942.10.13	10347 inscription
Unknown		1882.01.21	SLC	CT.Hartford	This is a	116:1945.04.19	09178
Unknown		1882.02.**	SLC	CT.Hartford	Very Truly Yours	CU-MARK(ph)	09319 inscription
Unknown		1882.02.19	SLC	CT.Hartford	The expression of	CU-MARK(ph)	02160
Unknown		1882.02.22	SLC	CT.Hartford	There isn't any	MiMtpT	09320 inscription
Unknown		1882.08.26	SLC	NY.Elmira	Truly Yours	C7	11076 inscription
Unknown		1882.08.26	SLC	NY.Elmira	I could not	CU-MARK(ph)	02255
Unknown		1882.08.26	SLC	NY.Elmira	Truly Yours	NjP	09323 inscription
Unknown		1882.11.25	SLC	CT.Hartford	Yrs Truly	107:1926.01.14	09572 inscription
Unknown		1883.01.05	SLC	CT.Hartford	If you would	ViU	10773 inscription
Unknown		1883.02.22	SLC	CT.Hartford	The man who	127:11f	09325 inscription
Unknown		1883.02.22	SLC	CT.Hartford	Form for Literary	CU-MARK	02349
Unknown		1883.04.24	SLC	CT.Hartford	This is to	CU-MARK(ph)	02374 typed
Unknown		1883.05.13	SLC	Unknown	Truly Yrs	155:1961.12.12	10438 inscription
Unknown		1883.06.**	SLC	Unknown	With pleasure	CU-MARK(ph)	10957 inscription
Unknown	o/a	1883.07.22	SLC	NY.Elmira	I send this	CU-MARK	02326 on Twichell July 22

ADDRESSEE	DATE	WRITER	PLACE	CUE	SOURCE	NUMBER/NOTES
Unknown	1883.09.**	SLC	Unknown	Pay no attention	NPV	09327
Unknown	1883.11.14	SLC	CT.Hartford	As I had	CU-MARK	02856 fragment
Unknown	1884.**.**	SLC	Unknown	Just enclose this	NPV	02882
Unknown	1884.01.14	SLC	CT.Hartford	Stephen--nothing became	CU-MARK(ph)	02575
Unknown	1884.05.11	SLC	CT.Hartford	I cannot remember	NN-B	02579
Unknown	1884.05.16	SLC	CT.Hartford	Very Truly Yours	CLU-S/C	02980 inscription
Unknown	1884.07.05	SLC	NY.Elmira	They are pirates	CU-MARK(ph)	10475
Unknown	1884.08.05	SLC	NY.Elmira	I apologize for	ODa2	09177
Unknown	1884.11.10	SLC	Unknown	Truly yours	MnU-Rb	09331 inscription
Unknown	1885.**.**	SLC	NY.Elmira	The name of	305:1911.01.18	09852
Unknown	1885.01.26	SLC	Unknown	None genuine without	Mo2	09335 inscription
Unknown	1885.02.13	SLC	Unknown	Sincerely Yours	CU-MARK(ph)	10565 inscription
Unknown	1885.02.21	SLC	NY.New York	With the best	105:1938.11.21	09650 inscription
Unknown	1885.03.01	SLC	CT.Hartford	Truly Yours	DLC	10787 inscription
Unknown	1885.03.21	SLC	NY.New York	To the General's	ViU	09336 inscription
Unknown	1885.03.28	SLC	CT.Hartford	The review came	Mo2	02422
Unknown	1885.04.01	SLC	CT.Hartford	Of course I	IEN	03202
Unknown	1885.04.15	SLC	CT.Hartford	I am just	NN	03217
Unknown	1885.05.13	SLC per JR	CT.Hartford	The subject is	OCIWHi	03225
Unknown	1885.05.27	SLC	NY.New York	This is to	NPV	03224
Unknown	1885.06.15	SLC	CT.Hartford	Truly yours	418:1974.11.19	09486 inscription; other sources
Unknown	1885.07.22	SLC	NY.Elmira	I thank you	272:1982.07.22	09189
Unknown	1885.07.30	SLC	NY.Elmira	Truly Yours	CtY	11047 inscription

Unknown	aft 1885.07.30	SLC	Unknown	It seems to	CU-MARK(ph)	03272
Unknown	1885.08.30	SLC	NY.Elmira	I said a	TxU	03281
Unknown	1885.09.23	SLC	CT.Hartford	Indeed I not	107:1924.03.10	09460
Unknown	1885.10.**	SLC	CT.Hartford	Truly Yours	305:1911.04.04	09737 inscription
Unknown	1885.11.**	SLC	Unknown	Truly Yours	CU-MARK(ph)	10560 inscription
Unknown	1885.11.01	SLC	CT.Hartford	I think you	CU-MARK(ph)	03302
Unknown	1885.11.20	SLC	NY.New York	When & where	CU-MARK	03311
Unknown	aft 1885.11.30	SLC	Unknown	who seem glad	CtHMTH	03320 fragment
Unknown	1885.12.**	SLC	CT.Hartford	There is not	105:1971.02.02	09689
Unknown	1885.12.14	SLC	Unknown	truly yours	110:1966.05.31	09716 inscription
Unknown	1885.12.26	SLC	CT.Hartford	You make me	NN-B	02625
Unknown	1885.12.26	SLC	CT.Hartford	The watch which	ViU	03344
Unknown	1886.**.**	SLC	CT.Hartford	Oh--so you	CCamarSJ	03658 unsent
Unknown	1886.01.17	SLC	CT.Hartford	please send me	107:1926.04.01	09569
Unknown	1886.02.02	SLC	CT.Hartford	I had very	ViU	03364
Unknown	1886.02.22	SLC	CT.Hartford	And yet it	CtY	03369 fragment
Unknown	1886.06.05	SLC	CT.Hartford	Mrs. Clemens--with	NNU-F	03406
Unknown	1886.06.06 & 1886.06.07	SLC	CT.Hartford	This appeared in	CU-MARK	03407 fragment
Unknown	1886.07.15	SLC	NY.Elmira	Your kind note	COMC	03419
Unknown	1886.08.21	SLC	Unknown	The confidence will	Mo2	02429 inscription
Unknown	1886.09.16	SLC	NY.Elmira	There are some	CU-MARK(ph)	03457 inscription
Unknown	1886.09.16	SLC	NY.Elmira	There are some	ODa2	10442 inscription
Unknown	1886.11.06	SLC	CT.Hartford	When the Lord	NN-B	09218 inscription

ADDRESSEE	DATE	WRITER	PLACE	CUE	SOURCE	NUMBER/NOTES
Unknown	o/a 1886.12.02	SLC	CT.Hartford	P.S. So it's	CU-MARK	03488 on Smith Dec 2
Unknown	1886.12.21	SLC	CT.Hartford	Just let it	TxU	03501
Unknown	1887.**.**	SLC	Unknown	I do not	CU-MARK	08733 on Loisette broadside
Unknown	1887.03.04	SLC	CT.Hartford	Prof. Loisette did	287	03535
Unknown	1887.04.25	SLC	CT.Hartford	I should very	IreDNL	09204
Unknown	1887.08.29	SLC	CT.Hartford	Yes, they are	IaU	03636
Unknown	1888.**.**	SLC	CT.Hartford	I shall be	110:1968.09.12	10350
Unknown	1888.07.12	SLC	CT.Hartford	I beg to	CtHMTH	03730
Unknown	1888.09.27	SLC	NY.New York	I desire to	MeHi	03793
Unknown	1888.11.23	SLC	CT.Hartford	I haven't a	IU-R	03836
Unknown	1888.11.30	SLC	CT.Hartford	He that would	CU-MARK(ph)	09341 inscription
Unknown	1889.**.**	SLC	CT.Hartford	No more these	105:1941.04.16	10351 inscription
Unknown	1889.01.24	SLC	CT.Hartford	my obligations are	110:1973.03.22	10353
Unknown	1889.03.09	SLC	Unknown	Truly Yours S.L.	122:1936.03.03	09739
Unknown	1889.04.10	SLC	CT.Hartford	I suppose you	CtY	03882
Unknown	1889.04.30	SLC	CT.Hartford	Mark Twain	CtY	11046 inscription
Unknown	1889.05.**	SLC	CT.Hartford	We have never	CU-MARK	03888
Unknown	1889.11.19	SLC	CT.Hartford	Telephoned at 6.30	CtHMTH	03971
Unknown	1889.12.06	SLC	CT.Hartford	A true date	Uk4	09494 deposit
Unknown	1889.12.16	SLC	CT.Hartford	I wish I	421:1917.02.20	10355
Unknown	1890.01.30	SLC	Unknown	If I had	412:1937.04.13	10354 inscription
Unknown	1890.03.17	SLC	CT.Hartford	I am not	ViU	04028
Unknown	1890.06.**	SLC	Unknown	Truly Yours	MH-H	10844 inscription
Unknown	1890.10.16	SLC	CT.Hartford	If this is	CU-MARK	04103

Unknown		1891.01.**	SLC	Unknown	A lie well	122:1934.12.05	09305 inscription
Unknown		1891.01.08	SLC per FGW	CT.Hartford	Thanks very much	CU-MARK	04156
Unknown		1891.02.12	SLC	CT.Hartford	Some day you	CU-MARK	04171
Unknown	ca	1891.02.14	SLC	CT.Hartford	A lie well	110:1965.09.30	10356 inscription
Unknown	aft	1891.02.28	SLC	Unknown	is so pitiably	CU-MARK	04176 fragment
Unknown		1891.03.07	SLC	CT.Hartford	I am very	NBu	04179
Unknown		1891.05.**	SLC	CT.Hartford	By the test	CtY	09307 inscription
Unknown		1891.05.11	SLC	CT.Hartford	I don't really	CU-MARK	04205
Unknown		1891.10.04	SLC	SW.Lausanne	I am not	CU-MARK(ph)	04242
Unknown		1891.11.27	SLC	GE.Berlin	No. 1 I	CCamarSJ	04257
Unknown		1891.12.22	SLC	GE.Berlin	Never put off	418:1975.12.17	04260 inscription
Unknown		1892.01.12	SLC	GE.Berlin	If it is	NN-B	04607
Unknown		1892.05.29	SLC	IT.Cadenabbia	You pay me	CU-MARK(tr)	04295
Unknown		1892.06.19	SLC	SH.Havel	You cannot imagine	Mo2	04300
Unknown		1892.08.**	SLC	Unknown	Yes indeed, &	CtY	09304 inscription
Unknown		1892.08.23	SLC	GE.Bad-Nauheim	I comply with	SwUU	01800
Unknown		1893.**.**	SLC	Unknown	In America my	107:1924.05.08	09550
Unknown		1893.02.12	SLC	IT.Florence	It is too	114:562	04338
Unknown		1893.02.27	SLC	IT.Florence	P.S. Feb. 27	NN5	04344
Unknown		1893.05.**	SLC	Unknown	With great pleasure	UkB	10655 inscription
Unknown		1893.06.**	SLC	Unknown	Also Truly Yours	C4	09302 inscription
Unknown		1893.09.19	SLC	NY.New York	I wish I	105:1945.01.23	09425
Unknown		1893.12.25	SLC	NY.New York	Dern that language	ViU	04539
Unknown		1894.**.**	SLC	NY.New York	The no-speech terms	441:1920.01.07	10352

ADDRESSEE	DATE	WRITER	PLACE	CUE	SOURCE	NUMBER/NOTES
Unknown	1894.03.05	SLC	Unknown	with the best	105:1971.05.18	09694 inscription; other sources
Unknown	1894.04.**	SLC	Unknown	Truly Yours	107:1918.03.06	09543 inscription
Unknown	1894.04.**	SLC	Unknown	Truly Yours	Mo2	09299 inscription
Unknown	1894.05.**	SLC	SH.New York	Thank you cordially	Mo2	11010
Unknown	1894.08.09	SLC	NY.New York	I do not	CAlb2	04777
Unknown	1895.**.**	SLC	Unknown	In my experience	175:1902.10.16	09856
Unknown	1895.02.09	SLC	FR.Paris	You will see	NN-B	04989
Unknown	1895.04.08	SLC	FR.Paris	The above signature	157:1924.11.10	09792 inscription
Unknown	ca 1895.04.08	SLC	Unknown	My share of	105:1941.01.08	04857
Unknown	1895.06.22	SLC	NY.Elmira	I am sorry	ViU	04896
Unknown	1895.06.25	SLC per OLC	NY.Elmira	It was a	MiD	04901
Unknown	1895.06.25	SLC	NY.Elmira	One thing I	105:1957.04.30	04899
Unknown	1895.06.25	SLC	NY.Elmira	I am ashamed	TxU	04900
Unknown	ca 1895.08.**	SLC	Unknown	The law recognizes	211:352	09067
Unknown	1895.08.22	SLC	Unknown	Truly Yours	ViU	10765 inscription
Unknown	1895.11.08	SLC	Unknown	Mark Twain (Educated	105:1947.12.01	09667 inscription
Unknown	1896.03.09	SLC per OLC	II.Jaipur	I am truly	UkB	10654
Unknown	bet 1896.08.01 & 1896.08.18	SLC	Unknown	They say Mrs.	CU-MARK	05090 on Freuling-huysen ca Aug 1
Unknown	1896.08.03	SLC	EN.Southampton	The books have	UPB	10865
Unknown	1896.08.28	SLC	EN.Guildford	Mr. Smythe asks	Mo4	05101 on printed broadside
Unknown	1896.10.15	SLC	EN.London	Can be used	MoHM	09408
Unknown	1897.**.**	SLC	AU.Vienna	Truly Yours	116:1950.04.06	09958 inscription

Unknown		1897.**.**	SLC	AU.Vienna	Truly Yours	ViU	11085 inscription
Unknown		1897.**.**	SLC	Unknown	Please make a	418:1975.04.30	09347 other sources
Unknown		1897.02.10	SLC	EN.London	until the hurt	155:1936.05.04	10450
Unknown		1897.03.13	SLC	EN.London	My stay in	NN-B	05506
Unknown		1897.05.31	SLC	EN.London	James Ross Clemens	CU-MARK(ph)	05196
Unknown		1897.07.**	SLC	Unknown	Universal brotherhood is	ODa2	11198 inscription
Unknown		1897.07.05	SLC	EN.London	Unfortunately our change	CU-MARK(ph)	05250
Unknown		1897.10.14	SLC	AU.Vienna	The old proverb	Mo2	05297 inscription
Unknown		1897.10.15	SLC	AU.Vienna	My wife &	ViU	05298
Unknown	aft	1897.10.25	SLC	Unknown	Private. Never mind	PBL	10942 on Oct 25 to Frisbie
Unknown		1897.12.12	SLC	AU.Vienna	The proper proportions	226:49	09350 inscription
Unknown		1898.**.**	SLC	AU.Vienna	I have secured	105:1963.10.08	09680 other sources
Unknown	ca	1898.01.01	SLC	AU.Vienna	What you have	ODa2	04708
Unknown		1898.04.29	SLC & OLC	AU.Vienna	Good friends, good	105:1938.11.21	09649 inscription
Unknown		1898.05.**	SLC	Unknown	Truly Yours	ODa2	11221 inscription
Unknown		1898.05.24	SLC	AU.Kaltenleut.	Yes, the sentence	NN-B	05490
Unknown		1898.05.24	SLC	AU.Kaltenleut.	Thank you very	ViU	05393
Unknown		1898.06.26	SLC	AU.Kaltenleut.	I thank you	IMacoW	05403
Unknown		1898.08.02	SLC	AU.Kaltenleut.	Truly Yours	CtHMTH	09355 inscription
Unknown		1898.08.11	SLC	AU.Kaltenleut.	I mailed that	ViU	05421
Unknown		1898.11.10	SLC	AU.Vienna	The Jew is	IU-R	05464 inscription
Unknown		1898.11.12	SLC	Unknown	Sign thanks splendid	CU-MARK(tr)	05584 telegram; SLC tr

ADDRESSEE	DATE	WRITER	PLACE	CUE	SOURCE	NUMBER/NOTES
Unknown	1898.11.15	SLC	Unknown	Never put off	CU-MARK(ph)	09357 inscription
Unknown	1898.12.02	SLC	Unknown	Yes, with pleasure	WaS	09358 inscription
Unknown	1898.12.12	SLC	AU.Vienna	Lacks 500	CU-MARK(tr)	05479 telegram; SLC tr
Unknown	1899.02.11	SLC	AU.Vienna	I should like	IU-R	05545
Unknown	1899.02.25	SLC	AU.Vienna	I very much	CU-MARK	08666
Unknown	1899.03.**	SLC	AU.Vienna	Be good &	CLU-S/C	09359 inscription
Unknown	1899.03.25	SLC	Unknown	It is best	105:1948.10.04	09360 inscription; other sources
Unknown	1899.03.27	SLC	HU.Budapest	It is not	C7	11088 inscription
Unknown	1899.05.05	SLC	AU.Vienna	No, of course	CU-MARK(ph)	05587
Unknown	1899.05.23	SLC	AU.Vienna	It is not	NEImC	09361 inscription
Unknown	1899.06.01	SLC	EN.London	If we try	NStBU	09713 inscription
Unknown	1899.06.11	SLC	EN.London	I have an	ViU	05638
Unknown	1899.06.21	SLC	EN.London	I shall try	ViU	05641
Unknown	1899.06.22	SLC	EN.London	If we try	105:1961.11.29	09703 inscription
Unknown	1899.07.05	SLC	EN.London	Don't risk the	NEImC	05650
Unknown	1899.08.03	SLC	SE.Sanna	of my series	CtY	11044 fragment
Unknown	1899.09.01	SLC	SE.Sanna	A thousand dollars	NN-B	05619
Unknown	1899.09.16	SLC	SE.Sanna	Truly Yours	116:1948.09.30	09959 inscription
Unknown	1899.10.19	SLC	EN.London	I understand, now	ViU	05692
Unknown	1899.11.08	SLC	EN.London	I don't want	CtY	11045
Unknown	1899.11.11	SLC	EN.London	The "Diary" has	NNU-F	05705
Unknown	1899.11.13	SLC	EN.London	Let us save	212:1942.02.28	09904 inscription

Unknown		1900.01.**	SLC	EN.London	We ought never	110:1964.05.21	09741 inscription
Unknown		1900.04.05	SLC	EN.London	by Yours Truly	CU-MARK(ph)	10556 inscription
Unknown		1900.04.24	SLC	EN.London	I am grateful	NvU	05798
Unknown		1900.04.28	SLC	EN.London	I perceive, now	CCamarSJ	08412
Unknown	ca to	1900.06.28 1900.10.06	SLC	EN.London	That's the address	ViU	09033
Unknown		1900.07.01	SLC	EN.London	This house, out	CU-MARK(ph)	09715
Unknown		1900.10.18	SLC	NY.New York	I would have	CBev2	05878
Unknown	bet &	1900.11.01 1901.06.21	SLC	NY.New York	Rockwood photographed me	441:1919.11.25	09993
Unknown		1900.11.21	SLC	NY.New York	From his oldest	CU-MARK(ph)	11089 inscription
Unknown		1900.11.30	SLC	NY.New York	I know I	114:702	05922
Unknown		1900.12.01	SLC	NY.New York	We ought never	C4	09265 inscription
Unknown	bef	1900.12.25	SLC	NY.New York	Prosperity and happiness	317:1901.01.25	05940 inscription
Unknown		1900.12.31	SLC	NY.New York	Give her soap	NN-B	09264 inscription
Unknown		1901.**.**	SLC	Unknown	The proof-slips are	122:1934.12.05	05953
Unknown		1901.**.**	SLC	Unknown	I remember Rameses	155:1930.07.28	10455
Unknown		1901.**.**	SLC	Unknown	come down &	165:1958.05.23	09861
Unknown		1901.01.10	SLC	NY.New York	Please wait a	CU-MARK(ph)	10575
Unknown		1901.01.10	SLC	NY.New York	I may have	RNR	05963
Unknown		1901.01.22	SLC	NY.New York	Truly Yours	107:1914.01.20	09423 inscription
Unknown		1901.02.16	SLC	NY.New York	I got great	182:107	06001
Unknown		1901.04.13	SLC	NY.New York	It is such	CU-MARK	06035
Unknown		1901.05.15	SLC	NY.New York	P.S. After filling	CU-MARK(ph)	06057
Unknown		1901.05.30	SLC	NY.New York	Please send me	NN-B	09044
Unknown	ca	1901.07.13	SLC	NY.Saranac Lake	I shall be	CU-MARK(tr)	06087

ADDRESSEE	DATE	WRITER	PLACE	CUE	SOURCE	NUMBER/NOTES
Unknown	1901.08.27	SLC	NY.Saranac Lake	In the list	OC	06120
Unknown	1901.10.**	SLC	Unknown	Mark Twain, October	107:1918.03.13	09546 inscription
Unknown	1901.10.19 or 1902.10.19	SLC	NY.Riverdale	your printers need	157:1915.05.20	09788
Unknown	1901.10.25	SLC	NY.Riverdale	For two hours	NN5	06165
Unknown	1901.10.29	SLC	NY.Riverdale	Plant acorns--extend	NN-B	08221 inscription
Unknown	1901.11.**	SLC	NY.New York	Ever so many	122:1934.05.09	06170 on Harper circular
Unknown	1901.11.01 or 1902.11.01	SLC	NY.Riverdale	I thank you	Mo2	08281
Unknown	1901.12.14	SLC	NY.Riverdale	In talk with	CU-MARK	09206 on Harper Dec 12
Unknown	1902.**.**	SLC	NY.New York	with the love	NBuU-PO	09371 inscription
Unknown	1902.02.15	SLC	NY.Riverdale	I am smoking	CU-MARK(tr)	06277
Unknown	1902.02.19	SLC	NY.Riverdale	One should not	233:1936.03.23	10368 inscription
Unknown	1902.02.19	SLC	NY.Riverdale	Only he who	305:1911.04.04	09368 inscription; other sources
Unknown	ca 1902.02.23	SLC	NY.Riverdale	Private. Will the	DLC(tr)	09037
Unknown	1902.02.27	SLC	NY.Riverdale	Yes, dear Madam	205:1931.04.29	09818 inscription
Unknown	ca 1902.03.15	OLC	Unknown	Mr. Clemens is	CU-MARK	06288
Unknown	1902.04.24	OLC	NY.Riverdale	Mr Clemens asks	ViU	06328
Unknown	1902.04.25 & 1902.05.16	SLC & OLC	NY.Riverdale	Let us save	205:1935.11.19	09814 inscription
Unknown	ca 1902.06.01	SLC	MO.Hannibal	I can't come	CU-MARK(tr)	06352
Unknown	1902.06.20	SLC	NY.Riverdale	Lately, by order	CU-MARK	06369
Unknown	1902.07.02	SLC	ME.York Harbor	I think that	CU-MARK(ph)	10577
Unknown	1902.08.07	SLC	ME.York Harbor	If I remember	CU-MARK	06402
Unknown	1902.08.29	SLC	ME.York Harbor	Ordinarily I might	ViU	06421

Unknown		1902.09.16	SLC	ME.York Harbor	That I am	NNC	06433
Unknown		1902.10.09	SLC	ME.York Harbor	All the letters	NvU	08867
Unknown		1902.11.25	SLC per IVL	NY.Riverdale	We have received	CU-MARK	06494
Unknown		1902.12.11	SLC	NY.Riverdale	I shall not	CU-MARK(ph)	06512 SLC tr
Unknown		1903.**.**	SLC	Unknown	Let us add	CU-MARK	06539
Unknown		1903.01.12	SLC	NY.Riverdale	The lady--in	CU-MARK(tr)	06557 SLC tr
Unknown		1903.01.16	SLC	NY.Riverdale	You have expressed	CCamarSJ	06566
Unknown		1903.03.20	SLC	NY.New York	Surely the Outlook	CU-MARK	06604
Unknown		1903.03.23	SLC	NY.Riverdale	I seldom go	C4	06608
Unknown		1903.04.30	SLC & IVL	NY.Riverdale	Work & Play	IaDmE	06641 inscription with IVL cover letter
Unknown		1903.06.30	SLC	NY.Riverdale	Work & Play	116:1952.11.06	09974 inscription
Unknown		1903.09.19	SLC	NY.Elmira	those two sittings	157:1912.01.29	09796
Unknown	bef	1903.11.01	SLC	Unknown	Mrs. Lyon &	CU-MARK(tr)	10811
Unknown		1904.01.08	SLC	IT.Florence	I am sorry	CU-MARK	06785 also in German
Unknown		1904.03.25	SLC	IT.Florence	I remember writing	124:218f	06815
Unknown		1904.06.12	SLC	IT.Florence	Truly Yours	CStoC	10804 inscription
Unknown		1904.06.19	SLC	IT.Florence	Ugo Piemontini, a	324:1932.10.13	06876 form letter; other sources
Unknown	ca	1904.06.21	SLC	IT.Florence	For what you	CtHMTH	06854 form letter
Unknown	ca	1904.06.21	SLC	IT.Florence	For what you	PP	06852 form letter
Unknown		1904.09.28	SLC	Unknown	Truly Yours	NN	10789 inscription
Unknown		1904.10.**	SLC	NY.New York	With the kindest	105:1962.10.16	09704 inscription

ADDRESSEE	DATE	WRITER	PLACE	CUE	SOURCE	NUMBER/NOTES
Unknown	1904.10.25	SLC	NY.New York	With the kindest	233:1932.05.03	09977 inscription
Unknown	1904.11.16	SLC	NY.New York	I desire to	CU-MARK	06951
Unknown	1904.11.26	SLC	NY.New York	I hardly need	ViU	06957
Unknown	1905.**.**	SLC per IVL	Unknown	Mr. Clemens directs	CU-MARK(dr)	07284
Unknown	1905.**.**	SLC per IVL	Unknown	Mr. Clemens directs	CU-MARK	06971
Unknown	o/a 1905.02.23	SLC per IVL	NY.New York	Still in bed	CU-MARK(dr)	07006 on Unknown Feb 23
Unknown	1905.03.15	SLC per IVL	NY.New York	Mr. Clemens directs	CU-MARK(dr)	07019
Unknown	1905.04.05	SLC per IVL	NY.New York	According to Dr.	CU-MARK	07025
Unknown	1905.05.**	SLC	NY.New York	Very Truly Yours	ViU	10771 inscription
Unknown	ca 1905.06.**	SLC per IVL	NH.Dublin	Mr. Clemens says	CU-MARK(dr)	07053
Unknown	1905.07.01	SLC	NH.Dublin	I am deeply	CU-MARK(dr)	07076
Unknown	1905.07.08	SLC	NH.Dublin	was trying to	107:1927.02.28	09571
Unknown	1905.08.06	SLC	NH.Dublin	There are two	PP	09625 inscription
Unknown	1905.10.**	SLC	Unknown	Taking the pledge	C4	09374 inscription
Unknown	1905.11.**	SLC	Unknown	There is no	InRE	09373 inscription
Unknown	aft 1905.11.08	SLC per IVL	NY.New York	Your letter of	CU-MARK(dr)	08703
Unknown	1905.11.30	SLC	NY.New York	Truly Yours	CtHMTH	09375 inscription
Unknown	1905.11.30	SLC	Unknown	Mark Twain	157:1909.03.08	09864 inscription
Unknown	1905.12.**	SLC	NY.New York	Necessity is the	122:1936.01.29	09376 inscription
Unknown	1905.12.**	SLC	Unknown	You may straighten	105:1964.06.17	09685 inscription

Unknown	o/a	1905.12.06	SLC	NY.New York	To you, &	C6	09440 form letter
Unknown		1905.12.29	SLC	NY.New York	Yes I did	NN-B(tr)	02181
Unknown		1906.**.**	SLC	NH.Dublin	I have: (1) Instalment	CU-MARK(dr)	07287
Unknown		1906.**.**	SLC	NY.New York	I thank you	ODa2	07292
Unknown		1906.01.**	SLC	NY.New York	Truly Yours	110:1968.09.12	10376 inscription
Unknown		1906.01.10	SLC	Unknown	If you mean	CU-MARK(tr)	07301 SLC tr
Unknown		1906.01.11	SLC per IVL	NY.New York	I thank you	ViU	07304
Unknown		1906.02.17	SLC	NY.New York	Truly Yours	CU-MARK(ph)	10492 inscription
Unknown		1906.02.24	SLC per IVL	NY.New York	I am old	CU-MARK(tr)	07354 IVL tr
Unknown		1906.03.**	SLC	NY.New York	Let us save	212:1945.05.26	09909 inscription
Unknown		1906.03.06	SLC	NY.New York	Truth is the	105:1971.04.04	09692 inscription
Unknown	o/a	1906.03.24	SLC	NY.New York	Her songs were	CU-MARK	07400
Unknown		1906.04.09	SLC per IVL	NY.New York	You must get	110:1964.05.21	09740
Unknown		1906.04.12	SLC per IVL	NY.New York	Mr. Clemens suggests	CU-MARK(tr)	07427
Unknown		1906.04.12	SLC	NY.New York	Let us save	NN	09247 inscription
Unknown		1906.04.12	SLC	NY.New York	Let us save	ODa2	11211 inscription
Unknown	bef	1906.04.14	SLC	NY.New York	We were quite	122:1936.01.29	09911 interview responses
Unknown		1906.09.03	SLC	NH.Dublin	Your favor of	MH-H	09050
Unknown		1906.09.17	SLC	Unknown	No, it is	153:20f	10991 inscription
Unknown		1906.10.**	SLC	Unknown	On the whole	CtHMTH	09249 inscription
Unknown		1906.12.**	SLC	Unknown	I am sorrier	131:1906.12.12	07583

ADDRESSEE	DATE	WRITER	PLACE	CUE	SOURCE	NUMBER/NOTES
Unknown	1906.12.18	SLC	NY.New York	I never did	CU-MARK(tr)	07599
Unknown	1907.**.**	SLC	Unknown	The bust is	RuM2	09378 inscription
Unknown	1907.01.21	SLC	NY.New York	Consider the proportions	ViU	10838 inscription
Unknown	1907.03.01	SLC	NY.New York	By the note	122:1937.11.11	07666
Unknown	1907.04.03	SLC	Unknown	A true copy	ViU	11099 inscription
Unknown	1907.04.10	SLC	NY.New York	This is the	ViU	07691
Unknown	o/a 1907.07.17	SLC per IVL	Unknown	Mr. Rogers sick	CU-MARK(dr)	07786 on Wendell July 17
Unknown	1907.08.**	SLC	NY.Tuxedo Park	Many gay &	CU-MARK	08678
Unknown	1907.09.19	SLC	NY.Tuxedo Park	S.L. Clemens	DLC	10788 inscription
Unknown	1907.10.**	SLC	Unknown	Let us save	CU-MARK(ph)	10557 inscription
Unknown	1907.10.17	SLC per IVL	NY.Tuxedo Park	I take pleasure	NHor2	07855
Unknown	1907.11.**	SLC	NY.New York	Mr. Samuel L.	CU-MARK(ph)	07866 form letter
Unknown	1907.12.25	SLC	NY.New York	Now that the	212:1946.11.16	09912 inscription
Unknown	1908.01.18	SLC	NY.New York	I am grieved	CU-MARK	07921
Unknown	1908.01.18	SLC	NY.New York	I do not	CU-MARK	07920
Unknown	aft 1908.02.20	SLC per IVL	NY.New York	Mr. Clemens's permission	CU-MARK(tr)	07944
Unknown	1908.05.**	SLC per IVL	NY.New York	I am just	CU-MARK(dr)	07989
Unknown	1908.05.**	SLC	NY.New York	I published this	ViU	11100 inscription
Unknown	1908.05.20	SLC per IVL	NY.New York	Mr. Clemens asks	NjP	08003
Unknown	1908.05.25	SLC per IVL	NY.New York	Mr. Clemens asks	NjP	08010
Unknown	1908.06.17	SLC	NY.New York	My charming niece	311:373	08032

Unknown	ca	1908.08.11	SLC per IVL	CT.Redding	Mr. Tallman should	CU-MARK(tr)	08081
Unknown		1908.08.28	SLC	CT.Redding	By "private," I	CU-MARK	08093
Unknown		1908.09.18	SLC	CT.Redding	Notice to the	NN-B	08102
Unknown	o/a	1908.10.07	SLC	CT.Redding	Greeting and Salutation	462:47	11162 form letter
Unknown		1908.11.06	SLC	CT.Redding	I note this	CU-MARK	08158
Unknown		1908.11.23	SLC	CT.Redding	bought the plates	105:1953.05.12	09666 inscription
Unknown		1908.11.30	SLC	CT.Redding	I like the	CU-MARK	08164
Unknown		1909.**.**	SLC	CT.Redding	I am sending	CU-MARK(dr)	10970 on 1909 to New York governor
Unknown		1909.01.04	SLC	NY.New York	Doubtless the work	MoHi	08309 typed
Unknown		1909.01.05	SLC	CT.Redding	Have we ever	205:1935.11.19	09813
Unknown	ca	1909.01.18	SLC per MLH	CT.Redding	X and say	CtHMTH(dr)	08334
Unknown	ca	1909.01.18	SLC per MLH	CT.Redding	X and thank	CtHMTH(dr)	08335
Unknown	ca	1909.01.18	SLC per MLH	CT.Redding	X in answer	CtHMTH(dr)	08323
Unknown	ca	1909.01.18	SLC per MLH	CT.Redding	X me to	CtHMTH(dr)	08321
Unknown	ca	1909.01.18	SLC per MLH	CT.Redding	X thank you	CtHMTH(dr)	08322
Unknown	ca	1909.01.18	SLC per MLH	CT.Redding	X to acknowledge	CtHMTH(dr)	08324
Unknown	ca	1909.01.18	SLC per MLH	CT.Redding	X to say	CtHMTH(dr)	08325
Unknown	ca	1909.01.18	SLC per MLH	CT.Redding	X to thank	CtHMTH(dr)	08326
Unknown	ca	1909.01.18	SLC per MLH	CT.Redding	X to thank	CtHMTH(dr)	08327
Unknown		1909.01.19	SLC per MLH	CT.Redding	X and say	CtHMTH(dr)	08317

ADDRESSEE	DATE	WRITER	PLACE	CUE	SOURCE	NUMBER/NOTES
Unknown	1909.01.29	SLC per MLH	CT.Redding	X you for	CtHMTH(dr)	08332
Unknown	1909.03.02	SLC	CT.Redding	I am very	CU-MARK(tr)	08357
Unknown	1909.03.23	SLC	CT.Redding	Mr. Sunderland built	414:1958.06.19	08376
Unknown	1909.06.14	SLC	CT.Redding	Yes, I remember	CU-MARK(ph)	08903
Unknown	1909.06.16	SLC	CT.Redding	Truly Yours	110:1966.11.03	10380 inscription
Unknown	1909.06.25	SLC	CT.Redding	I suddenly learn	ViU	08426
Unknown	1909.07.04	SLC	CT.Redding	Let persons devoid	MdU	09390 inscription
Unknown	1909.10.11	SLC per ABP	CT.Redding	You have located	CtY	08466
Unknown	1909.11.10	SLC	CT.Redding	What went with	CU-MARK	08488
Unknown	1909.12.26	SLC	CT.Redding	To all friends	ODa2(dr)	11212 dr of form letter
Unknown	1910.01.25	SLC	BE.Hamilton	Very Truly Yours	CU-MARK(ph)	09392 inscription
Unknown	1910.02.22	SLC	BE.Hamilton	Paine says he	CU-MARK(ph)	08563
Van der Wyde, W.M.	1906.09.21	SLC	NY.New York	Taking the pledge	111:326	09250 inscription
Van Dreele, Mr.	1904.07.22	SLC	MA.Lee	I & my	MiD	06898
Van Duzer, S.C.	1907.06.19	SLC per RWA	EN.London	Mr. Clemens directs	CU-MARK(tr)	07758 RWA tr
Van Dyke, Henry	1902.12.**	SLC	NY.Riverdale	It probably costs	437:218	06496
Van Dyke, Henry	o/a 1902.12.10	SLC per IVL	NY.Riverdale	For such reasons	CU-MARK	10910
Van Schuyver, Charles	1887.08.08	SLC	CT.Hartford	Please set me	CSmH	03619
Vanderbilt, Cornelius	o/a 1907.02.26	SLC per IVL	NY.New York	If I allow	CU-MARK(dr)	07665 on Vanderbilt Feb 26
Venable, William H.	1902.10.27	SLC	NY.Riverdale	I have only	OHi	06475
Verey, Joseph N.	bef 1890.07.19	SLC per FGW	NY.Tannersville	Clemens gave you	CU-MARK(dr)	06169 telegram
Vilas, Anna M.	1909.10.13	SLC	CT.Redding	I thank you	WHi	08469

Virginia City Terr.Ent.		1868.04.23	SLC	NV.Coburn's Sta.	I am doing	431:1868.04.24	00203 telegram
Virginia City Terr.Ent.		1869.02.17	SLC	PA.Titusville	I have pretty	431:1869.03.26	00256
Vitagraph Co.		1907.**.**	SLC	Unknown	I authorize the	265:76	07605
Volkhovsky, Felix		1900.01.29	SLC	EN.London	It breaks my	CU-MARK	05754
Von Oppen, Isabel		1890.01.03	SLC	CT.Hartford	Mr. Clemens offers	CU-MARK	04004
Wachschlager, Miss		1885.04.03	SLC	CT.Hartford	Ah, if I	105:1970.10.29	09339 inscription; other sources
Wagner-Smith, Miss	o/a	1906.12.12	SLC per IVL	NY.New York	Apply to Librarian	CU-MARK(dr)	07592 on Wagner-Smith Dec 12
Wagstaff, Alfred		1908.05.06	JC	CT.Greenwich	I am unaware	NN	10744
Wakeman, Edgar M.		1874.04.25	SLC	NY.Elmira	You know I	ViU	01079
Wakeman-Curtis, Minnie		1877.10.05	SLC	CT.Hartford	I can mention	439:12	01493
Walden, Frank		1870.03.04	SLC	NY.Buffalo	It was a	246:1935.03.06	00439
Walden, Frank		1901.03.04	SLC	NY.New York	I was glad	246:1935.03.06	06014
Walker, Bernard		1909.12.13	SLC	BE.Hamilton	Let us endeavor	NN-B	09645 inscription
Walker, John B.		****.**.**	SLC	NY.New York	Won't you name	C4	00398
Walker, John B.		1898.08.20	SLC	AU.Kaltenleut.	The second check	NN-B	05493
Walker, John B.		1898.09.19	SLC	AU.Kaltenleut.	Sure it's the	NN5	05435
Walker, John B.		1899.07.30	SLC	SE.Sanna	Do you want	CU-MARK	05658
Walker, John B.		1899.10.19	SLC	EN.London	By gracious but	CU-MARK	05693
Walker, John B.		1899.11.08	SLC	EN.London	At this rate	157:1908.05.15	09185
Walker, John B.		1900.03.02	SLC	EN.London	One thing didn't	IEN	05767
Walker, John B.		1900.04.07	SLC	EN.London	But you didn't	405:1910.04.24	05788 other sources
Walker, John B.		1900.09.27	SLC	EN.London	Your cable has	CtY	05872
Walker, John B.		1900.11.10	SLC	NY.New York	The world does	CSto3	05900
Walker, John B. & Page, Walter H.		1903.07.21	SLC	NY.Elmira	Although I have	NN-B	11121 also to others

ADDRESSEE	DATE	WRITER	PLACE	CUE	SOURCE	NUMBER/NOTES
Walker, Katherine K.	1881.10.28	SLC	CT.Hartford	You spoke rather	CU-MARK(tr)	02076
Walker, Katherine K.	1881.10.31	SLC	CT.Hartford	Come, now, please	CU-MARK(tr)	09233
Walker, Mr.	****.**.**	SLC	Unknown	Will Mr. Walker	CU-MARK(tr)	04174
Walker, Mr.	1890.03.17	SLC	Unknown	I thank you	CU-MARK(tr)	04026
Wall, Horace	bef 1889.06.21	SLC	Unknown	But not to	ViU(tr)	09181
Wallace, Elizabeth	1909.01.05	SLC	CT.Redding	You have overwhelmed	CSmH	08297
Wallace, Elizabeth	1909.04.22	SLC	CT.Redding	It is not	440:128	08387
Wallace, Elizabeth	pm 1909.04.25	SLC	CT.Redding	*	CSmH	10160 envelope only
Wallace, Elizabeth	1909.05.26	SLC	CT.Redding	It is indeed	CSmH	08403
Wallace, Elizabeth	1909.06.07	SLC	CT.Redding	I'm leaving home	CSmH	08418
Wallace, Elizabeth	1909.07.**	SLC	CT.Redding	Dear Betsy, it was	CSmH	08431
Wallace, Elizabeth	1909.08.27	SLC	CT.Redding	That rotten-hearted pair	CSmH	08446
Wallace, Elizabeth	1909.09.22	SLC	CT.Redding	It is a	CSmH	08457
Wallace, Elizabeth	pm 1909.11.09	SLC	CT.Redding	*	CSmH	10161 envelope only
Wallace, Elizabeth	1909.11.10	SLC	CT.Redding	Happily it is	CSmH	08487
Wallace, Elizabeth	1909.11.13	SLC	CT.Redding	No, I haven't	CSmH	08490
Wallace, Elizabeth	1909.12.**	SLC	BE.Hamilton	We all send	CSmH	08504
Wallace, Elizabeth	1909.12.17	SLC	BE.Hamilton	Merry Christmas &	CSmH	08511
Wallace, Elizabeth	1910.01.01	SLC	CT.Redding	I can't write	CSmH	08532
Wallace, Elizabeth	1910.01.26 & 1910.01.29	SLC	BE.Hamilton	No revelation--of	CSmH	08548
Wallace, Elizabeth	1910.03.12	SLC	BE.Hamilton	You "know there	CSmH	08570
Wallack, Lester	1887.01.14	SLC	CT.Hartford	I should be	MoSW	03507
Wallop, Beatrice M. & Wallop, Newton	1907.06.19	SLC per RWA	EN.London	Mr. Clemens begs	CU-MARK(tr)	07754 RWA tr
Wallop, Newton & Wallop, Beatrice M.	1907.06.19	SLC per RWA	EN.London	Mr. Clemens begs	CU-MARK(tr)	07754 RWA tr
Walton, W.S.	****.**.**	SLC	Unknown	The Sphynx has often	ODa2	11185
Ward, Elizabeth S.	ca 1904.06.21	SLC	IT.Florence	For what you	255:130	10373 form letter

Ward, L.P.	pm	1902.05.03	SLC	NY.New York	*	CAlb2	09439 envelope only
Ward, William H. or New York Independent		****.05.03	SLC	CT.Hartford	Although I have	CU-MARK(tr)	07672
Ward, W.R.		1887.09.08	SLC	NY.Elmira	And so it	CU-MARK	03773
Wardle, Elizabeth & Wardle, Thomas		1902.01.07	SLC & OLC	NY.Riverdale	S.L. Clemens	NcD	06225
Wardle, Thomas & Wardle, Elizabeth		1902.01.07	SLC & OLC	NY.Riverdale	S.L. Clemens	NcD	06225
Wardle, Thomas		1902.11.02	SLC	NY.Riverdale	I was deeply	NcD	06481
Wardle, Thomas		1904.05.04	SLC	IT.Florence	The whiskey arrived	CLSU	06829
Warfield, Edwin & Warfield, Mrs. Edwin		1907.11.27	SLC	NY.New York	Best thanksgiving wishes	CU-MARK(dr)	08742 telegram
Warfield, Mrs. Edwin & Warfield, Edwin		1907.11.27	SLC	NY.New York	Best thanksgiving wishes	CU-MARK(dr)	08742 telegram
Waring, George E. Jr.		1875.07.14	SLC	CT.Hartford	I am sorry	ViU	01250
Waring, George E. Jr.		1883.04.06	SLC	CT.Hartford	Of course I	ViU	02368
Waring, George E. Jr.		1886.11.06	SLC	CT.Hartford	I've written that	ViU	03477
Warner, Brainard		1898.06.28	SLC	AU.Kaltenleut.	I have waited	131:1898.07.24	05404
Warner, Charles D.		1872.04.22	SLC	NY.Elmira	We have read	CU-MARK	00744
Warner, Charles D.		1872.10.05	SLC	EN.London	By the enclosed	CU-MARK	00819
Warner, Charles D.		1873.05.13	SLC	NY.Elmira	There was no	PBL	00915
Warner, Charles D.		1873.05.17	SLC	SH.Batavia	Ask House to	CU-MARK	00917
Warner, Charles D.	ca	1873.07.11	SLC	EN.London	Livy says--& I	NjP	00951
Warner, Charles D.		1873.07.16	SLC per SCT	EN.London	I have just	CtY	00954
Warner, Charles D.		1873.12.30	SLC	EN.London	I have made	CU-MARK	01021
Warner, Charles D.		1874.05.05	SLC	NY.Elmira	Business. A San	CU-MARK	01082
Warner, Charles D.		1874.06.15	SLC	NY.Elmira	We are still	CU-MARK	01099
Warner, Charles D.		1878.06.16	SLC	GE.Heidelberg	We are mightily	CU-MARK	01572
Warner, Charles D.	ca	1878.08.01	SLC	Unknown	It certainly is	CtY	01581 fragment

ADDRESSEE	DATE	WRITER	PLACE	CUE	SOURCE	NUMBER/NOTES
Warner, Charles D. & Harris, Joel C.	1885.11.29	SLC	CT.Hartford	It was the	CLU-S/C	02420 also to Holmes & Stockton
Warner, Charles D.	1886.07.22	SLC	NY.Elmira	Lord, how do	418:1973.10.30	10349
Warner, Charles D.	1891.09.22	SLC	SW.Rhone River	I have been	CtHMTH	04231
Warner, Charles D. & Warner, Susan L.	1894.04.12	SLC	SH.New York	I couldn't get	NN-B	04909
Warner, Charles D.	1896.01.01	SLC	SH.Oceana	Just a line	122:1934.05.09	05008 other sources
Warner, Charles D.	1899.02.15	SLC	AU.Vienna	Oh, I hope	ViU	05546
Warner, George H.	1881.08.10	OLC	NY.Elmira	Many thank for	CtHMTH	01999
Warner, George H.	aft 1882.11.17	OLC	CT.Hartford	The jugs have	CtHSD	10608
Warner, George H.	1886.07.13	OLC	NY.Elmira	As usual I	CtHMTH	03414
Warner, George H.	1886.07.17	SLC	NY.Elmira	Thank you ever	CtHMTH	03424
Warner, George H.	1887.04.06	OLC	CT.Hartford	Thank you so	CtHMTH	03557
Warner, George H.	1891.12.01	SLC & OLC	GE.Berlin	My arm broke	CtHMTH	04258
Warner, George H.	1895.03.09	SLC	NY.New York	The first time	CtHMTH	04849
Warner, Lilly G.	****.**.**	SC	Unknown	In any form	CU-MARK	10426 poem inscription
Warner, Lilly G.	pm ****.08.14	OLC	NY.Elmira	I was so	CU-MARK	08640
Warner, Lilly G. & Twichell, Joseph H.	1874.04.14	SLC	CT.Hartford	Borrowed of the	297:35	11145
Warner, Lilly G.	1875.12.25	SLC	CT.Hartford	A Merry Christmas	CtHMTH	09297 inscription
Warner, Lilly G.	1880.04.13	SLC	CT.Hartford	With the friendly	ViU	11073 inscription
Warner, Lilly G. & Warner, Susan L.	1880.06.17	SLC	NY.Elmira	We came through	CU-MARK	01814
Warner, Lilly G.	1881.12.25	SLC	CT.Hartford	With kindest regards	ViU	11075 inscription
Warner, Margaret	1883.02.10	SLC	CT.Hartford	With the affectionate	ViU	11077 inscription
Warner, Margaret	1883.12.25	SLC & CC	CT.Hartford	Merry Christmas to	CtHMTH	09712 inscription

Warner, Margaret	1885.03.17	SLC	CT.Hartford	With the love	ViU	11079 inscription
Warner, Margaret	1889.12.25	SLC	CT.Hartford	with the warm	ViU	09414 inscription; other sources
Warner, Susan L.	****.**.**	SLC	CT.Hartford	You must forgive	CAlb2	09435
Warner, Susan L. & Twichell, Joseph H.	1878.11.20	SLC	GE.Munich	By George but	CtY	01608
Warner, Susan L. & Warner, Lilly G.	1880.06.17	SLC	NY.Elmira	We came through	CU-MARK	01814
Warner, Susan L.	1880.12.25	SLC	CT.Hartford	I beg to	NN-B	08919
Warner, Susan L.	1883.01.01	SLC	CT.Hartford	mit herzlichsten guten	157:1924.11.10	09766 inscription
Warner, Susan L. & Warner, Charles D.	1894.04.12	SLC	SH.New York	I couldn't get	NN-B	04909
Warren, George K.	1874.12.12	SLC	CT.Hartford	Be sure &	CU-MARK(ph)	03806
Washington, Booker T.	o/a 1908.01.08	SLC	NY.New York	Ah, I'd just	CU-MARK(dr)	07911 on Washington Jan 8
Washington Intell.	1868.01.11	SLC	DC.Washington	I am sorry	442:1868.01.11	00127 other sources
Waters, Mrs.	****.**.**	SLC & OLC	Unknown	Mr. & Mrs.	Mo2	10532
Watson, A.	1905.10.18	SLC	NH.Dublin	Please don't draw	CU-MARK	07181 telegram
Watson, Russell E.	bef 1900.12.24	SLC	NY.New York	The high compliment	316:1900.12.25	05938
Watt, Robert	1874.07.15 & 1874.07.16	SLC	NY.Elmira	The book has	CU-MARK(ph)	01111
Watt, Robert	1875.01.26	SLC	CT.Hartford	Your New Year	NN-B	02484
Watt, Robert	1875.03.08	SLC	CT.Hartford	I haven't any	ODa2	01206
Watterson, Henry	aft 1875.11.22	SLC	CT.Hartford	I guess this	DLC	11071
Watterson, Henry	1896.08.18	SLC	EN.London	Burn letter. Blot	CU-MARK(tr)	05089 telegram
Watts, F.H.	1889.**.**	SLC	Unknown	With compts of	NN-B	10798 inscription
Watts, W.H.	1908.08.15	SLC	CT.Redding	I highly prize	NN	08086

ADDRESSEE	DATE	WRITER	PLACE	CUE	SOURCE	NUMBER/NOTES
Wayland, Francis	1883.01.15	SLC	CT.Hartford	Mine is a	CU-MARK(tr)	02337
Wayland, Francis	1886.01.15	SLC	CT.Hartford	You catch my	325	09951
Wayland, Isabel S.	1909.09.29	SLC	CT.Redding	That bushel must	CU-MARK(ph)	10579
Wayland, John E.	o/a 1908.10.07	SLC	CT.Redding	Greeting and Salutation	283:5	10517 form letter
Webb, Charles H.	pm ****.11.08	SLC	NY.New York	*	ViU	10174 envelope only
Webb, Charles H.	1867.03.19	SLC	MO.St. Louis	Everything is going	ViU	00120
Webb, Charles H.	1867.11.25	SLC	DC.Washington	I send the	InU-Li	00160
Webb, Charles H.	1868.01.09	SLC	DC.Washington	Please send me	105:1940.10.30	00178 other sources
Webb, Charles H.	1868.01.15	SLC	DC.Washington	The books came	ViU	00181
Webb, Charles H.	1870.11.26	SLC	NY.Buffalo	Business first. I	ViU	00544
Webb, Charles H.	1871.01.14	SLC	NY.Buffalo	I dassent. I	MoSW	00558
Webb, Charles H.	1875.04.08	SLC	CT.Hartford	First--Bliss has	NBuU-PO	01219
Webb, Charles H.	1894.10.10	SLC	FR.Rouen	Betsy & I	122:1934.05.09	05246
Webb, Charles H.	1896.02.16	SLC	II.Darjeeling	Certainly write the	CtY	05021
Webber, Albert G.	o/a 1906.04.05	SLC per IVL	NY.New York	I wrote that	CU-MARK(dr)	07416 on Webber Apr 5
Webster, Annie M. & Moffett, Samuel E.	ca 1866.11.**	SLC	Unknown	will all come	NPV	00111 fragment
Webster, Annie M.	pm 1871.12.27	OLC	Unknown	We rec'd today	CU-MARK(ph)	00520
Webster, Annie M.	1872.05.17	SLC & OLC	NY.Elmira	I send you	NPV	00750
Webster, Annie M.	1876.09.01	SLC	NY.Elmira	I am right	NPV	01361
Webster, Annie M.	ca 1880.12.25	OLC	CT.Hartford	We thank you	NPV	01750
Webster, Annie M.	bef 1882.08.28	SLC	NY.Elmira	Charlie & I	CU-MARK	02256
Webster, Annie M.	1882.08.29	SLC	NY.Elmira	Your letters confirm	NPV	02258
Webster, Annie M.	o/a 1882.08.30	SLC	NY.Elmira	Well, Annie, you	NPV	10882 on Pamela Moffett Aug 30
Webster, Annie M.	1885.07.30	SLC	NY.Elmira	I enclose $250	NPV	03271

Webster, Annie M. & Webster, Charles L.	1885.10.25	OLC	CT.Hartford	I don't know	NPV	03295
Webster, Annie M.	1885.10.28	SLC	CT.Hartford	I started out	NPV	03298
Webster, Annie M.	1886.10.18	SLC	CT.Hartford	Will you &	NPV	03469
Webster, Annie M.	1891.04.26	SLC	CT.Hartford	There are no	NPV	04195
Webster, Annie M. & Moffett, Pamela A.	1893.09.21	SLC	NY.New York	Yes, I saw	NPV	04458
Webster, Annie M.	1894.11.28	SLC	FR.Paris	I have signed	NPV	04813
Webster, Annie M.	1905.02.18	SLC per IVL	NY.New York	Mr. Clemens has	CU-MARK	07003
Webster, Annie M.	1909.12.25	SLC	CT.Redding	I thank you	CU-MARK(dr) NPV	08517 NPV receipt telegram
Webster, Charles L.	****.**.**	OLC	CT.Hartford	I want to	NPV	10908
Webster, Charles L.	****.**.**	OLC	CT.Hartford	Will you find	NPV	10901
Webster, Charles L.	****.**.**	OLC	CT.Hartford	Will you please	NPV	10891
Webster, Charles L.	****.**.**	OLC	Unknown	The wine glasses	CU-MARK	08749
Webster, Charles L.	****.**.**	SLC per OLC	CT.Hartford	Mr. Clemens is	NPV	09010
Webster, Charles L.	****.**.**	SLC	CT.Hartford	I have attempted	NPV	10894
Webster, Charles L.	****.**.**	SLC	Unknown	All right--come	CU-MARK	08747
Webster, Charles L.	****.**.**	SLC	Unknown	I have "Hubbard's	NPV	09014
Webster, Charles L.	****.**.**	SLC	Unknown	If that letter	NPV	08587
Webster, Charles L.	****.**.**	SLC	Unknown	Charley, your	ODa2	11181
Webster, Charles L.	****.**.**	SLC	Unknown	C &. W., this to	ViU	10973 on n.d. to Miss Nichols
Webster, Charles L.	1881.04.26	SLC	CT.Hartford	All right. The	NPV	01942
Webster, Charles L.	1881.04.29	SLC	CT.Hartford	This is to	NPV	01940
Webster, Charles L.	1881.05.01	SLC	CT.Hartford	I have a	NPV	01944
Webster, Charles L.	1881.05.01	SLC	CT.Hartford	Suppose you get	NPV	01945
Webster, Charles L.	1881.05.02	SLC	CT.Hartford	Let Dan furnish	NPV	01947
Webster, Charles L.	1881.05.03	SLC	CT.Hartford	Isn't there a	NPV	01897

ADDRESSEE	DATE	WRITER	PLACE	CUE	SOURCE	NUMBER/NOTES
Webster, Charles L.	1881.05.06	SLC	CT.Hartford	All right--am	NPV	01948
Webster, Charles L.	1881.05.07	SLC	CT.Hartford	The fact that	NPV	01950
Webster, Charles L.	1881.05.14	SLC	CT.Hartford	Mr. Talbot's proposition	NPV	01953
Webster, Charles L.	1881.05.16	SLC	CT.Hartford	Yes, if we	NPV	01954
Webster, Charles L.	1881.05.19	SLC	CT.Hartford	Make a list	NPV	01956
Webster, Charles L.	1881.05.20	SLC	CT.Hartford	All right, now	NPV	01957 telegram
Webster, Charles L.	1881.05.20	SLC	CT.Hartford	Fraud no. two	NPV	01958 telegram
Webster, Charles L.	1881.05.30	SLC	CT.Hartford	Here are some	NPV	01962
Webster, Charles L.	1881.05.31	SLC	CT.Hartford	Mr Howells says	NPV	01963
Webster, Charles L.	1881.06.**	SLC	Unknown	Woodman--Davis former	NPV	10904
Webster, Charles L.	1881.06.05	SLC	CT.Branford	Yes, you did	ViU	01970
Webster, Charles L.	1881.06.17	SLC	CT.Hartford	If you can	NPV	01974
Webster, Charles L.	1881.06.17	SLC	CT.Hartford	I mail check	NPV	10881 telegram
Webster, Charles L.	1881.06.20	SLC	CT.Branford	Very good--am	NPV	01975
Webster, Charles L.	1881.06.21	SLC	CT.Branford	Please go to	NPV	01977
Webster, Charles L.	1881.07.09	SLC	CT.Branford	So it appears	NPV	01983
Webster, Charles L.	1881.07.10	SLC	CT.Branford	They look well	ViU	01984
Webster, Charles L.	1881.07.18	SLC	CT.Branford	Mr. Chas. L.	NcU	08911
Webster, Charles L.	o/a 1881.07.26	SLC	CT.Branford	Your K. ad.	NPV	09235
Webster, Charles L.	1881.08.12	SLC	NY.Elmira	I wish the	NPV	02002
Webster, Charles L.	1881.08.12	SLC	NY.Elmira	This is a	NPV	02003
Webster, Charles L.	1881.08.17	SLC	NY.Elmira	What I meant	NPV	02008
Webster, Charles L.	1881.08.23	SLC	NY.Elmira	I am returning	NPV	02014
Webster, Charles L.	1881.08.25	OLC	NY.Elmira	I am exceedingly	NPV	02016
Webster, Charles L.	1881.08.26	SLC	MA.Boston	Stop the nonsense	NPV	02017 telegram
Webster, Charles L.	1881.08.31	SLC	NY.Elmira	1. As soon	NPV	02020
Webster, Charles L.	1881.09.02	SLC	NY.Elmira	I am going	NPV	02022

Webster, Charles L.		1881.09.04	SLC	NY.Elmira	All right--go	NPV	02026
Webster, Charles L.		1881.09.04	SLC	NY.Elmira	It is better	NPV	02025
Webster, Charles L.		1881.09.06	SLC	NY.Elmira	Terms satisfactory	NPV	02029 telegram
Webster, Charles L.		1881.09.07	SLC	NY.Elmira	Renew the English	NPV	02031 telegram
Webster, Charles L.		1881.09.07	SLC	NY.Elmira	You won't need	NPV	02030
Webster, Charles L.		1881.09.09	SLC	NY.Elmira	Have just received	NPV	02033
Webster, Charles L.		1881.09.17	SLC	NY.Elmira	All right. I	NPV	02035
Webster, Charles L.	o/b	1881.09.19	SLC	NY.Elmira	Find Louis C	NPV	02039 Sept 19 to Tiffany enc
Webster, Charles L.		1881.10.02	SLC	CT.Hartford	It occurs to	NPV	02042
Webster, Charles L.		1881.10.05	SLC	CT.Hartford	Your letter reminds	CU-MARK(tr)	02044
Webster, Charles L.		1881.10.10	SLC	CT.Hartford	All right--hope	NPV	02051
Webster, Charles L.		1881.10.18	SLC	CT.Hartford	Mr. Wm. Hamersley	NPV	02055 misdated Monday
Webster, Charles L.		1881.10.25	SLC	CT.Hartford	How did you	NPV	02066
Webster, Charles L.		1881.10.26	SLC	CT.Hartford	Ah, but I	NPV	02072
Webster, Charles L.		1881.10.27	SLC	CT.Hartford	Have you this	250:1981.05	01965
Webster, Charles L.		1881.10.28	SLC	CT.Hartford	What--bleed me	NPV	02077
Webster, Charles L.		1881.11.15	SLC	CT.Hartford	If the brass	NPV	02086
Webster, Charles L.		1881.11.17	SLC	CT.Hartford	A simple electrotype	NPV	02090
Webster, Charles L.	o/a	1881.11.18	SLC	CT.Hartford	I said Yes	NPV	02092 on Ticknor Nov 18
Webster, Charles L.		1881.11.19	SLC	CT.Hartford	It would appear	NPV	02091
Webster, Charles L.		1881.11.22	SLC	CT.Hartford	Perfect the English	NPV	02097 telegram
Webster, Charles L.		1881.11.24	SLC	CT.Hartford	Nobody who knows	NPV	02098
Webster, Charles L.		1881.11.27	SLC	CN.Montreal	Hire a compartment	NPV	02102
Webster, Charles L.		1881.12.23	OLC	CT.Hartford	I am so P.S. The children	CU-MARK(tr) NPV	02125

ADDRESSEE	DATE	WRITER	PLACE	CUE	SOURCE	NUMBER/NOTES
Webster, Charles L.	1881.12.31	SLC	CT.Hartford	Take good care	NPV	02131
Webster, Charles L.	1882.01.02	SLC	CT.Hartford	Make me a	NPV	02141
Webster, Charles L.	1882.01.05	SLC	CT.Hartford	Hang it, I	NPV	02144
Webster, Charles L.	1882.01.10 & 1882.01.11	SLC	CT.Hartford	I want to	NPV	02148
Webster, Charles L. & Clemens, Jane L.	1882.01.21	SLC	CT.Hartford	Suppose you put	NPV	02152
Webster, Charles L.	1882.03.02	SLC	CT.Hartford	Hamersley was here	NPV	02168 typed
Webster, Charles L.	1882.03.20	SLC	CT.Hartford	The report of	NPV	02174 typed
Webster, Charles L.	1882.03.27	SLC	CT.Hartford	Come come my	NPV	02182 typed
Webster, Charles L.	1882.04.03	SLC	CT.Hartford	I send you	NPV	02195 typed
Webster, Charles L.	1882.04.12	SLC	CT.Hartford	What we want	NPV	02199
Webster, Charles L.	1882.04.17	SLC	CT.Hartford	I hope you	NPV	02201 typed
Webster, Charles L.	1882.05.29	SLC	CT.Hartford	Enclosed is a	NPV	02193
Webster, Charles L.	1882.06.03	SLC	CT.Hartford	I return Buckland's	NPV	02214
Webster, Charles L.	1882.06.05	SLC	Unknown	I wish you	NPV	02215
Webster, Charles L.	1882.06.07	SLC	CT.Hartford	I mail check	CU-MARK(tr)	02216 telegram
Webster, Charles L.	1882.06.12	SLC	CT.Hartford	You may send	NPV	02218
Webster, Charles L.	1882.06.15	SLC	CT.Hartford	When I got	NPV	02219 typed
Webster, Charles L.	1882.06.21	SLC	CT.Hartford	It was a	NPV	02223
Webster, Charles L.	1882.06.26	SLC	CT.Hartford	From force of	NPV	02226
Webster, Charles L.	1882.07.08	SLC	CT.Hartford	Hadn't you better	NPV	02234
Webster, Charles L.	1882.07.08	SLC	CT.Hartford	Yes the Bank	NPV	02232
Webster, Charles L.	1882.07.11	SLC	CT.Hartford	Ahern came to	NPV	02235 typed
Webster, Charles L.	1882.07.16	SLC	NY.Elmira	I found a	NPV	02138
Webster, Charles L.	1882.07.18	SLC	NY.Elmira	Don't forget to	NPV	02237

Webster, Charles L.	1882.07.24	SLC	NY.Elmira	Yes, I received	NPV	02240
Webster, Charles L.	1882.07.26	SLC	NY.Elmira	Dam--nation!	NPV	02241
Webster, Charles L.	1882.08.01	SLC	NY.Elmira	It is dismal	NPV	02247
Webster, Charles L.	1882.08.08	SLC	NY.Elmira	Go to Mr.	NPV	02249
Webster, Charles L.	1882.08.09	SLC	NY.Elmira	K. flourishes, better	NPV	02250
Webster, Charles L.	1882.08.15	SLC	NY.Elmira	There is no	NPV	02252
Webster, Charles L.	1882.08.20	SLC	NY.Elmira	Maybe you had	NPV	02253 telegram
Webster, Charles L.	1882.09.**	SLC	NY.Elmira	They are not	NPV	10938 telegram; fragment
Webster, Charles L.	1882.09.09	SLC	NY.Elmira	I want you	NPV	02268
Webster, Charles L.	1882.09.17	SLC	NY.Elmira	If Mr. Green	CU-MARK	08728 on Green bef Sept 17
Webster, Charles L.	1882.09.19	SLC	NY.Elmira	I want Messrs.	NPV	02272
Webster, Charles L.	1882.09.19	SLC	NY.Elmira	You did miraculously	NPV	02276
Webster, Charles L.	1882.09.21	SLC	NY.Elmira	Letter received result	NPV	02277 telegram
Webster, Charles L.	1882.09.23	SLC	Unknown	Is not using	295:200	02280
Webster, Charles L.	1882.09.24	SLC	NY.Elmira	Be sure to	NPV	02279
Webster, Charles L.	1882.10.03	SLC	CT.Hartford	You ask what	NPV	02285 typed
Webster, Charles L.	1882.10.06	SLC	Unknown	Find out, in	NPV	02287
Webster, Charles L.	1882.10.09	SLC	CT.Hartford	Here is a	NPV	02288 typed
Webster, Charles L.	1882.10.21	SLC	CT.Hartford	Please return this	NPV	02294 typed
Webster, Charles L.	1882.10.27	SLC	CT.Hartford	I inclose a	NPV	02298 typed; Abercrombie to OLC enc
Webster, Charles L.	1882.10.30	SLC	CT.Hartford	Give this man	NPV	02301 typed
Webster, Charles L.	1882.11.11	SLC	CT.Hartford	You can bring	NPV	02305 typed

ADDRESSEE	DATE	WRITER	PLACE	CUE	SOURCE	NUMBER/NOTES
Webster, Charles L.	1882.11.21	SLC	CT.Hartford	About Christmas you	NPV	02308
Webster, Charles L.	1882.11.22	SLC	CT.Hartford	There is a	NPV	02309
Webster, Charles L.	1882.11.25	SLC	CT.Hartford	I have found	NPV	02310 typed
Webster, Charles L.	1882.11.30	SLC	CT.Hartford	There's no sort	NPV	01986
Webster, Charles L.	1882.12.16	SLC	CT.Hartford	By and by	NPV	02318 typed
Webster, Charles L.	1882.12.30	SLC	CT.Hartford	Here is the	NPV	02317
Webster, Charles L.	1883.**.**	SLC	Unknown	If you are	NPV	02876
Webster, Charles L.	1883.**.**	SLC	Unknown	The board need	NPV	02360
Webster, Charles L.	o/a 1883.01.03	SLC	Unknown	If there are	NPV	02330 on Osgood Jan 3
Webster, Charles L.	1883.01.15	SLC	CT.Hartford	Hand the check	NPV	02338
Webster, Charles L.	1883.01.27	SLC	CT.Hartford	I think that	NPV	02340
Webster, Charles L.	1883.02.22	SLC	CT.Hartford	Read Mr. Perkins's	NPV	02348 typed
Webster, Charles L.	1883.03.09	SLC	CT.Hartford	Pay this check	NPV	02355
Webster, Charles L.	1883.03.23	SLC	CT.Hartford	Inclosed find check	NPV	02362 typed
Webster, Charles L.	1883.03.31	SLC	CT.Hartford	Inclosed find check	NPV	02365 typed
Webster, Charles L.	1883.04.16	SLC	CT.Hartford	All right, I	NPV	02370 typed
Webster, Charles L.	1883.04.24	SLC	CT.Hartford	Today or tomorrow	NPV	02376 typed
Webster, Charles L.	1883.05.01	SLC	CT.Hartford	I hope you	NPV	02378 typed
Webster, Charles L.	1883.05.07	SLC	CT.Hartford	I have paid	NPV	02383 typed
Webster, Charles L.	1883.05.17	SLC	CT.Hartford	I inclose a	NPV	02386 typed
Webster, Charles L.	1883.06.08	SLC	CT.Hartford	Go to the	NPV	01943
Webster, Charles L.	bet 1883.06.10 & 1883.06.18	SLC	CT.Hartford	Say nothing to	NPV(dr)	01888 telegram
Webster, Charles L.	1883.06.18	SLC	NY.Elmira	Say nothing at	NPV	02143

Webster, Charles L.		1883.06.20	SLC	NY.Elmira	All right. Tell	NPV	01562
Webster, Charles L.		1883.06.28	SLC	NY.Elmira	Good gracious, I	CU-MARK(tr)	02257
Webster, Charles L.		1883.06.29	SLC	NY.Elmira	All right. I	NPV	02273
Webster, Charles L.		1883.07.26	SLC	NY.Elmira	Run up here	NPV	02346
Webster, Charles L.	ca	1883.08.**	SLC	NY.Elmira	That's a more	CU-MARK(tr)	02122
Webster, Charles L.		1883.08.01	SLC	NY.Elmira	The implements of	NPV	02816
Webster, Charles L.		1883.08.03	SLC	NY.Elmira	Never mind about	NPV	02819
Webster, Charles L.	ca	1883.08.03	SLC	NY.Elmira	See Frank &	NPV	02820
Webster, Charles L.		1883.08.24	SLC	NY.Elmira	Pitch into Mills's	NPV	02825
Webster, Charles L.		1883.08.31	SLC	NY.Elmira	Orion has done	NPV	02827
Webster, Charles L.		1883.09.**	SLC	Unknown	The board is	NPV	02828
Webster, Charles L.	ca	1883.09.**	SLC	CT.Hartford	I enclose some	NPV	10809
Webster, Charles L.		1883.09.03	SLC	NY.Elmira	Mail the enclosed	NPV	02830
Webster, Charles L.		1883.09.09	SLC	NY.Elmira	Will see you	NPV	02831
Webster, Charles L.		1883.09.12	SLC	NY.Elmira	We shall arrive	NPV	10868
Webster, Charles L.		1883.09.22	SLC	CT.Hartford	I will write	NPV	02840
Webster, Charles L.		1883.09.22	SLC	CT.Hartford	Now by the	NPV	10805
Webster, Charles L.		1883.09.29	SLC	CT.Hartford	Please get that	NPV	02842
Webster, Charles L.	or	1883.10.03 1883.10.04	SLC	CT.Hartford	The board should	NPV	02845
Webster, Charles L.		1883.10.06	SLC	CT.Hartford	Did I tell	NPV	02848
Webster, Charles L.		1883.10.10	SLC	CT.Hartford	Proof received. That	NPV	02850
Webster, Charles L.		1883.10.15	SLC	CT.Hartford	Orion has been	NPV	08932
Webster, Charles L.		1883.11.26	SLC	CT.Hartford	The inclosed has	NPV	02859 typed
Webster, Charles L.		1883.11.30	SLC	CT.Hartford	Now that you	NPV	02860
Webster, Charles L.		1883.12.17	OLC	CT.Hartford	Mother is very	NPV	02864
Webster, Charles L.		1883.12.19	SLC	CT.Hartford	Enclosed is $271	NPV	02865
Webster, Charles L.		1883.12.19	SLC	CT.Hartford	It occurs to	NPV	02834
Webster, Charles L.		1883.12.20	SLC	CT.Hartford	Keep the fender	NPV	02878

ADDRESSEE	DATE	WRITER	PLACE	CUE	SOURCE	NUMBER/NOTES
Webster, Charles L.	1883.12.26	OLC	CT.Hartford	Get up here	NPV	10900 telegram
Webster, Charles L.	1883.12.27	SLC	CT.Hartford	We will lie	NPV	02875
Webster, Charles L.	1884.**.**	SLC	Unknown	You see, by	CU-MARK(tr)	03027
Webster, Charles L.	1884.**.**	SLC	Unknown	Charlie, the seasons	NPV	10899 fragment
Webster, Charles L.	1884.01.**	SLC	CT.Hartford	I want Louis	NPV	02869
Webster, Charles L.	1884.01.02	SLC	CT.Hartford	If the book	NPV	02885
Webster, Charles L.	1884.01.07	SLC	CT.Hartford	Am Pub check	NPV	02887
Webster, Charles L.	1884.01.11	OLC	CT.Hartford	I am in	NPV	02888
Webster, Charles L.	1884.01.17	SLC	CT.Hartford	Slote check for	NPV	02891
Webster, Charles L.	1884.01.20	SLC	CT.Hartford	You can come	CU-MARK(tr)	02893
Webster, Charles L.	1884.01.28	SLC	CT.Hartford	No, the actor	NPV	02897
Webster, Charles L.	1884.01.29	SLC	CT.Hartford	Get your old-book	NPV	02899
Webster, Charles L.	1884.02.03	SLC	Unknown	Do send me	NPV	02874
Webster, Charles L.	1884.02.08	SLC	CT.Hartford	The thing I	NPV	02912
Webster, Charles L.	1884.02.10	SLC	CT.Hartford	You may drop	NPV	02883
Webster, Charles L.	1884.02.18	SLC	CT.Hartford	See the enclosed	NPV	02920
Webster, Charles L.	1884.02.29	SLC	CT.Hartford	Let us canvass	NPV	02925
Webster, Charles L.	1884.03.**	SLC	CT.Hartford	Osgood probably goes	NPV	08828
Webster, Charles L.	1884.03.03 or 1884.03.04	SLC	CT.Hartford	If Prang's contract	NPV	02928
Webster, Charles L.	1884.03.05	SLC	CT.Hartford	Tell Mr. Prang	NPV	02929
Webster, Charles L.	1884.03.06	SLC	CT.Hartford	This is the	NPV	02930
Webster, Charles L.	1884.03.20	SLC	CT.Hartford	I wish you	NPV	02938
Webster, Charles L.	1884.03.27	SLC	CT.Hartford	The fact looks	NPV	02939
Webster, Charles L.	1884.03.31	SLC	CT.Hartford	Is that artist's	NPV	08829
Webster, Charles L.	1884.04.06	SLC	CT.Hartford	Yes, come up	NPV	02948
Webster, Charles L.	1884.04.12	SLC	CT.Hartford	Here is a	NPV	02950
Webster, Charles L.	1884.04.14	SLC	CT.Hartford	Keep it diligently	NPV	02951
Webster, Charles L.	1884.04.15	SLC	CT.Hartford	Send to the	NPV	02955

Webster, Charles L.	1884.04.16	SLC	CT.Hartford	Find out where	NPV	02956
Webster, Charles L.	1884.04.22	SLC	CT.Hartford	Yes, I think	NPV	02962
Webster, Charles L.	1884.04.25	SLC	CT.Hartford	Show him this	NPV	02963
Webster, Charles L.	1884.04.28	SLC	CT.Hartford	Call at Laurence	NPV	02964
Webster, Charles L.	aft 1884.04.28	SLC	CT.Hartford	Say to her	NPV	02965 on Beemer Apr 28
Webster, Charles L.	1884.04.30	SLC	Unknown	If Mallory still	NPV	02900
Webster, Charles L.	1884.04.30	SLC	Unknown	Put in an	NPV	02967
Webster, Charles L.	1884.05.07	SLC	CT.Hartford	I returned the	NPV	02972
Webster, Charles L.	1884.05.10	SLC	CT.Hartford	If you have	NPV	02973 on Howells May 10
Webster, Charles L.	1884.05.12	SLC	CT.Hartford	Parsloe & Aldrich	NPV	02976
Webster, Charles L.	1884.05.19	SLC	Unknown	I sold the	NPV	02981
Webster, Charles L.	1884.05.23	SLC	CT.Hartford	Accept Raymond's offer	NPV	02982
Webster, Charles L.	1884.05.24	SLC	CT.Hartford	Some of the	NPV	02984
Webster, Charles L.	1884.05.31	SLC	Unknown	The contracts you	NPV	02987
Webster, Charles L.	1884.06.06	SLC	CT.Hartford	The cheap book	NPV	02990
Webster, Charles L.	1884.06.08	SLC	CT.Hartford	No, I want	NPV	02992
Webster, Charles L.	1884.06.11	SLC	CT.Hartford	I have reshipped	NPV	02993
Webster, Charles L.	o/a 1884.06.11	SLC	CT.Hartford	Write Miss Mettie	NPV	02907 on Curry June 11
Webster, Charles L.	1884.06.12	SLC	CT.Hartford	Yes, Charles, I	NPV	02906
Webster, Charles L.	1884.06.24	SLC	NY.Elmira	I ran the	NPV	02913
Webster, Charles L.	1884.06.25	SLC	NY.Elmira	It occurs to	NPV	02995
Webster, Charles L.	o/a 1884.06.25	SLC	NY.Elmira	If the American	NPV	02997 on Webster June 25
Webster, Charles L.	1884.07.01	SLC	NY.Elmira	How much was	NPV	02413
Webster, Charles L.	1884.07.02	SLC	NY.Elmira	The Osgoods gave	NPV	02417
Webster, Charles L.	1884.07.05	SLC	NY.Elmira	As a general	NPV	02430

ADDRESSEE	DATE	WRITER	PLACE	CUE	SOURCE	NUMBER/NOTES
Webster, Charles L.	1884.07.05	SLC	NY.Elmira	Yes, let Raymond	NPV	08939
Webster, Charles L.	1884.07.06	SLC	NY.Elmira	Send to me	NPV	08930
Webster, Charles L.	1884.07.10	SLC	NY.Elmira	Bliss's ck rec'd	NPV	01369
Webster, Charles L.	1884.07.10	SLC	NY.Elmira	Didn't I send	NPV	02442
Webster, Charles L.	1884.07.10	SLC	NY.Elmira	It seems to	NPV	02927
Webster, Charles L.	1884.07.10	SLC	NY.Elmira	Our Wild Indians	NPV	01505
Webster, Charles L.	1884.07.10	SLC	NY.Elmira	Your aunt Livy	NPV	02460
Webster, Charles L.	1884.07.11	SLC	NY.Elmira	Am. Pub Co's	NPV	02942
Webster, Charles L.	1884.07.13	SLC	NY.Elmira	Our furnace at	NPV	01475
Webster, Charles L.	1884.07.13	SLC	NY.Elmira	When you strike	NPV	01374
Webster, Charles L.	1884.07.15	SLC	NY.Elmira	Draw up my	NPV	01499
Webster, Charles L.	1884.07.17	SLC	NY.Elmira	The Pacific Coast	NPV	01551
Webster, Charles L.	1884.07.22	SLC	NY.Elmira	Yes, this contract	NPV	01510
Webster, Charles L.	1884.07.24	SLC	NY.Elmira	Can you alter	NPV	02155
Webster, Charles L.	1884.08.07	SLC	NY.Elmira	I miscalculated my	NPV	01536
Webster, Charles L.	1884.08.11	SLC	NY.Elmira	Most of this	NPV	01516
Webster, Charles L.	1884.08.14	SLC	NY.Elmira	The missing galleys	NPV	02944
Webster, Charles L.	1884.08.16	SLC	NY.Elmira	Very good. Put	NPV	02947
Webster, Charles L.	1884.08.19	SLC	NY.Elmira	If you have	NPV	01474
Webster, Charles L.	1884.09.01	SLC	NY.Elmira	That question appears	NPV	01293
Webster, Charles L.	1884.09.05	SLC	NY.Elmira	Isn't this part	NPV	01300
Webster, Charles L.	1884.09.05	SLC	NY.Elmira	Please hand these	NPV	01449
Webster, Charles L.	1884.09.08	SLC	NY.Elmira	Here is a	NPV	01373
Webster, Charles L.	1884.09.08	SLC	NY.Elmira	I paid 39 1/2	NPV	01357
Webster, Charles L.	1884.09.09	SLC	NY.Elmira	Without a doubt	NPV	01363
Webster, Charles L.	ca 1884.09.13	SLC	NY.Elmira	The bust was	NPV	01334
Webster, Charles L.	1884.09.15	SLC	NY.Elmira	Hang Raymond, let	NPV	02954
Webster, Charles L.	1884.09.20	SLC	NY.Elmira	I would like	NPV	01325
Webster, Charles L.	1884.09.24	SLC	Unknown	I've waited a	NPV	02966

Webster, Charles L.		1884.10.**	SLC	CT.Hartford	Look into that	NPV	02514 telegram
Webster, Charles L.		1884.10.03	SLC	CT.Hartford	Instruct your clerks	NPV	03003
Webster, Charles L.	ca	1884.10.03	SLC	CT.Hartford	Charlie, when I	NPV	10876
Webster, Charles L.		1884.10.31	SLC	CT.Hartford	I have referred	NPV	02996
Webster, Charles L.		1884.10.31	SLC	CT.Hartford	I hear whispered	NPV	03014
Webster, Charles L.		1884.11.09	SLC	RI.Providence	Pond will presently	NPV	03031
Webster, Charles L.		1884.11.23	SLC	NY.New York	A most important	CtY	03036
Webster, Charles L.		1884.12.**	SLC	Unknown	Plucky lawyers are	NPV	03033
Webster, Charles L.		1884.12.10	SLC	CN.Fort Erie	The "Rose Publishing	NPV	03054
Webster, Charles L.		1884.12.14	SLC	MI.Grand Rapids	Get a copy	NPV	10853
Webster, Charles L.		1884.12.15	SLC	OH.Toledo	How in the	NPV	03063
Webster, Charles L.		1884.12.22	SLC	CT.Hartford	Call at Everett	NPV	03066
Webster, Charles L.		1884.12.23	SLC	CT.Hartford	I think you	NPV	03068 statement enc; on printed page
Webster, Charles L.		1884.12.23	SLC	CT.Hartford	Damn that Western	NPV	03067 telegram
Webster, Charles L.		1884.12.28	SLC	PA.Pittsburgh	We are a	NPV	03075
Webster, Charles L.		1885.**.**	SLC	CT.Hartford	Don't forget that	NPV	10897
Webster, Charles L.		1885.**.**	SLC	CT.Hartford	Please send Mum	NPV	03089
Webster, Charles L.		1885.**.**	SLC	CT.Hartford	What did you	NPV	03090
Webster, Charles L.		1885.**.**	SLC	Unknown	P.S. I forgot	NPV	10896
Webster, Charles L.		1885.**.**	SLC	Unknown	This house ought	NPV	03092 on printed flyer
Webster, Charles L.		1885.**.**	SLC	Unknown	When you come	NPV	03091
Webster, Charles L.		1885.01.04	SLC	OH.Cincinnati	All right--that	NPV	03102
Webster, Charles L.		1885.01.10	SLC	CT.Hartford	I am sorry	NPV	10313 misdated, see 1886
Webster, Charles L.		1885.01.13	SLC	IL.Quincy	Your letter should	NPV	03114

ADDRESSEE		DATE	WRITER	PLACE	CUE	SOURCE	NUMBER/NOTES
Webster, Charles L.		1885.01.15	SLC	IA.Keokuk	Your letter is	NPV	03117
Webster, Charles L.		1885.01.19	SLC	Unknown	Have you inquired	NPV	03122
Webster, Charles L.		1885.01.19	SLC	WI.Janesville	No, it is	NPV	10312 misdated, see Jan 20
Webster, Charles L.		1885.01.20	SLC	WI.Janesville	No, it is	NPV	03123 misdated Jan 19
Webster, Charles L.		1885.01.21	SLC	Unknown	Don't forget to	NPV	03126
Webster, Charles L.		1885.01.23	SLC	MN.St. Paul	A day or	NPV	03130
Webster, Charles L.		1885.01.23	SLC	MN.St. Paul	I see part	NPV	03129
Webster, Charles L.		1885.01.23	SLC	MN.St. Paul	P.S. Do you	NPV	10903
Webster, Charles L.		1885.01.25	SLC	MN.Minneapolis	Even $2 is	NPV	03134
Webster, Charles L.		1885.01.26	SLC	MN.Minneapolis	What is perdition	NPV	03137
Webster, Charles L.		1885.01.27	SLC	Unknown	The following is	NPV	03138
Webster, Charles L.	o/a	1885.01.28	SLC	Unknown	Charlie, drop in	NPV	03139 on Appleton bill Jan 28
Webster, Charles L.		1885.01.29	SLC	WI.Milwaukee	Yes draw five	NPV	03140 telegram
Webster, Charles L.		1885.02.**	SLC	NY.New York	Pond asks me	NPV	03064
Webster, Charles L.	ca	1885.02.01	SLC	Unknown	See fine notice	NPV	10898
Webster, Charles L.		1885.02.08	SLC	IN.Indianapolis	In 3 more	NPV	03157
Webster, Charles L.		1885.02.10	SLC	OH.Columbus	Glad to be	NPV	03162
Webster, Charles L.		1885.02.15	SLC	CN.Toronto	You may draw	NPV	03167
Webster, Charles L.		1885.02.17	SLC	MA.Brockton	I have paid	NPV	03170
Webster, Charles L.		1885.03.**	SLC	CT.Hartford	Leave 2 cloth	NPV	03177 fragment
Webster, Charles L.		1885.03.06	SLC	CT.Hartford	Make this note	NPV	03185
Webster, Charles L.		1885.03.13	SLC	CT.Hartford	My instructions--if	NPV	03189
Webster, Charles L.		1885.03.16	SLC	CT.Hartford	Your news is	NPV	03190
Webster, Charles L.		1885.03.18	SLC	CT.Hartford	The Committee of	CU-MARK	03192
Webster, Charles L.		1885.04.**	SLC	Unknown	I go home	NPV	03080

Webster, Charles L.		1885.04.**	SLC	Unknown	Warner finds that	NPV	03069
Webster, Charles L.		1885.04.04	SLC	CT.Hartford	Now the dam	NPV	03206
Webster, Charles L.		1885.04.04	SLC	CT.Hartford	The Advertiser &	NPV	03205
Webster, Charles L.	aft	1885.04.04	SLC	CT.Hartford	Livy forbids the	NPV	03207
Webster, Charles L.	ca	1885.04.06	SLC	CT.Hartford	Just take a	NPV	03204
Webster, Charles L.		1885.04.08	SLC	NY.New York	I hope it	NPV	03209
Webster, Charles L.		1885.04.11	SLC	CT.Hartford	Stop leaving those	NPV	03214
Webster, Charles L.		1885.04.11	SLC	CT.Hartford	Whatever work Alexander	NPV	03215
Webster, Charles L.		1885.05.**	SLC	CT.Hartford	I have watched	NPV	03085
Webster, Charles L.		1885.05.05	SLC	CT.Hartford	Osgood's busted, at	NPV	03223
Webster, Charles L.		1885.05.10	SLC	CT.Hartford	I meant to	NPV	03081
Webster, Charles L.		1885.05.13	SLC	CT.Hartford	I grow more	NPV	03226
Webster, Charles L.		1885.06.**	SLC	NY.Elmira	Stir up the	NPV	03231
Webster, Charles L.		1885.06.17	SLC	CT.Hartford	I enclose a	NPV	03242
Webster, Charles L.		1885.06.24	SLC	NY.Elmira	I have read	NPV	03244
Webster, Charles L.		1885.07.**	SLC	Unknown	When you get	NPV	08834
Webster, Charles L.		1885.07.27	SLC	NY.Elmira	The Western Union	NPV	10886 telegram
Webster, Charles L.		1885.07.28	SLC	NY.Elmira	I have been	NPV	03270
Webster, Charles L.		1885.07.28	SLC	NY.Elmira	I will write	NPV	10906 telegram
Webster, Charles L.		1885.07.28	SLC	NY.Elmira	Part of my	NPV	03269
Webster, Charles L.		1885.08.**	SLC	NY.Elmira	The letter concerning	NPV	03084
Webster, Charles L.		1885.10.**	SLC	CT.Hartford	Glad you've got	NPV	02419
Webster, Charles L.		1885.10.13	SLC	CT.Hartford	I mean to	NPV	03096
Webster, Charles L.		1885.10.22	SLC	CT.Hartford	It is proposed	NPV	03113
Webster, Charles L. & Webster, Annie M.		1885.10.25	OLC	CT.Hartford	I don't know	NPV	03295
Webster, Charles L.		1885.10.28	SLC	CT.Hartford	Beginning with November	NPV	03297
Webster, Charles L.		1885.10.30	SLC	Unknown	I wouldn't have	NPV	03300

ADDRESSEE	DATE	WRITER	PLACE	CUE	SOURCE	NUMBER/NOTES
Webster, Charles L.	1885.11.**	SLC	NY.New York	Please send your	NPV	03147
Webster, Charles L.	1885.11.02	SLC	CT.Hartford	We will let	NPV	03303
Webster, Charles L.	1885.11.10	SLC	CT.Hartford	Please send a	NPV	03128
Webster, Charles L.	1885.11.11	SLC	CT.Hartford	R.M. Daggett, late	NPV	03304
Webster, Charles L.	1885.12.16	SLC	CT.Hartford	I am plotting	NPV	03334
Webster, Charles L.	1885.12.16	SLC	CT.Hartford	I shall reach	NPV	03331
Webster, Charles L.	1885.12.17	SLC	CT.Hartford	Well, I am	NPV	03048
Webster, Charles L.	1885.12.18	SLC	CT.Hartford	The more I	NPV	03337
Webster, Charles L.	1885.12.20	SLC	CT.Hartford	It is important	NPV	03339
Webster, Charles L.	1885.12.21	SLC	NY.New York	If the first	NPV	02421
Webster, Charles L.	1885.12.28	SLC	CT.Hartford	Your letter looked	NPV	03345
Webster, Charles L.	1885.12.29	SLC	CT.Hartford	All right; that	NPV	03194
Webster, Charles L.	1886.01.03	SLC	CT.Hartford	I expect to	NPV	03353
Webster, Charles L.	1886.01.10	SLC	CT.Hartford	I am sorry	NPV	03354 misdated 1885
Webster, Charles L.	1886.01.13	SLC	CT.Hartford	But does not	NPV	03196
Webster, Charles L.	1886.02.01	SLC	CT.Hartford	I believe it	NPV	03363
Webster, Charles L.	1886.02.08	SLC	CT.Hartford	What do you	NPV	03273
Webster, Charles L.	1886.02.08	SLC	CT.Hartford	What is the	NPV	03367
Webster, Charles L.	1886.02.10	SLC	CT.Hartford	Gen. Grant seldom	NPV	03279
Webster, Charles L.	1886.02.13	SLC	CT.Hartford	For the first	NPV	02425
Webster, Charles L.	1886.03.19	SLC	CT.Hartford	It isn't good	NPV	03378
Webster, Charles L.	1886.03.27	SLC	CT.Hartford	The Hartford Canvasser	NPV	10895
Webster, Charles L.	1886.04.**	OLC	CT.Hartford	I want to	NPV	03379
Webster, Charles L.	1886.04.06	SLC	CT.Hartford	Did you see	NPV	02427
Webster, Charles L.	1886.04.12	SLC	CT.Hartford	Never mind about	NPV	03294
Webster, Charles L.	1886.04.14	SLC	CT.Hartford	I wish you	NPV	03384
Webster, Charles L.	1886.04.21	SLC	Unknown	This is a	NPV	03301
Webster, Charles L.	1886.04.22	SLC	CT.Hartford	I wish to	NPV	03385
Webster, Charles L.	1886.04.22	SLC	CT.Hartford	We are infinitely	NPV	03386

Webster, Charles L.	1886.05.25	SLC	CT.Hartford	I forgot to	NPV	03401
Webster, Charles L.	1886.06.06	SLC	CT.Hartford	Hadn't you better	NPV	03408
Webster, Charles L.	1886.06.11	SLC	Unknown	See that you	NPV	03313
Webster, Charles L.	1886.06.17	SLC	NY.Elmira	I have thought	NPV	03411
Webster, Charles L.	1886.08.06	SLC	NY.Elmira	Your letter is	NPV	03434
Webster, Charles L.	1886.09.03	SLC	NY.Elmira	I would make	NPV	03449
Webster, Charles L.	1886.10.05	SLC	NY.New York	Welcome home, to	NPV	08933
Webster, Charles L.	1886.10.10	SLC	CT.Hartford	We were very	NPV	03467
Webster, Charles L.	1886.11.13	SLC	CT.Hartford	All right, I	NPV	03479
Webster, Charles L.	1886.11.17	SLC	CT.Hartford	I should say	NPV	03482
Webster, Charles L.	1886.11.17	SLC	CT.Hartford	I wish you	NPV	03465 telegram
Webster, Charles L.	1886.11.29	SLC	CT.Hartford	Your check for	NPV	08835
Webster, Charles L.	1886.12.**	OLC	CT.Hartford	Thank you so	NPV	03486
Webster, Charles L.	1886.12.**	OLC	Unknown	I want to	NPV	03487
Webster, Charles L.	1886.12.06	SLC	CT.Hartford	Don't you think	NPV	03491
Webster, Charles L.	1886.12.11	SLC	CT.Hartford	Stanley wants to	NPV	03495
Webster, Charles L.	1886.12.14	SLC	CT.Hartford	When a stranger	NPV	03497
Webster, Charles L.	1886.12.26	SLC	CT.Hartford	Please send a	NPV	03500
Webster, Charles L.	1886.12.26	SLC	CT.Hartford	P.S. Livy wants	NPV	10892
Webster, Charles L.	1886.12.30	SLC	CT.Hartford	Mrs. Custer's book	NPV	03504
Webster, Charles L.	1887.01.04	SLC	CT.Hartford	Yes, 1/2 profits	295:373	03505
Webster, Charles L.	1887.01.13	SLC	CT.Hartford	Upon further reflection	NPV	03506
Webster, Charles L.	1887.01.19	SLC	CT.Hartford	$1000 to Pond	NPV	03513
Webster, Charles L.	1887.02.15	SLC	CT.Hartford	Mr. Howells wants	NPV	03528
Webster, Charles L.	1887.02.25	SLC	CT.Hartford	We all want	NPV	03533
Webster, Charles L.	1887.03.01	SLC	CT.Hartford	I think well	NPV	03534
Webster, Charles L.	1887.03.04	SLC per FGW	CT.Hartford	With regard to	CU-MARK(tr)	03536

ADDRESSEE	DATE	WRITER	PLACE	CUE	SOURCE	NUMBER/NOTES
Webster, Charles L.	o/a 1887.03.19	SLC	Unknown	Charlie, this is	CU-MARK	03544 on Warner Mar 19
Webster, Charles L.	o/a 1887.03.27	SLC	CT.Hartford	Answer to the	CU-MARK(dr)	10098 on Webster Mar 27
Webster, Charles L.	1887.03.28	SLC per FGW	CT.Hartford	In reply to	NPV	03551
Webster, Charles L.	1887.03.28	SLC	CT.Hartford	Get those people	NPV	03387 telegram
Webster, Charles L.	1887.03.28	SLC	CT.Hartford	The chances are	NPV	03550
Webster, Charles L.	o/a 1887.03.30	SLC	CT.Hartford	I approve the	CU-MARK(tr)	11117 SLC tr; telegram
Webster, Charles L.	1887.04.10	SLC	CT.Hartford	All right. Now	NPV	03559 telegram
Webster, Charles L.	1887.04.17	SLC	CT.Hartford	Good--it is	NPV	03412
Webster, Charles L.	1887.04.22	SLC	CT.Hartford	I am laid	NPV	03565
Webster, Charles L.	1887.04.25	SLC	CT.Hartford	Thank goodness the	NN-B	02658
Webster, Charles L.	1887.05.09	SLC	CT.Hartford	I expect Ned	NPV	03571
Webster, Charles L.	1887.05.11	SLC	CT.Hartford	Joe Jefferson has	NPV	03355
Webster, Charles L.	1887.05.25	SLC	CT.Hartford	The new contract	NPV	02943
Webster, Charles L.	1887.05.28	SLC	CT.Hartford	You can mail	NPV	08918
Webster, Charles L.	1887.06.16	SLC	CT.Hartford	We reach New	NN-B	02661
Webster, Charles L.	1887.06.20	SLC	CT.Hartford	Here is a	NN-B	02662
Webster, Charles L.	1887.07.24	SLC	NY.Elmira	Cable's address is	NN-B	03613
Webster, Charles L.	1887.08.03	SLC	NY.Elmira	I have to	NN-B	02667
Webster, Charles L. & Hall, Frederick J.	1887.08.15	SLC	NY.Elmira	Thank you very	NN-B	02668
Webster, Charles L.	1887.08.16	SLC	NY.Elmira	Oh, no, I	NN-B	02669
Webster, Charles L.	1887.08.23	SLC	NY.Elmira	The etching is	NN-B	02671
Webster, Charles L.	1887.09.05	SLC	CT.Hartford	I find a	NPV	03642
Webster, Charles L. & Hall, Frederick J.	1887.09.05	SLC	Unknown	You need to	NN-B	02672
Webster, Charles L.	1887.09.09	SLC	NY.Elmira	I hope to	NPV	03646

Webster, Charles L.		1887.10.19	SLC	CT.Hartford	Your letter received	NPV	03659
Webster, Charles L.		1887.10.27	SLC	CT.Hartford	The $5,000 has	NPV	03661
Webster, Charles L.		1887.12.28	SLC	CT.Hartford	I am quite	NPV	03685
Webster (C.L.) & Co.		****.**.**	SLC	Unknown	Instruct Chatto to	308:6	09008
Webster (C.L.) & Co.		****.**.**	SLC	Unknown	I am afraid	CU-MARK	08748
Webster (C.L.) & Co.		1886.01.14	SLC	CT.Hartford	Statements of Slote	NN-B	02630
Webster (C.L.) & Co.	o/a	1887.04.05	SLC per FGW	CT.Hartford	In response to	CU-MARK(tr)	11114 FGW tr
Webster (C.L.) & Co.		1887.04.18	SLC	NY.New York	I have none	CU-MARK	03562
Webster (C.L.) & Co.		1887.06.10	SLC	CT.Hartford	This is as	NN-B	02660
Webster (C.L.) & Co.		1887.09.18	SLC	CT.Hartford	Here is a	NN-B	02675
Webster (C.L.) & Co.		1887.10.14	SLC	CT.Hartford	You may write	NN-B	02676
Webster (C.L.) & Co.		1887.10.17	SLC	CT.Hartford	I should say	NN-B	02677
Webster (C.L.) & Co.		1887.11.03	SLC	CT.Hartford	Please keep a	NN-B	02678
Webster (C.L.) & Co.		1887.11.13	SLC	CT.Hartford	I believe it	NPV	03666
Webster (C.L.) & Co.		1887.11.15	SLC	CT.Hartford	No, a thousand	NPV	03667
Webster (C.L.) & Co.		1887.12.07	SLC	CT.Hartford	For a book	NN-B	02680
Webster (C.L.) & Co.		1887.12.24	SLC	CT.Hartford	That is a	NPV	03684
Webster (C.L.) & Co.		1888.07.15	SLC	NY.Elmira	Why are these	NN-B	02683
Webster (C.L.) & Co.	o/a	1889.01.09	SLC	CT.Hartford	Yours of Jan	NNC	03849
Webster (C.L.) & Co.		1892.04.20	SLC	IT.Rome	Close with Arnold	CU-MARK(tr)	04284 telegram; SLC tr
Webster (C.L.) & Co.	pm	1892.10.11	SLC	IT.Florence	*	DLC	10091 envelope only
Webster (C.L.) & Co.		1893.06.01	SLC	IT.Florence	Please send a	NN-B	04642
Webster (C.L.) & Co.		1893.08.16	SLC	Unknown	Summary. March 1.	NN5	04435
Webster, T.K.		1893.10.31	SLC	NY.New York	This is to	CU-MARK	04480
Welles, Carlotta		1907.06.**	SLC	SH.Minneapolis	Charlie, dear, you	CU-MARK(tr)	07779
Welles, Carlotta		1907.06.**	SLC	SH.Minneapolis	Please tell the	CU-MARK(tr)	07740

ADDRESSEE	DATE	WRITER	PLACE	CUE	SOURCE	NUMBER/NOTES
Welles, Carlotta	1907.06.17	SLC	SH.Minneapolis	There's many a	CU-MARK(tr)	09261 inscription
Welles, Carlotta	1907.07.05	SLC per RWA	EN.London	You didn't know	CU-MARK(tr)	08682
Welles, Carlotta	1907.07.08	SLC	EN.London	Didn't I say	CU-MARK(tr)	07781
Welles, Carlotta	1907.07.12	SLC	EN.London	Indeed you are	CU-MARK(tr)	07784
Welles, Carlotta	1907.12.30	SLC	NY.New York	Your letter has	CU-MARK(tr)	07899
Welles, Carlotta	1908.05.29	SLC	NY.New York	Dear Charley, I	CU-MARK(tr)	08018
Wells, Carolyn	1906.04.15	SLC	NY.New York	It is easier	147:230f	10941 inscription
Welsh, Herbert	o/a 1906.12.15	SLC per IVL	NY.New York	interests are full	CU-MARK(dr)	07594 on Welsh Dec 15
Werner, Selma	o/a 1907.08.18	SLC	NY.Tuxedo Park	Truth is the	CU-MARK(tr)	09231 inscription
West, Charles E.	1883.06.18	SLC	NY.Elmira	I should be	NBu	01686
West Point Mess & Battarns, Mr.	o/a 1907.01.22	SLC per IVL	NY.New York	I thank you	CU-MARK(dr)	10965
Western Union president	1902.08.**	SLC	ME.York Harbor	I desire to	CU-MARK	06397
Westland, Len G.	o/a 1905.09.04	SLC per IVL	Unknown	And I, also	CU-MARK(dr)	07128 on Westland Sept 4
Wetter	****.**.**	SLC	NY.New York	For your sake	NElmC	03218
Wheeler, Candace	****.**.**	SLC	NY.New York	Oh, dear, I	Mo2	08564
Wheeler, Candace	****.**.**	SLC	Unknown	with as much	ViU	11104 inscription
Wheeler, Candace	1885.08.30	SLC	NY.Elmira	It was the	445:337	03283
Wheeler, Candace	1885.10.03	SLC	CT.Hartford	Mrs. Clemens charges	Mo2	02426
Wheeler, Candace	pm 1885.10.08	SLC	CT.Hartford	*	Mo2	10072 envelope only
Wheeler, Candace	1888.04.19	SLC	CT.Hartford	It is most	ViU	03717
Wheeler, Candace	1888.05.25	SLC	CT.Hartford	Lord bless you	Mo2	02437
Wheeler, Candace	1890.10.13	SLC	CT.Hartford	It is a	Mo2	08937
Wheeler, Candace	1890.10.15	SLC	CT.Hartford	I am simply	Mo2	02448
Wheeler, Dora	1886.10.19	SLC	CT.Hartford	Of course I'll	Mo2	02432

Wheeler, Dora		1886.11.13	SLC	CT.Hartford	Prithee come right	Mo2	02433
Wheeler, Dora		1887.01.27	SLC	CT.Hartford	Bless your soul	Mo2	02434
Wheeler, Dora		1887.02.15	SLC	CT.Hartford	Oh, geewhillikins	CtHMTH	03530
Wheeler, Dora		1887.09.12	SLC	NY.Elmira	Alas, we dasn't	Mo2	02435
Wheeler, Dora		1889.05.16	SLC	CT.Hartford	Mrs. Clemens wants	Mo2	02439
Wheeler, Dora		1889.09.23	SLC	CT.Hartford	It is my	Mo2	02441
Whelpley, Albert W.		1872.12.05	SLC	CT.Hartford	Dan Slote tells	OCHP	00842
White, Ellen		1870.06.11	SLC	NY.Elmira	Send for us	212:1943.01.09	09890
White, Frank M.		****.**.**	SLC	EN.London	Will it answer	ViU	03001
White, Frank M.		1897.06.02	SLC	EN.London	Too bad you	CU-MARK(tr)	05520 telegram; SLC tr
White, Frank M.		1897.07.09	SLC	EN.London	Do you think	ViU	05259
White, Frank M.		1897.07.10	SLC	EN.London	Come down, now	ViU	05260
White, Frank M.	ca	1897.11.01	SLC	AU.Vienna	It is all	CU-MARK(ph)	05304
White, Frank M.		1897.11.04	SLC	AU.Vienna	Yesterday I mailed	ViU	05308
White, Frank M.		1897.12.26	SLC	AU.Vienna	There is nothing	ViU	05327
White, Frank M.		1898.01.06	SLC per OLC	AU.Vienna	Mr Clemens asks	ViU	05332
White, Frank M.		1898.01.11	SLC per OLC	AU.Vienna	Mr Clemens wishes	ViU	05335
White, Frank M.		1898.02.04	SLC	AU.Vienna	It wouldn't do	ViU	05341
White, K.W.		1874.10.05	SLC	CT.Hartford	I regret exceedingly	131:1874.10.09	10323 spurious, see Oct 9 to NY Times
White, Mr.		1893.06.10	SLC	IT.Florence	To my regret	TxU	04413
White, Willard M.		1873.03.03	SLC	CT.Hartford	There is nothing	CtY(tr)	00880
White, William A.		1906.06.24	SLC	NH.Dublin	Howells told me	CU-MARK(tr)	07465
Whitehead, Lucy P.	o/a	1905.02.09	SLC per IVL	NY.New York	Mr. Clemens directs	CU-MARK(dr)	06996 on Whitehead Feb 9

ADDRESSEE	DATE	WRITER	PLACE	CUE	SOURCE	NUMBER/NOTES
Whitehead, Lucy P.	o/a 1905.12.06	SLC per IVL	NY.New York	Be glad if	CU-MARK(dr)	07239· on Whitehead Dec 6
Whiteing, Richard	1879.05.17	SLC	FR.Paris	This,family all	DLC	01656
Whitford, Daniel	1885.08.14	SLC	NY.Elmira	These are piping	DSI	10441
Whitford, Daniel	1890.**.**	SLC	Unknown	The only reason	CU-MARK	04000
Whitford, Daniel	1890.02.27	SLC	CT.Hartford	It is no	CU-MARK	04023 unsent
Whitford, Daniel	1890.10.16	SLC	CT.Hartford	I have just	CU-MARK	04102
Whitman, Walt	1889.05.24	SLC	CT.Hartford	You have lived	CtY	03895
Whitman, Walt fund	1887.**.**	SLC	Unknown	What we want	104:1887.05.24	10851
Whitmore, Franklin G.	****.**.**	SLC	CT.Hartford	Program changed again	105:1963.12.03	09677 on form letter
Whitmore, Franklin G.	****.**.**	SLC	CT.Hartford	Hang it, every	CtHMTH	09846
Whitmore, Franklin G.	****.**.**	SLC	CT.Hartford	I think Clark's	CtHMTH	10975
Whitmore, Franklin G.	****.**.**	SLC	CT.Hartford	2 incandescents in	CU-MARK	08762
Whitmore, Franklin G.	****.**.**	SLC	CT.Hartford	Billiards put off	CU-MARK	08760
Whitmore, Franklin G.	****.**.**	SLC	CT.Hartford	Brer, the incandescent	CU-MARK	08759
Whitmore, Franklin G.	****.**.**	SLC	CT.Hartford	Can't seem to	CU-MARK	08763
Whitmore, Franklin G.	****.**.**	SLC	CT.Hartford	The Putnam com	CU-MARK	08766 on envelope
Whitmore, Franklin G.	****.**.**	SLC	FR.Paris	Please buy a	CU-MARK	08757
Whitmore, Franklin G.	****.**.**	SLC	NY.Elmira	I've gone to	CU-MARK	08756
Whitmore, Franklin G.	****.**.**	SLC	NY.Elmira	Oui--oui, pay	CU-MARK	08767
Whitmore, Franklin G.	****.**.**	SLC	Unknown	I was going	CtHMTH	08967
Whitmore, Franklin G.	****.**.**	SLC	Unknown	Brer, this is	CU-MARK	08752
Whitmore, Franklin G.	****.**.**	SLC	Unknown	don't pay Lewis's	CU-MARK	08753
Whitmore, Franklin G.	****.**.**	SLC	Unknown	Hearty thanks for	CU-MARK	08754
Whitmore, Franklin G.	****.**.**	SLC	Unknown	Let the government	CU-MARK	08765
Whitmore, Franklin G.	****.**.**	SLC	Unknown	Please express this	CU-MARK	08758
Whitmore, Franklin G.	****.**.**	SLC	Unknown	Please return this	CU-MARK	08755
Whitmore, Franklin G.	****.**.**	SLC	Unknown	P.S. What amount	CU-MARK	08761

Whitmore, Franklin G.		****.**.**	SLC	Unknown	What I'm after	CU-MARK	08687
Whitmore, Franklin G.		****.**.**	SLC	Unknown	Won't you invite	CU-MARK	08764
Whitmore, Franklin G.		****.01.01	SLC	Unknown	Can you come	Mo2	08589
Whitmore, Franklin G.	pm	****.11.01	SLC	CT.Hartford	Billiards Thursday night	CU-MARK	08768
Whitmore, Franklin G.		****.11.19	SLC	Unknown	Brer, when the	CU-MARK	08769
Whitmore, Franklin G.	pm	****.12.14	SLC	NY.New York	Please send me	CU-MARK	08770
Whitmore, Franklin G.		1880.**.**	SLC	Unknown	*	CU-MARK	10066 envelope only
Whitmore, Franklin G.		1880.05.18	SLC	CT.Hartford	Those delightful little	CtHMTH	01807
Whitmore, Franklin G.		1880.11.27	SLC	CT.Hartford	Ich bin Ihren	CU-MARK	01858 on form letter
Whitmore, Franklin G.		1880.11.30	SLC	CT.Hartford	How could you	CU-MARK	01860
Whitmore, Franklin G.		1881.08.06	SLC	NY.Elmira	Please send me	CtHMTH	01994
Whitmore, Franklin G.		1881.08.06	SLC	NY.Elmira	Broke an axle	CU-MARK	01993 telegram
Whitmore, Franklin G.		1881.08.08	SLC	NY.Elmira	Carrying Jean up	CtHMTH	01996
Whitmore, Franklin G.		1881.08.12	SLC	NY.Elmira	We will switch	CU-MARK(ph)	02004
Whitmore, Franklin G.		1881.08.18	SLC	NY.Elmira	I clear forgot	CtHMTH	09007
Whitmore, Franklin G.		1881.09.03	SLC	NY.Elmira	I owe you	CtHMTH	02024
Whitmore, Franklin G.		1881.09.10	SLC	NY.Elmira	All right, Brer	CU-MARK	02034
Whitmore, Franklin G. & Whitmore, Harriet E.	bef	1885.04.18	OLC	CT.Hartford	Mrs. S.L. Clemens	CtHMTH	06176
Whitmore, Franklin G.		1885.07.05	SLC	IA.Keokuk	The music scheme	CU-MARK	03250
Whitmore, Franklin G.		1886.02.11	SLC	CT.Hartford	Dank' schon! Es	CU-MARK	03368
Whitmore, Franklin G.		1886.06.15	SLC	NY.New York	I came off	CtHMTH	03410
Whitmore, Franklin G.		1886.06.20	SLC	NY.Elmira	Three boxes contain	157:1924.03.03 CU-MARK	10135 CU-MARK envelope
Whitmore, Franklin G.		1886.07.12	SLC	NY.Elmira	We are here	CtHMTH	03413
Whitmore, Franklin G.		1886.07.15	SLC	NY.Elmira	Please deposit enclosed	CU-MARK CtHMTH	03418 CtHMTH envelope
Whitmore, Franklin G.		1886.07.17	SLC	NY.Elmira	I am glad	CtHMTH	03423

ADDRESSEE		DATE	WRITER	PLACE	CUE	SOURCE	NUMBER/NOTES
Whitmore, Franklin G.	o/a	1886.07.22	SLC	NY.Elmira	Treat him kindly	CU-MARK	03426 on Hopson July 22
Whitmore, Franklin G.		1886.07.26	SLC	NY.Elmira	Let Will set	CU-MARK	03428
Whitmore, Franklin G.		1886.07.28	SLC	NY.Elmira	I am not	CtHMTH	03429
Whitmore, Franklin G.		1886.08.17	SLC	NY.Elmira	How is Will	CtHMTH	03440
Whitmore, Franklin G.		1886.08.19	SLC	NY.Elmira	Yesterday I joined	CU-MARK	03441
Whitmore, Franklin G.		1886.08.23	SLC	NY.Elmira	This is the	CtHMTH	09821
Whitmore, Franklin G.	pm	1886.08.28	SLC	CT.Hartford	*	ViU	10074 envelope only
Whitmore, Franklin G.		1886.09.01	SLC	NY.Elmira	I guess the	CU-MARK	03448
Whitmore, Franklin G.		1886.09.03	SLC	NY.Elmira	Thanks for the	CU-MARK	03450
Whitmore, Franklin G.		1886.09.07	SLC	NY.Elmira	Please safe-deposit	CU-MARK	03452
Whitmore, Franklin G.		1886.09.14	SLC	NY.Elmira	We leave here	CU-MARK	03455
Whitmore, Franklin G.	pm	1886.09.15	SLC	NY.Elmira	*	CU-MARK	10099 envelope only
Whitmore, Franklin G.		1886.09.16	SLC	NY.Elmira	Please pick me	CU-MARK	03458
Whitmore, Franklin G.	o/a	1886.09.29	SLC	CT.Hartford	Have you overlooked	CU-MARK	03461 on Bissell Sept 29
Whitmore, Franklin G.	o/a	1887.06.11	SLC	CT.Hartford	Tell him arrangements	CU-MARK	11116 on Walton June 10
Whitmore, Franklin G.	o/a	1887.06.19	SLC	CT.Hartford	Brer. W. please	CU-MARK	03584 on See June 17
Whitmore, Franklin G.	pm	1887.06.25	SLC	NY.Elmira	*	CtHMTH	09823 envelope only
Whitmore, Franklin G.	o/a	1887.06.27	SLC	Unknown	Brer. W., please	CU-MARK	03587 on Lippincott June 27
Whitmore, Franklin G.		1887.06.28	SLC	NY.Elmira	Please look in	CU-MARK	03588 Fairbanks June 21 enc
Whitmore, Franklin G.		1887.07.04	SLC	NY.Elmira	Did you frame	CU-MARK	03590
Whitmore, Franklin G.		1887.07.06	SLC	NY.Elmira	We can't require	CU-MARK	03593
Whitmore, Franklin G.		1887.07.08	SLC	NY.Elmira	Please finish filling	CtHMTH	09824

Whitmore, Franklin G.		1887.07.09	SLC	NY.Elmira	I have never	CU-MARK	03596 dr of form letter enc
Whitmore, Franklin G.		1887.07.11	SLC	NY.New York	I am send	CtHMTH	03600
Whitmore, Franklin G.		1887.07.12	SLC	NY.Elmira	I'm glad your	CU-MARK	03601
Whitmore, Franklin G.		1887.07.15	SLC	CT.Hartford	I have sent	CtHMTH	03603
Whitmore, Franklin G.		1887.07.15	SLC	CT.Hartford	P.S. Deposit this	CU-MARK	03605
Whitmore, Franklin G.		1887.07.21	SLC	NY.Elmira	Furnish to Paige	CU-MARK	03607
Whitmore, Franklin G.		1887.07.23	SLC	NY.Elmira	I am coming	CtHMTH	03608 telegram
Whitmore, Franklin G.		1887.08.05	SLC	NY.Elmira	As I understand	CU-MARK	03617
Whitmore, Franklin G.		1887.08.12	SLC	NY.Elmira	Consound it I	CU-MARK	03624
Whitmore, Franklin G.		1887.08.13	SLC	NY.Elmira	The eleventh-hour idea	CU-MARK	03626
Whitmore, Franklin G.		1887.08.14	SLC	NY.Elmira	Now suppose you	CtHMTH	03627
Whitmore, Franklin G.		1887.08.17	SLC	NY.Elmira	Do you mean	CU-MARK	03628
Whitmore, Franklin G.		1887.08.18	SLC	NY.Elmira	I signed &	CU-MARK	03629
Whitmore, Franklin G.		1887.08.22	SLC	NY.Elmira	Yes, I would	CtHMTH	03633
Whitmore, Franklin G.		1887.08.26	SLC	NY.Elmira	I didn't know	CU-MARK	03635
Whitmore, Franklin G.		1887.08.27	SLC	NY.Elmira	All right, then	CtHMTH	10488
Whitmore, Franklin G.		1887.08.29	SLC	NY.Elmira	If I've enclosed	CU-MARK CtHMTH	03637 CtHMTH envelope
Whitmore, Franklin G.		1887.09.03	SLC	NY.Elmira	I suppose the	CU-MARK	03641
Whitmore, Franklin G.		1887.09.10	SLC	NY.Elmira	Those people propose	CU-MARK	03647 telegram
Whitmore, Franklin G.	pm	1887.11.19	SLC	CT.Hartford	Please get Dr.	CU-MARK	03669
Whitmore, Franklin G.		1888.01.08	SLC	CT.Hartford	Please be here	CU-MARK	03696
Whitmore, Franklin G.	o/a	1888.02.04	SLC	CT.Hartford	I will not	CU-MARK	03701 on Spencer Feb 4
Whitmore, Franklin G.	o/a	1888.02.20	SLC	CT.Hartford	Please tell him	CU-MARK	08827 on Roberts Feb 10
Whitmore, Franklin G.		1888.07.16	SLC	NY.Elmira	It was eminently	CtHMTH	03734

ADDRESSEE		DATE	WRITER	PLACE	CUE	SOURCE	NUMBER/NOTES
Whitmore, Franklin G.		1888.07.18	SLC	CT.Hartford	No, I don't	CU-MARK	03736
Whitmore, Franklin G.		1888.07.18	SLC	NY.Elmira	Yes protest in	CU-MARK	03739 telegram
Whitmore, Franklin G.	o/a	1888.07.18	SLC	NY.Elmira	Did this check	CU-MARK	03735 on Bliss to Whitmore July 18
Whitmore, Franklin G.		1888.07.19	SLC	NY.Elmira	If they finally	CU-MARK	03742
Whitmore, Franklin G.		1888.07.25	SLC	NY.Elmira	Please copy and	CtHMTH	09826 July 25 to Bok enc
Whitmore, Franklin G.		1888.07.30	SLC	NY.Elmira	Please send this	CU-MARK	03745 July 30 to N. American Phono. enc
Whitmore, Franklin G.	pm	1888.08.04	SLC	NY.Elmira	*	CU-MARK	10136 envelope only
Whitmore, Franklin G.		1888.08.05	SLC	NY.Elmira	Yours received. Now	CU-MARK	03748
Whitmore, Franklin G.		1888.08.10	SLC	NY.Elmira	If you can	CtHMTH	03750
Whitmore, Franklin G.	pm	1888.08.12	SLC	NY.Elmira	*	CU-MARK	10137 envelope only
Whitmore, Franklin G.		1888.08.28	SLC	NY.Elmira	Please send me	CtHMTH	09827
Whitmore, Franklin G.		1888.08.30	SLC	CT.Hartford	Put no more	CU-MARK(tr) CU-MARK	03755 CU-MARK envelope
Whitmore, Franklin G.		1888.09.05	SLC	NY.Elmira	No, you may	CtHMTH	09828
Whitmore, Franklin G.		1888.09.06	SLC	NY.Elmira	Will the machine	CU-MARK	03771
Whitmore, Franklin G.		1888.09.07	SLC	NY.Elmira	I have sold	CU-MARK	03758
Whitmore, Franklin G.		1888.09.10	SLC	NY.Elmira	Please bank the	CtHMTH	03759
Whitmore, Franklin G.		1888.09.13	SLC	NY.Elmira	If, as you	CU-MARK	03762
Whitmore, Franklin G.		1888.09.17	SLC	NY.Elmira	If the machine	CtHMTH	03768
Whitmore, Franklin G.		1888.09.17	SLC	NY.Elmira	Please turn these	CU-MARK	03767
Whitmore, Franklin G.		1888.09.20	SLC	NY.Elmira	Please put this	CU-MARK	03770
Whitmore, Franklin G.		1888.09.22	SLC	NY.Elmira	The hat trunk	CU-MARK	03772
Whitmore, Franklin G.		1888.09.26	SLC	NY.New York	Please deposit the	CtHMTH	03775
Whitmore, Franklin G.		1889.02.14	SLC	NY.Albany	Please mail to	CU-MARK	03864

Whitmore, Franklin G.		1889.06.15	SLC	CT.Hartford	I have made	CtHMTH	03901
Whitmore, Franklin G.		1889.06.28	SLC	NY.Elmira	I expect a	CtHMTH	09829
Whitmore, Franklin G.		1889.07.02	SLC	NY.Elmira	Mr. Langdon says	CU-MARK	03907
Whitmore, Franklin G.		1889.07.08	SLC	NY.Elmira	Send all bonds	CU-MARK	03908
Whitmore, Franklin G.	o/a	1889.07.19	SLC	NY.Elmira	Please mail my	CU-MARK	10911 on Thornton July 19
Whitmore, Franklin G.		1889.07.29	SLC	NY.Elmira	Fred's progress is	CU-MARK	03917
Whitmore, Franklin G.		1889.08.**	SLC	NY.Elmira	I can have	CU-MARK	03919
Whitmore, Franklin G.		1889.08.03	SLC	NY.Elmira	Brer Whitmo' please	CU-MARK	03922
Whitmore, Franklin G.		1889.08.04	SLC	NY.Elmira	Don't let Fred	CU-MARK	03923
Whitmore, Franklin G.		1889.08.18	SLC	NY.Elmira	Please call at	CU-MARK	03928
Whitmore, Franklin G.		1889.08.20	SLC	NY.Elmira	There is but	CtHMTH	03930
Whitmore, Franklin G.		1889.08.27	SLC	NY.Elmira	I had a	CU-MARK	03932
Whitmore, Franklin G.	pm	1889.09.04	SLC	NY.Elmira	P.S. We leave	CU-MARK	03937
Whitmore, Franklin G.		1889.09.13	SLC	NY.Elmira	I have sent	CU-MARK	03940
Whitmore, Franklin G.	o/a	1889.09.14	SLC	CT.Hartford	Tell him I	CU-MARK	10912 on Butler Sept 14
Whitmore, Franklin G.	o/a	1889.10.10	SLC	CT.Hartford	I know of	CU-MARK	10935 on Drake Oct 10
Whitmore, Franklin G.	o/a	1889.10.12	SLC	CT.Hartford	please acknowledge this	CU-MARK	10211 on Kelly Oct 12
Whitmore, Franklin G.	o/a	1889.10.16	SLC	CT.Hartford	Brer W, say I	CU-MARK	10913 on Drake Oct 16
Whitmore, Franklin G.	o/a	1889.10.22	SLC	CT.Hartford	Please attend to	CU-MARK	09088 on Gerhardt Oct 22
Whitmore, Franklin G.	o/a	1889.11.22	SLC	CT.Hartford	Brer W., tell	CU-MARK	03975 on Unknown pm Nov 22
Whitmore, Franklin G.	o/a	1889.11.23	SLC	CT.Hartford	Brer W., please say	CU-MARK	03976 on Unknown pm Nov 23

ADDRESSEE	DATE	WRITER	PLACE	CUE	SOURCE	NUMBER/NOTES
Whitmore, Franklin G.	o/a 1889.11.26	SLC	CT.Hartford	Brer W, please thank	CU-MARK	10914 on Howard Nov 25
Whitmore, Franklin G.	o/a 1889.12.30	SLC	CT.Hartford	do the necessary	CU-MARK	10915 on Smith Dec 30
Whitmore, Franklin G.	1890.**.**	SLC	CT.Hartford	Brer, preserve letter	CU-MARK	04001 on Means 1890
Whitmore, Franklin G.	1890.**.**	SLC	Unknown	I have not	CU-MARK	04002
Whitmore, Franklin G.	o/a 1890.01.09	SLC	CT.Hartford	Brer W, the paper	CU-MARK	10917 on Pattison Jan 7
Whitmore, Franklin G.	o/a 1890.01.20	SLC	CT.Hartford	Brer, please tell him	CU-MARK	10918 on Algie Jan 18
Whitmore, Franklin G.	o/a 1890.01.22	SLC	CT.Hartford	Brer W, please explain	CU-MARK	10919 on Dawkins Jan 22
Whitmore, Franklin G.	o/a 1890.02.06	SLC	CT.Hartford	refer him to	CU-MARK	10920 on Scribners Feb 6
Whitmore, Franklin G.	1890.02.09	SLC	CT.Hartford	Please decline it	CU-MARK	10219
Whitmore, Franklin G.	o/a 1890.03.16	SLC	CT.Hartford	Brer, please tell	CU-MARK	10922 on Butchelder Mar 16
Whitmore, Franklin G.	o/b 1890.03.18	SLC	CT.Hartford	Brer, please tell	CU-MARK	10995 on Parvin Mar 14
Whitmore, Franklin G.	1890.03.19	SLC	CT.Hartford	Brer, please tell	CU-MARK	10923 on Green Mar 19
Whitmore, Franklin G.	pm 1890.03.19	SLC	NY.New York	Yes, send me	CU-MARK	04029
Whitmore, Franklin G.	o/a 1890.03.21	SLC	CT.Hartford	Brer, tell him	CU-MARK	10924 on Whitford Mar 25
Whitmore, Franklin G.	o/a 1890.03.23	SLC	CT.Hartford	Brer, please tell	CU-MARK	10921 on Johansen Mar 15
Whitmore, Franklin G.	o/a 1890.03.25	SLC	CT.Hartford	Brer, please tell	CU-MARK	10925 on Coit Mar 25

Whitmore, Franklin G.	o/a	1890.03.30	SLC	CT.Hartford	Brer, please tell	CU-MARK	10926 on Griffin Mar 29
Whitmore, Franklin G.	o/a	1890.03.31	SLC	CT.Hartford	please tell her	CU-MARK	10927 on Burgoyne Mar 30
Whitmore, Franklin G.	o/a	1890.04.**	SLC	CT.Hartford	Please acknowledge Brer	CU-MARK	10916 on Kelly Jan 13
Whitmore, Franklin G.	o/a	1890.04.19	SLC	CT.Hartford	Brer, tell him	CU-MARK	10929 on Hall Apr 18
Whitmore, Franklin G.	o/a	1890.04.26	SLC	CT.Hartford	Brer, please decline &	CU-MARK	10930 on Townsend Apr 25
Whitmore, Franklin G.	o/a	1890.05.12	SLC	CT.Hartford	Brer, tell him it	CU-MARK	10931 on Felt May 10
Whitmore, Franklin G.	o/a	1890.05.12	SLC	CT.Hartford	Decline for me	CU-MARK	10932 on Earll May 11
Whitmore, Franklin G.	o/a	1890.05.24	SLC	CT.Hartford	Tell him I	CU-MARK	10933 on Slattery May 23
Whitmore, Franklin G.	o/a	1890.05.26	SLC	CT.Hartford	Tell him I	CU-MARK	10934 on Christian May 26
Whitmore, Franklin G.		1890.07.06	SLC	NY.Tannersville	I want Ned	CtHMTH	10486
Whitmore, Franklin G.		1890.07.09	SLC	NY.Tannersville	You mention the	CtHMTH	09830
Whitmore, Franklin G.	pm	1890.07.10	SLC	NY.Tannersville	*	CU-MARK	10096 envelope only
Whitmore, Franklin G.	pm	1890.07.12	SLC	NY.Tannersville	*	CU-MARK	10139 envelope only
Whitmore, Franklin G.	bef	1890.07.19	SLC	NY.Tannersville	Yours received. Many	CU-MARK	04058
Whitmore, Franklin G.		1890.07.24	SLC	NY.New York	Have it moved	CU-MARK	04067 telegram
Whitmore, Franklin G.		1890.07.28	SLC	NY.New York	I tried to	MeWC	08914
Whitmore, Franklin G.		1890.07.29	SLC	NY.New York	Joe Goodman will	CU-MARK	04068
Whitmore, Franklin G.		1890.08.05	SLC	NY.Tannersville	If we find	CtHMTH	04072

ADDRESSEE	DATE	WRITER	PLACE	CUE	SOURCE	NUMBER/NOTES
Whitmore, Franklin G.	1890.08.05	SLC	NY.Tannersville	Tell me by	CU-MARK	04071 telegram
Whitmore, Franklin G.	1890.08.08	SLC	NY.Tannersville	I think we	CU-MARK	04075
Whitmore, Franklin G.	1890.08.08	SLC	NY.Tannersville	P.S. I forgot	CU-MARK	04076
Whitmore, Franklin G.	1890.08.09	SLC	NY.Tannersville	I want you	CU-MARK	04077
Whitmore, Franklin G.	1890.08.11	SLC	NY.Tannersville	I go to	CU-MARK	04079 telegram
Whitmore, Franklin G.	1890.08.13	SLC	NY.New York	It is all	CtHMTH	04080
Whitmore, Franklin G.	1890.08.14	SLC	CT.Hartford	Better fix up	CU-MARK	04081
Whitmore, Franklin G.	1890.08.21	SLC	NY.Elmira	Don't worry about	CtHMTH	09831
Whitmore, Franklin G.	1890.08.26	SLC	DC.Washington	You will have	CU-MARK	04086
Whitmore, Franklin G.	1890.08.27	SLC	DC.Washington	Please look in	CU-MARK	04087
Whitmore, Franklin G.	1890.08.31	SLC	NY.Tannersville	Please send me	CU-MARK	04089
Whitmore, Franklin G.	1890.09.01	SLC	NY.Tannersville	Please don't send	CtHMTH	09832
Whitmore, Franklin G.	1890.09.04	SLC	NY.Tannersville	Please send 3	CU-MARK	04092
Whitmore, Franklin G.	1890.09.11	SLC	NY.Tannersville	But you forgot	CU-MARK	04094 on envelope
Whitmore, Franklin G.	1890.10.01	SLC	DC.Washington	Turn in at	CU-MARK	04098
Whitmore, Franklin G.	1890.12.07 or 1890.12.08	SLC	CT.Hartford	Tell him go	CU-MARK	10928 on Kimball Dec 6
Whitmore, Franklin G.	1891.01.03	OLC	CT.Hartford	Susy was the	CtHMTH	04153
Whitmore, Franklin G.	1891.03.**	SLC	CT.Hartford	Brer, In Jan.	CU-MARK	04177
Whitmore, Franklin G.	bet 1891.05.25 & 1891.06.04	SLC	CT.Hartford	Will you see	CU-MARK	04214
Whitmore, Franklin G.	1891.07.18	SLC	FR.Aix-les-Bains	My arm is	CU-MARK	04221
Whitmore, Franklin G.	1891.08.24	SLC	GE.Marienbad	Yes, I would	CU-MARK	04225
Whitmore, Franklin G.	1891.09.23	OLC	SW.Ouchy	I never dreamed	CtHMTH	04232
Whitmore, Franklin G.	1891.10.16	SLC	GE.Berlin	Did you remember	CtHMTH	04246
Whitmore, Franklin G.	1891.11.09	SLC	GE.Berlin	I remembered, when	CtHMTH	04252
Whitmore, Franklin G.	1891.11.23 & 1891.11.28	SLC per OLC	GE.Berlin	When a bill	CtHMTH	04256
Whitmore, Franklin G.	1891.12.23	SLC	GE.Berlin	C.L. & W. pay	CU-MARK	04261

Whitmore, Franklin G.		1892.02.20	SLC	GE.Berlin	Oh yes, Br.	CU-MARK	04271
Whitmore, Franklin G.		1892.05.05	SLC	IT.Florence	Three good-sized	CU-MARK	04286
Whitmore, Franklin G.		1892.05.22	SLC	IT.Venice	Yes, I think	CtHMTH	04293
Whitmore, Franklin G.		1892.07.01	SLC	NY.New York	If Mrs. Clemens	CU-MARK	01586
Whitmore, Franklin G.		1892.07.02	SLC	CT.Hartford	P.S. July 2.	CU-MARK	08646
Whitmore, Franklin G.		1892.08.07	SLC	Unknown	Suppose you proceed	CtHMTH	09833
Whitmore, Franklin G.		1892.08.27	SLC	GE.Bad-Nauheim	When the cablegram	CU-MARK	01810
Whitmore, Franklin G.		1892.09.10	SLC	GE.Bad-Nauheim	You have a	CU-MARK	02084
Whitmore, Franklin G.		1892.09.17	SLC	SW.Lucerne	When Pratt &	CU-MARK	02117
Whitmore, Franklin G.		1892.09.29	SLC	IT.Florence	You may send	CU-MARK	04303
Whitmore, Franklin G.		1892.10.14	SLC	IT.Florence	Well, I swon	CU-MARK	00651
Whitmore, Franklin G.		1892.10.22	SLC	IT.Florence	As to that	CU-MARK	00736
Whitmore, Franklin G.		1892.10.31	SLC	IT.Florence	Please hand the	CU-MARK	08924
Whitmore, Franklin G.		1892.11.02	SLC	IT.Florence	Please notify our	CtHMTH	08923
Whitmore, Franklin G.		1892.12.02	SLC	IT.Florence	Have just received	CU-MARK	00777
Whitmore, Franklin G.	pm	1893.01.**	SLC	IT.Florence	*	CU-MARK	10138 envelope only
Whitmore, Franklin G.		1893.01.02	SLC	IT.Florence	Happy New Years	CU-MARK	04320
Whitmore, Franklin G.		1893.02.**	SLC	IT.Florence	I forgot to	CU-MARK	04331
Whitmore, Franklin G.		1893.03.02	SLC	IT.Florence	The Smiths are	CtHMTH	04347
Whitmore, Franklin G.		1893.03.08	SLC	IT.Florence	Yes, pay the	CU-MARK	04349
Whitmore, Franklin G.		1893.03.16	SLC	IT.Florence	I don't know	CtHMTH	04352
Whitmore, Franklin G.		1893.03.20	SLC	IT.Florence	I wish you	CU-MARK	04354
Whitmore, Franklin G.		1893.04.07	SLC	NY.New York	I didn't write	CtHMTH	09834
Whitmore, Franklin G.		1893.04.24	SLC	IL.Chicago	The Webster Co	CU-MARK	04384
Whitmore, Franklin G.		1893.05.01	SLC	NY.New York	I am pretty	CtHMTH	04392
Whitmore, Franklin G.		1893.05.05	SLC	NY.Elmira	I don't know	CU-MARK	04394
Whitmore, Franklin G.		1893.05.07	SLC	NY.Elmira	The railway trip	CU-MARK	04398
Whitmore, Franklin G.		1893.05.11	SLC	NY.New York	You can send	CU-MARK	04402

ADDRESSEE		DATE	WRITER	PLACE	CUE	SOURCE	NUMBER/NOTES
Whitmore, Franklin G.		1893.06.13	SLC	IT.Florence	I see that	CU-MARK	04416
Whitmore, Franklin G.		1893.07.03	SLC	GE.Munich	Please send the	CU-MARK	04420
Whitmore, Franklin G.		1893.09.13	SLC	NY.New York	I ran up	CtHMTH	04448
Whitmore, Franklin G.	pm	1893.11.14	SLC	NY.New York	Please look in	CtHMTH	04488
Whitmore, Franklin G.		1894.04.12	SLC	SH.New York	I shall arrive	CtHMTH	09835
Whitmore, Franklin G.		1894.08.03	SLC	NY.New York	Before I forget	CU-MARK	04770
Whitmore, Franklin G.		1894.10.07	SLC	FR.Rouen	Of whom do	CU-MARK	04794
Whitmore, Franklin G.		1894.10.23	SLC	FR.Rouen	We send our	CtHMTH	04801
Whitmore, Franklin G.		1894.10.23	SLC	FR.Rouen	In each &	CU-MARK	04802 on Whitmore Oct 11
Whitmore, Franklin G.		1894.11.06	SLC	FR.Paris	I note what	CU-MARK	04806
Whitmore, Franklin G.		1894.11.16	SLC	FR.Paris	Luck? Indeed it	CtHMTH	04811
Whitmore, Franklin G.		1895.01.08	SLC	FR.Paris	I have got	CtHMTH	04834
Whitmore, Franklin G.		1895.02.22	SLC	FR.Paris	I suppose John	CU-MARK	04845
Whitmore, Franklin G.		1895.03.24	SLC	NY.New York	Presently when you	CtHMTH	04854
Whitmore, Franklin G.		1895.03.27	SLC	NY.New York	In five minutes	CtHMTH	04855
Whitmore, Franklin G.		1895.04.07	SLC	FR.Paris	Mrs. Clemens says	CtHMTH	04863
Whitmore, Franklin G.		1895.05.25	SLC	NY.Elmira	Please look out	CU-MARK	04878
Whitmore, Franklin G.		1895.05.30	SLC	NY.Elmira	It isn't necessary	CtHMTH	04883
Whitmore, Franklin G.		1895.06.02	SLC	NY.Elmira	I enclose an	CU-MARK	04885
Whitmore, Franklin G.		1895.06.09	SLC	NY.Elmira	I am glad	CU-MARK	04887
Whitmore, Franklin G.		1895.06.18	OLC	NY.Elmira	I enclose you	CtHMTH	04893
Whitmore, Franklin G.		1895.06.25	OLC	NY.Elmira	Thank you for	CtHMTH	04902
Whitmore, Franklin G.	o/a	1895.06.29	SLC	Unknown	Please write him	CtHMTH	09844 on Horne June 29
Whitmore, Franklin G.		1895.07.06	SLC	NY.Elmira	Mrs. Clemens will	CtHMTH	09836
Whitmore, Franklin G.	pm	1895.07.13	OLC	NY.Elmira	You ask about	CU-MARK	04929
Whitmore, Franklin G.		1895.08.20	SLC & OLC	CN.Vancouver	It may be	CtHMTH	04955

Whitmore, Franklin G.	1895.10.07	OLC	AS.Melbourne	*	CtHMTH	04967 envelope only
Whitmore, Franklin G.	1896.04.05	SLC	SH.Wardha	In Ceylon, two	CtHMTH	05036
Whitmore, Franklin G.	1896.04.12	SLC	SH.Wardha	Do you remember	CU-MARK	05039
Whitmore, Franklin G.	bef 1896.05.22	SLC	Unknown	*	CU-MARK	10140 envelope only
Whitmore, Franklin G.	1896.09.10	SLC	EN.Guildford	I thank you	CU-MARK	05106
Whitmore, Franklin G.	1896.09.14	SLC	EN.London	Please give me	CtHMTH	05111
Whitmore, Franklin G.	1896.09.14	SLC	EN.London	Since writing this	CtHMTH	05112
Whitmore, Franklin G.	1896.09.23	SLC	EN.London	P.S. I forgot	CtHMTH	05115
Whitmore, Franklin G.	1896.10.11	SLC	EN.London	Yes, but you	CU-MARK	05126
Whitmore, Franklin G.	1896.10.13	SLC	EN.London	P.S. Please send	CU-MARK	05127
Whitmore, Franklin G.	1896.11.24	SLC	EN.London	I think you	CU-MARK	05147
Whitmore, Franklin G.	1896.12.09	SLC & OLC	EN.London	Mr Clemens wants	CU-MARK	05152
Whitmore, Franklin G.	1896.12.18	SLC	EN.London	I am glad	CU-MARK	05154
Whitmore, Franklin G.	1896.12.19	SLC	EN.London	P.S. I forgot	CU-MARK	05155
Whitmore, Franklin G.	1897.02.08	SLC	EN.London	You have not	CU-MARK	05177
Whitmore, Franklin G.	1897.07.29	SLC	SW.Weggis	Do not permit	CtHMTH CU-MARK	05273 CU-MARK envelope
Whitmore, Franklin G.	1897.12.11	SLC	AU.Vienna	My brother Orion	CU-MARK	05321
Whitmore, Franklin G.	1897.12.26	OLC	AU.Vienna	Mr Clemens rec'd	CU-MARK	05328
Whitmore, Franklin G.	1898.05.05	SLC	AU.Kaltenleut.	I have received	CU-MARK	05382
Whitmore, Franklin G.	1898.07.09	SLC	AU.Kaltenleut.	O come, what	CtHMTH	05410
Whitmore, Franklin G.	1898.07.20	SLC	AU.Kaltenleut.	I forgot to	CtHMTH	05413
Whitmore, Franklin G.	1898.08.20	SLC	AU.Kaltenleut.	I note that	CU-MARK	05423
Whitmore, Franklin G.	1898.09.01	SLC	AU.Kaltenleut.	Away I cannot	CU-MARK	05430 poem inscription
Whitmore, Franklin G.	1898.10.05	SLC	AU.Kaltenleut.	Quarles (of Texas	CU-MARK	08654 mislabeled Vienna

ADDRESSEE		DATE	WRITER	PLACE	CUE	SOURCE	NUMBER/NOTES
Whitmore, Franklin G.	pm	1898.10.30	SLC	Unknown	*	CU-MARK	10145 envelope only
Whitmore, Franklin G.		1898.11.06	SLC	AU.Vienna	I wish you'd	199:1949.05.28	04747
Whitmore, Franklin G.		1898.12.19	SLC	AU.Vienna	Your second disaster	CU-MARK	05482
Whitmore, Franklin G.	bet &	1899.01.** 1899.05.**	SLC	AU.Vienna	Quarles (of Texas	CU-MARK	05530
Whitmore, Franklin G.		1899.01.21	SLC	AU.Vienna	P.S. Please hurry	CtHMTH	05537
Whitmore, Franklin G.		1899.02.25	SLC	AU.Vienna	I told Bliss	CU-MARK	05549
Whitmore, Franklin G.		1899.04.05	SLC	AU.Vienna	Maybe I forgot	CU-MARK	05575
Whitmore, Franklin G.		1899.05.09	SLC	AU.Vienna	to expect a	CU-MARK	05589 fragment
Whitmore, Franklin G.		1899.06.07	SLC per OLC	EN.Broadstairs	As Mr Clemens	CU-MARK	05636
Whitmore, Franklin G.		1899.10.01	SLC	EN.London	Five years ago	MeWC	08915
Whitmore, Franklin G.		1899.10.26	SLC	EN.London	Such money as	CtHMTH	05695
Whitmore, Franklin G.		1899.11.18	SLC	EN.London	I enclose a	CU-MARK	05711
Whitmore, Franklin G.		1899.12.21	SLC	EN.London	Tell me definitely	CtY(tr)	05721 SLC tr with OLC note
Whitmore, Franklin G.		1899.12.22	SLC	EN.London	*	CU-MARK	10108 envelope only
Whitmore, Franklin G.		1900.03.30	SLC	EN.London	I left the	CU-MARK	05785
Whitmore, Franklin G. & Baird, Loni	ca	1900.04.08	SLC & OLC	EN.London	Regarding the main	CU-MARK	08719
Whitmore, Franklin G.		1900.06.04	SLC	EN.London	Have written Bliss	CU-MARK	05812
Whitmore, Franklin G.		1900.06.14	SLC	EN.London	Yours of the	CU-MARK	05824
Whitmore, Franklin G.		1900.06.27	SLC	EN.London	Mrs. Clemens &	CU-MARK	05826
Whitmore, Franklin G.		1900.08.17	SLC	EN.London	You may go	CtHMTH	09837
Whitmore, Franklin G.	pm	1900.10.22	SLC	NY.New York	I expect to	CU-MARK	05883
Whitmore, Franklin G.		1900.11.13	SLC	NY.New York	I cannot persuade	CtHMTH	09838
Whitmore, Franklin G.		1901.01.**	SLC	NY.New York	Mrs. Clemens has	ViU(tr)	05954
Whitmore, Franklin G.	pm	1901.01.25	SLC	NY.New York	*	CU-MARK	10144 envelope only
Whitmore, Franklin G.		1901.03.01	SLC	NY.New York	Please keep a	CU-MARK	06013

Whitmore, Franklin G.		1901.03.08	SLC	NY.New York	How is this	CU-MARK	06015
Whitmore, Franklin G.		1901.05.02	OLC	NY.New York	Thank you so	CtHMTH	06050
Whitmore, Franklin G.		1901.05.06	OLC	NY.New York	I shall be	CU-MARK	06053
Whitmore, Franklin G.		1901.05.09	OLC	NY.New York	I find that	CtHMTH	06055
Whitmore, Franklin G.		1901.05.20	SLC	NY.New York	I enclose check	CU-MARK	06059 typed
Whitmore, Franklin G.		1901.05.21	SLC	NY.New York	Pratt & Whitney	CU-MARK	06061
Whitmore, Franklin G.		1901.06.18	SLC	NY.New York	Enclosed is the	CU-MARK	06074
Whitmore, Franklin G.		1901.07.17	OLC	NY.Saranac Lake	Mr Clemens asks	CU-MARK	06090
Whitmore, Franklin G.		1901.08.27	SLC	NY.Saranac Lake	Whenever you have	CU-MARK	06122
Whitmore, Franklin G.		1901.08.27	SLC	NY.Saranac Lake	You can do	CU-MARK	06123
Whitmore, Franklin G.		1901.09.08	SLC	NY.Saranac Lake	Pay no further	CU-MARK	06133
Whitmore, Franklin G.		1901.09.29	SLC	NY.New York	Collect the within	CtHMTH	06147
Whitmore, Franklin G.		1901.10.04	SLC	NY.Riverdale	Yes, it is	CU-MARK	06152
Whitmore, Franklin G.		1901.10.15	SLC	NY.Riverdale	Our Hartford house	CtHi	06159
Whitmore, Franklin G.		1901.10.25	OLC	NY.Riverdale	Mr Clemens asks	CU-MARK	06166
Whitmore, Franklin G.		1901.10.26	SLC	NY.Riverdale	Don't do it	CtHMTH	06167 on Whitmore Oct 25
Whitmore, Franklin G.	pm	1901.10.28	SLC	NY.New York	*	CU-MARK	10143 envelope only
Whitmore, Franklin G.		1901.12.07	SLC	NY.New York	The madam won't	CU-MARK	06184
Whitmore, Franklin G.		1902.01.03	OLC	NY.Riverdale	Mr Clemens asks	CU-MARK	06219
Whitmore, Franklin G.		1902.01.25	SLC	NY.New York	All right, pay	CU-MARK	06253 typed
Whitmore, Franklin G.		1902.01.29	SLC	NY.Riverdale	Please meet me	CU-MARK	06257
Whitmore, Franklin G.		1902.01.30	OLC	NY.Riverdale	Mr Clemens asks	CU-MARK	06259
Whitmore, Franklin G.		1902.02.02	SLC	NY.Riverdale	Did you pay	CU-MARK	06265
Whitmore, Franklin G.		1902.02.09	OLC	NY.Riverdale	Mr Edward T.	CU-MARK	06273
Whitmore, Franklin G.		1902.02.27	SLC	NY.Riverdale	What did you	CU-MARK	06286
Whitmore, Franklin G.	&	1902.03.02 1902.03.03	SLC	NY.Riverdale	I am glad	CU-MARK	06290

ADDRESSEE		DATE	WRITER	PLACE	CUE	SOURCE	NUMBER/NOTES
Whitmore, Franklin G.		1902.03.04	OLC	NY.Riverdale	Mr Clemens asks	CU-MARK	06291
Whitmore, Franklin G.	pm	1902.03.05	SLC	NY.Riverdale	*	CtHMTH	09839 envelope only
Whitmore, Franklin G.		1902.05.19	SLC	NY.Riverdale	You are surprised	CtHMTH	06341 fragment
Whitmore, Franklin G.	pm	1902.05.21	SLC	NY.New York	*	CU-MARK	10148 envelope only
Whitmore, Franklin G.		1902.05.23	SLC	NY.Riverdale	Although "ridiculous" is	CU-MARK	06345
Whitmore, Franklin G.		1902.06.10	SLC	NY.Riverdale	Mrs. Clemens, I	CU-MARK	06359
Whitmore, Franklin G.		1902.06.14	SLC & OLC	NY.Riverdale	Indeed it looks	CU-MARK	06366
Whitmore, Franklin G.		1902.06.21	OLC	NY.Riverdale	I enclose you	CU-MARK	06373
Whitmore, Franklin G.		1902.07.03	SLC	ME.York Harbor	I've not cards	CtHMTH	06384
Whitmore, Franklin G.		1902.07.03	SLC	ME.York Harbor	I am very	CU-MARK	06383
Whitmore, Franklin G.		1902.07.28	OLC	ME.York Harbor	I enclose a	CU-MARK	06389
Whitmore, Franklin G.		1902.07.30	SLC	ME.York Harbor	The proposition to	CtHMTH	06394
Whitmore, Franklin G.		1902.08.02	SLC	ME.York Harbor	I have just	CtHMTH	09840
Whitmore, Franklin G.		1902.08.06	SLC	ME.York Harbor	The following shows	CU-MARK	06400 on Rogers Aug 5
Whitmore, Franklin G.		1902.08.21	SLC	ME.York Harbor	Mrs. Clemens was	CtHMTH	06409
Whitmore, Franklin G.		1902.08.30	SLC	ME.York Harbor	I enclose $100	CU-MARK	06422
Whitmore, Franklin G.		1902.09.26	SLC	ME.York Harbor	He offered me	CU-MARK	06445 on McVickar Sept 18
Whitmore, Franklin G.		1902.10.04	SLC	ME.York Harbor	Please send me	CU-MARK	06453
Whitmore, Franklin G.		1902.10.06	SLC	ME.York Harbor	If you could	CtHMTH	06455
Whitmore, Franklin G.		1902.10.08	SLC	ME.York Harbor	My recollection is	CU-MARK	06457
Whitmore, Franklin G.		1902.10.18	SLC	NY.Riverdale	Please look in	CU-MARK	06468
Whitmore, Franklin G.		1902.10.20	SLC	NY.New York	You may sell	CU-MARK	06470
Whitmore, Franklin G.		1902.10.21	SLC	NY.New York	If it is	CtHMTH	09841
Whitmore, Franklin G.		1902.10.23	SLC	NY.Riverdale	What I want	CU-MARK	06473
Whitmore, Franklin G.		1902.10.31	SLC	NY.Riverdale	This is private	CU-MARK	06478

Whitmore, Franklin G.		1902.11.05	SLC per IVL	NY.Riverdale	I shall prefer	CU-MARK	06482
Whitmore, Franklin G.		1902.11.05	SLC	NY.Riverdale	P.S. I have	CU-MARK	06484 misdated Nov 6
Whitmore, Franklin G.		1902.11.09	SLC	NY.Riverdale	Mrs. Clemens has	CU-MARK	06485
Whitmore, Franklin G.		1902.11.12	SLC per IVL	NY.Riverdale	Mr. Clemens wishes	CU-MARK	06486
Whitmore, Franklin G.		1902.11.24	SLC per IVL	NY.Riverdale	Mr. Clemens asks	CU-MARK	06493
Whitmore, Franklin G.		1902.11.24	SLC	NY.Riverdale	As soon as	CtHMTH	06492
Whitmore, Franklin G.		1902.12.09	SLC per IVL	NY.Riverdale	Mr. Clemens bids	CU-MARK	06507
Whitmore, Franklin G.		1903.01.01	SLC per IVL	NY.Riverdale	Your note came	CU-MARK	06545
Whitmore, Franklin G.		1903.01.05	SLC per IVL	NY.Riverdale	Mr. Clemens wishes	CU-MARK	06550
Whitmore, Franklin G.		1903.01.13	SLC per IVL	NY.Riverdale	Mr. Clemens tells	CU-MARK	06558
Whitmore, Franklin G.		1903.01.16	SLC per IVL	NY.Riverdale	Mr. Clemens comes	CU-MARK	06565
Whitmore, Franklin G.		1903.03.07	SLC per IVL	NY.Riverdale	Mr. Clemens wishes	CU-MARK	06592
Whitmore, Franklin G.		1903.03.09	SLC per IVL	NY.Riverdale	Mr. Clemens wishes	CU-MARK	06594
Whitmore, Franklin G.		1903.03.10	SLC per IVL	NY.Riverdale	Mr. Clemens bids	CU-MARK	06595
Whitmore, Franklin G.		1903.03.27	SLC per IVL	NY.Riverdale	Mr. Clemens wishes	CU-MARK	06609
Whitmore, Franklin G.		1903.04.05	SLC	NY.Riverdale	Our common everyday	CtHMTH	06615
Whitmore, Franklin G.	pm	1903.04.05	SLC	NY.Riverdale	*	CU-MARK	10142 envelope only
Whitmore, Franklin G.		1903.04.20	OLC per IVL	NY.Riverdale	Mrs Clemens has	CtHMTH	06628
Whitmore, Franklin G.		1903.04.24	SLC per IVL	NY.Riverdale	Mr. Clemens wishes	CU-MARK	06630
Whitmore, Franklin G.		1903.04.28	SLC	NY.Riverdale	Good. If Witherbee	CtHMTH	06638

ADDRESSEE		DATE	WRITER	PLACE	CUE	SOURCE	NUMBER/NOTES
Whitmore, Franklin G.	pm	1903.04.29	SLC	NY.New York	*	CtHMTH	09842 envelope only
Whitmore, Franklin G.	ca	1903.05.**	OLC	NY.Riverdale	I send you	CtHMTH	06543
Whitmore, Franklin G.		1903.05.02	SLC per IVL	NY.Riverdale	Mr. Clemens wishes	CU-MARK	06643
Whitmore, Franklin G.		1903.05.06	SLC per IVL	NY.Riverdale	Mr. Clemens is	CU-MARK	06647
Whitmore, Franklin G.		1903.05.06	SLC per IVL	NY.Riverdale	Mr. Clemens wishes	CU-MARK	06648
Whitmore, Franklin G.		1903.05.06	SLC	NY.Riverdale	Mrs. Clemens left	CU-MARK	06646
Whitmore, Franklin G.		1903.05.07	SLC	NY.Riverdale	He doesn't understand	CtHMTH	06650
Whitmore, Franklin G.		1903.05.09	OLC per IVL	NY.Riverdale	Mrs. Clemens wishes	CtHMTH	06653
Whitmore, Franklin G.	&	1903.05.09 1903.05.10	OLC	NY.Riverdale	Your letters were	CtHMTH	06654
Whitmore, Franklin G.		1903.05.09	SLC	NY.Riverdale	You'll remember there's	CtHMTH	06652
Whitmore, Franklin G.	pm	1903.05.11	SLC & OLC	NY.Riverdale	In realizing that	CtHMTH	06642
Whitmore, Franklin G.		1903.05.13	SLC	NY.Riverdale	What in the	CU-MARK	06657
Whitmore, Franklin G.		1903.05.14	SLC	NY.Riverdale	Mr. Reeves asked	CU-MARK	06660
Whitmore, Franklin G.		1903.05.15	OLC	NY.Riverdale	I want to	CtHMTH	06662
Whitmore, Franklin G.		1903.05.18	SLC	MA.Fairhaven	P.S. You know	CU-MARK	06658
Whitmore, Franklin G.		1903.05.20	SLC per IVL	NY.Riverdale	Mrs. Clemens begs	CtHMTH	06665
Whitmore, Franklin G.		1903.05.21	OLC per IVL	NY.Riverdale	Mrs. Clemens wishes	CU-MARK	06666
Whitmore, Franklin G.		1903.05.23	SLC per IVL	NY.Riverdale	Mr. Clemens wishes	CtHMTH	06667
Whitmore, Franklin G.		1903.05.29	SLC per IVL	NY.Riverdale	Mr. Clemens wishes	CU-MARK	06668
Whitmore, Franklin G.		1903.05.29	SLC per IVL	NY.Riverdale	Mr. Clemens would	CU-MARK	06669
Whitmore, Franklin G.		1903.06.01	SLC per IVL	NY.Riverdale	I expect to	CU-MARK	06671
Whitmore, Franklin G.		1903.06.02	SLC per IVL	NY.Riverdale	Mr. Clemens wishes	CU-MARK	06672

Whitmore, Franklin G.		1903.06.15	SLC per IVL	NY.Riverdale	Mr. Clemens came	CU-MARK	06679
Whitmore, Franklin G.		1903.06.29	SLC per IVL	NY.Riverdale	Mrs. Clemens wants	CU-MARK	06685
Whitmore, Franklin G.		1903.07.14	SLC	NY.Elmira	Please give me	CU-MARK	06698
Whitmore, Franklin G.		1903.10.01	SLC	NY.Elmira	In this envelop	Mo2	08885
Whitmore, Franklin G.		1903.10.14	SLC	NY.New York	P.S. Moreover, that	CU-MARK	06741
Whitmore, Franklin G.	pm	1904.06.22	SLC	IT.Florence	For what you	CtHMTH	06879 form letter
Whitmore, Franklin G.		1904.09.10	SLC	NY.New York	Where is the	CtHMTH	06920
Whitmore, Franklin G.		1904.10.28	SLC	NY.New York	If I remember	CtHMTH	06939
Whitmore, Franklin G.		1904.11.11	SLC	NY.New York	Thank you ever	CtHMTH	06949
Whitmore, Franklin G. & Whitmore, Harriet E.		1908.01.01	SLC	NY.New York	Happy New Year	CtHMTH	07908 inscription
Whitmore, Franklin G.		1908.05.21	SLC	NY.New York	I am unspeakably	CU-MARK	08004 telegram
Whitmore, Franklin G.		1909.06.21	SLC	CT.Redding	Have you our	CtHMTH	08423
Whitmore, Harriet E.		****.**.**	OLC	Unknown	I wish I	CtHMTH	08966
Whitmore, Harriet E.		1878.02.21	OLC	CT.Hartford	Can you meet	CtHMTH	01532
Whitmore, Harriet E.		1880.09.13	SLC	NY.Elmira	Mrs. Clemens is	CU-MARK(ph)	01832
Whitmore, Harriet E.		1881.05.18	OLC	CT.Hartford	Will you and	CtHMTH	01955
Whitmore, Harriet E.		1881.12.17	OLC	CT.Hartford	I want so	CtHMTH	02118
Whitmore, Harriet E.		1882.07.**	SLC	CT.Hartford	With the friendliest	CtHMTH	09322 inscription
Whitmore, Harriet E.		1882.11.18	SLC	CT.Hartford	If the dog	CtHMTH	09324 inscription
Whitmore, Harriet E.		1883.07.16	OLC	NY.Elmira	I rec'd your	CtHMTH	02451
Whitmore, Harriet E.	ca	1885.**.**	JC	Unknown	Thank you very	CtHMTH	03494
Whitmore, Harriet E. & Whitmore, Franklin G.	bef	1885.04.18	OLC	CT.Hartford	Mrs. S.L. Clemens	CtHMTH	06176
Whitmore, Harriet E.		1888.12.26	CC	CT.Hartford	I do thank	CtHMTH	03807
Whitmore, Harriet E.		1888.12.28	OLC	CT.Hartford	I can not	CtHMTH	03809
Whitmore, Harriet E.		1889.02.14	OLC	CT.Hartford	Thank you so	CtHMTH	03863

ADDRESSEE		DATE	WRITER	PLACE	CUE	SOURCE	NUMBER/NOTES
Whitmore, Harriet E.	pm	1889.09.13	SC	NY.Elmira	Mamma has been	CtHMTH	03935
Whitmore, Harriet E.		1890.**.**	JC	Unknown	I am sorry	CtHMTH	03999
Whitmore, Harriet E.		1890.12.03	IVL	Unknown	I cannot tell	CtHMTH	10985
Whitmore, Harriet E.		1892.05.05	OLC	IT.Florence	Your exquisite Easter	CtHMTH	04287
Whitmore, Harriet E.		1893.01.05	OLC	IT.Florence	I thank you	CtHMTH	04322
Whitmore, Harriet E.		1893.05.12	SLC	NY.New York	I'll deliver the	CU-MARK	04403
Whitmore, Harriet E.		1893.06.02	OLC	IT.Florence	Thank you so	CtHMTH	04409
Whitmore, Harriet E.		1893.12.25	OLC	FR.Paris	A Merry Christmas	CtHMTH	04535
Whitmore, Harriet E.		1896.04.09	OLC	SH.Wardha	I have just	CtHMTH	05038
Whitmore, Harriet E.		1897.04.22	OLC	EN.London	The dainty little	CtHMTH	05205
Whitmore, Harriet E.		1900.09.23	OLC	EN.London	Thank you for	CtHMTH	05866
Whitmore, Harriet E.		1900.10.21	CC	NY.New York	We all thank	CtHMTH	05880
Whitmore, Harriet E.		1900.12.15	OLC	NY.New York	How glad I	CtHMTH	05934
Whitmore, Harriet E.		1900.12.24	SLC	NY.New York	It arrived last	CU-MARK	05939
Whitmore, Harriet E.		1901.01.13	SLC	NY.New York	I saw Mr.	CU-MARK	05965
Whitmore, Harriet E.		1901.01.21	SLC	NY.New York	No, the earlier	CU-MARK	05976
Whitmore, Harriet E.		1901.11.20	OLC	NY.Riverdale	I am sorry	CtHMTH	06172
Whitmore, Harriet E.		1902.05.27	OLC	NY.Riverdale	How I wish	CtHMTH	06348
Whitmore, Harriet E.		1902.06.02	OLC	NY.Riverdale	I am so	CtHMTH	06353
Whitmore, Harriet E.		1902.06.20	JC	NY.Riverdale	I have been	CtHMTH	06371
Whitmore, Harriet E.		1902.06.21	OLC	NY.Riverdale	How can I	CtHMTH	06374
Whitmore, Harriet E.		1902.06.30	OLC	NY.Riverdale	Indeed I was	CtHMTH	06381
Whitmore, Harriet E.		1902.09.08	CC	ME.York Harbor	My mother wants	CtHMTH	06429
Whitmore, Harriet E.		1902.12.10	CC	NY.Riverdale	I want to	CtHMTH	06509
Whitmore, Harriet E.		1903.06.16	SLC	NY.Riverdale	Livy says she	CtHMTH	06680
Whitmore, Harriet E.		1903.07.18	SLC	NY.Elmira	If I wished	CtY	06702
Whitmore, Harriet E.		1903.07.25	SLC	NY.Elmira	Yes, put it	CtHMTH	06710
Whitmore, Harriet E.		1903.09.**	OLC	NY.Elmira	For weeks I	CtHMTH	06542
Whitmore, Harriet E.		1903.10.14	OLC	NY.New York	Thank you for	CtHMTH	06742

Whitmore, Harriet E.		1904.03.08	SLC per IVL	IT.Florence	Mr. Clements wants	CtHMTH	06807
Whitmore, Harriet E.		1905.01.08	IVL	NY.New York	Your sweet and	CtHMTH	10951
Whitmore, Harriet E.		1905.02.06	IVL	NY.New York	This is just	CtHMTH	10986
Whitmore, Harriet E.		1905.02.09	IVL	NY.New York	Thank you so	CtHMTH	11113
Whitmore, Harriet E.		1906.06.25	SLC	NH.Dublin	This with the	CtHMTH	09252 inscription
Whitmore, Harriet E.		1906.10.09	SLC per IVL	NH.Dublin	Mr. Clemens wishes	CtHMTH	07540
Whitmore, Harriet E.		1906.10.21	SLC per IVL	NY.New York	Mr. Clemens is	CtHMTH	07551
Whitmore, Harriet E.		1906.11.12	IVL	NY.New York	The darling wonderful	CtHMTH	10962
Whitmore, Harriet E.		1907.02.07	SLC	NY.New York	But the truth	CtY	07645
Whitmore, Harriet E.		1907.02.25	SLC per IVL	NY.New York	Mr. Clemens asks	CtHMTH	07663
Whitmore, Harriet E.		1907.03.04	SLC per IVL	NY.New York	Mr. Clemens doesn't	CtHMTH	07616
Whitmore, Harriet E.		1907.03.11	SLC per IVL	NY.New York	I'm quite sure	CtHMTH	07674
Whitmore, Harriet E.		1907.04.10	SLC per IVL	NY.New York	Mr. Clemens is	CtHMTH	07690
Whitmore, Harriet E.		1907.06.27	IVL	NY.Tuxedo Park	Please forgive this	CtHMTH	10988
Whitmore, Harriet E. & Whitmore, Franklin G.		1908.01.01	SLC	NY.New York	Happy New Year	CtHMTH	07908 inscription
Whitmore, Harriet E.		1908.08.17	IVL	CT.Redding	I'd have written	CtHMTH	10969
Whitmore, Harriet E.		1908.12.25	SLC	CT.Redding	I thank you	CtHMTH	08187
Whitmore, Harriet E.		1909.12.28	SLC	CT.Redding	She is out	CtHMTH	08526
Whitmore, Will	ca	1891.**.**	SLC	Unknown	Will, Let's have	IC3	09709
Whitney, Caspar		1900.03.09	SLC	EN.London	The trouble is	ViU	05186
Whitney, Mr.		1900.04.20	SLC	EN.London	The trouble is	ViU	05795
Whitney, William D.		1875.01.16	SLC	CT.Hartford	It seems that	CtY	08610
Whitney, William D.		1881.10.24	SLC	CT.Hartford	I want to	NPV	02062

ADDRESSEE	DATE	WRITER	PLACE	CUE	SOURCE	NUMBER/NOTES
Whyte, Frederic	1907.01.29	SLC per IVL	NY.New York	Mr. Clemens asks	CU-MARK(dr)	07632 on Whyte Jan 18
Wickham, Gertrude Van	1886.10.06	SLC	CT.Hartford	Although I can't	OClWHi	03464
Wiggin, James H.	1899.10.12	SLC	EN.London	I am very	CU-MARK(tr)	05688
Wiggin, Kate D.	****.01.17 or ****.02.08	SLC	NY.New York	You are just	122:1936.01.29	02813
Wiggin, Kate D.	1905.12.09	SLC	NY.New York	To you, &	CtY	07246 form letter
Wiggin, Kate D.	1906.12.07	SLC	DC.Washington	I have telegraphed	NN-B	08271
Wiggin, Kate D.	1907.06.19	SLC per RWA	EN.London	Mr. Clemens has	CU-MARK(tr)	07755 RWA tr
Wiggin, Kate D.	1907.11.22	SLC	NY.New York	It was a	447:139	10430
Wiggin, Kate D.	1908.02.11	SLC	NY.New York	A cow is	Mo2	09382 inscription
Wilbrandt, Mrs. Adolf	1899.03.10	SLC	AU.Vienna	I am rested-up	CU-MARK(ph)	05559
Wilder, Daniel W.	1881.11.02	SLC	CT.Hartford	I have just	CU-MARK(tr)	02082
Wiley, Louis	****.12.30	SLC	Unknown	I thank you	NRU	02823
Willard, Frank	1901.06.18	SLC	NY.New York	with the kindest	105:1965.10.05	09502 inscription; other sources
Willard, J.F. & Gorky, Maxim	1906.04.13	SLC	NY.New York	Mr. Willard, the	CU-MARK	07429
Willard, Mary B.	1891.12.25	SLC	GE.Berlin	with the sincere	NN-B	10814 inscription
Willard, Mary B.	ca 1894.12.25	SLC	FR.Paris	Merry Christmas &	NN-B	10810 inscription
Willard, W.A.	****.11.21	SLC	CT.Hartford	I might be	178:1978.03	07914
Willey, Charles	1893.12.01	SLC	NY.New York	I have great	CU-MARK(ph)	04515
Williams, Byron	o/a 1905.09.27	SLC per IVL	NH.Dublin	Mr. Clemens directs	CU-MARK(dr)	07149 on Williams Sept 27
Williams, H.A.	o/a 1906.03.05	SLC per IVL	NY.New York	2 o'clock Thurs.	CU-MARK(dr)	07364
Williams, Samuel	1868.04.14	SLC	CA.San Francisco	Please see that	Mo2	02781
Williams, Thomas	1892.01.25	SLC	GE.Berlin	I am sincerely	CtHMTH	04267

Williams, Walter		1889.04.10	SLC	CT.Hartford	Unquestionably I would	NcGr2	10737
Williams, Walter		1894.03.04	SLC	NY.New York	I shouldn't be	MoU	04705
Williamson, Mildred		1900.10.05	SLC	EN.London	with the compliments	116:1974.11.21	09967 inscription
Wilson, Albert L.	o/a	1905.12.06	SLC per IVL	NY.New York	Thanks for the	CU-MARK(dr)	07231 on Wilson Dec 6
Wilson, Clara M.		1880.10.27	SLC	CT.Hartford	Confidential. You being	CSadM	01847
Wilson, Erasmus	o/a	1906.02.08	SLC per IVL	NY.New York	Mr. Clemens's movements	CU-MARK(dr)	07334 on Wilson Feb 8
Wilson, Francis & Matthews, Brander		****.**.**	SLC	Unknown	He did	185	04426 telegram
Wilson, Francis		1893.11.01	SLC	NY.New York	Salutation and Best	173:1940.11.06	09899 inscription
Wilson, Francis		1893.11.15	SLC	NY.New York	with kind regards	173:1940.11.06	09900 inscription
Wilson, Francis		1894.02.06	SLC	NY.New York	Unto Francis Wilson	ViU	09902 inscription
Wilson, Francis	bef	1908.10.13	SLC	CT.Redding	In "Anne of	307	08116
Wilson, George T.		1907.05.23	SLC	NY.Tuxedo Park	Can you cable	CU-MARK	07728 telegram
Wilson, George T.		1907.05.23	SLC	NY.Tuxedo Park	I shall be	CU-MARK	07727 telegram
Wilson, George T.		1907.05.25	SLC	NY.Tuxedo Park	Please cable Secretary	CU-MARK	07729 telegram
Wilson, Harry L.		1902.06.23	SLC	NY.Riverdale	Read it? Indeed	CU-BANC	06376
Wilson, Harry L.		1902.06.28	SLC	ME.York Harbor	Between you &	CU-BANC	06378
Wilson, James G.		1868.12.25	SLC	Unknown	L.T.--First day	107:1924.11.24	09449 inscription
Wilson, Mr.		1894.06.16	SLC	FR.Paris	Thank you heartily but	ODa2	11204
Wilson, Mrs.	ca to	1910.02.01 1910.03.30	CC	CT.Redding	Thank you for your very	ODa2	11192
Winchell, R.		1901.02.12	SLC	NY.New York	Consider Mr Irving's	CU-MARK(ph)	05992 inscription

ADDRESSEE	DATE	WRITER	PLACE	CUE	SOURCE	NUMBER/NOTES
Windeyer, William C.	1895.12.24	SLC	SH.Oceana	I enclose a note	AuSN-M	10661 Dec 24 to Robinson & Hutton enc
Windmuller, Louis	1905.12.12	SLC	NY.New York	I have known	WU(tr)	07248
Wingate, Charles F.	1870.03.31	SLC	NY.Buffalo	I am grateful	NN	00451
Wingate, Charles F.	1873.04.02	SLC	CT.Hartford	I shall be	Mo2	00896 date uncertain
Winslow, Helen M.	1900.12.03	SLC	NY.New York	It is most	MB	05926
Winslow, Helen M.	1901.12.04	SLC	NY.Riverdale	If I were	MB	06183
Winter, Elsie L.	*	*	*	*	*	10996 see Leslie, Elsie L.
Winter, William	1879.12.05	SLC	CT.Hartford	I have been	ViU	01734
Winter, William	1890.11.05	SLC	CT.Hartford	I thank you	CU-MARK(ph)	08604
Winter, William	1901.12.**	SLC	NY.Riverdale	with the affectionate	441:1923.10.11	10367 inscription
Winter, William	1901.12.08	SLC	NY.Riverdale	I have examined	CU-MARK(ph)	06185
Winter, William	1902.02.15	OLC	NY.Riverdale	I am entirely	Mo2	08876
Winter, William	1902.03.14	OLC	NY.Riverdale	Mr Clemens is	Mo2	08877
Winter, William	1903.04.28	SLC	NY.Riverdale	Yes, indeed, that	DFo	06639
Winter, William	pm 1904.07.20	SLC	MA.Lee	For what you	CtY	06892 form letter
Winter, William	1905.07.07	SLC	NH.Dublin	We are too	CCC	07078
Winterburn, Florence H.	1901.**.**	SLC	NY.New York	In my case	PGC	05946
Wirt Fountain Pen	1898.10.11	SLC	AU.Kaltenleut.	With a single	CU-MARK(ph)	05447 mislabeled Vienna
Wirth, Bettina	1898.06.19	SLC	AU.Kaltenleut.	I sent the	Mo2	08851
Wirth, Bettina	aft 1898.11.25	SLC	AU.Vienna	I have cramped	NN-B	05497
Wister, Owen	1902.01.09	SLC	NY.Riverdale	As regards that	CU-MARK	06239 typed form letter
Wolcott, Ella	1870.09.07	SLC	NY.Buffalo	It always hurts	CU-MARK	00503
Wolf, Simon	****.**.**	SLC	Unknown	There is no	DJHi	10469 inscription

Wolf, Simon		1899.09.15	SLC	SE.Sanna	I wish to	OCAJA	05677
Wolf, Simon		1899.11.08	SLC	EN.London	In your introduction	142:183f	05700
Wolfe, Mr.		1902.05.13	SLC	NY.Riverdale	After endorsing your	PP	06334
Wolff, Victor	ca	1877.01.01	SLC per FCH	CT.Hartford	I accept with	NN	10739
Wolf-Kane, Margaret		****.**.**	SLC	Unknown	with the kindest	406:1979.05.17	09985 inscription
Wolseley, Lord		1909.04.17	SLC	CT.Redding	It is long	Uk3	08384
Wood, Charles E.		1882.02.21	SLC	CT.Hartford	Twichell's tribe and	ViU	02161 typed
Wood, Charles E.		1882.04.03	SLC	CT.Hartford	I inclose the	ViU	02196 typed
Wood, Charles E.		1882.08.**	SLC	NY.Elmira	I'd like it	ViU	02243
Wood, Charles E.		1884.07.24	SLC	NY.Elmira	Oh, the devil	CU-MARK(ph)	01297
Wood, Charles E.		1900.03.21	SLC	EN.London	I greatly need	CU-BANC	05779
Wood, Charles E.		1901.02.23	SLC	NY.New York	I am glad	CU-BANC	06009 typed
Wood, Charles E.		1901.06.07	SLC	NY.New York	I am so	CU-MARK(ph)	06071 typed
Wood, Charles E.		1901.06.24	SLC	NY.Saranac Lake	Good--I shall	CU-MARK(ph)	06079
Wood, Charles E.		1902.01.29	SLC	NY.Riverdale	Think it over	CU-MARK(ph)	06258
Wood, Charles E.		1904.10.31	SLC	NY.New York	I have read	CU-BANC(tr)	06941
Wood, Elizabeth S.		1904.08.08	SLC	MA.Lee	For what you	105:1938.11.02	09274 form letter
Wood, J.M.G.		1886.09.08	SLC	NY.Elmira	I wish I	NBuU-PO	03453
Wood, Mr.		1890.08.03	SLC	NY.Tannersville	I and the	134:1923.10.30	04070
Wood, Mr.		1905.**.**	SLC	NY.New York	I am pretty	N2	06964
Wood, Mr.		1905.**.**	SLC	NY.New York	The afternoon seems	N2	06965
Wood, Mr.		1908.11.30	SLC	CT.Redding	The beautiful mantel	WU(ph)	08165
Wood, Mrs. James		1891.12.23	SLC	GE.Berlin	Thank you over	176:14	04262
Woodford, Stewart L.		1882.12.14	SLC	CT.Hartford	The Brunswick is	InU-Li	10835

ADDRESSEE	DATE	WRITER	PLACE	CUE	SOURCE	NUMBER/NOTES
Woodruff, W.N.	o/a 1884.11.20	SLC	Unknown	I knew that	CU-MARK(dr)	03028 on Waller to Woodruff Nov 20
Woods, Ruth	1909.02.04	SLC	CT.Redding	Thank you ever	WvU	08340
Woolf, S.J.	ca 1909.01.28	SLC per MLH	CT.Redding	X is not	CtHMTH(dr)	08333
Woolley, William P.	1881.01.**	SLC	CT.Hartford	But you haven't	CU-MARK	09630 on Wooley bill ca Jan 1
Wright, Arthur H.	o/a 1888.11.05	SLC	CT.Hartford	But you quite	CU-MARK	03828 on Wright Nov 5
Wright, Charles	****.**.**	SLC	Unknown	P.S. If you	CU-MARK(tr)	02837
Wright, Howard	****.05.20	SLC	Unknown	150 cigars and	205:1935.11.19	09815
Wright, Jean W.	aft 1902.05.27	OLC	NY.Riverdale	As you are	CU-MARK	10705
Wright, Livingston	1903.04.17	SLC	NY.Riverdale	The MS., with	ODa2	06623
Wright, Mr.	1902.01.14	SLC per JC	NY.Riverdale	I forgot to	CtY(ph)	06246
Wright, William	1864.07.15	SLC	CA.San Francisco	Tell Dawson to	CU-BANC	00084
Wright, William	1864.09.17	SLC	CA.San Francisco	If you will	CU-MARK(ph)	00086
Wright, William	bet 1870.01.01 & 1870.01.05	SLC	NY.Elmira	Old Dan, my	CU-BANC	00399 on envelope
Wright, William	1875.03.24	SLC	CT.Hartford	I have just	CU-BANC	01215
Wright, William	1875.03.29 & 1875.04.04	SLC	CT.Hartford	publishing risks--Can't	CU-BANC	01218 fragment
Wright, William	1875.03.29	SLC	CT.Hartford	You have a	CU-BANC(tr)	01217 telegram
Wright, William	1875.04.29	SLC	CT.Hartford	Yours just rec'd	CU-MARK(tr)	01228
Wright, William	1875.05.01	SLC	CT.Hartford	Your second just	NvHi(tr)	01273
Wright, William	pm 1875.08.31	SLC	RI.Newport	We return home	CU-MARK	01258 deposit
Wright, William	1876.01.05	SLC	CT.Hartford	Yours of Nov.	NvHi(tr)	01296
Wright, William	1876.01.28	SLC	CT.Hartford	I have been	NvHi(ph)	01304
Wright, William	1876.02.08	SLC	CT.Hartford	I enclosed $1500	NvHi(tr)	01305

Wright, William	1876.03.01 or 1876.03.07	SLC	CT.Hartford	I supposed that	CU-MARK(ph)	01312
Wright, William	1876.03.26	SLC	CT.Hartford	I wasn't scolding	CU-MARK(ph)	01318
Wright, William	1876.11.29	SLC	CT.Hartford	Please sell that	NvHi(tr)	02466
Wright, William	1880.01.01	SLC	CT.Hartford	I send you	200:1880.01.16	09531 spurious, see Mar 6 to Clark
Wyndham, Edward	1874.02.02	SLC	CT.Hartford	from his friend	323:1981	09293 inscription
Yale Immortals	1888.06.26	SLC	NY.New York	To be made	117:1888.06.29	03725
Yale Phi Beta Kappa	1906.03.03	SLC per IVL	NY.New York	I thank you	CtY	11057
Yost, Mrs. Robert M.	1887.01.14	SLC	CT.Hartford	I enclose with	NN-B	02654
Young, John R.	****.**.**	SLC	NY.New York	Come here any	NjMo	10974
Young, John R.	1867.11.22	SLC	DC.Washington	I called at	DLC	00157
Young, John R.	1867.11.24	SLC	DC.Washington	Out of a	DLC	00159
Young, John R.	1867.11.25	SLC	DC.Washington	I have neglected	DLC	00161
Young, John R.	1867.12.01	SLC	DC.Washington	This is to	DLC	00164
Young, John R.	1867.12.04	SLC	DC.Washington	I thought Swinton	DLC	00168
Young, John R.	1868.02.01	SLC	DC.Washington	I smouched those	DLC	00188
Young, John R.	1869.03.07 or 1869.03.08	SLC	CT.Hartford	This is a	DLC	00270
Young, John R.	1874.01.06	SLC	EN.London	I have just	DLC	01016
Young, John R.	1881.02.21	SLC	CT.Hartford	It was mighty	DLC	01913
Young, John R.	1881.04.08	SLC	CT.Hartford	The General was	DLC(tr)	02412
Young, John R.	1881.04.29	SLC	CT.Hartford	Thanks for the	DLC	01941
Young, John R.	1882.01.09	SLC	CT.Hartford	The prospective pleasure	DLC	02146
Young, John R.	1882.02.03	SLC	CT.Hartford	Your beautiful volumes	DLC	02156
Young, John R.	1882.03.06	SLC	CT.Hartford	I am writing	DLC	02170 telegram
Young, John R.	1882.03.13	SLC	CT.Hartford	I was exceedingly	DLC	02171 typed

ADDRESSEE	DATE	WRITER	PLACE	CUE	SOURCE	NUMBER/NOTES
Young, John R.	1882.03.20	SLC	CT.Hartford	All right: you	DLC	02175 typed
Young, John R.	1882.04.25	SLC	AR.Arkansas City	I send a	DLC	02207 telegram
Young, John R.	1885.12.07	SLC	CT.Hartford	The main thing that	ODa2	11207
Young, John R.	1887.01.20	SLC	CT.Hartford	I am just	DLC	03514
Young, John R.	1890.07.13	SLC	NY.New York	I am ever	DLC	04063
Young, John R.	1890.07.14	SLC	NY.New York	Reconsider! Can't you	DLC	09116
Young, John R.	1890.08.06	SLC	NY.Tannersville	You sent it	DLC	04073
Young, John R.	1890.10.08	SLC	NY.New York	I shall be	DLC	04099 telegram
Young, John R.	1891.02.07	SLC	CT.Hartford	It is a	DLC	11160
Young, Mary D.	1901.09.29	SLC	NY.New York	I explained to	DLC	06148

Appendixes

Abbreviations

A&L -- Arts and Letters
ABP -- Paine, Albert B.
AF -- Africa
Africa -- AF
aft -- after
Apr -- April
AR -- Arkansas
Arkansas -- AR
AS -- Australia
Ashcroft, Ralph W. -- RWA
asterisk (*) -- unknown element
AU -- Austria
Aug -- August
Australia -- AS
Austria -- AU
Barr. -- Barrington
BE -- Bermuda
bef -- before
Bermuda -- BE
bet -- between
CA -- California
ca -- circa
Cable, George W. -- GWC
California -- CA
Canada -- CN
CC -- Clemens, Clara L.
CEP -- Perkins, Charles E.
Chaun. -- Chauncey
Ches. -- Chester
Clemens, Clara L. -- CC
Clemens, Jean (Jane L.) -- JC
Clemens, Olivia L. -- OLC
Clemens, Samuel L. -- SLC
Clemens, Susy (Olivia S.) -- SC
CLW -- Webster, Charles L.
CN -- Canada
Co. -- Company
Connecticut -- CT
Constantinop. -- Constantinople
CT -- Connecticut
CWS -- Stoddard, Charles W.
DC -- District of Columbia
Dec -- December
District of Columbia -- DC
dr -- draft
E# -- endorsement number
ed(s). -- editor(s)
Eliz. -- Elizabeth
EN -- England
enc. -- enclosed/enclosure
England -- EN
f -- facsimile
FAR -- unidentified amanuensis
FCH -- Hesse, Fanny C.
Feb -- February
FGW -- Whitmore, Franklin G.
FL -- Florida
Florida -- FL
FR -- France
France -- FR
GA -- Georgia
GE -- Germany
Georgia -- GA
Germany -- GE
GWC -- Cable, George W.
Hawaii -- HI
Hesse, Fanny C. -- FCH
HHR -- Rogers, Henry H.
HI -- Hawaii
Hist.Soc. -- Historical Society
Howden, Mary L. -- MLH
HU -- Hungary
Hungary -- HU
IA -- Iowa
II -- India
IL -- Illinois
Illinois -- IL
IN -- Indiana
India -- II
Indiana -- IN
Intell. -- Intelligencer

Iowa -- IA
IR -- Ireland
Ireland -- IR
IT -- Italy
Italy -- IT
IVL -- Lyon, Isabel V.
J. -- Journal
Jan -- January
JC -- Clemens, Jean (Jane L.)
JR -- Redpath, James
Kaltenleut. -- Kaltenleutgeben
Kentucky -- KY
Kingwilliams. -- Kingwilliamstown
KY -- Kentucky
LA -- Louisiana
Louisiana -- LA
Lyon, Isabel V. -- IVL
MA -- Massachusetts
Maine -- ME
Mar -- March
Maryland -- MD
Massachusetts -- MA
Mauritius -- MU
MC -- Monaco
MD -- Maryland
ME -- Maine
MI -- Michigan
Michigan -- MI
Minnesota -- MN
Missouri -- MO
MLH -- Howden, Mary L.
MN -- Minnesota
MO -- Missouri
Monaco -- MC
Montana -- MT
MT -- Montana
MU -- Mauritius
N. -- North
n.d. -- no date
Nevada -- NV
New Hampshire -- NH
New Jersey -- NJ
New York -- NY
New Zealand -- NZ
NH -- New Hampshire
NJ -- New Jersey
Nov -- November
NV -- Nevada
NY -- New York
NZ -- New Zealand
o/a -- on or after
o/b -- on or before
Oct -- October
OH -- Ohio
Ohio -- OH
OLC -- Clemens, Olivia L.
PA -- Pennsylvania
Paine, Albert B. -- ABP
Pennsylvania -- PA
Perkins, Charles E. -- CEP
ph -- photocopy
Phono. -- Phonograph
Pietermaritz. -- Pietermaritzburg
pm -- postmarked
PO -- Portugal
Port-de-Gros. -- Port-de-Groslee
Portugal -- PO
Pub. -- Publishing
Redpath, James -- JR
Rhode Island -- RI
RI -- Rhode Island
Rogers, Henry H. -- HHR
RU -- Russia
Russia -- RU
RWA -- Ashcroft, Ralph W.
SC -- Clemens, Susy (Olivia S.)
Scotland -- SK
SCT -- Thompson, Samuel C.
SE -- Sweden
Sept -- September
SH -- ship
SK -- Scotland
SLC -- Clemens, Samuel L.
SP -- Spain
Sp. -- Springs
Spain -- SP
Sta. -- Station
Stoddard, Charles W. -- CWS
SW -- Switzerland
Sweden -- SE
Switzerland -- SW
SY -- Syria
Syria -- SY
Tel. -- Telegraph
Tennessee -- TN
Terr.Ent. -- Territorial Enterprise
Thompson, Samuel C. -- SCT
TN -- Tennessee
tr -- transcript
TU -- Turkey
Turkey -- TU
VA -- Virginia
Vermont -- VT
Virginia -- VA
VT -- Vermont
WA -- Washington
Washington -- WA
Webster, Charles L. -- CLW
West Virginia -- WV
Whitmore, Franklin G. -- FGW
WI -- Wisconsin
Wilh. -- Wilhelm
Wisconsin -- WI
WV -- West Virginia

Cities and Ships

Adams -- MA
Adelaide -- AS
Agra -- II
Aix-les-Bains -- FR
Albany -- NY
Allentown -- PA
Allerheiligen -- GE
Amenia -- NY
Ampersand -- NY
Ann Arbor -- MI
Arkansas City -- AR
Arles -- FR
Ashford -- CT
Auburn -- NY
Auckland -- NZ
Aurora -- NV
Azores -- PO
Babylon -- NY
Baden -- AU
Baden Baden -- GE
Bad-Nauheim -- GE
Ballarat -- AS
Baltimore -- MD
Batavia -- IL
Batavia -- SH
Baton Rouge -- SH
Bayreuth -- GE
Beirut -- SY
Belfast -- IR
Benares -- II
Bennington -- VT
Berlin -- GE
Bethlehem -- PA
Bloemfontein -- AF
Bombay -- II
Boston -- MA
Branchville -- CT
Branford -- CT
Bremen -- GE
Broadstairs -- EN
Brockton -- MA
Bronx -- NY
Brooklyn -- NY
Bryn Mawr -- PA
Budapest -- HU
Buffalo -- NY
Cadenabbia -- IT
Cadiz -- SP
Cagliari -- IT
Cairo -- IL
Calais -- FR
Calcutta -- II
Cambridge -- MA
Cambridge -- NY
Canandaigua -- NY
Capetown -- AF
Carson City -- NV
Chambery -- FR
Champaign -- IL
Chicago -- IL
Christchurch -- NZ
Cincinnati -- OH
City of Ches. -- SH
Cleveland -- OH
Clinton -- MA
Coburn's Sta. -- NV
Columbus -- OH
Como -- IT
Constantinop. -- TU
Cradock -- AF
Cronenberg -- GE
Crookston -- MN
Curepipe -- MU
Cuxhaven -- GE
Danville -- IL
Darjeeling -- II
Davenport -- IA
Dayton -- OH
Deal -- NJ
Detroit -- MI
Dublin -- NH
Durban -- AF
East London -- AF
East Windsor -- CT
Edinburgh -- SK
El Paso -- IL
Elmira -- NY
Erie -- PA
Esmeralda -- NV
Etretat -- FR
Fairhaven -- MA
Florence -- IT
Fluelen -- SW
Fontainebleau -- FR
Fort Erie -- CN
Fort Monroe -- VA
Fort Plain -- NY
Fort Wayne -- IN
Frankfurt -- GE
Franklin -- PA
Franzensbad -- GE
Fredonia -- NY
Galena -- IL
Galesburg -- IL
Geneva -- NY
Geneva -- SW
Genoa -- IT
Gibralter -- SP
Gloucester -- MA
Gold Dust -- SH
Grand Rapids -- MI
Great Barr. -- MA
Great Neck -- NY
Greenwich -- CT
Guildford -- EN
Hamburg -- GE
Hamilton -- BE
Hannibal -- MO
Hannibal City -- SH
Harrisburg -- PA
Hartford -- CT
Havel -- SH
Haverhill -- MA
Heidelberg -- GE
Helena -- MT
Henry Chaun. -- SH
Hindhead -- EN
Holsatia -- SH
Holyoke -- MA
Homer -- NY
Honolulu -- HI
Hornellsville -- NY
Ilsenburg -- GE
Indianapolis -- IN
Interlaken -- SW

Ischl -- AU
Jacksonville -- IL
Jaipur -- II
Janesville -- WI
Jerusalem -- SY
Johannesburg -- AF
Kaiser Wilh. -- SH
Kaltenleut. -- AU
Kanawha -- SH
Kandersteg -- SW
Katonah -- NY
Keokuk -- IA
Kingwilliams. -- AF
Kittanning -- PA
Krankenheil -- AU
La Bourboule -- FR
La Voulte -- FR
Lafayette -- IN
Lansing -- MI
Lausanne -- SW
Lawrence -- NY
Lee -- MA
Leipzig -- GE
Leukerbad -- SW
Liverpool -- EN
Lockport -- NY
Logansport -- IN
London -- EN
Lowell -- MA
Lucerne -- SW
Mackinac -- MI
Madison -- NJ
Madison -- WI

Mararva -- SH
Marienbad -- GE
Marseilles -- FR
Maui -- HI
Melbourne -- AS
Memphis -- TN
Menton -- FR
Miami -- FL
Milford -- MA
Milton -- PA
Milwaukee -- WI
Minneapolis -- MN
Minneapolis -- SH
Minnehaha -- SH
Minnetonka -- SH
Montana -- SH
Montclair -- NJ
Monte Carlo -- MC
Montreal -- CN
Mt. McGregor -- NY
Munich -- GE
Muskegon -- MI
Napier -- NZ
Naples -- IT
New Boston -- CT
New Haven -- CT
New Orleans -- LA
New Saybrook -- CT
New York -- NY
New York -- SH
Newport -- RI
Nimes -- FR
Norfolk -- CT

Norman -- SH
Norwalk -- OH
Norwich -- NY
Oceana -- SH
Omaru -- NZ
Orange -- NJ
Ottawa -- CN
Ottawa -- IL
Ouchy -- SW
Oxford -- EN
Palm Beach -- FL
Palmerston N. -- NZ
Paris -- FR
Paris -- IL
Paris -- KY
Paris -- SH
Pawtucket -- RI
Philadelphia -- PA
Pietermaritz. -- AF
Pittsburgh -- PA
Port Eliz. -- AF
Port-de-Gros. -- SW
Portland -- ME
Postdampfers -- SH
Pretoria -- AF
Pretoria -- SH
Princeton -- NJ
Providence -- RI
Quaker City -- SH
Quebec -- CN
Queenstown -- AF
Quincy -- IL
Ravenna -- OH

Redding -- CT
Rhone River -- SW
Riverdale -- NY
Rochester -- NY
Rockford -- IL
Rome -- IT
Rouen -- FR
Salem -- OH
Salisbury -- EN
San Francisco -- CA
Sanna -- SE
Saranac Lake -- NY
Savannah -- GA
Scotia -- SH
Smyrniote -- SH
South Bend -- IN
Southampton -- EN
Spokane -- WA
Springfield -- MA
St. Augustine -- FL
St. Louis -- MO
St. Niklaus -- SW
St. Paul -- MN
Steamboat Sp. -- NV
Steubenville -- OH
Sydney -- AS
Syracuse -- NY
Tannersville -- NY
Tecumseh -- MI
Timaru -- NZ
Titusville -- PA
Toledo -- OH
Toronto -- CN

Trent -- AU
Troy -- NY
Tuscola -- IL
Tuxedo Park -- NY
Utica -- NY
Vancouver -- CN
Venice -- IT
Vernon -- CT
Victoria -- CN
Vienna -- AU
Virginia City -- NV
Wardha -- SH
Warrimoo -- SH
Washington -- DC
Webster -- MA
Weggis -- SW
Wellington -- NZ
West Point -- NY
Weybridge -- EN
Wheeling -- WV
Wiesbaden -- GE
Wilkes-Barre -- PA
Willesden -- EN
Windermere -- EN
Wooster -- OH
Worcester -- MA
Yalta -- RU
York -- EN
York Harbor -- ME

Source Names

Black (Robert K.) catalogs -- 179
Blumenfeld, R.D. In the Days of Bicycles & Bustles. 1930. -- 181
Bodleian Library, Oxford University, Oxford, United Kingdom -- UkOxU
Bodley Book Shop catalogs -- 182
Bodmeriana Library (Bibliothek Bodmeriana), Geneva, Switzerland -- SzG2
Bok, Edward W. Americanization of Edward Bok. 1922. -- 184
Bok, Edward W. Twice Thirty. 1925. -- 183
Bolton, Sarah K. Famous American Authors. 1940. -- 185
Bookman, The (London) -- 187
Boston Athenaeum, Boston, Mass. 02108 -- MBAt
Boston College, Chestnut Hill, Mass. 02167 -- MChB
Boston Daily Advertiser -- 189
Boston Evening Journal -- 190
Boston Evening Transcript -- 191
Boston Herald -- 104
Boston Public Library and Eastern Massachusetts Regional Public Library System, Boston, Mass. 02117 -- MB
Bowdoin College, Brunswick, Me. 04011 -- MeB
Bradford (Penn.) Reporter -- 192
Bridgeport Public Library, Bridgeport, Conn. 06603 -- CtB
Brigham Young University, Provo, Utah 84601 -- UPB
British Library, London, WC1B 3DG, United Kingdom -- Uk
British Library of Political and Economic Science, London, United Kingdom -- UkL2
Broadley, A.M. Chats on Autographs. 1910. -- 193
Brooklyn Daily Eagle -- 194
Brotherton Library, University of Leeds, Leeds, United Kingdom -- UkLe2
Brown, John Jr. and Forrest, D.W. Letters of Dr. John Brown. 1907. -- 195
Brown, Picton and Hornby Libraries, Liverpool, United Kingdom -- UkLi2
Brown University, John Hay Library of Rare Books and Special Collections, Providence, R.I. 02912 -- RPB-JH
Buffalo Express -- 196
Buffalo, State University of New York at. Poetry Library, Buffalo, N.Y. 14203 -- NBuU-PO
Buffalo and Erie County Historical Society, Buffalo, N.Y. 14216 -- NBuHi
Buffalo and Erie County Public Library, Buffalo, N.Y. 14203 -- NBu
Burdette, Clara B. Robert J. Burdette: His Message. 1922. -- 197
Calaveras County Museum & Archives Library, San Andreas, Calif. 95249 -- CSadM
California Book Auction Company catalogs -- 198
Cape Ann Historical Association, 27 Pleasant Street, Gloucester, Mass. 01930 -- MGlHi
Carnegie, Andrew. Autobiography of Andrew Carnegie. 1920. -- 188
Carnegie Book Shop catalogs -- 199
Carson Appeal (Carson City, Nev.) -- 200
Carson City (Nev.) Daily Independent -- 201
Carter, M.H. Cat Stories Retold from St. Nicholas. 1914. -- 202
Case Western Reserve University, Cleveland, Ohio 44106 -- OClW
Cat Stories Retold from St. Nicholas. Carter, M.H. 1914. -- 202
Central Michigan University, Mount Pleasant, Mich. 48858 -- MiMtpT
Central State Archive of Literature and Art, Moscow, Soviet Union -- RuM2
Chapin, Adele. Their Trackless Way. 1931. -- 203
Chapin Library, Williams College, Williamstown, Mass. 01267 -- MWiW-C
Chats on Autographs. Broadley, A.M. 1910. -- 193
Chattanooga (Tenn.) Republican -- 204
Chatto & Windus Archive, see University of Reading -- Uk4
Cheiro's Memoirs. Hamon, Louis. 1912. -- 244
Chemung County Historical Society, Elmira, N.Y. 14901 -- NElmHi
Chicago Book Auction catalogs -- 205
Chicago Herald -- 206
Chicago Public Library, Chicago, Ill. 60602 -- IC
Chicago Tribune -- 207
Childhood's Appeal (Boston) -- 208
Christian Union (New York) -- 209
Christie, Manson & Woods catalogs -- 210
Chubb, Edwin W. Stories of Authors: British and American. 1926. -- 211
Cincinnati Historical Society, Cincinnati, Ohio 45202 -- OCHP
Cincinnati and Hamilton County, Public Library of. Cincinnati, Ohio 45202 -- OC
City Book Auction catalogs -- 212
Claremont Colleges (Honnold Library), Claremont, Calif. 91711 -- CCC
Clark University, Worcester, Mass. 01610 -- MWC
Clark (William Andrews) Memorial Library, University of California, Los Angeles, Calif. 90024 -- CLU-C
Clemens, Clara. My Father Mark Twain. 1931. -- 293
Clemens, Clara. My Husband Gabrilowitsch. 1938. -- 294
Clemens, Cyril. Mark Twain: The Letter Writer. 1932. -- 297
Clemens, Will M. Mark Twain: His Life and Work. 1892. -- 296
Cohasco Inc. catalogs -- 213
Colby College, Waterville, Me. 04901 -- MeWC
Colfax Clipper (Iowa) -- 214
Colgate University, Hamilton, N.Y. 13346 -- NHC
Collecting Autographs and Manuscripts. Hamilton, Charles. 1961. -- 108
College of William and Mary, Williamsburg, Va. 23185 -- ViW
Columbia University, New York, N.Y. 10032 -- NNC
Coming Out, A Letter to a Rosebud. n.d. -- 216
Commercial Appeal (Memphis) -- 100
Concord Free Public Library, Concord, Mass. 01742 -- MCo
Congress, United States Library of. Washington, D.C. 20540 -- DLC
Connecticut Historical Society, Hartford, Conn. 06105 -- CtHi
Connecticut State Library, Hartford, Conn. 06115 -- Ct

Copley Newspapers Incorporated, James S. Copley Library, La Jolla, Calif. 92037 -- CLjC
Cornell University, Ithaca, N.Y. 14850 -- NIC
Cortissoz, Royal. Life of Whitelaw Reid. 1921. -- 217
Cosmos Club, Washington, D.C. 20008 -- DCos
Critic, The (New York) -- 219
Daniel Frohman Presents. Frohman, Daniel. 1935. -- 235
Dartmouth College, Hanover, N.H. 03755 -- NhD
Darwin R. Barker Library Association, Fredonia, N.Y. 14063 -- NFred
Davis, Sam. Short Stories. 1886. -- 125
Dawson's Book Shop catalogs -- 120
De Sormo, Maitland C. Summers on the Saranac. 1982. -- 221
Detroit Public Library, Detroit, Mich. 48202 -- MiD
Diary of a Book-Agent, The. Lindley, Elizabeth. 1911. -- 284
Dickinson College, Carlisle, Pa. 17013 -- PCarlD
Distinguished Authors. Sanborn, John W. 1920. -- 419
Doheny Collection, Saint John's Seminary, Camarillo, Calif. 93010 -- CCamarSJ
Duke University, Durham, N.C. 27706 -- NcD
Duschnes (Philip) catalogs -- 226
Duttons Inc. catalogs -- 227
Earlham College, Richmond, Ind. 47374 -- InRE
East Hampton Free Library, East Hampton, N.Y. 11937 -- NEh
East Sussex Record Office, Lewes, United Kingdom -- Uk2
Eau Claire Public Library, Eau Claire, Wis. 54701 -- WE
Eccentricities of Genius. Pond, James B. 1900. -- 408
Eighteenth Year Book 1919. Bibliophile Society. 1919. -- 228
Eighth Annual Dinner of the New York Press Club. 1881. -- 320
Ellsworth, William W. A Golden Age of Authors. 1919. -- 230
Elmira College, Elmira, N.Y. 14901 -- NElmC
Emory University, Atlanta, Ga. 30322 -- GEU
Enoch Pratt Free Library, Baltimore, Md. 21201 -- MdBE
Epoch: The Life of Steel MacKaye. MacKaye, Percy. 1927. -- 300
Fales Collection, New York University, New York, N.Y. 10012 -- NNU-F
Famous American Authors. Bolton, Sarah K. 1940. -- 185
Feldman, Lew David (House of El Dieff) catalogs -- 229
Finnish Literature Society (Suomalaisen Kirjallisuuden Seura), Helsinki, Finland -- FiH2
First Annual Meeting and Banquet of the Associated Pioneers of the Territorial Days of California. 1876. -- 170
First Decennium of the National Editorial Association. Herbert, B.B. 1896. -- 231
Folger Shakespeare Library, Washington, D.C. 20003 -- DFo
Forrest, D.W. and Brown, John Jr. Letters of Dr. John Brown. 1907. -- 195
Forum, The (New York) -- 232
Fourth Generation. Ross, Janet. 1912. -- 416
Frear, Walter F. Mark Twain and Hawaii. 1947. -- 124
Free Library of Philadelphia, Philadelphia, Pa. 19103 -- PP
Freeman (Samuel T.) & Co. catalogs -- 233
Freeman, William H. Press Club of Chicago: A History. 1894. -- 409
Friend, The (Honolulu) -- 234
Frohman, Daniel. Daniel Frohman Presents. 1935. -- 235
Genesee (Geneseo, N.Y.) Valley Herald -- 236
George Harvey. Johnson, Willis F. 1929. -- 268
George MacDonald and His Wife. MacDonald, Greville. 1924. -- 299
George Washington University, Washington, D.C. 20006 -- DGW
Georgetown University, Washington, D.C. 20007 -- DGU
Gettysburg College, Gettysburg, Pa. 17325 -- PGC
Gillis, William R. Gold Rush Days with Mark Twain. 1930. -- 237
Glimpses of Authors. Ticknor, Caroline. 1922. -- 121
Globe, The (Buffalo) -- 239
Gold Rush Days with Mark Twain. Gillis, William R. 1930. -- 237
Golden Age of Authors, A. Ellsworth, William W. 1919. -- 230
Goodspeed's catalogs -- 111
Grand Lodge of Iowa, Cedar Rapids, Iowa 52406 -- IaCrM
Grover Cleveland: The Man and the Statesman. McElroy, Robert. 1923. -- 303
Hallmark Cards, Kansas City, Mo. 64141 -- MoKHC
Hamilton, Charles. Collecting Autographs and Manuscripts. 1961. -- 108
Hamilton (Charles) catalogs -- 110
Hamilton and Kirkland Colleges, Clinton, N.Y. 13323 -- NCH
Hamon, Louis. Cheiro's Memoirs. 1912. -- 244
Hampden (Walter) Memorial Library, New York, N.Y. 10003 -- NNWH
Hannibal (Mo.) Daily Journal -- 245
Hannibal (Mo.) Daily Post -- 150
Hannibal (Mo.) Evening Courier Post -- 246
Hannibal (Mo.) Weekly Journal -- 247
Harper, J. Henry. House of Harper. 1912. -- 248
Harper's Monthly Magazine -- 101
Harper's Weekly Magazine -- 151
Harris (Doris) Autographs catalogs -- 250
Hartford Courant -- 117
Hartford Evening Post -- 251
Hartford Public Library, Hartford, Conn. 06103 -- CtH
Hartford Seminary Foundation, Hartford, Conn. 06105 -- CtHC
Hartford Times -- 252
Harvard University, Houghton Library, Cambridge, Mass. 02138 -- MH-H
Harvest, The. Tauchnitz, Bernhard. 1937. -- 106
Haverford College, Haverford, Pa. 19041 -- PHC
Hawaiian Annual -- 123
Hay (John) Library of Rare Books and Special Collections, Brown University, Providence, R.I. 02912 -- RPB-JH
Hayes (Rutherford B.) Library, Fremont, Ohio 43420 -- OFH
Henkels (Stan V.) catalogs -- 134
Henry E. Huntington Library, San Marino, Calif. 91108 -- CSmH
Henry Van Dyke: A Biography. Van Dyke, Tertius. 1935. -- 437
Herbert, B.B. First Decennium of the National Editorial Association. 1896. -- 231
Heritage Bookshop catalogs -- 255
Historical Society of Pennsylvania, Philadelphia, Pa. 19107 -- PHi

Historical Society of Western Pennsylvania, Pittsburgh, Pa. 15213 -- PPiHi
History of American Magazines. Mott, Frank L. 1938. -- 309
Historical Society of York County, York, Pa. 17403 -- PYHi
History of the Missouri Press Association. 1931. -- 133
History of the Ohio Society of New York. Kennedy, James H. 1906. -- 274
Hobart and William Smith Colleges, Geneva, N.Y. 14456 -- NGH
Hobbies--The Magazine for Collectors -- 256
Hofstra University, Hempstead, N.Y. 11550 -- NHemH
Honnold Library, Claremont, Calif. 91711 -- CCC
Horner, Charles. Life of James Redpath. 1926. -- 257
Houghton Library, Harvard University, Cambridge, Mass. 02138 -- MH-H
House of El Dieff (Lew David Feldman) catalogs -- 229
House of Harper. Harper, J. Henry. 1912. -- 248
Hove Central Library, Hove, United Kingdom -- Uk3
Howells, William D. My Mark Twain. 1910. -- 258
Hunley (Maxwell) Rare Books catalogs -- 260
Huntington (Henry E.) Library, San Marino, Calif. 91108 -- CSmH
Hutton, Lawrence. Talks in a Library. 1909. -- 261
In Memoriam, Peter F. Collier. 1910. -- 215
In Quest of the Perfect Book. Orcutt, William D. 1926. -- 145
In the Days of Bicycles & Bustles. Blumenfeld, R.D. 1930. -- 181
Indiana University, Lilly Library, Bloomington, Ind. 47401 -- InU-Li
Inland Printer, The (Chicago) -- 263
Institute of Russian Literature and Art, Leningrad, Soviet Union -- RuL2
International Copyright Association, Proceedings at the Meeting for the Foundation of the. 1888. -- 410
Iowa Grand Lodge, Cedar Rapids, Iowa 52406 -- IaCrM
Iowa Journal of History and Politics -- 264
Iowa State Education Assocation, Des Moines, Iowa 50319 -- IaDmE
Iowa State Historical Society, Iowa City, Iowa 52240 -- IaHi
Ireland, National Library of. Dublin, Ireland -- IreDNL
Jacobs, Lewis. Rise of the American Film. 1968. -- 265
Jenkins Company catalogs -- 266
Jerome, Robert D. and Wisbey, Herbert A. Mark Twain in Elmira. 1977. -- 142
Jewish Historical Society of Greater Washington, Washington, D.C. 20001 -- DJHi
Jewish National and University Library, Hebrew University, Jerusalem, Israel -- IsJJNL
John Kendrick Bangs. Bangs, Francis H. 1941. -- 140
Johnson, Robert U. Remembered Yesterdays. 1923. -- 267
Johnson, Willis F. George Harvey. 1929. -- 268
Joint Collection, Western Historical Manuscript Collection and State Historical Society of Missouri Manuscripts, Columbia, Mo. 65201 -- MoCoJ
Joint Free Public Library of Morristown and Morris Township, Morristown, N.J. 07960 -- NjMo
Joint University Libraries, Nashville, Tenn. 37203 -- TNJ
Jordan, Elizabeth. Three Rousing Cheers. 1938. -- 148
Journal Letters of Emily A. Severance. Severance, Emily A. 1938. -- 156
Journal of Society for Psychical Research (London) -- 269
Kansas City Star -- 461
Kansas City Star Magazine -- 270
Kansas City Times -- 271
Kate Douglas Wiggin. Smith, Nora A. 1925. -- 447
Kate Field: A Record. Whiting, Lilian. 1900. -- 446
Kelleher (Daniel F.) Co. catalogs -- 272
Keller, Helen. Midstream. 1929. -- 273
Kennedy, James H. History of the Ohio Society of New York. 1906. -- 274
Kent State University, Kent, Ohio 44240 -- OKentU
Keokuk (Ia.) Gate City -- 275
Keokuk Public Library, Keokuk, Iowa 52632 -- IaK
Keokuk Savings Bank & Trust Company, Keokuk, Iowa 52639 -- IaK2
Knox College, Galesburg, Ill. 61401 -- IGK
Koch, Robert. Louis C. Tiffany: Rebel in Glass. 1964. -- 276
Kongelige Bibliotek (Royal Library), Copenhagen, Denmark -- Dn
Koschal (Stephen) catalogs -- 277
Ladies' Home Journal -- 278
Langdon, Jervis. Samuel Langhorne Clemens: Some Reminiscenses. n.d. -- 102
Larrowe, Marcus D. (Loisette, Alphonse). Loisettian School of Physiological Memory. 1887. -- 287
Laurence and Eleanor Hutton: Their Books of Association. Wood, M.E. 1905. -- 451
Law, Frederick H. Modern Great Americans. 1926. -- 280
Leach (Ken) catalogs -- 281
Lehigh University, Bethlehem, Pa. 18015 -- PBL
Lenin Library, Moscow, Soviet Union -- RuM3
Leominster Historical Society, Inc., Leominster, Mass. 01453 -- MLeoHi
Letters of Dr. John Brown. Brown, John Jr. and Forrest, D.W. 1907. -- 195
Libbie (C.F.) & Co. catalogs -- 282
Library of Congress (United States), Washington, D.C. 20540 -- DLC
Library of New South Wales, Mitchell Library, Sydney, N.S.W., Australia -- AuSN-M
Library of Poultney Bigelow, Bigelow Homestead, Malden on Hudson, N.Y. 12453 -- N7
Life and Letters of Edmund Clarence Stedman. Stedman, Laura. 1910. -- 429
Life of James Redpath. Horner, Charles. 1926. -- 257
Life of Whitelaw Reid. Cortissoz, Royal. 1921. -- 217
Lilly Library, Indiana University, Bloomington, Ind. 47401 -- InU-Li
Lincoln (Louis A. Warren) Library and Museum, Fort Wayne, Ind. 46801 -- InFwLW
Lindley, Elizabeth. The Diary of a Book-Agent. 1911. -- 284
Lion Heart Autographs catalogs -- 283

Litchfield Historical Society, Litchfield, Conn. 06759 -- CtLHi
Living Leaders of the World. Wallace, L. 1889. -- 154
Log of an Ancient Mariner. Wakeman, Edgar. 1878. -- 439
Loisette, Alphonse (Larrowe, Marcus D.). Loisettian School of Physiological Memory. 1887. -- 287
Loisettian School of Physiological Memory. Larrowe, Marcus D. (Loisette, Alphonse). 1887. -- 287
London Borough of Richmond upon Thames, Richmond, Surrey, United Kingdom -- UkL4
London Morning Post -- 288
London Standard -- 289
London Times -- 457
Louis A. Warren Lincoln Library and Museum, Fort Wayne, Ind. 46801 -- InFwLW
Louis C. Tiffany: Rebel in Glass. Koch, Robert. 1964. -- 276
Louisiana State University, Department of Archives and Manuscripts, Baton Rouge, La. 70803 -- LU-Ar
Louisville Courier-Journal -- 290
Louisviller (Ky.) Anzeiger -- 103
Love Letters of Mark Twain. Wecter, Dixon. 1949. -- 456
Lowe (James) Autographs catalogs -- 137
Lucy, Henry W. Sixty Years in the Wilderness. 1909. -- 291
Lyceum Magazine (Boston) -- 292
M & S Rare Books catalogs -- 166
MacDonald, Greville. George MacDonald and His Wife. 1924. -- 299
MacKaye, Percy. Epoch: The Life of Steel MacKaye. 1927. -- 300
MacManus (George S.) Co. catalogs -- 301
Maggs Brothers catalogs -- 302
Maine Historical Society, Portland, Me. 04111 -- MeHi
Marietta College, Marietta, Ohio 45750 -- OMC
Mark Twain: A Biography. Paine, Albert B. 1912. -- 153
Mark Twain, Business Man. Webster, Samuel C. 1946. -- 295
Mark Twain Collection, University of California, Berkeley, Calif. 94720 -- CU-MARK
Mark Twain: His Life and Work. Clemens, Will M. 1892. -- 296
Mark Twain Journal -- 159
Mark Twain Library Association, Inc., Redding, Conn. 06875 -- CtRe
Mark Twain Memorial, Hartford, Conn. 06105 -- CtHMTH
Mark Twain Museum, Hannibal, Mo. 63401 -- MoHM
Mark Twain Returns to Hawaii. Wilson, Willard. 1969. -- 449
Mark Twain: The Letter Writer. Clemens, Cyril. 1932. -- 297
Mark Twain and Hawaii. Frear, Walter F. 1947. -- 124
Mark Twain and the Happy Island. Wallace, Elizabeth. 1913. -- 440
Mark Twain in Elmira. Jerome, Robert D. and Wisbey, Herbert A. 1977. -- 142
Mark Twain to Mrs. Fairbanks. Wecter, Dixon. 1949. -- 298
Mark Twain's Letters. Paine, Albert B. 1917. -- 114
Maryland Historical Society, Baltimore, Md. 21201 -- MdHi
Mason City Public Library, Mason City, Iowa 50401 -- IaMc
Massachusetts Historical Society, Boston, Mass. 02215 -- MHi
McElroy, Robert. Grover Cleveland: The Man and the Statesman. 1923. -- 303
McGill University, McLennan Library, Montreal, Que., Canada -- CaQMM
McGill University, Osler Library, Montreal, Que., Canada -- CaQMMO
McLennan Library, McGill University, Montreal, Que., Canada -- CaQMM
Memphis Avalanche -- 118
Merwin-Clayton Sales Company catalogs -- 305
Michigan State University, East Lansing, Mich. 48823 -- MiEM
Middlebury College, Middlebury, Vt. 05753 -- VtMiM
Midstream. Keller, Helen. 1929. -- 273
Millicent Library, Fairhaven, Mass. 02719 -- MFai
Mills College, Oakland, Calif. 94613 -- COMC
Minneapolis Public Library, Minneapolis, Minn. 55401 -- MnM
Minnesota Historical Society, St. Paul, Minn. 55101 -- MnHi
Miss Porter's School, Farmington, Conn. 06032 -- CtFP
Missouri Press Association, History of the. 1931. -- 133
Missouri State Historical Society, Columbia, Mo. 65201 -- MoHi
Missouri, State Historical Society of, and Western Historical Manuscript Collection (Joint Collection), Columbia, Mo. 65201 -- MoCoJ
Mitchell Library, Library of New South Wales. Sydney, N.S.W., Australia -- AuSN-M
Modern Great Americans. Law, Frederick H. 1926. -- 280
Monroe Country (Mo.) Appeal -- 306
Montana Historical Society, Helena, Mont. 59601 -- MtHi
Montgomery, L.M. Anne of Green Gables. 1908. -- 307
Moody, Eric N. Western Carpetbagger. 1978. -- 279
Moray District Council, Elgin, United Kingdom -- Uk6
Morgan (Pierpont) Library, New York, N.Y. 10016 -- NNPM
Morristown National Historical Park, Morristown, N.J. 07960 -- NjMoHP
Morristown and Morris Township, Joint Free Public Library, Morristown, N.J. 07960 -- NjMo
Mott, Frank L. History of American Magazines. 1938. -- 309
Mott (Howard S.) Inc. catalogs -- 308
Muscatine (Ia.) Journal -- 158
Muscatine (Ia.) Tri-Weekly Journal -- 310
Muzej Nikole Tesle (Tesle Museum), Belgrade, Yugoslavia -- YuB2
My Father Mark Twain. Clemens, Clara. 1931. -- 293
My Husband Gabrilowitsch. Clemens, Clara. 1938. -- 294
My Mark Twain. Howells, William D. 1910. -- 258
Myers & Co. catalogs -- 311
National Archives Library, United States National Archives and Records Service, Washington, D.C. 20408 -- DNA
National Library of Ireland, Dublin, Ireland -- IreDNL
National Library of New Zealand, Alexander Turnbull Library, Wellington, New Zealand -- NzW2
National Library of Scotland, Edinburgh, United Kingdom -- UkENL
National Register of Archives, Edinburgh, United Kingdom -- UkE2
Nevada State Historical Society, Reno, Nev. 89504 -- NvHi
Nevada State Library, Carson City, Nev. 89701 -- Nv
Neville (Maurice F.) Rare Books catalogs -- 323

New England Society, Seventy-second Anniversary Celebration of the. 1877. -- 109
New Jersey Historical Society, Newark, N.J. 07104 -- NjHi
New Orleans Times-Democrat -- 152
New South Wales (Library of), Mitchell Library, Sydney, N.S.W., Australia -- AuSN-M
New York Evening Mail -- 312
New York Evening Post -- 119
New York Graphic -- 313
New York Herald -- 314
New York Historical Society, New York, N.Y. 10024 -- NHi
New York Journal -- 315
New York Press Club, Eighth Annual Dinner of the. 1881. -- 320
New York Public Library, Albert A. and Henry W. Berg Collection, New York, N.Y. 10018 -- NN-B
New York Public Library, New York, N.Y. 10018 -- NN
New York State Library, Albany, N.Y. 12224 -- N
New York Sun -- 316
New York Times -- 131
New York Tribune -- 317
New York University, Fales Collection, New York, N.Y. 10012 -- NNU-F
New York Weekly -- 318
New York World -- 319
New Zealand, National Library of. Alexander Turnbull Library, Wellington, New Zealand -- NzW2
Newark Galleries catalogs -- 324
Newark Public Library, Newark, N.J. 07101 -- NjN
Newberry Library, Chicago, Ill. 60610 -- ICN
Newman (Marvin H.) catalogs -- 325
Northeast Missouri State University, Kirksville, Mo. 63501 -- MoKiU
Northwestern University, Evanston, Ill. 60201 -- IEN
Nye, Frank W. Bill Nye, His Own Life Story. 1926. -- 326
Ohio Historical Society, Columbus, Ohio 43211 -- OHi
Olana State Historic Site, Hudson, N.Y. 12534 -- NHudO
Omaha Public Library, Omaha, Neb. 68102 -- NbO
Orcutt, William D. In Quest of the Perfect Book. 1926. -- 145
Osler Library, McGill University, Montreal, Que., Canada -- CaQMMO
Otto, Curt. Verlag Bernard Tauchnitz. 1912. -- 327
Oxford University, Bodleian Library, Oxford, United Kingdom -- UkOxU
Pacific Northwest Quarterly -- 128
Packard's Short-hand Reporter & Amanuensis (New York) -- 328
Paine, Albert B. Mark Twain: A Biography. 1912. -- 153
Paine, Albert B. Mark Twain's Letters. 1917. -- 114
Paine, Albert B. Th. Nast: His Period and His Pictures. 1904. -- 321
Pall Mall Gazette (London) -- 400
Paris (Mo.) Mercury -- 401
Parke-Bernet Galleries catalogs -- 105
Pennsylvania, Historical Society of. Philadelphia, Pa. 19107 -- PHi
Pennsylvania State University, University Park, Pa. 16802 -- PSt
Pepper & Stern catalogs -- 402
Perkins School of Theology, Southern Methodist University, Dallas, Tex. 75222 -- TxDaM-P
Perspectivas (Universidad de las Americas) -- 113
Petoskey (Mich.) Record -- 403
Philadelphia Evening Bulletin -- 404
Philadelphia, Free Library of. Philadelphia, Pa. 19103 -- PP
Philadelphia Public Ledger -- 405
Phillips Academy, Andover, Mass. 01810 -- MAnP
Phillips catalogs -- 406
Pierpont Morgan Library, New York, N.Y. 10016 -- NNPM
Pike, Gustavus. Singing Campaign for Ten Thousand Pounds. 1875. -- 407
Pond, James B. Eccentricities of Genius. 1900. -- 408
Portraits and Autographs. Stead, William T. 1890. -- 132
Pratt (Enoch) Free Library, Baltimore, Md. 21201 -- MdBE
Press Club of Chicago: A History. Freeman, William H. 1894. -- 409
Princeton University, Princeton, N.J. 08540 -- NjP
Private Collector -- C2
Private Collector -- C3
Private Collector -- C4
Private Collector -- C6
Private Collector -- C7
Private Collector -- CAlb2
Private Collector -- CBev2
Private Collector -- CRc2
Private Collector -- CSj2
Private Collector -- CSto3
Private Collector -- CoAur2
Private Collector -- CtH2
Private Collector -- CtMy2
Private Collector -- CtNc2
Private Collector -- CtNh2
Private Collector -- F2
Private Collector -- FG2
Private Collector -- FSp2
Private Collector -- GMar2
Private Collector -- I2
Private Collector -- IC3
Private Collector -- IC4
Private Collector -- M2
Private Collector -- M3
Private Collector -- Me2
Private Collector -- MiK2
Private Collector -- Mo2
Private Collector -- Mo3
Private Collector -- Mo4
Private Collector -- MoFu2
Private Collector -- MoSw2
Private Collector -- N2
Private Collector -- N4

Private Collector -- N5
Private Collector -- N6
Private Collector -- NBron2
Private Collector -- NElm2
Private Collector -- NHor2
Private Collector -- NN2
Private Collector -- NN3
Private Collector -- NN4
Private Collector -- NN5
Private Collector -- NN7
Private Collector -- NPla2
Private Collector -- NWhp2
Private Collector -- NcGr2
Private Collector -- NjBern2
Private Collector -- NmA2
Private Collector -- NmR2
Private Collector -- ODa2
Private Collector -- PP2
Private Collector -- PP3
Private Collector -- PP4
Private Collector -- TxAu2
Private Collector -- TxAu3
Private Collector -- UkCo2
Private Collector -- ViAl2
Private Collector -- WRl2
Private Collector -- WRl3
Private Collector -- WaCheh2
Proceedings at the Meeting for the Foundation of the International Copyright Association. 1888. -- 410
Public Library of Cincinnati and Hamilton County, Cincinnati, Ohio 45202 -- OC
Punch Brothers Punch. Twain, Mark. 1878. -- 460
Purdue University, Lafayette, Ind. 47907 -- InLP
Putnam Museum, Davenport, Iowa 52804 -- IaDaPM
Rains Galleries catalogs -- 412
Reade, A. Arthur. Study and Stimulants. 1883. -- 430
Reception Given to Thurlow Weed. 1880. -- 444
Redding (Conn.) Times -- 414
Redwood Library and Athenaeum, Newport, R.I. 02480 -- RNR
Reed College, Portland, Or. 97202 -- OrPR
Remembered Yesterdays. Johnson, Robert U. 1923. -- 267
Remington Art Memorial Museum, Ogdensburg, N.Y. 13669 -- NOg2
Rendell (Kenneth W.) catalogs -- 415
Report of the Nineteenth Annual Reunion. Society of the Army of the Potomac. 1888. -- 424
Rice, Alice H. The Inky Way. 1940. -- 146
Richards, P. Zeichner und Geseichnete. 1912. -- 453
Richards (Paul C.) catalogs -- 127
Riksarkivet (Swedish Public Record Office), Stockholm, Sweden -- Sw2
Rise of the American Film. Jacobs, Lewis. 1968. -- 265
Robert J. Burdette: His Message. Burdette, Clara B. 1922. -- 197
Ross, Janet. Fourth Generation. 1912. -- 416
Routledge and Kegan Paul, London, United Kingdom -- UkL5
Royal Library (Kongelige Bibliotek), Copenhagen, Denmark -- Dn
Russell Sage College, Troy, N.Y. 12180 -- NTRS
Rutgers-The State University, New Brunswick, N.J. 08901 -- NjR
Rutherford B. Hayes Library, Fremont, Ohio 43420 -- OFH
S.L.C. to C.T. 1925. -- 433
Saint Bonaventure University, St. Bonaventure, N.Y. 14778 -- NStBU
Saint John's Seminary, Camarillo, Calif. 93010 -- CCamarSJ
Saint Mary's Seminary, Perryville, Mo. 63775 -- MoPeS
Samuel Langhorne Clemens: Some Reminiscenses. Langdon, Jervis. n.d. -- 102
San Francisco Alta California -- 417
San Jose State University, San Jose, Calif. 95192 -- CSjU
Sanborn, John W. Distinguished Authors. 1920. -- 419
Saturday Evening Post (Indianapolis) -- 129
Scott & O'Shaughnessy catalogs -- 421
Seattle Public Library, Seattle, Wash. 98104 -- WaS
Second Life Books catalogs -- 462
Self (K.C.) catalogs -- 422
Seventy Years: Being the Autobiography of Lady Gregory. Smythe, Colin. 1974. -- 144
Seventy-second Anniversary Celebration of the New England Society. 1877. -- 109
Severance, Emily A. Journal Letters of Emily A. Severance. 1938. -- 156
Short Stories. Davis, Sam. 1886. -- 125
Singing Campaign for Ten Thousand Pounds. Pike, Gustavus. 1875. -- 407
Sir Arthur Conan Doyle: Centenary. 1959. -- 224
Sixty Years in the Wilderness. Lucy, Henry W. 1909. -- 291
Sketch of the Celebration of the Sixty-First Birthday of Hon. Horace Greeley, LL.D. Wingate, Charles F. 1872. -- 450
Smith College, Northampton, Mass. 01060 -- MNS
Smith, Nora A. Kate Douglas Wiggin. 1925. -- 447
Smith, U.S. Up a Tree with Mark Twain. 1978. -- 143
Smithsonian Institution, Washington, D.C. 20560 -- DSI
Smythe, Colin. Seventy Years: Being the Autobiography of Lady Gregory. 1974. -- 144
Society of California Pioneers, San Francisco, Calif. 94102 -- CSfCP
Society of the Army of the Potomac. Report of the Nineteenth Annual Reunion. 1888. -- 424
Sotheby & Co. (London) catalogs -- 155
Sotheby Parke Bernet (New York) catalogs -- 418
Sotheby, Wilkinson & Hodge catalogs -- 425
Southeast Missouri State College, Cape Girardeau, Mo. 63701 -- MoCgS
Southern Illinois University, Carbondale, Ill. 62901 -- ICarbS
Southern Methodist University, Perkins School of Theology, Dallas, Tex. 75222 -- TxDaM-P
Spectator, The (London) -- 426
St. Louis Republican -- 428
Stanford University, Stanford, Calif. 94305 -- CSt

State Historical Society of Iowa, Iowa City, Iowa 52240 -- IaHi
State Historical Society of Wisconsin, Madison, Wis. 53706 -- WHi
State Library of Victoria, Melbourne, Vic., Australia -- AuMS
State University of New York at Buffalo, Poetry Library, Buffalo, N.Y. 14203 -- NBuU-PO
Stead, William T. Portraits and Autographs. 1890. -- 132
Stedman, Laura. Life and Letters of Edmund Clarence Stedman. 1910. -- 429
Stories of Authors: British and American. Chubb, Edwin W. 1926. -- 211
Stowe-Day Memorial Library and Historical Foundation, Hartford, Conn. 06105 -- CtHSD
Strand Magazine (London) -- 138
Strathclyde Regional Archives, Glasgow, United Kingdom -- UkG2
Study and Stimulants. Reade, A. Arthur. 1883. -- 430
Summers on the Saranac. De Sormo, Maitland C. 1982. -- 221
Suomalaisen Kirjallisuuden Seura (Finnish Literature Society), Helsinki, Finland -- FiH2
Swann Galleries Inc. catalogs -- 116
Swedish Public Record Office (Riksarkivet), Stockholm, Sweden -- Sw2
Syracuse University, Syracuse, N.Y. 13210 -- NSyU
Talks in a Library. Hutton, Lawrence. 1909. -- 261
Tauchnitz, Bernhard. The Harvest. 1937. -- 106
Telegrapher (New York) -- 459
Tennessee State Library and Archives, Nashville, Tenn. 37219 -- T
Tesla Museum (Muzej Nikole Tesle), Belgrade, Yugoslavia -- YuB2
Texas Christian University, Fort Worth, Tex. 76129 -- TxFTC
Th. Nast: His Period and His Pictures. Paine, Albert B. 1904. -- 321
The Inky Way. Rice, Alice H. 1940. -- 146
The Rest of My Life. Wells, Carolyn. 1937. -- 147
Their Trackless Way. Chapin, Adele. 1931. -- 203
Three Rousing Cheers. Jordan, Elizabeth. 1938. -- 148
Ticknor, Caroline. Glimpses of Authors. 1922. -- 121
Trailside Museum, Bear Mountain, N.Y. 10911 -- NBmtT
Trinity College, Watkinson Library, Hartford, Conn. 06106 -- CtHT-W
Tulane University, New Orleans, La. 70118 -- LNT
Tuolomne County Museum, Sonora, Calif. 95370 -- CSoM
Turnbull (Alexander) Library, National Library of New Zealand, Wellington, New Zealand -- NzW2
Twain, Mark. Punch Brothers Punch. 1878. -- 460
Twice Thirty. Bok, Edward W. 1925. -- 183
Union Art Galleries catalogs -- 436
United States Library of Congress, Washington, D.C. 20540 -- DLC
United States National Archives and Records Service, National Archives Library, Washington, D.C. 20408 -- DNA
Universitet i Uppsala (University of Uppsala), S-751 20 Uppsala, Sweden -- SwUU
Universitetet i Oslo (University of Oslo), Oslo, Norway -- NoOU
University of Arkansas, Fayetteville, Ark. 72701 -- ArU
University of California, Berkeley, Bancroft Library, Berkeley, Calif. 94720 -- CU-BANC
University of California, Berkeley, Mark Twain Collection, Berkeley, Calif. 94720 -- CU-MARK
University of California, Los Angeles, Department of Special Collections, Los Angeles, Calif. 90024 -- CLU-S/C
University of California, Los Angeles, William Andrews Clark Memorial Library, Los Angeles, Calif. 90024 -- CLU-C
University of Chicago, Chicago, Ill. 60637 -- ICU
University of Colorado, Boulder, Colo. 80302 -- CoU
University of Houston, Houston, Tex. 77004 -- TxHU
University of Illinois, Rare Book Room, Urbana, Ill. 61803 -- IU-R
University of Iowa, Iowa City, Iowa 52240 -- IaU
University of Kentucky, Lexington, Ky. 40506 -- KyU
University of Leeds, Brotherton Library, Leeds, United Kingdom -- UkLe2
University of Louisville, Louisville, Ky. 40208 -- KyLoU
University of Maryland, College Park, Md. 20742 -- MdU
University of Michigan, Ann Arbor, Mich. 48104 -- MiU
University of Michigan, Michigan Historical Collection, Ann Arbor, Mich. 48104 -- MiU-H
University of Minnesota, Rare Book Division, Minneapolis, Minn. 55455 -- MnU-Rb
University of Missouri, Columbia, Mo. 65201 -- MoU
University of Nevada, Reno, Nev. 89507 -- NvU
University of New Brunswick, Archives and Special Collections Department, Fredericton, N.B., Canada -- CaNBFUA
University of New Mexico, Albuquerque, N.M. 87106 -- NmU
University of North Carolina, Chapel Hill, N.C. 27514 -- NcU
University of Notre Dame, Notre Dame, Ind. 46556 -- InNd
University of Oslo (Universitetet i Oslo), Oslo, Norway -- NoOU
University of Pennsylvania, Philadelphia, Pa. 19104 -- PU
University of Pittsburgh, Pittsburgh, Pa. 15213 -- PPiU
University of Queensland, St. Lucia, Brisbane, Qld., Australia -- AuBrU
University of Reading, Reading, United Kingdom -- Uk4
University of Rochester, Rochester, N.Y. 14627 -- NRU
University of Southern California, Los Angeles, Calif. 90007 -- CLSU
University of Sussex, Brighton, United Kingdom -- Uk5
University of Texas, Austin, Tex. 78712 -- TxU
University of Texas at El Paso, El Paso, Tex. 79999 -- TxEU
University of Uppsala (Universitet i Uppsala), S-751 20 Uppsala, Sweden -- SwUU
University of Virginia, Charlottesville, Va. 22904 -- ViU
University of Wisconsin, Madison, Wis. 53706 -- WU
University of the Pacific, Stockton, Calif. 95204 -- CStoC
Up a Tree with Mark Twain. Smith, U.S. 1978. -- 143
Van Dyke, Tertius. Henry Van Dyke: A Biography. 1935. -- 437
Van Nosdall (G.A.) catalogs -- 438
Vassar College, Poughkeepsie, N.Y. 12601 -- NPV
Verlag Bernard Tauchnitz. Otto, Curt. 1912. -- 327

Victoria State Library, Melbourne, Vic., Australia -- AuMS
Victoria and Albert Museum, South Kensington, London, United Kingdom -- UkL6
Vienna State Library (Wien Stadt- und Landesbibliothek), Vienna, Austria -- As2
Virginia City Territorial Enterprise -- 431
Virginia Historical Society, Richmond, Va. 23221 -- ViHi
Wake Forest University, Winston-Salem, N.C. 27109 -- NcWsW
Wakeman, Edgar. Log of an Ancient Mariner. 1878. -- 439
Wallace, Elizabeth. Mark Twain and the Happy Island. 1913. -- 440
Wallace, L. Living Leaders of the World. 1889. -- 154
Walpole Galleries catalogs -- 441
Walter Hampden Memorial Library, New York, N.Y. 10003 -- NNWH
Washington Daily National Intelligencer -- 442
Washington State University, Pullman, Wash. 99163 -- WaPS
Washington University, St. Louis, Mo. 63130 -- MoSW
Watkinson Library, Trinity College, Hartford, Conn. 06106 -- CtHT-W
Webster, Samuel C. Mark Twain, Business Man. 1946. -- 295
Wecter, Dixon. Love Letters of Mark Twain. 1949. -- 456
Wecter, Dixon. Mark Twain to Mrs. Fairbanks. 1949. -- 298
Wellesley College, Wellesley, Mass. 02181 -- MWelC
Wells, Carloyn. The Rest of My Life. 1937. -- 147
West Virginia University, Morgantown, W.Va. 26505 -- WvU
Western Carpetbagger. Moody, Eric N. 1978. -- 279
Western Historical Manuscript Collection and State Historical Society of Missouri Manuscripts (Joint Collection), Columbia, Mo. 65201 -- MoCoJ
Western Illinois University, Macomb, Ill. 61455 -- IMacoW
Western Pennsylvania, Historical Society of. Pittsburgh, Pa. 15213 -- PPiHi
Western Reserve Historical Society, Cleveland, Ohio 44106 -- OClWHi
Wheeler, Candace. Yesterdays in a Busy Life. 1918. -- 445
Whiting, Lilian. Kate Field: A Record. 1900. -- 446
Wien Stadt- und Landesbibliothek (Vienna State Library), Vienna, Austria -- As2
Wilder's Boston Book Auction catalogs -- 448
Williams College, Chapin Library, Williamstown, Mass. 01267 -- MWiW-C
Wilson Bulletin for Librarians -- 463
Wilson, Willard. Mark Twain Returns to Hawaii. 1969. -- 449
Wingate, Charles F. Sketch of the Celebration of the Sixty-First Birthday of Hon. Horace Greeley, LL.D. 1872. -- 450
Wisbey, Herbert A. and Jerome, Robert D. Mark Twain in Elmira. 1977. -- 142
Wisconsin, State Historical Society of. Madison, Wis. 53706 -- WHi
Wood, M.E. Laurence and Eleanor Hutton: Their Books of Association. 1905. -- 451
Ximenes Rare Books catalogs -- 452
Yale University, New Haven, Conn. 06520 -- CtY
Yesterdays in a Busy Life. Wheeler, Candace. 1918. -- 445
York County, Historical Society of. York, Pa. 17403 -- PYHi
Zeichner und Geseichnete. Richards, P. 1912. -- 453
Zeitlin & Ver Brugge catalogs -- 454

Source Symbols

100 -- Commercial Appeal (Memphis)
101 -- Harper's Monthly Magazine
102 -- Langdon, Jervis. Samuel Langhorne Clemens: Some Reminiscenses. n.d.
103 -- Louisviller (Ky.) Anzeiger
104 -- Boston Herald
105 -- Parke-Bernet Galleries catalogs
106 -- Tauchnitz, Bernhard. The Harvest. 1937.
107 -- American Art Association catalogs
108 -- Hamilton, Charles. Collecting Autographs and Manuscripts. 1961.
109 -- Seventy-second Anniversary Celebration of the New England Society. 1877.
110 -- Hamilton (Charles) catalogs
111 -- Goodspeed's catalogs
112 -- Berkshire County (Mass.) Eagle
113 -- Perspectivas (Universidad de las Americas)
114 -- Paine, Albert B. Mark Twain's Letters. 1917.
116 -- Swann Galleries Inc. catalogs
117 -- Hartford Courant
118 -- Memphis Avalanche
119 -- New York Evening Post
120 -- Dawson's Book Shop catalogs
121 -- Ticknor, Caroline. Glimpses of Authors. 1922.
122 -- American Art Association--Anderson Galleries catalogs
123 -- Hawaiian Annual
124 -- Frear, Walter F. Mark Twain and Hawaii. 1947.
125 -- Davis, Sam. Short Stories. 1886.
127 -- Richards (Paul C.) catalogs
128 -- Pacific Northwest Quarterly
129 -- Saturday Evening Post (Indianapolis)
130 -- AB Bookman's Weekly
131 -- New York Times
132 -- Stead, William T. Portraits and Autographs. 1890.
133 -- History of the Missouri Press Association. 1931.
134 -- Henkels (Stan V.) catalogs
137 -- Lowe (James) Autographs catalogs
138 -- Strand Magazine (London)
140 -- Bangs, Francis H. John Kendrick Bangs. 1941.
142 -- Jerome, Robert D. and Wisbey, Herbert A. Mark Twain in Elmira. 1977.
143 -- Smith, U.S. Up a Tree with Mark Twain. 1978.
144 -- Smythe, Colin. Seventy Years: Being the Autobiography of Lady Gregory. 1974.
145 -- Orcutt, William D. In Quest of the Perfect Book. 1926.
146 -- Rice, Alice H. The Inky Way. 1940.
147 -- Wells, Carloyn. The Rest of My Life. 1937.
148 -- Jordan, Elizabeth. Three Rousing Cheers. 1938.
150 -- Hannibal (Mo.) Daily Post
151 -- Harper's Weekly Magazine
152 -- New Orleans Times-Democrat
153 -- Paine, Albert B. Mark Twain: A Biography. 1912.
154 -- Wallace, L. Living Leaders of the World. 1889.
155 -- Sotheby & Co. (London) catalogs

156 -- Severance, Emily A. Journal Letters of Emily A. Severance. 1938.
157 -- Anderson Auction Company catalogs
158 -- Muscatine (Ia.) Journal
159 -- Mark Twain Journal
160 -- Autograph Collector's Journal
161 -- American Literature
162 -- Adelaide Observer
163 -- Ainslee's Magazine
164 -- Altman (B.) & Co. catalogs
165 -- American Book Auction catalogs
166 -- M & S Rare Books catalogs
168 -- Argosy Book Stores catalogs
169 -- Army and Navy Journal
170 -- First Annual Meeting and Banquet of the Associated Pioneers of the Territorial Days of California. 1876.
171 -- Atlantic Monthly
173 -- Baker (G.A.) & Co. catalogs
174 -- Baldwin, James M. Between Two Wars. 1926.
175 -- Bangs & Co. catalogs
176 -- Batchelder (Robert F.) catalogs
177 -- Battan (David) Autographs catalogs
178 -- Benjamin (Walter R.) Autographs catalogs
179 -- Black (Robert K.) catalogs
181 -- Blumenfeld, R.D. In the Days of Bicycles & Bustles. 1930.
182 -- Bodley Book Shop catalogs
183 -- Bok, Edward W. Twice Thirty. 1925.
184 -- Bok, Edward W. Americanization of Edward Bok. 1922.
185 -- Bolton, Sarah K. Famous American Authors. 1940.
187 -- Bookman, The (London)
188 -- Carnegie, Andrew. Autobiography of Andrew Carnegie. 1920.
189 -- Boston Daily Advertiser
190 -- Boston Evening Journal
191 -- Boston Evening Transcript
192 -- Bradford (Penn.) Reporter
193 -- Broadley, A.M. Chats on Autographs. 1910.
194 -- Brooklyn Daily Eagle
195 -- Brown, John Jr. and Forrest, D.W. Letters of Dr. John Brown. 1907.
196 -- Buffalo Express
197 -- Burdette, Clara B. Robert J. Burdette: His Message. 1922.
198 -- California Book Auction Company catalogs
199 -- Carnegie Book Shop catalogs
200 -- Carson Appeal (Carson City, Nev.)
201 -- Carson City (Nev.) Daily Independent
202 -- Carter, M.H. Cat Stories Retold from St. Nicholas. 1914.
203 -- Chapin, Adele. Their Trackless Way. 1931.
204 -- Chattanooga (Tenn.) Republican
205 -- Chicago Book Auction catalogs
206 -- Chicago Herald
207 -- Chicago Tribune
208 -- Childhood's Appeal (Boston)
209 -- Christian Union (New York)
210 -- Christie, Manson & Woods catalogs
211 -- Chubb, Edwin W. Stories of Authors: British and American. 1926.
212 -- City Book Auction catalogs
213 -- Cohasco Inc. catalogs
214 -- Colfax Clipper (Iowa)
215 -- In Memoriam, Peter F. Collier. 1910.
216 -- Coming Out, A Letter to a Rosebud. n.d.
217 -- Cortissoz, Royal. Life of Whitelaw Reid. 1921.
219 -- Critic, The (New York)
221 -- De Sormo, Maitland C. Summers on the Saranac. 1982.
224 -- Sir Arthur Conan Doyle: Centenary. 1959.
226 -- Duschnes (Philip) catalogs
227 -- Duttons Inc. catalogs
228 -- Bibliophile Society. Eighteenth Year Book 1919. 1919.
229 -- House of El Dieff (Lew David Feldman) catalogs
230 -- Ellsworth, William W. A Golden Age of Authors. 1919.
231 -- Herbert, B.B. First Decennium of the National Editorial Association. 1896.
232 -- Forum, The (New York)
233 -- Freeman (Samuel T.) & Co. catalogs
234 -- Friend, The (Honolulu)
235 -- Frohman, Daniel. Daniel Frohman Presents. 1935.
236 -- Genesee (Geneseo, N.Y.) Valley Herald
237 -- Gillis, William R. Gold Rush Days with Mark Twain. 1930.
239 -- Globe, The (Buffalo)
244 -- Hamon, Louis. Cheiro's Memoirs. 1912.
245 -- Hannibal (Mo.) Daily Journal
246 -- Hannibal (Mo.) Evening Courier Post
247 -- Hannibal (Mo.) Weekly Journal
248 -- Harper, J. Henry. House of Harper. 1912.
250 -- Harris (Doris) Autographs catalogs
251 -- Hartford Evening Post
252 -- Hartford Times
255 -- Heritage Bookshop catalogs
256 -- Hobbies--The Magazine for Collectors
257 -- Horner, Charles. Life of James Redpath. 1926.
258 -- Howells, William D. My Mark Twain. 1910.
260 -- Hunley (Maxwell) Rare Books catalogs
261 -- Hutton, Lawrence. Talks in a Library. 1909.
263 -- Inland Printer, The (Chicago)
264 -- Iowa Journal of History and Politics
265 -- Jacobs, Lewis. Rise of the American Film. 1968.
266 -- Jenkins Company catalogs
267 -- Johnson, Robert U. Remembered Yesterdays. 1923.
268 -- Johnson, Willis F. George Harvey. 1929.
269 -- Journal of Society for Psychical Research (London)
270 -- Kansas City Star Magazine
271 -- Kansas City Times
272 -- Kelleher (Daniel F.) Co. catalogs

273 -- Keller, Helen. Midstream. 1929.
274 -- Kennedy, James H. History of the Ohio Society of New York. 1906.
275 -- Keokuk (Ia.) Gate City
276 -- Koch, Robert. Louis C. Tiffany: Rebel in Glass. 1964.
277 -- Koschal (Stephen) catalogs
278 -- Ladies' Home Journal
279 -- Moody, Eric N. Western Carpetbagger. 1978.
280 -- Law, Frederick H. Modern Great Americans. 1926.
281 -- Leach (Ken) catalogs
282 -- Libbie (C.F.) & Co. catalogs
283 -- Lion Heart Autographs catalogs
284 -- Lindley, Elizabeth. The Diary of a Book-Agent. 1911.
285 -- Arkansaw Traveler
287 -- Larrowe, Marcus D. (Loisette, Alphonse). Loisettian School of Physiological Memory. 1887.
288 -- London Morning Post
289 -- London Standard
290 -- Louisville Courier-Journal
291 -- Lucy, Henry W. Sixty Years in the Wilderness. 1909.
292 -- Lyceum Magazine (Boston)
293 -- Clemens, Clara. My Father Mark Twain. 1931.
294 -- Clemens, Clara. My Husband Gabrilowitsch. 1938.
295 -- Webster, Samuel C. Mark Twain, Business Man. 1946.
296 -- Clemens, Will M. Mark Twain: His Life and Work. 1892.
297 -- Clemens, Cyril. Mark Twain: The Letter Writer. 1932.
298 -- Wecter, Dixon. Mark Twain to Mrs. Fairbanks. 1949.
299 -- MacDonald, Greville. George MacDonald and His Wife. 1924.
300 -- MacKaye, Percy. Epoch: The Life of Steel MacKaye. 1927.
301 -- MacManus (George S.) Co. catalogs
302 -- Maggs Brothers catalogs
303 -- McElroy, Robert. Grover Cleveland: The Man and the Statesman. 1923.
305 -- Merwin-Clayton Sales Company catalogs
306 -- Monroe Country (Mo.) Appeal
307 -- Montgomery, L.M. Anne of Green Gables. 1908.
308 -- Mott (Howard S.) Inc. catalogs
309 -- Mott, Frank L. History of American Magazines. 1938.
310 -- Muscatine (Ia.) Tri-Weekly Journal
311 -- Myers & Co. catalogs
312 -- New York Evening Mail
313 -- New York Graphic
314 -- New York Herald
315 -- New York Journal
316 -- New York Sun
317 -- New York Tribune
318 -- New York Weekly
319 -- New York World
320 -- Eighth Annual Dinner of the New York Press Club. 1881.
321 -- Paine, Albert B. Th. Nast: His Period and His Pictures. 1904.
323 -- Neville (Maurice F.) Rare Books catalogs
324 -- Newark Galleries catalogs
325 -- Newman (Marvin H.) catalogs
326 -- Nye, Frank W. Bill Nye, His Own Life Story. 1926.
327 -- Otto, Curt. Verlag Bernard Tauchnitz. 1912.
328 -- Packard's Short-hand Reporter & Amanuensis (New York)
400 -- Pall Mall Gazette (London)
401 -- Paris (Mo.) Mercury
402 -- Pepper & Stern catalogs
403 -- Petoskey (Mich.) Record
404 -- Philadelphia Evening Bulletin
405 -- Philadelphia Public Ledger
406 -- Phillips catalogs
407 -- Pike, Gustavus. Singing Campaign for Ten Thousand Pounds. 1875.
408 -- Pond, James B. Eccentricities of Genius. 1900.
409 -- Freeman, William H. Press Club of Chicago: A History. 1894.
410 -- Proceedings at the Meeting for the Foundation of the International Copyright Association. 1888.
412 -- Rains Galleries catalogs
414 -- Redding (Conn.) Times
415 -- Rendell (Kenneth W.) catalogs
416 -- Ross, Janet. Fourth Generation. 1912.
417 -- San Francisco Alta California
418 -- Sotheby Parke Bernet (New York) catalogs
419 -- Sanborn, John W. Distinguished Authors. 1920.
421 -- Scott & O'Shaughnessy catalogs
422 -- Self (K.C.) catalogs
424 -- Society of the Army of the Potomac. Report of the Nineteenth Annual Reunion. 1888.
425 -- Sotheby, Wilkinson & Hodge catalogs
426 -- Spectator, The (London)
428 -- St. Louis Republican
429 -- Stedman, Laura. Life and Letters of Edmund Clarence Stedman. 1910.
430 -- Reade, A. Arthur. Study and Stimulants. 1883.
431 -- Virginia City Territorial Enterprise
433 -- S.L.C. to C.T. 1925.
436 -- Union Art Galleries catalogs
437 -- Van Dyke, Tertius. Henry Van Dyke: A Biography. 1935.
438 -- Van Nosdall (G.A.) catalogs
439 -- Wakeman, Edgar. Log of an Ancient Mariner. 1878.
440 -- Wallace, Elizabeth. Mark Twain and the Happy Island. 1913.
441 -- Walpole Galleries catalogs
442 -- Washington Daily National Intelligencer
444 -- Reception Given to Thurlow Weed. 1880.
445 -- Wheeler, Candace. Yesterdays in a Busy Life. 1918.
446 -- Whiting, Lilian. Kate Field: A Record. 1900.
447 -- Smith, Nora A. Kate Douglas Wiggin. 1925.
448 -- Wilder's Boston Book Auction catalogs
449 -- Wilson, Willard. Mark Twain Returns to Hawaii. 1969.
450 -- Wingate, Charles F. Sketch of the Celebration of the Sixty-First Birthday of Hon. Horace Greeley, LL.D. 1872.
451 -- Wood, M.E. Laurence and Eleanor Hutton: Their Books of Association. 1905.
452 -- Ximenes Rare Books catalogs

453 -- Richards, P. Zeichner und Geseichnete. 1912.
454 -- Zeitlin & Ver Brugge catalogs
456 -- Wecter, Dixon. Love Letters of Mark Twain. 1949.
457 -- London Times
459 -- Telegrapher (New York)
460 -- Twain, Mark. Punch Brothers Punch. 1878.
461 -- Kansas City Star
462 -- Second Life Books catalogs
463 -- Wilson Bulletin for Librarians
ArU -- University of Arkansas, Fayetteville, Ark. 72701
As2 -- Wien Stadt- und Landesbibliothek (Vienna State Library), Vienna, Austria
AuBrU -- University of Queensland, St. Lucia, Brisbane, Qld., Australia
AuMS -- State Library of Victoria, Melbourne, Vic., Australia
AuSN-M -- Library of New South Wales, Mitchell Library, Sydney, N.S.W., Australia
C2 -- Private Collector
C3 -- Private Collector
C4 -- Private Collector
C6 -- Private Collector
C7 -- Private Collector
CAlb2 -- Private Collector
CBev2 -- Private Collector
CCC -- Honnold Library, Claremont, Calif. 91711
CCamarSJ -- Saint John's Seminary, Camarillo, Calif. 93010
CLSU -- University of Southern California, Los Angeles, Calif. 90007
CLU-C -- University of California, Los Angeles, William Andrews Clark Memorial Library, Los Angeles, Calif. 90024
CLU-S/C -- University of California, Los Angeles, Department of Special Collections, Los Angeles, Calif. 90024
CLjC -- Copley Newspapers Incorporated, James S. Copley Library, La Jolla, Calif. 92037
COMC -- Mills College, Oakland, Calif. 94613
CRc2 -- Private Collector
CSadM -- Calaveras County Museum & Archives Library, San Andreas, Calif. 95249
CSfCP -- Society of California Pioneers, San Francisco, Calif. 94102
CSj2 -- Private Collector
CSjU -- San Jose State University, San Jose, Calif. 95192
CSmH -- Henry E. Huntington Library, San Marino, Calif. 91108
CSoM -- Tuolomne County Museum, Sonora, Calif. 95370
CSt -- Stanford University, Stanford, Calif. 94305
CSto3 -- Private Collector
CStoC -- University of the Pacific, Stockton, Calif. 95204
CU-BANC -- University of California, Berkeley, Bancroft Library, Berkeley, Calif. 94720
CU-MARK -- University of California, Berkeley, Mark Twain Collection, Berkeley, Calif. 94720
CaNBFUA -- University of New Brunswick, Archives and Special Collections Department, Fredericton, N.B., Canada
CaQMM -- McGill University, McLennan Library, Montreal, Que., Canada
CaQMMO -- McGill University, Osler Library, Montreal, Que., Canada
CoAur2 -- Private Collector
CoU -- University of Colorado, Boulder, Colo. 80302
Ct -- Connecticut State Library, Hartford, Conn. 06115
CtB -- Bridgeport Public Library, Bridgeport, Conn. 06603
CtFP -- Miss Porter's School, Farmington, Conn. 06032
CtH -- Hartford Public Library, Hartford, Conn. 06103
CtH2 -- Private Collector
CtHC -- Hartford Seminary Foundation, Hartford, Conn. 06105
CtHMTH -- Mark Twain Memorial, Hartford, Conn. 06105
CtHSD -- Stowe-Day Memorial Library and Historical Foundation, Hartford, Conn. 06105
CtHT-W -- Trinity College, Watkinson Library, Hartford, Conn. 06106
CtHi -- Connecticut Historical Society, Hartford, Conn. 06105
CtLHi -- Litchfield Historical Society, Litchfield, Conn. 06759
CtMy2 -- Private Collector
CtNc2 -- Private Collector
CtNh2 -- Private Collector
CtRe -- Mark Twain Library Association, Inc., Redding, Conn. 06875
CtY -- Yale University, New Haven, Conn. 06520
DCos -- Cosmos Club, Washington, D.C. 20008
DFo -- Folger Shakespeare Library, Washington, D.C. 20003
DGU -- Georgetown University, Washington, D.C. 20007
DGW -- George Washington University, Washington, D.C. 20006
DJHi -- Jewish Historical Society of Greater Washington, Washington, D.C. 20001
DLC -- United States Library of Congress, Washington, D.C. 20540
DNA -- United States National Archives and Records Service, National Archives Library, Washington, D.C. 20408
DSI -- Smithsonian Institution, Washington, D.C. 20560
Dn -- Kongelige Bibliotek (Royal Library), Copenhagen, Denmark
F2 -- Private Collector
FG2 -- Private Collector
FSp2 -- Private Collector
FiH2 -- Suomalaisen Kirjallisuuden Seura (Finnish Literature Society), Helsinki, Finland
GEU -- Emory University, Atlanta, Ga. 30322
GMar2 -- Private Collector
I2 -- Private Collector
IAurC -- Aurora College, Aurora, Ill. 60507
IC -- Chicago Public Library, Chicago, Ill. 60602
IC3 -- Private Collector
IC4 -- Private Collector
ICN -- Newberry Library, Chicago, Ill. 60610
ICU -- University of Chicago, Chicago, Ill. 60637
ICarbS -- Southern Illinois University, Carbondale, Ill. 62901
IEN -- Northwestern University, Evanston, Ill. 60201
IGK -- Knox College, Galesburg, Ill. 61401
IMacoW -- Western Illinois University, Macomb, Ill. 61455
IU-R -- University of Illinois, Rare Book Room, Urbana, Ill. 61803

IaCrM -- Grand Lodge of Iowa, Cedar Rapids, Iowa 52406
IaDaPM -- Putnam Museum, Davenport, Iowa 52804
IaDmE -- Iowa State Education Assocation, Des Moines, Iowa 50319
IaHi -- State Historical Society of Iowa, Iowa City, Iowa 52240
IaK -- Keokuk Public Library, Keokuk, Iowa 52632
IaK2 -- Keokuk Savings Bank & Trust Company, Keokuk, Iowa 52639
IaMc -- Mason City Public Library, Mason City, Iowa 50401
IaU -- University of Iowa, Iowa City, Iowa 52240
Ii2 -- American Studies Research Center, Hyderabad, India
InFwLW -- Louis A. Warren Lincoln Library and Museum, Fort Wayne, Ind. 46801
InLP -- Purdue University, Lafayette, Ind. 47907
InNd -- University of Notre Dame, Notre Dame, Ind. 46556
InRE -- Earlham College, Richmond, Ind. 47374
InU-Li -- Indiana University, Lilly Library, Bloomington, Ind. 47401
IreDNL -- National Library of Ireland, Dublin, Ireland
IsJJNL -- Jewish National and University Library, Hebrew University, Jerusalem, Israel
KyLoU -- University of Louisville, Louisville, Ky. 40208
KyU -- University of Kentucky, Lexington, Ky. 40506
LNT -- Tulane University, New Orleans, La. 70118
LU-Ar -- Louisiana State University, Department of Archives and Manuscripts, Baton Rouge, La. 70803
M2 -- Private Collector
M3 -- Private Collector
MA -- Amherst College, Amherst, Mass. 01002
MAnP -- Phillips Academy, Andover, Mass. 01810
MB -- Boston Public Library and Eastern Massachusetts Regional Public Library System, Boston, Mass. 02117
MBAt -- Boston Athenaeum, Boston, Mass. 02108
MChB -- Boston College, Chestnut Hill, Mass. 02167
MCo -- Concord Free Public Library, Concord, Mass. 01742
MFai -- Millicent Library, Fairhaven, Mass. 02719
MGlHi -- Cape Ann Historical Association, 27 Pleasant Street, Gloucester, Mass. 01930
MH-H -- Harvard University, Houghton Library, Cambridge, Mass. 02138
MHi -- Massachusetts Historical Society, Boston, Mass. 02215
MLeoHi -- Leominster Historical Society, Inc., Leominster, Mass. 01453
MNS -- Smith College, Northampton, Mass. 01060
MWA -- American Antiquarian Society, Worcester, Mass. 01609
MWC -- Clark University, Worcester, Mass. 01610
MWelC -- Wellesley College, Wellesley, Mass. 02181
MWiW-C -- Williams College, Chapin Library, Williamstown, Mass. 01267
MdBE -- Enoch Pratt Free Library, Baltimore, Md. 21201
MdHi -- Maryland Historical Society, Baltimore, Md. 21201
MdU -- University of Maryland, College Park, Md. 20742
Me2 -- Private Collector
MeB -- Bowdoin College, Brunswick, Me. 04011
MeHi -- Maine Historical Society, Portland, Me. 04111
MeWC -- Colby College, Waterville, Me. 04901

MiD -- Detroit Public Library, Detroit, Mich. 48202
MiEM -- Michigan State University, East Lansing, Mich. 48823
MiK2 -- Private Collector
MiMtpT -- Central Michigan University, Mount Pleasant, Mich. 48858
MiU -- University of Michigan, Ann Arbor, Mich. 48104
MiU-H -- University of Michigan, Michigan Historical Collection, Ann Arbor, Mich. 48104
MnHi -- Minnesota Historical Society, St. Paul, Minn. 55101
MnM -- Minneapolis Public Library, Minneapolis, Minn. 55401
MnU-Rb -- University of Minnesota, Rare Book Division, Minneapolis, Minn. 55455
Mo2 -- Private Collector
Mo3 -- Private Collector
Mo4 -- Private Collector
MoCgS -- Southeast Missouri State College, Cape Girardeau, Mo. 63701
MoCoJ -- Joint Collection, Western Historical Manuscript Collection and State Historical Society of Missouri Manuscripts, Columbia, Mo. 65201
MoFu2 -- Private Collector
MoHM -- Mark Twain Museum, Hannibal, Mo. 63401
MoHi -- Missouri State Historical Society, Columbia, Mo. 65201
MoKHC -- Hallmark Cards, Kansas City, Mo. 64141
MoKiU -- Northeast Missouri State University, Kirksville, Mo. 63501
MoPeS -- Saint Mary's Seminary, Perryville, Mo. 63775
MoSW -- Washington University, St. Louis, Mo. 63130
MoSw2 -- Private Collector
MoU -- University of Missouri, Columbia, Mo. 65201
MtHi -- Montana Historical Society, Helena, Mont. 59601
N -- New York State Library, Albany, N.Y. 12224
N2 -- Private Collector
N4 -- Private Collector
N5 -- Private Collector
N6 -- Private Collector
N7 -- Library of Poultney Bigelow, Bigelow Homestead, Malden on Hudson, N.Y. 12453
NAlf -- Alfred University, Alfred, N.Y. 14802
NBmtT -- Trailside Museum, Bear Mountain, N.Y. 10911
NBron2 -- Private Collector
NBu -- Buffalo and Erie County Public Library, Buffalo, N.Y. 14203
NBuHi -- Buffalo and Erie County Historical Society, Buffalo, N.Y. 14216
NBuU-PO -- State University of New York at Buffalo, Poetry Library, Buffalo, N.Y. 14203
NCH -- Hamilton and Kirkland Colleges, Clinton, N.Y. 13323
NEh -- East Hampton Free Library, East Hampton, N.Y. 11937
NElm2 -- Private Collector
NElmC -- Elmira College, Elmira, N.Y. 14901
NElmHi -- Chemung County Historical Society, Elmira, N.Y. 14901
NFred -- Darwin R. Barker Library Association, Fredonia, N.Y. 14063
NGH -- Hobart and William Smith Colleges, Geneva, N.Y. 14456

NHC -- Colgate University, Hamilton, N.Y. 13346
NHemH -- Hofstra University, Hempstead, N.Y. 11550
NHi -- New York Historical Society, New York, N.Y. 10024
NHor2 -- Private Collector
NHudO -- Olana State Historic Site, Hudson, N.Y. 12534
NIC -- Cornell University, Ithaca, N.Y. 14850
NN -- New York Public Library, New York, N.Y. 10018
NN-B -- New York Public Library, Albert A. and Henry W. Berg Collection, New York, N.Y. 10018
NN2 -- Private Collector
NN3 -- Private Collector
NN4 -- Private Collector
NN5 -- Private Collector
NN7 -- Private Collector
NNAF -- American Foundation for the Blind, New York, N.Y. 10011
NNAL -- American Academy of Arts and Letters, New York, N.Y. 10032
NNC -- Columbia University, New York, N.Y. 10032
NNPM -- Pierpont Morgan Library, New York, N.Y. 10016
NNU-F -- New York University, Fales Collection, New York, N.Y. 10012
NNWH -- Walter Hampden Memorial Library, New York, N.Y. 10003
NOg2 -- Remington Art Memorial Museum, Ogdensburg, N.Y. 13669
NPV -- Vassar College, Poughkeepsie, N.Y. 12601
NPla2 -- Private Collector
NRU -- University of Rochester, Rochester, N.Y. 14627
NStBU -- Saint Bonaventure University, St. Bonaventure, N.Y. 14778
NSyU -- Syracuse University, Syracuse, N.Y. 13210
NTRS -- Russell Sage College, Troy, N.Y. 12180
NWhp2 -- Private Collector
NbO -- Omaha Public Library, Omaha, Neb. 68102
NcD -- Duke University, Durham, N.C. 27706
NcGr2 -- Private Collector
NcU -- University of North Carolina, Chapel Hill, N.C. 27514
NcWsW -- Wake Forest University, Winston-Salem, N.C. 27109
NhD -- Dartmouth College, Hanover, N.H. 03755
NjBern2 -- Private Collector
NjHi -- New Jersey Historical Society, Newark, N.J. 07104
NjMo -- Joint Free Public Library of Morristown and Morris Township, Morristown, N.J. 07960
NjMoHP -- Morristown National Historical Park, Morristown, N.J. 07960
NjN -- Newark Public Library, Newark, N.J. 07101
NjP -- Princeton University, Princeton, N.J. 08540
NjR -- Rutgers-The State University, New Brunswick, N.J. 08901
NmA2 -- Private Collector
NmR2 -- Private Collector
NmU -- University of New Mexico, Albuquerque, N.M. 87106
NoOU -- Universitetet i Oslo (University of Oslo), Oslo, Norway
Nv -- Nevada State Library, Carson City, Nev. 89701
NvHi -- Nevada State Historical Society, Reno, Nev. 89504
NvU -- University of Nevada, Reno, Nev. 89507
NzW2 -- National Library of New Zealand, Alexander Turnbull Library, Wellington, New Zealand
OC -- Public Library of Cincinnati and Hamilton County, Cincinnati, Ohio 45202
OCAJA -- American Jewish Archives, Cincinnati, Ohio 45220
OCHP -- Cincinnati Historical Society, Cincinnati, Ohio 45202
OCIW -- Case Western Reserve University, Cleveland, Ohio 44106
OCIWHi -- Western Reserve Historical Society, Cleveland, Ohio 44106
ODa2 -- Private Collector
OFH -- Rutherford B. Hayes Library, Fremont, Ohio 43420
OHi -- Ohio Historical Society, Columbus, Ohio 43211
OKentU -- Kent State University, Kent, Ohio 44240
OMC -- Marietta College, Marietta, Ohio 45750
OrPR -- Reed College, Portland, Or. 97202
PBL -- Lehigh University, Bethlehem, Pa. 18015
PCarlD -- Dickinson College, Carlisle, Pa. 17013
PGC -- Gettysburg College, Gettysburg, Pa. 17325
PHC -- Haverford College, Haverford, Pa. 19041
PHi -- Historical Society of Pennsylvania, Philadelphia, Pa. 19107
PP -- Free Library of Philadelphia, Philadelphia, Pa. 19103
PP2 -- Private Collector
PP3 -- Private Collector
PP4 -- Private Collector
PPiHi -- Historical Society of Western Pennsylvania, Pittsburgh, Pa. 15213
PPiU -- University of Pittsburgh, Pittsburgh, Pa. 15213
PSt -- Pennsylvania State University, University Park, Pa. 16802
PU -- University of Pennsylvania, Philadelphia, Pa. 19104
PYHi -- Historical Society of York County, York, Pa. 17403
RNR -- Redwood Library and Athenaeum, Newport, R.I. 02480
RPB-JH -- Brown University, John Hay Library of Rare Books and Special Collections, Providence, R.I. 02912
RuL2 -- Institute of Russian Literature and Art, Leningrad, Soviet Union
RuM2 -- Central State Archive of Literature and Art, Moscow, Soviet Union
RuM3 -- Lenin Library, Moscow, Soviet Union
Sw2 -- Riksarkivet (Swedish Public Record Office), Stockholm, Sweden
SwUU -- Universitet i Uppsala (University of Uppsala), S-751 20 Uppsala, Sweden
SzG2 -- Bibliothek Bodmeriana (Bodmeriana Library), Geneva, Switzerland
T -- Tennessee State Library and Archives, Nashville, Tenn. 37219
TNJ -- Joint University Libraries, Nashville, Tenn. 37203
TxAu2 -- Private Collector
TxAu3 -- Private Collector
TxDaM-P -- Southern Methodist University, Perkins School of Theology, Dallas, Tex. 75222

TxEU -- University of Texas at El Paso, El Paso, Tex. 79999
TxFTC -- Texas Christian University, Fort Worth, Tex. 76129
TxHU -- University of Houston, Houston, Tex. 77004
TxU -- University of Texas, Austin, Tex. 78712
UPB -- Brigham Young University, Provo, Utah 84601
Uk -- British Library, London, WC1B 3DG, United Kingdom
Uk2 -- East Sussex Record Office, Lewes, United Kingdom
Uk3 -- Hove Central Library, Hove, United Kingdom
Uk4 -- University of Reading, Reading, United Kingdom
Uk5 -- University of Sussex, Brighton, United Kingdom
Uk6 -- Moray District Council, Elgin, United Kingdom
UkB -- Birmingham Public Libraries, Birmingham B3 3HQ, United Kingdom
UkCo2 -- Private Collector
UkE2 -- National Register of Archives, Edinburgh, United Kingdom
UkENL -- National Library of Scotland, Edinburgh, United Kingdom
UkG2 -- Strathclyde Regional Archives, Glasgow, United Kingdom
UkL2 -- British Library of Political and Economic Science, London, United Kingdom
UkL4 -- London Borough of Richmond upon Thames, Richmond, Surrey, United Kingdom
UkL5 -- Routledge and Kegan Paul, London, United Kingdom
UkL6 -- Victoria and Albert Museum, South Kensington, London, United Kingdom
UkLe2 -- University of Leeds, Brotherton Library, Leeds, United Kingdom
UkLi2 -- Brown, Picton and Hornby Libraries, Liverpool, United Kingdom
UkOxU -- Oxford University, Bodleian Library, Oxford, United Kingdom
ViAl2 -- Private Collector
ViHi -- Virginia Historical Society, Richmond, Va. 23221
ViU -- University of Virginia, Charlottesville, Va. 22904
ViW -- College of William and Mary, Williamsburg, Va. 23185
VtMiM -- Middlebury College, Middlebury, Vt. 05753
WE -- Eau Claire Public Library, Eau Claire, Wis. 54701
WHi -- State Historical Society of Wisconsin, Madison, Wis. 53706
WRl2 -- Private Collector
WRl3 -- Private Collector
WU -- University of Wisconsin, Madison, Wis. 53706
WaCheh2 -- Private Collector
WaPS -- Washington State University, Pullman, Wash. 99163
WaS -- Seattle Public Library, Seattle, Wash. 98104
WvU -- West Virginia University, Morgantown, W.Va. 26505
YuB2 -- Muzej Nikole Tesle (Tesle Museum), Belgrade, Yugoslavia